PROCEEDINGS of the
CONFERENCE on

COMMON PROPERTY RESOURCE MANAGEMENT

April 21-26, 1985

Prepared by
Panel on Common Property Resource Management
Board on Science and Technology for
International Development
Office of International Affairs
National Research Council

Washington, D.C., 1986
National Academy Press

The National Research Council was established by the National Academy of Sciences in 1916 to associate the broad community of science and technology with the Academy's purposes of furthering knowledge and of advising the federal government. The Council operates in accordance with general policies determined by the Academy under the authority of its congressional charter of 1863, which establishes the Academy as a private, nonprofit, self-governing membership corporation. The Council has become the principal operating agency of both the National Academy of Sciences and the National Academy of Engineering in the conduct of their services to the government, the public, and the scientific and engineering communities. It is administered jointly by both Academies and the Institute of Medicine. The National Academy of Engineering and the Institute of Medicine were established in 1964 and 1970, respectively, under the charter of the National Academy of Sciences.

These proceedings have been prepared by the Board on Science and Technology for International Development, Office of International Affairs, National Research Council, funded by the Agency for International Development under Grant No. DAN-5433-6-5-55-4059-00/R, the Ford Foundation under Grants No. 8550436 and 8550436A, and the World Wildlife Fund under Grant No. 6043/R.

Copies available from:
Board on Science and Technology
  for International Development
National Research Council
2101 Constitution Avenue, N.W.
Washington, D.C. 20418 USA

ISBN 0-309-04258-5
Library of Congress Catalog Card No. 86-636-60
Second Printing, July 1987

Panel on Common Property Resource Management

DANIEL W. BROMLEY, Department of Agricultural Economics,
    University of Wisconsin, Madison, Wisconsin, U.S.A.
    Chairman
DAVID H. FEENY, Department of Economics and Department of
    Clinical Epidemiology and Biostatistics, McMaster
    University, Hamilton, Ontario, Canada
JERE L. GILLES, Department of Rural Sociology, University
    of Missouri, Columbia, Missouri, U.S.A.
WILLIAM T. GLADSTONE, Southern and International Forestry
    Research, Weyerhaeuser Company, Hot Springs, Arkansas,
    U.S.A.
BARBARA J. LAUSCHE, World Wildlife Fund, Washington, D.C.,
    U.S.A.
MARGARET A. McKEAN, Department of Political Science, Duke
    University, Durham, North Carolina, U.S.A.
RONALD J. OAKERSON, Advisory Commission on Intergovern-
    mental Relations, Washington, D.C., U.S.A.
ELINOR OSTROM, Workshop in Political Theory and Policy
    Analysis, Indiana University, Bloomington, Indiana,
    U.S.A.
PAULINE E. PETERS, Department of Anthropology and Institute
    for International Development, Harvard University,
    Cambridge, Massachusetts, U.S.A.
C. FORD RUNGE, Department of Agricultural and Applied
    Economics, University of Minnesota, St. Paul,
    Minnesota, U.S.A.
JAMES T. THOMSON, Associates in Rural Development, Silver
    Spring, Maryland, U.S.A.

NATIONAL RESEARCH COUNCIL STAFF

JEFFREY A. GRITZNER, Senior Program Officer
F. R. RUSKIN, Editor
IRENE MARTINEZ, Program Assistant

FOREWORD
M. S. Swaminathan

People dependent upon renewable natural resources have
evolved ways of managing them properly. When they have
failed to do so, the people, the resources, or both have
disappeared. Communities have developed such institutionalized forms of control as irrigation councils in southern
Asia, forest-cutting controls in Nepal, wildlife utilization taboos and regulations in the Congo Basin, the hema
system of pasture protection in Arabia, fishermen's indigenous associations in western and southern Asia, and land
use management for conservation in Zimbabwe.

When practiced at the community level, this common
property resource management has often been successful, or
the resources would have vanished long since. In many
places, these systems, or remnants of them, still exist.
In others, the management systems are more recent but have
been adapted from traditional practices of other cultures
and have survived modernization. Examples of this sort are
the Zanjera irrigation system in the Philippines and the
Islamic practices relating to land use and water rights in
West Africa.

The papers in this volume, brought together as a result
of an in-depth process of expert consultation and debate by
the National Research Council, show an encouraging trend
among academic people for this rediscovery of very old
resource management practices and institutions existing
among many communities. Even more than that, they show us
as planners and development professionals that in many
places these institutions are still alive. This is a
hopeful sign, given the inability of many private and state
level resource management systems to come to grips with the
need for long-term sustainability of resource use issues.
Restoring to the community the responsibility that was
originally its own may be our only hope for the future

protection of our soil, water, fisheries, pastures, forests, and wildlife.

M. S. Swaminathan
Director General
International Rice Research Institute
    and
President
International Union for Conservation
    of Nature and Natural Resources

PREFACE

Economic well-being throughout the world is directly related to the management and productivity of environmental systems. As indigenous social systems are transformed, economic emphases altered, and land-use patterns modified, human adaptations and regulatory mechanisms that earlier maintained the balance between man and his environment break down, and use of renewable resources can no longer be prudently asserted. However, drawing on the adaptations of the past, as well as on contemporary scientific insight, management systems can be improved so that the resources basic to the availability of food, fuel, fodder, and shelter can be restored and exploited on a sustainable basis.

The note of urgency regarding issues of common property resource management emerged from a series of studies and associated deliberations conducted by the National Research Council's Advisory Committee on the Sahel. The Council's Conference on Common Property Resource Management was undertaken to assess systematically differing institutional arrangements for the effective conservation and utilization of jointly managed resources. The members of the Panel on Common Property Resource Management, recognizing the global dimensions of the current environmental emergency, selected case studies drawn from four continents and a broad range of cultural and environmental settings. It is hoped that the background papers, case studies, and conclusions of the conference will contribute substantively to efforts to rehabilitate and manage the soils, water resources, forests, rangelands, agricultural lands, and other jointly held resources that constitute the global commons.

The contributions of several individuals made the conference a reality. Financial support was provided by the National Research Council, the United States Agency for International Development, the Ford Foundation, and the World Wildlife Fund. The members of the panel were active in all phases of this effort. They contributed to the conceptualization of the conference, to the difficult task of selecting participants so as to provide appropriate geographical and topical balance, to the convening of pre-conference seminars to assist with the preparation of appropriately structured case studies, to the organization of the conference itself, and to the technical editing of the case studies. Many panel members also presented papers that appear in this volume. Emery Castle of Oregon State University, Adelaide Cromwell Gulliver of Boston University, and Robert Repetto of the World Resources Institute provided valuable criticisms and suggestions on various drafts of the proceedings.

Many other individuals contributed to this effort as well. Particular recognition must be given to Irene Martinez, whose concern, skills, and energy contributed significantly to the success of the conference and the preparation of the conference proceedings. Michael G. C. McDonald Dow frequently interrupted his own work to assist with the common property program. Other staff members who contributed to the program include Ann Harrington, who served as conference expeditor, and Hertha Hanu and Barbara Jones, who assisted with the preparation and reproduction of conference documents.

The enormous task of editing the proceedings volume fell to F. R. Ruskin, in collaboration with Patti Lowery. The final production of the proceedings was facilitated by the commitment and efforts of Susan Piarulli, Mark Dafforn, and Mary Lee Schneiders. Jeffrey A. Gritzner served as program director.

CONTENTS

Forest and Bushland Resources

PART THREE: CONCLUSIONS

PART ONE: **Background**

1

The Common Property Challenge*
Daniel W. Bromley

The degradation of natural resources in the tropics
must be stopped--not only for its own sake, but because
approximately 80 percent of the world's population depend
on these resources for their spare and precarious existence. If degradation problems are to be solved, they
must first be understood. If we are to understand
resource degradation, then we must understand human
behavior with respect to those resources. The behavior
that now threatens natural resources is the product of a
constellation of rules and conventions. To understand
resource degradation, then, we must first comprehend the
full array of these rules and conventions--incentives,
sanctions, rights, duties, and privileges. We must also
understand how these affect an individual's relationship
both to other individuals and to the group.
   At the end of this conference, we will be expected to
have developed several specific products. The first will
be a set of performance indicators that speaks both to
resource integrity and to the human dimension. That is,
we cannot recommend a resource management regime that precludes any human use of the ecosystem; practicality demands

*Opening comments prepared for the Conference on Common
Property Resource Management.

that we regard the social system and the ecosystem as equally important and then search for both management and use regimes that--almost as a compromise--allow both components to survive, if not prosper.

A second product will be that we have identified at least three major causes of success or failure in common property resource management situations. Therefore, as the week progresses, we should look for general principles that can be related to particular regimes. It may be that correlations are all we can acquire in this brief period. I would not despair if this were the best we could do. Causality comes dear to social scientists. A few well-founded correspondences are certainly to be preferred to even one mis-specified causal relationship. I urge caution here, and modest expectations.

As a third product, we will be expected to develop in some detail at least three major research undertakings that are the logical result of our conceptual and empirical deliberations. These research tasks should have as their central objective the greater elucidation and clarification of the relationships among: (1) the ecosystem; (2) technique; (3) the congeries of rules and conventions regarding resource use, as well as rules for making new rules; (4) the patterns of interaction among all members of the social system under study--but especially of the resource users themselves; and finally (5) the outcome or performance of this entire "going concern."

The fourth and final product we will develop consists of at least five major items for the action agenda of the development assistance agencies and the host countries with whom they cooperate. These activities must be programmatic in nature; they should not be specific projects. They will need to entail a major commitment of the host country and the donor agency in the country to be studied. And these activities must be designed and implemented so that the lessons learned can be readily transferred to other resource situations in other countries.

I suggest that the obvious starting place in our concern for common property resources is to understand the reasons in the first instance for the existence of joint-control arrangements as opposed to individual control. The anthropologist would likely suggest some survival explanation; the sociologist might look for reasons related to group cohesion; the economist might propose that joint control saves important scarce resources that might be required under atomistic control. The common thread, obviously, is that the group as a whole has some abiding interest in survival, in cohesion, in the benefits and costs attendant to a particular use regime, and in economizing on perceived scarcities.

Quite assuredly, joint control of one natural resource may be unrelated to the control of other natural resources, as well as of other objects significant to the groups. Put somewhat differently, the group develops differential decision domains over significant objects--both naturally occurring and manufactured--depending upon some calculus regarding practicality, risk management, equity, and the costs of making a wrong decision. This means that the group keeps a diverse "set of books" over its various assets, depending on the variables just described. For some objects, atomistic control is fine. For others, either because of the physical imperatives of the object, because of the technical imperatives of using that object, or because of the critical role that the object plays in the survival of the group, group control is required.

The structure provided by Oakerson in his presentation to us is rightly concerned with institutional change and adaptation. However, for now, we may have to be content with merely describing different situations, and with offering tentative hypotheses about what we observe; proposals for change may need to be deferred until some time in the future. Indeed, I urge that we not move too quickly to "solutions." Prescription must await explanation; after all, prescription is prediction, and we do not yet know enough to predict.

I suggest that our task will be complicated by the frequent incongruence between rules and conventions and the behaviors that derive from those conventions. Oakerson talks of reciprocity as it contrasts to a "free ride." I think there is an important elaboration to be made in that regard, and I ask you to consider both positive and negative reciprocity. Positive reciprocity might be thought of as an individual's doing something because it is understood that others will do the same. Negative reciprocity is, therefore, an individual's failing to do something because it is expected that others also will not do something. Both behaviors are reciprocal, they derive from expectations about the likely actions of others, and they are motivated by a desire on the part of the individual to "go along with the crowd"--for good or for ill. The free rider, on the other hand, avoids doing something because it is expected that others will do it. Altruism is the converse of free riding in that an individual does something because others are expected not to. In contrast to reciprocity (either positive or negative), the free rider or the altruist wants to "go it alone."

We will need to be sensitive to the conditions of reciprocity as well as to free riding, and we will need to look for indications of how incentives and sanctions for these behaviors are structured. But we must also understand that compliance with existing rules and conventions is not necessarily widespread--indeed, it may be the exception, as we will see in several of the case studies to be presented.

As we turn to that important task, we must all applaud the shift in focus away from natural resources as commodities, and toward management regimes, systems, and mechanisms. By saying that, I do not mean that the resources themselves are unimportant, but there can be no hope for progress in avoiding resource degradation if there is no progress in understanding management regimes and the rules and conventions that determine resource control.

The case studies to be presented are our data--they are means to an end. We must be both bold and cautious; bold in lumping, splitting, challenging, and searching for relations; and cautious in declaring that we have located truth. The future of donor-country/host-country relations in the domain of natural resource programs rests on what we do this week, and how we do it. I am aware of few other exercises in which pan-resource management regimes have been the object of such focused and intense analytic scrutiny by an interdisciplinary group of this stature.

Most exercises that have attempted to span several natural resources have been rather cosmic in nature-- claiming that we must stop this or that immediately if we are to avoid catastrophe. The unique aspect of our task is that we recognize--even insist--that the resource needs of human beings take center stage; we are denied the luxury of simple platitudes about denying current users any future access. Idealists will be critical because we did not condemn, for instance, swidden agriculture or proper solutions that ignore immediate human need.

But we start with several constraints. First, pragmatic policy for the rehabilitation and stabilization of degraded ecosystems requires that such programs proceed so that users are able to retain their current role in that ecosystem; we cannot expect to develop programs that evict people. Second, the relations between donor agencies and host countries--and so the prospects for success in resource degradation problems--will depend upon the depth of our understanding and analysis of the problems that we

will study over the course of our discussions. If we miss
essential ingredients in the diagnosis of current resource
situations, then programs that evolve will miss the mark--
and badly.

Let us search the case studies for lessons, for insights, for common elements, and also for their logical
inconsistencies. Let us finally, after several decades of
intellectual imperialism regarding the structure of natural
resource regimes in the tropics, be prepared to indicate a
few things that perhaps should not be done, a few things
that seem to be feasible options, and--yes--even a few
things that we do not yet know.

Resource management in the tropics will be much influenced by the document that is to come out of this conference; the imprimatur of the National Research Council
assures us of that. The document will be studied to see
whether our own framework of analysis has been sufficiently
consistent and rigorous; it will be scrutinized to judge
whether we have been properly circumspect in the conclusions drawn, and attentive to the imperatives of economic,
cultural, and political realities.

If we accomplish little else, I hope that we will use
this opportunity to give both scope and substance to the
questions that must be asked of all resource management
regimes in the tropics. This would provide a valuable
diagnostic framework that others might find helpful as they
ponder resource degradation in various settings. That
framework must be action oriented, and it must be rather
simple. We must develop a taxonomic structure of resource
management regimes that goes beyond the mere simplicity of
common property, private property, and open access. Along
with a taxonomy, we must develop a diagnostic process and
a set of operating procedures that will allow nonexperts
to gain a general understanding of resource management
regimes and problems.

I am pleased to be part of this important exercise, and
I am awed by the collection of talent represented in this
room. If we can but harness our collective experiences,
our complementary disciplinary skills, and our individual
dedication to the task before us, this conference cannot
fail.

2

Conference on Common Property Resource Management: An Introduction

David H. Feeny

THE ISSUE

Throughout the world today, various common property resource systems are coming under increased pressure, particularly in the tropics and subtropics. Rapid rates of population growth, technological change, increases in the size of markets, and cultural change, as well as uneven growth and persistent poverty, have often resulted in increased levels of utilization of various natural-resource-based systems. Forests are being cleared rapidly; groundwater is being pumped to the surface at an often alarmingly high rate; fish and wildlife populations are declining in the face of loss of habitat and high levels of harvesting; range and pasture lands are being overgrazed; and other examples abound. Because the exploitation of these resource systems represents an important component in the livelihoods of people throughout Africa, Asia, and Latin America, their degradation cannot be ignored.

Although resource degradation is an issue of great concern in the current scene, generalizations concerning worsening conditions or their causes cannot be universally applied. More specifically, there are no simple and valid generalizations concerning the relationship between resource degradation and the type of property-rights regime. Degradation as well as successful management occur in cases of private, state, and common property. In particular, several common property management regimes have functioned well and are still the preferred form of resource management in many places.

The basic question that motivated the organization of the Annapolis conference was how and why certain groups have been able to manage common property resources successfully while others have not. The focus was on the institutional arrangements that governed the relationships among people who were associated with each other through the use of the resource. The theme was an inquiry into the nature and causes of success and failure.

PLANNING FOR THE CONFERENCE

Planning for the conference began in the summer of 1983 and culminated in the first meeting of an ad hoc steering committee (that was later transformed into the Panel on Common Property Resource Management) in September 1983. The committee quickly reached consensus on several points. First, we were confident that there was a rich body of research on the management of common property resources in the tropics and subtropics. Second, we concurred that the existing literature needed to be identified, collected, and synthesized. Third, we agreed that by bringing the evidence together we would obtain a detailed and useful understanding of the operation of a wide variety of systems of resource management. Fourth, we felt that a barrier to the previous synthesis of this body of evidence was that it comprised a diverse set of studies that had been conducted by scholars from different disciplines, working in different regions of the world, on a wide variety of resource systems.

The committee therefore decided that a special effort would be required to identify investigators working in this field and to tap into the large body of existing evidence. To locate relevant work, a questionnaire initially was sent to a small group of investigators known to members of the committee; recipients were invited to suggest the names of other investigators. The result has been the development of the Common Property Resource Management Network, a body currently composed of more than 800 investigators who have responded to the questionnaire.[1]

The committee then decided to plan a conference on common property management that would be based on a collection of case studies and focused on the institutions of resource management. The original plan was to have a case

study on each of four resources (fish and wildlife, forests
and bushland, range and pastures, and water, both surface
water and groundwater) for each of four major world regions
(sub-Saharan Africa, Asia, Latin America and the Caribbean,
and North Africa and the Middle East). Relevant studies
were identified initially through the use of the network,
and authors were invited to submit abstracts.

A third major decision was to provide explicitly for a
comparison across case studies. A common framework for the
preparation of case studies was developed (see Oakerson,
Chapter 3). The use of the framework allowed the conference to move beyond the presentation and discussion of
high-quality case studies into comparative work and the
generation of inductive hypotheses (see, for instance,
Bromley, this volume, and Ostrom, this volume).

The selection of participants and case studies for the
conference was guided by the plan to achieve diversity
across regions and resource systems. Given the wealth of
abstracts submitted, we had little difficulty in obtaining
diverse and representative case studies with a range of
disciplinary approaches, and the submission of several
abstracts on the management of agricultural land led to its
inclusion among the resource categories represented. The
committee determined that the case studies that would be
presented at the conference should also represent a range
of outcomes from very successful management to examples of
limited success.

The committee then decided on the organization of
pre-conference workshops for case study presenters. It was
felt that a meeting largely focused on the discussion of
the framework (Oakerson, this volume) was needed to clarify
its use. The two workshops (approximately half of the case
study authors attended each) also allowed for a preliminary
discussion of each case study and greatly facilitated the
main event by familiarizing conference participants with
each other and each other's work. As a result, serious
discussion was possible from the very beginning of the
conference in Annapolis.

THE CONFERENCE

Drafts of the case study papers contained in this
volume were read by all participants before the conference.
During the conference, each author was given ten minutes to
present his case study. Sessions were organized around
each of the five major resource types. The brief presen-

tations were followed by active discussion. Additional
sessions and discussions were organized in small groups
around proposals for the research agenda, the policy
agenda, and three major issues (the effects of multiple
levels of management, the effects of group size, and
mechanisms for dispute settlement) that transcended
resources and regions.

The panel owes a debt of gratitude to all conference
participants who entered into lively, stimulating, and
informed discussions that cut across disciplinary and other
boundaries. Knowledge of how common property resource
management systems work, as well as the factors that appear
to influence success, or lack of it, in managing such systems was greatly enhanced by the conference. Important
items for the research and action agendas were generated.
In sum, the conference accomplished a great deal and laid a
solid foundation for future work.

NOTE

1. An associated common property resource management network newsletter is published by the Center for Natural
Resource Policy and Management at the University of Minnesota, in collaboration with the International Union for
Conservation of Nature and Natural Resources and the
National Research Council. Core support for the publication of the newsletter has been provided by the Ford Foundation.

3

A Model for the Analysis of Common Property Problems
Ronald J. Oakerson

The subject of this paper could be stated as a riddle:
how are forests, fishing grounds, pastures, parks, groundwater supplies, and public highways all alike? Answer:
each one is often--even typically--a "commons," a resource
or facility shared by a community of producers or consumers. The list of common property resources and facilities is highly diverse and could be greatly extended. A
commons can have a fixed location or it can occur as a
"fugitive" resource (fish and wildlife). Some commons are
renewable (grasslands), others are not (oil pools). Some
are both open access and indivisible and therefore must be
organized as common property, if organized at all (large
fishing grounds or large forests); others are treated as a
commons by choice (small pastures). All common property
nevertheless faces one common problem: how to coordinate
individual users to attain an optimal rate of production or
consumption for the whole community.

More precisely defined, a commons is an economic
resource or facility subject to individual use but not to
individual possession. It can be distinguished from both
collective consumption goods (also called "pure" public
goods) and private goods. The first are collectively consumed, as in the case of a street lamp, in the sense that
the rate of consumption is independent of the number of
consumers and the particular use made of the good. The

second is subject to the exclusive use and possession of individuals. With respect to a commons, the total rate of consumption varies with both the number of users and the type of use and, at the same time, use is joint in the sense that several individuals share the same resource or facility. Problems of coordination generally become apparent when there is some significant change in the pattern and/or level of use; such a change often is associated with increasing scarcity. If the community of users is unable to work through existing arrangements to respond appropriately to changes, destructive competition or conflict among users may follow. Resource depletion (or degradation of facilities) results--an eventuality characterized by Hardin (1968) as the "tragedy of the commons." In specific cases, the consequences may be soil erosion, overgrazing, diminishing fish harvests, disappearing species, nonrenewing woodlots, or impassable roads.

The purpose of this paper is to present a model that can be used to analyze common property problems whatever the particular resource or facility. Such a model must be specific enough to offer guidance in the field, yet general enough to permit application to widely variable situations. The trick is to develop concepts that identify key attributes shared broadly by common property problems and that can be treated as variables that take on different values from one circumstance to another. Relationships among these variables should be specified in a way that allows one to diagnose what is wrong and why in particular situations. On this basis, potential solutions can be offered.

A scholar or practitioner who is familiar with a certain problem situation will have access to a large body of technical, historical, cultural, economic, and political information concerning that situation. The model presented here invites the analyst to sort this body of information into four mutually exclusive subsets: (1) the technical and/or physical attributes of the specific resource or facility; (2) the decision-making arrangements (organization and rules) that currently govern relationships among users (and others relevant); (3) the patterns of interaction among decision makers; and (4) outcomes or consequences (V. Ostrom 1974:55; Oakerson 1981:81). Each subset is a separate component of the model. The plan of discussion, to follow, is to introduce each of the four components, to examine the relationships in the model among its components, and, finally, to suggest ways of applying the model iteratively to understand the impact of institutional change and adaptation.

COMPONENTS OF THE MODEL

Technical and Physical Attributes

All common property problems are rooted in some set of constraints either given in nature or inherent in available technology. The technical and physical constraints can be analyzed against three concepts drawn from economics literature: (1) jointness of consumption or supply, (2) exclusion, and (3) indivisibility. Each concept can be expressed as a variable, as indicated below.

Jointness

This concept was originally used to define a "pure public good" (Samuelson 1954). Jointness means that no single beneficiary of some good subtracts from the ability of others to derive benefits; it ordinarily refers to simultaneous use, but can be modified to include serial use. The opposite of jointness defines the case in which a single individual fully consumes (and destroys) a good. As a variable, jointness refers to degrees of subtractability (V. Ostrom and E. Ostrom 1978) in the use of common property. All common property falls, by definition, into the broad range of partial subtractability. Each individual user is potentially capable of subtracting from the welfare of other users; but, within limits, all users can derive benefits jointly. The analyst should specify, as precisely as possible, the limiting conditions within which jointness can be maintained. The relevant conditions include, for example, grazing limits in a commons pasture, trapping limits in a lobstery, and weight limits on a highway. These limits, established in nature or technology, provide essential information for devising rules to maximize the joint beneficial use of the commons. "Jointness can then characterize common property as it does a pure public good with this difference: one person's lawful use does not subtract from the lawful use of others" (Oakerson 1981). Given an appropriate set of rules, based on limiting conditions, the same economies of sharing that Samuelson demonstrated with respect to a pure public good may also be available to the users of common property.

It is important for the model, however, that limiting conditions be specified without respect to any rules in place. The relevant limits at this point in the analysis are those derived from nature or technology, not those derived from rules.

Exclusion

The "exclusion principle," also used by economists to differentiate private from public goods (Musgrave 1959), ordinarily refers to the ability of sellers to exclude potential buyers from goods and services unless they pay the stipulated price. The concept can be broadened somewhat to include the question of access to any good, including a commons. The opposite of exclusion is complete openness--unlimited access. Common property is not necessarily characterized by open access (Runge 1981). Access may be fully controlled on an individual basis or partially controlled and applied only to those outside the immediate community. As a variable, the degree of exclusion attainable depends upon both the physical nature of a resource (or design of a facility) and available technology. Historically, open range was difficult to fence; but the development of barbed wire greatly relaxed this limitation. Again, at this point in the analysis, one is interested not in an exclusion or nonexclusion policy, but rather in "excludability": the limiting conditions that apply to the possibility of exclusion--conditions established by nature and/or technology. Although common property problems do not depend upon the existence of difficulty with exclusion, these problems are clearly exacerbated by nonexclusion.

Indivisibility

Is the commons divisible? Could the property held in common feasibly be divided among private property holders? What would be the costs of doing so? If the commons is not divisible, what boundary conditions apply to its regulation? On what scale would regulation have to occur to be effective?

Underlying boundary conditions derive from nature or technology and should not be confused with legal boundaries, that is, boundaries imposed by rule. Consider the example of a groundwater basin. The common pool of water has a definite set of physical boundaries. The legal boundaries of a jurisdictional unit formed to deal with the groundwater problem may or may not correspond to the physical boundaries of the resource. Other common property resources may have less determinate physical boundaries; nonetheless, it still may be possible to assign boundaries based on physical or technical attributes of the commons.

The western range in the United States, for example, might superficially be viewed as a single commons; but variations in weather and soil conditions prompt the "division" of the range into much smaller units for management purposes.

The analysis must contain some sense of underlying boundary conditions, even if they are somewhat ambiguous. If the boundaries chosen for the purposes of analysis are too small, then relevant aspects of the problem will be left outside; if the boundaries are too large, then multiple problems may be compounded. If the precise boundary is somewhat arbitrary, the question is whether it lies within an acceptable range.

Together, the three concepts--jointness, exclusion, and indivisibility--provide a way of summarizing the physical and technical nature of a commons. In general, common property is characterized by partial jointness and the probability of some difficulty with exclusion within a limited set of boundaries. The precise conditions, of course, vary from one situation to another.

Decision-Making Arrangements

The second component of the model consists of rules-- those rules that structure individual and collective choices with respect to the particular "commons" defined by the first component. These arrangements may also be thought of as "organizational" or "institutional," as the reader prefers (the designation used here is intended to convey a very broad set of arrangements that are not confined to any single "organization" or "institution"). Parts of several institutions are generally implicated in the management or mismanagement of a commons.

In general, decision-making arrangements have to do with authority relationships that determine who decides what in relation to whom. In the discussion below, decision-making arrangements are sorted into three subsets: first, rules that establish conditions of collective choice within the group most immediately involved with the commons; second, "operational" rules that regulate use of the commons; and third, external arrangements, those decision structures outside the immediate group, that impinge on how the commons is used.

Conditions of Collective Choice

Rules that establish the ability of some group to act collectively (to make decisions common to the group), are especially relevant to the management of common property. Obstacles to collective choice are at the same time opportunities for individualistic choice--decisions that individuals can make on their own without the consent of others. When a group is unable to act collectively, individual members are left free to act separately. Four different relationships can be considered to affect the conditions of collective choice: (1) the capacity of individuals to act solely on the basis of personal discretion in matters of concern to others, perhaps preempting action by others or initiating an action that creates costs of opposition for others; (2) the availability of potential sources of remedy to individuals adversely affected by others; (3) the capacity of an affected population to relax the rule of willing consent and make a collective decision binding on all parties; and (4) the presence of potential veto positions in any process of collective decision making--opportunities for one or more decision makers to say "no."

Typically, common property arrangements give use rights to individuals. Hardin's "tragedy of the commons" occurs in a context of unrestricted individual rights to use the commons. Individuals may also, however, be vested with rights that protect them from injury caused by others. Remedies may be available through such "third-party" arrangements as courts. Beyond the domain of individual decision making, a community of users may be able to act collectively to establish limits on individual use. Some decision makers may enjoy a veto capability in this process, perhaps by virtue of official position.

Operational Rules

The content of collective choice is the "operational rules" that regulate use of the commons. Three types of rules can be distinguished, each related to one of the three technical and/or physical features found in the first component of the model. (1) Partitioning rules are those that serve to limit user behavior in the interest of jointness. Behavior is partitioned into subtractive and nonsubtractive sets. If more than one type of use is made of a commons, partitioning rules should take into account the relationships among those various uses. Some types of use may be compatible; others, sharply conflicting. At times a commons is physically partitioned for individual use without dividing it into separate parcels of property; the effect is to partially segregate different or incompatible uses (for example, a parking lot). (2) Entry and exit rules (E. Ostrom n.d.) are concerned with exclusion and seek to regulate access to a commons. This set of rules includes qualifications for participation in a community of users (entry) and whether membership in an organization of users is compulsory (exit). (3) Any organizational arrangement for governing a commons must stipulate a set of jurisdictional boundaries. These boundary rules, however, may be more or less congruent with the underlying boundary conditions determined by the technical and/or physical nature of the commons.

External Arrangements

Decision-making arrangements external to the community of users will also be relevant in most cases. The relevance, however, varies widely. Some external arrangements may be mainly constitutional in connection with the commons, establishing the capability of the community of users to act collectively. (For example, California enabling legislation that allows the formation of groundwater basin management districts.) At the other extreme, a community of users may be entirely dependent on external decision makers for the legislation and enforcement of operational rules. In this case, external arrangements are frequently bureaucratic, characterized by some combination of central rule making and field officer discretion. Third-party arrangements may also be available externally to consider disputes between users. Courts of law fall into this category, but so do such other arrangements as a bureaucratic hearing officer or a traditional local chief in areas with a tribal history. Finally, market arrangements external to the commons may be relevant in establishing economic parameters within which management of the commons can be undertaken. If there were no market in land, for example, those who use common land for grazing or agriculture would be affected differently than if land were scarce or in great demand.

Patterns of Interaction

Given the technical and/or physical features of a commons and the decision-making arrangements available to govern it, the next question concerns behavior: what patterns of interaction characterize the behavior of users and other decision makers in relation to the common? It is assumed that the important elements of individual behavior are interdependent (Runge 1981). What matters is how individuals choose to behave in relation to one another. Patterns of interaction derive from mutual choice of strategies; that is, each individual's choice of strategy (how to relate to others) depends upon individual expectations of others' behavior.

Choices are generally viewed in terms of a comparison of costs and benefits. These economic concepts, however, are very abstract. Behaviorally, a cost can be treated as any perceived obstacle to the choice of some alternative (Buchanan 1969). Conversely, a benefit is any perceived inducement to choose one alternative over another. Individual choices thus derive from a mental image of obstacles and inducements in one's environment. Patterns of interaction cannot be understood except in terms of these elements of choice.

The basic pattern of interaction on which successful joint use of the commons depends is reciprocity. In a pattern of reciprocity, individuals contribute (through mutual action or mutual forbearance) to each other's welfare, but without the interposition of an immediate quid pro quo. Instead, reciprocity depends on mutual expectations of positive performance (Oakerson 1983). Note that a pattern of reciprocity differs from exchange (Boulding 1972). Exchange is a fully contingent relationship with each transaction; but reciprocity is contingent only through time, as individuals learn what to expect from one another. What is ordinarily called "collective action" can be understood as the reciprocal interaction of individuals.

The abandonment of reciprocity is reflected in the development of free rider strategies. Free riding is the opposite of reciprocity: one fails to contribute with the expectation that others will contribute. The prospect of "riding free" on the contributions of others can be a considerable inducement; but an even more powerful obstacle to the choice of cooperative strategies may be the expectation that others will choose free rider strategies. Decision-making arrangements attempt to avoid inducements and obstacles to choice that lead persons to abandon a pattern of reciprocity.

Although cooperation and noncooperation among users are the primary strategies of interest, there are also important secondary strategies (which in turn affect the choice of primary strategies). Within the community of users, the degree to which individuals attempt to monitor one another's behavior and to hold one another accountable to common standards of behavior is a relevant variable. If decision-making arrangements provide for the enforcement of rules and application of sanctions, then the choice of enforcement strategies by officials may be critical (other decision makers, from bureaucrats to judges, may also play a role). In general, any assignment of a decision-making capability simply sets parameters within which individuals choose strategies.

If reciprocity among users is fully abandoned, what follows is some pattern of mutually destructive competition and/or conflict. Users may try to drive one another out to preclude mutually subtractive use. Or they may engage in a competitive race to exploit the commons without regard to an optimal rate of use. Relevant patterns of interaction may include concealment, deceit, intimidation, threats, and violence.

Outcomes

Patterns of interaction produce outcomes. To supply information for this fourth component of the model, the analyst is required to (1) stipulate the use of evaluative criteria and (2) search for consequences that affect users and decision makers (and others involved) in accordance with these criteria. The study of consequences is necessarily value laden. One cannot even distinguish relevant consequences without first having in mind evaluative criteria. The most commonly used criteria are efficiency and equity. The analyst, however, must somehow convert these abstractions into operational measures of social value that can be used to appraise specific outcomes.

Efficiency

Considerations of efficiency in the use of commons generally relate to the overall rate of use. Technical and physical attributes dictate some optimal rate. Excessive use leads to resource depletion or facility degradation. Inefficiency is also present if the resource or facility

is underutilized: closed commons can create as much
inefficiency as open commons. If it would be feasible to
develop a rule structure to sustain joint use with greater
openness, then excluding potential users is inefficient.
A plan of regulation should be evaluated in terms of the
value of uses foregone in addition to the value of uses
retained.

To conclude that there is inefficiency in the use of
common property, one should be able to use the test of
Pareto optimality: if at least one person could be made
better off, and no one worse off, by a modification in the
use of the commons, then present outcomes are inefficient;
conversely, the proposed change is efficient. The emphasis
here is on identifying Pareto-efficient changes, that is,
improvements in efficiency, rather than on the identification of a Pareto-optimum condition from which no further
improvement is possible. Information requirements are
reduced by seeking amelioration rather than optimization
per se.

Equity

Considerations of equity are, somewhat surprisingly,
closely related to efficiency concerns. The basic question
of equity is this: do individuals get a reasonable and
fair return on their contribution to a collective undertaking to regulate a commons? Inefficiency and inequity
are apt to be mixed together in common property problems.
Indeed the presence of inequities may lead to the collapse
of collective efforts, resulting in inefficiency. Equity
problems are exacerbated by asymmetries among users, which
create opportunities for some to benefit at others'
expense. This, in turn, can lead to costly conflict where
all parties lose. Such situations may still admit of
Pareto-efficient change. In any event, Pareto-efficient
changes satisfy a minimal standard of fairness: they do
no harm.

Other questions that arise from considerations of
equity include the possibility of arbitrary exclusion from
the common or selective enforcement of rules. Abuse of
authority and/or corruption may contribute to a pattern of
inequity.

RELATIONSHIPS IN THE MODEL

The first two components of the model can be thought of broadly as independent or exogenous variables in the short term. The third and fourth components are endogenous, the third intervening. The basic relationships are depicted in Figure 1 below:

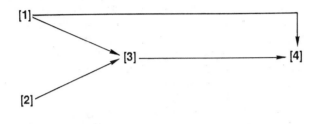

[1] **Technical/Physical Attributes**
[2] **Decision–Making Arrangements**
[3] **Patterns of Interaction**
[4] **Outcomes or Consequences**

FIGURE 1   Relationships among independent variables.

Individuals choose strategies in [3]. These choices reflect the combined set of constraints and opportunities found in [1] and [2]. The mutual choice of strategies comprises some pattern of social interaction. From interactions, consequences [4] follow, subject to evaluation.

The technical and physical characteristics of common property [1] affect outcomes [4] both through the mutual choice of strategies by relevant decision makers and independent of human choice. The constraints found in [1] are "hard" constraints. If ignored in the process of choice, constraints in [1] still affect outcomes in [4]. Decision-making arrangements in [2], on the other hand, have no effect on outcomes [4] independent of human choice and interaction [3]. Institutional constraints are "soft" constraints, made operative only through human knowledge, choice, and action. Rules found in [2] exist entirely in the realm of language, whether written or unwritten. Decision-making arrangements, therefore, need to be comprehended as commonly understood and applied by the relevant community of decision makers.

A good example of the way in which the physical nature of a resource affects individual strategies and social interaction is found in the case of Maine inshore lobster fisheries (Wilson 1977). Unlike schooling fish, the sedentary lobster inhabits small inshore areas. Thus, the fishing area is easily accessible and can be monitored daily by the community of lobstermen. Lobster traps are marked by each lobsterman in distinctive colors, so small communities of lobstermen can define and monitor exclusive fishing areas. Lobstermen from outside the community may lose their gear, but within the community mutual forbearance allows "locals" to leave their gear. This pattern of interaction allows the community to control access to the commons. Decision-making arrangements within the community are entirely voluntary. Those outside the community have no effective recourse to gain access. The physical nature of the resource sets the relatively small set of boundaries that defines each inshore area and makes it possible to exclude individual fishermen. Jointness is feasible so long as fishermen are willing to act with mutual forbearance.

Coal-haul roads in east Kentucky (Oakerson 1981) afford an example of how the distribution of decision-making capabilities [2] can affect the mutual choice of strategies [3]. Rural highway development, provision, and maintenance is largely a state government responsibility in Kentucky; but the application of criminal sanctions against violators of state-prescribed legal weight limits is in the hands of locally elected judges. Through the office of the county judge, local communities are able to maintain a free rider strategy in behalf of the coal industry. State efforts to respond with a strategy of withholding maintenance from coal-field highways proved politically infeasible because ordinary users were affected jointly with coal haulers. State highway officials nevertheless can and do reduce the maintenance efforts on selected coal-haul routes. The outcome is a highway system subject to severe overuse and inadequate maintenance.

Each component of the model separately summarizes some portion of a problem. When an outcome [4] is evaluated negatively, one should then work backward through the model to determine relationships. How do adverse consequences [4] flow from the prevailing patterns of interactions [3]? What strategies are inherent in those patterns? What structure of obstacles and inducements contributes to those choices? How does the structure of obstacles and inducements derive from elements of decision-making arrangements

[2] and the technical and physical attributes [1] of the commons?

Consequences disclose the effect [4] of a difficulty. The difficulty is manifest behaviorally in patterns of interaction [3]. The source of the difficulty, however, lies in some lack of symmetry or congruence between [1] and [2]--a mismatch between the technical and physical nature of a commons and the decision-making arrangements used to govern its use. The lack of a good "fit" between these two components of the model sets up a perverse structure of obstacles and inducements leading individuals into counterproductive patterns of interaction [3].

Incongruence between [1] and [2] is first apparent in the relationship between operational rules and corresponding technical and physical attributes of a commons. Partitioning rules should closely match underlying conditions of jointness; entry and exit rules must be related to conditions of exclusion (excludability); and boundary rules ought to reflect those boundary conditions inherent in the nature of common property. If efforts to adapt operational rules to technical and physical attributes have failed, and there is a general understanding in the relevant community of the relationships between attributes of the commons and specific operational rules, one can conclude that there is some problem with the organizational conditions of collective choice. Further, if efforts to adjust the conditions of collective choice in the community have failed, the difficulty may lie with external arrangements. At some point, an analyst may choose to arbitrarily close off the analysis, accepting some larger set of decision-making arrangements as given, and inquire into means of improvement within the established order.

Having diagnosed problem conditions by working backward through the model, one can turn to questions of design: how to rearrange decision making by adjusting rules to better fit the nature of a commons. Design requires that one work prospectively forward through the model. What do key features of the technical and physical component [1] require of operational rules and conditions of collective choice? What adjustments might be made in external decision-making arrangements? How would these changes in [2] affect the structure of obstacles and inducements to choice that face decision makers? What choice of strategies, and resultant patterns of interaction [3], would the analyst predict? How would predicted patterns of interaction affect users of the commons and others [4]? Rule changes produce different outcomes only to the extent that individual choices of strategy are modified.

A DYNAMIC MODEL

Often there are opportunities to study specific problem situations over a considerable period of time and thereby observe various efforts to resolve a difficulty. Each change in decision-making arrangements can be associated with changes in patterns of interaction and outcomes. Over time, changes can also occur in the technical and physical nature of a commons. In the short-run analysis, undertaken for a diagnostic purpose, both the nature of the commons [1] and decision-making arrangements [2] are assumed to be unchanging. A long-run analysis, however, must allow for change in both sets of variables. The model is modified by adding a set of long-term relationships, shown by the broken lines in Figure 2 below:

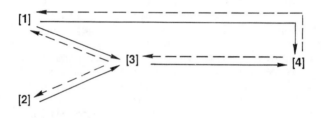

[1] **Technical/Physical Attributes**
[2] **Decision–Making Arrangements**
[3] **Patterns of Interaction**
[4] **Outcomes or Consequences**

FIGURE 2 Long-term relationships among independent variables.

One way to introduce a longer time horizon into the analysis is to apply the simpler (solid line) model iteratively. As changes occur in [1] and [2], changes in [3] and [4] are observed. This approach treats institutional change as exogenous to the model; the aim is simply to understand how changes in decision-making arrangements affect patterns of interaction and outcomes. Viewing change as exogenous, however, contributes nothing to an understanding of how change comes about.

The more complex model (with broken lines) introduces a set of relationships that are pertinent to understanding institutional change. Outcomes can affect patterns of interaction insofar as a process of learning occurs, causing individuals to modify their strategies. Instead of continuing to produce outcomes on the basis of decision-making arrangements as given, individuals may attempt to modify those arrangements to produce better outcomes. Similarly, individuals may invest in technological innovation that would change the technical and physical attributes of the commons. The latter may also be subject to change over time as an indirect result of strategies pursued in securing outcomes; this is easily seen if prevailing patterns of interaction result eventually in the destruction of a resource.

The effort to understand institutional change raises new issues. What opportunities are present for learning the consequences of one's action? How do existing decision-making arrangements constrain the individual's ability to make incremental adjustments in those same decision-making arrangements? This question touches upon the community's ability to make effective constitutional choices to modify perverse patterns of interaction. Moreover, what incentives promote investment in technological change?

CONCLUSION

The purpose of the model presented here is to aid in the collection and assimilation of case-by-case analysis. The ability to observe regularities across many different cases depends upon the use of a common framework for analysis. Some method is needed to array information into meaningful sets in order to examine relevant relationships in a particular case. Use of a common method by a community of scholars enhances the comparability of separate case studies. As scholars use and apply a model, and exchange ideas, the model, too, becomes the subject of change--elaboration or modification--in view of experience. The model developed here is therefore offered simply as a point of departure in a joint effort of scholarship and research.

REFERENCES

Boulding, K. E. 1972. The household as Achilles' heel.
    Journal of Consumer Affairs 6:111-119.

Buchanan, J. M. 1969. Cost and Choice. Chicago: Markham.

Crecine, J. P., ed. 1981. Research in Public Policy
    Analysis and Management. Greenwich, Connecticut: JAI
    Press.

Hardin, G. 1968. The tragedy of the commons. Science 162:
    1243-1248.

Hardin, G. and J. Baden, eds. 1977. Managing the Commons.
    San Francisco: W. H. Freeman.

Musgrave, R. A. 1959. The Theory of Public Finance: A
    Study in Public Economy. New York: McGraw-Hill.

Oakerson, R. J. 1981. Erosion of public goods: the case
    of coal-haul roads in eastern Kentucky. In Crecine
    1981: Vol. 2:73-102.

Oakerson, R. J. 1983. Reciprocity: The political nexus.
    Unpublished manuscript.

Ostrom, E. n.d. Strategy and the structure of decision-
    making mechanisms. Unpublished paper.

Ostrom, V. 1974. The Intellectual Crisis in American
    Public Administration. Rev. ed. University, Alabama:
    University of Alabama Press.

Ostrom, V. and E. Ostrom. 1978. Public goods and public
    choices. In Savas 1978:7-49.

Runge, C. F. 1981. Common property externalities:
    isolation, assurance, and resource depletion in a
    traditional grazing context. American Journal of
    Agricultural Economics 63:595-606.

Samuelson, P. A. 1954. The pure theory of public
    expenditure. Review of Economics and Statistics
    36:387-389.

Savas, E. S., ed. 1978. Alternatives for Delivering Public
    Services. Boulder, Colorado: Westview Press.

Wilson, J. A. 1977. A test of the tragedy of the commons.
    In Hardin and Baden 1977:96-111.

BIBLIOGRAPHY

Olson, M. 1965.   The Logic of Collective Action.
    Cambridge, Massachusetts: Harvard University Press.

4

Common Property and Collective Action in Economic Development

C. Ford Runge

INTRODUCTION

In much of the developing world, common property provides a complex system of norms and conventions to regulate individual rights to use a variety of natural resources, including forests, range, and water. These arrangements closely resemble those that dominated the early stages of European economic development, where institutional rules specifying joint use by a village or other well-defined group prevailed as a form of resource management for at least a thousand years. With the forced enclosure movements of the fifteenth and sixteenth centuries, the common property typical of early Western Europe declined, although it did not disappear. Many localities maintain complex arrangements of joint tenancy. Common property institutions continue to be observed, for example, on Swiss grazing lands and elsewhere in Europe (Netting 1978; Rhodes and Thompson 1975).

The European experience with enclosure provides a rich background for this study. The immediate purpose of the study, however, is to explore contemporary problems of common property resource management in developing countries. Although common property has proved a stable form of resource management in some traditional societies, the combination of population growth, technological change, climate, and political forces have destabilized many exist-

ing property institutions.[1] A fundamental issue in much
of the developing world is the degree to which resource
mismanagement has actually been caused by common property
arrangements. In the Sahel and southern Africa, for example, serious misuse of resources has been alleged to be the
direct result of traditional common property institutions
(see Hitchcock 1981; Picardi and Seifert 1976; Glantz
1977). In response, Western economic consultants and
planners have called for the imposition of private property
rights (Johnson 1972; Picardi 1974).

Similarly motivated private property schemes have been
attempted throughout the developing world. Many, perhaps
most, have failed to stop overuse, and in many cases may
have contributed to even more rapid degradation of
resources and to increased inequality in already unequal
distributions of wealth. Not unlike the European experience with enclosure, lands formerly held in common are
often transferred to individuals (such as high-ranking
government bureaucrats) who can exercise influence in the
allocation of use rights. These individuals have then
failed to manage these resources effectively.

Despite this record, such policies are often supported
by those who argue on theoretical grounds that individual
incentives inevitably lead common property to be mismanaged. Modern economists often refer to this as the
"free rider" problem. When applied to resource management,
the free rider problem leads to the conclusion that common
property is not a viable institutional alternative.

This paper presents an alternative perspective. It
describes a number of reasons why common property may be as
viable as private property on grounds of both efficiency
and equity. Rather than representing an atavistic arrangement of rights that inevitably results in inefficient
resource use, common property institutions may actually
contain much that is valuable, and new institutional
arrangements with common property characteristics may also
be worthwhile. In many cases, these institutions may play
a key role in the effective management of scarce natural
resources, complementing and combining with private rights.
What follows is thus neither an attack on private property
nor a wholesale endorsement of common property. It is an
argument in favor of institutions that are well-adapted to
the particular resource constraints facing villages and
groups in developing countries. In this sense, it stems
from the work on institutional constraints and innovation
developed by Hayami and Ruttan (1985).

As an institution, common property is to be dis-

tinguished from free and open access, where there are no
rules regulating individual use rights (Ciriacy-Wantrup and
Bishop 1975). Often, what appears to the outside observer
to be open access may involve tacit cooperation by individual users according to a complex set of rules specifying
rights of joint use. This is common property. Empirically, it is crucial to distinguish between open access and
common property if appropriate policy is to be formulated.
Problems of open access arise from unrestricted entry,
whereas problems of common property result from tensions
in the structure of joint use rights adopted by a particular village or group. These tensions may arise from a
variety of complex causes, including population pressure,
changes in technology, climate, or political forces. The
thesis of this article is that too often these causes have
been confused, and the problem ascribed simply to the
"tragedy of the commons" (Hardin 1968), in which the misuse
of resources is attributed to the institution of common
property itself. The problems with this view, and an
alternative competing hypothesis, are investigated below.

[handwritten margin note: Are common property arrangement inherently subject to destabilization]

COMMON PROPERTY AND THE VILLAGE ECONOMY

To appreciate the traditional role of common property
resource management, three stylized characteristics of village life in less developed economies must be understood.
The first, which follows almost from the definition "less
developed," is relative poverty. Evidence of low incomes
and levels of living are obvious enough conditions of poverty. What is less obvious is that this poverty, by imposing
a strict budget constraint, also eliminates myriad opportunities for many villagers acting alone and many villages
acting collectively. These limitations can make a joint
use rights a necessity, not simply a virtuous bit of cooperation. In particular, the transactions costs of well-
defined and enforced private property typical of the West
may simply be too great for a subsistence economy to bear.
Consider the capacity for enforceable claims of private
property, crucial to the flexibility and acceptance of such
a system. Private rights--individual rights to exclude
others--must be based on clear definition and assignment
in connection with the thing owned, together with a mechanism to adjudicate disputes when they arise. The more
things for which exclusive rights are assigned and defined,
the greater must be the social investment in assignment,
definition, and adjudication. If common property--the

individual right to joint use--is the norm, comparatively fewer claims must be assigned and defined. Less clarity in the assignment of rights (at least by Western standards) may also result. However, this is balanced against reduced social costs of assignment and definition. Naturally, some enforcement and adjudication of even these claims is necessary.

In developed economies of the West, the substantial social overhead necessary for a system of private rights is often hidden from view, except when one faces court costs or becomes directly involved in titling or litigation. Even then, the social overhead required by assigned, defined, and transferable private property rights, and the capacity to support this superstructure through legal fees and taxes, often goes unrecognized. This capacity is difficult to maintain without an expensive support structure capable of effectively recording, administering, and adjudicating local disputes over these claims.

In a poor, developing economy, a malfunctioning approximation to a Western bureaucratic system would likely be based on incipient titles promulgated by a centralized authority that is only dimly aware of local conditions. Such a situation may be worse than continued dependence on local level common property rules. The fair enforcement of formalized private rights and duties may be prohibitively costly compared with customary arrangements. These customary arrangements may involve some private rights that are enforced locally, as well as common rights and a wide variety of "mixed" arrangements. To suppose that these results of poverty are in fact its cause is a heroic claim, although one that has been made in studies of privatization (North and Thomas 1977).

A second characteristic of life in a village economy is that it is critically dependent on a local agricultural and natural resource base. That a majority of the work force moves away from direct dependence on this base is indeed a mark of development; as this happens, higher value-added goods are produced with inputs from points removed from the local economy, and become the primary outputs of the society (see Johnston and Mellor 1961). Because the distribution of basic natural resources such as soil or water (including rainfall) is often quite random over both time and space, the assignment of exclusive use rights to a given land area can yield an inherently unfair distribution of resources, as compared to the more equitable results of assigning joint rights of access to these resources. Such distributions may tend to become further

skewed as individuals with an advantageous initial endowment acquire more resources over time. Such increasing
inequality may have dynamic destabilizing effects that are
ultimately very costly to efficient local resource use.

A third characteristic of life in a developing economy
is a consequence of the first two. Poverty, together with
a dependence on low value-added outputs and relatively
randomly distributed natural resources, results in a high
degree of uncertainty with respect to income streams.
Poverty eliminates the cushion against adversity represented by accumulated wealth. The random element in
natural resource allocation introduces additional uncertainty for those whose income depends on the rain's falling
or the hunt's succeeding. In contrast, much more of the
randomness of nature is under control in a developed
economy, whether due to irrigated crop production, feedlot
livestock operations, or a highly developed food distribution chain, which allows local risks to be shared and
hence reduces uncertainty.

In the face of the uncertainty characteristic of life
in a developing economy, no individual can be assured that
he or she will be spared failure. Given the intimate connection between basic resources and subsistence, unpredictable events such as floods or drought may bring disease
or death. In the face of this environmental uncertainty,
common property institutions may be created; rather than
emphasizing the right to exclude some, these institutions
provide instead for the right of many to be equally included as a hedge against uncertainty. The expectation is that
when one is in need, aid will be forthcoming from others in
return for a like commitment; this may indeed be more
agreeable than "going it alone" in the face of nature.[2]
This "insurance" against environmental uncertainties
complements the relative efficiency of common property,
especially in pastoral situations where rainfall,
rather than land, is a scarce resource.

Poverty, natural resource dependency, and resulting
uncertainties thus create an incentive structure that may
make common property a comparatively rational solution to
certain problems of resource management. In what follows,
I will call this a solution to the "assurance problem," one
in a class of coordination problems in which individuals
organize their behavior by reference to a particular rule
or norm. Sometimes, this rule may be based on joint use.
Before developing the argument for common property institutions along these lines, however, it is necessary to
examine current approaches to common property institutions

and their limitations. While capturing certain truths in the history of resource management, much current literature leads to the false conclusion that common property is universally mismanaged. This conclusion is not always valid, suggesting the need for a more complete explanation of incentives and choices in resource management.

THE FREE RIDER PROBLEM

The free rider problem results when an individual shirks responsibility to the community or group. It is often argued that the incentive for this behavior is logical from the point of view of narrow self-interest. Such narrow logic leads to an outcome in which the group as a whole is made worse off. An often-cited parable used to illustrate this behavior is the "tragedy of the commons," in which the private benefit of grazing an additional head of cattle on a common range exceeds the private cost, because the costs of maintaining range quality can be shifted to the group as a whole (Hardin 1968). The "tragedy" of overgrazing results from each person's incentive to free ride regardless of the expected actions of others. Even if an agreement is struck that specifies that all will refrain from further grazing, the strict dominance of free rider strategy makes such a contract unstable.

Some argue that the proper solution for overgrazing a common range is therefore to "internalize" its costs by making the public aspects of the range private. Instituting a scheme of such rights, if they are properly enforced, is argued to be a necessary (though not a sufficient) condition for creating a market for private grazing rights. This approach has led a number of economists to argue that the mere existence of common property rights over a scarce resource will lead to a tragedy of the commons (Demsetz 1967; Cheung 1970; Furubotn and Pejovich 1972; North and Thomas 1977).

As noted above, this position ignores considerable historical and empirical evidence to the contrary and is due in part to a lack of familiarity with common property in practice, and the associated failure to distinguish problems of free and open access from those of common property.[3] However, the fundamental problem is that free rider behavior is assumed to be a dominant motive, against which the group is defenseless.[4]

This motive is often described by reference to the "prisoner's dilemma," a simple game in which collective

decisions produce outcomes harmful to the group as a whole
without intervention by some higher authority. The
two-person prisoner's dilemma is illustrated in the
following gain-loss table.

Cooperate or defect represent the choices (or strategies) open to each of two prisoners. The ordered pairs
indicate the payoffs that will result from a particular
coincidence of choices by each person; the first number

TABLE 1 The Prisoner's Dilemma.

First Person	Second Person	
	Cooperate	Defect
Cooperate	(1, 1)	(-2, 2)
Defect	(2, -2)	(-1, -1)

represents the payoff to the first person, the second number for the second person. Imagine that the prisoners are
interrogated separately. Both know that if they cooperate
with each other and neither confesses, they will receive
suspended sentences (1, 1); if one defects and turns
state's evidence, he will be paid and released, and the
other will receive a heavy prison term (2, -2) (-2, 2).
If both defect, each gets a prison sentence (-1, -1).
Assuming mutually disinterested motivation, the course of
action represented by the pair (1, 1) is not an equilibrium. To protect himself, if not to further his own
interests, each has a sufficient reason to defect, whatever
the other does. "Rational" decisions by each prisoner
individually make both worse off. Even if communication
between the individuals results in an agreement to cooperate, both have an incentive to break it. Therefore, the
noncooperative pair, (-1, -1) is an inferior Nash equilibrium.

Now imagine a village of n individuals who must graze
cattle on a common range of fixed size. Each individual
must choose to do one of two things. One is "stinting,"
or cooperative grazing on the commons. The second is
grazing at a level that, while advantageous to the
individual, ultimately results in exploitative overuse of
the commons. This defection strategy is the free rider
option. The cost of grazing to each individual is a function of the grazing decisions of all n individuals. If all

cooperate, then the common range is preserved and cattle remain healthy. But if the prisoner's dilemma logic accurately portrays the incentives of the village, no one will have an incentive to cooperate and all will defect, leading to overgrazing.

This analysis of overgrazing may be generalized as a "binary choice with externalities," of which the multiperson prisoner's dilemma (MPD) is one example (Schelling 1973; Runge 1985). The decision whether to cooperate with others in observing a stinting rule, or to defect, is binary when the choice is between cooperation and defection (C and D) and it has external effects when it alters consumption of the resource by other agents. (In trivial cases, the resource is so abundant that no negative external consumption effect occurs.) If agents derive payoffs from cooperation or defection based on the number of other agents who also choose either C or D, then among $n + 1$ individuals there are $2n$ possible configurations of choice, depending on how many choose C or D. The decisions of all agents result in a particular physical product of the resource (for example, "total forage availability") from which each agent derives positive utility.

I will first consider this binary choice in terms of a uniform MPD, then extend the analysis to include multiple equilibria and the absence of dominant strategies, which I have argued elsewhere may better approximate actual common property resource decisions (Runge 1981, 1984a). This approach provides a theoretical basis for empirical testing of complex incentive structures in various resource regimes.

THE MULTIPERSON PRISONER'S DILEMMA (MPD)

The MPD is characterized by n agents, each with the same binary choice and the same payoffs. As noted above, each agent has a dominant choice, whatever others do, which is dominant for all n agents. Each also has a dominant preference for the other's choices. These preferences go in opposite directions: each prefers that all others cooperate while he himself defects; so defection strictly dominates cooperation, leading to a unique, Pareto-inferior Nash equilibrium. However, there is some number, $k > 1$, such that if k individuals cooperate and the rest defect, those who cooperate are still better off than if they had all defected. If we explicitly assume the uniformity of agents, k is independent of the particular agents who cooperate or defect, eliminating the possibility (at this level of analysis) of "leadership." Below, this assumption will be relaxed. For now, the number k represents the minimum coalition that can make positive gains by cooperating with the rule even though others do not. Where k = n, no one gains from cooperation unless cooperation is universal and there are no free riders (a coalition of the whole). Where k < n, some free riders (n - k) can be tolerated while the k cooperators gain, although the n - k free riders benefit more than do the cooperators.

Consider Figure 1(a), in which two linear payoff curves are drawn for a village population of n + 1, reflecting the benefits of cooperation and defection in an interdependent decision framework to the (n + 1)th agent, where n equals the number of other resource users. The upper curve corresponds to the dominant choice of defection, D. Its left end is labeled O, the open access equilibrium, in which no agents cooperate and rents are driven to zero. The D curve rises monotonically to the right. Below it is the dominated cooperation strategy C, which also begins at the open access equilibrium O, rises monotonically and crosses the axis at point k where positive gains to cooperation begin. The number choosing to cooperate with the proposed rule in Figure 1 is denoted by the distance along the horizontal axis.

The vertical axis of Figure 1 shows the payoff to cooperation by agent (n + 1) when a certain number of others choose to cooperate and the remainder defect. At k = n/2 in Figure 1(a), for example, positive gains are made by cooperators whenever at least half of the other agents cooperate by stinting. Because D lies everywhere above C, it is a strictly dominant strategy. Monotonicity of both curves in the same direction implies that cooperation leads to uniformly positive externalities, and defection to uniformly negative externalities. The C curve is higher on the right than the D curve on the left, reflecting the Pareto-inefficiency of the dominant defection strategy. The dotted lines show total (or average) values corresponding to the number of agents choosing the two strategies, and point m represents the maximum collective payoff for the group. The slope of these schedules may be interpreted as the marginal payoff to defection and cooperation.

In Figure 1(a), D rises more rapidly than does C, indicating that the more agents who join the cooperative coalition, the greater is the advantage of defecting. The collective maximum at point m is achieved with some agents choosing D and some C. Point m falls to the right of k on the horizontal axis. This implies that collective gains are greater when there are more than k cooperators, and that these gains reach a maximum at point m, and diminish thereafter.

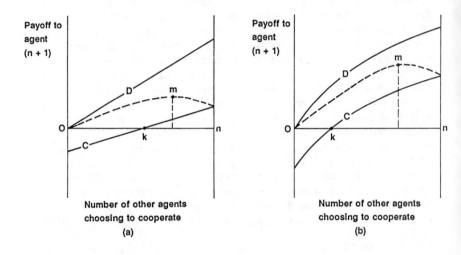

FIGURE 1 Relationships between benefits and cooperation.

In Figure 1(b), the slopes of the C and D functions reflect an alternative incentive structure: the proposed rule achieves most of its benefits after about half of the population participates, after which benefits grow at a decreasing rate and ultimately decline after reaching a maximum of m. The collective maximum occurs at about two-thirds participation, with room for gains to cooperators from point k to point m along the horizontal axis. Cases 1(a) and 1(b) represent two of an infinite number of possible variations on the MPD theme, a distinguishing feature of which is that defection strictly dominates, making some form of coercion necessary to solve the problem of collective action. Restrictive rules and the level of coercion accompanying them alter the payoffs of the C and D schedules, and thus their level and shape.

In the MPD model of common property, each individual

has an incentive to free ride and graze heavily in the
near-term, thereby overexploiting the range. Each believes
that he will receive a higher payoff from defecting rather
than from cooperating. The incentive structure is such
that it does not matter which strategy the others choose.
Therefore, defecting or free riding strictly dominates
cooperative stinting for each individual. Hardin, in his
original article on the tragedy of the commons, wrote:

> The rational herdsman concludes that the only sensible
> course for him to pursue is to add another animal to
> his herd. And another.... But this is the conclusion
> reached by each and every rational herdsman sharing the
> commons. Therein is the tragedy. Each man is locked
> into a system that compels him to increase his herd
> without limit--in a world which is limited. (Hardin
> 1968:1244).

The main features of this view of common property are:

o   Inferior outcome. Each individual will choose
     "rationally" to defect and graze at an exploitative
     level, leading to a situation in which all are made
     worse off. All are led toward this noncooperative
     equilibrium.

o   Strict dominance of individual free rider strategy.
     The result of overgrazing arises independent of
     the expectations of each individual regarding the
     actions of others. Because the choices of each
     are unaffected by the choices of the others,
     defecting is a dominant strategy, and uncertainty
     with respect to the behavior of others does not
     pose a problem.

o   Need for enforcement. Even if an agreement is
     struck that specifies that all will stint on the
     range, the strict dominance of individual strategy
     makes such cooperation unstable. Without compul-
     sory enforcement imposed by an outside authority,
     any such agreement is unstable because each prefers
     that the others stint while he or she defects and
     grazes exploitatively (Sen 1967).

In the MPD framework, individuals may attempt to
develop cooperative common property rules to enforce
stinting, but they cannot resolve their problem because no

one has an incentive to keep such agreements. As a result, an enforceable rule must be imposed from outside. In this sense, property institutions are viewed as exogenous. Private property rights are argued to be consistent with this formulation because they can be imposed from outside, as were systems of enclosure. Because this approach starts from the presupposition that individuals pursue strategies regardless of the expected actions of others, the appropriate decision unit is the private individual user. A somewhat contradictory result, especially when the argument is used to support privatization, is that the strict dominance of individual free rider strategy is argued to be accompanied by rational individuals who will husband and conserve their own private range area at a rate more consistent with the preferences of society as a whole. If this formulation is correct, then only by imposing private property rules from outside can the group optimize its grazing. Any other alternatives are unstable because of the strict dominance of defecting behavior.

Three key difficulties with this model render it unreasonable on empirical grounds. First, its assumption of dominant free rider behavior leaves no place for cooperative rules unless they are imposed and enforced from outside. Second, the dominant strategy mechanism, by ruling out the importance of changing expectations of others' behavior, fails to capture the interdependence of decisions in a village economy. Third, by sidestepping the importance of mutual expectations in the formulation of individual strategy, it fails to deal explicitly with the problem of uncertainty regarding the actions of others (Runge 1981).

These objections raise questions over this theoretical approach, which is founded on the restrictive view that free riding is a dominant strategy, that private property is uniquely suited to optimal resource allocation, and that common property rules cannot be solutions to problems of resource use in developing economies. By restricting our view of the institutional opportunity set, it fails to consider a variety of institutional alternatives.

THE ASSURANCE PROBLEM AND COMMON PROPERTY

The view of common property outlined above, with its underlying premise of dominant free rider behavior, has been widely used to explain overgrazing, deforestation and other abuses of natural resources. What is striking is the extent to which resulting policies of privatization have

been driven by the unproven premise that free rider
behavior dominates and the accompanying view that the
expected behavior of others is irrelevant to this choice.
Where there are no dominant strategies, a variety of alternative outcomes are possible, depending on the structure
of mutual expectation and resulting patterns of strategic
choice. This situation seems to fit most closely with
empirical studies of common property. Several authors have
argued that it may fit public goods and collective choice
situations in general (Kimber 1981; Wagner 1983; Runge
1984a).

The very nature of village-level decisions makes
dominant free riding implausible. Such decision making
involves interdependent choices in which the benefits and
costs of resource use are not only a function of the total
actions of the group, but in which decisions to use (or
overuse) resources will be affected by the expected
decisions of others. If the use of common resources is
conditional on these expectations, this interdependence
places a premium on mechanisms that coordinate community
decisions. The key observation that bears emphasis is that
such mechanisms tend to arise from several different rules,
customs or conventions, of which private exclusive property
is only one example.

Consider the more complex and arguably more realistic
case in which neither C nor D represents a strictly dominant strategy. Figure 2 shows a situation in which a linear D curve dominates a linear curve C until point y, after
which C dominates D. The absence of a dominant strategy
raises the problem of coordinating the expectations of a
"critical mass" of agents around a particular rule change.
In Figure 2, there are two equilibria: one at O and one at
z. The problem of coordination is to achieve the
Pareto-superior equilibrium at z. In cases such as these,
the coalition must move beyond k to the switch point y;
otherwise, defection will dominate and lead to the Pareto-
inferior equilibrium at O. Unlike the MPD, in which defection dominates at all levels of participation, implying a
continual need for outside coercion, this situation rests
on the contingent strategies of agents. If enough people
in a village are assured that others will cooperate, then
z will emerge as the equilibrium. However, if a Pareto-
inferior open-access equilibrium has become established,
no agent will decide to join a coalition subscribing to a
restrictive rule unless he expects a sufficient number of
others to do so. Achieving a Pareto-superior solution
will require an organized change in behavior leading a
critical mass to cooperate with the rule.

Achieving this level of cooperation may require some
kind of enforcement mechanism. If the situation resembles
Figure 2, however, relatively little enforcement may be
necessary to organize a change in behavior. Voluntary
cooperation with rule restrictions may even be sufficient
to organize this change. As Hayek (1948) argued, sponta-
neous recognition of the need for organized collective
action in many cases occurs on the part of the affected
group simply because the payoff to such organization is
substantial.

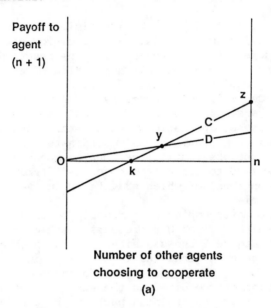

FIGURE 2 Number of agents choosing to cooperate.

In the case of a village economy, the structure of
incentives may well be of this sort, and villagers will
seek a rule coordinating the resource use of all villagers.
This search for "coordination norms," to use Schelling's
(1960) phrase, is an endogenous adaptive response to the
demand for scarce information about the likely behavior of
others. By providing the assurance that others will not
misuse common resources, common property institutions can
make it rational for the individual to respect them.
Although expectations of widespread free rider behavior may
be quite likely to provoke a corresponding response, leading to a downward spiral of overuse, the multiple possible
outcomes suggest that careful attention also be given to

institutions that promote a critical mass of resource-conserving behavior.[5] There is no reason to suppose that these do not include institutions of joint use.

This problem may be described in terms of an alternative to the MPD game, the "assurance problem" (Sen 1967), one in a class of "coordination problems" (Schelling 1960). The problem shown in Figure 2, where cooperation continues to refer to stinting together, and defection to overgrazing, leads to an ordering of alternatives in which a villager (n + 1) benefits most when everyone stints, but also benefits when a critical mass cooperates with a stinting rule, even though everyone does not. It is precisely the role of village-level conventions, including common property institutions, to reinforce expectations of collective behavior leading a critical mass of individuals to adopt such a solution as a cooperative strategy (see Hardin, R. 1982). If they function optimally, common property institutions can lead to equilibrium outcomes in which each individual is assured that a critical mass of others will cooperate, so that they will have an incentive to do so too. This is in marked contrast to the MPD, in which no one would contribute even if everyone else did. Of course, common property institutions do not always provide this assurance. The approach developed here, like other more formal approaches, emphasizes that the village can get locked into an equilibrium in which the range is over-exploited, because a requisite level of assurance is not achieved.[6] The model says that the free rider problem can be solved--not that it will be solved.

When elaborated to describe problems of resource management, this model provides an intuitively appealing way of looking at common property as a solution to coordination problems. First, coordinated strategies can evolve inside the structure of the game, rather than always being imposed from without. In this sense, such strategies model innovative, endogenous property rules initiated by a village or group. By providing security of expectation, property institutions are responses to the uncertainty of social and economic interaction (see Schotter 1981; Johnson and Libecap 1982). Second, the model places central emphasis on the interdependence associated with group decision making, and the multiple outcomes possible when agents are engaged in a search for rules of coordination when there are no dominant strategies. It allows for either cooperation or free riding, rather than saying that free riding will dominate. Third, it emphasizes the key obstacle of uncertainty, emphasizing the fact that opportunity costs must be paid to develop support for new rules or norms of coordination.

Approaching common property in this way provides some interesting perspectives in both analytical and policy terms. In contrast to the results of the MPD, the strict dominance of the free rider strategy no longer holds. Rather, expectations of others' choices must be entered as a formal part of the determination of one's own choice. No individual can decide on a preferred strategy until it is known whether a sufficiently large group of others will cooperate. An inferior outcome is no longer inevitable; if everyone is assured that a critical mass of others will obey a common property agreement, then it is in each person's individual interest to do likewise, since this outcome is preferred.

In more complex cases faced in actual situations of resource management, the lack of a dominant strategy for each individual means that the particular outcome will depend on individual's bargaining power, the initial endowment of resources, the culture, climate, and so on. Thus, the assumption that individuals are identical and face identical constraints must be relaxed. Sugden (1984) has argued that the more homogeneous a community, the more likely are optimal outcomes; the more heterogeneous, the more difficult coordination becomes. As the heterogeneity of the group increases, and as the resource constraints facing it become more severe, common property rules (indeed, any rules) may become increasingly difficult to maintain (see Johnson and Libecap 1982). Given a heterogeneous community, however, coordination norms offer their own incentive to be kept. Naturally, some enforcement of these agreements is likely to be necessary. However, this enforcement may readily emerge from inside the group, as well as being imposed from outside it. The key element that determines the success or failure of institutions is therefore the extent to which the institutions foster coordinated expectations in relation to a particular physical and social environment (Ullman-Margalit 1977).

In this framework, it is easier to see how internal group incentives to maintain and enforce common property rights may be as strong, if not stronger, than those restricted to private exclusive use. Suppose that tradition--the result of longstanding agreement--is such that each grazer on a common range is expected to stint at an arbitrary level. The result of this property rule is to formalize the expected actions of others. If each expects all others to graze at this level, there is an incentive to do the same, since the rule extends the set of superior allocations available to the group by preserving the range. Because the communication and transactions needed to achieve common property rules are not costless, agreement on the particular rule for grazing provides a further incentive to be retained as tradition. The social overhead costs required to maintain common property rules may be substantially lower when they are already a part of the customary structure of rights and duties. In a village economy, the benefits possible from free riding in the short term may be more than offset by costs imposed on those who break the rules. Recognized interdependence makes the costs of reputation loss high, much like losing one's credit rating in a developed economy. Other, more severe sanctions may be imposed by the village on its own noncooperative members. These costs, coupled with reductions in overall free riding if such antisocial behavior sets a trend for others, plus the opportunity costs of implementing innovative rules, may well exceed the cost of continuing to observe the common property rule.[7]

Moreover, where the resource endowment of the group or village is highly randomly distributed, additional incentives may exist to adopt a rule of joint use. In the Kalahari Desert of Botswana, for example, rainfall is both scarce and highly variable. Rather than demarcating the range and hoping that rain will fall on one's own parcel, traditional common property institutions have been reinforced by the ecological imperative to move from one area to another. The relative access afforded to scarce resources under this arrangement is both more efficient and a better form of insurance against adverse individual outcomes than a system in which a few are blessed by rain while the majority face drought-like conditions (Peters 1983).

Finally, the fairness implicit in joint access may prove a highly assuring feature of common property agreements, even if the relative benefits accruing to individual members of the group on average are somewhat less than under a system of exclusive use-rights. The expropriation of common property, as Dasgupta and Heal note, "...while blessed at the altar of efficiency[,] can have disastrous distributional consequences..." (1979:77). Since these consequences may in turn give rise to instability and lead to breakdowns in efficient use, questions of equity, efficiency and assurance are closely connected in practice over time.

This does not deny that enforcement from outside may help achieve improvements in the institutions, if the costs of such enforcement are affordable. Where local level rule making has broken down, such interventions may be necessary. In many cases, local interests may request assistance in enforcing property rights, including private rights, which local authorities alone cannot guarantee. The lesson of the assurance problem is simply to let individuals have full freedom to create self-binding property rules that best serve their needs before adding enforcement mechanisms from outside. Property rules will be better suited to these needs and more likely to succeed if they are based on this premise. These rules may come in many shapes and forms, including various agreements to use resources under some type of common property arrangement.

Furthermore, enforcement of private property rights from outside the group or village is not a sufficient condition for optimal resource utilization. Not only are the costs of such "top-down" enforcement likely to be high; they also may lead to attempts to impose patterns of land use incompatible with local needs, causing lands to be brought into or taken out of production based on criteria developed at "the top" rather than the village level (see Bromley and Chapagain 1984). This may be especially true when control over land use is in the hands of those with fewer incentives for efficient and equitable local management, such as absentee owners. Any enforcement mechanism that operates from outside and above village level institutions and that is designed to coerce local action is thus likely to involve high costs and uncertain benefits.

In summary, the analysis above suggests that common property institutions may be well adapted to problems of resource management in developing economies. Its major implication is that inferior outcomes, such as overgrazing, do not necessarily arise from the strict dominance of free rider strategy (although resource misuse may still occur) but from the inability of interdependent individuals to coordinate and enforce actions in situations of strategic interdependence (see Runge 1984b). Successful responses to these situations may be made even more difficult if property institutions developed in response to conditions in the West are imposed on the village economies of the developing world.

COMMON PROPERTY MANAGEMENT

If a variety of responses to problems of resource
management are possible, the incentives leading to a particular institutional choice must result from the physical
and social environment in which this choice is made. The
arguments of the preceding sections may be brought together
with the three characteristics of village life in a less
developed economy identified above. Each suggests a reason
for the comparative institutional advantage of joint use
rights. First, low levels of income imply that formalized
private property institutions that involve high transactions and enforcement costs are often outside the village-
level budget for resource management. Even if a system of
private use rights is affordable, common property alternatives can be relatively less costly to maintain and
enforce and better adapted to local conditions. Since
common property rules are generally enforced locally,
abuses of authority, if they occur, may be less widespread
than under a centralized program of privatization.

A second reason for the survival and utility of common
property is that close dependence on natural resources
makes survival more subject to a variety of unpredictable
natural events that are likely to fall unequally in both
time and space on the local population. If this inequality
is threatening to a sufficiently large proportion of the
group, incentives may exist to guarantee access to certain
resources held in common rather than to restrict access
through exclusive use. By institutionalizing a degree of
fairness in the face of random allocation, common use
rights may contribute to social stability at the same time
that they promote efficient adaptation to changing resource
availability over time.

Common property may be an appropriate institutional
adaptation to resource management at the village level for
a third reason: the right to be included in a group provides a hedge against individual failure. This hedge will
be likely to grow in significance as the overall level of
risk to group members increases. In this sense, the combination of relatively high levels of poverty, relatively
high levels of randomness in allocation of natural resources, and resulting uncertainty in individual levels
of welfare are all mutually reinforcing explanations for
the appropriateness of common property institutions.

A more general reason for continued common property
management is that the opportunity costs associated with
changing established practices are high. Despite attempts

to break down traditional common property institutions, these rules are tenacious. As Malinowski observed:

> [W]hile it may seem easy to replace a custom here and there or transform a technical device, such a change of detail very often upsets an institution without reforming it, because...beliefs, ideas and practices are welded into bigger systems (1961:52).

The tenacity of traditional institutions cannot be explained simply as the manifestation of "backwardness" or "irrationality." A more logical explanation is that rational individuals are not inclined to relinquish institutional arrangements that have promoted survival, even if survival has not been especially comfortable. This implies that economic development efforts should involve not only attempts to break down belief in and observance of old rules, but also promote institutions that are consistent with the physical and social environment in which resource management is to occur. In some cases, this will involve the development and promotion of private, exclusive use rights. But in many cases it will involve elaborations of common or joint use. The sooner this is recognized, the sooner problems of resource management can be addressed in a fashion consistent with the incentives of village-level decision making.

THE NEED FOR EMPIRICAL RESEARCH

The abstract observations made in the previous sections require examination and empirical testing in specific settings. While a number of recent analyses have pointed to the erroneous conclusions of the "tragedy of the commons," only a few well-documented studies of modern common property management have entered the literature. These include examples reported by Gilles and Jamtgaard (1981) and by others of pasture management in Peru (see Browman 1974; Orlove 1977, 1980), African grazing and forest management (see Legesse 1973; Horowitz 1979; Thomson 1980; Hitchcock 1981; Peters 1983); Japanese forestry (McKean 1982); and the aforementioned case of Swiss grazing (Rhodes and Thompson 1975; Netting 1978).

In the historical literature, recent research on the common field systems replaced by 18th century enclosures continues to break down the conventional wisdom that enclosure was a prerequisite to the adoption of advanced agricultural methods. "Open field" farmers in fact adopted modern practices without changes in property rights (Yelling 1977). Recent empirical research by Allen (1982:950) concludes that "...the major economic conse- quence of the enclosure of open field arable in the eigh- teenth century was to redistribute the existing agricul- tural income, not to create additional income by increasing efficiency." Much more attention in research needs to be given, however, to the rich variety of contemporary re- source management strategies that result from alternative environmental conditions and constraints.

In this volume, participants in the National Research Council-sponsored Conference on Common Property Resource Management have presented the first in a series of case studies specifically designed to explore the role of common property institutions and resource management in developing countries. These studies, dealing not only with range resources but with forestry, agricultural lands, fisheries, and water, can begin a much more detailed process of investigation focused on specific common property issues. In this way, a priori theorizing can give way to empirical investigations of whether certain resources (for example, water versus forests) are more or less likely to be suc- cessfully managed as common property, private property, or some combination.

This discussion, while essentially theoretical, directs attention to the specific resource constraints faced by groups at the local level. Rather than invoking the general superiority of one type of property institution, this analysis suggests that different institutions are responses to differing local environments in which insti- tutional innovation takes place. Such innovations are likely to range along a continuum of property rights, from pure rights of exclusion to pure rights of inclusion, depending on the nature of resource management problems (Runge 1984b).

Institutional innovation, like technological innova- tion, is responsive to the relative abundance of different factors, and the resulting costs and benefits of alterna- tive strategies (Hayami and Ruttan 1985). As Randall states:

> The fact that different configurations of property
> rights have different impacts on both allocation and
> distribution illustrates the need for understanding the
> impact of specific configurations of rights. Collec-
> tive decision making procedures must select appropriate

configurations of rights, not only specifying rights
in complete and nonattenuated form but also selecting
that particular bundle of rights which will provide the
correct incentive structure to achieve the collective
goal. (1974:53-54)

The task of identifying the appropriate configuration
of rights begins with a recognition that private exclusive
property is not always comparatively advantageous in the
villages of less developed economies. The search for
appropriate institutional responses must respect both the
traditions and the constraints of local needs in specific
choice environments. There are no universal prescriptions
for efficient and equitable resource management.

NOTES

1. Useful historical perspective on current privatization
efforts in other parts of the world is offered by the
English case. Cromwell's success at rallying popular support early in the English Civil War was based in part on
the strenuous objections of commoners to the enclosure of
wetlands or "fens" that provided rich hunting and fishing
resources. The king financed groups, called "adventurers,"
to enclose and drain these open meadows, in return for
which one-quarter to one-half of the lands were granted as
private preserves. The result was to provoke riots, which
Cromwell exploited in organizing a base of opposition to
royal authority. This pattern was repeated throughout the
English enclosure movement. A similar process of land
acquisition in the North of England and in Ireland can be
seen as a partial cause of the "Irish problem" (see Darby
1940; Albright 1955; Fraser 1973:73-77). A recent comparison of the English experience with that of herders in the
Andes of South America is provided by Campbell and Godoy
(this volume).

2. This is the argument described in John Rawls' (1971)
analysis of the "original position," in which players in a
game of decision making under uncertainty must formulate
rules about the distribution of primary resources. The
result of a high level of risk aversion is that equality is
favored, together with a stipulation (the "difference
principle") that inequality must favor those who find
themselves worst off. It is also the foundation for a
variety of real world voluntary associations, including
volunteer fire departments, in which the possibility that
one agent might face disaster is mitigated by a joint contract of mutual aid. There are also numerous historical
examples from seventh to twelfth century Europe of feudal
institutional arrangements driven by what Duby (1974) terms
"les générosités nécessaires."

3. North and Thomas, for example, describe the economic
state of traditional societies as one in which "[t]he
natural resources, whether the animals to be hunted or
vegetation to be gathered, were initially held as common
property. This type of property right implies free access
by all to the resource" (1977:234).

4. The logic underlying this argument in Hardin's (1968)
"Tragedy of the Commons" parable is formally explicated by
Muhsam (1977). The errors, logical and otherwise, of the
parable are increasingly recognized by economists. Partha
Dasgupta, in a recent examination of its impact on resource
management, observes that "It would be difficult to locate
another passage of comparable length and fame containing as
many errors...." (Dasgupta 1982:13).

5. Axelrod (1984), Taylor (1976), and R. Hardin (1982)
have shown that cooperation is consistent with self-
interested behavior, even inside the MPD framework, if
repeated plays are allowed. Repeating the game opens the
door to expectations of others' behavior. The conditions
for cooperation then turn on whether the players are
sufficiently forward-looking and formulate a "tit-for-tat"
rule, motivated by expectations of others' cooperation and
fear of retaliation in the case of noncooperation. Similarly, Sugden (1982; 1984) has noted that a "principle of
reciprocity" may operate in actual situations of collective
choice. This principle does not say that one must always
contribute or cooperate, but that one must not free ride
while others are contributing. The individual villager has
obligations to the group from whose efforts he derives
benefits. The model of reciprocity that Sugden develops is
based on commitment to a rule of behavior, conditional on
the expectation that a sufficiently large group of others
also will adhere to it. This is the same concept as the
"critical mass" discussed earlier.

6. Sugden (1984) and Runge (1981) emphasize that
(a) equilibrium exists; (b) it is not unique; (c) one
equilibrium is Pareto-efficient; and (d) other equilibria
involve undersupply of the collective good.

7. Maintaining rules or norms such as common property may
generate second-order collective action problems. However,
the rewards and punishments underlying property institutions, once in place, may be less susceptible to defection
because the costs of sanction are small in relation to the

benefits of maintaining the rule. Naturally, these rules
can, and do, break down. I am grateful to a reviewer for
these observations.

REFERENCES

Albright, M. 1955. The Entrepreneurs of Fen Draining in
    England under James I and Charles I: An Illustration
    of the Uses of Influence. Explorations in
    Entrepreneurial History. Volume 8. Cambridge,
    Massachusetts: Harvard University Press.

Allen, R. C. 1982. The efficiency and distributional
    implications of 18th century enclosures. The Economic
    Journal 92:937-953.

Axelrod, R. 1984. The Evolution of Cooperation. New
    York: Basic Books.

Bromley, D. W. and D. P. Chapagain. 1984. The village
    against the center: resource depletion in South Asia.
    American Journal of Agricultural Economics 66:868-873.

Browman, D. L. 1974. Pastoral nomadism in the Andes.
    Current Anthropology 15:630-634.

Cheung, S. N. S. 1970. The structure of a contract and
    the theory of nonexclusive resource. Journal of Law
    and Economics 13:49-70.

Ciriacy-Wantrup, S. V. and R. C. Bishop. 1975. Common
    property as a concept in natural resource policy.
    Natural Resources Journal 15:713-727.

Darby, H. C. 1940. The Draining of the Fens. Cambridge:
    Cambridge University Press.

Dasgupta, P. S. 1982. The Control of Resources. Oxford:
    Basil Blackwell.

Dasgupta, P. S. and G. M. Heal. 1979. Economic Theory and
    Exhaustible Resources. Cambridge: Cambridge Univer-
    sity Press.

Demsetz, H. 1967. Toward a theory of property rights. American Economic Review 57:347-359.

Duby, G. 1974. The Early Growth of the European Economy: Warriors and Peasants from the Seventh to the Twelfth Century. Ithaca, New York: Cornell University Press.

Fraser, A. 1973. Cromwell: The Lord Protector. New York: Dell Publishing Company.

Furubotn, E. and S. Pejovich. 1972. Property rights and economic theory: a survey of recent literature. Journal of Economic Literature 10:1137-1162.

Gilles, J. L. and K. Jamtgaard. 1981. Overgrazing in pastoral areas: the commons reconsidered. Sociologia Ruralis 21:129-141.

Glantz, M. H., ed. 1977. Desertification: Environmental Degradation in and around Arid Lands. Boulder, Colorado: Westview Press.

Hardin, G. 1968. The tragedy of the commons. Science 162: 1243-1248.

Hardin, G. and J. Baden, eds. 1977. Managing the Commons. San Francisco: W. H. Freeman.

Hardin, R. 1982. Collective Action. Baltimore, Maryland: Johns Hopkins University Press.

Hayami, Y. and V. W. Ruttan. 1985. Agricultural Development: A Global Perspective. Baltimore, Maryland: Johns Hopkins University Press.

Hayek, F. A. 1948. Individualism and Economic Order. Chicago, Illinois: University of Chicago Press.

Hitchcock, R. K. 1981. Traditional systems of land tenure and agrarian reform in Botswana. Journal of African Law 24.

Horowitz, M. M. 1979. The sociology of pastoralism and African livestock projects. Washington, D.C.: U.S. Agency for International Development Program Evaluation #6.

Johnson, O. E. G. 1972. Economic analysis, the legal framework and land tenure systems. Journal of Law and Economics 15:259-276.

Johnson, R. N. and G. Libecap. 1982. Contracting problems and regulation: the case of the fishery. American Economic Review 72:1005-1022.

Johnston, B. and J. Mellor. 1961. The role of agriculture in economic development. American Economic Review 51: 566-593.

Kimber, R. 1981. Collective action and the fallacy of the liberal fallacy. World Politics 33:178-196.

Legesse, A. 1973. Gada: Three Approaches to the Study of African Society. London: Collier McMillan.

Malinowski, B. 1961. The Dynamics of Culture Change. New Haven, Connecticut: Yale University.

McKean, M. A. 1982. The Japanese experience with scarcity: Management of traditional common lands. Paper presented at the Conference on Critical Issues in Environmental History, University of California-Irvine, January 1-3.

Muhsam, H. V. 1977. An algebraic theory of the commons. In Hardin and Baden 1977.

Netting, R. M. 1978. Of men and meadows. Strategies of alpine land use. Anthropology Quarterly 45:123-144.

North, D. C. and R. P. Thomas. 1977. The first economic revolution. Economic History Review 30:229-241.

Orlove, B. S. 1977. Alpaca, Sheep and Men. New York: Academic Press.

Orlove, B. S. 1980. Pastoralism in the Southern Sierra. Andean Peasant Economics and Pastoralism, Publication 1, Small Ruminants CRSP. Columbia: Department of Rural Sociology, University of Missouri.

Peters, P. 1983. Cattlemen, Borehole Syndicates and Privatization in the Kgatleng District of Botswana. Ph.D. thesis. Boston: Boston University.

Picardi, A. C. 1974. A systems analysis of pastoralism in the West African Sahel. Framework for Evaluation, Long-Term Strategies for the Development of the Sahel-Sudan, Annex 5, Center for Policy Alternatives. Cambridge: Massachusetts Institute of Technology.

Picardi, A. C. and W. W. Seifert. 1976. A tragedy of the commons in the Sahel. Technology Review 78:42-51.

Randall, A. 1974. Coasean externality theory in a policy context. Natural Resources Journal 14:35-54.

Rawls, J. 1971. A Theory of Justice. Oxford: Clarendon Press.

Rhodes, R. E. and S. J. Thompson. 1975. Adaptive strategies in alpine environments: beyond ecological particularism. American Ethnologist 2:535-551.

Runge, C. F. 1981. Common property externalities: isolation, assurance and resource depletion in a traditional grazing context. American Journal of Agricultural Economics 63:595-606.

Runge, C. F., 1984a. Institutions and the free rider: the assurance problem in collective action. Journal of Politics. February. Pp. 154-181.

Runge, C. F. 1984b. Strategic interdependence in models of property rights. American Journal of Agricultural Economics 66:807-813.

Runge, C. F. 1985. The innovation of rules and the structure of incentives in open access resources. American Journal of Agricultural Economics 67:368-372.

Schelling, T. 1960. The Strategy of Conflict. Cambridge, Massachusetts: Harvard University Press.

Schelling, T. 1973. Hockey helmets, concealed weapons and daylight savings: a study of binary choice with externalities. Journal of Conflict Resolution 17: 381-428.

Schotter, A. 1981. The Economic Theory of Social Institutions. Cambridge: Cambridge University Press.

Sen, A. K. 1967. Isolation, assurance and the social rate of discount. Quarterly Journal of Economics 81:112-124.

Sugden, R. 1982. On the economics of philanthropy. Economic Journal 92:341-350.

Sugden, R. 1984. Reciprocity: the supply of public goods through voluntary contributions. Economic Journal 94: 772-787.

Taylor, M. 1976. Anarchy and Cooperation. New York: John Wiley and Sons.

Thomson, J. T. 1980. Peasant perceptions of problems and possibilities for local-level management of trees in Niger and Upper Volta. Paper presented at the African Studies Association Meetings, October 15-18.

Ullman-Margalit, E. 1977. Coordination norms and social choice. Erkenntnis 11:143-155.

Wagner, R. H. 1983. The theory of games and the problem of international cooperation. American Political Science Review 77:330-346.

Yelling, J. A. 1977. Common Field and Enclosure in England, 1450-1859. Hamden, Connecticut: Archon Books.

PART TWO: **Case Studies**

Marine Inshore Fishery Management in Turkey[1]
Fikret Berkes

INTRODUCTION

Third World fisheries suffer from two interrelated and worldwide problems: the failure of modernization efforts, and the conflict and allocation problems involving the inshore and offshore sectors. This paper attempts to deal with both of these issues in the context of the common property resource theory, and more specifically, in terms of the control of the resource base by fishing communities. It deals with the relative efficacy of small-scale organizations and the conditions under which fisheries can be self-managed successfully.

Many of the programs to "modernize" or to "develop" fisheries have failed. Emmerson (1980) and Panayotou (1982) have attributed this largely to the development planner's preoccupation with technology and economic rationalization, at the expense of understanding the inner logic of the existing artisanal or small-scale fisheries. "While small-scale fisheries still employ over 90 percent of all fishermen and contribute about half the edible world catch ... the emphasis has been on the development of industrial fisheries...." (Panayotou 1982:49).

To remedy this situation, there has recently been a modest shift of interest in international circles towards small-scale fisheries. For example, the 1984 report, "FAO World Conference on Fisheries Management and Development,"

states that "there is widespread recognition by governments and donor agencies of the need to support development
of marine and inland small-scale fisheries" (p. 26). It
refers to the "continued and assured share of the fisheries
resources for small-scale producers and their active involvement in the management of the resources" (p. 26).

This last point hints at the second crisis in Third
World fisheries. Throughout the world, small-scale inshore
fisheries are in conflict with the expanded fleets of
large-scale fisheries. Allocation problems often develop
when large-scale operators are forced inshore following the
depletion of offshore fish stocks. Thomson (1980) gives
examples of such conflicts from Yemen, Indonesia, Thailand,
India, and the Philippines--only a small sample of the
global conflict between the two sectors. Many researchers
have attempted to analyze and to resolve the problem. One
of the more exhaustive studies of the conflict was carried
out in San Miguel Bay, the Philippines (for a summary, see
Smith and Pauly 1983; Cruz, this volume).

McGoodwin (1980) described the conflict between coastal
shrimp fishermen in Mexico and the offshore shrimp trawling
fleet that had developed with government assistance. The
two sectors exploited the same stocks, first inshore and
later offshore, as the shrimp grew larger and moved into
deep waters during their life cycle. To protect the yield
of large shrimp caught offshore by the trawlers, the Mexican government curtailed the inshore fishery; thus, "the
development of the trawling industry has brought about a
parallel underdevelopment of the inshore fisheries"
(McGoodwin 1980). A common course of events in the conflict between the inshore sector and the offshore sector
is described by Dasgupta (1982:17) with reference to a
case in India:

> For marine fisheries with free entry the ... problem
> can arise via a seemingly convoluted process. In free
> waters, where historical rights to the traditional
> fishermen are not respected, it can happen that large
> firms enter with modern fishing vessels. For the short
> run, unit harvesting costs are thereby dramatically
> reduced, thus exacerbating the tendency towards
> overfishing. Meanwhile, the traditional fishermen,
> unable to compete with such equipment, are left im-
> poverished for want of any catch. But in the long run,
> as a consequence of continual overfishing, harvest
> costs increase, despite--one should say, because
> of--the use of modern harvesting techniques.

The significance of common property institutions in Third World fisheries is related to these two questions:

(1) Can an understanding of common property institutions in Third World fisheries provide one of the missing ingredients towards successful economic development?

(2) Can these institutions be used to resolve the conflict and allocation problems involving the inshore and the offshore sectors?

In addressing these questions, it is necessary first to have some empirical information as to how these common property institutions operate. Further, it is important to know the conditions under which these institutions can exist and successfully operate, as opposed to conditions under which they cannot.

THE STUDY AREAS AND THE STATUS OF THE FISHERIES

All five of the study areas are located in the southern seas of Turkey, the Aegean, and the Mediterranean; their fisheries share a number of common characteristics by virtue of their location: they operate in biologically poor waters and utilize a diverse assemblage of bottom-dwelling species that are of limited abundance but relatively high market value. Most of these fisheries are artisanal operations that use simple fishing gear and return daily to home port.

The role of the southern seas in the overall Turkish fishery production is relatively minor. The Aegean region accounts for only about three percent of the total catch of close to one-half million tons annually, and the Mediterranean region only about two percent (DPT 1985; TCZB 1982). The greatest part of the total yield is landed in the eastern Black Sea, a biologically productive area dominated by pelagic (surface dwelling) species and schooling species such as the anchovy. The Aegean and the Mediterranean are technically oligotrophic marine environments in which the low level of nutrients in the water is translated through the food web into low levels of fish productivity (Gulland 1971).

Most of the commercially utilized fish species of the Aegean and the Mediterranean are bottom-dwelling (demersal) species. The fish fauna is highly diverse, but none of the individual species is particularly abundant. However, many of them have a high market value, as elsewhere in the Mediterranean. Charbonnier (1977) observed that the prices for the Mediterranean fish (demersal and pelagic together) were five times higher than the average world price, and for the demersal species alone, seven times higher.

The standard small-scale operation in Turkish coastal fisheries is a 2-man, 8 m boat equipped with a 10-25 HP inboard diesel engine; some are 3-man, 10 m boats. The standard fishing equipment is the trammel net, a gillnet-like set net that captures fish by entangling them. Long-lines or a series of baited hooks on a main line attached to a float are also used. Both types of equipment are used in exploiting a diverse fauna of demersal species dominated by sea breams, basses, mullets, and groupers.

Larger-scale operations include trawlers, purse seiners, and beach seiners. Trawlers drag a bag-shaped net for demersal fish. In the Aegean and the Mediterranean, they average 15-25 m with a crew of 7 or 8. Purse seiners catch pelagic species using a net that hangs from the surface by its attached floats. The bottom of the net may be closed off like a purse when a school of fish has been surrounded. Purse seine boats average 15 m and carry a crew of 10. Beach seiners, 10-15 m boats with a crew of 5, drag nets while anchored in shallow areas.

As may be seen from the description above, the larger-scale fisheries that operate in the Turkish Mediterranean and Aegean are really not large-scale fisheries by international standards or even by the standards of the Turkish Black Sea. They may best be identified as medium-scale operations. Three of the fisheries in the study area consist only of small-scale operations; two consist of both small-scale and medium-scale.

The study area is shown in Figure 1. Three of the fisheries are located north of Cyprus on the eastern Mediterranean coast of Turkey, and two on the southern Aegean coast. Some of the characteristics of each of the five fisheries in the study area are shown in Table 1. The first three of the areas (the coastal lagoon near Adana, Tasucu near Silifke, and Alanya) were chosen for the study because they were known from previous surveys by the author to be well-run, successful fisheries. The fourth (Bodrum) was chosen as an example of a previously successful fishery that had overcapitalized (overexpanded the fleet) in the early 1970s. The fifth (Bay of Izmir) was chosen as an example of an intensive fishery in a multiple-use area adjacent to a large urban center.

In contrast to the first three fisheries, which are used by single groups of small fishermen, the last two areas are used by medium-scale operations as well. Further, in Bodrum and the Bay of Izmir, there are relatively large groups of casual or sport fishermen; however, Table 1 accounts for only the registered commercial fishermen.

The data in Table 1 were collected in 1983. These

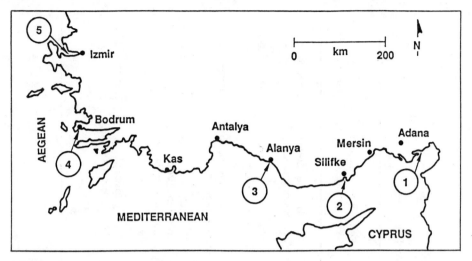

FIGURE 1   The Study Area.

five areas were selected from among some 50 fishing
communities first investigated by the author in 1976-78;
they are not a random selection, nor are they meant to be
representative of all Turkish coastal fisheries.

USE OF THE OAKERSON FRAMEWORK: THE OUTCOME

In this paper, the Oakerson framework will be used
diagnostically, beginning with the "outcome" and working
backwards to investigate the reasons behind the outcome.
It is therefore important to specify at the outset the
criteria by which the outcome has been evaluated in this
paper. Basically, four criteria are appropriate measures
for this work, two from the Oakerson framework (efficiency,
equity), and two additional criteria, sustainability and
the expression of satisfaction or dissatisfaction by the
users themselves. The latter two criteria are meant to
address, respectively, the ecological and the social dimensions of the outcome. The last criterion may perhaps also
provide a composite measure of the outcome as perceived by
the fisherman.

Efficiency, defined as Pareto optimality, cannot be
worked out because of lack of suitable data on individual
yields and incomes in the study area. In any case, there
may be serious complications in the application of the
Pareto optimality approach to resources in which there are
large year-to-year variations in productivity, and where
short-term efficiency undermines long-term sustainability.

TABLE 1 Description of the Five Fisheries in the Study Area, Southern Turkey, 1983.

The Fishery	Area Used (approximate km^2)	Number and Type of Boats	Number of Registered Fishermen	Cooperatives and User Groups	Outcome
(1) The Coastal Lagoon	20	43 small inboard 80 non-motorized	103	All in one coöp; one user group	Successful
(2) Tasucu	150	90 small inboard	140	All in one coöp; one user group	Successful
(3) Alanya	80	45 small inboard	100	Half in one coöp; one user group	Successful
(4) Bodrum	(overlapping with other communities in the area)	11 trawlers 2 purse seiners 9 bottom seiners 100 small inboard	80 20 45 250	No active cooperatives; six user groups	Unsuccessful
(5) Bay of Izmir	400	27 purse seiners 30 bottom seiners 700 small inboard	300 150 1400	Many cooperatives; five user groups	Unsuccessful

Equity, as with efficiency, is difficult to calculate. It can be evaluated indirectly, however, from the general conduct of the five fisheries. In the first and third areas, there were explicit sharing mechanisms to ensure equity. In the second area, all fishermen had access to bank credit of the equivalent of U.S. $3,000 (1983 dollars) through their cooperative society. By contrast, in the last two areas, there were no mechanisms by which a certain basic fishing income or other benefits could be obtained.

The sustainability of the harvest is an important criterion often used to evaluate the success of common property resource use. Together with other biological criteria, measures of sustainability have been incorporated into a current and ecologically up-to-date definition of conservation by several international agencies (Talbot 1980). There are insufficient data, however, to test fully whether any of the fisheries in the study area are sustainable.

Perhaps the most suitable measures of outcome in the present study are the usual bioeconomic criteria of success used in fisheries science: evidence of overfishing and overcapitalization (Gulland 1974). These criteria have the added advantage that they represent rough indicators of efficiency and sustainability. Together with a measure of equity, as done above, and an expression of satisfaction or dissatisfaction of the users themselves, these criteria should provide a suitably complete assessment of the outcome.

Using these three criteria, the first three study areas--the coastal lagoon, Tasucu, and Alanya--represent successful fisheries: there is no decrease in overall catches over the years, no sharp drops in the catch per unit of effort, no evidence for increasing scarcity of the more valuable species, no obvious overcrowding in the fishing area, and no indication of vessels and fishermen dropping out of the fishery. In these areas, the fishermen indicated that conflicts were largely resolved internally; the great majority of them expressed general satisfaction with the fishery.

By contrast, the last two areas--Bodrum and the Bay of Izmir--represent unsuccessful fisheries. While there has probably been no decrease in the overall yield over the years, there has been a sharp decline in the catch per unit of fishing effort. The more valuable species have all but disappeared. There are too many fishermen and too many boats chasing too few fish. In the Bodrum area, many fishermen have become occupational pluralists, catering to tourists in the summer and fishing part-time opportunis-

tically. The larger vessels have left Bodrum for lack of
fish. In 1983, all but one of 11 Bodrum-based trawlers
operated outside the area, and one had dropped out of the
fishery. In the Bay of Izmir, many of the small fishermen
of the area were forced to travel north to the outer bay,
even though this meant much higher operating costs. The
more valuable species were so scarce that it was said that
a fisherman could more than recoup his daily expenses if he
could catch a single good-sized specimen of Dicentrarchus
labrax (a type of white bass) and sell it to a restaurant
in Izmir. In these two areas, fishermen either talked
bitterly of the conflicts or refused to talk at all.
Although some expressed general satisfaction with the
fishery, many said they were dissatisfied with the outcome.

TECHNICAL AND PHYSICAL ATTRIBUTES OF THE RESOURCE

The techno-environmental attributes of the resource
base are much the same in the five study areas, with a few
notable exceptions. Jointness is a problem in all areas:
each individual user is potentially capable of subtracting
from the welfare of other users, even when fishing law-
fully. Certain illegal practices (such as the use of dynamite and nets with sub-legal mesh sizes) exacerbate the
problems. In theory, all users can derive benefits from
the use of the resource, within certain limits. To ensure
this, however, it is necessary to institute limited entry
or license limitation programs so that the number of fishermen exploiting the resource can be matched to the ability
of the resource to sustain them. This, in most fisheries,
is the limiting condition under which jointness can be
maintained (Gulland 1974; Pearse 1980).

Excludability poses a serious problem in all of the
five study areas. In general, access to a fishery is difficult to restrict. The first study area (coastal lagoon)
is perhaps the easiest one in which to apply the exclusion
principle because of its small size and geographical location. The next three coastal fisheries are less easy to
defend because they are conducted along a stretch of the
shoreline, and the fifth (Bay of Izmir) is much the same.

Divisibility poses both a theoretical and a practical
problem. The resource itself, the fish stock, is indivisible; it cannot be divided up among private property
holders. The fishing areas, however, can be divided up by
using landmarks and the usual measures of location finding
among coastal fishermen (triangulation). The problem in
dividing up the fishing grounds is that no fish remain in

one place for long. Moreover, all of the stocks fished in
the study areas range beyond the actual areas fished by the
fishing communities in the study. In some open ocean
fisheries, relatively few stocks (subpopulations of a species that can be considered a management unit) are quantitatively important. In such fisheries, it is theoretically possible to manage each stock. But in Mediterranean
coastal fisheries with a large number of species, it is
virtually impossible to manage the fishery on a stock-by-
stock basis; this condition is generally true for subtrop-
ical and tropical fisheries (Pauly and Murphy 1982). In
the study area, each major species has a different migratory behavior, and it would not be possible to match the
management area to the geographical range inhabited by each
stock.

Last, the techno-environmental attributes of the
resource may include some measure of the potential demand
for the resource by the human population who live in the
area. On this count, there are major differences among
the five study areas. The Bay of Izmir fishery is near a
metropolitan area of over one million. This fishery and
the one in Bodrum (a tourist center) are in areas in which
there is a large recreational demand; the other fisheries
are not.

DECISION-MAKING ARRANGEMENTS

Rules and institutions governing fishery resource use
include laws issued by the central government and operational rules instituted locally. The Government of Turkey
regulates fisheries through the Aquatic Resource Act
No. 1380 of 1971 (1380 Sayili Su Ürünleri Kanunu). The
following restrictions and conditions are provided under
the Act:

o   Licensing of commercial fishermen (but not license
    limitation)
o   Prohibition of destructive practices
o   Regulation of a minimum mesh size for nets
o   Prohibition of trawling within three miles of the
    coast and within bays
o   Restriction of fishing during the spawning period
o   Prohibition of the taking of undersized individuals
    of certain relatively rare species (such as
    sturgeon)
o   Dumping of substances deleterious to the aquatic
    environment.

The actual regulations under the Act are communicated to fishermen and the public at large through fisheries circulars that are issued annually and that specify such provisions as the length of the closed season, the names of species on the restricted species list, and the details of the restrictions for chemical pollutants.

The Ministry of Agriculture has jurisdiction over fisheries but employs no fishery conservation officers. The provisions of the Act and its regulations, such as the three-mile limit, are enforced by the coast guard and the rural police (the gendarme) of the Ministry of the Interior.

Operational rules instituted locally are one of two kinds. In areas in which the fishermen belong to fishermen's cooperatives, such operational rules are subject to the conditions of the charter of the local cooperative. The constitution, in turn, is subject to the regulations of the Government of Turkey that govern producers' (agriculture and fish) cooperatives. For example, the rules on membership allow for no discrimination on an ethnic basis but do allow for residency requirements in the local community.

Other operational rules are those that exist without any reference to formal government legislation. The rule that establishes the condition of collective choice within the group involved with the fishery is willing consent. The actual operational rules that emerge by the application of the rule of willing consent differ from fishery to fishery in the five study areas, even though "the general rules of the game" or the constraints that shape the management choices are the same. The more pertinent operational rules regarding common property management are summarized below for the five study areas.

The Coastal Lagoon Fishery at Ayvalik-Haylazli

As with all lagoon fisheries, use-rights are established by the lease of the lagoon from the Government of Turkey. Thus, members of the cooperative, all of whom come from three neighboring villages, have exclusive and legal rights to the fish of the lagoon and the lagoon's adjacent waters. All fishermen are cooperative members, and all cooperative members are active fishermen. They protect their rights by patrolling the boundary of their fishing area and chasing off or apprehending intruders. (Three outside fishing boats were apprehended in 1983.) Rules for membership are stated in the charter of the cooperative and include six months of residency in one of the

three villages. The other important condition is that no
one earning wages from employment is eligible for membership.
    Of the five fishing areas in the study, perhaps the
clearest operational rules are found in this fishery
because the mechanisms for establishing use-rights and
membership are legally defined.

Tasucu

    All fishermen are small-boat inshore fishermen and all
belong to the local cooperative. The right to fish is not
restricted to membership in the local cooperative, but cooperative membership has the attractive features of bank
credit for members and a year-round guaranteed price that
is seasonally adjusted. Fishing rights of the group are
protected by the three-mile limit for trawlers. Boats
other than trawlers may come into the area fished by Tasucu
fishermen, but apparently do not because the adjacent areas
are less heavily fished and therefore more attractive than
in Tasucu Bay.

Alanya

    Another small-boat coastal fishery, Alanya, differs
from the others in that half the fishermen belong to the
local cooperative, and half do not. This fishery is
located on the edge of a deep basin, and the inshore zone
suitable for setting nets is very limited. The operational
rules for the use of this zone are established on the basis
of willing consent, and organized by the community of
fishermen informally.

o   Each September, a list of eligible fishermen is
    prepared, consisting of all licensed fishermen in
    Alanya, regardless of cooperative membership.
o   Within the area normally used by Alanya fishermen,
    all usable fishing locations are named and listed.
    These spots are spaced so that the net set in one
    does not block the fish that should be available at
    the adjacent spot.
o   These named fishing locations are in effect from
    September to May, and the practice applies to the
    use of the large mesh (80 mm) nets for bonito and
    large carangids (Sarda sarda and Lichia spp.).
o   In September, the eligible fishermen draw lots and
    are assigned to specific fishing locations.

o   From September to January, each fisherman moves
     each day to the next location to the east. After
     January, the fishermen move west. This gives each
     fisherman an equal opportunity at the stocks that
     migrate east to west between September and January,
     and reverse their migration from January to May
     through the area.

These operational rules are based on a broad interpretation of the Aquatic Resources Act, which states that
the cooperatives have jurisdiction over "local arrangements." They are enforced by having each fisherman endorse
the list of fishing locations, and depositing copies of the
agreement with the mayor and the local gendarme. Violations of the rule of assigned locations are dealt with by
the fishing community at large, in the coffee house. Violators may come under social pressure and, on occasion,
threats of violence. The threat of removing the violator's
name from the list, to our knowledge, has never been
carried out. (The organizers concede privately that such
an action would not be supported by the government.)
Alanya is unusual in that there are no problems with
trawlers. The coastal zone is steep and deep enough
(1,000 m deep at 1 km out in some places) to discourage
trawlers. There are no known operational rules to deal
with small fishermen of adjacent communities and with the
increasing flux of spear-fishermen and sport fishermen.

Bodrum

In this area, the traditional small-boat fishery
collapsed after the development of a trawl fleet in the
1970s that coincided with the development of Bodrum as a
tourism center. A local cooperative tried unsuccessfully
through the 1970s to mediate between small boats and
trawlers; by 1983, the cooperative had completely disappeared. No single organization is likely to speak for all
fishermen and organize the consensus necessary to establish
operational rules because in 1983 there were six distinct
groups of fishermen: (1) small-scale coastal fishermen,
(2) larger-scale operators including trawlers and beach-
seiners, (3) semiprofessionals who obtain their own fish
and sell the occasional surplus, (4) large numbers of unskilled sport fishermen, (5) spear-fishermen licensed as
sponge fishermen but who sell fish on the open market, and
(6) charter boat operators who fish to feed their clients
and occasionally sell the surplus.

Bay of Izmir

This fishery differed from the Bodrum fishery by the
presence of two large cooperatives, both based at the Izmir
fish market, one representing small-scale fishermen, the
other comprising large-scale fishermen; there were also
several local cooperatives within the bay area. The Bay of
Izmir was similar to Bodrum with respect to the presence of
several distinct groups of fishermen: (1) purse seiners,
(2) small-scale gillnetters, (3) small-scale liftnetters,
(4) larger-scale beach seiners, and (5) sport and semiprofessional fishermen from the urban metropolitan area of
Izmir. Each of these groups reportedly conflicted with at
least one other group, and in some instances, with more than
one. There were no operational rules in place to allocate
the fish, to reduce the conflicts, or to limit crowding.

PATTERNS OF INTERACTION

The use of the resources in the five study areas is
under somewhat similar constraints with respect to technical and physical attributes of the resource and decision-
making arrangements for the use of the resource. Yet the
outcomes are different, perhaps partly due to differences
in urban and recreational demands on the resource. Alanya
is different from the others because the narrowness of the
continental shelf in this area restricts possible fishing
sites. To explore these differences further, each of the
five fisheries will be described in terms of patterns of
interaction of the users.

The Coastal Lagoon Fishery at Ayvalik-Haylazli

In this successful fishery, the fishermen have taken
good advantage of the options open to them. The cooperative was established in 1974 to make a bid for the lease
of the lagoon, which had previously been operating under a
private company. A few of the members had been employed
as laborers by the company. Taking advantage of a provision under the Aquatic Resources Act to give priority to
cooperatives in the leasing of lake and lagoon fisheries,
the Ayvalik-Haylazli Cooperative was successful in its bid.
Even though very few of the members had fishing experience,
they were able to run the lagoon profitably. The cooperative initially included members from a nearby town and
those who held wage employment. Subsequently, the cooper-

ative interpreted its charter more strictly and expelled
members who lived elsewhere and who could not choose between fishing and wage employment. However, many of the
1983 members were themselves part-time fishermen: some
80 percent were part-time farmers and only 20 percent
full-time fishermen. To maintain the profitability of the
fishery, they have rejected requests for membership from a
large nearby village. The relatively small size of the
area makes it possible for the cooperative to police the
boundary of its fishing area.

The limitation of membership makes it possible for the
cooperative to capture a larger resource rent than would
be possible. As compared with other fisheries, the cost
of fishing is kept low by the use of rowboats. Fishermen
work in groups of four, using two rowboats and one motorized vessel per group. The rowboats are towed to the
fishing area, and the motor boat then anchored, thus
saving fuel. Each group owns its means of production
collectively and splits the income equally. Cooperative
officers take turns in accompanying the cooperative truck
to the city of Adana, a large market only one hour away by
truck.

Aside from the occasional problem of sales accounting
(which seems to be so common with cooperatives), and aside
from the discontent of those excluded from the fishery,
the operation appears to be a successful example of common
property resource management. Even though the membership
is open to all residents of three villages (combined population 2,500), the organizers do not foresee a crowding
problem in the near future.

Tasucu Fishery

The Tasucu Fishing Cooperative is often cited as an
example of a producer's cooperative that works. There is
a substantial literature on it in Turkish, including a book
(Ozankaya 1976), and the head of the cooperative is somewhat of a folk hero. At the time the cooperative was established in 1968, there were two motorized fishing boats
in Tasucu and five rowboats. Most of the others who made
their living from fishing used dynamite. The cooperative
banned dynamite-fishing and promised fishermen financial
help to allow them to obtain proper means of production.
In 1970, the growing cooperative confronted trawlers that
operated (illegally) within Tasucu Bay, and chased them off
with shotguns (Ozankaya 1976). By 1971, cooperative members owned 40 inboard boats and controlled their fishing
area. Membership appears to have reached a peak of 180 in

1975 (Ozankaya 1976), and then declined through the loss of members from adjacent communities who formed their own associations.

The cooperative appears to have been exceptionally successful in fighting competing users. In 1983, it was preparing to go to court over allegedly illegal night fishing with scuba equipment, and also to block the relaxing of the three-mile limit to allow trawlers to fish shrimp inshore for two months. Cooperative members, meanwhile, were developing techniques to fish shrimp from small boats.

The cooperative has also been successful as a marketing enterprise, perhaps because its leader is a successful local businessman. By operating a large freezer facility, the cooperative has been able to stabilize and control the market and guarantee the price of fish for the producers. Further, the cooperative has been able to obtain for its members a bank credit of $3,000, sufficient capital for a new fisherman to buy the essential equipment. The cost of most two-man boats averaged about twice that amount. Some fishermen have apparently made enough to pay off the loan in a year: $2,800 is probably a reasonable estimate of the mean annual gross income (200 fishing days per year times 10 kilograms per day times $1.40 per kilogram).

This cooperative was thus able to build up the membership, a strong financial position, and political power. The leadership did not appear to be concerned about overcapacity and stock depletion, arguing that the Bay of Tasucu could probably support some 300 boats, provided that destructive practices (trawling, night fishing with scuba) are controlled.

Alanya Fishery

The fishery at Alanya emerged from its "dark ages" when the fishermen decided to cooperate with one another for the use of the limited number of fishing spots. The rotation system they developed by trial-and-error over 15 years is based on the principle of preventing fishermen from cutting off one another's "rightful supply of fish." This is done by spacing the fishermen sufficiently far apart so that they would not intercept each other's fish between September and May when migratory fish dominate the harvest. The system has the support of the great majority because it optimizes production at the best fishing sites, and in turn allocates these sites by lottery, with a rotation provision that ensures all fishermen an equal chance to fish these best spots. According to fishermen, the most desirable feature of the system is that it reduces conflict.

Thirty seven boats were on rotation in 1983 (three others were not fishing for various reasons). There were 34 named fishing locations, including two prime sites and five sub-prime sites. When a boat finished its turn at each of the 34 sites, the fishermen had the option of repairing equipment or going long-lining in deeper waters or simply tying up for three days. After May and through the summer months, fishermen sought large and valuable members of the Sparidae family and red mullet (<u>Mullus</u> <u>barbatus</u>), all nonmigratory species for which the rotation system was not deemed necessary.

All of those eligible were licensed fishermen; none appears to have been excluded in 1983. However, membership into the fishing community probably required more than the acquisition of a valid license. A fisherman who wants to participate in the system has to know the rules of the game and the named fishing spots. (As one fisherman put it, "Suppose some guest worker comes from Germany in his Mercedes car and wants to fish, do you think we would allow him? No way.")

The organizers of the rotation system had sufficient support from the community of fishermen as a whole to supervise it because the system benefited everyone except those who once monopolized the prime sites. The organizers were cooperative members, but the cooperative was not formally involved in the rotation system. Yet the organizers often cited the legal authority of cooperatives over "local arrangements" to legitimize the system. The reasons for this contradiction are not clear. Some of the differences between Alanya and, for example, Tasucu may be due to the lack of a strong cooperative organizer and to a greater sense of individual entrepreneurship in Alanya. (Again, a fisherman: "Fixed prices as in Tasucu? Well, our fishermen in Alanya would never stand for that. We are individualists; we sell to whomever offers a better price.")

About half of the Alanya fishermen were not members and sold their catch through buyers who were able to offer a slightly better price than the cooperative ("by evading municipal taxes," according to the cooperative secretary). The nonmembers were thus preventing the cooperative from building a stronger financial base and accumulating political power. The cooperative was therefore unable to offer its members the kind of service the Tasucu cooperative was able to give.

Bodrum and the Bay of Izmir Fisheries

Both of these fisheries were overcrowded and the stocks overexploited. In the case of Bodrum, the overfishing appeared to be due to the financial success of trawlers in the early 1970s, a success that attracted new entries until the cost of fishing exceeded the revenues of the fleet as a whole--a textbook example of rent dissipation in a fishery (for example, Gulland 1974). Most of the trawlers then abandoned the area, leaving the depleted stocks to small-boat fishermen. The spokesmen for the trawlers expressed dissatisfaction with this turn of events, not so much because the stocks had been depleted, but because the trawlers had become very restricted in their area of operation. According to trawlermen, in the 1970s the government had encouraged them to build the new vessels and had rarely enforced the three-mile limit, much to the anger of the small fishermen. However, with tighter regulations on trawling, trawlers could no longer make a living in the Bodrum area and went to the shrimp grounds near Mersin.

Meanwhile, in Bodrum, conditions had become no better for the small fishermen. The booming tourist trade resulted in higher prices for fish, but this also brought a great many part-time fishermen and charter boats into the fishery, and created apparently insurmountable problems of conflicts within user groups.

A similar situation with conflicts within user groups also existed in the Bay of Izmir, although the line-up of groups was somewhat different. But here the problem was not the trawlers (none were allowed in the bay). Rather, the problem was due to the proximity of a large urban center, a lucrative market but also a source of large numbers of semiprofessional fishermen. Unlike Bodrum, cooperatives did exist in this case, but represented only the narrow interest of various groups competing over the share of the markets.

With over 750 licensed commercial boats (Table 1) and a great many semiprofessional fishermen, the area was so crowded that it was simply not possible for any group to defend a fishing area. In fact, many trammel net fishermen found it difficult even to defend their own nets. This explains the existence of liftnet fishermen as a distinct group. The liftnet fishermen do not set and leave the net in the water to be retrieved later, but rather set and lift the net repeatedly over a wide area and look for visual evidence of such fish as the gray mullet (Mugil cephalus).

CONCLUSIONS

Fishing is a zero-sum game in which the limiting
condition under which jointness can be maintained is to
match the fishing pressure with the ability of the stock
to sustain it. Since there is no license limitation in
Turkish fisheries, overcapitalization develops if the
demand is high enough (Bodrum and the Bay of Izmir case
studies). However, if the local community has sufficient
control over the resource base and can also act cooperatively, the problem can be avoided by instituting closed-
access conditions (the case studies of the lagoon fishery,
Tasucu, Alanya). Thus, it appears from the case studies
that the most important condition under which coastal
fisheries can be self-managed successfully is local
control.

This also is the key to solving the conflict and
allocation problems involving the inshore and offshore
sectors. The development of large-scale offshore operations is encouraged by the government so that supposedly underutilized offshore stocks can be fished. The
biological reality is that, except for extensive shallow
seas and a few upwelling areas such as that off Peru,
offshore waters are biologically unproductive and therefore
costly to fish. In many cases, the "offshore fleet" ends
up coming inshore and conflicting with the coastal fishery
(Thomson 1980; Dasgupta 1982; Panayotou 1982). Thus, the
historical and traditional fishing rights are relevant for
the solution of this allocation conflict (Dasgupta 1982),
and the protection of these rights becomes a necessity
(Thomson 1980). There is a fairly large literature on this
(for example, Berkes 1985).

This study shows that the presence of cooperatives or
"traditional" fishing communities are not necessary pre-
conditions for successful self-management. Local "operational rules" for resource management can evolve relatively
quickly: 15 years in Alanya and Tasucu and 9 years in the
coastal lagoon fishery. The presence of producers' cooperatives is not a necessary condition for successful fisheries management, but it certainly helps if the cooperative
is able to act as a management institution in making sure
that "common property" is not "open access." Whether or
not this can be done depends not solely on the technical/
physical nature or the decision-making arrangements or the
actual behavior of the users, but a combination of these.

NOTE

1. I am grateful to fishermen and cooperative officials in
the study areas for their cooperation. Several colleagues at the Annapolis Conference and members of the
Panel on Common Property Resource Management made valuable
comments, including Daniel Bromley, David Feeny, Ronald
Oakerson, Margaret McKean, Wilfrido Cruz, and Jere Gilles.
The study was supported by the Social Sciences and Humani-
ties Research Council of Canada (SSHRC) as part of a larger
comparative study on small-scale fisheries.

REFERENCES

Berkes, F. 1985. Fishermen and "the tragedy of the commons." Environmental Conservation 12:199-206.

Charbonnier, D. 1977. Prospects for fisheries in the Mediterranean. AMBIO 6:374-376.

DPT 1985. Besinci Bes Yílík Kalkínma Planí. Su Ürünleri ve Su Ürünleri Sanayii. Özel Ihtisas Komisyon Raporu. TC Basbakanlík Devlet Planlama Teskilatí, Ankara. (The Fifth Five Year Plan. Aquatic Resources Expert Committee Report. State Planning Agency, Ankara. In Turkish.)

Dasgupta, P. S. 1982. The Control of Resources. Cambridge, Massachusetts: Harvard University Press.

Emmerson, D. K. 1980. Rethinking Artisanal Fisheries Development: Western Concepts, Asian Experiences. Washington, D.C. World Bank, Staff Working Paper No. 423.

FAO World Conference on Fisheries Management and Development. 1984. Rome: Food and Agriculture Organization of the United Nations. (26).

Gulland, J. A. 1971. The Fish Resources of the Ocean. C. Mediterranean and Black Sea. Rome: Food and Agriculture Organization of the United Nations.

Gulland, J. A. 1974. The Management of Marine Fisheries. Seattle: University of Washington Press.

McGoodwin, J. R. 1980. The human costs of development. Environment 22(1):25-31.

Ozankaya, O. 1976. "Kooperatif Kur, Sefaletten Kurtul"
    Türkiye'de Kooperatifçilik. Milliyet Yayínlarí,
    Istanbul. ("Start a Co-operative and Escape Poverty."
    Co-operatives in Turkey. In Turkish.)

Panayotou, T. 1982. Management concepts for small-scale
    fisheries: economic and social aspects. FAO Fisheries
    Technical Paper 228.

Pauly, D. and G. Murphy, eds. 1982. Theory and Management
    of Tropical Fishery. Manila: ICLARM.

Pearse, P. H. 1980. Regulation of fishing effort: with
    special reference to Mediterranean trawl fisheries.
    FAO Fisheries Technical Paper 197.

Smith, I. R. and D. Pauly 1983. Resolving multigear
    competition in nearshore fisheries. ICLARM Newsletter
    6(4):11-18. Manila.

TCZB 1982. Su Ürünlerini Artírma ve Kredileri Yönlendirme
    Sempozyumu. TC Ziraat Bankasí Su Ürünleri Kredileri
    Müd. Yayínlarí No. 4. (Symposium on Fishery
    Production and Fishery Investment Policies. State
    Agricultural Bank. In Turkish.)

Talbot, L. M. 1980. The world's conservation strategy.
    Environmental Conservation 7:259-268.

Thomson, D. 1980. Conflict within the fishing industry.
    ICLARM Newsletter 3:3-4. Manila.

Sea Tenure in Bahia, Brazil

John C. Cordell
Margaret A. McKean

INTRODUCTION

Property institutions--systems of rules specifying permissible and forbidden actions and the rights and obligations of individuals and groups with respect to the resources in question--are potent forces in social evolution (Bromley 1978; Runge, this volume). Knowledge of the formation and functions of property systems, however, is largely confined to studies of terrestrial economies, western countries, or legal institutions. There have been few inquiries into the nature of sea ownership or fishing rights aside from theoretical or public policy studies and ongoing debates over the international law of the sea. Even less is known about matters of "sea rights" in the Third World, of de facto fishing property arrangements, and of hereditary claims in small-boat fishing communities. Curiously, the issue of customary sea rights and laws--a paramount concern for many coastal fishing peoples--has almost never been raised by anthropologists otherwise interested in the territorial rights observed by indigenous and traditional cultures (e.g., Bodley 1981).

In recent years, however, ethnographers have begun to investigate the neglected domain of customary property relations in maritime fisheries and have discovered "sea tenure"--collectively managed informal territorial use rights in a range of fisheries previously regarded as

unownable (Johannes 1978; Acheson 1981; Christy 1982;
Cordell 1986). Sea tenure is concerned with ways in which
inshore fishermen perceive, name, partition, own, and
defend local sea space and resources. Western authorities
have conventionally viewed coastal sea space and fishing
grounds as resources to which no property rights are
attached, where the "commons" are open to all comers, and
where fishermen engage in unrestricted competition for a
limited product (Christy and Scott 1965; Gulland 1974;
Crutchfield 1982). Because no single user has exclusive
use rights in the resource or any right to prevent others
from sharing in its exploitation (Christy and Scott
1965:6), individual users have no incentive to restrain
production (Christy 1964:2). No consideration is given
to the possibility that certain arrangements of property
rights, jurisdiction, or ownership might be able to reduce
resource use (Christy 1982). Where these authorities do
admit the existence of cooperation in maritime communities,
they see exclusively selfish motives (Muir and Muir 1982).

> It is worth noting that maritime networks for all their
> egalitarianism are not based on friendship. Friendship
> implies an emotional relationship which supersedes
> economic advantage. You'd give a friend the shirt off
> your back. That makes a friend an economic liabil-
> ity ... maritime networks don't rely on trust or the
> emotional bonds of friendship (Muir and Muir 1981).

Moreover, the well-entrenched "culture of poverty" school
of thought on Latin America construes social marginality as
a foremost obstacle to any adaptive community organization
or stable resource management (Lewis 1952; Varallanos 1962;
Oberg 1965; cf. Pearlman 1973; cf. Lobo 1982). From this
perspective, the marginal fishermen of Bahia would be
especially incapable of regulating their own fishing
behavior and protecting the ecology of tropical marine
resources.
    These conventional views fail us in two respects:
first, they cannot account for the allocation of exclusive
joint use rights that we find in traditional inshore fishing regimes. Second, they fail to take into account the
powerful currency of reciprocity and cooperation--even
generosity in poverty--or their mollifying effects on
potentially destructive competition and their capacity to
assist in sustaining and regulating fisheries and other
renewable resources. In fact, many maritime communities
have "informal" systems of rights to resources and sea

territories that are supported by unwritten laws and subtle interpersonal relationships within close-knit communities. Even if they are not evident to the outside, these arrangements are just as real, socially binding, and ecologically consequential as standard catch quotas, seasons, and selective licensing programs used by governments to manage fisheries for sustained yields. Indeed, in certain non-industrial inshore settings they are more effective.

This paper looks outside mainstream Euro-American definitions of fishing rights to document fishermen's sea tenure in shallow, near-shore waters in Bahia, Brazil. Southern Bahia is one of the few tropical coasts where traditional sea tenure has been sufficiently documented for us to perceive its social logic, ecological basis, and strategic role as a resource management institution. In view of the well-known difficulties of designing and enforcing regulations in fishing, valuable lessons may be learned from traditional "unofficial" management practices. This ethnography of Brazilian sea tenure suggests some of the benefits of studying and working to maintain local tenure and customary fishing rights in the marine commons.

Four salient features of sea tenure in peasant communities of rural Bahia are discussed: (1) physical and technical attributes--the environmental parameters conducive to subdivision of the fishing grounds into "closed community" territories; (2) the decision-making arrangements--the rules and mechanisms of collective action and group sanction that work to legitimize and uphold the tenure system; (3) the patterns of interaction--the social contexts in which sea rights are extended, in which disputes arise, and in which conflict is resolved; and (4) outcomes--the problems of uncontrolled coastal belt and fishery development that undermine village solidarity and break down territorial autonomy in local fishing, with detrimental impacts on the equity among fishermen and also on long-term efficiency and productivity of inshore fisheries.

PHYSICAL AND TECHNICAL ATTRIBUTES

Throughout the Latin American tropics are many impoverished fishing peoples who have not made the transition to modernity. Among the poorest are the fisherfolk or beirados (shore dwellers) of southern Bahia in the Brazilian Northeast. Fishing for subsistence or for a small cash or supplementary income has long been a critical livelihood

alternative for the poor in this region. Today's
predominantly black maritime communities developed as
successive generations of hinterland plantation laborers
lost out in the wider economy and took refuge in the mangrove swamps that no one else had the need or stamina to
exploit. These fishermen still work from dugouts, slogging
through the mangroves day after day, often with little more
to eat than the crab bait left over from their traps and
trotlines. There is no upward mobility out of swamp fishing into the Brazilian economic mainstream. The Bahian
canoe fishing population has no stable market involvement
and at times even suffers the failure of its "last-resort"
fishing strategies. There is an unmistakable decline in
living standards at the landward edge of the swamps where
a majority of fishermen live.

In the Brazilian economic hierarchy, fishing has low
visibility: in 1976, revenue from fishing was 1.31 percent
of the gross national product and only 2.5 percent of total
agricultural production (Morris 1979). Traditional fishermen, assumed to be primitive and inefficient, are often
blamed for the low productivity of the industry. Yet
Bahia's traditional marginal fishermen still land roughly
70 percent of the catch on the southern coast (Silva 1979),
and thus contribute substantially to the area's interna-
tionally acclaimed cuisine, help to sustain the vital
tourist industry, and seasonally stock the domestic seafood
market with fresh fish. They are struggling to maintain
control of their mangrove, estuarine, and coral reef sea
territories as large seafood companies, high-tech fleets,
and export and interstate markets increasingly dominate both
inshore and offshore fishing in most other parts of Brazil.

The Bahian coastline is indented by estuaries, swamps,
and tidewaters dotted with sedimentary and coral reefs.
These comparatively sheltered waters seem conducive to
marking off micro-habitats for fishing claims. In addition, the proximity of fishing grounds to home ports affords
the fishermen great ease in guarding their territory.
Typically, the inshore fishing pattern centers around local
plantation ports and provides coastal and immediate
hinterland markets with fresh catches. Day-trip operations
and many traditional methods (e.g., the calao, a purse
seine) have changed remarkably little since their introduction by sixteenth century Portuguese settlers. Fishermen on the southern Bahian coast still work mainly from sail
canoes, using customary lines, nets, traps, and corrals to
harvest more than 200 different species of fish and shellfish. They lay claim to extensive fishing grounds in the

1,000 kilometer strip of shallow waters between Salvador and the Abrolhos Banks (see Figure 1).

The calao is a shallow-water purse seine, finely adapted to catching large schools of estuarine-spawning fish; it is operated by eight-man crews from dugout canoes 6 to 10 meters long. New nets may cost from $200 to $700, depending on size, quality, and elaborateness of mesh; few caloes are bought brand new. They are usually inherited in various advanced states of use and have been extensively repaired. Owning such a net is a fishermen's foremost economic aspiration and a mark of high social standing. A 200- to 300-meter calao typically represents the investment of a fishing captain's life savings.

Purse seining must conform to the intricate tidal changes along Bahia's estuaries and creeks that wind back into the mangrove swamps. A system of reckoning tides based on phases of the moon enables the canoe bosses (mestres) to monitor closely the behavior, migratory routes, and life cycles of fish (Cordell 1974). Seining and nearly all canoe fishing moves in a circuit: at neap tide, fishermen concentrate along the northeastern shores; as the tide begins to rise, they move inward into the main body of the fishing grounds. At spring tide, activity shifts to the southern reaches, and finally, as the tide falls, boats move back up into the main channels. The contours of the estuary are affected by currents, so a spring tide in the inner reaches of the fishing ground is like a neap tide in the outer reaches and vice versa. The result is that fishermen can use most of their techniques every day, as long as they choose fishing spots appropriate to the day's current regime.

Favorably located water space becomes valuable, and netcasting spaces are ranked according to criteria such as ease of access during foul weather, distance from port, past production history, and so on. Because fish and fishermen alike must move from spot to spot, it is neither possible nor desirable to create physical barriers around each fishing territory, so rules must substitute for fences to exclude interlopers from each spot. The elaborate system of rules and enforcement mechanisms that has evolved then allows the fishermen to maintain considerable jointness of use of the inshore fishery as a whole. In sum, whereas in most fishing systems, including those of Bahia, the limiting condition on production is ultimately resource availability, a more immediate check on sea tenure relations is the waterspace opportunity configuration for purse seines.

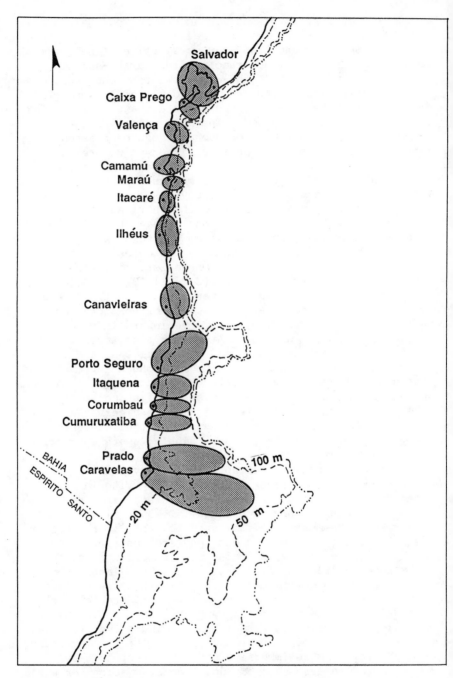

FIGURE 1 Fishing territories of Southern Bahia.

Decision-Making Arrangements

It is important to note at the outset that the forms
of sea tenure practiced in rural Bahia are not acknowledged
by any formal governmental body; in fact, they contradict
national fishing codes that stipulate that Brazilian territorial waters are public property. As far as the
national government is concerned, any Brazilian boat
registered in a national port can move anywhere and take
any amount or species of fish. SUDEPE, the fisheries
bureaucracy, simply does not have the capability to play a
significant managerial role in fishing. The fact that
Bahian and other similar fisheries in the Northeast exist
outside the purview of the national fisheries administration poses critical questions for marine resource use:
What happens when fishermen are left to their own devices?
Are resources and fishing activities essentially unmanaged?
Do local fishermen share the government's view of their
resources as available to all? Is fishing destined to
degenerate into what Hardin (1968) calls the "tragedy of
the commons"? What happens when traditional fishing col-
lides with modern markets and fleets that penetrate previously isolated fishing grounds?

Bahian canoe fishing systems reveal a number of para-
doxes and hidden strengths of life within the confines of
marginality. Within their inshore domain, Bahia's rural
fishermen, even those heavily dependent on creditors and
middlemen, are their own bosses. They take advantage of
the screen of geographical and cultural marginality to work
unencumbered by government regulation. They are able to
avoid purchasing licenses for their boats and gear or paying dues to the corrupt local fishing guilds, and they
instead market a large portion of their catch clandestinely
to avoid special docking and municipal fisheries tariffs.
Though they do not have to deal with national regulations
and laws, they do not live in local anarchy; rather, they
create, maintain, transfer, and defend an elaborate system
of fishing rights outside the written law of the sea.
Thus, the destitute and politically powerless fishing
population of Bahia can own large stretches of shoreline
sea that Brazilian law regards as open-access public
property.

It is impossible to determine with any finality how and
when sea tenure evolved or how canoe bosses consolidated
control over premium water space in Bahian canoe fishing.
There are no court records or laws to support fishermen's
claims. Yet sea tenure in the form of space controlled by

the community, by individuals, and by social networks has
existed over the span of the oldest net bosses' memories,
including their knowledge of fishing in previous generations. It is a century-old tradition at the very least.
Fishing grounds range from 400 km^2 to 600 km^2 and are
restricted in size by how species are distributed close to
shore, by the fact that the sail canoes (even if motorized)
cannot effectively carry ice or maneuver at sea, and by the
rhythm of markets in local ports and the hinterland, where
consumers demand a daily supply of fresh fish.

In the northern part of the fishery around the port of
Valena there are 258 traditional net-casting spots
(pesqueiros), each accommodating a range of methods (hand
lines, trotlines, set nets, traps, and seines). To prevent
people using different techniques from interfering with
each other, pesqueiros are subdivided into nonoverlapping
lanos, or minimal water spaces, as determined by fort-
nightly current changes, daily tide-level changes, lighting
conditions during different phases of the moon, position
of the lano relative to the shore slope, bottom conditions,
and the interactions of wind and current. Names are
bestowed on the spots by fishing captains who exercise
exclusive use rights over these tiny chunks of lunar-tide
fishing space.

Tenure may vary from sequential net-casting claims on
migratory species lasting hours or a few days to long-term
private claims covering brackish water spawning grounds,
reefs, and net fishing spots defined by the lunar-tide
cycle (cf. Forman 1967; Cordell 1974). Relative mobility
of gear and fishing craft, seasonality, micro-environmental
zones, life cycles of fish, and a whole host of social
variables enter into the constellation of tenure arrangements found in a given locale. Rights to fish are
characteristically transmitted in limited numbers of
apprenticeships, kinship, and other long-term social relations connected to the work setting.[1]

Tenure-holding units vary from loosely allied groups
of fishing captains, families, or informal partnerships to
extended ritual kin groupings and individual canoe fishing
captains who monopolize clusters of net-casting locations.
Knowledge of how to fish under this system is passed on in
a limited number of apprenticeships; these may last as long
as 10 or 15 years. Not all apprentices become proficient
net-casting specialists and equipment owners, and consequently do not inherit rights of access to the most valued
fishing grounds.

Marginal areas of the fishing grounds also include

areas of essentially unclaimed sea space where new fishing
spots are discovered and staked out from time to time.
There is also a series of intervillage buffer zones, where
rights are defined loosely, if at all. Yet even in the
most marginal waters, special agreements exist for exercising well-ordered, sequential temporary claims to
net-shooting areas. This system of property rights and
rules has evolved slowly and only as a response to endogenous competitive pressures; there is no formal assembly of
all rights holders, nor are there constitutional rules
(rules for making rules) by which rights holders may con-
vene to change the operational rules for fishing the
inshore sea. Instead, existing kinship and other social
relationships provide the arena in which rules are
enforced.

Patterns of Interaction

Purse-seining is the occasion for much social drama.
These large, encircling caloes are thought to be particularly deadly for the catfish, which is greatly prized
locally for its flavor and tenderness, though worth relatively little on the official market. Thus, a good calao
catch reaffirms a man's faith that God will continue to
send him runs of fish. A captain can take great pride in
bestowing these fish on friends and relatives, paying off
debts to middlemen, and holding beer-drinking fests. A bar
floor littered with broken beer bottles at dawn is a sure
sign that a fishing captain has been celebrating great good
fortune and skill: empty beer bottles are valued storage
containers in swamp-fishing neighborhoods, and to break
them is considered extravagant.

Purse-seining gives people a special opportunity to air
their grievances through soap box oratory, to bestow or
withhold favors, to praise or ostracize their companions,
and to mobilize participants in social networks. It is
necessarily a cooperative enterprise, as many people may
be involved in a single net-casting sequence--sometimes
several crews of eight to ten men each--and catches are
shared. Risks are great because there is often precious
little time to deploy and haul a net against the tidal flow
and get the fish back to market without ice at peak hours
before they spoil (Cordell 1974). And it is naturally
conducive to conflict because the stakes are high relative
to the catch and earning potential of other techniques.
Fishermen spend many hours debating and analyzing what goes

on in <u>calao</u> fishing. What is condensed here of their
storytelling and fussing illustrates how sea space is
named, owned, partitioned, and governed by an implicit
social contract or reciprocity and an ethical code of
<u>respeito</u> (respect); this constellation of techniques reg-
ulates access to premium net-casting locations and
minimizes conflict.

Cooperation

The ethical code associated with <u>respeito</u> is much more
encompassing than is superficial fishing etiquette, and far
more binding on individual conscience than any government
regulations could ever be. Where material wealth is
scarce, debts obviously arise from reciprocal exchanges
among fishermen, and the <u>respeito</u> that ensures that these
debts will be honored is the measure of a person's worth.
It is impossible to fish for long in a given community
without receiving and showing <u>respeito</u>. People honor each
other's claims because of <u>respeito</u>, which is created,
bestowed, and reaffirmed through sometimes trivial and
sometimes substantial acts of benevolence bordering on
self-sacrifice. Fishermen need not be physically present
to defend their territories or to make them real. Shore-
side economic necessities continually reinforce cooperation.

Marketing fish, obtaining bait, building canoes, borrowing and lending equipment, mending nets and sails,
locating crew, and acquiring information on weather and
catches create opportunities to perform small favors,
building up dependencies for future exchanges. Some favors
up the ante: giving tows, helping someone string a trot-
line, or bringing special wood of the white mangrove to
form crossbeams for a house. Gifts of fish, income from
the catch, and shares taken filter down through the neighborhood and village networks. All these exchanges set up
comfortable interdependencies that carry over into fishing
and make it a distinctly sociable undertaking.

Perhaps the most explicit show of cooperation and
<u>respeito</u> is made during the peak catfishing season in June
and July. Good net-fishing spaces are narrow due to tidal
fluctuations, so the chance of conflict over water space
is great. To relax spatial access codes in the lunar-tide
property system during this time, fishermen enter into
temporary partnerships that are dissolved when the spawning
runs subside. This turns out to be a very practical

scheme, since catfish are liable to enter the estuary in
such large schools that a single boat and crew cannot possibly catch all the available fish. If the catch is too
large to fit into several boats, one crew's net is used to
construct a temporary fish corral out on the tidal or reef
flats. Once the main catch is delivered, more live fish
are retrieved from the corral net.

Another important occasion for bestowing favors
involves marketing fish. Some captains double as fish
hawker-gamblers (pataqueiros). These people are supposed
to be officially licensed by the mayor's office, but there
is considerable moonlighting, and it is difficult to bring
the activities of hawkers under the control of the local
prefecture that oversees the operation of the fish market.
Fishermen can always find black market buyers who usually
pay slightly less than the going rate in the official market. But selling fish to a hawker enables one to avoid
paying a weight and class-specific tax and eliminates the
annoyance of going upriver into the market to unload fish.
Hawkers have a clientele in mind, and they have a fairly
good idea of what the demand will be for the fish available. The problem with selling to hawkers is that they
seldom have cash on hand for an on-the-spot transaction.
A fisherman, then, may choose to sell to a hawker on
credit.

A great deal of mutual trust must accompany such
transactions: selling on credit is a vote of confidence
in the hawker's reputation. Another fisherman and his
hawker provide an audience for the display of respeito.
When a price is agreed on and a transaction falls through,
the hawker must cover the loss himself. If the hawker
fails to fulfill his end of the deal, witnesses to it can
usually bring enough pressure to bear by way of gossip and
verbal censure to extract the amount due.

For Bahian purse-seiners, the ultimate test and
strongest demonstration of the cooperative ethic occurs in
the context of godparenthood networks, with their distinctive rituals and obligations. As summer weather opens up
the outermost ocean-beach fishing spots, boats from ports
upriver and in the swamp fan out to the ends of their territories, and intervillage conflicts can arise over
net-casting space and schools of fish. Becoming a godparent is one strategy to gain access to new territory and
to fish safely in waters of an adjoining community. The
first step is to arrange to sell a catch to hawkers in
neighboring territories, to make gifts of fish all around,
and if the catch is good, to pay for a beer-drinking ses-

sion. After initially displaying good will, the visiting
captain may either volunteer or be asked to be a godparent
to another fisherman's child. These relationships are
frequently established after only a brief acquaintance, and
a major benefit is to confer summer fishing rights. These
ongoing rights may endure for many years, reinforced by
other types of cooperation.

Alternatively, a captain planning to fish close to
another community's sea space will arrange to take along a
crew member who has a local friend. This is a necessary
precaution to ensure that his crew will receive good treatment if they have to go ashore, and to avoid the threat of
competition during net-casting sequences. Some people will
venture into interstitial areas to fish only when they have
a network of friends or actual kin in adjoining villages.

The phenomena of becoming a godparent and establishing
networks of informal contracts to ensure sea rights result
in wide-ranging circles of fishermen bound by respeito, and
also account, in part, for the cooperative extension of sea
tenure within a community. Canoe fishermen, purse-seiners
in particular, have huge personal networks with many godparent connections that often run through a series of villages. Such ritualized extension of sea rights restores
an element of flexibility in fishing opportunities where
waters are otherwise exclusively used and claimed by single
villages.

Another tactic is used to minimize the possibility of
competitive encounters: when a captain wishes to fish in
a particular spot outside the system of lunar-tide property
rights, he announces his intention--including what tide
level or series he will use in casting nets--several days
in advance at a local bar where fishermen like to congre-
gate. All that is required is for another fisherman to be
present as a witness. To ensure the claim, the captain
must follow his proclamation by going to the chosen spot
the day before fishing to leave a canoe anchored with pad-
dles sticking up in the air. This forewarns competitors
that the casting space has been taken. Fishing captains
go to considerable lengths to support each other in this
routine, which is part of the sea tenure politics that
shore up the entire fishing system.

A cogent illustration of the honor code is the way
fishermen cope with potential and actual competitive
encounters while fishing the intervillage buffer zones.
What often happens to create territorial conflict in
unclaimed or less-fished waters is the simultaneous arrival
of several boats, sometimes from different ports, to go

after a sizable school of fish when the tide offers room
and time for only one optimal net cast. Net bosses follow
a standard procedure of drawing lots to decide who will
cast first. Once an order is established, a tide marker,
usually a pole stuck in the bank, dictates a sequence of
net-shooting rights. Not more than one tide-level change
is allowed each boat. On this basis, captains decide
whether to remain. Sometimes this queuing pattern works
out well, but often a boat will not close its seine and
draw in the catch in the specified time. If the next boat
in line begins its operations regardless, the two nets can
become fouled.

Within a community's fishing grounds, where tenure
privileges to lunar-tide space are clear-cut, accidents
happen. Although units of net-shooting space have been
worked out over time so boats can operate at a safe distance from one another, one prime casting space will
occasionally overlap with another immediately upstream or
downstream that belongs to a different phase of the tide
cycle. In this case, fishermen may observe spatial boundaries correctly but miscalculate time boundaries. The
resulting territorial infringements might appear trivial,
but nonetheless have the potential to disrupt fishing
operations and social relations.

Bahian fishermen take a certain amount of competition
and boundary fuzziness for granted. The limits that people
will tolerate depend on the extent to which potential competitors are linked by the honor code. Within these
limits, which vary between individuals and social networks,
people try to get away with whatever scheme will increase
their fishing success. Canoes, for instance, have a way
of disappearing before a critical fishing expedition and
later turning up adrift on the tide. Nor is it unusual to
find a fishing captain buying drinks for a competitor's
crew, in hopes of getting them too drunk to leave in the
time required to reach a mutually desirable fishing spot.

In any of the above situations, however, where there
is a potential conflict over a fishing claim as a result
of net crossing, most captains would rather act deferen-
tially toward a competitor than force the issue. At first
glance, the rationale for this ostensibly one-sided con-
cession may appear self-defeating. However, the posture
of noninterference increases a skipper's respectability,
upholds the cooperative ethic, and sets up reciprocal debts
of gratitude to be paid at a later date. As a captain goes
out to work borderline fishing grounds, it is especially
important to know who can and who cannot be trusted to stay

within acceptable bounds of competition and honor the prior occupancy rule.

Failure to cooperate in these practices can be much more devastating for a fisherman than would be breaking a government law. Respeito is a cognitive reference point to the community conscience. It influences how fishermen evaluate each other's actions on and off the fishing grounds. It is a yardstick for measuring the justice of individual acts, especially in conflicts. Collective social pressure to conform to the ethics of fishing is reflected in the ôlho do povo (watchfulness of the community's eye, or sense of justice), reminiscent of the forceful moral and ethical standard in Palauan fishing, "words of the lagoon" (Johannes 1981). Reputations rise and fall in terms of the ôlho do povo. The ôlho do povo determines whether territorial competition in fishing is deliberate or accidental, and whether it is antagonistic enough to require counteraction.

Conflict

Just as the community confers rewards on those who follow respeito, it may withdraw the benefits of exchange and reciprocity from people who consistently create conflict in fishing. The most severe gesture occurs when an entire network of fishing captains decides to deny territorial use rights to a troublemaker who does not respect their lunar-tide claims. They can do this by sabotaging equipment, disavowing the prior occupancy rule and competing fiercely for space, engaging in deliberate net crossing, or boobytrapping net-casting spaces. These strategies and withdrawal of cooperation on shore are powerful incentives for renegade fishermen to mend their ways or leave the community.

From time to time, competition within the traditional community gets out of hand and escalates into disputes, calling into play a coercive and punitive set of social controls on fishing. Most captains espouse an "eye-for-an-eye, tooth-for-a-tooth" brand of swamp justice. They recognize a danger in letting someone get away with violations of claims or codes and consider it their prerogative to redress grievances so no one will become addicted to wrongdoing.

But the backup social controls are also strictly channeled. In cases of serious rifts, certain individuals are

called upon as mediators (<u>aconselheiros</u>). Were it not for
the concerted efforts and personal examples set by these
key individuals, the cooperative ethic might remain more
symbolic than real as a binding force in social relations.
Mediators are people to be emulated. They epitomize
<u>respeito</u> in all they do. They are usually retired fishing
captains, or in some cases fishermen's widows. These
individuals take an active interest in the welfare of the
fishing community and are constantly sought out for advice
and to exhort fishermen to maintain <u>respeito</u> in times of
controversy.

Although more or less deliberate incursions into private fishing space are a common feature of disputes, they
are seldom the root cause. Conflicts of this sort usually
have a long history. Mediators must be able to comprehend
and soothe social relationships that have fluctuated and
festered over a long period of time. Prolonged disputes
resemble the legendary Appalachian feuds: they reach
across several generations and are marked by vengeful acts
and general hostility among coalitions of fishermen and
their families and friends. Most fishermen's disputes
begin with rifts onshore and carry over into fishing with
its peculiar competitive possibilities. Contesting captains may try to claim each other's fishing slots by force.
The victims are likely to retaliate by poaching, stealing
equipment, sinking canoes, or boobytrapping fishing spots
with jagged tree trunks and boulders capable of ripping an
intruder's net to shreds. In extreme cases, people fight
with machetes. Disputes over fishing claims frequently
result from family quarrels over infidelity, wife-beating,
or inheritance of assets (such as a house or fishing equipment). Once a confrontation (such as ramming a canoe)
occurs on the fishing grounds, much drama in the fishing
neighborhoods is bound to arise, especially if anyone is
physically hurt. The heated public exchanges, threats, and
counter-threats that follow surely have reverberations in
subsequent fishing trips.

There is only one way to end a state of disunion among
fishing captains, crews, and families once grievances have
escalated to violence: the combatants must be willing to
air their grievances before a mediator. To promote reconciliation, the mediator must invoke <u>respeito</u>, the cooperative ethic, as it is reflected in the <u>ôlho</u> <u>do</u> <u>povo</u>, and
bring it to bear on individual consciences.

Thus, the way out of a dispute is not to fix blame and
then to punish the wrongdoer, but to negotiate reunion (by
appealing to the sense of justice) and to restore equality.

A simple face-saving gesture by either one of the parties
will suffice for openers. This involves humbling oneself
and showing that one no longer wishes to carry a grudge.
If successful, this strategy will lead to an exchange of
favors or kindness. The conciliatory gesture may consist
of a gift, perhaps a fish or a tow in from fishing in bad
weather, which might otherwise seem insignificant. Through
an exchange of just such small favors and concessions,
fishermen are frequently able to come to terms, reestablish
respeito, renew cooperative relations, and reaffirm the
value of honor and deference in avoiding water space challenges.

In most cases, fishermen involved in disputes not only
feel justified in selective acts of reprisal, but consider
themselves immune from punishment by police in nearby
towns. At the request of the local sheriff, civil dis-
orders are usually handled by state military police who
have garrisons in the major seaports along the southern
coast. Fishermen see little threat from these authorities,
however, because they contend that their swamp neighborhoods are outside the jurisdiction of the state and local
townships. They believe that their homes and fishing
grounds come under the control of the Brazilian navy and
federal jurisdiction.

Under Brazilian law, there is in fact such a separation
in authority over land and sea, and the navy historically
has been the central figure in regulating fishermen's
activities and registration in professional organizations.
But most of these regulations never penetrate the mangrove
swamps, and fishermen's only contacts with naval authorities are with indifferent local port captains who for the
most part leave fishermen alone. Because of their periph-
eral social status and dissociation from government,
fishermen believe that they cannot be prosecuted on land
for illegal acts committed in fishing. Taking advantage
of the thinness of national political and legal authority
in rural coastal fishing areas, a fisherman charged with a
serious crime will flee to the recesses of the swamp until
things blow over, because he will be on federal territory
and supposedly safe from prosecution. Accordingly, fishermen exercise their own brand of "bush" justice in the
course of fishing disputes, most of which are ultimately a
response to harmful acts committed on shore. This
laissez-faire situation underscores the marginality of
traditional swamp fishing with respect to modern Brazilian
politics and the legal system, and it allows Bahian fishermen to create and enforce their own rules for sea tenure.

OUTCOMES

For many years, Bahia's inshore sea tenure traditions
operated smoothly. There was no evidence that coastal
fisheries were being exploited in an ecologically damaging
manner, indicating that the practices described above were
a successful arrangement for managing common property
resources. A true self-regulated fishery presumes that
fishermen know both the limits of their resources and the
impact of their equipment on resource availability, and
furthermore that they have the ability to keep their rates
of exploitation in line with the productive capacity of the
environment. It is doubtful that there is a traditional
system anywhere that would meet this presumption. Many
commercial species are transboundary or highly migratory,
and no group of inshore fishermen can manipulate the fate
of entire species over their life cycles (cf. Johannes
1981).

Yet this is not to say that deliberate conservation
strategies do not occur or that fishermen cannot assess the
effects of their gear on resources and accordingly adjust
their fishing efforts. Captains possess various means to
gauge how much their production system can safely expand
(Cordell 1977). Perceptions of what constitutes a "safe"
number of people on fishing grounds, however, are primarily
based on acceptable levels of boat crowding rather than on
estimates of the reproductive reserves of fish that are
necessary to sustain certain levels of production.

Resource management in purse seining is socially diffuse and does not involve decisions by a controlling group
or individual; neither does the configuration of territorial ownership control fishing. Rather, fishing is controlled by the special cooperative relationships fishermen
develop with one another. Sea tenure is an extension,
almost an epiphenomenon, of these personal networks.
Within their sea tenure networks, fishermen exercise controls on participation in fishing that may directly or
indirectly limit the intensity of exploitation. Apprenticeships and associated channels for the recruitment and
mobility of fishermen serve to limit entry to the fisheries
in question, in turn curtailing fishing pressure. Although
there is no evidence that tenure patterns were intentionally elaborated for conservation purposes, fishermen have
species-specific knowledge of reproductive and migratory
behavior and display a sophisticated and biologically
well-founded perception of the natural limits to their
production system.

The sea territories are collectively defensible, and only local fishermen know how to work them safely and productively on a sustained basis--both of which discourage encroachment. Left to their own devices, local fishermen can enforce their territorial claims against competitors of similar economic means. However, since sea tenure is legitimized only by internal mechanisms like respeito, it can easily be subverted by the modernization of fishing technology and the expansion of markets. Traditional fishermen are extremely vulnerable to territorial displacement, loss of sea rights, and resource "piracy." All that is required to shatter the balance is for an external power to assert domain--easily done in Brazil because of national laws declaring the shore to be public property--or for a local enclave to begin using competitive technology. Local fishermen cannot cope indefinitely with entrepreneurs who have more capital or with nonresident vessels that have no respect for local customs and no need to cooperate because they will move on after they deplete local resources. At that point, the internal code among local fishermen loses its own raison d'être and breaks down; there is no longer anything for the local fishermen to gain through cooperative fishing or respect of traditional authority or autonomy.

Such encroachment by inappropriate gear and nonresident boats began in the early 1970s, when nylon nets started to compete with traditional gear for identical species and water space; the consequences for traditional fishing were very destructive. We do not have the statistical data on costs and catches for different fishing methods that would be needed to evaluate the efficiency of different techniques, but we do know that overfishing of certain species and areas has occurred since 1970, and that traditional fishermen are even poorer in relative terms than they used to be. Hundreds of monofilament nylon gill nets and seines were introduced by the fisheries agency (SUDEPE), which provided loans and tax incentives for investors.[2] Affluent strangers using nylon nets were unable to coexist peacefully with the established purse seiners, and cutthroat competition for limited net-casting spaces began in earnest. This rivalry has altered the distribution of equipment in Valença and the concentration of ownership in the different categories represented. There is a tendency for traditional nets to be abandoned in favor of secondary methods, such as mobile trotlines and fish corrals, which have a fixed seasonal location and an uncontestable exclusive or even private tenure status. By far the greatest

reduction of gear has occurred in the category of traditional natural-fiber nets. On the whole, net fishing has
been in decline since 1970; but traditional purse seining,
which is remarkably well adapted to estuarine fishing and
to the social organization and redistributive food networks
of poorer neighborhoods, has been making a slight comeback
since 1976.

As a result of encroachment, rich nursery-area fisheries have been gravely damaged, and short-term speculation
and overcapitalization have led to sudden overfishing of a
number of native estuarine and reef species. Previous
studies of the Valença Delta (see Figure 1) have recorded
the debilitating changes in canoe fishing society that were
set in motion with the arrival of nylon gear (Cordell 1973;
1978). Since 1970, conditions have worsened in the Valença
Delta and along the southern coast of Bahia, as far as the
Abrolhos Archipelago. Uncontrolled exploitation of land
and sea resources in the coastal zone has reached a critical intensity (cf. Kottak 1983). Over the past 15 years,
investors and economic planners have targeted the southern
shore for every conceivable kind of development--not just
fisheries but also oil exploration, shipbuilding, tourism,
lumber, agriculture, aquaculture, mining, and heavy metal
processing. New roads have been built into the region,
making it accessible from the large urban centers of
southern Brazil and the state capital, Salvador.[3] The
greatest exploitation of fisheries has been near the major
cities and near shore. A critical area of actual and
potential overfishing now extends from the landward range
of mangrove swamps out to a depth of 50 meters, which
roughly corresponds to the limits of most inshore fishing
gear.

Two of the most visible and possibly destructive pressures on inshore species are the aforementioned use of
monofilament nylon nets and the "pirating" of peasant
fishing territories by out-of-state trawlers and long-
liners. The unregulated use of nylon gear--a single vessel
may set several kilometers of nets--is implicated in territorial conflicts, equipment foul-ups, and reduction of
catches from traditional gear. The blockade effect of gill
nets stretched across a channel may also adversely affect
spawning runs. There has been a continuous escalation of
trawling in waters with depths between 20 and 50 meters.
Large power boats with tiny meshed seines for shrimp kill
many other demersal species. In general, modern trolling
and trawling interfere with the operation of traditional
methods and can irreparably damage the set gear of small-

scale fishermen. Particularly during spawning runs, they
compete for the same spots and species.

In Valença and other southern ports, excessive netting
of major commercial varieties of finfish has produced a
spillover effect on shellfish. Many local fishermen work
the mangrove shellfish habitats, and migrants to and from
cities often settle in the swamp areas to scavenge. More
and more fishermen who conventionally work in the estuaries
and farther offshore with large encircling and dragged nets
have been forced to turn to the swamp for survival. Recent
studies indicate that the intensity of foraging for some
mollusks and crustacea exceeds the sustainable-yield levels
(Cordell 1973; Blanco 1978). Near Valença, swamp-fishing
settlements must shift frequently to achieve a satisfactory
ratio of work-to-production from shellfish-collecting
ranges. Change in these fishing communities has taken
different forms and has differing effects on the economy
and the power structure.

Nylon nets have been selectively introduced in parts
of the delta fishing community; other parts still use traditional technology. Some communities have switched their
economic dependence from the traditional power base of
captains and middlemen to factory bosses, wealthy merchants, and speculators from the Salvador fish and grain
markets. This new power base purchases nylon gear and
canoes for a small segment of townspeople, some of whom
have little or no fishing experience but are desperate
enough to work at fishing for very low fixed wages. Traditional captains must be conservative with their equipment
(usually representing a lifetime's investment), unlike
their competitors with nylon, who can afford to precipitate
spatial conflict that destroys gear. The chaotic expansion
of a nylon-outfitted fishing enclave in the narrow corridor
of brackish water between land and sea marks the end of an
era in which marginality was the small-scale fishermen's
hedge against encroachment and overexploitation of the
fish.

Today in Brazil, capital is available in unprecedented
amounts to fund the expansion of interstate seafood markets, and developers are reaching out with advanced technology to capture even the most residual supplies of fish
and shellfish. They are diverting local food supplies,
which the coastal poor have always fallen back on for subsistence in times of scarcity, to elite urban and foreign
markets. Technical innovation per se is not destructive.
But the way in which change proceeds does disrupt customary
sea tenure and removes the informal spatial and political

autonomy local groups must enjoy if they are to fish sustainably and without conflict. Escalating conflict in Bahia's fisheries demonstrates that the tragedy of the commons is catalyzed when institutions break down that have supported traditional sea tenure. Indeed, traditional sea tenure seems to prevent the tragedy.

CONCLUSIONS

Both the conventional view that fisheries are invariably open-access resources and the argument that poverty inhibits constructive collective action fail to account for what we find in Bahian fishing communities before the arrival of outsiders: the successful management of inshore fisheries resources by marginal, traditional fishermen. Both theories assume that there is no relatedness or strategic interdependence among people who use resources jointly (cf., Runge, this volume). Both contain a certain cynicism about human nature; neither allows for community. Fishing in Brazil, if anything, indicates that cooperative sea tenure is a logical mechanism for allocating perilously scarce resources, and that poverty strengthens these incentives to cooperate all the more. Sea tenure, legitimized through respeito and reciprocity, is embedded in the culture; what has been all too casually deemed self-regulation in small-scale fishing (e.g., Acheson 1981) is actually a subterranean economic system that overflows into every facet of social life.

With extended maritime jurisdiction, many countries, including Brazil, assume sweeping new powers and responsibilities for managing resources without any coherent frame of reference or forum to evaluate fishing claims, particularly traditional ones, or to define and justify new allocations of use rights. Arguments concerning the relative superiority of public or private ownership ignore the value and legitimacy of a third category, that of collective ownership. This study shows that there are practical reasons for the development of inshore tenure. Fishing productively and sustainably near shore requires regulation of access (cf., Stiles 1976). Governments might support such traditional institutions by giving fishermen something approaching guarantees of exclusive community tenure and recognition of the importance of their customary, limited-entry recruitment procedures.

If Brazil and other tropical countries are to begin serious long-range management of their marine resources, they must be prepared to take into account a wide range of customary rights and claims to the sea that they do not now acknowledge. The real managerial strengths in Third World coastal fisheries are indigenous, vested not in the state or its bureaucracies but in fishermen's own informal institutions, norms, and cooperative organizations.

It is difficult to convince fishery authorities that traditional sea tenure even exists in places like Bahia, much less that it is worth preserving. Fishermen's laws are nontechnical and, admittedly, somewhat intangible to the uninitiated. Sea tenure is a kind of invisible wealth, created and maintained for both material and nonmaterial ends. Yet beneath the ragged, impoverished exterior of swamp-fishing communities are rational and proven solutions to problems of sharing, partitioning, and maintaining the fishery. In a traditional context, these solutions minimize conflict and ease fishing pressure by limiting the number of people and types of boats and gear that can fish compatibly in fixed territories close to the shore. Together with fishermen's extensive ecological knowledge of the sea, the tenure arrangements are valuable resources in themselves, worthy of some type of formal protection.

Fishing is one of the few economic alternatives available to the coastal poor in Bahia and other parts of northeastern Brazil. Establishing sea tenure through their own unwritten laws helps local fishermen transcend the misfortune of being born "marginal." Sea rights, in place of land rights that seem forever beyond their reach, give fishermen a group identity, honor, some sense of security, and a chance to own something in the highly class-stratified society of northeastern Brazil. Paradoxically, the marginality that keeps them poor also allows people the independence to invent and speak boldly of their "sea rights," and sometimes to sing like birds and dance as they walk.

NOTES

This research builds on Cordell's earlier fieldwork in
Bahia, Brazil, (Cordell 1973, 1974, 1978), but is principally based on materials collected on the southern coast
during an 18-month marine conservation survey sponsored by
the World Wildlife Fund in the U.S. in 1982-1983. For
assistance in preparing this study, Cordell gratefully
acknowledges the support of the World Wildlife Fund and a
fellowship awarded by the Social Science Research Council.

1. Studies elsewhere in northeastern Brazil (Kottak 1966;
Forman 1967, 1970; Robben 1984) contain valuable clues and
observations concerning the emergence of territorial
systems among similar groups of small-scale fishermen.

2. For the past 25 years, Brazil has pursued policies of
unrestricted fishery development, encouraged by a number of
fiscal incentives for entrepreneurs and investors.
Decreto-Lei 221/67 provided tax exemptions of 25 to
75 percent on personal income invested in fishing; it
suspended both import tariffs on fisheries technology and
craft and various federal taxes on catches destined for
luxury internal and export seafood markets. These incentives supersede the 1938-39 fisheries codes (Codigos de
Pesca), which contained some potentially useful, though
unenforceable, management concepts (such as exclusive zones
for fixed-territorial methods like fish corrals). The tax
incentives remain in effect at this writing, and will probably be prolonged despite recent sobering catch statistics.
    Falling catches are illustrated by changes in shrimp
and several other major species. With one of the most
extensive coasts in the world (nearly 8,000 kilometers) and
a favored climate, Brazil ranks among the 10 largest
shrimp-producing countries. However, the total shrimp
harvest, which reached a high of 129,000 tons in 1972, had
decreased to 79,000 tons in 1979 (Silva 1979). Exports
rose somewhat during this period from 6,783 to 7,172 tons,
but per capita consumption decreased from 0.506 kg to

0.197 kg (Silva 1979), due to steep increases in the price
of shrimp on the domestic market. Overall, catches in
Brazil rose from 280,000 tons in 1960 to 816,000 tons in
1974 (Anuario Estatistico do Brasil 1976:158). This growth
was largely spurred by tax incentives (Silva 1979:28-43).
Between 1974 and 1979, the total catch only increased from
816,000 to 858,000 tons (Anuario Estatistico do Brasil
1981:354-355), indicating a nationwide leveling-off of
production. The five principal species caught--tuna, cor-
vina, shrimp, lobster, and sardines--have been in a state
of decline since 1979 (Nascimento 1982).

3. Additional impacts on coastal fishery resources that
are difficult to quantify are: stepped up drilling and
exploration by the Brazilian oil company, PETROBRAS; bio-
cide runoff from plantations in the littoral zone; increasing landfill for highways, resorts, and other construction;
and widespread extraction of coral for cal, lime manufac-
ture. Dynamite is heavily employed in this mining process,
and according to coral-reef specialist Laborel (1969) who
worked in Bahia, the Itaparica reefs in Salvador Bay were
practically dead due to the extraction of lime-rich
deposits.

REFERENCES

Acheson, J. M. 1981. Anthropology of fishing. Annual
    Reviews of Anthropology 10:275-316.

Anuario Estatistico do Brasil. 1976:158.

Anuario Estatistico do Brasil. 1981:354-355.

Blanco, M. 1978. Race and face in Bahia. Unpublished
    Ph.D. dissertation. Stanford, California: Department
    of Anthropology, Stanford University.

Bodley, J. 1981. Victims of Progress. Menlo Park,
    California: Cummings Press.

Bromley, D. 1978. Property rules, liability rules, and
    environmental economics. Journal of Economic Issues
    12:43-60.

Christy, F. T. Jr. 1964. The exploitation of common
    property natural resource: the Maryland oyster
    industry. Unpublished Ph.D. dissertation. Ann Arbor,
    Michigan: University of Michigan.

Christy, F. T. Jr. 1982. Territorial use rights in marine
    fisheries: definitions and conditions. FAO Technical
    Papers, No. 227. Rome: Food and Agriculture
    Organization of the United Nations.

Christy, F. T. Jr. and A. Scott. 1965. The Common Wealth
    in Ocean Fisheries. Baltimore, Maryland: Johns
    Hopkins University Press.

Cordell, J. C. 1973. Modernization and marginality.
    Oceanus 17:28-33.

Cordell, J. C. 1974. The lunar-tide fishing cycle in
    northeastern Brazil. Ethnology 13:379-392.

Cordell, J. C. 1977. Carrying capacity analysis of fixed territorial fishing. Ethnology 17, No. 1.

Cordell, J. C. 1978. Swamp fishing in Bahia. Natural History, June:62-74.

Cordell, J. C. 1986. A Sea of Small Boats: Customary Law of the Sea and Territoriality in the World of Inshore Fishing. Cambridge, Massachusetts: Cultural Survival Report 26 (in press).

Crutchfield, J. 1982. The economics of fisheries management. In Howe 1982.

Forman, S. O. 1967. Cognition and the catch: the location of fishing spots in a Brazilian coastal village. Ethnology 6:405-426.

Forman, S. O. 1970. Jangadeiros: Raft Fisherman of Northeastern Brazil. Bloomington: Indiana University Press.

Gulland, J. 1974. The Management of Marine Resources. Seattle, Washington: University of Washington Press.

Hardin, G. 1968. The tragedy of the commons. Science 162: 1243-1248.

Howe, C. W., ed. 1982. Managing Renewable Natural Resources in Developing Countries. Boulder, Colorado: Westview Press.

Johannes, R. E. 1978. Traditional marine conservation methods in Oceania and their demise. Annual Review of Ecological Systems 9:349-364.

Johannes, R. E. 1981. Words of the Lagoon: Fishing and Marine Lore in the Palau District of Micronesia. Berkeley, California: University of California Press.

Johnston, D. M., ed. 1976. Marine Policy and the Coastal Community. New York: Saint Martins Press.

Kottak, C. 1966. The structure of equality in a Brazilian fishing community. Ph.D. thesis. New York: Department of Anthropology, Columbia University.

Kottak, C. 1983. Assault on Paradise. New York: Random House.

Laborel, J. 1969. Les peuplements de Madréporaires de côtes tropicales du Brasil. Annales de l'Université d'Abidjan (Ecologie) 2, No. 3:1-261.

Lewis, O. 1952. Urbanization without breakdown. Scientific Monthly 75, No. 1:31-41.

Lobo, S. 1982. A House of My Own: Social Organization in the Squatter Settlements of Lima, Peru. Tucson, Arizona: University of Arizona Press.

Morris, M. 1979. International Politics and the Sea: The Case of Brazil. Boulder, Colorado: Westview Press.

Muir, B. and M. Muir. 1981. Where've you been, stranger?: disintermediation in the maritimes. Coevolution Quarterly, Summer:74-77.

Muir, B. and M. Muir. 1982. Think its breezin' up? Coevolution Quarterly, Summer:40-43.

Nascimento, I. A. 1982. Cultivo de camaroes marinhos no Brasil. Boletim de Pos-Graduaao e Pesquisa. (Universidade Federal de Bahia, Brazil) 2, No. 1:5-11.

Oberg, K. 1965. The marginal peasant in Brazil. American Anthropologist 67:1417-1427.

Pearlman, J. 1973. Rio's favelados and the myth of marginality. Institute of Urban and Regional Development, Working Paper, No. 222. Berkeley, California: University of California.

Robben, A. C. 1984. Entrepreneurs and scale: interactional and institutional constraints on the growth of small-scale enterprises in Brazil. Anthropological Quarterly 57, No. 3:125-138.

Silva, S. B. 1979. Consideracoes sobre a pesca baiana no contexto da pesca Brasileira. Boletim Baiano de Geografia. XII, No. 18, Vol. 11:28-45.

Stiles, G. 1976. The small maritime community and its resource management problems. In Johnston 1976.

Varallanos, J. 1962. El cholo y el Peru: introducción
al estudio sociológico de un hombre y un pueblomestizo
y su destino cultural. Buenos Aires: Imprensa Lopez.

BIBLIOGRAPHY

Acheson, J. M. 1972. Territories of the lobstermen.
    Natural History 81:60-69.

Acheson, J. M. 1975. The lobster feifs. Human Ecology
    3:187-207.

Ciriacy-Wantrup, S. and R. Bishop. 1975. Common property
    as a concept in natural resources policy. Natural
    Resources Journal 15, No. 4:713-727.

Cordell, J. C. 1983. Sea tenure and marginality in
    Brazilian fishing. Occasional papers in Latin American
    studies, No. 6. Latin American Studies Association,
    Stanford University and the University of California at
    Berkeley. Stanford, California: Stanford University
    Press.

Cordell, J. C. 1986. A Sea of Small Boats: Customary Law
    of the Sea and Territoriality in the World of Inshore
    Fishing. Cambridge, Massachusetts: Cultural Survival
    Report 26 (in press).

Dasgupta, P. 1982. The Control of Resources. Oxford:
    Basil Blackwell.

Fenn, P. 1926. The Origin of the Right of Fishery in
    Territorial Waters. Cambridge, Massachusetts: Harvard
    University Press. (Reprinted in 1974 by Crofton:
    Newton, Massachusetts.)

Hardin, G. and J. Baden, eds. 1977. Managing the Commons.
    San Francisco: W. H. Freeman.

International Union for Nature and Natural Resources. 1980.
    The World Conservation Strategy. Gland, Switzerland.

Lomnitz, L. 1977. Networks and Marginality: Life in a Mexican Shantytown. New York: Academic Press.

McCay, B. 1978. Systems ecology, people ecology, and the anthropology of fishing communities. Human Ecology 6, No. 4:397-422.

McCay, B. 1986. The culture of the commoners. In Cordell 1986.

Musham, H. 1977. An algebraic theory of the commons. In Hardin and Baden 1977.

Nader, L. and H. Todd, eds. 1978. The Disputing Process in Ten Societies. New York: Columbia University Press.

Yngvesson, B. 1978. The Atlantic fishermen. In Nader and Todd 1978.

Overfishing and Conflict in a Traditional Fishery: San Miguel Bay, Philippines[1]

Wilfrido D. Cruz

INTRODUCTION

San Miguel Bay in the Camarines Sur province of the Philippines is a major fishing ground on the country's Pacific coast. The bay, located on the Pacific coast of Luzon island, is relatively shallow and very productive. While a great variety of fish make up the aggregate catch, shrimp are the most important in terms of economic value. Apart from its productivity (and consequently its economic relevance), the bay is instructive as a case study because it is a very well-defined fishery where the patterns of technical change and resource overexploitation may be clearly identified.

Government intervention in increasing the amount of fishing and the introduction of nontraditional techniques have triggered instances of conflict that cannot be resolved in the current institutional context of traditional fisheries in the Philippines. While the exploitation of the coastal fishery would be better controlled with the introduction of common property approaches to management, the formal institutional structure for resource use does not recognize the common property attributes of the fishery. Government policy therefore treats the resource management problem in much the same way as a conventional private property problem--merely a case of enforcing fishery access rights. The result is that the management system fails to address the growing problems of fishery overexploitation and conflict among different groups of resource users.

After presenting the data sources and describing the physical and technical characteristics of the bay fishery, the paper will relate how government intervention and the introduction of new technology (specifically, trawling gear) have engendered conflicts that transcend the changes that will result from the increasing population pressures in the area. The discussion highlights the presence of a resource sustainability threshold beyond which transitions are neither gradual nor peaceful; indeed, they are characterized by conflict.

DATA SOURCES

San Miguel Bay is located in the Camarines Sur province in Region V (Bicol) of the Philippines (see Figure 1). The primary data on this area is based on fieldwork in four municipalities of Camarines Sur that border the bay: Sipocot, Cabusao, Calabanga, and Tinambac. Most interviews were conducted during 1981, but follow-up fieldwork was done in 1984.

Interviewees were chosen to ensure that all the important fishing gear types and the complex of institutional arrangements governing the utilization of these gears would be sampled. Gear was ranked according to popularity of use in the area based on the results of a major survey of the bay conducted by the University of the Philippines Institute of Fishery Development and Research (IFDR) and the International Center for Living Aquatic Resource Management (ICLARM) in 1980 and 1981. (See Smith, et al. 1983 for a full description of this research.) Thereafter, the relative popularity of each of the ten types of gear in each of the survey villages was determined by dividing the number of a particular gear type by total number of fishing households in the barrio. The listing of the top ten gears and their relative popularity is presented in Table 1.

The primary technique used in the investigation was unstructured interviews with informants involved in the relevant fishing activity in each of the villages. The choice of the informant was based on his familiarity (as ascertained by barrio captains and IFDR-ICLARM field researchers) with the history, the operation, and the institutional arrangements pertaining to a particular gear. (See Appendix for the list and description of respondents.)

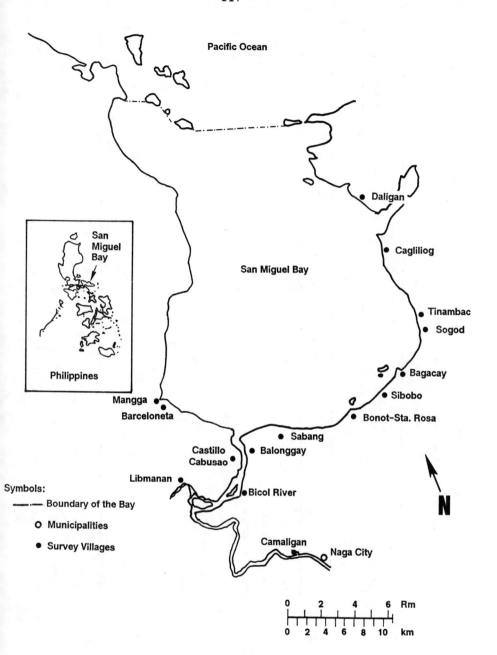

FIGURE 1 San Miguel Bay.

TABLE 1 Ranking of Gear Types and Their Relative Popularity in San Miguel Bay Communities.

					Rank of Gear					
	1	2	3	4	5	6	7	8	9	10
Gear[a]	Gill net	Sakag	Banwit	Baby trawl	Kitang	Bocatot	Itik-Itik	Bubo	Sagkad	Biacus
Number Used[b]	486	105	68	62	55	47	44	31	18	17
Relative Popularity[c] (%)										
Sipocot Mangga	91	23				5			2	
Cabusao Castillo	71	71	2	1			29		1	8
Calabanga Sabang	37	27	1	27			44			
Balonggay	27	27	71		2				7	27
Bonot-Sta. Rosa	58	68	10		5	62	2	2	2	
Sibobo	81	53						12	15	
Tinambac Sogod	21		61			5	6			
Daligan	47		22		1			52		18
Bagacay		75		9						
Cagliliog						52				

[a]See Table 2 for a description of gear types.

[b]Number of each corresponding gear reported in use the bay from IFDR-ICLARM survey.

[c]Relative popularity computed as number of particular gear divided by number of fishing households in the community; data based on IFDR-ICLARM community inventories.

RESOURCE ATTRIBUTES AND FISHING TECHNOLOGY

Because of its location, San Miguel Bay is only fished during certain seasons. From April to September, the period of the southwest monsoon (amihan), the entire bay is fairly well-protected. However, very little fishing activity can take place (except along the Tinambac village side) during the northwest monsoon (habagat) from October to March.

The bay itself covers approximately 840 square kilometers with a modal depth of less than 7.2 meters.[2] The bottom of the bay is generally muddy, which makes it an ideal trawling ground.

Consistent with the multispecies nature of the fishery, a great variety of fish make up the aggregate catch; shrimp are the most important, but croakers, anchovies, sardines, and mullets are also found along with such trashfish as undersized slipmouths and goat fish.

The resource is clearly renewable. The Bicol River introduces large quantities of freshwater into the bay, giving the fishery estuarine characteristics and very high productivity. It has recently been estimated that the aggregate catch is 19,000 tons (Smith et al. 1983) of which shrimps make up the most part (South China Sea Program 1978).

Exclusion is very difficult except along the river and the shore where the right to set fixed gears has traditionally been allocated by informal village resource managers called amoionadors (boundary setters).[3] While the fishing activity itself is essentially open, a potential exclusion point is at the fish landings since the catch, in the absence of ice storage in most of the boats, must be disposed of immediately, and there are limited landing areas (normally one per village).

Fishing Technology

A great variety of fishing gear is used in traditional small-scale fisheries, due to the different fishing environments exploited and to the presence of many different types of fish. Even within a household, more than one gear is available, at least for the different fishing seasons during the year.

The villages are located in diverse ecological areas, so there are variations in the types of species and their seasonality. These variations result in differing choices

and uses of gear. While such choices are necessitated by
the resource environment, the prevailing techno-
institutional context tends to impose basic similarities
in resource use that cut across the different gears. On
the whole, gears are simple and usually constructed by the
household. Accordingly, access to the technology is quite
easy for most members of the fishing community (see
Table 2);[4] the capital required to acquire gear is low,
consistent with the generally low levels of accumulation
that obtain in the fishing community. Another aspect of
the prerequisite of techno-institutional consistency may
be pointed out: with respect to the marketing channels for
excess production, the low volumes of catch and the important species in the catch are associated with a particular
type and level of development of product distribution and
processing. Consequently, attempts at innovation require
a sensitivity to a much broader range of problems and
potentials than is generally recognized.

This concept of techno-institutional consistency
pointed out above allows us to group the variety of gears
in use into two major types. From Table 2 we may note that
the "baby trawlers" (medium and small), characterized by
high energy use, large capitalization (relative to labor
absorption), and a primarily market-oriented level of catch
represent an essentially capital-intensive technique of
resource exploitation. On the other hand, the proliferation of all the other gears generally represents a strategy
of exploiting different species in as many locations and
during as many months of the year as possible--an extensive
form of resource use. Capital requirements for some of
these traditional gears have recently risen because boats
(used for operation of gill nets, lift nets) have been
motorized, the costs of traditional construction materials
(especially for stationary gear) are very inflated, and
synthetic materials have been substituted for traditional
ones (especially for nets). Thus the construction of traditional gears has changed--somewhat improving efficiency--
but their basic ability to exploit the resource has not
changed. More important, their use is not as dependent as
the baby trawler system on markets for factor inputs
(especially fuel) and for specialized fish or shrimp
harvests.

TABLE 2   Gear Description and Requirements.

Gear Type	Description	Capitalization in Pesos[a]	Number of Employed	Marketing[b]
Stationary:				
Bocatot	Stationary lift net that works best in sheltered shallow waters (characteristic of Cagliliog); requires a maestro skilled in operating lights and lifting the net	6,400-9,700	4-5	Specialized handling of significant volumes of anchovies
Biacus	Filter net requiring placement against a current, usually set at the mouth of a river (typical of Daligan and Balonggay)	2,200-3,300	1-2	
Sagkad	Fish corral needing shallow, sheltered water	2,000-4,000	1-2	
Net:				
Gill net	Drift or set gill net	1,100-3,800	2	
Trawl:				
Itik-itik	Very small trawl, usually run by a 16 hp engine; operates in shallow water	4,300-7,100	2	Specialized markets for balao
Baby trawl	Small trawler weighing about 3 G.T.; uses a 190-240 hp engine	44,500-59,300	4-6	Large volume of catch to be marketed
Others:				
Banwit	Hook and line used for large fish species in rocky or coral-bottomed areas; requires knowledge of good fishing ground	500-3,200	1-2	
Kalikot	Hand-operated scissors net used in shallow muddy water	30-50	1	
Bubo	Fish traps used for large fish species in rocky or coral-bottomed areas	300-3,400	1	

[a] Capitalization figures are approximate ranges for 1981 based on experience and observations of informants. Gill net and bocatot costs include motor boat (10-16 hp and 5-16 hp, respectively). Biacus and sagkad costs include non-motorized boat. The upper limits for banwit and bubo represent inclusion of small motor (about 5 hp).

[b] Unless specified in marketing requirements column, specific gear needs no special marketing capability.

Overfishing and Conflict

Standard overfishing occurs when both increasing fishing effort and declining catch are observed in a fishery. This is based on Gordon-Schaefer models of the relation between effort and catch.

Before the 1950s, population growth rates for the Bicol region, the Camarines Sur province, and the San Miguel Bay were generally above Philippine rates (see Tables 3 and 4). Presumably, the demands of the growing communities surrounding the bay were also increasing in this period. Since the 1950s there has been a decline in population growth rate for San Miguel Bay (relative to regional and national rates); this may be due to the limited absorption capacity of the area's economic base--the fishery. Fish catch information for both periods, however, is not available, so it is not possible to make any definite conclusion on whether overfishing occurred.

While the role of population pressure in natural resource exploitation is potentially significant, its importance in San Miguel Bay has been overshadowed since the 1970s by technical changes that have exacerbated trends toward fishery overexploitation that followed population growth. This is due to two specific developments. The first is the government's program, initiated in the mid-1970s, to upgrade fishing technology by offering low-cost loans for motorizing fishing boats. In San Miguel Bay, 1,206 municipal fishermen received loans of about P4.5 million (Philippine pesos) for this upgrading program (Smith et al. 1983). At about the same time, an unusual form of technical innovation--the baby trawler--was introduced in the fishery. Capitalized at about P50,000 each in 1981, these are shallow-draft boats powered by diesel engines (of 200 or more horsepower) that allow the boats to pull trawl nets. They were designed to meet the small-scale classification (less than 3 gross tons) so that they could trawl within coastal waters. These two factors have substantially changed the level of resource exploitation and the pattern of distribution that has resulted in conflict in the fishery by the early 1980s.

DECISION-MAKING ARRANGEMENTS AND PATTERNS OF INTERACTION

The appropriateness of decision-making arrangements regarding access to or control of resources needs to be evaluated in the context of available resources and growing

TABLE 3   Population Growth Rates for the Philippines, the
           Bicol Region, Camarines Sur Province, and Four San
           Miguel Bay Survey Municipalities, 1918-1975.

	Place	Annual Growth Rates					
		1918	1939	1948	1960	1970	1975
1	Philippines	1.92	2.22	1.91	3.06	3.01	2.79
2	Bicol Region	1.75	2.38	2.21	3.13	2.25	1.48
3	Camarines Sur	0.81	2.74	4.10	3.72	1.47	1.54
4	Four SMB Municipalities	0.00	3.51	4.82	4.65	1.49	0.99

Basic Source of Data: Republic of the Philippines, Bureau
of Census and Statistics, 1975.

interdependence among resource users. The fisheries of San
Miguel Bay, like other coastal fisheries of the Philippines, were traditionally characterized by open access
exploitation.
     With an abundance of fishery resources (relative to the
demands of a small population), the degree of specific
institutional controls on decision making and interaction
was quite limited. The notable exception was that
near-shore areas were allocated to specific families for
exclusive use for fixed gear, due to the limited availability of such sites even during periods of relative
abundance. In general, therefore, as long as basic rights
were respected (e.g., the right not to be disturbed once
one's boat and gear have been set for the particular day's
fishing), there was much room for individualistic decision
making.
     Aside from this environmental and demographic context,
which was conducive to individualistic decision-making
arrangements, the technical nature of the fishing activity
itself contributed to this pattern. In contrast to rice
farming communities--where intravillage work is closely
coordinated through exchange labor groups, irrigation
associations and village councils--the traditional fishing

TABLE 4 Population Densities for the Philippines, the Bicol Region, Camarines Sur Province, and Four San Miguel Bay Survey Municipalities, 1903-1975.

Place	Land Area (km^2)	Population Density						
		1903	1918	1939	1948	1960	1970	1975
1 Philippines	300,000	25.2	34.4	53.3	64.1	90.3	122.3	140.2
2 Bicol Region	17,632	36.5	47.6	76.4	94.5	134.0	168.3	181.1
3 Camarines Sur	5,267	36.8	41.6	73.2	105.1	155.6	180.1	194.4
4 Cabusao	47	66.1	54.4	100.9	109.2	170.6	193.2	219.1
5 Calabanga	164	43.6	48.5	92.0	132.9	173.6	211.7	233.7
6 Sipocot	212	13.2	12.9	37.4	85.3	172.9	180.0	191.8
7 Tinambac	316	16.8	17.4	34.6	44.6	91.5	115.1	108.9
Sum of 4-7	739	25.0	25.4	52.4	80.0	138.1	160.1	168.1

Basic Source of Data: Republic of the Philippines, Bureau of Census and Statistics, 1975.

village exhibits relatively few instances of institutional
control. In general, the organization of work in fisheries
is characterized by fewer interdependencies among production units so that traditionally basic rules (e.g., constraining the use of destructive fishing techniques) have
sufficed for resource management.

However, when population growth increases the competition for fixed fishery resources, arrangements for access
to or control of such resources may become quite complex.
It is necessary to distinguish between the degree of control over the resource and the form that such control
takes. While the tendency for resource control tends to
be monotonic (generally increasing), the same cannot be
said for the form of control. In some fishery case studies
(Forman 1970; Cordell 1980; Spoehr 1980), it has been shown
that decision making and control tend to be cooperatively
done so that the resource management system follows the
common property model. In other instances, a more formal
government role is introduced with population growth, and
the fishery becomes part of the public domain. The
government then allocates the use of the resource through
licensing or leasing systems.

In the Philippines, the current system follows the
second pattern: public ownership of the fishery is divided
between the off-shore resource, which is directly under the
national government's jurisdiction, and the coastal fishery, which is assigned to municipalities. The boundary
between these fisheries has been set at three nautical
miles from the shore. Additional depth limitations are set
for the use of trawling equipment: trawlers of more than 3
gross tons may operate only in waters more than 7 fathoms
deep, while the lighter ones may operate to as shallow a
depth as 4 fathoms.

In the case of San Miguel Bay, based on charts of the
Philippine Bureau of Coast and Geodetic Survey for the area
of the four municipalities, maximum water depth in no
instance exceeds 5 fathoms. In fact, only very small portions of the area exceed 4 fathoms in depth (mostly off
Cagliliog in Tinambac). Thus, not even municipal trawling
is legal in most areas.

Implications for Patterns of Interaction

The problem with this system is that while the apparent
control of fishery resource use is assigned to government

policymakers, the de facto system of exploitation of offshore fisheries is closer to open access. Indeed, even the
coastal fishery rules are difficult to enforce with the
limited resources available to most municipalities. In
this situation, there arises a large discrepancy between
the formal decision-making system that is supposed to
govern resource use and the actual pattern of interaction.

This underscores the fact that formal decision-making
rules comprise only one set of determinants of the pattern
of interaction that prevails. At least two other sets are
important in San Miguel Bay as well as in other coastal
fisheries--the first encompasses the informal rules that
are based on local beliefs or practices; the second has to
do with the differential technical capabilities of users in
exploiting the resource. The relative importance of these
two latter groups of factors can have critical implications
for the pattern of interaction that may arise.

A useful way of distinguishing between interaction
patterns is to determine whether they are primarily
conflict-oriented or cooperative. In the bay, cooperative
forms are characteristic of the traditional fishery, while
the relationships between the traditional and the trawl
fishermen are conflict-oriented.

In the case of the traditional fishery, conflict as a
pattern of interaction did not arise, even when external
regulation from government was very limited. In the period
of growing population pressure (since the 1950s), interaction within the traditional sector has nonetheless been
characterized by coordination or cooperation, even in the
face of declining average catch.

For example, UPCF-ICLARM survey data show that in spite
of the increasing pressure on resources and growing interdependencies, the majority of fishermen considered traditional techniques not to be destructive of the resource.
Almost a quarter of all fishermen linked declining catch
with the growth of effort in the fishery. However, almost
a third believed that the destructive activity was due only
to the operation of trawlers in traditional grounds.

Informants in Castillo say that fishermen from the
neighboring municipality of Mercedes seasonally transfer
to Castillo for the balao (tiny shrimp) season late in the
year, yet no apparent conflicts have developed, suggesting
the efficacy of traditional rules of access in coordinating
these traditional activities.

On the other hand, in the case of the entry of commercial trawlers, the pattern of interaction has tended to be

largely conflict-oriented. In the first place, the destructive technical capability of trawlers in overexploiting the resource is very different from that of traditional
gears that are quite selective with respect to catch.
Indeed, some fishermen reported that trawlers are not only
destructive of the resource but also of other gears. Nets
and traps, for example, are often damaged by indiscriminate
trawling activities. The operation of trawlers therefore
runs counter to traditional perceptions vis-à-vis destructive fishing techniques.

And in the second place, trawlers demand an unusually
large capital investment, meaning that only those who are
economically well off will benefit from the fishery resource; an unusually large proportion of catch is therefore captured by the very small group of wealthy fisherman
who can afford to purchase and operate the trawlers. This
undermines the more equitable sharing patterns that are
characteristic of traditional fisheries.

Moreover, and to compound the problems thus far described, traditional fishermen are aware that the operation of the trawlers within municipal waters is often not
legal. The effect is widespread friction between the traditional fishermen and the trawlers.

OUTCOMES AND IMPLICATIONS FOR MANAGEMENT

When resources were abundant, fishery catch was dependent primarily on the level of technology and not on differential access or endowments of rights to the resource
(except for the case of near-shore fixed gear locations).
Income distribution was therefore interesting only in terms
of fishermen's access to technology and not in terms of
resource endowment.

The growth of population pressure from the 1950s did
not necessarily bring with it widespread dissatisfaction
with resource management practices. While the overall
catch in the area might have been stable (or might have in
fact slowly increased), there is no doubt that average
catch started to decline in this period. The distribution
of the catch among traditional gears, however, did not
significantly change. Indeed, easy access to the different
low-cost gears must have been an important factor in
stabilizing income distribution.

The increase in effective effort (since the mid-1970s)
coupled with the entry of the trawling fleet (in the late

1970s) radically changed both overall catch and distribution conditions. Latest estimates for the fishery (by
Smith et al. 1983) show that of the 19,000 tons total catch
in 1981, the 5000 or more small-scale fishermen caught only
60 percent of the total while the 95 trawlers in the bay
got the rest. The situation is worse when reported in
terms of the value of catch: the baby trawlers, which
represented only 3 percent of fishing units and employed
only 7 percent of labor, got 42 percent of the P53.5 million worth of catch and over 50 percent of resource
rents.[5]

Because of the rapid pace at which this transition has
occurred (trawlers were introduced not more than 5 or
6 years before this 1981 estimate), and because of the
unusual inaccessibility of this technology, this trend
toward resource overexploitation and increasing concentration of the benefits of resource use has led to widespread
dissatisfaction among traditional fishermen over the
inability of current institutional arrangements to control
trawling.

Inadequate enforcement of municipal fishery regulations
has fueled a growing discontent among traditional fishermen
who complain not only of the indirect effect of trawling
in terms of decreased catch but of numerous instances where
trawlers have destroyed nets and traps. Cases of violent
confrontations between trawlers and traditional fishermen
have been reported. Active organizational work among traditional fishermen has occurred especially in the communities in the eastern side of the bay where municipal leaders
have tended to take the side of the small fishermen versus
the owners of the trawlers.

Implications for Management

A program of fishery management for the bay needs to
address the problem of growing interdependence (and conflict) due to: (1) a general increase in population levels
leading to more potential conflict among traditional
fishermen, and (2) a sharp increase in effective effort
linked to the greater role of commercial trawlers in
near-shore areas.

These two concerns point to the need for greater control and management of the fishery on the basis of
techno-institutional and environmental considerations.
With the growing interdependencies in fishing activity--

both among traditional fishermen and between the commercial and traditional sectors--the community will be forced to evolve essentially new forms of cooperation for management of the resource--forms that may require greater interaction within the village level and more formal means of assuring access to resource use.

On an essentially technical level, near-shore fisheries need to be demarcated from offshore fisheries with the distinction being based on the technical capacity for resource exploitation of the traditional versus the commercial sector.

By reserving near-shore resources according to the capability for exploitation by the traditional sector, the community is allowed a greater opportunity for internally generated adjustments, and the potential is reduced for both recruitment and growth overfishing in the coastal areas (which principally arises from commercial intrusion). At the same time, if commercial fleets (primarily trawlers) are limited to the offshore areas that cannot be exploited by traditional techniques, capital will be channeled to the resources where the traditional fishery cannot intensify its efforts.

Because the determination of access to near-shore resources is tied to the capability of traditional techniques, such a program will be acceptable both in terms of historical access and current regional programs that implicitly differentiate access to fishing grounds by techniques used. Indeed, this approach may be interpreted as a rationalization of current trends; however, it also introduces the main advantage of providing a theoretical (versus arbitrary) basis for the regulation of techniques of capture.

It can be shown that this approach represents a rare case in which less developed countries' apparently conflicting national goals for fishery development of increasing production and promoting maritime community assistance (Emmerson 1980) can both be adequately met. With respect to assistance, preventing commercial trawlers from exploiting near-shore resources will undoubtedly have beneficial implications for employment in the traditional fisheries.

Although not as obvious, it is also the case that the limitation of technology in near-shore areas does not imply any long-term decrease in output potential. It merely suggests the imposition of a particular distribution of income because the maximum sustainable yield of the multi-species fishery is essentially fixed; the real question is who can appropriate the catch. Given the presumption that, without management, the commercial fishery will not only monopolize the catch but deplete the stock as well, this program of management not only contributes to a viable fishery but assigns the problem of exploiting the more inaccessible grounds and adjusting to a smaller proportion of catch to the commercial sector. With the flexibility and resources that such adjustment requires, the commercial sector will be in a better position than are traditional fishermen to make the investment or to find alternative income sources.

Apart from the technical aspect, a major problem remains the failure of municipal fishery officials to recognize the inadequacy of current institutions that are expected to govern the bay. In the current setup, the common property attributes of the fishery and the potential for interdependent decision making and action cannot be exploited because the regulatory mechanism uses a licensing system that is dependent on centralized enforcement. Because such enforcement (given the extensive nature of the resource and the limited funds available to municipal authorities controlling the bay) does not work, there is a clear need to establish regulatory mechanisms that can utilize instead of ignore the common property attributes of the fishery. To be sure, the growing interaction within villages and organizational efforts of local fishermen point to local participation that is just waiting to be harnessed.

For example, municipal governments (while retaining their jurisdiction over current traditional fishing grounds) may increasingly formalize systems of village control over fishing grounds and fish landing sites. Especially in the case of landing sites, local sanctions against catching immature fish or against the use of illegal gears may be established through the local village organization. The specific form of organization should be determined from a detailed management study. On the one hand, the structure may require nothing more than a variation of cooperative organization. On the other hand, it may require separate legislation that assigns to the village explicit legal rights and obligations for fishery management.

Survey Areas, Sample Size, Description
of Respondents, and Topics Discussed

Location	n	Informant	Topic
Sipocot Mangga	1	Pangke (gill net) operator	
Cabusao: Castillo	3	Municipal Development Officer	General conditions of enforcement of fishing laws and problems of fishermen in Cabusao
		Fish buyer	Systems of marketing and gill net fishing in Castillo
		Itik-Itik (mini trawl) operator	
Calabanga: Sabang	12	Baby-trawl owner	History of trawling in San Miguel Bay: operation of gear
		Trawl-net maker	Design, measurements of different trawl types
		Kuto-Kuto (mini trawl, Itik-Itik) operator	
		Baby-trawl operator	
Bonot-Station Rosa		Bocatot (lift net) operator	
		Kalikot (scissors net, sakay) operator	

Survey Areas, Sample Size, Description
of Respondents, and Topics Discussed

Location	n	Informant	Topic
Calabanga (continued):			
Sibobo		Pangke (gill net) operator	
		Sagkad (fish corral) operator	
		Bubo (fish trap) operator	
Balonggay		Banwit (hook and line) operator	
		Biacus (filter net) operator	
		Bintol operator	
Tinambac:	7	Acting Municipal Mayor	Lift net fishing conditions; trawler, gill net operation; conflicts
Sogod		Banwit operator	
Daligan		Biacus operator	
		Bubo operator	
Bagacay		Kalikot (scissors net variant) operator	
		Baby-trawl operator	
Cagliliog		Bocatot operator	

Notes: For the different gear operators, the interview guide was use
These are detailed interviews; short interviews with minor informants
are not listed here.

NOTES

1. This paper draws on information gathered for the
author's dissertation research (during which he benefited
from the scholarly generosity of the staff of the Institute
of Fishery Development Research and Management) and more
recent data from an ongoing project funded by the International Development Research Centre (Project 3-A-83-4926).
The author, of course, retains sole responsibility for the
contents of the paper.

2. Much of the discussion of the characteristics of the
bay is taken from Vakily (1980).

3. The amoionador loosely translates as "the one who sets
the boundary." According to informants, they were primarily respected elders in the community who had a good grasp
of the history of family claims on fishing sites and whose
primary duty was to regulate the entry of new gear to
ensure the least interference on the activity of existing
gears.

4. Before the entry of commercial fleets and government
gear upgrading programs, very few boats were motorized, and
consequently even these were inexpensive.

5. Trawler ownership is concentrated among very few
families who are resident in the municipalities and who
also control a substantial part of the fish marketing and
processing activities.

REFERENCES

Cordell, J. 1980. Carrying capacity of fixed
    territorial fishing. In Spoehr 1980.

Emmerson, D. K. 1980. Rethinking Artisanal Fisheries
    Development: Western Concepts, Asian Experiences.
    Washington, D.C.: World Bank Staff Working Paper
    No. 423.

Forman, S. 1970. The Raft Fishermen: Tradition and
    Change in the Brazilian Peasant Economy. Bloomington:
    Indiana University Press.

Smith, I. R., et al. 1983. Small-Scale Fisheries of San
    Miguel Bay, Philippines: Options for Management and
    Research. Manila: International Center for Living
    Aquatic Resources Management.

South China Sea Program. 1978. Report of the BFAR/SCSP
    Workshop on the Fishery Resources of the Pacific Coast
    of the Philippines. Naga City, Philippines: South
    China Sea Program.

Spoehr, A., ed. 1980. Maritime Adaptations: Essays on
    Contemporary Fishing Communities. Pittsburgh,
    Pennsylvania: University of Pittsburgh Press.

Vakily, J. M. 1980. The Exploitation of a Fishing Ground
    in the Philippines. Kiel, Federal Republic of
    Germany: Institut für Meereskunde an der Christian-
    Albrechts-Universität Keil.

BIBLIOGRAPHY

Crisostomo, C. and R. Barker. 1973. Growth Rates of
    Philippine Agriculture, 1948-1971. East-West Center
    Conference on Agricultural Growth in Japan, Korea, and
    the Philippines. Honolulu, Hawaii: East-West Center.

Economic and Social Commission for Asia and the Pacific.
    1978. Populations of the Philippines. Bangkok:
    United Nations.

Forman, S. 1980. Cognition and catch: the location of
    fishing spots in a Brazilian coastal village. In
    Spoehr, A., ed. Maritime Adaptations: Essays on
    Contemporary Fishing Communities. Pittsburgh,
    Pennsylvania: University of Pittsburgh Press. 1980.

Larkin, P. 1982. Directions for future research in
    tropical multi-species fisheries. In Pauly and Murphy
    1982.

Pauly, D. and G. Murphy, eds. 1982. Theory and Management
    of Tropical Fisheries. Manila: International Center
    for Living Aquatic Resources Management.

A Social Dilemma in a Less Developed Country: The Massacre of the African Elephant in Zaire[1]

Emizet Kisangani

INTRODUCTION

The recent interest in management of common property resources has been greatly stimulated by Hardin's classic article, "The Tragedy of the Commons" (1968). Applied to the hunting grounds of elephants (<u>Loxodonta</u> <u>africana</u>) in Zaire, the economic analysis of the tragedy of the commons (or social dilemma) proceeds from the fact that open access to elephants within the context of applicable law creates a situation in which ivory hunting is encouraged.[2] Personal benefits exceed personal costs.

This paper investigates the manner in which open access to the hunting grounds has emerged, and it examines the types of regimes that have controlled elephant hunting grounds in Zaire, especially in the northeastern regions. It is suggested here that, since the commons is potentially characterized by exclusion, the right to use or exploit it is ultimately founded on the ability to forcefully or contractually exclude potential competitors. The first section discusses the nature of the hunting grounds in which elephants are established and the nature of the elephants themselves. The second section examines hunting activities in the traditional setting. Subsequent sections provide an empirical investigation of the political processes that have resulted in the sequential shifts in ownership of the hunting grounds from indigenous groups to

colonial settlers, and then from settlers to a currently
ambiguous public trust.

NATURE OF THE HUNTING GROUND
AND OF THE ELEPHANT

Zaire is a country of approximately 30,261,000
inhabitants, and occupies an area of approximately
2,344,885 square kilometers. The terrain is undifferentiated, with some scattered hills--largely outliers of the
highlands of Shaba and the eastern borderlands. The
country is wholly tropical, with abundant rainfall (more
than 1,500 mm per annum) and broadleaf evergreen forest
characterizing the Congo Basin and ample, but more
seasonal, rainfall and savanna dominated by broad-leaved
deciduous trees typical of the surrounding uplands.
Elephants are actively hunted in more than half the
country, and are particularly vulnerable in areas where
the relatively poor distribution of water supplies results
in seasonal migration and congregation.

An elephant drinks an average of 52 gallons of water
daily and consumes at least 400 pounds of food (Offermann
1951). The way this mammal feeds is devastating to its
natural habitat: it breaks down trees, pushing them over
to obtain leaves and roots, and debarking them, and its
weight (4.5 short tons for an average elephant) damages
younger trees and inhibits regeneration.

Elephants live in family units of anywhere from 2 to
20, led by old females (Laws 1970), but on occasion, larger
aggregates of 25 to 40 may form. Bulls tend to live
separately in small groups or alone with short-term associations with family units when a female is in estrus
(Croze 1974). A given herd may be composed of 50 percent
nonadults and 50 percent reproductive adults in which
20 percent are males and 30 percent are females (Offermann
1951).

The elephant's gestation period averages 22 months.
The calf is nursed for about 2 years, and becomes sexually
mature between the age of 8 and 19 (Laws and Parker 1968).
On average, an adult female reproduces every 4 years; thus,
maintaining the sustainable yield of elephants requires
harvesting no more than 5 percent annually (Offermann
1951). Laws and Parker (1968) point out that after the
elephants reach maturity, the proportion of pregnant
females increases to a maximum of 43.2 percent in the

31-35 age group, but subsequently declines to 8.3 percent
in the 51-55 age group, and falls to zero thereafter.

The African species, Loxodonta africana, of both sexes
have tusks (by contrast, the Asian female has none), making
the African species more attractive to ivory hunters than
are its Asian congeners.

Given the nature of the forest and size of the
elephant, the fear of hunting alone has made hunters
operate in groups. Moreover, hunting in groups was enhanced by a strong belief in traditional Zairian communities that the hunting ground must first benefit the whole
community, even at the expense of the individual. This
belief was institutionalized through mythological and
ritual emphasis of the need to respect nature as the source
of life. In the long run, however, the introduction of new
technology for hunting game (for instance, motorized
vehicles and guns) and an expanding human population have
provided individual users both the capability and motivation to exploit the hunting ground for personal profit.

Excludability, on the other hand, has also been a major
attribute of the hunting ground as different actors compete for its products. For centuries, the hunting tribes--
the BaMbuti pygmies--have been effective owners of the
hunting ground because of their familiarity with the forest
and other tribes' fears of getting lost. With the arrival
of Europeans and their technology, selective exclusion
became more difficult.

Another physical attribute of the resource is divisibility. Although the hunting ground may be divisible among
users, the elephants may be difficult to divide because
their migratory movements transcend regional boundaries.
Nevertheless, the fact that the elephants may live in herds
near rivers may create temporary ownership of a given herd
by a hunting group living close to the area. Here again,
technological means such as guns, motorized vehicles, small
airplanes, or helicopters may assign a given group in the
community some advantage in keeping a number of herds in
specific locations, whereas in a traditional setting, the
hunting tribes had to pursue the elephants wherever they
migrated.

The hunting grounds of the elephants became more
accessible to the technologically superior Europeans, who
were able to exclude the natives. The hunting ground has
also become subject to relatively high divisibility and
subtractability. In the short run, the technological and
structural attributes of the hunting ground may be as sig-

nificant as the extent of the area occupied by the elephants, particularly as their range is reduced through environmental degradation. Water availability remains the main factor affecting migration, herd size, mating, and reproduction.

Three different periods related to the management of the hunting ground of the elephants are discussed in the following sections: the traditional setting, the colonial era, and the post-colonial period.

MANAGEMENT OF THE HUNTING GROUND
IN THE TRADITIONAL SETTING

Until the colonization of the Congo in the 18th century, the natives of Zaire hunted the elephants primarily for food: one elephant could furnish meat for an entire village. Ivory had only limited use and exchange value. For instance, ivory was used as a hammer by the BaBira tribesmen, but had no direct use for the BaMbuti pygmies, although they traded it for metal, agricultural crops, and protection from their powerful Bantu neighbors. The patron-client relationships between the BaMbuti and their Bantu and Sudanic agricultural and pastoral neighbors had begun in the 12th century (Turnbull 1965). These relationships resulted in the adoption of a patron language by the BaMbuti, but did not influence other aspects of their lives or livelihoods.

Decision-Making Arrangements

As hunters, the BaMbuti may be divided into net-hunters and archers. This technological distinction has shaped their social, economic, and political organization with respect to the management of the hunting grounds.

The net-hunting bands were much larger, 15 to 30 families, because the use of the net to capture the elephant required more cooperation, whereas the archer hunting bands were much smaller, ranging from 7 to 15 families. In the net-hunting groups, women and children were usually associated with hunting activities, whereas in the archer bands they specialized in gathering operations. Thus, the lack of specialization in net-hunting technique was associated with a social system that was more egalitarian than that of the archers (Turnbull 1965).

While both categories of hunters respected the elderly, individual skill in the archer bands was a sign of maturity; a skillful young archer could gain a voice in the council of elders in vetoing a decision or in conflict resolution. Mutual trust and mutual cooperation, enhanced by the small size of the hunting bands, sustained intra-group cohesion and harmony; obligation to the community was balanced against self-interest, and the elders were seen as the source of wisdom and hence authority. (There were no formal or elected chiefs.)

Another mechanism in resolving conflict was an institutionalized system of flux that always occurred either in the beginning or at the end of an arbitrarily determined period called the "honey season." Flux may be understood as the constant changeover of personnel between local groups and the frequent shifts of campsites through the seasons (Turnbull 1968).

For the net-hunters, the honey season was the period of plenty and the time to dissociate antagonistic members. At the end of this season, the bands reformed, avoiding unreconciled members. The archers, on the other hand, hunted together in the honey season, which for them is a period of poor hunting, and split into small groups thereafter. In both groups, ostracism was the solution of last resort to resolve conflict.

In the traditional hunting society of the BaMbuti, informal rules arising from the technological capabilities of the hunters, and from traditional beliefs, regulated exit and entry into the hunting grounds. For example, the net-hunting technique produced the surest and largest supply of meat, but it frightened the animals, while the archer's technique usually did the opposite. Therefore, the former technique necessitated frequent changes of site resulting in a limited system of inheritance and little personal ownership. The archers, on the other hand, were more attached to their hunting grounds. In both cases, however, every band possessed at least several hundred square miles of forest territory for hunting and gathering operations (Turnbull 1965), usually separated by natural obstacles or by the proximity of agricultural tribes.

The net-hunters and the archers believed that while they held an ancestral, and therefore inalienable, right to the hunting grounds, an elephant became property only when killed. This belief regarded the forest as the only constant in their lives--more important even than social relations--because of its life-giving qualities, providing

them with a strong feeling of attachment towards the
forest. Fluctuating social relations served not only to
resolve conflict, but also deemphasized stability in
personal relations and weakened the concepts of unilinear
descent and affiliation.

Furthermore, the fact that the surrounding tribes
feared the forest made the BaMbuti less open to external
control in their exploitation of the hunting grounds of
the elephants. However, the patron-client relationship
established through the centuries in which the Bantu and
Sudanic villages provided metal, food crops, and protection to the pygmies in exchange for elephant meat and
ivory, encouraged the Bantu to try to impose control over
the Sudanic villages. One major way the patrons exerted
their influence was to take a leading role in the arrangement and financing of intra-pygmy marriages. Through this
relationship, the patrons claimed hereditary rights over
pygmy offspring through patrilineal descent (Turnbull
1965). But the BaMbuti developed devices to evade the
system either by changing bands during periods of flux or
by calling for villager specialists to perform magic in
the forest to improve hunting. (The pygmies themselves
hardly believed in magic.) Calling for the magicians was
merely a political maneuver to avoid total commitment to
trade, because by doing so they could persuade their
patrons that the Bantu magic had failed and, consequently,
they had very little to trade, even though their hunting
efforts were in reality highly successful.

Patterns of Interaction

Patterns of interaction existed here at four levels:
(1) within a given hunting band, (2) between bands using
the same techniques, (3) between bands using different
hunting techniques, and (4) between hunting tribes and
their patrons.

Intraband patterns of interaction were characterized
by reciprocity. Hence, the lack of anonymity in hunting
made free-riding behavior a very costly choice. In
addition, mutual trust and mutual cooperation through
consanguineal ties provided the individual hunter a sense
of membership and made each individual believe in the
ability of others to extract a livelihood from the
environment.

The second and third types of interaction were charac-

terized by lack of competition. The system of flux has
permitted different bands to exchange members, thereby
resolving interband animosity. If joint hunting was rare,
interband cooperation was encouraged by attending another
band's dances and festivities. These activities were
regulated by the lineage elders (Schebesta 1941).

Finally, the trade between the patrons and their
clients involved another type of reciprocity. Unlike
close kinship ties that elicit cooperation in which
reciprocities are long-term and often intangible, relations
between patrons and clients were distant and generally
tangible. Being non-kin relatives, they involved short-
term reciprocities and voluntary cooperation only as long
as protection was provided by the patrons. In other words,
close consanguineal bonds are perpetual and based on
affiliative obligation regardless of choice, whereas non-
kin bonds are of varying duration and based on self-
interest.

Outcomes

In the traditional setting, the sustainable yield of
the elephants was in no way threatened. Primitive hunting
techniques and belief systems kept the hunting tribes'
consumption patterns at a level that corresponded with
their daily needs, either through trade with their patrons
or through their flux system. Some observers (among them
Sahlins 1968) have even argued that hunting communities
were affluent societies.

The exchange patterns made the traditional system
operate efficiently through specialization. That is, the
hunting ground was left to the hunting tribes and arable
land left to the patrons for agricultural purposes. In
both cases, trade was highly valued. Trade allowed the
patrons (unfamiliar with the forest) to avoid the high
cost of being lost or killed that are associated with
hunting, and allowed the pygmies to avoid the high cost,
to them, of settling down to a sedentary agricultural life.

The pygmy system of reciprocity was noteworthy insofar
as sick or weak individuals were never deprived of their
benefits as members of the community. For example, after
an elephant was killed, sick and weak hunters were given
their shares before active hunters received theirs
(Turnbull 1965).

These traditional patterns of exchange began to

disintegrate around the second half of the 18th century
when ivory became an object of intensive trade. It is
reported that only ivory and slaves were traded for
turkedi (textiles).[3] Four attractive turkedi were worth
a slave or four 55-pound (30-kilogram) pieces of tusk.
That also meant that for four 55-pound (30-kilogram)
pieces of tusk, any slave trader in West Africa could
purchase a slave if he wished. Thus, the massive arrival
of European settlers during the 1800s had two impacts on
the hunting grounds and the tribes exploiting them. First,
it unbalanced the traditional regime in the composition of
its population, in its consumption patterns, in its group
size and composition, and in its technology. Second, an
increasing demand for ivory created a discrepancy between
the demand for elephant meat and its supply.

EARLY BELGIAN RULE IN ZAIRE: THE LEOPOLDIAN REGIME[4]

Decision-Making Arrangements

The clash between Europeans and the natives in the
late 19th century brought animosity. The agricultural
tribes resisted the invaders, and the hunting tribes that
could locate the elephants in the forest refused to
cooperate with the alien hunters. Confronted with this
behavior, the Belgian settlers faced occupational difficulties in the Congo Basin. Their first reaction was to
break up traditional family ties and patron-client relationships associated with the hunting grounds through the
introduction of a coercive labor system for hunting and
gathering operations. This was coupled with per capita
taxation in natural commodities. Ivory became the principal commodity with which the citizens could fulfill this
obligation.

This move meant that hunting and gathering activities
were no longer the monopoly of the hunting tribes. With
the increase in the size of the hunting population and the
disruption of social ties and obligations, individuals
began acting on the basis of personal interest in order to
pay their taxes and survive.

The second European reaction in the face of occupational difficulties was Leopold II's decree of July 1,
1885, expropriating the land from the natives. In the
absence of any judicial court system in the early colonial
period, compensation for expropriation was unlikely. Thus,

expropriation enabled the Leopoldian representatives to begin selling the land at 1.6 Belgian francs an acre (4 francs per hectare) with ulterior preemption rights over the surrounding areas (Merlier 1962). The new owner--being either an individual settler or a charter company--also received the monopoly on hunting and gathering products from these areas. (For more information concerning the charter companies, see Merlier 1962: chapters 1 through 6.)

The new system was totally alien to the natives, for whom land was not a marketable commodity. To gain the natives' compliance, the Leopoldian bureaucrats began appointing chiefs who were willing to cooperate with the settlers, thus eliminating those who were resistant to the new system. Indeed, the death sentence was invoked when cooperation could be obtained no other way.

The Leopoldian regime was thus an increasingly powerful and barbaric centralized bureaucracy (see James 1943) that took considerable discretion with respect to land use as they implemented laws drawn up in Belgium to regulate the hunting grounds in Zaire.

Patterns of Interaction

Relationships between the bureaucrats and the new charter companies were cooperative insofar as the charters' interests were safeguarded. The first opposition broke out, however, after Leopold II established the monopoly on ivory by the domainal decree of 1891, through which he became the sole owner of ivory. The charter companies opposed this decree and those who tried to implement it.

On the other hand, patterns of interaction between the settlers and the natives were those associated with dominant/subordinate relationships. So far as interaction among the natives themselves was concerned, compulsory taxation based on individual responsibility made the individual native try to maximize his acquisition of ivory, whereas in the traditional setting the individual acted as part of a corporate group.

Rural discontent rose as individuals became more isolated and were subjected to forced labor and coercive taxation. In 1895, several native revolts broke out in protest against the Leopoldian system. These revolts subsided in 1911 after more than 15 million natives were massacred (James 1943).[5]

Outcomes

The Europeans brought to Zaire a new technology (gunpowder) and various sophisticated means of transportation, which together destroyed the equilibrium that had existed in the feudal and tribal economies. The destruction had three important manifestations. First, the increasing size of the European population meant a reduction of the number of hectares of arable land per native, and encroachment into the hunting grounds by human settlement and agriculture. Second, communication between traditional patrons and the new settlers was unsatisfactory, since the latter spoke only French. Third, the arrival of Europeans fragmented the group at the tribal level and gave a new, and more limited, meaning to the concept of "family."

This disequilibrium had two consequences. First, the introduction of trade with the accompanying money economy required Zairians to adopt conflicting strategies to survive. That is, they had to maintain their agricultural cycle and, at the same time, they had to manipulate new markets as much as they could to avoid becoming totally dependent on the new means of exchange. Second, the introduction of compulsory taxation and unpaid labor forced the Zairian men off their land, leaving the subsistence agriculture to women and children.

If the Pareto optimality test were applied to determine efficiency and equity, then the Leopoldian regime would be both inefficient and unfair. That is, it heavily favored the minority Belgian settlers at the expense of the majority natives in its laws regarding the use of the hunting grounds. In addition, the supply of elephant meat exceeded its demand, because the increased acquisition of ivory also resulted in the increased availability of meat. In fact, in only 23 years (1885-1908), at least 200,000 elephants were killed for the ivory trade (Fallon 1944). This killing yielded almost 2 million short tons of meat. Furthermore, if "abuse of authority and arbitrary exclusion from the common property resource" (Oakerson, this volume) are used as criteria to assess equity, the Leopoldian system would again be unfair. It is, indeed, Leopold II's abuse of authority and selective enforcement of rules by his bureaucrats that led to the arbitrary exclusion of the natives from their land and precipitated their revolts, revolts that were not subsequently crushed without bloodshed. The awakening of metropolitan concern hastened the demise of the Congo Free State, which was terminated through the annexation of the Congo to Belgium on November 4, 1908.

In brief, the establishment of new uses for, and exploitation rights of, the hunting grounds was motivated neither by scarcity due to market pressures nor by an increase in population. The elephants were plentiful and roamed almost everywhere. The native population dropped by more than half during the period described. The European settlers represented approximately 4 percent of the total population. So we see that it is not always accurate to associate the formation of new property rights with scarcity as Levi and North (1982) have argued. Scarcity may be the effect of a law that modifies property rights in an attempt to overcome environmental and internal constraints such as unknown customs, uncooperative behavior, and the like, or a law that intends to enrich one individual, or a group, at the expense of the majority.

THE POST-LEOPOLDIAN REGIME:
COLONIAL MOVES

The annexation of the Congo to Belgium was the beginning of a new form of exploitation. Indeed, despite this annexation, the colony was forced to be self-financing, and ivory became one of the main currencies in achieving this goal, in lieu of such mineral resources as gold. Ivory was no longer employed for the payment of taxes. The system of forced labor permitted the Belgian settlers to collect ivory without incurring any monetary costs.

Decision-Making Arrangements

The first colonial move toward managing the hunting ground of the elephants came 26 years after the colony was established, by the decree of November 26, 1934, that created the Institut des Parcs Nationaux du Congo Belge. This decree established the limits of the first national parks, in which hunting, fishing, and tree felling were prohibited. (Note that the parks covered an area of 17,380

square miles [45,026 square kilometers], whereas the
elephant reserves spread over 6,000 square miles [15,544
square kilometers] in 1940). This decree also placed a
fine of $169 to $845.70 per elephant and a two-month prison
sentence for the killing of elephants already living in
the parks. The prison sentence and the fine were more
severe for hunters who had no licenses for hunting
elephants.

The hunting licenses were regulated by the decree of
April 21, 1937, that required a nonrefundable $2.00 deposit
for a one-year license to be issued by the state, as well
as a tax of $5.00 for every mature elephant killed outside
the parks. This tax increased to $20.00 in 1956. Thus,
the tax requirement automatically excluded the majority of
natives from hunting activities; this amount was beyond
their yearly income.

A third move carried out by the colonial rulers in the
1930s was the domestication of elephants and their use for
farming in the environs of Gangala na Bodio. The cost of
maintenance and domestication was valued at $25,372 per
year for 80 elephants. This domestication of the elephants
helped the Belgian rulers to justify the protection of
these mammals, and hence to press for money through an
increase in per capita taxation of the natives.

To carry out these policies, a corps of Belgian
officers and native employees was created in 1937 by the
decrees of September 27, December 23, and December 26.
This corps had to prevent people from killing elephants
either in forbidden zones or during the rainy season--the
period during which elephants reproduce in the savanna
zone.

Unlike the embryonic Leopoldian bureaucracy, the
colonial regime was a vertically centralized bureaucracy
with Belgians occupying all the positions from the top to
the bottom within the administrative hierarchy. In this
context the villages were no longer autonomous entities,
but rather became executory agents of the colony.

Patterns of Interaction

The colonial regime was a coercive system ruled by
three interconnected entities: the administration, responsible for the enforcement of the law; the capitalist
economy, which commercialized ivory; and the Catholic
church, which was responsible for reporting all illegal

activities. The natives, furthermore, were considered to
be second-class citizens without legal rights to the
hunting ground. The coercive nature of the system and
cooperation between the charter companies and the church
elicited native cooperation and sharply reduced any
incentive for smuggling.

Outcomes

The creation of national parks and the regulation of
hunting grounds were justified by the colonial rulers as
being necessary to maintain the elephants at carrying
capacity through a culling system. The goal of culling
herds in the national parks was twofold: first, to prevent
the overpopulation of elephants to avoid the destruction
of woodland and forest; and second, to allow natural forces
in the parks and reserves to operate to the fullest extent
possible in creating and maintaining a dynamic equilibrium.
Within that context, the Belgian authorities decided that
each year some of the mature elephants would have to be
cropped to satisfy the national meat market as well as the
international ivory markets and zoological gardens. Theoretically, this annual crop was supposed to be less than
5 percent, an amount large enough to relieve pressure on
the ecosystem but small enough to allow time to study the
biology of the elephant. Practically, from 1937 to 1959,
at least 200,000 elephants were killed and almost 69 million pounds of ivory were exported (Jeannin 1947; Institut
National de la Statistique 1950-1959; Offermann 1951).

The result of colonial policies after 1936 is outlined
in Figure 1. First, the largest quantity of ivory exported
was from the mature group of elephants (which also included
nonreproducing females), that is, elephants over 55 years
of age, bearing two tusks each weighing at least 33 pounds
(15 kilograms). Second, the minimal years in ivory exports
were either years during which the colonial authorities
issued few shooting licenses, or years that followed
decrees increasing the tax for every elephant killed outside the parks. Third, the low level of ivory exports
from every reproductive age group between 18 and 55 years--
in contrast to the exports from the 56-and-over age group--
may be attributed to the fact that the colonial rulers
rarely allowed the registration of ivory exports from these
three groups.

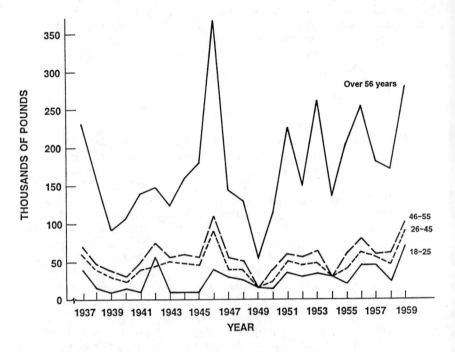

FIGURE 1 Exports of ivory per age group of elephants.

Source: Institut National de la Statistique 1950-1959;
Jeannin 1947; Offermann 1951.

    Because of the coercive colonial regime, the elephants
were rationally utilized in farms and killed when mature;
the colonial regime may have been efficient, but it was
also an unfair regime.
    The creation of national parks gave the Belgian
authorities an alibi for excluding the natives from the
land without any compensation, and this move forced the
natives into mining and plantation agriculture. This was
usually accompanied by bitterness and frustration arising
from separation from the family and the village. Prohibition on hunting, fishing, and tree felling in the parks and
reserves extended over an area of 11 million acres
(4,455,000 hectares), 8.2 million acres (3,321,000
hectares) in the northeastern regions. Any native caught
in these areas was beaten to death. Merlier (1962) reports

that for the sake of saving the flora and the fauna in
Albert National Park (now Virunga Park) in the Kivu region,
five villages were erased from the colonial map for having
hunted there, thirty for having fished, forty-two for
having illicitly circulated, and four for allegedly having
set fires.

The goal of colonial law was to induce native cooperation by force, and to transform the structure of property
rights to justify the exploitation of common property
resources by the politically dominant group, the Belgian
settlers. For instance, in looking at 1946 and 1959 (see
Figure 1), no proposition of effectively protecting the
elephants is tenable. Ivory exported from young elephants
in 1946 rose 300 percent over the previous year, which can
be explained only by the effort of the Belgians to recon-
struct their postwar economy. An increase in the hunting
of the same group of elephants in 1959--just one year
before the impending Zairian independence--surely had no
connection with the preservation of the herds.

Another effect of colonial rule was that most Zairians
had limited access to the reserves and parks, and no access
at all to the private and public decision-making bodies
that created and maintained these areas. Therefore, it can
be inferred that the colonial conservation policy was
unilaterally designed to serve the recreational and
economic interests of European settlers. With the
declaration of political independence on June 30, 1960,
the natives gained a measure of access and political
control over the parks, reserves, and hunting grounds.

THE POST-COLONIAL REGIME I: THE NATIONAL BUREAU
FOR IVORY AND MANAGEMENT OF COMMON PROPERTY RESOURCES

Between 1960 and 1972, the degree of exploitation of
the elephants in Zaire is almost unknown. Assessing the
number of elephants killed becomes more difficult because
of a lack of data and also because no policy was formulated
regarding elephants during that period. It can, however,
be reasonably asserted that the political and economic
instability that has followed Zairian political independence encouraged an erratic exploitation of the elephants.
The first post-colonial policy was the decree of January 5,
1973, which established a monopolistic agency called the
National Bureau for Ivory (NBI). It survived for only
three years.

Decision-Making Arrangements

The law creating the NBI explicitly recognized the common property character of the hunting grounds: it specified that the exclusive goal of the agency was to buy ivory from native hunters and sell it on international markets. As the law was mute about the content of colonial decrees, the elephants living in the parks were still protected by the state. Accordingly, the creation of the NBI gave rise to two types of resources. The first, public in character, were the various national parks, from which no one could be excluded; moreover, these parks were indivisible among users.

The second, the hunting grounds of the elephants that had been erratically exploited after the Belgian departure, could not be controlled by the mere act of creating the NBI. Besides, the government system of price controls over ivory was similar to colonial controls insofar as the law did not differentiate licensed hunters from hunting tribes. For the agency, anyone desiring to hunt elephants had to possess a hunting license, without which any possession of ivory was a crime subject to prison sentence and fine.

So the response of the Zairian government, fearing local initiative and decision making, was to impose control from the center upon local authorities. Licensed hunters were simply instructed to sell ivory at the fixed price of 3 zaires ($6) a pound and the government would buy it. This law prohibited the hunting tribes from living their traditional life. But fear of the forest made licensed hunters rely on the hunting tribes for information on locating the elephants.

Furthermore, local bureaucrats of the NBI were supposed to act as channels of communication between different communities and the state government, but instead they acted in their self-interest. As Crowe (1969) has asserted, there is considerable evidence that when national regulatory agencies are utilized as the only administrative apparatus for dealing with common property resources, small, highly organized groups have subverted the regulatory process to their own advantage. Whereas the formal decision rules proscribe work outside of one's bureaucratic functions or for personal gain, the NBI bureaucrats became involved in smuggling activities and the agency became the instrument of those in power.

Patterns of Interaction

The ceiling price instituted by the NBI--which in microeconomic terms was below equilibrium price--increased illegal poaching and smuggling of ivory. Furthermore, because the fine and prison sentence were not prohibitive (gain from smuggling or poaching illegally exceeded the cost of bribing a customs official or police officer), smugglers easily crossed the Zairian borders to trade ivory in exchange for new Toyota pickups and Fiat trucks in the neighboring Sudan.

The increase in smuggling activities that has followed the 1973 decree clearly indicated that the colonial decrees were obsolete. First, unlike the colonial regime, the post-colonial superstructure lacked the united tripartite structure that had shaped the colony (the bureaucracy, the capitalist economy, and the Catholic Church). Second, the NBI was designed to solve the problem of regulating ivory activities rather than managing the hunting ground of the elephants. Third, the use of the state apparatus for personal gains has led even high-ranking officials to hunting activities, and the result was the politicization of the NBI.

Outcomes

The main result of the creation of the NBI has been the proliferation of bribes in hunting activities, and hence a tremendous increase in elephant hunting operations. For instance, the police are paid to look the other way when illegal pieces of tusks are being unloaded. They also make a habit of not studying a ship's manifest, which might prove that a tusk was obtained illegally or from the parks. Police behavior may be explained by the fact that their real wages have fallen below subsistence level, so bribes have become a quasi-institutionalized way of distributing income. For all of the groups involved in ivory activities, the government controls favoring some segments of the populace were discriminatory. Complying was analogous to conditions during the colonial period when people were required to render service for the colonizer.

This situation has made the state's control of ivory activities inoperative in and out of the national parks. In 1976, the NBI was reduced to an agency without any ivory

to sell in international markets: more than 90 percent of
the ivory sold was reportedly smuggled (Banque du Zaire
1976). In the same year, the Zairian authorities opted for
liberalizing all ivory activities by abolishing the NBI.
To use the evocative metaphor borrowed from d'Arge and
Wilen (1974), the prey (the hunters) became so big they
ate the predator (NBI).

THE POST-COLONIAL REGIME II: THE AFTERMATH
OF THE SUPPRESSION OF THE NBI

Decision-Making Arrangements

The law abolishing the NBI was meant to induce Zairians
to create small cooperative hunting groups that would
harvest the mammals and would also have an incentive to
conserve them as their source of income. Unfortunately,
this law was unclear on how to achieve these private but
collective arrangements. The result was the emergence of
an open access system[2] for harvesting the elephants
living outside parks. But as the NBI was also the official
enforcer for protecting the parks, the massacre of elephants began with those living in the parks as well.

In the absence of any agency regulating the use of the
hunting ground, the local authorities were left to act
according to their discretionary power. In the Upper Zaire
and Kivu regions, the "official reproduction period" of
the elephants was not decided according to the climate
(reproduction usually occurred during the rainy season)
but according to the mood of the regional governor or of
his directors of environmental or economic affairs. Anyone
caught with ivory in the decreed reproduction period could
be jailed if the price of bribing an official was not
right. An alarming report in 1978 (Departement de l'Economie 1978) made the Zairian central government prohibit
the sale of ivory in April 1979. (Note that ivory exports
had been banned in 1978.) Unfortunately, the government
had failed to prohibit the consumption of elephant meat,
so the acquisition of meat became the ruse by which hunters
circumvented the ivory law.

Patterns of Interaction

In analyzing social formations as a combination of
capitalist (market) and noncapitalist (nonmarket) modes of

production in which capitalism dominates, Wolpe (1980) points out that the conditions of this domination tend to be left unspecified so that the conservation of noncapitalist modes appears to be explained in terms of the functions performed for capitalism. Accordingly, the vagueness of the law abolishing the NBI may be seen as the result of the coexistence of the noncapitalist mode of production of elephant meat/ivory and the capitalist mode of distribution. First, ivory is produced either illegally by the hunting tribes or through poaching, and is then distributed in the capitalist economy, where high prices in Zaire ($12 per pound in 1981) command huge profits. These high prices are also the major cause of smuggling activities in Sudan where a Zairian smuggler with one ton of ivory can obtain a large new Fiat truck (the unit net price, including cost, insurance, and freight, at the Zairian main port, Matadi, was $40,000 in 1981).

Second, the coexistence of these modes of production shapes patterns of interaction that result in one's being able or unable to exploit the hunting grounds of the elephants; who you know seems to be the critical consideration. In 1979, ivory activities were prohibited, but because the consumption of elephant meat was not forbidden, hunting the elephants for the national meat market became a de facto way of selling ivory. In this context, those with connections (kin or friendship relation and the like) with top-ranking officials or enough money to bribe police or custom officers are not severely sanctioned when caught with ivory; but sanctions are meted out to the less well-connected who break the law. So connections and money provide Zairians an unequal access qualification with respect to the hunting grounds of the elephants. In other words, while poaching and smuggling ivory are independent of the state, they are connected to it by the fact that to hold government office means having access to the hunting ground. Paradoxically, the present erratic exploitation of the elephants is well-organized in the sense that only the presidential clique, the presidential brotherhood, a few members of the new aspiring bourgeoisie, and those who are connected to these groups are highly involved in hunting the elephants. What can be expected from this free-riding behavior of the ruling group? Olson (1982) provides a general answer: he argues that the tendency of special interests to free ride on national economies always results in the decline of the entire economic and political system.

Outcomes

The ivory rush after the abolition of the NBI has increased the hunting activities to such a great extent that one could have expected the extinction of the elephants in Zaire. However, despite this massacre, the elephants can be found in herds of 4 to 18 in some parts of northeastern Zaire. This capacity for survival may be attributed to the reproductive capacity of the animal itself and to the belief by some Zairian tribes that wildlife should not enrich people or be worn as a jewel. But the recent increased use of poison to kill the elephants for ivory is threatening their reproductive capacity. Poisoning water and fruits kills not only mature elephants, but also kills female elephants and calves.

In addition to human predation, increased demand for land and crops (as well as drought) in some areas of Zaire has seriously reduced the range within which the elephants used to live. Independent Zaire inherited approximately 150,000 elephants in 1960, scattered all over the country; by 1976, these mammals had disappeared in several districts (for instance, South Kivu, Lualaba, and North Shaba) and in some reserves (Epulu, Djungu, and Faradje). This is a clear indication of overexploitation.

Finally, the decrees written since the abolition of the NBI had but one purpose: to eliminate competition for the well-organized, well-capitalized, well-connected hunters. These decrees have failed to specify boundaries within which the rights of the hunting tribes (or others) must be exercised; thus, the politically and economically powerful groups have used the state apparatus for excluding the least fortunate Zairians from the hunting ground of the elephants.

CONCLUSION

This paper has attempted to provide a relevant perspective on the process by which different regimes in Zaire have tried to profit from the hunting grounds of the elephants. Accordingly, this study has shown how different laws regulating common property resources have discouraged cooperative behavior by increasing the feelings of anonymity and invincibility of the individual, leading him to focus his attention upon himself and relieving him of the consequences of his own actions. The outcome has been the

conception of bureaucracy as a tool not for the execution
of national or community objectives but for the fulfill-
ment of ethnic loyalties. Externally induced, directed,
and imposed laws without any internal support are bound to
be dysfunctional in the short run as well as in the long
run. Therefore, the only way that common property
resources can benefit the community is through structural
arrangements starting from the unit at which the individual
is more at ease, that is, at the level of the community.

NOTES

1. Thanks to C. Ford Runge, Gatsinzi Basaninyenzi, John Orbell, William Mitchell, and two anonymous readers for their comments on an earlier version.

2. This paper refers to the elephants now living in Zaire as a nonexclusive resource, and as such they are characterized by open access that arises from unrestricted entry to the hunting grounds.

3. The turkedi were the largest hand-made textiles in the 18th century. See the link between turkedi, ivory, and slaves in West Africa in Jeannin (1947:92-93).

4. By the General Act of Berlin, February 26, 1885, signed at the conclusion of the conference held in Berlin in late 1884, the European powers agreed that activities in the Congo Basin should be governed not only by freedom of trade and navigation but also by principles of neutrality in the event of war, suppression of slave trade traffic, and improvement of the condition of the indigenous population. The conference recognized Leopold II of Belgium as the sole sovereign of the new Congo Free State. He later became involved in one of the bloodiest operations ever known. For more details, see James (1943).

5. According to James (1943:305), this estimate varies from 11,500,000 to 31,500,000 deaths.

REFERENCES

Banque du Zaire. 1976. Rapport Annuel. Kinshasa, Zaire.

Crowe, B. L. 1969. The tragedy of the commons revisited. Science 166:1103-1107.

Croze, H. 1974. The Seronera elephant problem I: the bulls. East African Wildlife Journal 12:1-28.

d'Arge, R. C., and J. E. Wilen. 1974. Governmental control of externalities, or the prey eats the predator. Journal of Economic Issues 8:353-372.

Département de l'Economie. 1978. Conjoncture Economique. Kinshasa, Zaire.

Fallon, F. 1944. L'éléphant africain. Mémoires de l'Institut Royal Colonial Belge. Collection 8, Vol. 13, No. 2:1-51.

Hardin, G. 1968. The tragedy of the commons. Science 162: 1243-1248.

Institut National de la Statistique. 1950-1959. Brussels, Belgium: Commerce Extérieur du Congo Belge et du Ruanda-Burundi.

James, S. 1943. South of the Congo. New York: Random House.

Jeannin, A. 1947. L'éléphant d'Afrique. Paris: Payot.

Laws, R. M. 1970. Elephants as agents of habitat and landscape change in East Africa. Oikos 21:1-15.

Laws, R. M. and I. S. C. Parker. 1968. Recent studies on elephant population in East Africa. Proceedings of Zoological Society 21:319-359.

Lee, R. B. and I. DeVore, eds. 1968. Man the Hunter. Chicago: Aldine Publishing Company.

Levi, M., and D. C. North. 1982. Toward a property rights theory of exploitation. Politics and Society 11:315-320.

Merlier, M. 1962. Le Congo: De la Colonisation Belge à l'Indépendance. Paris: Maspero.

Offermann, P. 1951. Les éléphants du Congo. Service des Eaux et Forêts, Chasse et Pêche 9:15-95.

Olson, M., Jr. 1982. The Rise and Decline of Nations: Economic Growth, Stagflation and Economic Rigidities. New Haven, Connecticut: Yale University Press.

Sahlins, M. D. 1968. Notes on the original affluent society. In Lee and DeVore, 1968.

Schebesta, P. 1941. Die Bambuti-Pygmaen von Ituri: Die Wirtschaft der Ituri-Bambuti. Mémoire de l'Institut Royal Colonial Belge, Section Sciences Morales et Politiques 2, Vol. 2:1-284.

Turnbull, C. M. 1965. The Mbuti pygmies: an ethnographic survey. Anthropological Papers of The American Museum of Natural History 50 (Part 3):145-282.

Turnbull, C. M. 1968. The importance of flux in two hunting societies. In Lee and DeVore, 1968.

Wolpe, H. 1980. Introduction. In H. Wolpe, ed. The Articulation of Modes of Production: Essays from Economy and Society. London: Routledge and Kegan Paul.

Common Property Management of Water in Botswana

Louise R. Fortmann
and Emery M. Roe

INTRODUCTION

In 1974, the Botswana Ministry of Agriculture established a policy of constructing small dams that would be
managed by groups that had (before construction) agreed to
stock limitations and management rules. The policy was
intended to prevent overstocking, overgrazing, and improper
dam maintenance. The groups would have the right to use
the dam if they abided by the conditions of the initial
agreement. By 1980, the policy was considered a failure:
the dams were overstocked and overgrazed and group management was nonexistent. Much of this alleged failure was
attributed to people's treating their dams as if they were
open-access property free for anyone to abuse. This study
of the use and management of these dams will show otherwise.

BACKGROUND INFORMATION

Definitions

Excluding a few large villages, the communal areas of
eastern Botswana contain approximately 20 percent of the
country's land, 60 percent of its human population, at
least 40 percent of its cattle, and most of its crop

production. Tribal land, statutorily defined as land
under the allocative and adjudicative control of government land boards, comprises the majority of this area.
It is commonly considered to be communally held, since it
cannot be owned on a freehold basis. Communal areas include
small villages, cultivated areas, and cattleposts on tribal
land. "Lands" denotes both cultivated fields and the
general area where they are found. "Cattlepost" means both
the places where livestock are penned and the adjacent
grazing areas. The major water sources include boreholes,
open wells, and surface water catchments, namely dams,
haffir-dams and haffirs.

Seasonal Cycles

Water management in rural areas reflects the interrelated changes in residence and activities associated
with the seasonal cycles of agricultural production and
rainfall. Highly variable, average annual rainfall in
eastern Botswana averages between 350 and 500 mm. Unreliable rainfall makes crop failure probable once in four
years.

Seasonal rainfall determines which sources contain
water. The agricultural season generally begins with the
rainy season; the timing of the agricultural season in
turn affects where people and their cattle will locate and
the nature of their water needs. Water use in a given
locality varies with these changes in residence.

When the first rains fall, people move to the lands
and start farming. Convenient lands water supplies are in
great demand at the beginning of the cropping season, the
busiest time of year for most farmers. Once harvesting is
finished, the scarcity of surface water at the lands and
cattleposts drives many household members back to their
villages. After the harvest, there is an increased demand
for water for making beer, which also supports the residential shift back to the better watered villages.

Each village, lands, and cattlepost has its own seasonal
resource base and activities. Its social and economic
activities may change over the course of the year. For
example, after harvest, a number of lands become grazing
areas and villages, places for celebrations and social
gatherings. These interrelated places and population shifts
make the multiple locality (the village and its lands and
cattleposts) the most appropriate unit of analysis for rural
land and water use.

The Fallback Strategy

The seasonal water use pattern for livestock can be seen in increased reliance on groundwater sources in the dry season as surface water use declines (Bailey 1982:174). Shifting water sources reveal a highly adaptive household fallback strategy of water point use and management to ensure a reliable supply over time for household purposes. The sensible household has a flexible backup system of water supplies. As one water point goes dry or breaks down, the household shifts to other, sometimes less convenient, but more reliable water points.

Water Point Typologies

Rural water supplies may be typified by four characteristics: (1) their locational frame of reference; (2) the interaction between their physical structure and the degree of seasonality of use and management; (3) the distinction between management of the water point and management of its use; and (4) the types of management.

The Locational Frame of Reference

Water management involves four locational frames of reference: the water point site; the locality; the multiple locality; and the rural water sector as a whole. For example, a borehole plays multiple roles in an area because of this locational frame of reference. At the point, the borehole is or is not used for domestic and/or livestock purposes. In the locality, the borehole may be the village water supply free to all. Within the multiple locality, it may serve as the drought fallback water point, the use of which is rationed during the drought. Within the sector, the borehole's operation may be hampered by the government's limited recurrent budget for all of its boreholes.

Water Point Structure and Season

Knowledge of resource availability underlies the temporal mobility and flexibility that is at the heart of the household fallback water strategy. As seen in Table 1, this in turn is affected by whether the water point structure is fixed and whether use and management occur seasonally or year-round.

TABLE 1 A Typology of Water Point Structure, Use and Management.

Water Point Use and Management	Water Point Structure	
	Fixed	Unfixed
Seasonal	Many dams	Emphemeral puddles
Permanent	Some wells and boreholes	Sandriver (wadi) pits redug in different sites of the same riverbed

The Management Matrix

"Water management" blurs the distinction between water point management and water use management. The examples in Table 2 make this distinction and indicate how easily different types of open-access resources can be confused. To some, open access water means case 4; others would add cases 2 and 3; a few would call case 1 open access if the water were public property.

TABLE 2 A Typology of Water Use and Management.

The Water Point	Water Use	
	Managed	Unmanaged
Managed	1. Managing operation of some dams and boreholes	2. Unherded cattle breaking through a dam's bush fence
Unmanaged	3. Cattle herded into open-access dam or river for drinking	4. Cattle freely watering from puddles and pits

Management Type

Classifying a water point by management type is complicated. A group-operated, government-owned borehole may be managed as if it were a private borehole, i.e., a single person or family dominates. A privately owned well may be used by residents of a locality as if it were a communally held open-access facility. It is not uncommon to find a water point with a different owner and manager or being used in a way not originally intended by either.

Thus, it is useful to classify water point management in three ways: (1) by owner, (2) by manager, and (3) by the kind of access locality members actually have to the water point. Owners and managers can be separated into four categories: (1) private individuals or families; (2) small non-kin groups; (3) government authorities; and (4) communities. Access to a water point is defined by whether its use is open or restricted in practice.

In general, community owned and managed natural water sources are open access. But there is no one-to-one association between private ownership, private management, and restricted access. A group-managed water source can be managed as a restricted access water source.

THE CASE STUDY: AN APPLICATION OF THE OAKERSON FRAMEWORK

Physical and Technical Attributes of Small Dams

Small dams, with steep walls and deep excavation pits, appear to have structural aspects that affect the jointness, exclusiveness, and indivisibility of their water supply. But, as seen in Table 1, water point structure cannot be isolated from factors that make its access and operation variable over time and place. While the structural features of water point technology are fixed, almost all of their effects are variable.

The constraining effects of water point technology depend on location, when the water is available, how is it made available, and how the source is managed. The availability, quantity and quality of labor used to draw water bear profoundly on the bundle of physical constraints associated with the use and management of a particular dam. The same dam, with the same amount of water, presents a fundamentally different set of physical constraints to users in the month before and after a harvest.

Decision-Making Arrangements: The Theory

Here we consider the rules people were to follow for
the Ministry of Agriculture's small dams; these are discussed according to our locational frame of reference. At
the dam, group behavior was to be guided by the terms of
agreement the group signed with the government as the
condition for takeover of the dam. Within the locality
and multiple locality, a major rule used by land boards
required that there be at least 8 kilometers between
livestock watering points to minimize the potential for
overgrazing between them. The water sector was affected by
traditional norms defining and regulating common property land and water resources. Finally, the formulation
and implementation of the dam policy were conditioned by
broader institutional and national concerns.

At the Dam: The Terms of Agreement

Under the dam policy, the dams were to be primarily
for stock watering in the lands and cattleposts; they were
not intended to provide domestic (human drinking) water to
villages. A dam group was to consist of approximately 15
members, who, on average, owned fewer than 20 adult cattle
each, with no single person allowed to water more than 50
head. Each group, consisting of farmers who wanted the
dam and were "willing to control their grazing," was to be
formed before the dam was constructed and was to sign
standard terms of agreement as a precondition to handover.
The major conditions in the agreement were threefold:
(1) group members would maintain and repair the dam;
(2) each member would pay an annual fee per adult animal
to provide revenue for dam maintenance and repair; and
(3) no more than the equivalent of 400 adult cattle would
water at the dam.
It is unclear whether the terms of agreement were a
binding legal document, although they included a clause
enabling local government authorities to take "appropriate
action" if conditions were not fulfilled.

Within the Locality and Multiple Locality: The Eight-Kilometer Rule

Whether any official government document ever stipulated an 8-kilometer spacing between livestock watering

points is unclear. Yet, both inside and outside
government, the widespread impression is that land boards
should follow such a rule as an unofficial policy. The
assumption has been that this rule was appropriate for
spacing permanent livestock watering points for between 300
and 500 head of cattle. The rule applied to the spacing of
small dams built under the 1974 policy.

Within the Sector: Differing Norms and Institutional
Concerns

     Traditional common property norms in Botswana often
contrast sharply with the Ministry of Agriculture's institutional objectives. The expatriate planners of the 1974
dam policy appear to have been unaware that many users
perceive dams--especially those built by the government--
as common property facilities (Schapera 1943). The
government believed water scarcity justified a flat-rate
water charge to discourage overutilization of the dam.
This ran counter to the traditional norm that all who
needed it could use surface water, particularly when it
was scarce. Officials argued that water prices were
necessary to impress water scarcity upon dam users, failing
to recognize that water was scarce only seasonally and
that traditionally the Batswana had managed scarce common
property resources without resorting to explicit prices.
     Moreover, at least since the 1960s drought, many
government authorities have considered forage the first
limiting factor in tribal area livestock production. In
this view, livestock deaths (including drought deaths)
were caused by lack of grazing due to excessive overstocking around permanent water supplies. So making
government water point development conditional on user
stock limitations appealed to many officials. The small
dam policy was justified as a lever for obtaining better
grazing control, both through constructing new dams in a
more dispersed fashion and through stock control measures.
But surveys suggest that rural households see grazing land
as a seasonally renewable resource, not as a limiting
factor, and they attribute overgrazing to poor rainfall
rather than to overstocking.
     There is also a subtle difference in perceptions about
the extent to which access to new grazing areas is restricted by the lack of man-made watering points. Some
Ministry of Agriculture staff believe that the development
of livestock watering points in a new grazing area

increases that area's effective carrying capacity. But
the availability of "frontier" grazing and water sources
has probably worked against the more efficient use in the
older established areas, and has undermined the stated
government intention of treating water and grazing as
scarce resources, because Botswana stockholders believe it
is cheaper to get forage and water in new areas than to
manage them more effectively in old areas.

Finally, small dam policy reflected three strong
Ministry of Agriculture institutional biases at the
national level. These are described next.

Anti-overstocking Bias Sensitive to charges that earlier
large dams had encouraged overgrazing and overstocking,
officials tried to control stocking rates at the 1974 dams
through stock restrictions in the terms of agreement and
by designing smaller dams with lower watering capacity.

Sandveld (Desert) Bias Extending livestock water supplies
into the sandveld areas has been a major government objective since at least the 1950s. The view of isolated desert
boreholes operating far from alternative water sources led
some government staff to the erroneous assumption that
reliable livestock watering sources were similarly spaced
everywhere and that therefore existing points would be
managed.

Reliability Bias The small dams were intended to be
managed year-round, with the assumption that water supply
reliability is the single most important factor in rural
water demand.

Decision-Making Arrangements: The Practice

In practice, the realization of the decision-making
arrangements described above was substantially different
from the original intent.

Patterns of Interaction at the Dam

Information on the terms of agreement was collected on
24 of the estimated 99 small dams constructed under the

policy between 1974 and 1980. Of these, 21 had some sort
of group management in the form of maintenance, regulation,
and/or revenue-collection activities.

Maintenance Functions Dams require no technically complicated maintenance unless they collapse or silt up, reasonably infrequent events in Botswana. Maintenance is largely
preventive and its absence is not immediately apparent.
About half of the groups did some maintenance. No dam
group did all stipulated maintenance. Most maintained the
fence enclosing the dam wall and reservoir, less to
lengthen dam life than because regulation of use depended
on them.

Regulatory Functions All groups tried to regulate the use
of their dams. As the alternative water sources began
drying up, the groups began restricting access to the
dams. The regulations did not always follow government
forms (no dam group set stock limits), but they did lead
to water management. Four kinds of regulation were common:

o   Limiting Numbers of Users. Managers generally
    turned away outsiders, even those willing to pay
    fees, rather than nonpaying members of the group
    or of the same locality.

o   Restricting Types of Use. Some dams were limited
    to domestic purposes only, either permanently or
    seasonally as other sources went dry. The success
    of such limitations depended on the availability of
    alternative and fallback water points.

o   Controlling the Manner of Use. Limiting direct
    cattle access into the reservoir was generally
    found at dams used for domestic purposes.
    Ironically, this regulation desired by the
    government occurred mainly in conjunction with a
    use for which the dams were not primarily intended.

o   Regulating the Time of Use. Some dams are closed
    completely at certain seasons. In some cases, dams
    were used as back-up points for other water points
    subject to breakdowns, such as boreholes. Other
    dams were part of the sequential system of fallback
    points.

Revenue-Generating Activities Dams have few, if any,
operating costs, so dam users perceived less need for fees
than did those who used such water points as boreholes
with obvious and compelling operating and maintenance
costs. Nine groups said they charged fees; none used the
recommended flat-rate fee for livestock. Revenue was
generated in response to specific needs, often as a
contribution, e.g., paying a caretaker for the dam. It
was the rare case when lack of funds prohibited a group
from taking essential action.

The next section examines why groups did what they
did. Since much of their behavior is explained by operating norms and perceptions within the water sector as a
whole, discussion of the use of the eight-kilometer rule is
deferred until later.

Patterns of Water Sector Interaction: Dam Operating in
Perspective

Why People Followed Some Government Management Procedures
Dams served a useful purpose. But, contrary to the
ministry's perception, dam users valued convenient and
cheap water supplies, not just reliable ones. Since time
and money invested in transporting water could be applied
elsewhere, it was worthwhile to protect and preserve a
nearby supply. Fences were maintained because people saw
their effectiveness as management tools. Similarly, when
the water in a dam came under stress within a fallback
system, its use was regulated. The rest of the year the
dry dam was of little interest to its users.

Why People Did Not Follow Other Government Management
Procedures Both technical and social organization factors
seemed to have encouraged groups to depart from the terms
of agreement.

    o   Technical Factors

        --   The Small Capacity of the Dams. Dams were
              intended to provide water through the dry
              season given adequate rainfall. But even
              given sufficient rain, many small dams cannot
              provide water because of improper siting or
              the pressure of an excessive number of stock.
              If a dam is perceived by its users as likely

to go dry, it makes sense to "mine" the water
while it is there, especially if other water
points are available.

The small capacity was the result of a
Ministry of Agriculture's decision to opt for
smaller dams to prevent overstocking. But by
choosing smaller dams, the Ministry reduced the
dam's reliability for year-round livestock
watering, and thus decreased the incentive for
permanent management.

-- Dams as Low Maintenance Facilities. Many
    people favor dams precisely because maintenance
    requirements are perceived to be low, and the
    need to pay fees is minimal.

-- The Role of Dams in the Fallback System.
    During the rainy season (when water is
    plentiful) and often during the late dry
    season (when many people have returned to
    the villages), dam management does not pay.
    Management makes sense only when the dam is
    used as a fallback point or needs repair. If
    fees are collected, it is typically at this
    time. Management occurs under stress at the
    time when dam water is critical.

-- Dams as Multipurpose Water Points. If
    livestock access to dam water is restricted,
    users are more likely to use the water for
    domestic purposes. Twenty of the twenty-four
    dams surveyed were used for drinking water.
    Management of dams providing both domestic and
    livestock water often differed from those used
    for livestock only. For example, users looked
    upon domestic water charges with even less
    favor than livestock watering fees, since
    domestic water was supplied free of charge in
    most villages.

o   Social Organization Factors

-- Shortage of Labor. Dam use was affected by a
    perceived shortage of agricultural labor,
    especially for cattle-herding. Herders would
    much rather open a gate and allow cattle to
    water freely than pump water into a trough.

Labor-intensive dam maintenance activities may not
be done for lack of labor. Indeed, the very lack
of fences and deep reservoirs may have increased
the value of some smaller dams to labor-short
stockholders who only used them to water livestock. This, however, ensured that these dams
would not be managed as required by government.

-- Local-Level Perceptions Affecting Dam Use.
Government dams are generally considered to be
government property, the local feeling sometimes
being that the government should take care of them
as it does its other property. The policy of
group formation prior to construction--meant to
foster a sense of local ownership--did not always
succeed. Because of the traditional norm of open
access to many surface water sources, a small dam
was commonly perceived as belonging either to the
government or to the people of the locality in
which it had been sited; rarely was it seen by
residents as belonging exclusively to a small
group of people in that area, even if they had
been registered by the government.

-- Dam Groups as a Government Creation. Dam groups
had little or no basis of local legitimacy. The
official members were not particularly deserving
of a dam; they were simply in the right place at
the right time. From the government's viewpoint,
the group had been given the right of exclusive
use of the dam and the responsibility to manage it
properly. But other residents of a locality were
often not prepared to recognize this "right." The
communal land on which the dam was built
"belonged" to all residents, including the
neighbors of group members. The dam itself was
constructed by the government at no cost to the
group. The water was rain water. This
distinguishes the dam groups from individuals
whose private right to wells or dams comes from
the labor or capital invested in their
development. Dam groups cannot draw on
traditional norms to support their claims.
Moreover, as long as there is mutual assistance
among neighbors, dam group members hesitate to
turn away people who might help them in other
circumstances.

-- <u>The Declining State of Self-Help</u>. The absence
   of community sanctions against those who did
   not support the management of a dam might have
   reflected the low priority that all self-help
   activities received in an area. An increasing
   lack of trust and cooperation in some
   localities may explain why some elected to not
   contribute to dam management.

-- <u>Insiders Versus Outsiders</u>. Rural Batswana
   consider their major water and land
   difficulties in the communal areas to lie less
   in developing or managing the resources
   directly than in managing the conflict caused
   by differential access to and control over
   these resources. People complain about their
   neighbors being uncooperative in assisting in
   the operation of a water point. Others
   complain about marauding "outsiders" who come
   in and use locality resources without
   permission. There is conflict at all levels
   over the use and management of tribal land and
   water resources in many parts of eastern
   Botswana, where determining who is an insider
   and who are outsiders to a locality and its
   land and water is fast becoming the central
   feature of this conflict.

Patterns of Interaction in the Locality and Multiple
Locality: The Eight-Kilometer Rule

The small dams at the survey sites were often closer
than eight kilometers to other permanent water sources,
and in four sites dams were less than eight kilometers
from each other, indications of the many exceptions made to
the eight-kilometer rule.

<u>Technical Ambiguities in the Rule</u>. The rule was intended
to prevent exceeding the carrying capacity of the rangeland through the spacing of permanent water points with
capacities of up to 500 adult cattle. There are a number
of technical problems with its underlying assumptions.

o   <u>Carrying Capacity</u> A key problem is using a
    450-500 kg animal as the standard of carrying

capacity. Because of local production strategies, cattle in these areas often weigh considerably less.

o   Grazing around the Water Point Since existing livestock watering points in the east are often nearer than eight kilometers to each other, grazing does not always improve with distance from a water point.

o   Watering up to 500 Head Stocking rates are difficult to assess since they usually vary by season. Comparing two watering points with numerically equivalent stocking rates at different seasons of the year would require normalizing stocking rates and estimating equivalencies for seasonally variable forage conditions.

o   Eight-Kilometer Spacing This rule implicitly requires an animal to trek eight kilometers or more a day although this is inadvisable for certain types of animals at certain times of the year. Hydrological and topological conditions also affect the practicality of standard spacings.

The Political Mandate for the Eight-Kilometer Rule Despite these technical difficulties, it is precisely the technical aura of the rule that is politically appealing to land boards. The Tribal Land Act gave land boards statutory authority over land and water allocation and adjudication, but left them with the task of establishing the legitimacy of their exercise of that authority. The rule represents a resource (Comaroff 1978) that can be manipulated to assert a land board's claim over regulating the use of a site. Closer spacing is often allowed when an appeal is made to other "rules" the land board claims it can also apply to govern land and water use (cf., Roe and Fortmann 1982:132-133).

Outcomes

Equity

The government's program of building and operating village boreholes for drinking water has clearly helped both rich and poor users (Fortmann 1981:57; Fortmann

and Roe 1981). But the dam-building policy, intended
primarily for stock watering, may have excluded the poor
who have no livestock.

Using a Guttman scale of relative wealth, Fortmann
found no statistically significant difference between the
richer and poorer households in their domestic use of dams
and haffir-dams (Fortmann 1981:57; Fortmann and Roe
1981). All households using the small dams, whether for
livestock or domestic purposes, benefited from the
generally free water.

Data on use of government-provided livestock watering
points (including a few boreholes) show that the very
poorest cattle holders used such sources to a greater
extent than did other economic classes. (Small sample
sizes argue for caution in interpretation.) Collapsing
economic classes into two categories showed, however,
that, while some poorer cattle-holding households had
access to government-provided sources, a greater proportion of the richer cattle-holding households used them.
Since this comparison is based on cases of use,[1] it is
not known how many head each economic category watered at
such sources or how crucial they were for each class.
Still, the larger percentage of richer cattle holders
using these sources indicates that they benefited more for
cattle watering purposes. While the dams were not intended
for domestic use, it is probably the case that this use not
only led to much of the observed management at the dams,
but also made the overall effect of the dam policy more
equitable.

Efficiency

To determine whether small dams had encouraged overstocking and overgrazing, dry season and wet season counts
of livestock numbers (converted into standard livestock
units) were taken at 39 regularly monitored water points
at 12 sites; and a dry and wet season range condition was
scored at 46 points, with 34 water points common to both
surveys. Nonparametric statistical tests of significance
were used to measure differences between physical and
management types.

Few significant differences were found among the range
scores of different physical types. Small dams were not
noticeably better or worse than other water point types.
In contrast, group-owned and managed water points did have
significantly better dry season range conditions than did

privately operated sources. Type of access accounted for
the greatest statistical difference. Restricted access
water sources had clearly better range conditions than did
open access sources, particularly in the wet season.
(These results are more fully described in Roe 1985.)

This evidence strongly suggests that group-operated
small dams were in fact less intensely grazed than were
open access sources. Many of the private water sources
were open access or operated for longer periods of time
than the group dams, which often were restricted access
and were not in operation throughout the year. In fact,
since use of these dams typically occurred within a fallback system, livestock watering numbers rarely exceeded
the limitation of the terms of agreement. Only 12 percent
of the recorded daily counts at the 15 government small
dams monitored were over 400 livestock units, and most of
these counts were recorded at one dam. Contrary to the
ministry's view, these dams were probably no more intensively grazed than were other water sources.

In a sense, though, the ministry was correct. There
was overgrazing around the dams. But there was overgrazing (often relatively worse) around almost every other
water point. Statistical tests should not detract from
the fact that the absolute values of the range scores were
often less than half of what the ministry thought appropriate for the area.

Such evidence simplifies measuring the costs of overgrazing induced by dam development, since it suggests that
at the margin, the addition of one dam in an overgrazed
area will only slightly worsen range conditions. The
conservation loss due to increased degradation probably is
small compared to the dam's capital and operating costs and
potential benefits.

While a new dam may have little impact on the conservation efficiency where grazing has already exceeded
maximum sustainable yield, overgrazing does affect the
economic efficiency of livestock feeding off that grazing.
Outside the experiment station, it is next to impossible to
measure the marginal productivity of water for livestock
production controlling for all the factors. Nonetheless,
the figures in Table 3 suggest that the more water points
per unit of land area, the greater the overstocking,
associated overgrazing, and liveweight losses.

The recorded weights are less than expected for a
450 kg beast (around 240 kg), illustrating some of the
loss incurred by the poor grazing as well as the
production strategy that emphasizes numbers. Still,

variability in range condition and stocking rates tied to
water point density probably does have an economic cost in
terms of cattle condition.

A rough estimate indicates that building a new dam in an
area will, on average, lead to a 1 percent decrease in carcass weight for each stock unit (SU)[2] which, if aggregated
over the life of the dam and converted into livestock units,
would represent a loss of about 3 SU over 15 years, at about
5 cents per cubic meter of water in the average dam. Even
if this figure were doubled, it is a relatively small
increment to the total cost of water. Bailey (1980, 1982)
estimated that at a 12 percent interest rate and assuming

TABLE 3   Dry Season Carcass Weight and Indicators of Range Pressure.

Village	1979 Dry Season Carcass (wgt/kg)[a]	1979 % Households Grass Problems[b]	1979 Range Score (dry)[c]	Stocking Ranges (ha/SU)[d]	Water Point (Density/km^2)[e]
1	207.8 (178.3)	41.2%	19.2	8.8	0.03
2	179.7 (150.8)	53.3%	9.9	5.4	0.06
3	163.3 (106.6)	94.4%	14.6	3.3	0.17

[a]Carcass weight figures in parentheses include
condemnations. Data are from three livestock marketing
cooperatives selling cattle in September and October 1979.

[b]Percent who had trouble only with grazing (Bailey
1982:116).

[c]Figures are 1979 dry season lower layer species scores.
The higher the value, the better the range (Fortmann and Roe
1981:91).

[d]SU are standard livestock units equivalent to 450 kg.
(Bailey 1982:107). In reality, an adult animal is smaller.

[e]Based on the area and numbers of water points mapped for
each village water use area using Bailey's estimates for
available grazing area (Fortmann and Roe 1981:158-160).
Water point types were standardized for the percentage of
total livestock months spent at each type by the households
sampled (Bailey 1982:136-137).

a service life of 15 years, the annualized unit cost of a
cubic meter of water from a government dam was around
$2.20, a figure probably on the low side since dam water is
less available than originally intended. At a 2 percent
interest rate, the cost would be around $1.20/m3 in
1979/80 prices. His computations for boreholes and open
wells show that, on cost effectiveness grounds, small dams
are comparatively cheaper.

In a number of mixed lands and cattleposts, the dams
have become a major part of the fallback water point
strategy. They allow households to arrive early and leave
the lands later, which can lead to increased crop production. They provide a more convenient source of both
domestic and livestock water for a number of households
when convenience and reliability are at a premium. As
such, a cubic meter of dam water probably represents a cost
of between $1.25 and $2.25 for those communities that find
it a strategic water source. Indeed, the intensity of some
dam management is the best indication that willingness to
"pay" exists for such sources.

                          CONCLUSION

We have presented a bare-bones analysis of communal
water use and management in Botswana. It has been shown
that villagers manage water in a systematic and rational
fashion, although not necessarily in the way the government
thinks is right and proper. It has also been shown that
the factors affecting water management differ according to
the level of social and spatial organization. A complete
analysis of any water use and management system therefore
will require careful data collection at a number of levels.

NOTES

1. "Cases of use" is the sum of all water points used by all households in the survey. If one household used two water points and a second household used three water points, there are five cases of use represented by those two households even if they are using some of the same water points. This does not measure volume of water used or frequency of use.

2. A stock unit is a standardized measurement equal to a mature zebu cow with calf at foot.

REFERENCES

Bailey, C. 1980. Keeping Cattle and the Cost of Water in Eastern Botswana. Gaborone, Botswana: Ministry of Agriculture.

Bailey, C. 1982. Cattle Husbandry in the Communal Areas of Eastern Botswana. Ph.D. dissertation. Ithaca, New York: Cornell University.

Comaroff, J. 1978. Rules and rulers: political processes in a Tswana chiefdom. Man (N.S.), 13.

Fortmann, L. 1981. Do the poor benefit from publicly provided water in the rural areas? Botswana Notes and Records 13.

Fortmann, L. and E. Roe. 1981. The Water Point Survey. Gaborone, Botswana: Ministry of Agriculture.

Roe, E. 1985. Range conditions around livestock watering points in Botswana and Kenya. Rangelands.

Roe, E. and L. Fortmann. 1982. Season and Strategy: The Changing Organization of the Rural Water Sector in Botswana. Special Series on Resource Management, Rural Development Committee. Ithaca, New York: Cornell University.

Schapera, I. 1943. Native Land Tenure in the Bechuanaland Protectorate. Alice, South Africa: The Lovesdale Press.

Private Rights and Collective Management of Water in a High Atlas Berber Tribe[1]

Mohamed Mahdi

This paper discusses the forms of water management utilized by the Erguita mountain tribe in Morocco.[2] The Erguita consider water a collective good; its management links the various social groups composing the tribe and reveals the links among them. The use of the term "collective good" to describe water must be understood in context.

Water is a collective resource in the sense that its management is the business of the community, an <u>affaire de tous</u>. It is also an object of private ownership. The double identity that characterizes the regulations surrounding water use is a topic of primary concern here. Another concern is the specific manner in which the water is managed. In fact, the original objective here, in addition to analyzing the process of water management, was to understand the organization of the Erguita through their management of water.

As precise and as complicated as they appear, the systems of water sharing serve only as theoretical guides to the actual distribution of water among rights holders. In fact, the strict observance of these rules is often constrained by social tension and disorder. As ingenious as it might be, any rule is subject to the caprice of men. The same Berber who enthusiastically describes the delicate system of water sharing that controls his life will also, with good humor, explain how the system can be circumvented, as getting around the rules is seen as merely another way of dealing with water shortages. In reality, the different systems passed down from father to son are neither rigid nor blind to circumstance. In practice, they are often corrected and adapted to the difficulties of a particular moment. A harmonious existence of brothers is more important than rules, and recourse to a rigid adherence to the rules signals a crisis in the group; rules and systems are seen as solutions to practical problems of the past, and are not necessarily valid for contemporary circumstances.

Rules may conform to normal practice, but they are ignored periodically or temporarily to deal with unforeseen events. The system serves as a foundation, but it is supplemented by improvised rules and daily adjustments in situations not addressed by the rules. These adjustments are not part of traditional law but are derived from local folkways and mores. Not surprisingly, then, it is difficult to understand how water is distributed on a daily basis. These complications are such that the tribesmen prefer to discuss their system in the ideal terms of "water rights" instead of actual utilization of the resource.

Water rights may be seen as private property, but they are not as precise and clear as land rights. Property implies fixed limits, but water rights are confined and limited in a complex system of social relationships. The oral history of water use is the key to the operation of the system. This knowledge is held by specialists who distribute water and by notables of the village. By virtue of being monopolized by a few, this knowledge can be manipulated on occasion. The status of those who share water and the balance of power within a group are factors that determine how water rights are interpreted and enforced, but these factors are never constant. Hammoudi (1982) emphasizes that one must distinguish between water as a substance and water rights as a relationship among group members:

> If I call substance all that is tangible (in known quantity), limited, fenced (land), or measured, it is evident that the property in water rights that an individual possesses is not a substance. All that he possesses is opposed to substance. It is a relationship measured in time with other users. It is by the intermediary of the irrigation system, and by the fruit of collective labor that a person obtains the water to irrigate his properties.

PHYSICAL AND TECHNICAL ATTRIBUTES

We will attempt to show how physical and technical constraints lead to a joint use of water by groups, while at the same time these constraints exclude outside groups from using it. This will give a unique meaning to the concept of indivisibility.

The mobilization and use of water cannot be seen as an individual activity. The difficult physical and technical conditions affecting irrigated agriculture in the region can only be overcome when individuals unite their efforts; this need for cooperation applies equally to both stream irrigation and basin irrigation.

Stream irrigation involves taking water directly from the stream using a fragile diversion dam constructed of rocks and branches. Originating at the dam, a dirt canal winds along the slopes above the streambed and the terraces.[3] Along this canal, turnouts serve secondary distribution canals. These, in turn, serve the ditches that irrigate each small parcel. Stream irrigation is not common among the Erguita.

Basin irrigation relies upon spring water. A spring feeds a large accumulation basin constructed below it. The spring itself is venerated and is the object of a sacrifice of blood each year just after the maize harvest, called the "sacrifice of the spring."

Clearly, the physical and technical environment requires joint use of water, and thus leads to the social and communal aspect of water management. The co-users are the members of groups within the tribe. The Erguita tribe consists of nine rather large groups or fractions, each of which can be divided into several villages. Each village is a conglomeration of lineages made up of several extended households. Each fraction is identified with a specific territory whose limits are known and recognized by neighboring groups. Each of these can be viewed as an independent mountain "island" whose inhabitants share a community of interest.

In adapting to its valley, each group appropriates the natural resources found there. Each fraction has three facets--one of territory, one of common social origins, and one of mutual defense. As a result, the members of a fraction share a strong social identity.

The fraction exercises its jurisdiction over the water of its valley. It assures defense against the ambitions of neighboring groups and also is responsible for managing water for the benefit of its members. This results in a

system of group opposition and interdependency that is
fundamental to understanding the management of water among
segmentary groups such as the Erguita. This system will be
more comprehensible when we discuss the relation of groups
within the fraction.

We have talked about water as a collective, indivisible
resource that is the property of a group. We will now
discuss the impacts of tribal structure on this group
property, and the concept of indivisibility.

Among the Erguita, two theoretical models of communal
ownership of water coexist: property of the fraction and
that of the village. The fraction normally has the responsibility for the management of water. But there are
exceptions. The spring, the diversion dam, the basin, and
the canals are the property of the four villages that
constitute the Tamadgost fraction; another village not of
the fraction is also a co-proprietor. This village belongs
to a neighboring fraction; its right to use the system was
acquired by the force of arms several generations ago
(demonstrating that topographic frontiers are not inviola-
ble). Thus we see that a group's water rights may be the
result of geographical, historical, or military factors, or
any combination thereof.

In some instances, a single village has full rights to
an irrigation system. The cases of the village of
Tigouliane of the Id Waftkout fraction and Bitaljane of
the Ait Makhloui fraction will serve as examples. Such
exclusive use is normally justified when a village uses
large amounts of water and/or has a high population
density.[4] But these villages are, in many ways,
pseudo-fractions, "islands" that coexist along with other
villages within their fraction. At other times, two or
more villages within a fraction may manage water together.

This collective ownership of water changes its form as
one goes from very large social groups to smaller ones. It
is possible to distinguish between the water rights of a
fraction, those of one or more douars (villages), those of
one or several lineages, and even those of an extended
family. Within the fraction, the opposition to the rights
of various groups is often manifested between the lineage
and village groups. The douar transcends the lineages
within--members of one douar will coalesce to meet a threat
imposed by other douars. Similarly, the lineage transcends
individual families in conflicts with other lineages.

The water management system of mountain tribes is
characterized by the appearance and disappearance of the
rights of various groups. Water may be the property of
those who possess it by virtue of their location below a

spring or along a stream, but in reality it is the relationship between villages that actually determines water rights. At the village level, water is appropriated according to which part of the _fraction_ (quarter) the villages belong. Within these divisions, the lineage rises to claim its water rights, thus eclipsing the rivalries.

Paralleling the collective "ownership" of water is ownership of hydraulic equipment (diversion dams, canals, and basins) that is constructed and maintained by groups in order to distribute water to fields. Whether the group utilizes streams directly or uses the basin has important sociological implications. Direct appropriation of water from the stream itself requires a constant mobilization of human energy--a continuous relay system and detailed supervision among users. It requires specific methods of water distribution as well as rather strong social ties among the groups that are engaged in the maintenance and construction of collective works.

The basin method does not require continuous action because of the waiting time involved while the basin fills, but maintaining the system does require collective work. The tank was constructed by the ancestors, but its care is an obligation of all males who have reached the age of fasting irrespective of the quantity of irrigated land or the water rights their families claim. Males who fail to participate in system maintenance are punished by a fine (equal to one day's wage) levied by the assembly of the group.

The technical requirements for the collection and utilization of water influences the organization of groups and the rules surrounding water use. Each group confirms its identity by emphasizing its ownership of water from a spring or basin (for example, the water of a spring belongs to the Ait Tamadgost). At the level of the spring or the basin, water is still appropriated in the name of the entire group.

MANAGEMENT POSSIBILITIES AND THE PLACE OF RULES

The group must face a dual challenge in managing its water: that posed by the natural environment (which the group overcomes by using its technical knowledge), and that posed by other groups who compete for water. Water management is also constrained by judicial and technical rules and norms of social conduct. The response to all of these demands affects how a group will choose between two

water management strategies available: (1) a collective
option centered on the problem of collective irrigation;
and (2) a private option that requires complicated rules
of division and distribution among rights holders.

The Collective Option

We must reemphasize a basic point central to our
preceding discussion of water as property. Above a system
of canals, water management is collective. It is only
below the basin that it becomes a "private affair." The
community can, however, extend its prerogatives beyond the
basin and substitute itself for individuals to manage water
in their place. When this happens, we have collective
irrigation.

Even though collective irrigation does not normally
occur, it is a well-elaborated system. It is defined by
the type of contract that establishes it, by the institutions it requires, and by the collective solidarity it
realizes. Collective irrigation is chosen when conditions
favor it. In the main, these conditions involve:

o   The availability of water: the scarcity of water,
    (especially in summer) causes co-users to carefully
    oversee the minute details of water distribution
    and to engage in disputes over water with their
    neighbors. Abundance of water permits the
    collective utilization of water.

o   The level of social tension: even when water is
    abundant, the level of social tension among group
    members will determine whether they are willing to
    irrigate collectively.

The choice made by individuals or subgroups in favor
of either individual or collective irrigation depends upon
the importance assigned to each of the above factors. The
decision to irrigate collectively is made at a meeting of
an assembly of representatives of each lineage in a group.
In reality, however, this council's deliberations are open
to all male members of the group that the assembly
represents.

Collective water management leads to collective
irrigation, which is the responsibility of specially
designated officials who are charged by the community to
service all of its irrigated fields. These irrigators are

called _imazzalen_. The institution of _imazzalen_ appears in humid years when the water available exceeds the quantity of recognized water rights. In such cases, the complicated rules governing the partitioning of water disappear. The _imazzalen_ are put in charge of the irrigation and the maintenance of individual parcels. There are no water allotments to distribute, and no rotations to observe. It is a gentlemanly system where the social and economic distinctions that normally influence the management of water are reduced; even those who have virtually no water rights can benefit. The rigid observation of minute water shares (and the rationing of parcels that results from it) are suspended; everyone can farm at will.

To examine the organization of the _imazzalen_ institution, we will use the example of the _douar_ of Tagadirt. Tagadirt is divided into four quarters. The members of the village "own" two days of water from the basin called _timansakht_, which belongs to them and the _fraction_ of Tamadgost. Each quarter contains two or more lineages. The division into quarters reflects an old but careful decision to maintain an equilibrium of power among various lineages. This division is important to understanding collective irrigation because each quarter provides two _imazzalen_, making a total of eight for the village.

A second division is on a territorial basis and is as important as the first. Land to be irrigated is divided into two halves corresponding to the two days of water rights that belong to the village. Formally, each half receives one day's water. The system is further complicated by the fact that each half is divided again into the land served by a single canal. Each half of the village land is served by four canals. The number of _imazzalen_ corresponds to the number of canals. The social divisions of the group and the physical division of its territory determine the number of irrigators.

Compensation of the _imazzalen_ poses a problem. Their nomination is proceeded by long debates among representatives of each quarter and lineage over the criteria to be used for the compensation of irrigators. Three possible criteria are discussed: percentages of harvest, water rights possessed, and by number of _takatines_ (extended households). Landholders with large parcels obviously reject any compensation based upon the amount of water rights possessed and prefer payment based on the household. A levy based on the number of couples in a _takat_ will treat the rich and the poor equally. A compromise involves payments based on a percentage of the harvest. These quarrels are repeated each time the imazzalen are named.

Determined by local custom, the "law of water" in the mountains cannot be understood simply by referring to concepts of jurisprudence originating from either the Muslim or Roman tradition. We must add that water is a resource without precise limits or shapes. Concepts more appropriately drawn from sociology than from jurisprudence better illuminate our understanding of the rules of water distribution. Erguita water rights would fall into the category of "collective regime," where each individual rights-holder has his share of water because of his membership in a particular group. Water rights are mediated by other factors. In order to exercise his rights, a person must refer to certain rules that authorize him to use his rights and that define the relationship of one proprietor to other proprietors in a system of collectively appropriated water. Water rights, then, are best understood through the rules that govern the division and distribution of water.

The rights-holder has been defined as a social unit, to whom a quantity of water is allocated in a block--such as a day of water, a night of water, a portion of a day or night--and may be shared by other units. The more we descend through the hierarchical structure of the tribe from larger to smaller units (especially to lineages and households), the smaller water shares become, and the more difficult it becomes to identify them. We will discuss below how water shares are allocated to each individual taken separately as rights-holders. Water is defined as quantifiable so that it can be distributed.

Private Option

Water is divided into a specific number of parts or water turns. The groups of the Tamarout taqbilt will illustrate the manner in which water turns are distributed among douars, then between lineages, and finally between lineages and takatines (plural of takat).

The water turns of each village have names. There are eighteen of them at Ifri Quassif, a basin belonging to the four douars of Tamarout. Every turn is divided into two periods to increase the number of turns to thirty six. These turns are subdivided into halves, thirds, quarters, or eighths.

The appropriation of water by a village poses no problems. The villages (rights-holders) and the water turns assigned to them are easy to identify. It is within the douar, once the first stage of distribution has been passed, that the distribution of small quantities of water becomes problematic. At the level of divisions of water between douars, one is still at the level where the ownership of water turns is collective. It is only at the lower levels (lineages, households) that property becomes real and is subject to minuscule division.

Water Turns: Lineages, Sublineages, Families

Just as at the douar level, water is allocated to each lineage (ikhs) in a block. The Ifri n'barr Wamane basin is a case in point. Water of this basin is the property of the lineage "Two Halves," which makes up the village of Assif Quagadir. As above, each water turn is identified by name. There are thirty-one water turns in this case. The odd number of turns resolves the delicate problem of which users have daytime water turns and which have night turns. All of the odd numbered turns will be daytime turns for one cycle and night turns in the next cycle.

It is the sharing of water among members of the same lineage that poses the greatest problem. The water turns identified by name are subdivided in order to be distributed among households. At this level, it is the flow in one's ditches that counts rather than some abstract right.

The initial division of water reflects the history of lineages. For example, water is divided into three parts that correspond to the three extended families making up the Ihouline lineage--Ait Said, Ait Bella, and Ait Abderrahman--and their three water turns. The Ihouline takatines will say that their water is divided into talt or mtalta (both of which mean thirds). In doing so, they are referring to this first partition, which corresponds to the geneology of the lineage.

The partition of water derived from the first level partition, here the second and third degree partitions, are more complex. The thirds are redistributed among members of each of the three takatines. New rights-holders appear at each step in the evolution of the groups and it becomes even more complicated as right-holders not belonging to the lineages begin to appear (heirs, spouses, etc.). Each of the original thirds is further subdivided into thirds or

fifths (khomes). These divisions represent the history of
the group and the modifications of the shares held by each
right-holder in the course of a lineage's historical
evolution.

The "ownership" of water among the lineages, however,
does reflect the lineage's actual informal composition and
present organization. The formal unity of the lineage is
counterbalanced by the particular interests of those who
compose it--not only those of extended families and households, with all the individual rights-holders, but also with
absentee members. For example, women born into the lineage
but living elsewhere still maintain their rights
in the lineage's territory.

Systems for Partitioning Water

Water must be measured if it is to be distributed to
those with rights to a particular share. Several systems of
measurement are practiced in the various taqbilt of the
Erguita. Each system has its own units of measurement. At
least four distinct systems are currently in use:

The Solar System. A brief description of this system
will make the solar system of measurement intelligible and
may help to explain the complex approach to water use that
is its corollary. (There is an interesting variation to the
method of collecting water in a basin that is found in the
Tamarout fraction.)

This system is referred to as the solar system because
it relies on the movement of the sun (which is tracked on a
rock or other visible protrusion--called an azmaz) to signal
whose turn it is to use the irrigation water. Those who
make use of this solar system rely on two basins--one that
collects the stream flow and is therefore the principal
source of irrigation water, and a second (also known as an
azmaz) that recollects the water once it has been released
from the principal basin. When the water is released from
this secondary basin, the process is referred to as azmaz.
When the sun hits the azmaz (rock), the person using the
principal basin opens it to flood his crops; this is also a
signal that the azmaz (the secondary basin) is to be closed.

As is the case with the concept of "azmaz," "imdal" and
"timane" are also terms used to refer simultaneously to a
unit of time and a volume of water (that is, the volume of
water that can be released during the measure of time

designated by either word). Moreover, the last unit of
time/volume of water (timane) is also coordinated with the
hours of prayer, and thus these become the demarcations for
the flow of water when the sky is overcast. These three
time/volume divisions (azmaz, imdal, and timane) represent
the points on an imaginary triangle carved into a
mountain's slope, each of which point is reached by the
rays of the sun at regular intervals.

   The Gauge System of Measurement. In general, this
system of measurement utilizes a notched stick to indicate
the different shares of water. The unit of measure utilized is called the takarroubt, which is the equivalent of
one-eighth the content of a basin. Eight principal notches
are marked on the basin to indicate these divisions. At
Tigouliane, each takarroubt is 20-22 cm--and is, in turn,
marked again in both thirds and eighths. Other measures
include the hand (afous) and the finger of water (addad
n'wamane). A finger of water is obtained by placing the
four fingers of the hand on the measuring stick (the thumb
folded on the palm) and marking the two sides of the hand
on the stick. Each takarroubt is divided into three
fingers and the number of fingers in the basin is thus
twenty-four.
   If the owners of a day of water are all members of the
same lineage who agree to use water together, the use
rarely poses problems. This system can establish fair
distribution for the multiple users of a day of water. In
addition, those who are the first to use water in one
rotation of irrigation water (which is seven days at
Tigouline) will be the last to have a turn in the next
cycle.

   The Tattast System of Measurement. The same can be
said for the system of the tattast. The tattast is a
copper bowl with a small hole pierced in the bottom. When
this vessel is placed in a bucket of water, it slowly sinks
until it is totally submerged. A tanast corresponds to the
quantity of water that flows from a basin or a stream
during the period that it takes the tattast to sink.
Sub-units of the tattast (halves, thirds, quarters, and
eighths) are marked inside the container. A conversion is
possible between the takarroubt and tattast systems. A
quarter of a takarroubt is the equivalent of one tanast.

Time Measurement. Only one taqbilt of the Erguita uses a clock to measure water. The introduction of this system is due to unique circumstances. This taqbilt once had a system of water distribution similar to those described above but, over time, the system was altered in favor of a local chief (Id l'Houssein) who had increased his appropriation of water through forced purchases. After independence, the peasantry demanded that their property be restored to them. The Moroccan authorities were overwhelmed by the difficulties of restoring the old order, so chose a simple option. They decreed that each extended household in the taqbilt receive one-and-one-half hours of water. It is the only example among the Erguita where the state intervened to change water rights inherited from the colonial period.

INTERACTION BETWEEN THE COMPONENTS OF THE SYSTEM

Constraints imposed by both the physical and social environments influence an individual's choice between individual and collective forms of water management. The physical environment so severely limits the choice of action that to act as an autonomous individual would be suicidal.

The consequent need to act collectively gives water its communal characteristic. But strong group affiliations add impetus to the move for collective management; an individual's membership in the group gives him access to communal resources. This membership creates a sort of interdependence among group members and promotes the idea of a community of interests. The first community interest is the respect for things that are communal or collective.

Individual behavior, as such, does not exist; the individual always operates from within a group. Even though the group may be very small, such as an extended household, it nevertheless controls the individual. Indeed, the option of ostensibly private water management has its "group" side. Many forms of exchanges among co-users are required if the system of individual water rights is to operate properly; water turns are exchanged and are lumped together, and agreements are made over which blocks will be irrigated to reduce water loss that would occur if isolated plots were irrigated. At times, parcels may be temporarily exchanged to permit better use of scarce water.

By belonging to a group, a person is required to obey

all of the rules governing it--moral, social, and
technical. Violation of one category of rules by the theft
or abusive use of water may lead to social stigma and
negative sanctions. These are reinforced under many
circumstances--at celebrations, meetings, and at certain
sacrifices where young people do satiric mimes of one's
actions during the past year (that are forms of symbolic
punishment).

Social disapproval may be coercive. Even though
banishment is no longer practiced, one can still hear the
words "go away from the people of this country" pronounced
against those who violate customs. Social coercion is
especially evident in the way village notables resolve
conflict, and in the way they testify if resolution of the
conflict should go before government authorities. The
rules of water sharing, as described above, help to constrain individual behavior.

Thus, two sets of factors influence the decision about
individual or collective water management. These factors
are the relative scarcity or abundance of water, and the
amount of conflict or consensus within a group. As
Bouderbala et al. (1984) put it, "everywhere that water is
scarce, we find a strong belief in individual appropriation, regardless of the type of system and the characteristics of water users." Scarcity stimulates the desire
for private control, and leads to a proliferation of regulations. These rules disappear in times of abundance, but
one must qualify these statements. As we saw during our
discussion of the distribution of water, the smaller the
social units or the shares of water, the more likely it is
that the share of each individual is insignificant. At
such a level, the scarcity of water encourages cooperation
and leads to joint actions.

Conflict and consensus are not eternal conditions.
Both are temporary states that will be transcended by
brotherhood, which usually prevails and is kept in reserve
by the group to regulate tension. It is the principal tool
for keeping a group's internal contradictions within
reasonable limits.

RESULTS AND EVALUATION OF THE SYSTEM

Is the system of water management among the Erquita
efficient and equitable? Certain canals (tiny ones of
course) gather their water from seepage out of uphill
canals. The existence of a series of such canals along a

valley attempts to prevent all such losses. Irrigation
among the Erguita is a struggle to benefit from even the
smallest amount of water. The current practice of lining
canals with concrete is a manifestation of the ancient
concern about waste, but it creates its own problems:
lining a canal means that certain other canals will be
deprived of water.

In addition to the purely hydraulic measures of
efficiency, the impact of irrigation on the surface over
which this water is distributed must be considered. Even
if all arable land were served by one canal, a minimum of
cooperation between irrigators would be required in order
for all to subsist or for water to be available. Thus
appears the need for informal arrangements. In times of
shortage, these may lead to quarrels, but they can also
favor tighter cooperation. Collective irrigation creates a
kind of equality among users and is an efficient form of
water management.

From an equity standpoint, it must be pointed out that
Berber society is hierarchical and inegalitarian. This
inequality is the result of unequal population growth and
of the status differentials of each group.

The different participants in the system must deal with
the inequalities of fate. When we look at the shares owned
by each takat and by each lineage, we can see that
inequalities exist not only between various groups, but
also within groups. An individual takes part in the
construction and maintenance of the irrigation system not
as an individual but as a member of a group (lineage). The
balance between the contribution of an individual to the
maintenance of the common irrigation system and the
benefits that an individual takes from using the system
cannot be simply evaluated on an individual basis. Equity
of distribution is contingent both upon the distribution of
water within a group and upon the unequal distribution of
resources between them.

NOTES

1. The research that served as a basis for this article
was conducted for a doctoral thesis that was defended June
1983 at the Faculté des Sciences Juridiques, Economiques et
Sociales, Casablanca. It is based on two visits to the
Erguita, the first for one month in December of 1981 and
the second for three months during the summer of 1982. The
fact that my parents are both from this group facilitated
the work. I would like to thank Richard Riddle and Jere
Gilles for translating this article into English.

2. A tribe in the Western High Atlas Mountains north of
Taroudant. The Secretary General of the Ministry of
Interior furnished us with the following statistical
information on the "tribe":

  Population: in 1971: 11,319; est. 1980: 13,647
  Number of villages: 46
  Land area possessed: 200 square kilometers
  Lands possessed: 1,195 hectares cultivated (475 hect-
  ares irrigated, 1,519 unirrigated) 9,770 hectares of
  forest.
  Livestock owned: 1,287 cattle, 3,081 sheep, 12,066
  goats, 34 camels, 1,165 horses, donkeys and mules.
  There are 531 members of the tribe who have emigrated
  to Europe and many more have gone to Moroccan cities.

3. The water coming from a small ravine may be water of an
extended household or even of an isolated family. Here we
only speak of the larger (village or intervillage) systems
of irrigation.

4. The spatial organization and the dimensions of such a
village reproduce that of the fraction. The lineages are
scattered in space in the image of the villages in a fraction but at the same time they maintain common interests in
the management of such common resources as water and sacred
objects.

REFERENCES

Bouderbala, N., J. Chiche, A. Herzenni, P. Pascon. 1984.
   La question hydraulique. Rabat: Institut Agronomique
   et Vétérinaire Hassan II.

Hammoudi, A. 1982. Droits d'eau et société: la vallée du
   Dra. Hommes, terres et eaux, No. 48 (September).

BIBLIOGRAPHY

Berque, J. 1978. Structures sociales du Haut Atlas.
Paris: Presses Universitaires Françaises.

Dresch, J. 1939-1941. Les procédés d'irrigation dans le
massif central du Grand Atlas. Association Française
pour l'Avancement des Sciences, 63ième assemble, Liège
1939-1941: 1045-1049.

El Alaoui, M. 1979. Aspect du régime juridique de la
propriété, de l'exploitation et de la gestion des eaux
et des réseaux d'irrigation au Maroc. Hommes, terres et
eaux, No. 33 (July-August).

El Hallani. n.d. Organization de la gestion, de
l'entretien des réseaux dans le périmètre de
Tessaout-Amont.

Geertz, C. 1966. Person, Time, and Conduct in Bali: An
Essay in Cultural Analysis. New Haven, Connecticut:
Souteast Asia Studies, Yale University.

Mahdi, M. Essai monographique sur une tribu du Haut
Atlas: Erguita. Mémoire de DES. Rabat: Faculté des
Sciences Juridiques, Economiques et Sociales, Hassan
II.

Meunie, J. 1951. Greniers, citadelles au Maroc. Paris:
Publications des Hautes Etudes Marocaines Vol. LII.

Sonnier, A. 1933. Le régime juridique des eaux au Maroc.
Paris: Institut des Hautes Etudes Marocaines. Recueil
Sirey.

Canal Irrigation in Egypt: Common Property Management [1]

Robert C. Hunt

A geographic territory contains many different materials, sources of energy, and spaces. A resource is created only when a technology and the intention to exploit the resources come into being and are brought to bear on the territory. For the purposes of this paper, the territory involved is the Nile Valley from the Aswan High Dam to the mouth of the Nile Delta.

The technology includes dams, canals, and water lifting devices, domesticated plants and animals, and the industrial inputs for agriculture, including fertilizers, insecticides, improved seeds, fossil fuel, tractors, etc. Unlike marginal situations, here we are involved with a stable and deeply organized capital-intensive form of resource exploitation.

The resource is water for irrigation. Virtually all of the fresh water for Egypt derives from the Nile, and most of it from the river's headwaters. Since the 1960s, Egypt has had over-year storage of Nile water behind the Aswan High Dam, and during this time period the volume of irrigation releases from the dam have been virtually identical from year to year. The water stored in Lake Nasser has multiple uses, including hydroelectricity, drinking water, navigation, and industry, in addition to irrigation of plants.

The Ministry of Irrigation (MOI) receives water from the dam, and distributes it throughout the irrigated

territory by means of barrages, canals, and gates. The
water flows year-round, to about 2.6 million hectares of
irrigated fields (except for the shut-down for maintenance
in January). MOI engineers are responsible for operating
and maintaining these structures. In Egypt, cropping
discipline and the supply of water are dominated by the
national government.

Irrigators must submit to cropping discipline by
mutually coordinating plant-growth cycles. Where farmers
get water from a common canal, there are serious consequences if the crops grown by one farmer do not need
water at the same time as the crops grown by another. For
the allocation system to work smoothly, some sort of
cropping discipline must ensure that the water needs of
the plants are coordinated with the schedule of water
delivery, and that the plants are coordinated from one
field, and one farm, to another.

The cropping discipline in most of Egypt is provided
by a complex set of arrangements designed and operated by
several national ministries. Every year, the Ministry of
Supply determines how much of several commodities the
country is to produce (cotton, wheat, rice, etc.). These
amounts are communicated to the Ministry of Agriculture
(MOA), which calculates the amount of land, seed, fertilizer, etc., needed and then draws up a plan and a timetable
for the country (Alderman et al. 1982).

A major feature of the agricultural plan is the administration by the agricultural cooperatives (Harik 1974).
In principle, every farmer belongs to some cooperative;
the cooperative receives its quota of crops to be produced
from the MOA, and then sets about the job of assigning
particular crops to particular fields with a timetable.
There is some negotiation, but essentially the plan comes
down from above. The MOA plan is also communicated to the
MOI, which designs water delivery schedules according to
the agricultural plan. Crop discipline then is officially
imposed by the national government, and there should be a
good fit between the timing and distribution of the plants
in the fields and the timing and distribution of the irrigation water (Alderman et al. 1982).

The MOI extracts water with barrages on the Nile and
sends it down the MOI canals. In the district (the lowest
MOI level), the water is rotated from one canal to another
on a regular and stable schedule. The mesqa is a ditch
that receives water from the MOI canals, and from which the
farmers draw most of their irrigation water. Short,

shallow, and small, compared with the MOI canals, mesqa usually serve fewer than 100 farmers. The system is designed so that when the MOI district canal has water, the perpetually open outlet allows water into the mesqa at the same time on the rotational schedule. Each one is supposed to get the same amount of water per feddan (Egyptian measure of area, = 1.04 acre) of agricultural field (Mehanna et al. 1983). A study conducted by the Egypt Water Use and Management Project (EWUP) determined that some upstream mesqa may get more water per hectare of irrigated land than would some downstream (Wolfe et al. 1979:16). Each farm within a mesqa is supposed to get the same amount of water per hectare. Skold et al. (1984) argue that there may be differential distributions here as well.

Most mesqa in the delta, and some in Upper Egypt, are below the surface of the fields, so that the water must be lifted 50-100 cm. Three ancient devices are used to lift water: the shadouf, a counterweighted bucket, the tambour or Archimedean screw, and the saqia, a wheel powered by animals. Large steam-driven pumps were introduced in the 19th century (Hopkins n.d.), and portable diesel-engine powered pumps recently have been included in the water lifting technology. In the Fayum, there are a number of gravity-flow mesqa.

COMMON PROPERTY MANAGEMENT OF IRRIGATION[2]

In common property management, there are local groups that have rights to the resource; the groups are organized to manage the use of that resource, and individuals within those groups enjoy individual rights to the benefits arising from the joint use. Two such groups are visible in irrigation in rural Egypt. One is associated with the mesqa, and one with the saqia (the wheel). The resource managed by common property institutions is the water that small groups of farmers acquire from the MOI canal system, and that they then divide up among themselves.

Most of the thousands of mesqa in Egypt are below field level, and apparently have no formal organization. They each have a score or more of saqia, which are formally organized. In the Fayum, which has a relatively large amount of topographic relief, the mesqa are formally organized; this organization is discussed here.

The mesqa is said to be a private ditch, and to be totally under the control of the farmers (Wolfe et al.

1979:6-7). The farmers who draw water from it are responsible for operating and maintaining it. Since the water is
available only part of the time (due to rotation among MOI
canals), the farmers must arrange to use the water while it
is available. The formally organized mesqa in the Fayum
(munawaba) has a chief executive officer (ra'is), and
subdivisions (taraf) that also have officers (Mehanna et
al. 1983:66-7, 77). These officers have lists of
water-rights-holders, how much water each is to receive,
and where in the intra-mesqa rotational system the farmer's
turn occurs, and they are responsible for administering
allocation turns within the mesqa.

Maintenance of the mesqa is the responsibility of the
farmers who draw water from it (Wolfe et al. 1979). Maintenance is organized by the officers, and all farmers are
supposed to provide able-bodied workers. Some do the
maintenance work themselves, while others hire substitutes.

Conflict within the mesqa is handled by the mesqa
organization itself. As in most stratified agricultural
economies, however, whatever disputes this group cannot
handle by itself will be dealt with by a series of notables, who may or may not be members or officials of the
group. Some breaches of the norm (violence, killing)
automatically call in the conflict resolution offices of
the state.

Access to mesqa water is supposed to be proportional to
the amount of land owned that is watered by the mesqa. In
the one studied in the Fayum, it was said to be common
knowledge that the shares of water were not proportional to
land; notables had much more than their share of water
(Mehanna et al. 1983). Membership in the mesqa group is a
function of owning land watered by the mesqa. It is clear
who are members and who are not. The group vigorously
objects to nonmembers who try to take water that belongs in
(and to) their mesqa. The mesqa group manages the behavior
of the members with respect to the resource (water) and
with respect to the technology (the mesqa) itself.
Internal sanctions are available for use against breaches
of the norms.

It is not clear how effective the sanctions are against
free riders. When the call for group participation in
maintenance comes, it is a major notable of the village who
makes the call, not officers of the mesqa, and there are
always some members who do not turn out (Mehanna et al.
1983).

The saqia, a pump driven by a cow or water buffalo, is

designed to lift water 50-100 centimeters from the below-field-level mesqa. Saqia ownership is divided into 24 equal shares (qirat); the ownership of 1 qirat entitles one to 1/24th of the water, and obliges one to pay for 1/24th of the expenses. Each farmer may have one or more qirats in one or more saqias, and must either power the device with his own animal or rent the time of someone else's animal. It is almost always the case that a saqia has two or more participants. Most below-grade mesqa have a score or more of saqia.

Each saqia has a formal leader, usually a relatively rich and senior cultivator who lives near the saqia. He keeps an essential part of the machinery in his house, arranges turns on it, organizes for maintenance and collects the relevant fees, and resolves conflict (Mehanna et al. 1983). The leader of the saqia is responsible for seeing to it that every member gets his share of saqia time. There is no discussion of recruitment to saqia membership in the literature. Presumably a person either inherits a set of shares, or is able to buy in.

Accounts of saqia operation in the 1980s report no trouble. However, it is said that before 1979, time on the saqia was a serious constraint and there was much conflict. Now with the availability of portable diesel pumps, this time constraint problem has been solved (Mehanna et al. 1983). It is also reported, however, that one consequence is increased tension over scarcity among saqia on the same mesqa (Harik 1974). This implies that the saqia group did not always manage to control competition for access to the technology, and thus to the resource.

DISCUSSION

Each of the farmer groups that allocates access to the mesqa and saqia does so in terms of a rule of fairness. Each feddan is supposed to get as much water as any other feddan. Each share in a saqia is supposed to get as much water as any other share.

The outcomes would seem to be largely good ones. Egyptian agriculture is generally quite productive and environmentally stable. Crop yields are very respectable by world standards (Dotzenko n.d.:2), and there is no evidence of environmental degradation in the old agricultural lands (Hunt 1985b).

It is clear that both the formally structured mesqa and the saqia groups are organized local groups successfully using a common pool resource by means of common property management. Before proceeding to a further stage of the argument, several features of this Egyptian case need to be highlighted.

First, the common property management group is appropriating the common pool resource from another social institution, not from "nature." The water is extracted from nature at the Aswan High Dam by the national government. Water for irrigation is taken from the Nile by the MOI, and is controlled by that ministry until it is released into the mesqa. The mesqa, and subsequently the saqia, then, acquire the water from the MOI. There is a change in the management principles of the common pool resource, water, at the point where it is transferred from the MOI to the mesqa. Most examples of common property management involve the acquisition of the common pool resource from nature (as in the case of forest, or mountain pasture, or fish). In the case of irrigation in Egypt, it is most emphatically different. Common property managers do exist for irrigation water, but they are downstream from other institutions.

Second, the analysis of the notion of property needs to be given more attention. In discussions of common property, "common" receives the lion's share of the discussion, and there is often little or no analysis of the "property" involved. We need to know more about property rights in the territory, the resource, and the technology. A detailed analysis of the property involved, including what is owned, what the rights and duties are, under what conditions those rights and duties may be alienated, and whether the "owning" entities are individuals, groups, partnerships, etc. remains to be worked out.[3]

In canal irrigation, the physical facility for managing irrigation water (the technology) and the water (the resource), have been referred to in property terms. Irrigation water can be owned as private property. (In some irrigation systems, water can be bought, sold, rented, and inherited. Cf. Maass and Anderson 1978.) Most empirical descriptions of irrigation systems contain references to water rights that clearly are not private property. Rarely, however, is there any discussion of what the rights are, how such rights are created, whether they can be alienated, and if so how. There is, in short, very little discussion of the property aspects of the irrigation water itself.

Our understanding of property rights in the physical facility has begun to improve. Coward (1983, 1985) has recently pioneered a focus on property in the physical facility, and argues that the viability of local irrigators' groups may well be intricately connected with these property rights. This new thrust of research is very welcome.

Several issues need further research. In Egyptian irrigation, we would like to know whether there are contexts in which water for irrigation is defined as property. Does the MOI have property rights in irrigation water? What are the conditions for appropriation and transfer of water if and when it can be property? In the case of the technology (mesqa, saqia), these facilities may be common property if they are property in the legal system of the surrounding nation, or if the local appropriation, as if it were property, is effectively ignored by the nation. Property rights in the saqia are probably clear to the participants, although they have not been discussed in the literature. The mesqa is another matter. It has been referred to as a "private ditch," yet some agricultural cooperatives and the MOI both assume some oversight responsibilities (Wolfe et al. 1979; Mehanna et al. 1983). Much is yet to be learned about the mesqa, and not just with respect to property. In the context of canal irrigation generally, a much more detailed and focused account is needed of local and national property concepts in the water source, the water once extracted, and in the physical facility.

Third, in terms of outcomes, the Egyptian mesqa and saqia do not work perfectly. There is evidence of free riders (Mehanna et al. 1983), of unequal access to shares of the commons (Mehanna et al. 1983; El-Din and Dardir, n.d.; Skold et al. 1984), and of conflict (Mehanna et al. 1983). The widespread assumption is that successful common property management will motivate all members in such a way that breaches of omission and commission will tend to be eliminated. Some analysts seem to feel that conflict is less in local irrigation groups than it is elsewhere. There is no authenticated report of an irrigation system that totally lacks conflict. Any such claim, if it is to be reasonably lacking in uncertainty, must first solve the problem of measuring relative amounts of conflict in different irrigation systems. Such measurements do not exist now, and they are exceedingly difficult even to think

about. The long-range goal should be to develop measures
of nonparticipation, and apply them to empirical cases.
Then we will be in a position to test empirically the
proposition that positive motivation has better outcomes
than does coercion. I would not expect that common
property managers of irrigation water would be without
conflict, would have no free-riders, or otherwise be
problem-free.

IMPLICATIONS

Does the Resource Determine Its Management?

Comparative study of irrigation organization shows
quite clearly that several different forms of organization
are possible, and indeed are found quite widely distributed
(Hunt n.d.a, n.d.b). The entirety of a canal irrigation
system can be managed by common property principles, or the
entirety of a system can be managed by a bureaucracy of the
state, or there can be a variety of mixtures of the two
principles. There is nothing inherent in the resource,
or in the technology, that forces a particular form of
management.

Some canal irrigation systems are under fiercely local
control by the farmers themselves. One can refer to Japan,
Spain, and the western part of the United States for convenient examples. In all three nations, systems of substantial size (up to 20,000 hectares) are owned, managed,
and operated by an organization of the farmers. These
farmers manage the headgate, operate the canals and gates,
do the maintenance, the conflict resolution, and the
accounting. They acquire the common pool resource from
nature and convert it into property at that point. Irrigation communities are operating with many or all of the
common property institutions (Beardsley et al. 1959; Glick
1970; Maass and Anderson, 1978; Kelly 1982; cf. Hunt,
n.d.a, n.d.b).

Some canal systems have been organized by a central
authority that is responsible for everything down to the
delivery of water to the farm gate. There are no common
property elements in the management or organization of such
systems. The Gezira scheme under British management is the
prime example of this, and there are many examples in
Mexico as well (Farbrother 1973; Hunt 1985a).

Some canal irrigation systems have a mixture of the two

principles, usually with an irrigation community at the farmer's end of things, and a bureaucracy at the top end. Southern Iraq as described by Fernea (1970) is a prime example: the British and national canal authorities managed the level of water in the major canals, and were responsible for operation and management down to the outlet pipe into small ditches. These ditches were the responsibility of small groups of farmers, who are also sets of kinsmen. These latter are organized in terms of irrigation communities, and operate with a commons.

These cases demonstrate that irrigation does not demand a particular kind of management regime.

Convergent Development

There appears to be a convergence of thinking about the social organization of canal irrigation. For some years, scholars have been working on the organizational features of small-scale traditional irrigation systems (cf., Millon 1962; Hunt and Hunt 1976; Coward 1977). From another point of view, there has been much interest in promoting water users associations for organizing small groups of farmers within larger bureaucratically managed canal systems (cf., Bromley et al. 1980; Wade 1980; Montgomery 1983; Steinberg 1983). With the essays on irrigation in this volume, common property management joins the fold and adds another perspective. All share a concern with the organization of local groups, and with motivations for getting work done.

Coward and I have been particularly interested in the comparative analysis of "traditional" or "indigenous" irrigation systems (cf., Coward 1977; Hunt 1979). Out of this work has come a clear recognition of several crucial principles that characterize what I have called the irrigation community (a local group with rights to water that are enforceable in the courts of the nation, with a locally chartered executive officer, and with a system of rights and duties). The irrigation community is a system of tasks and roles. The group itself has enforceable rights to receive water, and once the water is received the group has rights to distribute that water within the group. The leadership is accountable to the users of the water, as Coward (1979) has shown, and the leadership roles are organically connected to a system of tasks (Hunt n.d.b). Recently, Coward (1983, 1985) has argued that such groups have a property interest in the facility (due to having invested in the construction), and that this property interest is probably connected to the enduring and successful operation of these systems.

What is striking about the common property management literature is how closely it approaches the concept of the irrigation community. The common property management model includes local groups with rights to the resource, who will manage it jointly, carefully, and efficiently, control free riders, and spread benefits around equitably. All of these features usually characterize the irrigation community. The common property tradition adds a focus on the property dimension of these irrigation systems.

There is a third tradition for thinking about the local organization of irrigators, that of farmers' participation. In the development community, there is a general position that it would be beneficial if the farmers in large bureau-cratically run irrigation systems could be organized in small groups to manage the tail-ends of the systems. These groups are usually referred to as water users associations (WUA). The benefits to the farmers are supposed to be a more reliable supply of water for a larger number of farmers and more control over their own destiny. Few attempts to construct such groups have been successful. The findings of those interested in irrigation communities, and in common property, are relevant to the WUA problems. I have demonstrated that the WUA is based on a very weak analogy with what I have called the irrigation community (Hunt 1985a). Irrigation communities have control over the water once it is delivered to the group, and provide an arena for negotiating effectively with the system-wide authorities over problems in the delivery of water to the local group. All irrigation community systems so far examined own their own water and control how it is to be allocated.

In general, these WUA are expected to perform the maintenance and to control the problem of free riders. However, the articulation of the WUA with the rest of the system is seldom examined, nor is there any consciousness of a system of tasks and roles. The WUA are not supposed to have final control over the allocation of the water, and there is no attempt to conceptualize, much less solidify, the rules by which the WUA can ensure delivery of water by the system.

We have then three fairly distinct sets of propositions about the effective management of irrigation water at the

farmer level. The common property tradition encourages a
focus on the property relations. The irrigation community
emphasizes the internal systems of the local groups. Both
traditions have largely ignored the problems involved in
attaching such groups to larger, often bureaucratic,
organizations, and this subject needs careful and concentrated investigation as well. This is a convergence
that appears to be interesting and productive. What is
needed is a deeper look at local groups for irrigation,
combining the most productive aspects of these three
converging traditions.

NOTES

1. Fieldwork in Egypt in 1984 was funded by a grant from the Whiting Foundation, by a grant from the Sachar Fund of Brandeis University, and aided by a sabbatical from Brandeis University. I am grateful to Nicholas Hopkins for reading two versions of the paper. The manuscript has benefited greatly from the editorial judgments of David Feeny and Daniel Bromley. The opinions presented here are mine, and do not reflect the position of any of the supporting institutions.

2. I was very fortunate while in Egypt in 1984 to receive the full attention and generous sharing of information on the part of Professor Nicholas Hopkins of the American University, Cairo, and of Layton and Naguib of the Egypt Water Use and Management Project (EWUP), jointly sponsored by the MOI Egypt and Colorado State University. When I arrived in Egypt, I was handed a draft copy of the Social Research Council (AUC) monograph on the local organization of canal irrigation in Egypt (Mehanna et al. 1983), and was also privileged to be able to walk the canals in Upper Egypt and the Delta with an AUC group. EWUP personnel have been generous with their time, and have in addition shared with me a large number of research reports. Without these two sources, this paper could not have been written. I hope that I have done them justice.

3. On property, see Appell (1974); on corporate and corporation, see Dow (1973); on the relationships between forms of property and groups, see Appell (1983).

REFERENCES

Alderman, H., J. von Braun and S. A. Ahmed. 1982. Egypt's food subsidy and rationing system: a description. Research Report 34. Washington, D.C.: International Food Policy Research Institute.

Appell, G. 1974. The analysis of property systems. Prepared for the 1974 Conference of the Association of Social Anthropologists on Social Anthropology and Law. Unpublished.

Appell, G. 1983. Methodological problems with the concepts of corporation, corporate social grouping, and cognatic descent group. American Ethnologist 10:302-311.

Beardsley, R. K., J. Hall and R. Ward. 1959. Village Japan. Chicago: University of Chicago Press.

Bromley, D., D. Taylor and D. Parker. 1980. Water reform and economic development: institutional aspects of water management in the developing countries. Economic Development and Cultural Change 28:365-387.

Coward, E. W. Jr. 1977. Irrigation management alternatives: themes from indigenous irrigation systems. Agricultural Administration 4:223-237.

Coward, E. W. Jr. 1979. Principles of social organization in an indigenous irrigation system. Human Organization 38:28-36.

Coward, E. W. Jr. 1983. Property in action: alternatives for irrigation investment. Paper prepared for the Workshop on Water Management and Policy, Khon Kaen University, Thailand.

Coward, E. W. Jr. 1985. Property, persistence and partic-
   ation: the state and traditional irrigation systems.
   Paper prepared for the 1985 Meeting of the Society for
   Economic Anthropology, "The Development Process."

El-Din, K. and A. Dardir. n.d. Survey of outlets on Dakalt
   Canal downstream of Helal regulator, Abo Raia, Kafr El
   Sheikh. Staff Paper No. 50. Cairo: Egypt Water Use
   and Management Project.

Dotzenko, A. D. n.d. Response of rice, wheat and flax to
   zinc applications on the soils of the Nile Delta. Staff
   Paper No. 38. Cairo: Egypt Water Use and Management
   Project.

Dow, J. 1973. On the muddled concept of corporation in
   anthropology. American Anthropologist 75:904-908.

Farbrother, H. G. 1973. Annual report 1970-1971. Wad
   Medani, Sudan, Gezira Research Station, pp. 36-99.
   Cotton Research Reports, Republic of the Sudan.
   London: Cotton Research Corporation.

Fernea, R. 1970. Shaykh and Effendi. Cambridge,
   Massachusetts: Harvard University Press.

Glick, T. 1970. Irrigation and Society in Medieval
   Valencia. Cambridge, Massachusetts: Harvard University
   Press.

Harik, I. 1974. The political mobilization of peasants--a
   study of an Egyptian community. Bloomington: Indiana
   University Press.

Hopkins, N. n.d. Irrigation, mechanization, and the state
   in upper Egyptian agriculture. Paper prepared for a
   volume on farming systems, edited by Brush and Turner.

Hunt, R. C. 1979. The comparative method and the study of
   irrigation social organization. Cornell Rural Sociology
   Bulletin Series, No. 97. Ithaca, New York: Cornell
   University.

Hunt, R. C. 1985a. Appropriate social organization? Water
   users associations in bureaucratic canal irrigation
   systems. Paper delivered at the Annual Meeting, Society
   for Economic Anthropology.

Hunt, R. C. 1985b. Ecology of development: the Aswan high dam and Egyptian agriculture. Paper delivered to the Columbia Ecology Seminar. New York: Columbia University.

Hunt, R. C. n.d.a. Measurement of the organization of authority and scale in canal irrigation systems. Unpublished manuscript.

Hunt, R. C. n.d.b. Water work: the social organization of canal irrigation. Unpublished manuscript.

Hunt, R. and E. Hunt. 1976. Canal irrigation and local social organization. Current Anthropology 17:389-411.

Kelly, W. 1982. Water control in Tokugawa Japan: irrigation organization in a Japanese river basin 1600-1870. East Asia Papers Series. Ithaca, New York: Cornell University China-Japan Program.

Maass, A. and R. Anderson. 1978. And the Desert Shall Rejoice: Conflict, Growth, and Justice in Arid Environment. Cambridge, Massachusetts: MIT Press.

Mehanna, S., R. Antonius, R. Huntington, M. Fahim and M. El-Kadi. 1983. Water Allocation among Egyptian Farmers: Irrigation Technology and Social Organization. Cairo: Social Research Center, American University.

Millon, R. 1962. Variations in social responses to the practice of irrigated agriculture. In Woodbury 1962:56-88.

Montgomery, J. D. 1983. When local participation helps. Journal of Policy Analysis and Management 3:90-105.

Skold, M. D., S. El Shinnawi and M. Nasr. 1984. Irrigation water distribution along branch canals in Egypt: economic effects. Economic Development and Cultural Change 32:547-567.

Steinberg, D. I. 1983. Irrigation and AID's experience: a consideration based on evaluations. AID Program Evaluation Report No. 8. Washington, D.C.: U.S. Agency for International Development.

Wade, R. 1980. Water user associations: sociological principles and government practice. Unpublished manuscript.

Wolfe, J., F. Sahin and M. Issa. 1979. Preliminary evaluation of Mansouria canal system, Giza Governorate, Egypt. EWUP Technical Report No. 3. Cairo: Egypt Water Use and Management Project.

Woodbury, R., ed. 1962. Civilizations in Desert Lands. Anthropological Papers, No. 62. Salt Lake City, Utah: Department of Anthropology, University of Utah.

Tank Irrigation in India: An Example of Common Property Resource Management

K. William Easter
and K. Palanisami

INTRODUCTION

Although most of the tanks (small reservoirs) of South India are nominally the responsibility of government, in practice they are managed as common property resources. These tanks irrigate anywhere from a few hectares to about 1,000. In the southernmost state of India, Tamil Nadu, nearly 40,000 tanks are used to irrigate 910,000 hectares (rice during the wet season and, in some cases, a dry season crop.) Most of these tanks have been in use for almost a century.

The effectiveness with which the tank water is used varies widely. Most of the irrigation facilities are in some degree jointly operated, but cooperation is necessary if one farmer's overuse or misuse is not to subtract from another's water supply. Problems of coordination and cooperation generally become apparent when significant changes occur in the pattern or level of water use. These changes are often associated with increased water scarcity. With regard to many of the tanks, water scarcity and the need for cooperation are the rule rather than the exception.

If the users are unable to cooperate in the use of the resource, then competition emerges; the resulting conflict quickly exhausts the water supplies. Several attributes and relationships bear on the use of tank water and influence the overall management of the tank systems. In

this chapter, these attributes and relationships are
analyzed in terms of the four components of Oakerson's
framework (this volume). Each component is analyzed using
the tank management characteristics of 10 tanks in South
India (Tamil Nadu State).

TECHNICAL AND PHYSICAL ATTRIBUTES

Each farmer in the tank command area is eligible to
receive water from the tanks in proportion to the size of
his farm until the tank supply is exhausted. The water
supply is quite variable; it is limited by the tank's
storage capacity and the quantity of water available to
fill the tanks; some tanks are filled more than once a year
while others may be completely filled only once in every
four or five years.

Siltation and agricultural encroachment in the foreshore area have reduced the storage capacity of many of the
tanks, thus reducing farmers' water supplies. The location
of the sluices (outlets) in the tank, whether upper or
lower, also affects the amount of water delivered to
farmers (the upper sluices in the silted tanks cannot
provide water unless the tank water level is high). In
years when the tank water supply is inadequate, farmers
served by upper sluices may get little or no water.

In years of water shortages, farmers at the outer
reaches of the system are excluded by virtue of being located at a great distance from the tank. What little water
they receive will arrive late. Sometimes this exclusion by
location is due to poor engineering rather than distance:
two of the ten tanks we studied were constructed based on a
faulty design; the sluice gates were placed below the level
of the upper command area. Thus the farmers in the upper
command area are excluded because of their location even
though there is ample water to serve them.

The source of water is another physical constraint that
influences both the water supply and the degree of
exclusion because of location. The primary tanks have
water rights on such perennial sources of water as large
rivers or reservoirs and have adequate water supplies to
irrigate one crop for all farmers in the command area. In
contrast, supplementary tanks suffer frequent water shortages since their main source of water is runoff from rainfall. Consequently, farms irrigated by supplementary
tanks, particularly those in the tail-reaches, are
frequently excluded because of location.

The installation of private and community wells in the
tank irrigated areas have helped overcome some of the water
supply constraints. Return flows from surface irrigation
and the tanks themselves recharge groundwater. The wells
allow farmers to recapture some of the water lost through
excessive irrigation.

The tank investment is a typical indivisible large
investment. However, the rights to the water in the tank
can be subdivided and those rights can be either public or
private. Thus, the indivisibility aspect does not necessarily pose any special problems to resource management
once the tank and its subsidiary systems are built. Canal
maintenance is the one exception: responsibility for
maintenance of canals that serve more than one farmer must
be agreed upon and enforced. Must the person at the end of
the canal maintain the whole canal while those at the head
only maintain its upper part? How should the responsibilities be divided to maintain this indivisible asset?
These problems plague irrigation systems all over the
world.

Finally, the boundary of the resource demand is defined
on the physical side by soil, hydrology, and the construction of the tank and canals. The irrigated area must be
downhill and a reasonable distance from the tank and the
canals. On the supply side, the resource is defined by the
capacity of the tank and the source of water. The capacity
of the canals can also limit who gets water during peak
irrigation periods. But when the source of water is a
large river, and the delivery system is ample, then there
are few water supply constraints, except in extreme drought
years, and jointness in supply exists. In contrast,
supplemental (rainfed) tanks frequently suffer water
shortages and jointness poses a problem since one farmer's
use subtracts from the supplies of others.

DECISION-MAKING ARRANGEMENTS

Collective Use

Decision-making arrangements and rules result mainly
from the nature of technical and physical constraints and
from the farmers' primary goal of obtaining their share of
the tank water supplies; these have evolved both at the
tank and farm level.[1] The conditions for collective use
arise when the scarcity of tank water forces farmers to

compete for their share of water; informal water users'
organizations (WUO) develop to handle such situations, and
there is a high correlation between the degree of water
scarcity and the level of activity in the WUO. Even in the
primary tanks, where water is usually not scarce, farmers
cooperated during the 1983 drought by implementing a water
rotation schedule to conserve their limited tank water
supply.

A second condition that encourages collective use at the
tank level is the probability of a reasonably uniform
distribution of benefits. One measure of this uniformity is
the amount of variation in the size of farms in the tank
command area: the smaller the variation in farm size, the
greater the likelihood that farmers will participate in
organization decisions and form a WUO (see Table 1) because
they believe that they will obtain approximately equal
benefits and have equal influence on the allocation of
inadequate water supplies. Trusted leadership is a key
factor in the success of a WUO, and hence in the efficient
use of tanks. The leadership must successfully organize
community irrigation activities and be honest in handling of
community funds used for irrigation. Both inadequate funds
and the misuse of finances have caused a WUO to fail or
become inactive (see Russell and Nicholson 1981; Tubpun
1981).

The president of the WUO informally nominates one farmer
in each distributory (secondary canal) to monitor the water
distribution and collect fees and solicit labor for canal
and tank maintenance. These representatives report to the
president if any problems arise. The WUO members usually
meet once every two weeks during the irrigation season to
deal with problems. The frequency of meetings usually
increases during the end of the cropping season when the
water supply is low and irrigation critical.

Operating Rules

The collective use of tank water in our study involved
the following operating rules: (1) rotation schedules for
tank water and individual canals; (2) water release and
closing dates at the tank; (3) a minimum water level in the
tank for fish production; (4) canal maintenance charges in
rupees and/or man days of labor to be provided by each
farmer according to the farmer's location and area owned[2];
and (5) sanctions and penalties against farmers who violated
the tank water management rules.

Table 1 Tank Management in Relation to Farm Size Variation, Water Supply and Farmer Organization, South India, 1982.

Tank number	Average farm size (acres)	Farm size variation[a] (percent)	Water supply level	Active water users' organization	Overall tank management[b]	Water management expenditure Rs./acre[d]	Net benefits from water management Rs./acre[f]
1.	2.0	31	Low	Yes	Good	9.8	70
2.	3.1	66	High	No	Adequate[c]	0.3	--
3.	2.5	51	High	No	Adequate[c]	0.2	--
4.	1.3	24	Low	Yes	Good	4.7	43
5.	2.0	86	High	No	Poor	0.4	--
6.	1.9	72	High	No	Poor	0.5	--
7.	1.9	91	Low	No	Poor	2.2[e]	14
8.	1.9	91	Low	No	Poor	2.7[e]	15
9.	1.1	33	Low	Yes	Good	7.4	73
10.	2.3	104	Medium	No	Poor	1.8	--

[a]This is the coefficient of variation in farm size.

[b]Overall tank management is based on a subjective judgment of the tank's operation in terms of water storage, water allocation, water conflicts and crop yields. It is a comparative judgment among all tanks in our study.

[c]Tanks 2 and 3 are primary tanks and have surplus water in most years. Thus, little water management was required to achieve high yields in 1982.

[d]Rs. = rupees.

[e]Funds were used to help convey a request to the government for additional water as specified in previous agreements.

[f]Benefits from additional water equals the cost of buying well water in the tank area.

Source: K. Palanisami and K. William Easter 1983a.

Several additional rules were introduced during periods of extreme drought: (1) rules for sharing well water when demand exceeded capacity; and (2) priority concerning tank water use for those who could not obtain well water because of their location.

The rules for tank water rotation were usually acti-vated once the tank supplies were known to be inadequate. In general, the operating rules did not exist in cases where: (1) farmer conflicts prevented cooperation (as was the case for tank 10); and (2) there was a surplus of tank water supply (tanks 2 and 3 in 1982).

All five of the operational rules were in effect in only three of the tanks; these were the three tanks that had WUOs. However, farmers in most of the tanks did establish water release dates and collect money for main-tenance. For one of the two primary tanks, farmers estab-lished a minimum water level for fish production.

Sanctions and penalties were used only in tanks with a WUO. Those who violated the water management rules were deprived of tank water or required to pay a fine of Rs. 20-30 per acre. When police cases were filed by farmers against violators, the leaders of the WUO usually interceded and resolved the problem.

External Arrangements

After India's independence in 1947, ownership rights to private tanks were abolished and the government of India expropriated them from the Zamindars. The tanks became a common property resource; farmers who own land in the area served by each tank have the right to use the tank water. The tank restoration scheme, which was established to survey and improve each physical tank structure, helped to fix standards for future structural improvements. The government also provides grants for periodic tank mainten-ance above the outlet; maintenance below the outlet is the responsibility of the farmers. However, government funds available for maintenance cannot meet all the needs, in part because there is no relationship between the water fees the government collects from farmers and the budget allotted for maintenance of each tank. The fees go into general government revenues and maintenance funds are allocated to each administrative division of the public works department on an arbitrary basis. The funds tend to be allocated to each division for emergency repair needs while minor repairs are neglected.

The government of Tamil Nadu has issued patta (rights to land) to encroaching farmers, has introduced social forestry activities inside the tank water storage area, and has instituted tank rehabilitation measures. Encroachment on the tank foreshore area is a very common and serious problem in tanks that do not fill to capacity in most years. Farmers have gradually cultivated as much as 20 to 50 percent of the foreshore (water storage area) areas of many tanks. After they have had growth crops in the fore-shore area for several years, cultivators begin establishing their rights to these lands (Department of Agricultural Engineering 1982). The cultivators petition the government requesting that they be allotted the foreshore lands, arguing that the lands are idle. The government, after receiving a number of petitions from cultivators, issued patta to these farmers. This right, called kulamkorvai patta, legally changed the tank foreshore lands to cultivated lands (Palanisami and Easter 1983a). The government's decision encouraged encroachers to expand their cultivation of the foreshore areas. In one of the tanks in our study, this generated conflicts between encroachers and farmers who irrigated from the tanks, and resulted in inefficient tank water distribution and low crop yields.

The government also intervenes in tank management through the farm forestry program on vacant lands, including the water storage area. Currently, this program is initiated by the government of Tamil Nadu through the state forestry department with funds from the Swedish International Development Agency (SIDA). Acacia nilotica trees are grown on a 10-year rotation. Farmers believe that in about 10 years the trees will be large enough to reduce the tank water storage capacity and make it difficult to desilt tanks, a belief that is being ignored by the Tamil Nadu state forestry department.[3] The social forestry program may thus have some negative impacts on tank irrigation.

In recent years, there has been more interest in improving crop production from tank irrigated areas. Since many tanks are supplemental tanks, various measures are being tried to increase the water supply delivered to the farmers' fields. The government has introduced rehabilitation measures in selected tanks; these include lining the main canals and the provision of community wells. Community wells have been installed in two of the ten sample tanks, and canal lining was completed in another. All of these investments had rates of return equal to or better than investments in the private sector (Palanisami and Easter 1984).

Patterns of Interaction

Given the technical and physical constraints and the decision-making arrangements for tank management, it is important to identify the patterns of interaction that characterize the farmer's behavior in tank management. The primary pattern of interaction in the successful joint use of tank water is reciprocity, which depends upon mutual expectations of positive performance.

Some of the patterns adopted involved a direct substitution of management for scarce water. In three of the tanks studied, serious efforts were made to substitute management (which required cooperation) for scarce water. This occurred in tanks 1, 4, and 9, where the amount spent to improvement management was Rs. 9.8, 4.7, and 7.4 per acre, respectively. The net benefits due to additional irrigation (achieved as a result of improved management) ranged from Rs. 14 to Rs. 73 per acre, or an average of Rs. 43 per acre (see Table 1).

Farmers also interact to increase water supplies. Farmers who own wells have established an informal organization that determines the price of groundwater based on the expected demand for and supply of groundwater during the season.[4] In several cases, tank farmers got together and contributed to a common fund for diverting extra water from other (upper) tanks or streams. The funds collected were used to make diversion channels and to clean the existing channels. In one tank, farmers diverted water illegally from a nearby canal when the water supply in the tank was low during the middle of the crop season. In certain tanks, private pumping is allowed from within the tanks, particularly when the water in storage has fallen below the level of the sluice gates.

The government provides loans and installs community wells to supplement tank water supplies in the wet season and for full irrigation in the dry season. The farmers who benefit from the wells must pay the operating, maintenance, and investment costs. During the wet season, a well irrigates around 40 acres, but during the dry season only a limited number of farmers can obtain water due to the capacity constraint.

Farmers have organized both to support and to oppose the idea of connecting a series of tanks to a nearby large reservoir. Currently, there is no connecting channel and water flows from one tank to another in an inefficient manner. In fact, a number of the lower tanks now receive less runoff than they did before the large reservoir was built. Farmers from the lower tanks organized to recommend to the irrigation department that it construct a separate canal to deliver water to all tanks simultaneously; in this way, upper tanks would get less water but lower tanks would get more, and the improved water distribution would provide a larger effective water supply and total production would increase. This could be construed as a Pareto-efficient change by only redistributing excess water from the upper tanks. But, as should be expected, upper tank farmers organized to oppose the plan since they could not be assured that they would get adequate water supplies, particularly in drought years.

In a number of cases, farmers have also organized at the tank level to ask the government to remove the trees growing in the tanks. This runs counter to the government's program of social forestry, but farmers feel trees reduce the water supply and make desilting difficult.

In several tanks where the farmers are not organized, the free rider problem is apparent. For example, in tank 10, the water supply was reasonably adequate for the crop season, but due to conflicts and lack of cooperation, the water supply was exhausted through repeated unauthorized opening of the sluice gates. Operators farming the fore-shore area (encroachers) opened the gates at night to release water and make more foreshore land available for crop production. This caused drainage problems for the farmers in the head-reaches of the command area and low yields throughout the irrigated area. Because of these unauthorized releases, some of the farmers in the tail-reaches only received two irrigations as compared to eight in the head-reaches.

When water is scarce, as it is in many of the tanks, mutual action is required. To allocate water other than by continuous flow requires mutual action and forbearance: when water is scarce, farmers next to the canals must allow water to flow by their fields and go to their neighbors. Finally, mutual action is the basis for obtaining addi-tional water through water diversion activities, through the creation of channels, and/or through improved system maintenance.

Outcomes

The effects of technical and physical attributes of the tank area, of the decision-making arrangements involved in tank use, and of the patterns of interaction can be seen in the average size of crops of farmers who irrigate with tank water and the percent of the tank command area that is actually irrigated.5 Both efficiency and equity or fairness can be achieved in tanks where the management level is high; these tanks should achieve higher crop yields and a larger irrigated area, other things being equal, through timely and uniform water delivery. Equity is achieved in tanks where farmers with approximately equal holdings cooperate in the distribution of water supplies based on farm size (this assumes that the numbers of landless laborers is small).

Equity or fairness problems arise when a few large farmers try to dominate water deliveries. Inefficient water use results when head-reach farmers overuse water; lower-reach farmers suffer water shortages. Finally, the tragedy of the commons occurs in tanks where water is scarce and the level of the tank management is poor. The end result involves losses in both efficiency and equity.

The water management strategies adopted by the farmers in certain tanks show how both equity and efficiency can be achieved through improved tank management. The technical and physical attributes of the tanks, the decision-making arrangements, and patterns of interaction decide the equity and efficiency levels that can be achieved. These relationships suggest that to achieve a better outcome (area irrigated and crop yield), these three sets of variables should be studied in detail.

The relationships among rice yield, area irrigated, and the management variables can only be shown qualitatively (see Table 2). In general, tanks 1, 2, 3, and 9 had relatively high performance in terms of yield and area irrigated. For two of these tanks, 1 and 9, the performance required good decision-making arrangements and patterns of interaction to overcome physical and technical water supply constraints. In the two primary tanks (2 and 3), the same level of decision-making arrangements and patterns of interaction were not needed to achieve high performance because there were no physical or technical constraints in 1982. Tank number 10 is an interesting example of a tank with few physical and technical constraints but low performance--the lack of cooperation among farmers led to a misuse of the abundant water supply, which resulted in relatively low yields. In tank 4, the severe water supply constraint kept yields low even though decision-making arrangements and patterns of interaction were good. For tanks 5 and 6, the performance was poor because of design problems that prevented irrigation of the full command area. Finally, farmers served by tanks 7 and

TABLE 2 Tank Performance and the Level of Water Management, South India, 1982.[d]

Tank number	Physical/ technical constraints	Decision-making arrangements	Patterns of interaction	Percent of command area receiving water	Rice yield in metric tons/ha[b]
1.	Medium	Good	Active	84	3.41
2.	Low	Adequate	--	99	4.13[c]
3.	Low	Adequate	--	97	3.58[c]
4.	High	Good	Active	85	2.72[d]
5.	High	Poor	--	58	3.90
6.	High	Poor	--	21	3.66
7.	High	Poor	--	88	2.74
8.	High	Poor	--	90	2.87
9.	Medium	Good	Active	93	3.58
10.	Low	Poor	--	88	3.11

[a]The grouping of the variables low, medium, and high, and good, adequate, and poor are based on their overall performance during the 1982 study. The grouping is based on factors discussed in the Palanisami and Easter report, 1983a.

[b]The yields are for the area irrigated and not the total command area.

[c]These tanks are primary tanks and receive additional water from perennial sources.

[d]The yield is low due to very low 1982 rainfall. The community well in this tank covers only a small area in the total command area.

Source: K. Palanisami and K. William Easter 1983a.

8 faced a water supply constraint and were able to obtain an additional water allocation; even so, they could not organize to make better use of the available water.

CONCLUSION

Management of the tank irrigation systems is influenced by technical and physical factors. Several decision-making arrangements (rules) are required to manage the tanks effectively as a common property resource. Farmers' interactions to adopt decision rules are needed to achieve equity and efficiency in water use and management, which in turn results in higher crop yield and a larger area that is irrigated. The following actions could be taken to help improve the management of tanks as common property resources:

o   Identifying the technical and physical constraints for each tank or group of tanks so that efforts to improve tank management could focus on strategies to relax these constraints through appropriate planning and investment

o   Encouraging formal and informal water users' organizations by providing incentives in terms of technical assistance, training, legal authority, and funds for organization

o   Transferring ownership of tanks from the government to farmers once they are organized into viable WUO.

This can reduce the government's burden in collecting water fees from the farmers and in allocating funds (which are currently inadequate) for tank management. Such a decision will represent a property-enhancing strategy at the community level. By assisting the local community in its property-enhancing strategy, the government could induce farmers to make more investments in the tank system.

1. Share is usually defined in terms of the acreage irrigated. Thus, farmers with the largest acreage generally receive the largest shares.

2. Originally, the contribution of labor by the farmers for tank maintenance and repair was a regular feature (called kudimaramathu, which means cooperative repair work), but it is not prevalent among Indian tank users today.

3. Both the encroachment and the problems created by farm forestry might be eliminated if the WUOs had legal status. If they were considered legitimate by the government, then they could more effectively argue their cases against the misuse of farm forestry and encroachers. Currently, only one of the three WUOs is a legal entity; its tank is the most effectively managed of all we studied.

4. The well owners are the most influential farmers in the tank command area. They influence such matters as opening and closing of the sluices, water allocation schedules, and common fund collections. In times of scarcity, they even give away their share of the tank water to others. But in several tanks, the well owners constrained tank management with a view to selling their groundwater for a longer period at a high price. (For details, see Palanisami and Easter 1983b).

5. An analysis of rice production in the area served by the ten tanks suggests that fertilizer is the other major input besides water that influences yields. However, the use of a simultaneous equation model shows that tank and well water influence the level of fertilizer applied. Thus, it appears that in this area of uncertain rainfall, water availability and its use are the key determinants of fertilizer use and crop production (Palanisami and Easter 1983a). Consequently, crop yield and the percentage of

command area irrigated should be a good measure of tank
performance, when the comparison is made among tanks having
about the same per-acre water supply. Thus, primary tanks
2 and 3 should be compared with each other, but they should
not be compared with supplementary tanks, which have lower
water supplies. When crop yields and/or the percentage of
command area irrigated are relatively low, then performance
or outcome is low.

REFERENCES

Department of Agricultural Engineering. 1982. Development
    and Optimization in the Use of Irrigation Water under
    Ex-Zamin Tanks in Ramanathapuram District, Preliminary
    Report. Madras, India: Government of Tamil Nadu.

Palanisami, K. and K. W. Easter. 1983a. The Tanks of South
    India--A Potential for Future Expansion in Irrigation.
    Department of Agricultural and Applied Economics,
    Economic Report, ER83-4. St. Paul: University of
    Minnesota.

Palanisami, K. and K. W. Easter. 1983b. The Management,
    Production and Rehabilitation in South Indian
    Irrigation Tanks. Department of Agricultural and
    Applied Economics, Staff Papers Series, P 83-21.
    St. Paul: University of Minnesota.

Palanisami, K. and K. W. Easter. 1984. Irrigation tanks of
    South India: management strategies and investment
    alternatives. Indian Journal of Agricultural Economics
    39, No. 2:214-223.

Russell, C. and N. K. Nicholson, eds. 1981. Public
    Choice and Rural Development, Research Paper P-21.
    Washington, D.C.: Resources for the Future.

Tubpun, Y. 1981. Economics of Tank Irrigation Projects in
    Northeastern Thailand. Ph.D. thesis. St. Paul:
    Department of Agricultural and Applied Economics,
    University of Minnesota.

REFERENCES

Common Property Resource Management in South Indian Villages[1]

Robert Wade

INTRODUCTION

How do Indian villagers manage such common pool resources as canal irrigation water and grazing lands? In
one small area of South India, villages vary remarkably in
the degree to which they organize themselves to undertake
such management. Some are more highly organized than
anything hitherto reported in the literature on (nontribal)
Indian villages; others, perhaps only a few miles away,
have no village-level organization at all. This paper sets
out in broad terms an explanation of this variation.

The presence or absence of village-level organization
has a great deal to do with the degree of risk of crop
loss faced by many or most farmers of the village; this
risk is in turn related to ecological conditions of soil
type and water scarcity. These conditions influence the
demand for joint management of some common pool resources.
Within the limits of the sample studied here, it seems
that some villages are organized and others are not because
of variations in the demand for common pool resource management rather than variations in the village's capacity
to supply such management. This does not mean that the
sorts of supply-side obstacles to collective action emphasized by the public choice theorists are irrelevant in
these villages. What it means is that such obstacles as
the free rider problem have been effectively checked or

bypassed by a series of ingenious institutional arrangements. To extend the argument beyond the sample, however,
one needs both a theory of demand and a theory of supply to
explain the presence or absence of common property resource
management institutions.

"Indian society today," says the sociologist V. R.
Gaikwad, "is an atomized mass, composed of individuals
who are not in any organized fold except the family and
the extended kin-groups which form the sub-caste" (1981:
331). Much the same has been said not just of Indian
peasants, but of peasants in general. Such writers as
Foster (1965) and Popkin (1979) have given great emphasis
to the unimportance of the village as a focus of collective
action and sentiment. This theme of the peasantry literature resonates with a theme of the "public choice"
literature, which stresses the difficulties of voluntary
collective action in any kind of society other than,
perhaps, certain kinds of communes. Common sense would
suggest that people who perceive a joint interest will join
together to pursue this interest, and hence that a perceived common interest is a basic element in explaining
collective action.

The public choice theorists say that common sense is
misleading. The rational individual, they say, will not
voluntarily contribute to a common goal if the group is
large and if he or she cannot be excluded from enjoying the
benefit. The individual will, instead, seek a free ride.
As a result, any collective action (in other than very
small groups) that is not based on coercion or on the
availability of selective incentives tends to be fragile,
and tends to supply fewer public goods than the members
would be prepared to pay for on the market--if the market
were an option (Olson 1965).

Not everyone would agree that collective action and the
voluntary supply of public goods must be explained only in
terms of the behavior of rational, self-interested
individuals. We do, after all, observe a good deal of
voluntary collective action that seems on the face of it
difficult to explain simply in terms of the selective
benefits provided to participants (ecological lobby groups,
for example; see Kimber 1981). In any case, whether or not
the axiom is accepted, there remains the empirical question
of the conditions in which varying types and degrees of
collective action are found. Yet questions of degree and
difference have been overlooked by many writers on
peasantry because they have been so concerned to emphasize
the difficulties of collective action.

Much of the literature on collective action and public choice has dealt with the question of what conditions propel individuals to make voluntary financial contributions to the provision of a public good. We can turn the same kind of analysis to common pool resource management by rephrasing the question as: under what conditions will individuals formulate, and agree to abide by, a rule of restrained use of common pool resources? In this case too, as in the case of financial contributions to the provisions of a public good, there seem to be built-in incentives for the rational, self-interested individual to free ride--to cheat on the rule of restrained use while everyone else abides by it, on the assumption that others will not notice; so there seems to be an inner imperative for regression from abiding by the rules to unrestrained use. Certainly the literature describes many violations of rules of restrained use of common pool resources (such as grazing, irrigation water, and trees) that deplete the resource. But the literature also contains many cases of local groups that have been able to agree upon rules of restrained use and have enforced the rules using authority from within the group rather from outside (e.g., government). In these cases, we can talk of a "public realm" within the group, which consists of the rules and roles involved in common pool resource management.

Indian Villages

The conventional understanding of Indian villages is that they do not have any real public realm. A number of men are usually regarded as "big men," as being in some sense first in the village. But there is no clearly defined social domain or institution separate from state authority where activities of a "public" nature are carried out, no center of community management other than the bottom levels of the state apparatus itself, and no machinery for raising resources for public (village) purposes other than through state-sanctioned taxation.

My research suggests a more complex picture. I compared forty-one villages in an upland part of South India in terms of the range and strength of their public realm. Thirty-one of the villages are irrigated from a large canal system; ten are dry. A significant number of the forty-one do show a common purposefulness and ability to provide public goods and services. The arrangements are local and autonomous. They are not integrated with, initiated, or sustained by outside bodies, whether government or voluntary agencies. The scope and degree of local collective action in these villages exceeds that reported previously in the literature on Indian (nontribal) villages. On the other hand, such villages are not in a majority; most villages in my sample do fit (roughly) the "atomized mass" characterization, and only a few miles may separate a village with a substantial amount of corporate organization from others with none.

The Public Realm

The public realm consists of four main institutions:

(1) a village council (quite distinct from the statutory panchayat of local government legislation, which is moribund in all villages in my area);

(2) a village standing fund (distinct from local government moneys);

(3) a work group of village field guards, employed by the council to protect the crops from the depredations of livestock and thieves; and

(4) a work group of "common irrigators," employed by the council to distribute water through the government-run irrigation canal.

The council, and through it the field guards and common irrigators, are loosely accountable to an annual meeting of all the village's cultivators. In addition to the central services of crop protection and water distribution, the council also organizes the supply of many other public goods and services, such as well repairing, monkey catching (to rid the village of monkeys), donations to help meet the cost of a new primary school or of a building where sick animals can be treated, and so on.

All these services except water distribution are financed from the village standing fund, which the council administers; the standing fund is fed by a variety of income-raising devices that the council also administers.

Take K village as an example. It has a population of just over 3,000. Its council generally consists of nine members; the number is fixed for any one year, but varies slightly from year to year. Together they have authority to make decisions affecting all the village. The village's standing fund spends about rupees (Rs.) 10,000 a year in

an economy where a male agricultural laborer gets about
Rs. 4 a day outside of seasonal peaks. The standing fund
pays the salaries of the field guards. Four field guards
are employed full-time for most of the year, and another
two to four are added near harvest time. As for those who
work as common irrigators, about 12 are employed for up to
2.5 months, to cover about 1,200 acres of first-season
rice. At harvest time, the common irrigators, no longer
needed for water, supplement the field guards, giving K a
total of some 20 village-appointed men for harvest crop
protection.

In the sample of 31 canal-irrigated villages (all in
the Kurnool district of Andhra Pradesh), eight villages
have all four of the main corporate institutions--council,
fund, field guards, common irrigators; 11 have some but not
all; and 12 show no trace of any of them. The sample was
not drawn randomly but rather with an eye to ease of access
and a representative range of water supply situations, so
no conclusions can be drawn from these proportions about
how frequent the corporate forms are in the area as a
whole. But they are clearly not rare. Moreover, many
dry villages have some of the same institutions. In a
sample of 10, 8 have field guards, 6 have a village
council, and 6 have a village fund. So some of the dry
villages have a more clearly defined center of community
management than do some of the wet villages.

Kurnool district is semiarid--its rainfall averages
620 mm per year in a unimodal distribution. Population
density averages 105 people per square kilometer (1971),
up from 53 in 1870. Seventy percent of the cultivated
area is under food crops; only 12 percent of the gross
cultivated area is irrigated. Thirty-four percent of
villages are supplied with electricity (1971). There
is one tractor per one or two irrigated villages, and many
fewer in rainfed villages (1980). Most variation in real
wage rates is contained within the range of 3 $\pm$ 1.5 kilograms of food grain per day. It is a poor district, and in
no way atypical.

RESOURCES AND DECISION-MAKING ARRANGEMENTS

The irrigated villages have two main types of commons: grazing land and canal irrigation water. The
grazing land is of two types: year-round grazing along
the verges of roads and fields as well as on the
(relatively small) areas not under cultivation, and the

stubble area left after the crop harvest. Both water and grazing land are commons in the sense that many people share the use of the same resource, and each individual user can reduce the welfare of other users. When water is scarce, one person's use may reduce the amount available to others. When crops are still standing, grazing by one person's (mobile) animals poses risks to the owners of standing crops nearby. Privatization as a means of reducing these "externalities" is made difficult by the nature of the resource and the technology: running water is inherently difficult to privatize, and the cost of fencing precludes privatization of the verges or the stubble.

The impetus for central control at the village level, therefore, comes from a demand for protection against the externalities of others' decision making with respect to water and grazing. In those villages that have them, the collective rules are intended to limit individualistic choice on how much care to put into shepherding one's own animals, and on when and how much water to take for one's paddy. If the rules are enforced, their effect is to assure each decision maker that others will restrain their behavior too, so that if restraint is exercised one will not be duped (Runge 1984).

An organization is required to decide the rules and provide enforcement. If, as in these villages, enforcement is by the employment of specialized work groups, the work groups must be recruited, empowered, and paid. Procedures to settle disputes must be established. These requirements are met by a village council.

The authority of the council derives largely from the wider stratification order of caste and private property, its membership being drawn from the dominant caste and the wealthier landowners of the village. However, the users of the commons do not depend on external decision makers for enforcement, and in that sense the external dimension of this arrangement is unimportant.

Cross- or sub-village units of collective action are also unimportant, which in part reflects features of land tenure and canal layout. There is relatively little cross-village land holding (a person living in one village will have little or no land within the boundaries of another village), and the canals are designed so that most outlets serve the land of only one village. That sub-village units of collective action are not important partly reflects economies of scale in monitoring and enforcement, economies that are especially valuable to ensuring cost savings.

Field guards must be paid, and payment by means of a levy on each protected acre is vulnerable to free riding. The "corporate" villages are those with all or most of the corporate institutions, and they generally have devised a number of ways of raising income to pay the field guards, all of which depend on the village's acting as a unit. For example, the village council may restrict the right of access to a resource or profit opportunity, and then sell that right to an individual or small group. The money from the sale of the franchise goes to the village fund, and the individual or small group keeps the profit between what they paid for the franchise and what they earn from it. The most important resource that is subjected to this franchise is the stubble left on the harvested area. But a variety of other resources within the village boundary may also be so treated--the council might sell the right to collect tamarind nuts, or dung dropped in public places, or fish in the village tank. These constitute another category of common pool resources in addition to those discussed above, in that they permit exclusive use by an individual; consequently, the body that is able to sanction that exclusion can therefore use the resource to raise revenue. In addition, the council may also raise money for the village fund by selling the franchise to a profit opportunity based on something other than natural resource use--the right to collect a commission on all sales of grain from the village, or the right to sell liquor. With some of these revenue-raising arrangements in place, the council may be able to supply tangible pub- lic goods and services rather than just ensure a reduced risk of water scarcity or of animal damage to standing crops.

I now describe these arrangements in more detail, taking K village by way of example.

THE MANAGEMENT OF GRAZING

K has a population density of 159 people per square kilometer. Boserup (1981) predicts that with this density one would expect to find a farming system characterized by annual cropping (at least one crop per plot per year) and multiple cropping where irrigation permits. Indeed, this is the case in K. Little waste or yearly fallow land is left; the village has no "common" in the sense of a large

area available for common grazing for a year or more. But
oxen and buffalo are needed in this agriculture for traction, and they must be fed.

During the crop growing season, the animals must graze
close to standing crops on the verges or on small areas of
fallow, which are treated as commons. With no fencing,
crop protection is accomplished through shepherding or
tethering. The problem is that the incentives for careful
shepherding or tethering are distinctly asymmetrical: I
may not be unhappy to see my animals getting fat on your
grain. The open-field system of husbandry familiar during
the medieval and early modern period in Europe was a
response to the same problem. But whereas the open-field
system operated primarily by regulating the cropping, these
Indian villagers regulate the livestock. The rationale of
the field guards is to make the incentives on tethering and
shepherding less asymmetrical.

The field guards patrol the village area and make sure
no animal is grazing a standing crop. If they catch an
animal in the act, they take it to the village pound,
where it remains until its owner pays a fine. If just
a few animals are involved, the fine is a flat rate per
head-- Rs. 2 during the day, Rs. 4 at night, with the
council setting the rate. The field guards collect and
keep the fine, dividing it equally amongst themselves so
that the arrangements contain a built-in incentive for
enforcement. If large numbers of animals are involved,
the council decides the fine case-by-case; the fine may
run into hundreds of rupees in some instances. The field
guards collect the fine, keep 25 percent, and hand over the
balance to the standing fund. (In most villages, the owner
of the damaged crop is not compensated.) Notice that the
field guards do not enforce "stinting." The decision about
how many animals to own and graze is left to each individual.

Limited year-round grazing in the village or its
environs means that most of the village's grazing animals
are "big" stock--oxen and buffalo needed primarily for
draught power. Relatively small numbers of "small" stock--
sheep and goats--are owned by villagers. However, after
most of the rainfed crops are harvested in February, large
areas of stubble become available for grazing. Note that
all the irrigated villages have some area under rainfed
crops as well, and in most irrigated villages the area
under rainfed crops is larger than the irrigated area. It
would be possible for each landowner to reserve the stubble
on his own land for his own animals or for others he would

allow in. The owner could do so by posting guards around
each field, or by fencing. However, the cost of either
method of exclusion--the cost of privatizing the stubble--
is very high; all the more so given that (as is commonly
the case in peasant societies) any one landowner has
holdings divided into a number of scattered plots
(McCloskey 1975). So, as in the open-field system of
Europe, the stubble is put in common, and private rights
to the product of the land extend only to the crop, not to
the crop residues.

How is this commons managed in the "corporate" villages? Recall that the village's own stock of animals
is adjusted to the year-round grazing, which is much less
than the grazing that becomes available after the harvest
of the rainfed crops. There is thus an opportunity for the
village--for a village authority--to earn revenue by renting out the village's surplus grazing. Large tracts of the
district are hilly and arid, covered in scrawny scrub, and
unsuitable for more than desultory cultivation of sorghum
and millet. Herding sheep and goats is a major source of
income for the local residents. After the harvest of the
rainfed crops, they come down into the irrigated tracts
seeking grazing for their livestock. The herders want the
grazing and water, while the farmers want their fields
manured and cleared of stubble.

The market for grazing and manure is organized in two
distinct ways. In the first, a small group of herders
comes to a village and bargains with the village council
for exclusive access to the village's grazing.[2] The
agreement states how many sheep and goats they will bring,
when they will come, how long they will stay (in terms of a
date before which they will not leave and a date by which
they will be gone), and most important, how much they will
pay for the franchise. Once the agreement is made, that
group of herders has exclusive claim to the village's
grazing, and other herders can enter only as some leave.
Their flocks graze over the stubble by day. By night, when
the animals drop most of their manure, they are folded,
flock by flock, on the plots of particular landowners, who
pay them an agreed rate per head for the manure. So the
herders as a group pay the village fund a lump sum for
access to the commons; and they individually get back part
of what they pay through the sale of manure.

The second method (used in K and other villages) is
more complex. A group of herders, as before, obtains
exclusive access. But instead of a group entry fee or
rent, an auction is held at a regular interval (every four

days in K) to decide who will have each flock on his land
at night until the next auction. The auction is arranged
by the village council. Half the amount of the winning bid
for each flock is then paid to the herder, and half goes to
the village fund.

In K, between 9,000 and 13,000 head commonly enter the
village at this time. They graze the stubble on that part
of the 4,000 arable acres of land that is not still growing
a crop. The village fund commonly gets about Rs. 5,000 in
return, in the space of about six weeks.

However, the entry of such a large number of animals at
a time when some crops (mainly the irrigated ones) are
still standing poses a serious risk of loss for the owners
of those crops. The response is to tighten the regulation
of the livestock in two ways. One is to stipulate a set of
rules for both herder and landowner. The second is to
appoint full-time field guards. A village's rules of
grazing are read out at the first auction of every year,
and may be read out again if there are infringements. They
are worth giving here, because they tend to contradict the
belief that Indian villages show no deliberately concerted
action.

The rules for the herder: (1) He must take the flock
to the designated field by 6:30 p.m. and keep it there
until 8:00 a.m. (2) He must not allow the flock to graze
standing crops. (3) Half of the amount he is to be paid
for the first "turn" (four nights) must be put on deposit
with the council. If he leaves before four turns (16
nights) have been completed, he forfeits this amount to
the village fund. (This structure is to discourage the
herders from leaving early before the farmers have had
their fields manured and cleared of stubble.) (4) The
herder must stay within the village boundary; if the farmer
asks him to go to a field outside the village boundary, he
must refuse.

The rules for the farmer: (1) He must keep the flock
within the village boundary. (This rule is to ensure that
the farmers of the K village, rather than those of some
other village, get their fields cleared of stubble. It
also helps to reduce the conflict between villages, because
if a farmer from K brought a flock into another village
where he owned or rented lands, he might ignore that village's own implicit or explicit rules about grazing and
be less subject to formal or informal sanctions.) (2) If
he wishes to pay the fund or the herder in kind rather
than in cash, he must make the conversion at the rate of
Rs. 1.25 per measure of hybrid sorghum or Rs. 1.50 per

measure of "local" sorghum (early 1980 price). (3) He
must send men to help the herder guard the flock at night,
at the rate of two men per 2,000 head. If hired, the
men must be paid Rs. 3 per night, or grain equivalent
(to prevent the farmer from sending non-ablebodied men,
who could be paid less).

Such tight specification of responsibilities by the
council reflects the real danger of loss to standing crops
on unfenced fields. Rules of this kind, however, are not
self-enforcing. Any one farmer would have an incentive to
cheat by failing to provide the stipulated number of herd
guards or by bringing the flock to his field outside the
village boundary. So the second intensification of joint
regulation is by means of village-appointed field guards
to monitor observance of the rules.

Field guards must be paid a salary, however. It would
be possible for the council to lay down a flat rate, so
much per cultivated acre, that each landowner would have
to pay the field guards. But this arrangement is vulnerable to free riding. A farmer may delay payment indefinitely, expecting that others will not similarly delay;
in this way he can continue to benefit from the general
discipline of livestock that the field guards provide
while not himself having to pay a part of their cost.
Most villages address the free rider problem by finding a
method of raising income for the field guards' salaries
that does not depend on individual contributions. The
chief source of revenue is the one we have been considering: namely, the income from renting out the
village's grazing. Once a village decides to rent out
its grazing, the amount of money that can be earned is
much more than is needed to provide a guard force for the
period when large numbers of outside stock are in the
village. Here, then, we see the impact of the free rider
problem: in the context of field guarding it is a serious
matter, and institutions are designed to avoid it by
divorcing the supply of the public good from individual
contributions. However, the bypass institutions are more
costly to administer, and in small villages (500 people or
less) farmers will often try to institute the individual
payment method for meeting the field guards' salaries.
Recurrent free rider problems then tend to force villages
towards a more complex arrangement like selling the
franchise to the grazing.

Indeed, the "corporate" irrigated villages tend to
have several sources of revenue for the standing fund,
almost all of them based on the sale of council-sanctioned

franchises. One income source is the franchise to sell
liquor in the village. Some villages auction the right to
collect a commission on all grain sales from the village.
Still others may have an irrigation "tank" (small reservoir) within their their boundaries; each year the council
stocks it with fish, and later in the year auctions the
franchise to catch the fish, the money going to the fund.
The income sources vary considerably, but the grazing
franchise is the most common. With a standing fund in
surplus above the field guards' salaries, the fund can then
be used to provide additional public goods and services,
such as those mentioned earlier.

In short, the main advantage to the farmers of organizing the sale of such franchises is that they then
benefit from the supply of collective goods and services
made possible by the sales. Of these, the most important
is crop protection provided by the field guards, and the
most important franchise (in terms of revenue) is the sale
of the stubble. By organizing to control access to the
village's stubble, the farmers are able to raise income for
the immediate purpose of employing a work force to protect
those amongst them whose crops would be endangered by the
arrival of large numbers of free-ranging animals; the
income raised, once the franchise is organized, is
sufficient to provide crop protection for all the farmers
for most of the year. The alternative would be for each
farmer to arrange crop protection individually or in small
groups of field neighbors. The village-wide arrangements
allow economies of scale in providing monitoring and
policing of the grazing animals, and also save on transaction costs.[3]

THE MANAGEMENT OF IRRIGATION

Irrigation is the second source of conflict and
possible production loss. In any irrigation system where
water is scarce, there is an inherent conflict between
"upstream" and "downstream" farmers. Upstream farmers have
first access and their supply is relatively abundant; their
water use determines how much water those downstream will
get. Without the intervention of regulation and rules of
restrained access, constant conflict and crop loss are
likely.

The villages under study are fed from large-scale
government-run irrigation canals. Paddy is the only
significant first (wet) season crop, being transplanted in

late July or early August, and harvested in December or
January. By the end of September, the heavy rains have
normally stopped, and the crop is dependent largely on
canal water. The common irrigators are appointed shortly
thereafter, and do the job full-time until the harvest.
Their job is to allocate the scarce and fluctuating supply
of canal water over the village's land; they also help
procure more water for the village from the government-run
supply, by one means or another (such as surreptitiously
blocking the outlets of higher up villages). The irrigators are not normally employed in the second (dry)
season, however, when little paddy is grown.

Two things are to be noted about this arrangement.
First, the common irrigators do not influence decisions
about how much land will make a claim to the irrigation
water--those decisions are left in the hands of individual
cultivators, as are decisions about how many animals to
graze. Second, once the common irrigators are appointed,
they take very important irrigation decisions out of the
hands of individual farmers, in the name of a village-wide
authority.

Each field is entitled to be "adequately wetted" and
it cannot then receive water until all the other fields
beneath that outlet have also been adequately wetted.
This is quite different, then, from the open access,
first-come-first-served rule that prevails before the
common irrigators are appointed. Adequately wetted is
also quite different from the basic criterion of water
distribution in Northwest India, where canal water is
constantly scarce. There, a "fixed-time-per-acre" principle is used, such that during a fixed period of the week
any one field may receive whatever water is flowing in the
watercourse--but cannot receive water again until its
fixed time of the week comes around. The difference
presumably relates to the difference in the crop-water
response function for rice and all other crops.[4] If
rice gets less water than potential evapotranspiration,
the falloff in yield is much more severe than for other
crops. Adequately wetted at least ensures that each time
around some fields will be saturated, and whose fields
they are depends simply on their position in relation to
the fields that were saturated the last time around.

This difference in rules of water allocation illustrates an important supplemental factor. Whereas "fixed
time per acre" is self-policing (the next farmer in line
knows exactly when his turn should start), the judgment
of adequately wetted cannot be left to each individual

irrigator. Use of this criterion requires a superordinate
authority to make the judgment in the common interests. And
so we find an intriguing transition: water that was previously allocated by an open-access, first-come-first-served
rule becomes, after the common irrigators are appointed,
allocated by a village-wide authority. Plants show a
somewhat similar transition: crops are privately owned,
but what is left behind after the crops are gone from the
land becomes subject to the rules of the same village-wide
authority. As the season progresses, water shifts from
open access to common property; crops cease to be private
property as crops and become common property as residues.

Individual irrigators who steal water--who try to
influence how much water they get once the common irrigators have been appointed--are liable to be brought before
the council and fined. During a drought, when the common
irrigators are "spreading water like money" (to use a
village phrase), the fines may run between Rs. 20 and 50
per offense; but the main penalty is the loss of reputation
that results when the offender is dressed-down in front of
the council.

The common irrigators are paid at harvest time by means
of a levy on each irrigator (so much per irrigated acre),
not from the village fund. The rate is set by the council. Is this not vulnerable to free riding? The short
answer is no, because the collection is made at the time
of harvest, in kind, the one time of the year when every
irrigator patently has no excuse to delay payment in kind.
More important, however, common irrigators not paid one
year can more readily damage the nonpayer the next year.
The withdrawal of common irrigator services from one
individual's land has more serious implications than does
the withdrawal of field guarding services from that
individual's land. So again the free rider issue is
relevant; the fact that financial free riding could be more
easily punished in the irrigation case, and that if others
were to follow the example the consequences of widespread
free riding would be serious for a downstream free rider,
means that the council does not have to extend itself to
raise more revenue for the fund so as to pay the salaries
of common irrigators as well as field guards.

THE ECOLOGICAL BASIS OF COMMON PROPERTY RULES

I have discussed how things are done in the "corporate"
villages, those that have all or most of the four corporate

institutions. Although most of my detailed information
comes from K village, there is in fact remarkably little
variation in the principles of organization of the four
key institutions from village to village, even though the
institutions evolved autonomously and were not imposed
from above. However, many villages have no corporate
organization: there is no village council and no standing
fund; the villages have no village-appointed field guards
(though private landowners may sometimes appoint their
own, occasionally coming together into small groups to
do so), and no common irrigators. Here the rule of open
access to irrigation water continues through the irrigation
season, though informal turn-sharing may develop along some
watercourses. Here uncoordinated groups of herders may
enter a village's land at will (they may have the permission of the headman for which they have paid nothing),
and will negotiate individually whose fields they use to
fold their flocks, and for how long each time. Often the
farmer does no more than provide the herder with meals.
Why the difference between the "corporate" and "non-
corporate" villages?

The first point to note is that the corporate irrigated villages are located towards the tail-end of
irrigation distributories (roughly, the bottom one-
third of the length, where typical distributories may
be 5 miles long or more). The second point is that
the corporate dry villages tend to be located in black
soil rather than red soil areas. The third point is that
in the semiarid tropics generally, black soil areas tend
to be lower down a watershed than red soil areas. So
irrigated villages towards the tail-end of a distributory (given that distributories run from higher to lower
ground) also tend to have a higher proportion of black
soil areas.

Black soils are more water-retentive than red soils,
and permit a wider range and higher yield of rainfed
crops. Black soil villages thus have a more abundant
and more varied supply of stubble after the harvest of
the rainfed crops. More herders want to bring their sheep
and goats to graze in them. With unrestrained access, too
many animals might come in, causing the soil to become
excessively impacted. But also, with more herders wanting
to come in, the opportunity for earning money with which to
pay for field guarding (not just while the animals are at
large but also through the rest of the year) is more
attractive. Moreover, the risks of crop loss are higher:
in the more varied black soil cropping pattern, large

areas of stubble from the early harvested crops will become
available while later harvested crops are still standing.
With higher risks of crop loss, the premium on being able
to organize a regulation of the livestock is also high.
This provides the impetus to field guards and a sanctioning
village council in the black soil areas, while the herders'
willingness to pay for good black soil grazing provides a
way to finance the field guards.

This causal nexus operates in all black soil villages
whether irrigated or not (recall that most irrigated
villages also have a large area under rainfed crops). It
is then reinforced in tail-end irrigated villages by water
scarcity, and the consequent risk of conflict and crop
loss. Of course, if the power structure of the village
were such that no collective action could be sustained
without the agreement of small number of households, and if
these households held all their land close to the
irrigation channel, then they would have no interest in
rules of access. In practice, however, holdings are
typically scattered about the village area in small
parcels, partly to diffuse risk and partly because of
inheritance practices: a landowner with a plot close to
one irrigation outlet may have another plot close to the
tail-end of a block fed from another outlet. This greatly
helps the consensus on the need for rules and joint
regulation. It may be that the degree of scattering is
greater in black soil than in red soil villages, perhaps
because owners wish to utilize the greater variety of soils
in the black soil areas so as to spread risks. The
movement of water laterally through the soil and subsoil
profile is also more complex in black soil areas--so it is
not always the case that land closer to the irrigation
outlet is more desirable than land further away.

Areas of rainfed cultivation higher up a distributory
have more red soil than those lower on the path. Since red
soil dries out sooner after the rains stop, these areas
support less stubble, and so herders are less interested in
grazing there. And higher-up irrigated areas tend to be
under paddy in both seasons; but sheep and goat manure is
wanted mainly for non-paddy, so both the demand and supply
of animals and grazing is less in higher-up villages. In
higher-up villages, also, canal water is more plentiful and
less fluctuating.

Thus both sources of conflict and crop loss are
stronger in villages lower down a watershed than in
villages higher up. The evidence of my sample suggests
that lower down villages are very likely to have a

differentiated public domain in which the appointment, supervision, and payment of specialized work groups are carried out, and in which rules of common pool use are decided upon and enforced. The existence of this sort of organization does not seem to be very sensitive to variations in the standard sociological variables, such as caste structure, factions, and the like. Common need--or demand--seems to be an almost sufficient condition, in contrast to the argument of the "public choice" literature. Free rider problems remain, and they do shape the organization of the supply of public goods; but they do not generally destroy it.

At the same time, however, my evidence also questions the common generalization that irrigation per se induces a more clearly defined pattern of community management. Some of the dry villages have more corporate organization than any of the abundantly irrigated villages. The social response is not to irrigation per se, but to risk of conflict and crop loss. Where water is abundant, that risk is small.

What about the effects of the rules of restrained access on resource use? This question turns out to be exceedingly difficult to answer, in particular because of the difficulty of finding pairs of villages that have similar ecological conditions, but dissimilar corporate institutions (meaning, essentially, that one has such an institution and the other does not). All one can say with some confidence is that both production and equity are higher in the villages with these rules and institutions than they would have been in those same villages in the absence of the rules and institutions. Whether the current levels of provision of public goods and services are in some sense "optimal," given the transaction and enforcement costs of the village-level institutions, is a question that must be raised, but that my data cannot answer.

My explanation for presence and absence uses a simple combination of individuals' self-maximization interests joined with variations in ecological risk. I say that where there are substantial individual benefits from joint action, that action is likely to be forthcoming. This is not to say that the free rider problem, the temptation for self-interested individuals to go for immediate gain, is minor. The need to respond to the free rider problem has a basic effect on the organizational design. We have seen how it affects the amount of revenue the council must raise by means other than individual contributions. But we also noted that the council has developed formidable mechanisms

for enforcing the rules, for precisely the purpose of
convincing individuals that other people will probably
abide by the rules, so that if they too abide by the rules
they will not be the loser. These expectations come not
only from the enforcement mechanisms. They come also from
the social composition of the council, an elite body with
no pretense at "representation," which draws upon the power
and prestige of its individual members to bolster its
legitimacy in the resource management sphere. And they
come from the length of time that the council and its
rules have been operating, which is, in all these villages, several decades at least.

So an assumption of methodological individualism is
used to explain why certain resource management rules have
emerged in some villages but not in others. That is to
say, I do not think a sense of obligatory group membership,
or a belief in "cooperation" as a desirable way to live,
are important factors. There are no grounds for thinking
that general social norms of solidarity and cooperation
vary amongst the villages in the study area. On the other
hand, the rules and institutions I have tried to explain
are distinctly "second order," not first order; they
presuppose a wider and more fundamental set of rules and
norms making for a general pattern of social order. I do
not believe that these first order rules and institutions
can be explained in the same sort of terms, that is, as the
result of earlier rounds of individual maximizing (Field
1984).

LESSONS FOR ORGANIZATIONAL DESIGN

Suppose local common interest groups are to be deliberately induced by an outside authority (the "water users
associations" or other kinds of normal rural cooperatives)? What design principles does this study of autonomously evolved groups suggest? The first is that, in the
South Indian context at least, villagers are likely to
follow joint rules and arrangements only to achieve
intensely felt needs that could not be met by individual
responses (Johnston and Clark 1982). These are likely to
be concerned primarily with the defense of production
(avoidance of crop or animal loss), secondarily with the
enhancement of income, and finally (and a long stretch from
the first two), with education, nutrition, health, and
civic consciousness. The opportunities for avoiding losses

or making income gains by collective action will only
be taken if the losses or gains are large. This is the
significance of the fact that, of the irrigated villages
in my sample, corporate organization to manage common
property is found, with hardly any exceptions, only towards
the tail-ends of distributories (where resources are most
scarce).

The second principle is that the generation of authority (the right to decide for others) is likely to be
problematic within such common interest organizations, and
if the organization is to be sustained it should draw on
existing structures of authority. In practice, this means
that the council will be dominated by the local elite,
which is a disturbing conclusion for democrats and egali-
tarians. Would it not be better to prescribe a representa-
tional rule and/or a majority vote rule for selection of
decision makers?

If the experience of these Indian villages is a guide,
the answer is no. One reason is that such rules carry
little legitimacy in the eyes of the powerful. But more
importantly, the robustness of the organization depends on
its councillors' all having a substantial private interest
in seeing that it works; and for the kinds of functions we
are considering here, that interest is greater the larger
a person's landholding (assuming that landholdings are
typically in scattered parcels). By including on the
council only those who have a substantial private interest
in seeing that the collective good is provided, the council itself comes close to becoming the minimum coalition
whose members find it in their private interest to bear
the transition costs of organizing others to share in the
costs of providing the collective good (a modified version
of Olson's "privileged" group: 1965:50). This effect is
then greatly reinforced by the greater power of the elite
councillors versus the mass of the population; the tendency of the non-elite to cheat, hoping that because of large
numbers no one else will notice, can be checked by sanctions contained in the wider order of property and stratification. Without these wider sanctions, the formal
penalty mechanism would in all likelihood constitute
an inadequate barrier to cheating. This is a point
that the "public choice" literature tends to overlook
because it assumes a context of free and equal individuals.

One specific implication is that, where water users
associations are to be deliberately fostered, the village
rather than the water unit is likely to be a more viable

unit of organization. The attempt to induce irrigators
who depend on one canal outlet to form a water users
association (an outlet-based group) is likely to be
fragile if such a group has not already been mobilized
for other purposes. It will simply not contain enough
authority. Yet many programs for irrigation improvement
in India assume that the "natural" unit organization is
the outlet.

If the elite run the organization, will the organization not become another instrument of exploitation? That
it does not become so in these Indian villages reflects
the third basic principle: the council is concerned only
with benefits or costs that cannot be privatized. It is
not involved in input supply other than water. It is not
involved in settling disputes unrelated to the husbandry
of water. It does not try to compensate the owner of
animal-damaged crops using the fine levied upon the animal
owner, for that would generate conflict about privatizable
value. In K village, the one time the council tried to
intervene in the allocation of privatizable goods--namely,
in allocating rationed sugar from the state--the conflicts
over who got it became so strong that the organization
almost ceased to function. The council eventually
resolved that henceforth it should have nothing to do with
rationed sugar. All the activities it is involved in
(with this one temporary exception) are characterized by
strong publicness, and most also have important externalities.

But the restrictions on scope go much further. Several
kinds of decisions with important externalities do not
involve the council: notably, each village household's
decision about how many livestock to hold, and each farming household's decision about how much paddy area to
plant (that is, the council is not involved in "stinting,"
and not involved in restricting claims to irrigation
water). To become involved in such issues would evidently
require the council to wield a great deal more authority
than it does at present. The implicit rule of selective
involvement within the set of issues with strong externalities may be: do not become involved in households'
investment decisions, even in ones with strong externalities; but do organize ways of mitigating the externalities generated by those investment decisions.

The fourth principle is that the council will add
on other, less vital functions only as it becomes well
institutionalized in the performance of the vital

functions. In all the study villages, the less essential
things (well repairing, monkey catching, and so on) are
only done by a village-wide organization when that organization also does the core activities of field guarding
and common irrigating; but only a few of those organized
to do the essentials also do many of the less essential
tasks.

The fifth principle is to keep the techniques of calcu-
lation and control simple. When the councils intervene to
mitigate the externalities of households' investment decisions (with respect to livestock and paddy), they do so by
using rules that are simple, easily monitored, and consistent with general notions of equal treatment. They would
probably withdraw from involvements where this principle
could not be met. At the same time, however, all the
councils have some procedures for record-keeping and
accountability, so as to "institutionalize suspicion," in
Ronald Dore's phrase (1971). The procedures only make
sense on the assumption that the treasurer, for example,
might have stolen some funds. But it is in the interests
of the treasurer, as well as the contributors, to follow
procedures that would tend to expose his stealing. In this
way, the suspicion that the treasurer might have stolen is
given regular, institutionalized expression. In these
Indian villages, the annual general meeting of all
cultivators to discuss the forthcoming season, ratify the
new council, and receive nominations for field guards is a
simple technique of this kind. So also is the rather
simple kind of record-keeping on standing fund income and
expenditure, which is read out at the general meeting.
Meetings of the council are held in the open, and anyone
who passes by can listen in.

Governments and voluntary agencies can perhaps help to
promote local collective action by measures that reduce the
transaction costs of establishing and operating arrangements such as those described here. Enabling legislation,
permitting devolution of limited fiscal powers to local
communities in specified conditions, is one step. Another
is to promote knowledge among farmers of the various sorts
of arrangements that have been autonomously designed. Any
more active promotion measures should be targeted at areas
where there is a good chance that farmers will respond--
areas that can be identified by means of the kind of
analysis illustrated here.

CONCLUSIONS

I have examined spatial variation in common pool
management within an area of South India small enough
for technology, tastes, and general social norms to be
constant, while resources, notably soil and water, are
varied. The central conclusion is that village-wide
institutions are only likely to be formed and sustained
when the risks of loss are relatively high; but within
the limits of the sample, the chances that such institutions will exist in the relatively high-risk situations
are good. That is, the relationship between risk and
social response seems to be an almost sufficient one (risk
and social organization are almost always related to one
another in the predicted way). The conclusion is thus in
line with the argument of several economists writing about
induced institutional innovation, such as Coase (1960),
Hayami and Ruttan (1971), and North and Thomas (1973), who
have tended to argue that when the benefits of institutional change exceed the costs, change will occur.

However, the limits of the sample are very narrow.
Wider testing will almost certainly show that the relationship between risk and social organization is affected
by numerous contingent conditions, variations in which
will cause the risk/social organization relationship to
vary also. The structure and functioning of power is the
most obvious contingency that can be expected to have an
important effect on the social response to opportunities
for risk reduction. In these villages, it is very important that the most powerful households tend also to have
scattered holdings, which gives them an interest in what
happens over the whole village area. What the councils do
is certainly in the interests of the elite, but the fact
of scattered holdings helps to ensure that the councils'
actions also promote the common interest of landowners.
*Such factors as the government's workable authority in
the countryside might also be important: where the
irrigation agency is more effective at spreading water
scarcity evenly down a distributory, there would be a less
close relationship between village location and corporate
organization. I suspect that the contingencies are not so
strong within India as to make the occurrence of this type
of corporate organization rare; I suspect that much more
autonomous local group organization for resource management exists in the Indian countryside than is generally
thought. In the general case, one has to recognize that
risk reduction is only one kind of benefit. Other

benefits in other situations may also create a demand for collective arrangements.

Finally, I wonder whether we can learn something about the conditions for the original formation of states from the study of autonomous local group organization. We see in these Indian villages a clear example of how in some circumstances individuals can agree to assure mutual cooperation via mutual coercion (with some individuals more coerced than others). If, with some political theorists, we look upon the state as based on a conjunction of contract and coercion, and if we think of the first states as constituting a relatively advanced stage of evolution of a public realm in local communities, we might then draw on an understanding of how the conjunction of contract and coercion is sustained in these Indian villages today for insights about how it emerged in the agricultural communities of pristine states.[5]

NOTES

1. This paper is based on a forthcoming manuscript
provisionally titled, Peasants and Public Choice:
Group Action in Irrigated Open-Field Villages of South
India, Cambridge University Press, to which the reader
is referred for more details and references. The paper
has benefited from the editorial suggestions of David
Feeny.

2. I know little about how the herder groups are
organized. At the start of the stubble grazing, K
normally admits a group of 8 to 10 herders, each with a
flock ranging from 800 to 4,000 head. Some come from as
far as 50 miles away, but most live within 30 miles. About
half the herders who come in one year will have come the
previous year.

3. There might also be benefits to the farmers derived
from bilateral monopoly in bargaining with the herders (a
point I owe to David Feeny). But such benefits are checked
by the mobility of the herders--they can decide to go to
other villages without controlled access. However, the
quality of the grazing and the availability of water matter
more to the herders than their net payment per head of
livestock. In K's auctions of 1980, the price paid by
farmers per head of stock per night averaged Rs. 0.038, of
which half went to the herder; this represented the
herder's net profit, because he did not pay to come into
the village.

4. Rice is the traditional first irrigated crop in the
area of my study, but it has not until recently been grown
in the northwest.

5. The first test would be how well the argument made here
fits with accounts of the evolution of states in South
India itself. My argument seems to be consistent with

Stein's account (1980) of the formation of the "peasant
state" in medieval South India.

REFERENCES

Boserup, E. 1981. Population and Technology. Oxford: Blackwell.

Coase, R. 1960. The problem of social cost. Journal of Law and Economics 3 (October):1-44.

Dore, R. 1971. Modern cooperatives in traditional communities. In Worsley, 1971.

Dore, R. and Z. Mars, eds. 1981. Community Development: Comparative Case Studies in India, the Republic of Korea, Mexico and Tanzania. London: Croom Helm.

Field, A. J. 1984. Microeconomics, norms, and rationality. Economic Development and Cultural Change 32(4):683-711.

Foster, G., 1965. Peasant society and the image of limited good. American Anthropologist 67.

Gaikwad, V. R. 1981. Community development in India. In Dore and Mars 1981.

Hayami, Y. and V. W. Ruttan. 1971. Agricultural Development: An International Perspective. Baltimore, Maryland: Johns Hopkins University Press.

Johnston, B. and W. C. Clark. 1982. Organization programs: institutional structures and managerial procedures. In Redesigning Rural Development: A Strategic Perspective. Baltimore, Maryland: Johns Hopkins University Press.

Kimber, R. 1981. Collective action and the fallacy of the liberal fallacy. World Politics 32, No. 2.

McCloskey, D. 1975. The persistence of English common fields. In Parker and Jones 1975.

- 256 -

North, D. C. and R. P. Thomas. 1973. The Rise of the
    Western World: A New Economic History. Cambridge:
    Cambridge University Press.

Olson, M. 1965. The Logic of Collective Action.
    Cambridge, Massachusetts: Harvard University Press.

Parker, W. and E. Jones, eds. 1975. European Peasants and
    Their Markets: Essays in Agrarian Economic History.
    Princeton, New Jersey: Princeton University Press.

Popkin, S. 1979. The Rational Peasant: The Political
    Economy of Rural Society in Vietnam. Berkeley,
    California: University of California Press.

Runge, C. F. 1984. Institutions and the free rider: the
    assurance problem in collective action. Journal of
    Politics 46:154-181.

Stein, B., 1980. Peasant State and Society in South
    India. Delhi: Oxford University Press.

Worsley, P., ed. 1971. Two Blades of Grass. Manchester,
    England: Manchester University Press.

BIBLIOGRAPHY

Ault, W. 1973. Open-field Farming in Medieval England: A Study of Village By-laws. London: George Allen and Unwin.

Runge, C. F. 1984. The innovation of rules and the structure of incentives in open access resources. Department of Agricultural and Applied Economics, Staff Papers Series, September. St. Paul: University of Minnesota.

Management of Common Grazing Lands: Tamahdite, Morocco

Neal E. Artz
Brien E. Norton
James T. O'Rourke

INTRODUCTION

The purpose of this paper is to apply the common resource model proposed by Oakerson (this volume) to analyze
shifts in institutional regulation of grazing on a unit of
common grazing land in Morocco. The information presented
was generated in the course of a two-year study of the development implications of heterogeneity in a pastoral population (Artz, forthcoming). The study site was a portion
of an administrative unit, the Rural Commune of Timahdite,
in Morocco's Middle Atlas Mountains. Its roughly 20,000
hectares contain: state domain forested with cedar, oak,
and juniper; privately owned fields producing winter wheat
and barley, potatoes, and corn; and about 13,500 hectares
of collective grazing land, ceded to the area's tribal
inhabitants, which support several grass and shrub
complexes. This analysis focuses on the collective land.

Elevations range from 1,800 to 2,100 m. The climate is
semiarid with hot summers (August mean highs of 31°C) and
cold winters (January mean lows of -3°C). Annual precipitation is extremely variable, with annual averages ranging
from 350 to 800 mm across the area, most of it occurring in
spring and fall. Snow falls for between 15 and 40 days
each winter.

The area's inhabitants are the Aït Ben Yacoub, a
Berber <u>fraction</u> or tribal subgroup numbering about 2,000.

- 259 -

The _fraction_ is further subdivided into four sub-_fractions_,
the smallest units above the nuclear family in an agnatic
lineage extending to the tribal level. Some are farmers,
others herders, but most engage in both activities.

Until the 1930s, the Aït Ben Yacoub had no permanent
dwellings and few cultivated fields. They followed a
transhumant cycle with their herds, wintering with neighboring tribes on the _azaghar_, an adjacent, lower-lying
area, and passing the rest of the year in the mountainous
area they inhabit today. As cultivation of lower areas
spread, and as government policies to settle the Berbers
became effective, the old reciprocal agreements with
neighboring tribes broke down. The Aït Ben Yacoub were
confined to their current territory.

Most continue to follow a seasonal circuit, but it is
much reduced from earlier times. They winter their herds
near their homes; the herds graze nearby fields and uncultivated areas and are given varying levels of supplemental
feeds. Herds are stabled at night and during inclement
weather. When spring weather permits, herds are moved out
onto the collective, usually accompanied by the herd owner
or a herder and tent-dwelling family. Herds range from a
few head to about 300, but individuals own as many as
several thousand head divided among a number of herds. The
area currently supports approximately 40,000 sheep, 2,000
goats, and 1,000 cattle. The most pressing problems
manifested are the most fundamental ones: overstocking and
improper seasonal use.

TECHNICAL AND PHYSICAL ATTRIBUTES

The physical nature of this common grazing resource and
the level of available technology constrain institutional
regulation of grazing. These constraints are consolidated
as three variables drawn by Oakerson from economics
literature: jointness of consumption, exclusion, and
divisibility.

Jointness

Joint use of common grazing lands can be maintained
only as long as the grazing capacity of the land is not
exceeded for a significant period of time by the cumula-
tive herd of the joint tenants. However, the deceptive
simplicity of that statement becomes evident when the

concept of grazing capacity is examined. Grazing capacity
is not a biological constant, but an abstract management
concept. A plant produces a certain amount of forage
across a given season that can be consumed by herbivores
without reducing the plant's productive potential; that
amount, however, especially when measured in terms of
animal requirements, is a function of many variables, both
physical and technical: When in its growth cycle is the
plant grazed? By what herbivore(s)? What parts are
removed? How frequently and intensely is it grazed? How
do climatic patterns, the plant's growth cycle, and these
grazing management variables interact? Is a conservative
or an opportunistic grazing strategy being pursued? What
products are desired from the land supporting the plant?
Each of these variables affects the amount of grazing a
plant can tolerate without suffering a loss of productivity. When they are multiplied across countless plants of
different species forming diverse communities the complexity we attempt to encapsulate in an estimate of grazing
capacity is daunting: this study identified 13 vegetation
types on the Aït Ben Yacoub collective.[1]
    Grazing capacity can realistically be approximated only
over time, climatic variation, stocking rate and other
management variables; vegetation condition also must be
constantly monitored. Since such monitoring has not been
done on the collective, we can only study the available
records on grazing history and the current status of the
vegetation to conclude that the grazing capacity has been
exceeded in some areas, and that the common resource has
begun to be degraded. How grazing capacity might be
affected by alternative management strategies remains an
empirical question, but current conditions clearly threaten
jointness.

Exclusion

    No natural barriers separate this collective from other
lands, but the boundary is marked on maps and known to
pastoralists in the region. By law, tribal groups must
keep their herds within the limits of their own collectives
unless special arrangements have been made, but some trespassing in both directions across the collective boundary
is tolerated. For example, one of the region's important,
dry-season springs lies several kilometers inside the
northern limit of the collective, but herds from adjoining
areas are allowed to water there. Also, Aït Ben Yacoub

herdsmen who live near the western boundary graze the
adjacent Ain Leuh collective before Ain Leuh's herds are
moved up from lower elevations in the spring.

Trespass, whether tolerated or not, is easily detected
by the herdsmen who spend most of their time on the
collective and know with whom they share it. For government officials, the task is more difficult because the
collective is large, herds of sheep look similar, and
trespassing herders can claim local origins when questioned by an outsider. To facilitate exclusion, a development project in the area has proposed to fence each
collective unit.[2] But fences are neither common nor
popular among Berber pastoralists, and if they are not
desired by the groups they separate, their costs may well
exceed their benefits.

We conclude that the physical nature of the collective
and the limits of available technology combine to make
exclusion of illegitimate users problematic. Currently,
trespass could only be controlled if the Aït Ben Yacoub
would actively cooperate.

Divisibility

Nothing in the physical and technical setting precludes
dividing the collective into private holdings. In more
arid, Saharan zones of Morocco and other countries, factors
such as climatic variability make division untenable; where
precipitation is low in quantity and extremely variable in
spatial and temporal distribution, forage becomes almost a
fugitive resource, impractical to harvest from a small,
fixed plot. Under prevailing conditions in the Timahdite
region, precipitation and forage production are sufficiently uniform to allow the division of common grazing
areas into private parcels.

Such a shift in property rights would be expensive in
terms of the technical inputs required to divide the land,
fence the parcels, and develop the facilities required by
private ranching operations. The potential social costs
are also enormous. Physical and technical limits would
determine whether enough viable, private production units
could be created to allow those who currently hold grazing
rights to own a private parcel. Even if enough units
could be created, the issue of equality would make
allocation a nightmare. The equality issue might be
defused somewhat by creating larger private holdings and
ceding them to groups rather than to individuals--indeed,

the collective is already partitioned de facto among the four sub-<u>fractions</u>.

The point to be made is that, within certain limits, the effect of physical and technical constraints on boundary conditions is negligible. We chose to focus on the Aït Ben Yacoub collective in this analysis, but the analysis would not be substantially changed if the focus were shifted down to the sub-<u>fraction</u> level or up to the tribal level. The collective constitutes the smallest legally recognized unit of common grazing land. Problems evident at this level are characteristic of the system from a physical and technical perspective.

DECISION-MAKING ARRANGEMENTS

Radical changes in the institutional regulation of grazing on the Aït Ben Yacoub collective have occurred since the French Protectorate government undertook to settle the Berbers of the Atlas Mountains in 1912. The changes can be summarized as a steady erosion of traditional, endogenously generated and enforced controls paralleled by the evolution of a strong central government. The inability of the vestigial traditional institutions to protect Morocco's common grazing lands spurred the central government to intervene in their management. The form of that intervention described in the <u>Dahir</u> (royal decree of 1969[3]) has been difficult to implement. The Aït Ben Yacoub are left today with bits and pieces of traditional institutions and the poorly understood prospect of state control over their use of the collective. While the current situation is the focus of this analysis, some description of history will help set the stage. We employ Oakerson's (this volume) breakdown of decision-making arrangements: conditions of collective choice, operational rules, and outside regulations.

Conditions of Collective Choice

Rules that established the ability of these herdsmen to act collectively were the essence of the traditional institutions. Decision-making mechanisms were similar at the level of the sub-<u>fraction</u>, the <u>fraction</u>, and the tribe or confederation of tribes; at the level of the sub-<u>fraction</u>, decisions involved such day-to-day management issues such as dates of camp displacement, while larger problems (such as how to acquire additional grazing areas) were decided at the tribal level.

Each of the four Aït Ben Yacoub sub-fractions had a jmaa or council of elders that was the forum for managing most of the group's affairs. The jmaa selected an amghar n'tougga, literally a chief of grass, to make final decisions on the regulation of common grazing. His tenure lasted as long as consensus supported him. His decisions involved, among other things, the timing and location of transhumant movements, the timing and location of deferred grazing areas (called agdals), and the granting of grazing rights to outsiders recruited into the group. Decisions were binding on the entire group, and those who broke the rules were brought before the jmaa to be judged and punished--typically, minor infractions were reconciled by the accused's preparing a feast for the elders. Rules were made, infractions detected, and judgment passed all within the group.

This began to change when the protectorate government, with its primary mandate to pacify the Berbers, altered the structure of things. The French were determined to install a strong central government with as little bloodshed as possible. Toward this end, they attempted to maintain le droit coutumier, the traditional laws, while still ensuring peace. They placed collective lands and their management under the guardianship of the Conseil de Tutelle, a national council created by the Ministry of the Interior, and made the traditional offices of sheikh and moqqadem, at the fraction and sub-fraction levels respectively, salaried posts of the ministry and part of a bureaucracy stretching to the capital. Finally, they created the Ministry of Justice, which set about developing a penal code.

Although the traditional institutions were maintained to preserve order, they were weakened. Herdsmen, especially those who had cooperated with the state, began to perceive options and to realize that they need not be bound by the old institutions. Mutually dependent relationships developed between herdsmen and agents of the central government, and those herdsmen could effectively bypass the traditional strictures. Recourse to outside institutions began to disarm endogenous authority. As time passed, different institutions developed different clienteles: some herdsmen adhered to the weakening traditional institutions; others opted to ally themselves with the state; others looked to Islam to sanction their activities; and some chose to operate alone, seeking no one else's support.

This process, described in more detail later, degraded the ability of the Aït Ben Yacoub to act collectively. Today, no single institution binds all the herdsmen, and collective action is a rare occurrence.

The situation can be summarized by addressing the four relationships identified by Oakerson (this volume) as affecting the conditions of collective choice. (1) The process described above has increased the capacity of individuals to act solely on the basis of personal discretion in matters regarding use of the collective. (2) The immediate sources of remedy that had previously been available to individuals who had been adversely affected by the actions of others have been replaced by less sure, non-local sources. (3) The old institutions were based more on binding, collective decisions than on willing consent, but collective decisions are no longer the norm. (4) In the same vein, it seems that under current conditions any herdsman can veto collective decisions. Decisions are now voluntary rather than binding and collective.

Still, the situation may not be as grim as it seems. Recent legislation[4] provides incentives for collective action, encouraging the formation of milk and wool marketing cooperatives, supplemental feed cooperatives and livestock producer associations. Most of the Aït Ben Yacoub seem to appreciate the need for some collective action. Moreover, vestiges of traditional institutions remain, and the state is most interested in fostering cooperation. Taken together, then, these three conditions create the potential that the group's capacity to act collectively in managing their shared resources will be reactivated and institutionalized.

Operational Rules

The operational rules that currently regulate use of the collective are a combination of surviving remnants of traditional institutions and those that have been formalized in law. Following Oakerson (this volume), these operational rules are segregated into three categories that relate to the three technical and physical variables described in the first section.

Partitioning Rules

These rules, implemented to maintain jointness of use of the collective, take several forms, as illustrated by the following three examples.

By law, all Aït Ben Yacoub have the right to graze where they choose on the collective; there are no legally recognized internal boundaries. By convention, however, the area is divided among the four sub-fractions according to traditional patterns of use. Some of the internal limits are disputed, unclear, or ignored, but all herdsmen recognize their existence.[5] Generally, the sub-fractions have access to portions of the collective nearest to their settlements and cultivated areas. The four portions are not equal in size or in abundance of forage or stock water. Use rights to the collective are thus unequally partitioned among the four subpopulations of users.

The construction of houses, stables or any other permanent structures on common lands was forbidden under traditional rules. However, when the Aït Ben Yacoub were confined year-round to what had been their summer range, they were obliged to alter their management strategies to deal with mountain winters. Livestock shelters were essential, and some herdsmen chose to construct stables on the collective. From about the end of World War II until the mid 1960s, when the state put a halt to such construction, about 25 Aït Ben Yacoub herdsmen built complexes of houses and stables in some of the most desirable areas of the collective. This provided those few herdsmen with increased access to common forage resources. Other herders avoid grazing in the vicinity of someone else's dwelling, and the herds stabled on the collective can graze adjacent areas when inclement weather keeps other livestock close to shelter outside the collective boundary. Such construction yields differential use rights, affording the fortunate few the opportunity to extract more benefit, in terms of space and time, from the commons than can their peers.

Traditional institutions include a rather sophisticated measure for controlling the use of key areas of the collective; agdals are areas closed to grazing, or open only to certain types of livestock, during specific seasons. On this collective, agdals are typically adjacent to fields and/or dry-season stock water. They are closed to grazing, or open only to draft animals and sometimes dairy cattle, from the time snow melts off distant, higher areas of the collective until harvest time or until

ephemeral water sources dry up in the higher regions.
Three benefits result: forage availability near fields is
assured when the harvest demands all the family's labor;
forage availability in the vicinity of permanent water is
assured when no stock water is available elsewhere; and use
of some of the most heavily grazed parts of the collective
is deferred, allowing plants to reproduce and restore
carbohydrate reserves. The closure of agdals is decided at
the sub-fraction level, is binding on all herdsman, and
must be registered and approved by the Ministry of the
Interior's local agents. Unfortunately, this practice is
becoming rare, for reasons detailed in the section on
interactions.

Entry and Exit Rules

Traditional rules regulating entry, and thus exclusion,
have remained basically intact and been formalized under
law. Only members of the Aït Ben Yacoub fraction, of that
agnatic lineage or who have been officially accepted into
the fraction, have the right to graze the collective. In
the past, herdsmen employed from the outside or marrying
into a local family might petition the jmaa for acceptance
into the group, but this practice is no longer possible.
Grazing rights holders are currently defined as those heads
of household whose names appear on a list compiled by each
moqqadem, the sheikh and local Ministry of the Interior
officials. While some outside herders who remain in the
service of powerful Aït Ben Yacoub herdsmen appear on the
list, others whose great-grandfathers worked their way out
of such servitude long ago are excluded. Aït Ben Yacoub
who might be working in France or in the military employed
as herders elsewhere, or even in prison retained grazing
rights whether they used them or not. Recent legislation
will change that by reserving grazing rights for those who
depend on pastoralism for their livelihoods. There are no
exit rules.

Boundary Rules

While the elders (the jmaa) of the sub-fractions still
meet, especially on weekly market days, to discuss the
group's affairs, they seem to have lost any capacity to
regulate use of the collective under their traditional
jurisdiction. In most respects, the collective and the

four subdivisions it comprises have become the jurisdiction
of the individual herdsmen who use them.

Outside Regulations[6]

The first important piece of legislation affecting
Morocco's common grazing lands was the Dahir of 1919, the
protectorate government's first move toward settling the
Berbers. It called for the delimitation of collective
lands, ceded them inalienably to the tribal group using
them at the time, and placed them under the guardianship of
the Ministry of the Interior and the Conseil de Tutelle.
After several decades, however, legislation had been
passed that permitted the alienation of tribal lands for
use by colonial farmers and stockmen. Those laws were
rescinded as Moroccan nationalism began to grow. Seven
years after independence, the Dahir of 1963 ordered tribal
groups down to the level of sub-fractions to select nuab,
representatives who would speak for the group when the
state dealt with affairs involving collective lands.
The next important piece of legislation was the Dahir
of 1969; this defined the state's involvement in the
management of collective lands. It was enacted to halt
degradation and improve the management of those lands. It
called for the creation of pastoral improvement perimeters
and charges various agencies of the Ministry of Agriculture
with the design and implementation of management plans for
them. These plans were to be based on the Western, state-
of-the-art range management techniques; the perimeters were
to be fenced, divided into pastures and provided with
physical improvements such as roads, water points, houses
for Ministry of Agriculture technicians, forage store-
houses, livestock shelters and parasite dips. Vegetation
manipulation was to include clearing undesirable plant
species, planting improved forage species and windbreaks,
and fertilizing seeded and natural vegetation. Rotational
grazing systems were to be implemented, and up to one-fifth
of each perimeter could be closed to grazing to allow
natural regeneration or seeding establishment. A list of
grazing-rights holders was to be compiled for each
collective. Those individuals were to be issued cards
identifying them as rights holders and specifying the
number and type of livestock, and the time period they
would be allowed on the collective. The legislation
outlawed arrangements under which rights holders could
herd animals belonging to others for a share of the

profits unless the animals' owners were also rights holders on the same perimeter.

It called for the formation of local pastoral improvement commissions responsible for determining stocking rates on the perimeter and for regulating management based on rotational and deferred grazing. The commissions were to be composed of the provincial governor, a magistrate designated by the governor, the president and two other members of the provincial assembly, three representatives of the Ministry of Agriculture, a representative of the national agricultural credit organization, a representative of the Ministry of Finance, the caids and supercaids (local officials of the Ministry of the Interior) within whose jurisdictions the perimeter is located, and one representative from each tribal group that uses the collective.

The legislation identified which costs of development would be borne by the state and which would be repaid by the pastoral beneficiaries. Finally, it specified which articles of the national penal code would apply to various infractions of rules regarding the management of the perimeter.

Some rules regarding marketing of livestock have been instituted sporadically over the last several years when drought conditions prevailed. In three of the last five years, the King forbade the ceremonial slaughter of rams for the feast of aid Adha (aid el Kbir), a Moslem ritual. Other controls kept reproductive ewes from being sold. The intent was to maintain the largest possible reproductive herd on the country's rangelands to permit a rapid recovery of productivity after the drought.

PATTERNS OF INTERACTION

The Arab sociologist and historian Ibn Kaldoun described the 14th century inhabitants of the Atlas Mountains as vicious and untrustworthy, and Berbers have ever since been characterized as contentious. Prior to the formation of the modern Moroccan nation, Berbers were unconquered and never unified, living in a state of siba, best defined as institutionalized dissidence. However, they have historically demonstrated the capacity to organize themselves effectively for defensive or offensive purposes.[7] Large-scale threats--impending regional power struggles--typically spurred the alignment of tribal and social groups that were anything but allies during peaceful times. Once the danger was passed, the hierar-

chical organization broke down to component parts on the
scale necessary to contend with lesser problems. It seems
that Berber social institutions evolved to counter some
deep-seated love of dispute, and allowed the society to
function in an environment requiring cooperation.

The Evolution of Destructive Interactions

The traditional institutions to regulate communal
grazing were generally organized according to the following description. The jmaa council was the forum for
discussion of management decisions, but those decisions
were ultimately made by the amghar n'tougga. He served at
the discretion of the group, but his decisions were binding
as long as he served. Hard rules were in place to provide
herdsmen assurance regarding the expected actions of others
using the shared resource. There seem to have been few
avenues of appeal, little access to higher authority. One
obeyed the rules or swiftly and surely suffered known
consequences.

The inducements and obstacles that shaped behavior
under traditional institutions seem to have fostered
generally efficient, reciprocal interaction among the
herdsmen involved in managing the collective grazing area
in the past. Two conditions in particular seem to have
been essential to the functioning of traditional institutions. First, affiliation with a strong and cohesive
social network was a great advantage, if not a necessity,
for a herdsman. Second, all the rules regulating use of
the common resource were produced and enforced by the
immediate group. The incentive structures faced by
herdsmen were clear, palpable and similar across the group,
and expectations and actions were coordinated within the
group.

These conditions, as well as others that bear less
critically on this situation, have changed since the imposition of a central government, beginning with the French
protectorate and continuing since independence in 1956.
Some of the traditional institutions (such as the amghar
n'tougga) have disappeared or have been abolished at some
fixed point in recent history. Others (such as the jmaa)
continue to exist, though their authority and power have
eroded significantly. Further, rapidly increasing human
and animal populations have stressed most pastoral
production systems. The two conditions that were noted
above as being essential to the functioning of the tradi-

tional institutions are no longer in place. The old social
network now provides little protection or sustenance--
beyond the grazing rights conferred by tribal affiliation--
to herdsmen, and, as more and more traditional authority
and power have been co-opted by the central government,
incentive structures have become complicated, extending
beyond the immediate and comprehensible realm of the
herdsman, and ultimately differentiated across the group.
The net result has been a progressive fragmentation of the
society. Each level of the social hierarchy have become
less important to the level below. At the bottom, changing
conditions have presented individuals with progressively
more inducements to "ride free" or otherwise pursue narrow
individual strategies, competing rather than cooperating
for the good of the group. A few examples will illustrate
this process and the sorts of behavior it has produced.

Early in the protectorate period, the government
dispatched officers to the Berber tribes; the officers were
to argue the case of the French government quietly and
identify sympathetic leaders and groups who would ease the
establishment of a strong central power. In the Timahdite
area, these agents were resisted by the group in power at
the time. While the largest, most respected and powerful
of the four sub-fractions became involved in extended
guerilla warfare against the French, another sub-fraction
took the opportunity to work with the foreign power and
profited from the association. By the time the resistance
was crushed, a few members of the latter sub-fraction had
gained private use rights to areas that were formerly used
collectively by the resistant sub-fraction. They inserted
themselves in areas of the collective not traditionally
accessible to them, vastly increased their land and
livestock holdings, and established a sort of patron-client
relationship with the central government that continues
today. Those herdsmen saw inducements in the changed
milieu to break from the group, ally themselves with the
exogenous power structure, and conduct their affairs as
individuals rather than as components of the traditional
social network.

Another sub-fraction had traditionally used the
southern part of their portion of the collective as an
agdal. It was close to their fields and to permanent
water, so they closed it to grazing in the spring, obliging
everyone to move north to an area where the forage
was better but water was sparse. With this institution in
place, the sub-fraction could be confident that, when the
ponds and seeps in the north dried in June or July and the

harvest required all of a family's labor, both forage and
water would be available adjacent to the cultivated areas.
However, the agdal was effective only if respected by
everyone. As the sanctions of the traditional system
weakened, some individuals of this sub-fraction and of
neighboring ones opted to take the risk of grazing the
closed area. Periodic droughts exacerbated the problem,
making it more difficult to keep herds off the agdal when
no forage was available elsewhere. After all, on paper the
whole collective was open all the time to all members of
the fraction. In the end, the sub-fraction gave up the
practice. While a majority of the herdsmen said the agdal
was a good idea, they felt it could continue to function
only if everyone agreed to respect it, and that had become
impossible.[8] In this case, the traditional mechanisms
for enforcing collective management decisions had eroded to
the point that the regulations could be ignored with
impunity. Free riding, and the expectation of free riding
by others, undermined the efficacy of the agdal and, thus,
constituted an obstacle to a cooperative strategy.

The story of the sheikh of the fraction provides an
example of the lengths to which an individual free rider
strategy can be successfully pursued. This traditional
authority is now salaried by the Ministry of the Interior;
his selection is negotiated by the powerful members of the
community. As background, it is important to know that
irrigation water is a common resource in this society, and
its allocation is supervised by a chief selected by the
group, the amghar ou asif, whose role parallels that of the
amghar n'tougga who managed use of collective lands in the
past. At a weekly market, the sheikh was hounded by a
throng of irate neighbors who claimed he had kept the water
turned on his fields for two days when he was entitled to
only a half day. They demanded he respect the rules. The
amghar ou asif, who happened to be of the sheikh's
sub-fraction, was summoned, but he offered to resign rather
than to try to force the sheikh to obey the rules. The
neighbors then demanded that the sheikh accompany them to
the office of the supercaid, the Ministry of the Interior
official responsible for the entire administrative unit,
located 35 km away. The sheikh accepted happily, offering
to drive everyone in his truck, so sure was he that the
supercaid would support him. The neighbors, seeing no
further option, desisted. The sheikh, a major player in
collective decision making, could evidently opt to ignore
those same decisions and appeal to a sympathetic, outside
authority.

The Situation Today

Management of the collective along traditional lines
has not degraded as far toward anarchy as might be thought.
Outsiders are not free to graze; construction on the
collective is again prohibited, and the informal division
of the collective among sub-fractions is in force, with
some exceptions.[9] However, the traditional institutions,
with the alterations imposed on them by the state, were not
able to allay degradation under the pressures of
modernization. The state was thus compelled to intervene,
creating new management institutions as detailed in the
Dahir of 1969.

The state's commitment to improving the management of
the collective increased the number and diversity of
persons involved and produced new interactions among them.
The most telling of these are described below, starting at
higher administrative levels and finishing with the
herdsmen themselves.

Before many of the pastoral improvement perimeters can
be laid out, the boundaries of units of collective land
they encompass must be delimited. As noted, this activity
was legislated and begun in 1919, but still has not been
completed. Two large sectors of the Aït Ben Yacoub
collective's boundary, and therefore the boundary of the
improvement perimeter containing the collective, have been
disputed for years and are not yet fixed. This demonstrates the difficulty in achieving agreement about even
the most simple aspect of collective grazing areas, their
boundaries.

The perimeter development strategy has likewise
proceeded slowly. Since 1969, 29 perimeters have been
identified, but work is underway on only a handful. The
Timahdite perimeter was among the first to be identified.
A pastoral research station was appropriated from the
collective land, an act legitimized by the 1969 Dahir.
Development of the station was begun in 1977. The station
provided a site for studies of optimal stocking rates and
soil and vegetation manipulations, adaptability of
improved forage species, sheep diets and the impact of
grazing on natural vegetation. A house for a Ministry of
Agriculture range management specialist and a storage
facility for supplemental feed were constructed in 1980,
but no range specialist has been induced to live at the
station, and no feed has yet been placed in the still
roofless storage hangar. Ministry of Agriculture staff
from Meknes are assigned to work at the perimeter, 100 km

to the north, but provided less than $10 per month for
gasoline, not enough for one round trip. Clearly, the
current rate of progress is tortoise-like, mobilizing field
staff is difficult, and funds to support field operations
are quite scarce.

The herdsmen themselves, most of whom have only a
distorted, second-hand understanding of the planned perimeter, are divided in their response to it. Those who have
profited by collaborating with the government in the past,
and thus may be better informed about current plans than
are their peers, give rubber stamp approval. Those who by
their own choice or the design of others have historically
been left out of state-run programs have no opinion except
that they will continue to be left out. Herdsmen who have
suffered from past interventions are more active in their
distrust of the proposed scheme, refusing to attend any
functions associated with it or participate in any way.
The research station, in the opinion of most herdsmen, is
simply 200 hectares of their land expropriated by force by
the state for its own unknown purposes.

These examples illustrate the difficulties the state
faces in attempting to secure the future of its communal
grazing lands and pastoral people by creating new management institutions to replace what are perceived to be
archaic and ineffective ones. The plan outlined in the
1969 legislation is ambitious, especially in view of the
progress made to date. The plan requires massive expendi-
tures of manpower and capital, which are currently in
severely limited supply. Further, it requires that the
gulf of ignorance and mistrust that separates state
policymakers and their agents from the herdsmen be
bridged. If that could be done, the policymakers might
perceive some advantage in creating an institutional
setting that would induce the fragmented Aït Ben Yacoub
society to reconsolidate, cooperate rather than compete,
and devise and enforce rational management strategies with
state assistance, rather than forcing the state to develop
an entire exogenous regulatory system that will be expensive and ineffective.

OUTCOMES

The criteria used to evaluate the outcomes of this
situation are those suggested by Oakerson, efficiency and
equity. Given the number and diversity of players involved
in the management of this collective, it is probable that

the two criteria would be assessed quite differently depending on the perspective of the evaluator. For example, recent Moroccan land reform activities indicate that an immediate reduction in the rate of urban migration is a top state priority. Therefore, management institutions that keep the Aït Ben Yacoub at Timahdite might be perceived by some as more efficient than institutions that maximize the sustainable rate of output of animal products from the collective. Given the purpose of this analysis, efficiency is assessed according to the latter measure, and equity is appraised according to equality of access to the collective under different institutional forms.

Efficiency

As noted in the introduction, the issue of efficiency is a delicate one partly because of the complex nature of the physical resource base, and also because of the lack of consensus among range scientists about generalities regarding optimal grazing management. Nonetheless, efficient grazing management requires two conditions: the capability to monitor closely and continuously the status of vegetation and livestock, and the means to control grazing by adjusting its timing, intensity and duration, in response to shifts detected by monitoring the system. Traditional systems that meet these requirements can function efficiently, while technically sophisticated systems that do not meet them will fail. These two factors are therefore the principal criteria used to judge the relative efficiency of the grazing management institutions on the Aït Ben Yacoub collective.

Traditionally, all decision makers were herdsmen in close, daily contact with their land and livestock. Monitoring the workings of the system was a natural consequence of their livelihood. We have described some of the traditional, endogenous controls over grazing and their decline under the pressures of modernization. The system seems to have functioned efficiently in the past when the demands on common grazing resources were low. As the demand grew with increasing human and animal populations, traditional regulations were weakened, primarily by the development of a strong central government. Inefficiency, in the form of degradation of the collective resource base, resulted from overstocking and intense, season-long grazing, but it cannot be attributed to the failure of traditional institutions that were no longer allowed to function.

The traditional regulatory system has some obvious benefits when efficiency is considered. Since herdsmen are in constant contact with their grazing lands, livestock and each other, and stand to profit most from efficient management, they are potentially the best monitors of any management system. They are also best equipped to detect infractions of exclusionary and operational rules. We can conclude that the information needed to maintain efficient grazing management institutions is available at least cost to the herdsmen themselves. The free flow of that information among decision makers was one of the great strengths of the traditional institutions.

Some weaknesses are equally evident. As the traditional institutions deteriorated, they no longer adequately controlled grazing. That failure is the institutional explanation for the degradation evident today. Another weakness of the traditional system is the lack of any formal means of introducing new technical improvements.

The modern alternative outlined in the 1969 Dahir also has strengths and weaknesses regarding efficiency, and in many ways they complement those of the traditional institutions. The interventions described are based entirely on technical criteria developed outside the indigenous production system. The value of some of the interventions, particularly the insistence on rotational grazing, may be questionable from a technical standpoint.[10] The great potential strength is the degree to which grazing timing, intensity and duration could be controlled if the management institution existed and operated as intended. But that capacity is remote at this juncture. In the 15 years since this legislation was enacted, virtually nothing has been done to put new regulatory institutions in place, but degradation of the collective has become evident as the old institutions grow ever weaker. The fact that the new system would be monitored by outsiders constitutes another weakness.

In terms of efficiency, the current situation is grim. Management of the collective suffers the weaknesses of both the traditional and the proposed modern institutions, and the strengths of neither can be brought to bear. Any institutional change that would enhance the capacity of the Aït Ben Yacoub to collectively control grazing or that would speed implementation of the government's plans and increase its monitoring capability would improve efficiency. In the long term, optimal management institutions would combine the two options, capitalizing on the strengths of both. In the short term, given the relative costs in time, money and manpower, changes of the former sort seem preferable.

Equity

We noted above that Berber society has always been characterized as contentious. It is also characteristically inegalitarian. This study revealed rapid shifts in the fortunes of individuals, families and sub-<u>fractions</u>. The traditional grazing management institutions seem to have provided a number of opportunities for a herdsman to improve his position by conducting his affairs wisely. Other constraints, particularly stronger reciprocal social arrangements and labor efficiency, helped limit the amplitude of fluctuations of wealth in the community; 50 years ago, a poor herdsman had more animals and a rich one many fewer than they have today.[11] More recently, a few individuals have been able to secure disproportionately large benefits from the collective and to assure their ability to keep securing those benefits. The shift from collective to individual strategies increased the degree of inequality while limiting the opportunities for the non-elite to better their positions.

The effect of the 1969 legislation on equity is uncertain. It depends entirely on how the restructured use rights are distributed. If they were to be allocated on the basis of the current distribution of wealth, current inequalities might be perpetuated. If use rights were equitably distributed again, then institutional avenues might be opened to allow the old flux of relative benefits to begin again. The legislation does not describe how the issue of equity is to be addressed.

NOTES

1. Carrying capacity, grazing capacity, and related terms are defined and discussed in Heady (1975:114-116).

2. This is one of many technical interventions to be undertaken by the Middle Atlas Project, a cooperative effort of the Food and Agriculture Organization of the United Nations and the World Bank designed in 1979. It is an integrated natural resource project encompassing five adjoining rural communes including Timahdite.

3. The development of pastoral improvement perimeters is legislated in Dahir no. 1-69-171, Décret no. 2-69-312 and Arrêté no. 349-69 of the Code des Investissements Agricoles, a compilation of Moroccan agricultural law.

4. The formation of cooperatives was legislated by Décret no. 2-69-39 of the Code des Investissements Agricoles.

5. Some of the units of collective land used by the Aït Ben Yacoub are legally open to the other fractions of the Aït Arfa du Guigou tribe of the rural commune of Timahdite. However, as these areas are adjacent to Aït Ben Yacoub's private lands and used almost exclusively by this group, they are lumped with the Aït Ben Yacoub collective lands for this analysis.

6. This section presents only a few of the most important pieces of legislation affecting grazing on collective lands. All pertinent legislation has been compiled in La Legislation des Parcours Collectives et Forestieres, National School of Agriculture, Meknes.

7. Some of the effects of such organization are described in Halstead (1969). Some mechanisms for such organizations are described in Gellner (1969).

8. The Aït Bouatiya sub-<u>fraction</u> was the last of the four
to regularly create an <u>agdal</u>. The last occasion was 1980.
Since then, the group has not united in support for the
practice.

9. According to a 1968 decision of the Conseil de Tutelle,
the Aït Kessou sub-<u>fraction</u> has no right to graze parcel
295, which constitutes the majority of the Aït Ben Yacoub
collective. Their collective is in the mountains to the
east. Since the sub-<u>fraction</u> has settled among the Aït Ben
Yacoub and become powerful--the current <u>sheikh</u> is Aït
Kessou--they do use the collective.

10. Some inconsistencies in the findings of grazing
research, particularly regarding the benefits of rotational
over continuous grazing, are reviewed in Sims et. al. 1982.

11. In the past, herds of over 300 sheep were practically
unknown. Currently, a handful of Aït Ben Yacoub own more
than 1,000 head, and one more than 4,000.

REFERENCES

Artz, N. E. Forthcoming. The development implications of
heterogeneity in Moroccan communal grazing systems.
Ph.D. dissertation. Logan, Utah: Department of Range
Science, Utah State University.

Gellner, E. 1969. Saints of the Atlas. Chicago:
University of Chicago Press.

Halstead, J. P. 1969. Rebirth of a Nation: The Origins
and Rise of Moroccan Nationalism, 1912-1944.
Cambridge, Massachusetts: Harvard University Press.

Heady, H. F. 1975. Rangeland Management. New York:
McGraw-Hill Book Company.

Sims, P. L., R. E. Sosebee, and D. M. Engle. 1982. Plant
and vegetation response in grazing management. In the
Proceedings of the National Conference on Grazing
Management Technology. College Station, Texas: Range
Science Department, Texas A&M University.

Oukaimedene, Morocco: A High Mountain *Agdal* [1]

Jere L. Gilles
Abdellah Hammoudi
Mohamed Mahdi

INTRODUCTION

About one-fifth of the world's surface is currently
threatened by desertification (McGuire 1978). Most of
this land is now used for grazing domesticated animals.
If wide-scale environmental deterioration is to be
prevented, the management of world rangelands must be
improved, but to date virtually every attempt to manage
Third World rangelands has failed. Setbacks have been so
frequent that agencies that fund development programs have
begun to consider pastoral development too risky for
further investments (Little 1983). In large part, the
failure of pastoral development programs can be traced
to a failure to understand the complexity of traditional
pastoral production systems. Planners often assume that
the seemingly "primitive" techniques used by pastoralists
were unproductive and poorly adapted to semiarid environments. However, closer examination of these production
systems reveals that they are as productive as modern
ranching systems in North America and Australia.

The failure of most government-sponsored range management programs and the relative efficiency of traditional
pastoral systems suggest that indigenous approaches to
pasture management can be used to protect the world's
fragile rangelands. One of the few successful government-
sponsored pastoral development programs is based on such an

approach (Draz 1983). The Syrian government and the
Food and Agriculture Organization (FAO) were able to create
pastoral development cooperatives based upon a traditional
system of pasture reserves known as the "hema system."
While it may not be possible to manage rangelands using the
hema system everywhere, the Syrian experience illustrates
the importance of understanding traditional range
management systems (Eighmy and Ghanem 1982).[2]

An indigenous system of range management, known as the
agdal system, survives in many remote parts of Morocco. An
agdal may be defined as a "collective pasture with rigid,
fixed opening and closing dates" (Hart 1981), or any grassy
area whether collectively or privately owned from which
grazing animals are excluded (Geist and Gregg 1984).[3]
The focus of this paper is the collectively managed agdal
with collectively defined opening and closing dates. Such
agdals exist at many levels of society--some are shared by
members of a single hamlet, others by groups of villages,
and still others by whole "tribes." The agdal of
Oukaimedene described in this paper is shared by two
sedentary tribes--the Ourika and the Rhiraya.

The Oukaimedene agdal is located in the Western High
Atlas Mountains about 60 kilometers from Marrakech. A
stable institution dating from the 17th century, it is
notably free of the high degree of conflict surrounding
those in the Central High Atlas such as Talmest, the site
of "an annual brawl which occurs as regularly as clockwork,
one which neither the French nor the Moroccan government
since independence in 1956 has been able to solve...."
(Hart 1981:7). The stability of the Oukaimedene agdal
gives us an opportunity to identify the elements of an
appropriate range management system.

                    BERBER SOCIAL ORGANIZATION

Before we can discuss the use of Oukaimedene by the
Rhiraya and Ourika tribes, it is necessary to have some
understanding of the social organization of Berber society,
which turns on a notion of segmentation that is associated
with ties of solidarity within groups and among allied
groups, and also with serious conflict between groups and
between alliances (Hammoudi 1974). Kinship (real or
mythical) is the organizing principle of segmentary groups.

The basic building block of society is the household
(takat), which may include more than 50 members. House-

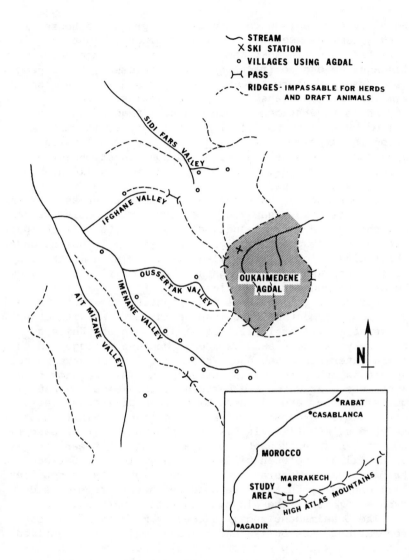

FIGURE 1   Location of the Rhiraya territory and
            Oukaimedene agdal.

holds in turn belong to lineages, or groups of households
with a common ancestor. Villages (douars) might contain
more than one lineage, and often share a common ancestor.
Lineages belong to fractions. In some cases, the lineages
of a fraction share a common ancestor and the fraction is
similar to the "clans" in other societies. Other fractions
may be confederations of nonrelated lineages that are
united by ancient political and military alliances. A
tribe is composed of fractions that may share common
ancestors or may be long-standing confederations of
unrelated fractions. The Rhiraya and the Ourika are
confederated groups.

Berber society, particularly in settled areas like the
Rhiraya, is also organized on a territorial basis: steep
mountain valleys create natural social units. In the past,
valleys or groups of valleys were politically united under
chieftains. Today, the village is a social unit that controls water and pasture rights. Territorial units may cut
across the boundaries of lineages or fractions.

For our purposes, it is important to remember that each
unit in a segmentary group can be in conflict with other
units at a similar level. Each valley in the Rhiraya
territory can be viewed as a unit because villages in them
share water resources and territory and often have to rely
upon each other for mutual protection. At the same time,
conflicts over water and pastures within a valley can be
quite intense, and villages might form alliances (leffs)
with outside groups to protect themselves against their
neighbors. Conflict is likely within any unit of Berber
society--between households in a lineage, between lineages
in a village, between villages in a valley, or between
tribes in a confederation. However, subunits in conflict
will generally unite to respond to threats from outside
groups. This is the classic segmentary pattern.

The Oukaimedene agdal is used by members of two confederations, the Ourika and Rhiraya, which are organized
along both kinship and territorial lines. With the exception of a few watchmen who protect the property in a
small ski station located at Oukaimedene, there is no
permanent population on the agdal. Before the French came
to ski in the late 1930s, the valley probably had no
year-round residents. Although both the Ourika and Rhiraya
participate in the opening ceremonies of the agdal, the
pasture is clearly divided between the two tribes, and each
tribe confines its animals to one of Oukaimedene's two
watersheds. At present, the "Ourika side" of Oukaimedene

has 115 corrals and shelters, while the "Rhiraya side" has 195. The two tribes belong to different administrative subdivisions. The authors did not have official permission to work among the Ourika, so this paper will concentrate on the Rhiraya and their use of Oukaimedene.

The Rhiraya are agro-pastoralists who have private lands outside the agdal. They cultivate barley and wheat on unirrigated terraces carefully carved out of steep mountain slopes. But they have developed an elaborate system of irrigated terraces that has allowed them to cultivate maize, potatoes, a variety of vegetables, and walnuts; in recent years, orchards of apples and cherries have been added. The stark beauty of the rocky canyons and of the carefully manicured terraces attracts hikers and mountaineers from throughout North Africa and Europe, and one has the impression that every possible resource is being exploited. The reality, however, is that even with extensive terracing, less than 10 percent of the territory can be used for crops: most of it is steeply sloped, and many areas are denuded of vegetation. Nonetheless, the valleys inhabited by the Rhiraya are heavily populated for such a marginal region--the average density is 55 persons per square kilometer (Chami 1982). The population of the Rhiraya is estimated at about 36,000 persons or about 2,800 households (Chami 1982), but only a small proportion of the Rhiraya tribe actually bring their animals to Oukaimedene. While all members of the tribe have some "right" to place their animals on the agdal, the physical and social constraints outlined below prevent most of them from doing so.

PHYSICAL AND TECHNICAL ATTRIBUTES OF THE AGDAL

The agdal of Oukaimedene is located in the highest part of the Western High Atlas mountains abut 16 kilometers from Jebel Toubkal, the highest peak in North Africa. Oukaimedene's elevation varies from 2,600 meters at its lower end to 3,260 meters atop Jebel Oukaimedene. Oukaimedene is a treeless valley, 4.5 kilometers long and 4 kilometers wide at its broadest point, divided into two watersheds separated by a low grass-covered mountain. These watersheds meet at the end of the valley at the entrance of a narrow gorge. With the exception of the granite cliffs of Angour and Jebel Oukaimedene, the valley is characterized by steep grass-covered slopes. A strip (1,000 meters long

and 150 meters at its widest point) of naturally subirrigated pastures runs along the valley floor; the peaty soil
is rich in organic matter, moistened by underground
seepage, and capable of supporting plants that can be cut
for hay and reserved for cattle. A number of small permanent springs are scattered throughout the valley; herders
have built stone corrals and stone huts or shelters next to
these sources of water. Ascending from the valley floor,
the mountain slopes have fine-textured soils in their lower
reaches and coarse alluvium in higher areas. The rain-fed
slopes provide pasture for sheep and goats.

Detailed climatic data on the agdal do not exist. The
average minimum winter temperatures for December, January,
and February are approximately -3°C. Precipitation is
estimated to be 500 to 600 millimeters per year, most of it
in winter and early spring, with virtually no rainfall
during the months of June and July. The usually heavy
snowpack at Oukaimedene precludes grazing during winter
months, but is sufficient to permit alpine skiing.

The agdal is only one of the forage resources used by
the people of the region. The local population classifies
its pastoral resources into five components: (1) the asif
or streambanks, (2) the adrar or mountain, (3) l'rabit or
forest, (4) the uta or plain, and (5) the agdal or closed
reserve. The streambanks are the focus of economic
activity, since they provide both the arable land and
sources of crop residues, hay, and pasture for cattle. The
mountain slopes are common grazing lands (especially for
sheep and goats), generally used by people from one
village. Although the forest is legally state property
from which the state is entitled to exclude people, local
groups still manage to exercise their traditional usufruct
rights. The plains are the territory of other groups, but
many Rhiraya have reciprocal arrangements that permit them
to graze their animals on the plains during winter months.

The streambanks and the mountain slopes are the most
important forage resources because they comprise the majority of any village's land and they can be used throughout
the year. Nonetheless, the agdal's pastures are highly
coveted because they provide high-quality forage at a time
when grass is in short supply everywhere else.

The use of the agdal is affected by climate, technology, the distance between Oukaimedene and one's village,
family size, the size and composition of the family's herd,
and the family's eligibility to use an overnight shelter on
the agdal. Thus, while a fairly large group of people are

theoretically entitled to the area, the above factors
sharply reduce the number of families who can in fact make
profitable use of the land. Oukaimedene's elevation
prevents it from being a permanent settlement, given traditional technology and housing. The growing season is too
short for most subsistence crops, and even though the
majority of the agdal's area is desirable pasture for sheep
and goats, the winters are too severe to permit year-round
pasturing. High elevation and low temperature prevent
goats from using the pasture except in the hottest months
of the summer, as these animals are more sensitive to cold
than are sheep or cattle. Sheep are more resistant to
cold, so they can utilize the agdal for several months, but
even they are forced to leave when the heavy snows arrive.
Forage suitable for cattle is limited to the small
subirrigated portions of the agdal, and because so many
cattle are taken to the agdal, the area can provide them
adequate food for only two to four weeks.

The remoteness of the agdal from village settlements
also affects its utilization. Two to three hours are
needed to herd animals to the agdal from the nearest
villages, and up to two days from more distant hamlets.
Only those who have successfully negotiated for the right
of transit may cross the territory of other groups that lie
between their own village and the agdal. The agdal is too
remote to permit herds to move back and forth between
pastures and the village on a daily basis, so herders must
remain with their animals on the agdal overnight. Considerable amounts of time and labor must be devoted to
ferrying supplies between the villages and the agdal, so a
family using the agdal must have enough labor to simultaneously maintain households in the village, care for the
herd at Oukaimedene, and go back and forth with supplies
for the shepherds on the agdal. Finally, in order to
maximize the quantity of hay available to the cattle,
families find it necessary to harvest hay from the
subirrigated areas of the agdal rather than allow the
cattle to roam loose and trample their own food. Thus only
families with labor to spare are able to make use of the
agdal for feeding their cattle. This is a burden for most
families, as the average number of animals per household is
quite small, yet it is also a necessary one, as virtually
all families have cattle and therefore value the agdal's
usefulness as a cattle pasture. Nearly every family in the
region owns one or two head of cattle, but herds of over
five cattle are quite rare. Many families also own goats,

but a substantial minority do not, and even fewer have sheep.

Because of the low nighttime temperatures and the importance of corralling one's herd for the night, Oukaimedene is effectively available only to those who have access to shelters or camps there. And since most shelters are located in the sites favored with a source of water and a hay meadow for cattle, eligibility to use a shelter is also crucial in obtaining access to the agdal's resources. Shelters and corrals are owned by individual families, so someone wishing to use the agdal must belong to a group that regularly uses the agdal and thus exercises its usufruct rights, and must either own his own shelter or enter into a cooperative arrangement with someone who does.

The characteristics of jointness, excludability, and indivisibility described by Oakerson (this volume) apply differently to each part of the agdal and to different groups of users. The hay meadows on the subirrigated portions of the agdal are small enough and valuable enough to make division into individual fields feasible--as with the land at lower elevations--but the isolation of the agdal from human settlements makes the enforcement of private property rights utterly impractical. Families and even villages simply cannot afford to post guards on the meadows year-round to ensure that the proper people and animals are using the proper piece of land. However, a collective agreement to close the agdal completely can be enforced even without such on-the-scene monitors. Grazing animals and intruders can easily be detected--though their identity and precise location cannot be pinpointed--from a distance of several kilometers, and the fact that they are violating the closure of the agdal is instantly apparent. Thus the Rhiraya maintain jointness of use of the hay meadows, as well as the other resources of the agdal, through collective regulation.

The dry uplands of the agdal are extensive, but have a relatively low productive value per unit of area. Individual appropriation of such lands is neither technically feasible nor desirable (Gilles and Jamtgaard 1981). The costs of dividing land among hundreds of co-owners and maintaining so many boundaries would exceed the benefits derived from private pasture ownership, especially given the small number of animals held by each family. Collective ownership is beneficial because it spreads the risks

inherent in extracting resources from a relatively fragile
and often-changing ecosystem and also allows individual
households to change the size and composition of their
herds without worrying about whether their particular
private pasture is suited in a particular year for the herd
they happen to have that year. Yet the total number of
animals brought to the agdal each year could easily destroy
its pastures if grazing were uncontrolled, so collective
regulation is needed to maintain jointness of use for the
tribe as a whole.

The remote location of Oukaimedene, on the frontier of
several rival Berber groups and closer to the territory of
the Ourika tribe than of the Rhiraya tribe, also encourages
collective management of the agdal. When the Ourika and
Rhiraya tribes established the agdal at Oukaimedene, the
possibility of bloody confrontations among users and raids
by rivals dictated that herders band together for mutual
protection to use the agdal. A group of shepherds from a
single village would be too vulnerable to attack, so
alliances among villages resulted.

DECISION-MAKING ARRANGEMENTS

The Oukaimedene agdal is closed to grazing from March
15 until August 10. According to tradition, these dates
(and other institutions surrounding the use of Oukaimedene)
were created by a Muslim saint who lived in the late 17th
or early 18th century--Sidi Fars, patron saint of the
Rhiraya tribe.[4] The agdal itself is considered to be
holy ground "belonging" to Sidi Fars.

A day or two before the August opening date, family
members with mule loads of personal effects arrive at the
agdal, but herds do not enter the valley until about 7 in
the morning of August 10. Some family members precede
those driving the herds to repair the rock shelters and
corrals where they and their animals will pass the nights.
The Rhirayas who use the agdal come from villages in the
five valleys of the Rhiraya area that possess corrals and
shelters; they are therefore the principal users of the
pasture. These valleys, in the order of their distance
from Oukaimedene, are Oussertak, Imnane, Ifghane, Aït
Mizane, and Sidi Fars.

Herds from the most distant locations arrive the night
of August 9 and camp near the passes that open into the

pasture. In earlier times the regulations concerning order of entry were more complex, specifying the sequence by household. There is still a definite order of entry, with people from Oussertak beginning and those from other valleys following. Cattle enter the agdal first, followed by herds of sheep and goats.

Immediately after the opening, the principal activity is hay cutting in the subirrigated meadows. All members of the family participate: women and children do most of the cutting and men transport the hay to the camps. Among rights holders, hay is cut on a first-come-first-served basis, so that those families with the largest labor force harvest the most hay. Cattle, mules, and horses could be left to graze in the hay meadows, but people prefer to cut as much of the choicest grass as quickly as possible to reserve it for their dairy cows. Rules require that this hay be consumed at Oukaimedene and not be transported back to the village, preventing anyone from cutting more hay than the animals can consume while they are on the agdal. Cutting the hay by hand produces a larger hay crop than if the animals graze directly and trample part of the grass underfoot, and thus prolongs the period of time that the agdal is useful as pasture. Sheep and goats are not per- mitted to graze the meadows but instead graze the mountain slopes adjacent to them.

Following the opening of the agdal, groups of women from specific valleys and villages participate in cere- monies at various springs and other sacred spots. On the first Friday after the opening of the agdal, the festival of the spring of Sidi Fars takes place. Young men and women from both the Ourika and Rhiraya groups hold a dance adjacent to the spring, which is protected by a small shelter and is visited by women who want to receive the blessings of Sidi Fars. Money collected at this time is used to compensate one of the herders for an animal that will be sacrificed at the zaouia (shrine of Sidi Fars and lodge of his disciples). Two weeks after the opening of the agdal, another celebration marks the departure of most of the people and animals.

PATTERNS OF INTERACTION

In principle, all members of the Rhiraya group have the right to graze their animals at Oukaimedene once the pasture is opened, but it is clear that not everyone exercises this right. To use the agdal, one needs access to a campsite with a shelter and a corral for the animals, located near a hay meadow and a source of drinking water. Although exact population figures for the Rhiraya are not available, even conservative estimates indicate that no more than 16 percent of the Rhiraya households actually have camps at Oukaimedene. The total number of families using the agdal is substantially higher than the number of campsites because other families place their animals in the care of a neighbor or relative. In 1983, for example, all of the families residing in the Oussertak valley sent some animals to the agdal; those without camps of their own added their animals to the herds their relatives took to camps on the agdal. The campsites used by households from the five valleys of the Rhiraya are shown in Table 1 below by valley of origin, with the closest first.

TABLE 1   Number of Camps by Valley of Origin (percentages are rounded).

Valley	Number of Camps	Percentage of All Camps on Agdal	Percentage of Households from Each Valley Owning Camps
Oussertak[a]	56	29	66
Imnane	83	43	22
Ifghane[a]	27	14	38
Aït Mizane	7	4	5
Sidi Fars[a, b]	22	11	22 (of households from the 3 villages in the valley that send animals to the agdal)
			10 (of households from all 9 villages in the valley of Sidi Fars)
TOTAL IN RHIRAYA	195	101	16

[a]Protectors and retainers of Saint Sidi Fars.

[b]Direct descendants of Saint Sidi Fars.

Several points are worth noting about the relative size and distance from the <u>agdal</u> of the various valleys of the Rhiraya tribe. First, families from the relatively nearby valleys of Oussertak and Imnane, with 72 percent of all of the shelters on the <u>agdal</u>, prevail among Rhiraya families who actually maintain corrals and shelters there. This is quite understandable, since such families face the lowest transport costs for using the <u>agdal</u>. Similarly, there seems to be a rough association between proximity to the <u>agdal</u> and the likelihood that a family will go to the trouble of maintaining a shelter there, doubtless also because of transport costs. However, the households from the three villages that send animals to the <u>agdal</u> from the most distant valley of Sidi Fars deviate from this rule somewhat by maintaining a larger presence on the <u>agdal</u> than their distance from the <u>agdal</u> would appear to warrant.

The existence of a convenient modern road traversing part of the distance between the valley of Sidi Fars and Oukaimedene reduces the effective distance and associated transport costs for families from Sidi Fars. But religious factors also give extra benefits to the Sidi Fars families who use the <u>agdal</u>: the fact that they claim to be the servants of Saint Sidi Fars--and that some of the families from the valley of Sidi Fars also claim direct descent from the saint himself--gives these households, along with those from Oussertak and Ifghane (who also claim to be protectors of Saint Sidi Fars) what we can call senior rights (extended or full rights) to the <u>agdal</u>. As we will see below, they may graze their animals anywhere on the <u>agdal</u> and are entitled to stay longer than the families from Imnane or Aït Mizane. These extra benefits from using the <u>agdal</u> presumably make using the <u>agdal</u> worthwhile even for families who face somewhat higher costs. The claim by some families from the valley of Sidi Fars to direct descent from the saint, as well as their right to command a "gift" (a payment or a tax) from all other Rhiraya households that use the <u>agdal</u>, may also be important in reinforcing their rights of access to the <u>agdal</u>. The Oussertak, who live closest to the <u>agdal</u> and could conceivably exclude all others from the <u>agdal</u> if they chose to, legitimize their own access to the <u>agdal</u> by their affiliation with Sidi Fars. They are therefore in no position to deny similar access to other groups able to claim connections with the saint.

The various ethnic divisions of the Rhiraya have access to different springs and hay meadows. Shelters and corrals

are located in proximity to these resources in campgrounds
or clusters known as azibs. There are three main Rhiraya
azibs: Dou Fatfira azib (approximately 90 camps), occupied
mostly by households from the valleys of Oussertak and
Ifghane; Assif n'Aït Irene azib (approximately 70 camps),
occupied primarily by families from Imnane and Aït Mizane;
and Imine Taghya azib (approximately 20 camps), occupied by
herders from Sidi Fars. Within each of these larger areas,
there are smaller groups of camps adjacent to particular
hay meadows or watering sites, often occupied by people
from a single village.

People from the valleys of Oussertak, Ifghane, and Sidi
Fars have more extensive rights than those from Imnane and
Aït Mizane. Senior rights holders are allowed to cut hay
in the large meadow just below the sacred spring of Sidi
Fars and to graze their animals in the well-watered areas
nearby. Junior rights holders (whose rights are limited
but not necessarily any more recent in origin) must put
their campsites above the spring and graze their animals in
this drier, less-favored, upper zone of the watershed.
They also leave Oukaimedene soon after the festival that
takes place on the 15th day after the opening of the agdal,
after which time the senior rights holders may then allow
their herds to graze the upland areas vacated by the junior
rights holders. Shepherds from Oussertak may stay until
snowfall or until the pastures are exhausted, and they may
also return in late February to pasture their sheep in
years when the snowfall is light.

These two classes of users disagree with each other
over the rules concerning the exact time of departure from
the agdal. Such disagreements probably reflect fluctuations in the power of various groups. The senior rights
holders, claiming to be protectors and descendants of Saint
Sidi Fars, argue that the others are required to leave the
agdal after the 15th day--that is, immediately after the
closing ceremony--and that the senior rights holders
generously allow the others to extend their stay for
another few days until the grass supply runs out. In
contrast, the junior rights holders argue that there is no
difference at all in their rights and that they are not
expected to leave on the 15th day, but that within a few
days of that time the grass for their herds is exhausted
anyway and it makes no sense to stay longer. In fact, once
a substantial number of people leave the agdal, the
camaraderie and the temporary traveling marketplace for
bread and supplies evaporate, and the attraction of

remaining on the agdal declines even for those who insist
that they are entitled to stay. Moreover, the grass supply
diminishes and the weather becomes more severe.

Ethnic identity not only creates a hierarchy of rights
among users but is also important in extending rights to
new users and denying rights to others. Reciprocal
arrangements through relatives permit people without camps
to use the camps of others or to construct a new corral and
shelter adjacent to those of their kinsmen--as long as the
kinsmen or others with camps in the same azib do not
object. Those with objections can take them to the jmaa,
the council of people with corrals in a particular azib.
Wherever there is a collective resource, a council composed of one adult male per household that is empowered to
enforce the rules and resolve conflicts among users can be
established. All members of a council are theoretically
equal, although representatives from rich families usually
have considerable power. Nonetheless, a learned or articulate representative from a poor family occasionally can be
persuasive and influence council decisions. Members of a
community normally oppose the effort by an "outsider"--
say, a member of a village that has no azib--who attempts
to construct a camp. The council is also likely to deny
permission to use water points or to build corrals even to
other members of the Rhiraya who theoretically have the
right to use the agdal.

Rights to a corral and shelter can be maintained only
through regular use. In a real sense, the only title one
can have to a camp is the historic fact that one's family
has always come to Oukaimedene and used its corrals and
shelters. We know that villages that do not currently use
the agdal used it in the past and possessed corrals and
camps there. Informants from the villages of Imlil and
Aremd in the Aït Mizane valley could point out their former
corral sites, though no physical evidence remains. If a
family fails to use its camp, others slowly pilfer the
rocks from the stone walls of the unused corrals. The
theft is hardly noticeable at first, but the corrals may
literally disappear in a few years' time. Those who build
new corrals and encounter no objections can eventually
claim that the silent compliance of their fellows confers
permission. Thus actual use over the years determines the
ebb and flow of rights to the agdal.

Finally, particular and idiosyncratic circumstances
have given many people rights to corrals that are not
located in the azib "belonging" to their community or

valley. A substantial number of households from the valleys of Sidi Fars and Imnane have corrals and shelters in the Dou Fatfira azib, which is otherwise limited to households from the Oussertak valley. The Dou Fatfira azib is particularly desirable because it is adjacent to the largest hay meadow and is close to a modern ski resort that provides some temporary winter employment. Some families may have acquired rights there when the original sites of their camps were leveled to make way for the ski resort and ski lift. Other people may have constructed shelters to live in while they worked at the resort, expanding these later to include corrals. Still others may have "inherited" rights from in-laws. Recently, however, this proliferation of camps at Dou Fatfira has been stopped. Although the Oussertak insist that they still have the right to construct new corrals there, the Moroccan government has forbidden the construction of new camps.

People from other tribes and from communities not possessing azibs in the agdal may still use it by asking or buying permission from a "friend" to share the friend's corral. Such transactions require approval by the council of users. Many people at Oukaimedene have been allowed such reciprocal grazing arrangements, but "strangers" are often denied permission and asked to leave. The council determines who is able to construct and occupy the corrals and azibs, and deals with objections raised by users to others' efforts to construct new corrals. The council functions on the basis of consensus, and Moroccan government authorities normally will respect and enforce a consensual decision.

Such councils may levy fines and exclude intruders from the agdal, but the major sanctions against illegal use of the agdal appear to be supernatural. Because Saint Sidi Fars or his spirit supposedly watches over the pasture, those who violate the rules are expected to become the victims of natural disasters and disease. Similarly, the councils at Oukaimedene cannot easily alter the fundamental rules of use as long as these are believed to be the sacred heritage handed down by Saint Sidi Fars. The opening and closing dates for the agdal, supposedly set over two centuries ago by Sidi Fars, are universally observed and not easily amended. Other rules not as closely associated with Sidi Fars are stretched or their very existence debated.

OUTCOMES AND EQUITY

As a resource management system, the agdal of
Oukaimedene is a reasonable success. Even an untrained eye
can detect the difference between the quality of pastures
at Oukaimedene and pastures beyond the agdal's boundaries.
Several desirable forage species that exist at Oukaimedene
have disappeared entirely in adjacent valleys. The August
opening date appears to ensure that most of the major
forage species have time to produce seed before they are
grazed.

Resource conservation is probably not the main reason
for the creation of Oukaimedene or other agdals. Equity
among various user groups was probably the main motivation.
Without regulation at Oukaimedene, the people from Oussertak could easily use the resources of the whole pasture
each year before other groups could get there. Similarly,
without regulation of grazing by sheep and goats, the meadows would not produce hay for cattle. Since virtually all
families in the tribe own cattle, but the poor generally
lack sheep or goats, these constraints on sheep and goats
actually favor the poorer families. Similarly, since the
race to harvest hay favors families with large amounts of
labor relative to the number of cows they possess, the
regulations on grazing that maximize hay production also
protect the poor families, which have the largest numbers
of people and the smallest numbers of cattle.

CONCLUSIONS

If everyone with rights to use Oukaimedene were
actually to exercise them, Oukaimedene would be devoid of
vegetation. The survival of the agdal is due largely to a
combination of technical and social factors. First, the
agdal's isolation and distance from villages make its use
extremely costly for shepherds from the Aït Mizane and Sidi
Fars valleys, so that only large, relatively rich households from these valleys can profitably use the agdal. As
a result, a larger proportion of families from nearby
valleys use the pasture than do those from distant
valleys. In addition to the technical prohibitions on
use, there are sociopolitical constraints. A person must
either belong to a village that has maintained usufruct
rights to corrals and campsites, or have a relative in
such a village in order to have access to hay and drinking

water. An individual from a village not possessing an azib
will have difficulty establishing a camp. The problems of
group membership and the physical characteristics of the
agdal serve to limit the number of rights-holders who
actually use the pasture.

We studied the Oukaimedene agdal in order to understand this pasture management institution and its implications for resource conservation in Morocco and elsewhere.
The closing of the agdal preserves plant cover and protects
some desirable forage species. In order to discuss
implications of this study for resource management in
general, we must first describe some of the differences
between Oukaimedene and other agdals.

The first reason for the stability at Oukaimedene is
the sacred nature of the agdal as the land of Saint Sidi
Fars. Many Moroccan agdals are similarly sacred, but
others are primarily secular institutions. In the latter,
where the rules are entirely in the hands of the community
of users, attempts to change the rules and conflicts over
these attempts frequently occur. The poor often try to
privatize land suitable for cultivation or hay production,
or the groups that live closest to an agdal may reduce the
access of more distant users (Bourbouze 1982; Geist and
Greg 1984). The councils overseeing the use of agdals are
consensual bodies that cease to operate in the context of
non-negotiable conflicts, which were traditionally settled
by force of arms, but today invite government intervention.
In such cases, the state may impose an arbitrary solution
that is inevitably unacceptable to some, freezing a conflict in place without permitting the emergence of the new
consensus that is essential to the functioning of group
decision making.

Another factor that may contribute to the stability of
the agdal at Oukaimedene is, oddly enough, the presence of
a ski resort. The ski season coincides with the period
when it is impossible to use Oukaimedene for pasturing, so
in one sense skiing is a complementary resource use. However, conflicts in land use do exist: a ski slope may be
an excellent pasture, but stone corrals and shelters are
dangerous obstacles to skiers. In addition, there may be
conflict over water. Some land that is not now subirrigated has peaty soils, indicating that they were once
moist. The large well that serves as the water supply for
the ski resort may have altered the hydrology of the lower
part of the agdal and thus reduced the size of hay
meadows. Thus further expansion of the resort would

threaten the pastoral users of the agdal and would not
necessarily benefit any of them.[5]

How then does this potential conflict affect the
stability of the agdal? Berber society is segmentary, made
up of tribes that are conglomerates of many smaller groups
(fractions, sub-fractions, villages, lineages, and extended
households), among which conflict is frequent.
Traditionally, the various components of society were held
together by the need for allies in case of conflict with
other groups, but the arrival of the French protectorate at
the beginning of the twentieth century reduced intergroup
conflict--at least at the inter-tribal level--and thereby
reduced the social significance of tribes and similar large
groups. Supravillage organizations still have some
importance, however, because the boundaries of
administrative units in rural areas still largely coincide
with the territory of a tribe or a fraction. Conflict at
lower levels, among lineages and villages, still continues,
so such groups continue to have a high degree of
solidarity. In the case of Oukaimedene, the external
threat posed by resort development may contribute to the
solidarity of those who use the agdal and thus to the
agdal's ecological stability.

The Oukaimedene agdal illustrates some management principles for communal pastures. There are many ways to manage a rangeland--through rest, rotation, deferment and
control over the timing and intensity of grazing. The case
of Oukaimedene suggests that deferment is a desirable
approach. If a pasture is visible to users, and if unfa-
vorable weather conditions end the grazing period, it is
relatively easy to set opening and closing dates. After a
deferment period is set, constant evaluation of pasture
quality is not required, and the rights concerning use of
the pasture can also be quite flexible. Thus, those without rights may use the pasture occasionally, and likewise
the Rhiraya will sometimes graze lands belonging to other
groups.

A possible barrier to the extension of these traditional resource management institutions is the fragility of the
councils that govern them. These councils are largely consensual bodies that depend on a certain degree of group
solidarity. As society changes, Berber groups become
increasingly differentiated and it becomes difficult for
the councils to operate, particularly when the central
government claims a superior right to decide resource use
questions. Today, an "injured" minority that objects to a

decision of the council may appeal to government authorities, who will sometimes contravene council decisions that are not accepted by all, and who will even ignore unanimous decisions that interfere with the central government's plans for development. Such intervention can only undermine further the legitimacy of local institutions, already a serious problem because the local councils' decisions have no legal status and are only advisory. The fact that council decisions have no official recognition makes it likely that the councils will be supplanted by the state in regions where economic development is a high priority. If the _agdal_ concept is to be used as the basis for rangeland conservation in Morocco, the legal status of the _agdal_ councils must be clarified and strengthened.

1. The order of authorship is alphabetical and does not indicate degree of contribution. Field research was begun in the summer of 1983 by Mohamed Mahdi under the direction of Abdellah Hammoudi and Jere Gilles and has continued to the present date. Beginning in June of 1984, Lloyd Mendes joined the team to conduct range and animal husbandry research. Research on the Oukaimedene _agdal_ in was part sponsored by the Small Ruminant Collaborative Research Program, U.S. Agency for International Development Grant No. DSAN/VII-G-0049.

2. Recently, Eighmy and Ghanem (1982) have called into question the utility of the _hema_ system. They imply that the success of efforts in Syria may be due to unique local conditions.

3. The origins of the word _agdal_ are obscure. David Hart defines an "agudal" (plural, "igudlan") as "collective pasture with rigid, fixed opening and closing dates." This is normally what is meant when the word _agdal_ is used in the anthropological literature. Although this is the sense of the word that is most of interest to us here, this is not the only one. _Agdal_ (or _agudal_) is more often used as a verb to denote the exclusion of grazing animals from a piece of pastureland. Geist and Gregg (1984) note that during the season when pasturing is permitted on an _agdal_, there is no _agdal_. A second sense of the word used among traditional agro-pastoralists of the Western and Central High Atlas is that of a meadow or a prairie. In the Rhiraya Valley and in adjacent areas, small private hay meadows are also given the name _agdal_. Thus the word _agdal_ can be the act of exclusion or a particular place, and its use in everyday speech seems to combine both of these.

4. Muslim holy men played an important role in maintaining the structure of Berber society. Successful ones (saints) founded religious lodges (_zaouia_) that were houses of

learning and places of mediation for various Berber
groups. These lodges were generally located between the
territories of tribes or <u>fractions</u>. One way in which land
could be made open to two conflicting groups was to make it
sacred land "belonging" to a saint--like the Oukaimedene
<u>agdal</u>.

5. The only way that those using the <u>agdal</u> might benefit
from the expansion of the resort would be if the site of
their corrals and shelters could be developed for the
construction of a ski chalet.

Bourbouze, A. 1982. Déplacements des troupeaux et
utilization des parcours dans le Haut Atlas Central.
Production Pastorale et Société 10:34-45.

Chami, M. 1982. Productions animales et systèmes
alimentaires des troupeaux du Haut Atlas Central.
Mémoire du Troisième Cycle. Rabat: Institut
Agronomique et Vétérinaire Hassan II.

Draz, O. 1983. The Syrian Arab Republic: rangeland
conservation and development. World Animal Review
47:2-14.

Eighmy, L. J. and Y. S. Ghanem. 1982. Prospects for
traditional subsistence systems in the Arabian
Peninsula. Culture and Agriculture 16:10-15.

Geist, A. and G. Gregg. 1984. Tinguerf/Ait Dadd Ou Ali:
Observations of an 'agudalled' pastureland. Report
prepared for the Food and Agriculture Organization of
the United Nations, Rabat, and the USAID-sponsored Utah
State University range management project.

Gilles, J. L. and K. Jamtgaard. 1981. Overgrazing in
pastoral areas: the commons reconsidered. Sociologia
Ruralis 21:129-141.

Hammoudi, A. 1974. Segmentarité, stratification sociale,
pouvoir politique et sainteté: réflexions sur les
thèses de Gellner. Hesperis Talmuda 15:147-179.

Hart, D. 1981. Dadda 'Atta and his forty grandsons: the
social organization of the Aït Atta of Southern
Morocco. Boulder, Colorado: Westview Press.

Hyder, D. H., ed. 1978. Proceedings of the First
    International Rangelands Congress. Denver, Colorado:
    Society for Range Management.

Little, P. D. 1983. Businessmen and part-time
    pastoralists: some factors affecting drought and
    overgrazing in Baringo District, Kenya. Paper
    presented at the 149th meeting of the American
    Association for the Advancement of Science, May 26-31,
    1983 in Detroit, Michigan.

McGuire, J. R. 1978. Rangelands, fulfilling the promise
    through planning. Pp. 2-3 in Hyder 1978.

BIBLIOGRAPHY

Breman, H. and C. de Wit. 1983. Rangeland productivity
    and exploitation in the Sahel. Science. 221:1341-
    1347.

Couvreur, G. 1968. La vie pastorale dans le Haut Atlas
    Central. Revue Géographique du Maroc 13:3-54.

Gellner, Ernest. 1969. Saints of the Atlas. London:
    Weidenfeld and Nicolson.

Socioecology of Stress: Why Do Common Property Resource Management Projects Fail?
Anil K. Gupta

INTRODUCTION: A SOCIOECOLOGICAL PERSPECTIVE

In a stratified rural society, different classes of
landless pastoralists or cultivators-cum-pastoralists can
be expected to have varying stakes in protecting the
environment. They also have differing expectations of the
kinds of assurances (see Runge, this volume) that they
should receive from the various institutions that control
resource use. These expectations may vary over time
depending on the extent to which the availability of the
resource is affected by environmental change. However,
other factors, separate from the vicissitudes of the
environment, also alter expectations: accumulated deficits
or surplus in household budgets, mobility patterns, and
simultaneous operations in factor and product markets alter
the amount of insurance that different classes seek to
cover risks in the future supply of common resources. The
implication is that "assurance" institutions that serve
different classes, and hence that have varying obligations,
do not emerge only through changes in factor prices alone.
The central question thus is how such assurance was
provided in traditional societies and why modern projects
frequently fail to provide it.

This paper offers a brief discussion on the socio-
ecological perspectives for explaining differential stakes
of various classes in environmental management. Then,

using the conference framework, a case study is presented,
followed by some tentative policy implications as well as
questions for further research. The focus is on agricultural endeavors in drought-prone regions.

The key ecological and institutional characteristics of
drought-prone regions are listed below:

o   Low population density
o   High risks inherent in various crop, livestock,
    craft enterprises
o   Current level of farmers' technology generally
    geared towards risk minimization rather than profit
    maximization.
o   Uncertainty of rainfall and lack of local
    employment opportunities that invariably lead to
    seasonal (or to some extent permanent) migration
    with the implication that often the households are
    managed by the women or the old people
o   The capital absorption capacity is very low with
    the result that the institutional infrastructure is
    very poor
o   Social and cultural networks are characteristi-
    cally different from the irrigated regions,
    particularly with regard to the extent of tra-
    ditional forms of cooperation and pooling of
    resources that exist in such regions to augment the
    extended family systems.

The key element of the socioecological perspective
is that the ecology defines the mix of economic enterprises
that different classes of farmers have found to be sustainable in a given environment. Different classes operate
different enterprises at varying scales, depending on their
respective access to credit, product, and labor markets.
Thus, when we find larger farmers owning predominantly
high-value grazers, while the poor own browsers (as was
the case in our study), it is not difficult to deduce the
amount of access and resource use options accorded to
each. Not surprisingly, each group had different perceptions of and responses to risks. It appeared thus that
different classes of farmers used different measures
(i.e., discount rates and time periods) to appraise their
returns in various resource markets depending upon their
knowledge, skills, resource advantage, and future expectations as well as their current or projected surplus,
subsistence, or deficit budget conditions. The cash
flows resulting from the risk-return trade-offs might

be more unstable for some than for others; some households
accumulated surpluses while others became chronically in
debt. The decision-making options of such farmers were
obviously different, as were their investments in the level
of productivity of the environment.

One of the characteristic responses of different
classes to changes in the environment (availability of dry
matter from common grazing lands to supplement the fodder
from private lands) has been to modify the livestock/space
mix, which often exacerbates ecological imbalance. Studies
have shown that in the event of drought, farmers-cum-
pastoralists tried to dispose of heavy grazers (cattle and
buffalo) first and browsers (sheep and goats) last (Gupta
1984a). Consequently, a region that has faced successive
droughts may well become biased in favor of browsers
instead of grazers, particularly if large-scale population
migration is prevented through public investments in
drought relief.

When we summarize the important bearing of this
approach on the Oakerson framework, the policy implications
become richer:

o   The fact that livestock species-mix is class-
     and eco-specific implies that in any region
     the technical and physical conditions of re-
     sources endowment would be defined differently
     by different classes. In other words, the
     catchment area where the dry matter is derived
     for sustenance of the livestock would vary in
     a characteristic manner for different classes.

o   In view of the above, the village common
     lands' vulnerability to degradation would
     also be different. At the same time, rich and
     poor may be disinterested in protecting common
     land for very different reasons. The rich have
     access to dry fodder from crop residues; in the
     main, they own grazers that do not migrate
     widely, hence their dependence on commons is
     relatively small. The poor, on the other hand,
     own smaller individual herds biased in favor of
     browsers that demand extensive labor mobility;
     their payoff from the increased dry matter
     supply from the village's commons is therefore
     not significant. However, in cases where
     male members migrate from an area and the
     households are headed by females or older

people (which is quite common in drought-prone
regions), the commons may become seriously
degraded without much concern from the herders,
whose household cash flow is never great and who
would require a significantly higher payoff to
be induced to change their habits of resource
use.

o   The discrepancies in access to commons as well
as to such private lands such as fallows (which
were generally used as common grazing land in
the dry season) require that the Oakerson
framework be applied from the perspective of
those who are losers in the game, instead of
from a holistic or a community perspective.

SHEEP AND PASTURE DEVELOPMENT PLOTS: A CASE STUDY

Under a World Bank project (World Bank 1974) for
development of drought-prone areas, 100-hectare sheep and
pasture development plots were established in 1974 in the
Jodhpur district of Rajasthan state, an area of 222,860
sq. km, and population (in 1971) of 1.152 million. The key
objectives were the conversion of lands not used for
agriculture, the maximum utilization of rainwater, the
prevention of migration of people and animals in famine
years and, to achieve all of these, the organization of a
cooperative of the weaker sections of sheep breeders.
These plots thus were to provide demonstrations of technological alternatives for better rangeland management and
possibilities of group action through the organization of
sheep growers' cooperatives.   In all, 49 plots of 100
hectares each were developed between 1974 and 1984.

Jodhpur district had a livestock population of
1.89 million in 1971. The mean rainfall ranges from 425 mm
in the southeast to about 200 mm in the northwest.
Traditionally, the private fallow lands were also treated
as common land, although this practice is becoming more and
more restricted. Cultivators have begun objecting to the
use of their fallow lands by other pastoralists, sometimes to the point of violence in many parts of the
country.

The pasture plots were to cover only a fraction of the
total waste common lands in the district; nonetheless, the
expectation was that once local people were convinced of
the utility of restricted grazing they might choose to

develop institutional alternatives for conserving the
village common land and private wastelands as well. The
program was to organize cooperatives that would buy share
capital (preferably in kind, i.e., sheep). In general, the
most degraded land was selected for initial improvement.
It was expected that after the full development of the
plots, a maximum of 400 sheep could be maintained on a
year-round basis in each plot.

One of the first pasture plots established on degraded
auran lands in Bhawad village was selected for detailed
analysis. (The word auran is derived from the Sanskrit
word aranya, meaning forest. Historically, auran was a
traditional institution signifying the concern of the
people towards conservation of common lands.) In these
lands, grazing was restricted; not even twigs from dead
trees were collected for domestic consumption. People were
restrained from using auran land for any individual
purposes because the land was dedicated to various gods or
goddesses respected in the region; the use of any water
source was also restricted. In general, the carrying
capacity of a plot could never increase beyond 33 adult
cattle because of successive droughts.

The soils at the study site are shallow, poorly
drained, severely eroded, saline and alkaline in nature,
and have very low organic matter. The temperature ranges
between 2°C and 45°C, and the rainfall pattern is extremely
erratic, with an annual average of around 300 mm. Because
of excessive grazing pressure, such coarse grasses as
Aristida spp. and other useless herbs (such as Techrosis
spp.) had been dominant in the area (Joshi and Jain 1979).
Cenchrus ciliaris grass was seeded in the plot.

The plot is located at the intersection of two
different ecological units. (The village of Bhawad is
situated in ecological unit number one and borders on
ecological unit two.) The southern part of the district
has a high aridity index, shorter crop sowing season, and
low rainfall probability; the result is that the cultivable
area is suitable generally for short-duration pulse crops.
Longer duration millets could be cultivated in the northern
ecological unit. Population density, livestock
species-mix, settlement patterns, and institutional
arrangements for resource use and conservation were
different in each part of the plot. In the region having
higher stress, (i.e., ecological unit number two), the
settlements were scattered, population density was lower,
the proportion of browsers (in particular, goats) was
higher, and reliance on non-farm activities, (including

drafts) was also greater. Interestingly, it appeared that
auran had survived more influentially as a mechanism for
managing common lands in ecological unit number two.

Other distinctive features of technical and physical
attributes of the total plot were as follows:

o   The proportion of goats in the total livestock had
    increased from 16.6 percent in 1951 to 35.6 percent
    in 1971; cattle and sheep had declined over the
    same period from 32.1 percent and 45.0 percent to
    22.5 percent and 36.1 percent, respectively (CAZRI
    1982).

o   The fodder deficit during the same period was
    estimated to have increased from 44 percent to
    55 percent (Gupta 1984b).

o   The population of cattle, buffalo, sheep, and goats
    had changed between 1951 and 1971 by 7.96, 17.3,
    23.39, and 229.89 percent, respectively. The
    dynamics of degradation thus were reflected in the
    changed species-mix of livestock. Goats were much
    more widely distributed amongst economic classes
    and ecological regions than were sheep, which were
    restricted more to the poor in the arid west (Gupta
    1984b).

Formal decision-making arrangements were based on
complex processes and requirements as described below.
A member of a sheep and pasture development project was
required to be a resident of the village where the project
operated and had to be a sheep breeder. His written
application had to be approved by the majority of the
management committee, and he should purchase at least one
share. No one would be admitted who had been convicted
on any criminal charge (per the provision of Rajasthan
Cooperative Society Act and Rules). A preference was
to be given to small, marginal farmers and agricultural
laborers (for example, sheep owners who would like to
purchase equity with specified livestock). A guaranteed
return of 25 percent was assured to every shareholder.
Individual members provided a sheep in lieu of the share
capital so that they would have greater attachment to
the project. The sheep and wool department of the state
government had appointed stockmen at each plot to take
care of the health of the animals and to protect against
unauthorized intrusions. Although each plot was fenced

with barbed wire, it was not uncommon to find the fence broken.

The president of the management committee of the pasture plot was one of the richest persons in the area. The members of his family owned about 25 percent of the total land and 45 percent of the cultivable land. They also had the most livestock, and a very high proportion of cattle. All of the good tube wells in the village belonged to this family (a total of six). The president of the sheep and pasture development society was also the village head-man, vice president of the dairy cooperative, and exercised influence over almost every other social activity. He belonged to the Rajput caste, which, although not the leading caste in sheep production, dominates the panchayat.

In the beginning, the "advance" team (organized by the department of sheep and wool development) was to try to persuade people (particularly those who owned sheep and goats) of the advantage of developing common land into pastures through cooperative societies. But in the push to launch the project and under political pressure from the Rajputs, the major objective of having the poorest shepherds form societies and nominate their management committee was sacrificed. Moreover, the project failed to consider that access to the common lands differs on the basis of social class. The land closest to the village was selected, although it was not representative of the worst parts of the common lands.

The management group, composed of three government representatives and four members of the society, was supposed to be representative of and accountable to all the members, yet most members could not explain anything about the actual decision-making processes or how they received income from the sale of their grass seed, sheep, and wool.

Many of those who were eligible to become members did not even know about the society when it was started, and others were skeptical about the benefits of participating in such a small project: even if the plot could carry 400 sheep belonging to 34 members, it could only deal with a fraction of the total problem. In fact, the village did not agree to fence the common land through collective decision making. The political dominance of the panchayat by the Rajputs ensured that the plot would be established in spite of opposition.

The plot should have been handed over to the people after four years of operation--that should have been in

1982--but it continued to be managed by the department, who feared the total disintegration of the plot.

The fence had been intact in the earlier years, but had broken down at several places over the life of the project. Several explanations were put forward:

o   Many people in the village were upset because they had not been included in the cooperative society but felt they deserved to be included.

o   The two watchmen posted at the plot could not effectively guard the 100-hectare plots.

o   Since the plot was located just next to the village, the farmers who had their fields on the other side of the plot had to take much longer routes to reach their fields. They felt that they did not gain anything by cooperating and protecting the fence.

o   Some people said that before the plot was fenced everybody grazed their animals on the common lands, but once the plot was developed, the benefits accrued only to the members.

It is difficult to isolate the contribution each factor made to the deterioration of the fence. It is important to note that most of the plots where fences remained intact were located in the ecological unit number two, where environmental stresses were higher.

The pattern of interaction can be studied by first determining the relative importance of livestock and land in the household enterprises of different classes. The households having more land than animals would have different perceptions of the benefits and costs of cooperating to preserve the commons than would those with the opposite situation. The landed class, in view of its access to fodder from private land, did not feel vulnerable even if the commons were degraded. On the other hand, those whose wealth lay in livestock found that the commons provided a very small share of their total grazing requirements. The lack of cooperation to protect the commons thus emerged for different reasons; this is one aspect of the tragedy of the commons that remains understudied.

It is also important to note that successive droughts in this region, coupled with excessive grazing (even if in the short run) have effected changes in the successional

profile of biomass. During monsoon, such species as
Tephrosia spp., Indigofera spp., Crotalaria spp., Cyperus
spp., and Cenchrus biflorus suppress the development of
perennial species. Many of these species are of very low
nutritive value, and being annual, leave soil bare and
subject to wind erosion for the greater part of the year
(Jodhpur Team 1980). The implication is that once the
degradation has reached a particular level, mere conservation or restraint would be insufficient to provide the
necessary regeneration of perennial and desirable grass
species; a technological change--seeding proper species--
would be required. Therefore, management of such commons
must not merely reinforce controlled grazing but should
also devise a strategy for sharing the costs of instituting technological change. Often, these costs have been
borne partly or fully by the state. However, in providing
these funds, the state failed to assure that (1) alternative sources of fodder and water would be available during
the stress period, and (2) the value added through government investment and supply of restraint would be shared
equitably among different classes and not merely in proportion to respective stocks as is often done.

In contrast to these formal decision-making arrangements and patterns of interaction, the traditional approaches to managing auran land invoked religion and moral
sanctions to effect the desirable collective behavior.
These sanctions could not be questioned while the rules of
the game were evolving.

Pasture plots unquestionably resulted in increased
grass cover and in conservation of water in the underground tanks. But the costs of conservation were very
high--the iron fencing was expensive, and the project
required a heavy investment of manpower to supervise the
arrangement. As a consequence, the project, and hence its
benefits, are difficult to replicate.

During the past decade, only a fraction of the total
land has been conserved by this arrangement, and wherever
management has actually been handed over to the people, the
fence has broken down. The basic question of equity--
reasonable and fair return to respective contributions--
could be answered with a statement from Oakerson (this
volume): "Indeed the presence of inequity may lead to the
collapse of collective efforts, resulting in inefficiency.
Equity problems are exacerbated by asymmetries among users,
which create opportunities for some to benefit at others'
expense."

The basic purpose of 100-hectare sheep and pasture

plots was "to demonstrate [to] the farmers how the carrying
capacity of the existing degraded land could be increased
by adopting scientific methods and utilizing the moisture
for longer periods, thus increasing the productivity of
[the] same lands substantially....[as well as] to
demonstrate...[that] adopting sheep husbandry practice
[could] increase the income without...any further
[investment]" (Jodhpur Team, n.d.)

Indeed, if the purpose of these plots (and other
extension measures) was to demonstrate that restricted
grazing would lead to increased grass cover, one must
acknowledge that the project succeeded admirably well.
However, the fact that <u>auran</u> land in many villages was not
only better conserved, but still had much denser growth of
trees, bushes and grass, should have provided the same
demonstration. Thus, the appropriate question for the
sheep and wool department to address should have been:
"why did traditional decision-making arrangements generate
diverse outcomes like protected <u>auran</u> land in some villages
and degraded common lands in other villages?" Yet, such a
question was neither explicitly raised nor implicitly
answered. Instead, it was assumed that people in arid
regions did not know the advantage of restricted grazing.

There also remained a case for improving veterinary
practice and enhancing the common lands (with better grass
seeds), both of which would have reduced sheep mortality.
But in a system already as iniquitous as this one, and one
that had no mechanism for keeping disparities in check,
technological changes that improve returns on existing
investments (in this case, sheep) only widen the gap
between "haves" and "have nots.". The uncertainties leading
to individually optimal but collectively suboptimal
outcomes were not reduced. The official review of the
pasture and sheep development program acknowledged some of
these problems:[1]

> o   "In the village there is a tough competition
>   between cattle versus sheep for grazing. Because
>   of lower socioeconomic status of the sheep
>   breeders, most of the grazing facilities in the
>   community grazing lands are utilized by the cattle
>   breeders for their cattle and buffaloes. Sheep
>   population is forced to the rocky and most unpro-
>   ductive areas and the Gochars and other productive
>   pastures are allotted to them after they have been
>   consumed by the cattle. In such a situation, it is
>   very difficult to teach the whole of the village

people to offer their community grazing land
patches...[as] sheep pastures (only for a
particular society's livestock)." (Jodhpur Team
n.d.)

o   The total production on the 100-hectare plots was
     very low and could not sustain a large number of
     animals. Further, because of low rainfall and
     longer periods of dry spell, the establishment of
     perennials posed serious problems.

o   In whichever case, the plots had a better grass
     cover compared with the adjoining community lands,
     but the fences were broken and frequent conflicts
     ensued between owners of plots and villagers.

o   As a result of frequent droughts, unpalatable
     shrubs (like Tephrosia) have come to dominate
     the plots and further reduced the grazing
     potential.

o   Because the government was not sure whether it
     wanted to continue the scheme (or even expand it
     with modifications), members of the society were
     reluctant to use their sheep as share capital on
     the plot.

o   Management problems, already severe, were
     exacerbated because the village extension
     workers in charge of the plots were often
     transferred.

The initial phases of establishing the pasture plots
were often marked by resistance from the villages (so much
so that in some cases the fencing had to be abandoned even
after the pillars were erected), yet no effort was made to
study the farmers' response systematically. This project
suffered from a typical development problem: technical
solutions were offered for what were basically institutional difficulties; not surprisingly, such pilot projects
have never been replicated.
     Using Oakerson's framework to analyze the lack of con-
gruence between the physical and technical resources and
the decision-making arrangements, we can see how counterproductive patterns of interaction led to undesirable
outcomes. Even more disturbing is the fact that the
national grazing policy (Ministry of Agriculture 1984)

evidences no appreciation for the potential conflicts
inherent in any strategy to manage common property.

The report of the Task Force to Study All Aspects of
Grazing and Fodder to Evolve a National Grazing Policy
includes the familiar recommendations (Ministry of
Agriculture 1984):

o   The number of livestock should be reduced and
     unproductive animals should be replaced with
     productive animals so that the land use plan could
     be developed for both community and waste land. In
     the scarcity-prone areas, arrangements should be
     made for maintaining fodder banks.
o   Migration of livestock should be stopped; the
     herdsman should be held responsible for any damage
     caused to the agricultural fields and various
     plantations.
o   Nomadic tribes should be permanently settled.
o   People should be encouraged to adopt the system of
     stall feeding.
o   The panchayats should take responsibility for
     ensuring rotational grazing on common lands.
o   Regional fodder depots should be established.
o   Critical areas (e.g., the catchments of major
     rivers) should be closed to grazing.
o   Sheep and goats should be prohibited in the forest
     areas.
o   Extension programs should be initiated to inculcate
     public awareness leading to cooperation.

These suggestions do not incorporate any attempt to
understand and address conflicts that have arisen from
historic inequities in the pattern of resource ownership
and their implications for the management of the commons.
It has been assumed that the landless communities, faced
with the degraded commons, irrationally concentrated on
raising sheep and goats because these animals require less
fodder than do cattle or buffalo. Yet the landless were
also confronted with two other problems: the intensified
use of private cultivated lands by the landed communities
(which reduced their access to private fallows) and the
increasing price of dry fodder. It may be that raising
sheep and goats was entirely sensible under the
circumstances.

The problem of degradation of commons should not be
considered in isolation of changes in private lands or in
the variations in the availability of dry fodder. A dry

fodder market has emerged in the few years consequent to
the large-scale efforts to encourage livestock development
in nontraditional irrigated cash crop regions. As a result, dry fodder has moved from one place to another, thus
restricting local supplies, particularly in drought years,
and intensifying the pressures on the commons. Recent
government efforts to encourage afforestation by closing
the roadsides or other areas where moisture retention may
be higher has further increased the demand for commons use.

FUTURE OPTIONS

Basically, four parameters influence the extent to
which any value-adding cooperative enterprise will generate
socially desirable outcomes:

o   The proportion of value addition that is used as
    dividend, replacement cost, maintenance fund, and
    most importantly, risk fund to ensure the risks
    that poor people take when they pool in the
    enterprise.

o   The share of value addition that is used to
    diversify the resource management strategy so that
    the skills or resources of the poor members of the
    cooperative are used in higher proportion.

o   The extent to which the transfer pricing
    arrangement is used to reduce the income dispari-
    ties (by charging, for example, higher prices for
    the same services--e.g., veterinary services--to
    wealthy members and lower prices to the poor
    members). It may be added here that the differen-
    tial pricing of services is easier than is
    differentially pricing the various inputs.

o   To the extent to which the pooling is independent
    of redistribution.

It must be appreciated that in any state intervention, the
case for pricing mechanisms that bias the outcomes of the
intervention in favor of the poor are justified by constitutional obligations in most developing countries. These
obligations are embodied in the socialistic objectives to
which many developing countries have subscribed. It must
also be noted that market forces will always try to

intensify the inequities in a manner in which the resource-use options would invariably be different for different classes of producers. Finally, if the development of common lands is intended to expand the decision-making horizon of the poor and to constrict or equalize the influence of the wealthy, then one cannot belittle the role of assurance mechanisms as argued by Runge (this volume). Given the class conflict in the rural society, these assurances would work only if different rations of assurance were properly accorded to different sections of the society, and the supply of restraint expected from these classes were specified.

These assurances must take cognizance of the varying levels of risk in different resource markets. The same risk phenomenon is subjectively perceived as being different by different classes of users of a resource depending upon their access to institutions and their historical experiences with the way the state and market forces respond to scarcity. Thus, different classes will require different degrees of assurance before they will invest in a common property resource. Classes that are less vulnerable to deprivations resulting from a degraded commons may need only minimal assurance about their future returns from restrained exploitation. On the other hand, the classes that are more vulnerable will want assurance of alternative means of subsistence in the short run and and high degrees of long-term assurance about sustained supply of resources from the common property. It is our contention that the kinds of institutional innovations that would provide these different degrees of assurance likely will not come about through the play of market forces alone; positive state action that draws upon the principles of traditional resource management very likely will be necessary; clearly, the institutional arrangements in this case did not in any way provide disproportionately higher returns to the poor landless shepherds.

Because the reasons for noncooperation by the poor and by the rich are different, it is important that one take into account the implication of these differences for any institutional solution. Using a multi-market socio-ecological framework with proper recognition of historic inequities in resource use might sharpen the Oakerson framework in such a way that new and viable options could be discovered.[2]

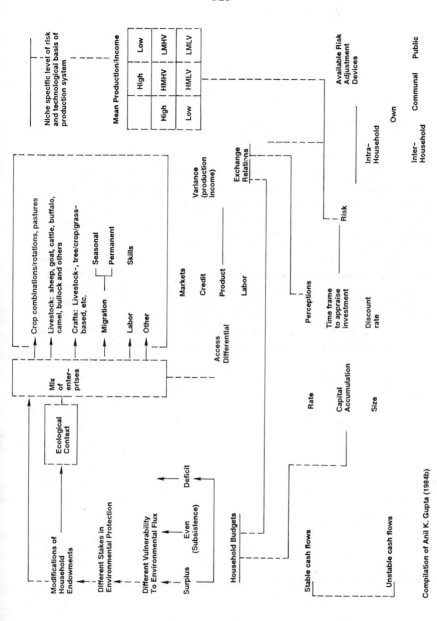

FIGURE 1 Socioecological framework for analyzing household economy.

NOTES

1. It is obvious that the conflict that was finally
recognized after 10 years of project operation could have
been anticipated from the beginning, yet neither the World
Bank report (in 1974) on the subject nor any other
evaluation except by the author (Gupta 1981) noticed the
conflict so as to modify the project design.

2. The theoretical implications of various aspects of
common property management are briefly discussed in a
separate paper (Gupta 1985). Managing common properties:
some issues in institutional design. The concept of
scarcity, role of redundancy in rule making, and the role
of state vis-à-vis assurance mechanism are discussed.

REFERENCES

CAZRI. 1982. Basic and Human Resources of Jodhpur District (Rajasthan). Jodhpur: CAZRI.

Gupta, A. K. 1981. Farmers' response to cooperative project implementation: cases in dairy and pasture development in arid regions. Paper presented at the XIIth UAES Congress, Amsterdam.

Gupta, A. K. 1984a. Dynamics of access differential in semi-arid regions. Invited paper for the Second International Rangeland Congress, Adelaide.

Gupta, A. K. 1984b. Small Farmer Household Economy in Semi-Arid Regions. Ahmedabad: CMA, IIM.

Gupta, A. K. 1985. Managing common properties: some issues in institutional design. Unpublished.

Jodhpur Team. 1980. Review note on sheep and pasture development programs under DPAP.

Jodhpur Team. n.d. Short note on pasture and sheep development programme under DPAP, Jodhpur, 1974-75 to 1983-84.

Joshi, B. R. and H. K. Jain. 1979. Structure, Function and Economics of 100-Hectare Pasture Plot in Village Bhawad, District Jodhpur and Its Impact on Village Community--A Case Study. Jodhpur: District Project Planning Cell, DPAP.

Ministry of Agriculture. 1984. Report of the Task Force to Study All Aspects of Grazing and Fodder to Evolve a National Grazing Policy. New Delhi: Government of India.

World Bank. 1974. Appraisal of Drought Prone Areas
    Project--India. Washington, D.C.: The World Bank.

Commonfield Agriculture: The Andes and Medieval England Compared

Bruce Campbell
Ricardo A. Godoy

INTRODUCTION

Commonfield agriculture is one of the most distinctive and the most intriguing manifestations of common property resource management--distinctive because of its peculiar blend of private and communal endeavors and its complex patterns of decision making and interaction; intriguing because farmland is inherently divisible, there being no technical or physical reason why individual holdings should not be managed on an entirely private basis. That this has not been the case in many parts of the world over remarkably long periods of time is consequently a matter of very considerable interest.

Four key attributes define the core dimensions of commonfield agriculture (Thirsk 1964). First, the holdings of individual cultivators comprise many separate parcels scattered among unenclosed commonfields. Second, after the harvest, and usually during fallow years, these commonfields revert from private farmland to communal pasture ground, as all villagers exercise their customary right to graze their animals on the herbage temporarily available on the arable land. Third, common rights extend beyond mere stubble grazing: in commonfield agrarian regimes, villagers also enjoy the collective right to gather peat, timber, and firewood from common pastures and fallow fields. Finally, regulation and supervision of the entire system is provided by an "assembly of cultivators."

Any of these features may be found in isolation in other farming systems. Many pastoralists, for instance, graze their stock communally. Village councils rule Himalayan, Swiss, Andean, Japanese, and Vietnamese peasant communities (Rhoades and Thompson 1975; Popkin 1979). The simultaneous occurrence of all four traits, however, is more rare; we see it only in selected parts of Europe, New England, the central Andean highlands, Mesoamerica, India, the Middle East, and West Africa.[1] The two- and three-field system of England is probably the best known of these systems and certainly one of the most systematized and regularized. In its case, historians now believe that the four elements noted above only coalesced after a long gestation period, possibly in the 10th and 11th centuries. Thereafter, the system endured in some parts of the country until well into the 19th century.[2]

No single definition is likely to capture all the subtleties of an agrarian system found over so wide a geographical area and so long a period of time. Nor is any one theory likely to explain the causal factors responsible for the emergence of such a complex system in so many geographical areas and sociopolitical environments. What this exploratory essay therefore offers is a systematic comparison of the technical and physical attributes, the decision-making arrangements, and the patterns of interaction among users of commonfield systems found in two widely separated parts of the world: the Central Andean highlands and medieval England. This comparison is less far-fetched than might at first appear for, despite vast difference in the material underpinnings of these two commonfield regimes, they manifest striking similarities in their functional attributes, demographic patterns, and evolutionary trajectories.

Current knowledge and understanding of Andean commonfield systems may be deficient, but, as Marc Bloch once remarked, there are times when synthesis, comparisons, and the formulation of interesting problems contributes more to an understanding of cultural phenomena than would further detailed case studies. Accordingly, this essay is offered as a first step in the development of a genuinely cross-cultural understanding of commonfield systems.[3] It also serves the more immediate function of helping to frame questions and rank priorities for further research. Above all, in the wider context of the present volume, it furnishes two very illuminating cases of highly developed and successful common property management systems.

HISTORICAL BACKGROUND OF THE TWO SYSTEMS

English and Andean commonfields are far removed from
each other in time and in space. In England, commonfield
farming is a thing of the past. Today, only a solitary,
deliberately preserved, commonfield township survives--at
Laxton in Nottinghamshire (Anonymous 1980). In contrast,
in Peru and Bolivia, commonfield farming continues to be
practiced over an extensive geographical area.

Precisely when and how commonfield farming came into
being in England remains a matter of considerable debate.
Nevertheless, there is general agreement that the system
reached its heyday during the early Middle Ages, from
approximately the 10th to the 14th centuries. Throughout
that period, commonfields were expanding and developing;
by its close, approximately two-thirds of England's population lived in commonfield townships (Baker and Butlin
1973; Dodgshon 1980; Campbell 1981a; Rowley 1981). Thereafter, the prevailing trend, with certain exceptions, involved increasing consolidation and enclosure, so that by
the close of the 17th century England had become a country
in which farming in severalty (i.e., with land held by an
owner in his own right and not jointly or in common with
others) predominated (Wordie 1983).[4]

It was at this same time that a fully fledged commonfield system seems to have been crystallizing in the Andes,
as native systems of husbandry were transformed under
Spanish colonial influence. Almost everything remains to
be learned about the history of these commonfields, but
fragmentary evidence suggests that it was during the 17th
and 18th centuries that the system became most widespread
(Chevallier 1953:60; Gade 1970; Custred and Orlove 1974;
Malaga Medina 1974; Gade and Escobar 1982). Since then,
these commonfields have also begun to succumb to alternative methods of land management.

TECHNICAL AND PHYSICAL ATTRIBUTES
OF ENGLISH AND ANDEAN COMMONFIELDS

Entirely different though their respective
chronologies of development may be, both commonfield
systems share the same fundamental physical attribute:
arable fields made up of myriad unenclosed and intermixed
parcels. This is the one abiding feature of all commonfield systems and it is from this that associated decision-
making arrangements and patterns of interaction spring.

Thus, rights of stubble grazing and the communal regulation of cropping are most satisfactorily interpreted as responses to the problems of farming in subdivided fields. That being said, subdivided fields could exist quite independently of such rights and regulations: the latter were by no means axiomatic upon the former.

In Andean and medieval English commonfields, the degree of subdivision was often extreme. The community of Irpa Chico in Bolivia, for instance, possesses six great fields in which Carter and Mamani (1982:26-27) noted some 11,000 separate parcels. These mostly ranged from 1,200 to 3,000 square meters, with some diminutive plots, and others as large as 24,000 square meters. In England, the size range of plots was narrower, although some diminutive plots did exist. At Martham, in Norfolk, for example, the land held by the peasantry was divided into at least 2,500 separate plots at the end of the 13th century, with an average plot size of 2,000 square meters and a significant number of plots measuring 1,000 square meters and less (Campbell 1980).

There has been much discussion of the reasons for this most distinctive form of field layout. It has recently been suggested that dispersed holdings may represent a strategy of risk minimization. The Andean evidence lends some support to this interpretation, insofar as plot scattering increases with altitude, which is positively linked to higher natural risk factors (McCloskey 1976; Dodgshon 1980:22-25 and 45-46; Figueroa 1982:127, 129, 132; McPherson 1983). Yet, although plot scattering may reduce the risk of wholesale crop failure, there is no unequivocal empirical evidence to show that it was actually undertaken with this express purpose.[5] Indeed, it may have arisen from entirely different motives. Thus, in England, several studies have demonstrated that piecemeal colonization by groups of cultivators, together with the repeated partitioning of holdings between heirs, and the sale and exchange of portions of land between different cultivators, were all capable, over a period of time and under conditions of population growth, of creating subdivided fields from formerly consolidated holdings (Bishop 1935; Baker 1964; Sheppard 1966; Campbell 1980). When the rules governing the transference of land permitted, population growth was likely to lead at one and the same time to an extension of the cultivated area and the fragmentation of established holdings. As population expanded, so holdings proliferated, individual parcels became smaller, and the degree of scattering increased.

In this context, it is significant that partible inheritance, whose contribution to the formation of subdivided
fields in medieval England is now well established, is
still practiced in many Andean commonfield communities
today. Other things being equal, such inheritances are
likely to ensure the persistence of a highly subdivided
field layout.[6]
Notwithstanding the high degree of parcellation in
both English and Andean commonfields, it would be misleading to represent their physical appearance as at all
similar. The shape of the parcels and the way in which
they were organized into fields differed due to the
contrasting technological and ecological circumstances
under which the two systems evolved.
English commonfields were developed for the most part
on level or gently undulating terrain and in conjunction
with a plow technology and mixed grain and stock economy.
Indeed, the plow was arguably the single most formative
influence upon the morphology of English commonfields. As
Langdon has shown, three main types of plow were in use by
the 13th century: the wheeled, foot, and swing varieties
(Langdon 1983).
Wheeled plows were more likely to be drawn by horses
than were the other varieties (on the lightest soils, a
team of only two horses would sometimes suffice), and in
distribution were confined to the southeastern counties and
parts of East Anglia. This pattern is partly a function of
soil conditions, but it also reflects social, economic, and
institutional factors, insofar as the adoption of horse
traction entails a greater emphasis upon the production of
fodder crops, notably oats; this, in turn, is associated
with higher labor inputs and the kind of intensive cultivation systems that, at this date, were only found in
conjunction with the more loosely regulated commonfield
systems.[7]
Elsewhere in the country, swing and foot plows
predominated, the ox was the principal plow beast, and
plow teams were often large--usually eight animals, but
sometimes ten, or even as many as twelve. Again, this is
partly because of physical conditions, as large, slow ox
teams were a necessity on the heavy clay soils of much of
lowland England; but it also correlates with lower population densities and cultivation systems that placed greater
emphasis upon fallowing, with a corresponding dependence
upon natural rather than produced fodder. These conditions
obtained in much of those parts of central and southern
England where commonfield farming was most strongly

developed, so there was a general association between
foot and swing plows, large ox teams, and regular commonfield systems. Finally, it was for the simple but obvious
reason that these large teams were cumbersome to manage and
awkward to turn that individual parcels within the commonfields acquired their characteristically long, sinuous, and
strip-like shape (Eyre 1955).

The prevailing plow technology can also be credited
with creating the equally characteristic micro-relief
pattern known as ridge and furrow. This resulted from the
repeated turning of the sod inwards, towards the center of
the strip, which the fixed mold-boards (it was the mold-
board that turned the sod) of medieval plows made unavoid-
able. The boundaries between strips thus became marked by
furrows, which had the additional advantage on heavy soils
of assisting drainage (Beresford 1948; Kerridge 1951). A
buildup of soil also resulted at the end of each strip from
the action of turning the plow: the resultant "headlands"
often became so massive that they may still be identified
from aerial photographs, even where the associated strip
pattern has long since been plowed out (Hall 1981).

Land hunger during the 13th century pushed the
cultivated area of most commonfield townships to its
physical limit, so that property boundaries became
clearly demarcated (double furrows, grass balks, and
marker stones and posts were all used for that purpose)
and property rights--private as well as communal--became
jealously guarded.[8] Odd patches of ground were sometimes
left untilled within the commonfields for reasons of shape,
accessibility, or soil conditions; these were usually utilized as a valuable supplement to the otherwise meager
pasturage resources. For the most part, however, commonfields were very regular and only appeared fragmented and
haphazard in areas of broken relief, poor soil, or bad
drainage (Elliott 1973). Even then, they still bore
little physical resemblance to the commonfields of the
Andes.

Andean commonfields occur in high mountains, where
the terrain is extremely fractured, and where cattle, and
especially plow oxen, have difficulty in adapting to the
altitudes. The commonfields are distributed over a very
extensive geographical area: they have been found as far
north as Huanuco in Peru and as far south as Macha,
Department of Potosi, in Bolivia. Within this zone, they
lie at 3,000-4,000 meters above sea level on both the
eastern and western flanks of the Andes, including the
altiplano.

Throughout this area, yoked oxen are employed for
plowing only in the lands surrounding Lake Titicaca,
and on the flatter patches of the Bolivian plateau.
Elsewhere, plow animals are precluded by the rugged
topography, easily degradable soils, and risk of hypoxic
stress (Guillet 1981). For these reasons, and partly
because the principal crops are roots and tubers (notably
potatoes), the predominant tool of cultivation is not the
plow but the digging stick (chakitaclla), supplemented by
picks, shovels, and scythes for planting and harvesting
(Gade and Rios 1976). Individual parcels of land are
therefore free to assume every conceivable size and shape,
a phenomenon that is encouraged by the steep and broken
slopes and stony soils.

In consequence, the typical appearance of Andean
commonfields is a mosaic of irregular parcels, many of them
Lilliputian in scale. The boundaries between these parcels
are often vague; they include natural features, untilled
land, marginal pasture grounds, and upended sod blocks.
The same applies to the commonfields themselves and the
boundaries between them, which tend to be zones rather than
precise lines and are usually demarcated by small piles of
stones (mojones) or natural landmarks (Godoy 1985). This
endows commonfield agriculture with an element of flexibility, for cultivation can be expanded or contracted as required according to demographic changes and altered land
requirements (Mamani 1973:93). It also produces a different agricultural landscape from the neatly aligned
arable strips of lowland England.

DECISION-MAKING ARRANGEMENTS IN ENGLAND AND THE ANDES

Pronounced though outward differences may have been,
both English and Andean subdivided fields presented their
dependent cultivators with the same basic problem: how
were cropping and grazing to be organized in fields that
were so parcellated? In particular, how was advantage to
be taken of the valuable opportunity that fallow land
afforded for feeding livestock and fertilizing soils? In
medieval England, the need to utilize the fallow grazings
was especially acute, for in many townships (especially in
the counties of the East Midlands) the area of arable land
had been so expanded that permanent grassland was in very
scarce supply (Fox 1984). Yet livestock remained an
indispensable adjunct of arable production both for
traction and manure. In the plowless Andes, the need was

different. What was important here was the conservation
of soil fertility in a mountain environment where soils are
deficient in nitrogen, phosphate, and potassium and easily
degradable (Crawford et al. 1970; Eckholm 1976; Orlove
1977:119; Ravines 1978a:3-74; Thomas 1979; Brush 1980).
Indeed, adequate dunging of the soil (usually by flocks
of sheep and llamas), is essential to the successful
cultivation of one of the region's main staples, the potato
(LaBarre 1947; Winterhalder et al. 1974; Camino et al.
1981; Browman n.d.).

It is in the context of these ecological requirements
that the adoption of communal decision-making arrangements
must be interpreted. The precise nature of these arrangements depended upon environmental, technological, demographic, and sociopolitical circumstances, which is why
England, for example, contained so many different types of
commonfield systems (it remains to be established whether
the same applied in the Andes, although this is a priori
likely).[9] These systems differed from one another in
both form and function, possessed distinctive geographical
distributions, and followed separate chronologies of
development. Apart from subdivided fields that were devoid
of communal decision-making arrangements, two basic generic
types of field systems can be identified: irregular
commonfield systems and regular commonfield systems.
Within the former category, further distinctions can be
drawn among systems in which there was no regulation of
cropping, systems in which there was some regulation of
cropping, and those where, very occasionally, there was
complete regulation of cropping. This last feature was,
however, more typical of regular commonfield systems,
whose distinctiveness lay in the superimposition of
communally enforced rotations upon a regular layout of
holdings.[10]

Although many different commonfield types existed, it
is important to recognize that there have always been some
subdivided fields within which individual holdings have
been managed without reference to any wider framework of
decision making. Thirsk believed that attempts to herd and
farm in subdivided fields were so prone to conflict that
"the community was drawn together by sheer necessity to
cooperate in the control of farming practices" (Thirsk
1964:9). In fact, this was by no means necessarily so,
as England and the Andes both demonstrate.

Examples may be found in both countries of intensely
subdivided fields with little or no communal regulation of

cropping and herding. This was particularly the case in
environmentally favored areas of relatively high population density and intensive agriculture. A high population
means that labor is available for the fencing and policing
of individual plots and private tethering, herding, and
folding of livestock. More to the point, intensive cultivation means that the area left fallow is usually either
small or nonexistent.

The husbandry systems where this occurred in medieval
England--notably in parts of Sussex, Kent and Norfolk--
were characterized by the cultivation of fodder crops and
associated stall-feeding of livestock, coupled with labor-
intensive methods of fertilizing the land. When fallowing
occurred, its sole purpose was to cleanse the land of weed
growth by means of multiple plowings, a practice that would
have been in direct conflict with any attempt to utilize
fallows as a source of forage. Wherever these husbandry
methods were employed, rights of common grazing on the arable fields were therefore either restricted to the period
immediately after the harvest (the one time in the year
when the fields were free from standing crops) or absent
altogether (Baker 1973; Campbell 1981c; Campbell 1983).

In the Andes, the counterpart of these intensive
grain-producing districts are the areas of irrigated
maize production, at lower altitudes than the main area
of commonfields, where a warmer and more stable climate
and a more benign topography permit a greater intensity of
cultivation and correspondingly higher densities of population. Here, too, the organization of cultivation is
largely on an individual basis, as communal supervision of
grazing is precluded by the intensity of cropping (Donkin
1979:120; Guillet 1981; Platt 1982). Cultivators make
their own private arrangements for feeding the plow oxen
employed in these areas.

The opposite extreme is represented by the classic
commonfield system of the English midlands. Here, demographic, economic, and environmental circumstances were
less conducive to the kind of intensification of production outlined above, with the result that there were both
greater incentives and fewer obstacles to the adoption of
collective controls upon agriculture. In fact, communal
management of an integrated system of cropping and grazing
was taken further in this system than in any other. What
made this possible was an artificially regular layout of
holdings, whereby an equal amount of land was held in each
of the commonfields of the township. This was essential

since a regular, and communally enforced, rotation of crops was superimposed upon the entire arable area.

The furlong--a bundle of adjacent strips--was the basic unit of cropping, with the result that individual commonfields frequently carried a range of different crops. Nevertheless, when it came to fallowing, the field retained a central place in the whole system of rotation: "Whatever changes in cropping were rung on the furlongs of the sown field or fields, the fallow field remained inviolate." (Fox 1981:74). Under the two- and three-field system, each field was fallowed either every second or third year. The basic rotation was either winter corn (wheat, rye, maslin, winter barley) followed by fallow; or winter corn, spring corn (barley, oats, dredge, legumes), and then fallow. The purpose of the fallow was to rest the soil so that it might recuperate its fertility, to allow the land to be fertilized with the dung of grazing livestock, and, above all, to supply the livestock with forage, which was in such short supply in many of the townships that followed this system. Since the need to find grazing for the livestock was the raison d'être of the entire system, there was no question of subjecting the fallow to repeated plowings: on the contrary, it was left to sward over with weeds and grasses and only put back under the plow shortly before it was returned to cultivation.

Andean commonfields share many affinities with these English arrangements, and display the same association with a moderate density of population and intensity of land use. They, too, employ communal controls to rationalize the distribution of sown and unsown plots, thereby facilitating common grazing of the fallows. On the other hand, the crops involved are very different from those grown in medieval England, as are the functions and organization of fallows. These differences ensure that Andean commonfields possess considerable individuality in their decision-making arrangements and attendant patterns of interaction.

Within the Andes commonfield, lands are generally sown for up to four consecutive years. There is no distinction between winter-sown and spring-sown crops and the normal rotational sequence is: first, potatoes fertilized with llama or sheep dung; second, native chenopods (quinua and canahue) and tubers (ocas and ullucus); and then cereals and leguminous crops in the third and fourth years. Having deep roots, the cereals and legumes seek nutrients below the shallow surface layer of the soil, whose

fertility is rapidly depleted during the first two years
of cropping (Freeman 1980). Thereafter, soil nutrients are
allowed to build up because the fields are allowed to rest
for as long as thirty years, but the mean fallow duration
is three or four years. The length of fallows is never
fixed, but varies according to soil conditions and cropping requirements, and this provides the key to the whole
system. The higher the altitude, the longer the fallow
period, owing to reduced soil fertility and slower rates
of growth (Caballero 1981).

In very few cases are fields sown for more than five
consecutive years, or fallows reduced to one year. The
exceptions include areas undergoing intensification, or
those communities situated on the shores of Lake Titicaca
that, owing to a more benign climate and richer soils,
plant on what approaches a continuous basis (Carter 1964;
Mamani 1973:89, 110; Urioste 1977:43; Lewellen 1978:16, 49;
LeBaron 1979; Godoy 1985). It remains to be established
how far such intensifications of production have led to
modifications in conventional Andean commonfield arrangements and to what extent they have led to irreversible
ecological degradation. Nevertheless, that intensification has occurred at all does demonstrate that commonfield
systems are nowhere a direct adaptive response to environmental factors--various nonecological considerations have
always been important.

Once a field is designated for cropping, the precise
pattern and sequence of crops sown is a matter of individual choice. There is thus no Andean equivalent of the
furlongs found in medieval England. The range of crops
grown within any field is usually quite wide, as cultivators tend to diversify their pattern of planting as a
hedge against environmental hazards and the risk of wholesale harvest failure (Brush 1981:71). Nevertheless, as far
as the decision-making arrangements of these commonfields
are concerned, it is not so much what crops are sown that
matters but, rather, which fields are to be left fallow
and for how long. Such important decisions are taken at
a village level. To accommodate the relatively long
fallow period required in this high mountain environment, the arable land of each community will usually be
divided into at least seven or eight commonfields, and
sometimes as many as fifteen. Whenever any of these
fields lie fallow, villagers exercise a customary entitlement to pasture their livestock, collect firewood,
and cut turf. At the same time, arrangements are made
for the systematic dunging of the land by sheep and llamas

penned in movable folds. This ensures that all the land is adequately manured before it is eventually returned to cultivation: the dung, urine, and treading of the animals are all highly beneficial to these upland soils. Analogous arrangements occurred in certain English commonfield systems on the light soils of East Anglia, where there was likewise a tendency for fallow periods to be of several years' duration (Postgate 1973).

Two aspects of these Andean arrangements require further comment. The first concerns the household's entitlement to common pasturage. In some cases, households have rights to graze only portions of the stubble of the commonfields and when this occurs the location of this grazing ground is often independent of the distribution of parcels making up the holding. Carter has described this distinctive arrangement (Carter 1964:68; Platt 1982; Godoy 1983). According to him, the section of the commonfields reserved to each household as pasture for its flocks is known as an unta, which is a prolongation of the houseplot into the commonfields. This unta privilege (literally meaning "that which one can see") directly overlays the normal rights of cultivation that apply to individual plots in the fields and sometimes applies to such uncultivable land as mountaintops or swamps. Such demarcation of each family's own grazing zone within the village's territory is an Andean peculiarity and reflects a desire for private control of their own animals by individual community members. It finds no counterpart in the more emphatically arable farming commonfield villages of lowland England, with their scarcer pasturage and much smaller flocks and herds.

A second, and much more significant characteristic of Andean arrangements is that a communally determined system of cropping and fallowing coexists with an irregular layout of holdings. Such a state of affairs carries with it the obvious penalty that each year some households will be obliged to leave a disproportionate amount of their land uncultivated. There is thus an inherent inequity within the system, a deficiency that is avoided in the English midland system by the equal distribution of a holding's strips among all the fields of a township.[11] Such a regular layout of holdings would be of no practical advantage in the Andean situation where the timing and duration of fallows are, perforce, subject to much flexibility. It is certainly true that (as in those few English instances where there was a similar mismatch between holding layout and rotations) Andean people are sometimes able to use

land held outside the commonfield system to offset the
inequities arising within that system. Thus all commonfield holdings include a house plot that is held in
severalty and capable of intensive cultivation. Although
such plots are occasionally quite substantial, most have
been much reduced in size through the application of a
custom of male partible inheritance (Carter 1964:65;
Heath et al. 1969:177; Rodriguez-Pastor 1969:84-86). For
 the tenants of these diminutive house plots, the most
effective supplements to commonfield land are therefore
valley plots. Not only are the latter not subject
to communal decisions, they are also environmentally
more favored and can consequently be cropped much more
intensively than the commonfields (Guillet 1981; Platt
1982).

When house plots, valley lands, and pasture grounds are
all taken into account, it transpires that commonfields
generally constitute between 20 and 70 percent of total
land holdings, the proportion rising with altitude
(Figueroa 1982:133). Nevertheless, many individuals remain
dependent upon the commonfields for the basic staples of
daily life. For them, the only solution when they are
temporarily disadvantaged by the system is to come to some
kind of reciprocal arrangement with those who are
temporarily advantaged. It is upon this kind of social
exchange between members of the same agricultural community
that the commonfield system ultimately depends for its
success.

The nearest equivalent in England was the commonfield
system of parts of East Anglia, noted above. A similar
coexistence of common rotations was found in this system in
the form of flexible cropping shifts, with an irregular
layout of holdings. The object of the cropping shifts was
likewise to concentrate fallow strips for sheep folding.
Since this periodically placed certain individuals at a
disadvantage, successful operation of the system, as in the
Andes, depended upon the establishment of a satisfactory
method of compensation. As control of the system was
vested in the manorial lord (who, as principal flockmaster,
was also usually the major beneficiary of it), a tenant
thus placed might receive part of the lord's crop, temporary use of a portion of the lord's demesne, or financial
compensation in the form of a cash handout or rent rebate.
Even so, this system was particularly prone to conflict,
as is testified by the large number of resultant court
cases (Allison 1957; Allison 1958; Simpson 1958; Postgate
1973).

On the whole, both English and Andean commonfield
systems made good practical sense in a situation where
land was cropped with only moderate intensity, and where
population levels were such that substantial dividends were
to be derived from pooling scarce labor and organizing
basic farming tasks in common. Savings were obviously
to be made by eliminating the need for fencing and by
appointing a few guards to watch over the fields and
stock of all the villagers. Moreover, information and
transaction costs were reduced when decisions were taken
at a village level as to when and where to plant and
pasture.

Such arrangements may also have proved advantageous
to subjects faced with heavy labor-tribute liabilities, a
relevant point in both a medieval English and an Andean
context. In the former, lords were entitled to exact labor
services from their tenants through the institution of
serfdom; these services characteristically assumed the form
of agricultural work on the lord's demesne. In fact, under
the conditions of labor scarcity that probably prevailed
when serfdom was first instituted, lords would have had a
vested interest in promoting the development of a system of
husbandry that enabled them to redeploy labor to their own
ends. There is certainly a striking coincidence between
the areas of strongest lordship and most fully developed
commonfield systems.[12]

Likewise in the Andes, the Spanish instituted a
system of forced-labor to work the silver and mercury
mines of Potosi and Huancavelica. This assumed the form
of an annual migration of able-bodied males (the mita)
drawn from a very extensive area. At the end of the 16th
century, this migration totaled some 13,000 workers per
year, some of whom came from so far away that they had to
walk for an entire month to reach the mines. As Tandeter
has pointed out, a migration on this scale must have had
major repercussions for the accumulation and reproduction
of the communities that were being exploited, the more so
as these heavy labor demands coincided with a prolonged and
massive reduction in population (Tandeter 1981).[13] It
seems, therefore, that in the Andes, too, there is a
coincidence between the area of heaviest labor-tribute
liabilities and the area where commonfield agriculture
appears to have attained its most complex form and survived
the longest.

PATTERNS OF INTERACTION

The common denominator of all these commonfield systems is a reversion from private use to till the soil to communal rights to graze on the herbage of the fallow fields. This communal arrangement places a premium upon the collective management of resources. For instance, since commonfields remain unfenced, individual house-holders face incentives to steal crops from adjacent plots and encroach upon neighboring lands. This potential threat fosters collective action, as isolated households by themselves would be less effective in opposing inter-lopers (Gade 1970:51; Orlove 1976:213; Albo 1977:23; Platt 1982:45). Hence the phenomenon of village-appointed guards and other officials. Furthermore, the movement across time and space of different flocks and herds, and the designation of fields to be sown and fallowed, involve complex scheduling problems affecting all villagers.

These logistical problems are therefore frequently de-cided upon by village assemblies; it is they who determine the date and place of planting, harvesting, and grazing. In the Andes, these village councils, as noted by McBride, constitute the "de facto government of a community, though its operation is so silent and its deliberation so careful-ly guarded that its existence is seldom even suspected" (McBride 1921:9). Much the same is true of similar assemblies in England, whose existence is often barely hinted at in the historical record. Yet, although there is a clear association between commonfield agriculture and strongly developed corporate village communities, the precise causal connection between them is enigmatic. At any event, the outward physical expression of the strong corporate character pos-sessed by these commonfield communities in both countries is the nucleated village. In contrast, more dispersed forms of settlement--loosely clustered hamlets, isolated farmsteads, and a mixture of villages and scattered messauges--tend to prevail in non-commonfield areas.[14]

The Andean evidence demonstrates that the corporate sense of these commonfield communities is usually suffi-ciently strong to override even quite substantial inequal-ities of holding size among cultivators.[15] As is to be expected, the larger landholders do tend to exert a dis-proportionate influence within village assemblies and dominate the principal village offices. On the other hand, all household heads serve as field guards by yearly turns. This rotational incumbency possibly had colonial origins, but it still functions (Rasnake 1981).

These officers, known variously as pachacas, campos, muyucamas, arariwas, camayoqs, or regidores de varas, are in charge of supervising fields, preventing animals from straying onto cultivated lands, guarding against crop theft and trespass, punishing and levying fines on miscreant shepherds, and performing rituals to protect crops when hail, drought, and other natural calamities threaten. Their honesty is ensured because they are answerable to the higher level village authority and charged with responsibility for any crops stolen from the fields. In recompense, if the harvest proves successful, they receive the produce of a few furrows from each family, or are allowed to plant in uncultivated plots of the commons.

As Thomas observes, this system of incumbency by yearly turns symbolizes total community involvement in the decision-making process of the entire community (Gade 1970:12; Degregori and Golte 1973:42; Preston 1973; Thomas 1979:161; Fujii and Tomoeda 1981:54). Household heads also sponsor village festivals at one or more times in their life cycle: these festivals confer prestige upon those who sponsor them, but are also essential for validating the individual household's right of access to village assets in the eyes of the community (Platt 1982; Godoy 1983).

The need to establish who belongs to a community and has a stake in its resources is critical: that it is perceived as such is demonstrated by the symbolic reapportionments and public reconfirmations of a household's rights to land that hacienda officials continue to supervise.[16] If anything, the issue of who is entitled to land rights has become more prominent in recent years as expanding populations have brought resources under increasing pressure.

Today, as in the past, a pronounced social stratification is apparent within many of these villages. In Bolivia, the true insiders (originarios) tend to have more parcels within the commonfields than do later arrivals (agregados). Below these two groups lie the kantu runas (people of the margin), peasants who settled in the village during the 19th century and who obtained indirect access to common land in exchange for services rendered to wealthier households (Platt 1982; Godoy 1983).[17] These divisions tend to be perpetuated by rules that proscribe the renting or selling of commonfield land to outsiders, although they permit cultivators to rent or mortgage their parcels to other members of the community (McBride 1921:14; Metraux

1959; Carter 1964:68; Custred 1974:258; Guillet 1979; Fujii and Tomoeda 1981:53; Godoy 1985). Such entry and exit rules are enforced by the village council, which, if need be, employs expulsion as the ultimate sanction against recalcitrant behavior. That village councils should have acquired such powers is a function of the historic weakness of national power structures in the areas of commonfield agriculture.

In medieval England, the administrative structure and patterns of interaction of these commonfield communities are more difficult to ascertain, filtered as they are through the historical record. Most of what is known is provided by the proceedings of manorial courts (the lowest level of courts with legitimate legal jurisdiction). It was in these courts that commonfield bylaws were enacted and enforced, and their proceedings usually record innumerable boundary disputes and prosecutions for trespass and crop theft (Ault 1965). The election of village officials was also usually enrolled in the courts. Some of these officers, like the pinder and hayward, are close equivalents of the Andean field guards. They watched over the livestock feeding on the commons, and when necessary impounded them and assessed the damage done by cattle and trespassers, after which a fine was imposed by the manor court on those responsible. Effective operation of these courts was obviously partly a function of the strength of seignorial authority, but it also depended upon the cooperation of the village community. Although a good deal of friction often existed between the villagers and their lord, they obviously derived considerable benefits from such ready access to a means of resolving local disputes.

The role of the manor court was important in the operation of the commonfield system, but the prerogative of overseeing the regular routine of commonfield husbandry and ensuring that cultivators conformed to its discipline was probably reserved to informal village assemblies.[18] Effectively, all those who owned land in the commonfields had a say in their management and enjoyed an entitlement to the appurtenant common rights usually in proportion to the size of their landholding. The only exceptions were various landless but long-established families within the community who sometimes retained a customary claim upon its resources through retention of the ancient house plot. All those holding such rights were known as commoners.

On the large Worcestershire manor of Halesowen, there were no less than 12 separate commonfield communities, each of which was represented in the central manor court

by two villagers elected by its members, an arrangement
that implies that they must each have possessed some kind
of well-organized self-governing machinery. As in the
Andes, these "assemblies" were almost certainly dominated
and run by the richer peasants, for it was they who usually
fulfilled the majority of manorial offices. Patterns of
social and economic interaction reconstructed by Razi from
these court records indicate a high incidence of reciprocity between peasants, its precise nature varying according
to socioeconomic status. It is his view that in the late
13th and early 14th centuries the manor of Halesowen was
characterized by "a high degree of cohesiveness, cooperation and solidarity as a result of the requirements of
an open-field husbandry, a highly developed corporate
organization, and a sustained and active resistance to the
seigneurial regime" (Razi 1981).

Nevertheless, the strong corporate sense manifest by
these commonfield communities should not be mistaken for
rural egalitarianism. Nor should commonfields be regarded
as an expression of such principles.[19] Cooperation, a
shared identity, and a sense of common purpose at a village level were perfectly compatible with the existence of
sharp inequalities between peasants and marked intragroup
rivalry. Moreover, in the long term, these internal divisions were potentially disruptive to the commonfield
regime, particularly given any changes in the wider
political and/or economic context.

Documentation of the long-entrenched social stratification that existed within these rural communities
is now becoming increasingly available (Dewindt 1972;
Britton 1977; Smith 1979; Razi 1980). Thus, Halesowen
village society may have functioned as a community but
it was also highly monetized and competitive. From his
reading of the evidence, Razi was in no doubt that the
well-to-do vil- lagers were exploiting the needs of their
less well-off neighbors to maximize their profits. Equivalent studies of villages in other parts of England have
come to much the same conclusion. There was no question of
arable land's being periodically reallotted (all attested
cases of reallotment relate to meadow land, a common
resource, like most other sources of herbage). From at
least the middle of the 13th century, it is plain that
peasants had attached strong individual ownership rights
to their land. According to customary law, even villein
land descended according to the prevailing rules of
inheritance within the same family: only in default of
heirs did it revert to the lord, who might then reallocate

it among his tenants. Moreover, an active market in peasant land was already established by this date in much of lowland England. Its effect was generally to encourage the emergence of socioeconomic differences between individual peasant families (Smith 1984b; Harvey 1984). Moreover, through the observation of certain common-sense safeguards, this land market proved in no way inimical to the effective operation of the commonfields.

CONCLUSIONS

That two commonfield systems with such a strong functional affinity should have developed under such fundamentally different technological conditions is highly significant, for several writers on the origin of English commonfields have placed great stress on the role of technology. Seebohm (1883) and Orwin and Orwin (1967), for instance, all have attributed the creation of commonfields to the practice of co-aration or joint plowing using a heavy mold-board plow (Dodgshon 1980:30-34). Yet the culture that evolved such similar agricultural arrangements in the Andes was effectively plowless.

Environmentally, too, there was a vast difference in the circumstances under which these two commonfield systems developed. However, despite the obvious physical differences between the high Andes and lowland England, both environments presented cultivators with an analogous problem. In each case, the productivity of the agricultural system rested upon the maintenance of a delicate ecological balance that required the reconciliation, on the same land, of the conflicting requirements of animal and pastoral husbandry. The need to supply forage to the animals and dung to the soil was the link between them. Even so, that the same basic need should have elicited such a similar institutional response says as much about the sociopolitical conditions prevailing when commonfields emerged, as it does about environmental considerations per se.

As has been shown, English and Andean commonfields only make complete sense when viewed in the context of a specific combination of economic, demographic, social, and political circumstances. The connection between cultivation practices at one extreme and sociopolitical institutions at the other may be difficult to demonstrate empirically, but we believe that it was a real and vital link in both of the cases discussed above.[20] Such a conclusion is not merely of relevance to students of com-

monfield systems: it also provides a warning against
adopting an approach to the whole question of common
property resources that is either too environmentally or
economically deterministic.

These two cases also demonstrate the capacity of common
property resource management systems to take on an
existence of their own, independent of the circumstances
that may have led to their creation. Commonfield systems
were self-perpetuating. This was partly because the system
could only be dismantled if the common rights that applied
to it were dissolved first, and the dissolution of such
rights required a consensus that was particularly difficult
to obtain where there were so many vested interests. The
process of parliamentary enclosure in England provides a
graphic illustration of this and demonstrates that the
intervention of a superior legal authority was sometimes
required before long-established common rights could be
finally extinguished (Tate 1967; Yelling 1977; Turner
1984).

Inertia also derived from the strict adherence to a
specific agricultural routine that a commonfield system
tended to impose upon a community. It was not that
progress was impossible--the system could not have survived for so long had this been the case--but rather that
changes were cumbersome to achieve (Havinden 1961; Dahlman
1980:146-199). Communal consent was required before any
deviations could take place from established crop rotations, or before alterations could be made in the existing
ratio of pasture to tillage. Radical changes in the techniques and intensity of cultivation were consequently to be
avoided. For these various reasons, commonfield systems
had a bias towards the maintenance of the economic and
demographic status quo, and their dependent communities
adopted social and cultural values and demographic
strategies that actually retarded population growth and
technological change (Homans 1941; Howell 1975; Goody et
al. 1976). The resultant symbiosis between commonfield
regime and sociodemographic behavior sometimes endured for
centuries.

Nevertheless, commonfield systems were by no means
immutable. Over time they furnish much evidence of adaptation to new technologies and socioeconomic circumstances.
Parcels have been altered in shape and size, and fields in
layout; new crops have been incorporated into rotations,
and increases made in the number of rotational courses;
livestock stints have been reassessed; and modifications
have been made to the management of fallows.[21] Provided

that the pace of change has been gradual, it has usually been possible for commonfields to adapt themselves to it.

However, problems have arisen when the pace and nature of change have been more revolutionary. In England, for instance, although economic and technological developments rendered commonfield agriculture increasingly anachronistic from the 15th century onwards, so that enclosure by agreement began to make quiet but steady progress, the final demise of the system did not come until the 19th century. Even then, it took powerful economic forces, combined with the facility of enclosure by act of parliament, before the last bastions of the system fell. During this final period, commonfield agriculture was much castigated by agricultural writers so that it became widely regarded as a moribund and inefficient system: recently compiled statistics show a 24.5 percent advantage in crop yields in enclosured, as compared with unenclosed parishes, suggesting that such views were not without practical foundation.[22] This specific historical experience from the last years of an otherwise extremely long-lived institution has tended to color contemporary western attitudes to communally managed resources in general and has been used to support a strong preference for privatized property systems in particular.

Yet in the Andes, the question of enclosure remains very much a live issue. Much privatization of former commonfield land has already taken place, by one means or another, in those areas where agriculture has been most strongly exposed to commercial penetration (Heath et al. 1969:192; Rodriguez-Pastor 1969:86; Mamani 1973:87-88; Preston 1974:247; Mayer 1981:82; Figueroa 1982:133). But away from the influence of the Peruvian coastal cities and the chief towns and mining centers of the Bolivian interior, traditional commonfield agriculture continues largely unaffected. Coincidentally, it is in these same areas that the terrain is most rugged and rural poverty greatest, and this poses a major dilemma for those working in development (Eckholm 1976; Thomas 1979; Guillet 1981; Godoy 1983). Should contemporary Andean commonfields be condemned, like their erstwhile English counterparts, as an obstacle to progress and a cause of rural poverty and backwardness? Or should stress be placed upon the delicate ecological balance that they undoubtedly help to maintain in this high mountain environment, and the sense of corporate identity and solidarity that they nurture in these isolated, materially deprived, and agriculturally dependent communities?

NOTES

1. For the European distribution, see Bloch (1967:
69). For the commonfields in New England, see Walcott
(1936:218-252) and Bidwell and Falconer (1925). For
Andean commonfields, see Godoy and Orlove (forthcoming).
Mesoamerican systems are briefly discussed in Wolf
(1966:20-21). Indian commonfields are described in Wade
(this volume). Middle Eastern systems are discussed in
Goodell (1976:60-68) and in Poyck (1962).

2. For an up-to-date review of the literature on English
commonfield origins, see Fox (1981:64-111). For a
comprehensive treatment of the development of English
commonfields, see Baker and Butlin (1973).

3. Pleas for comparative research in commonfield systems
have been made by Bloch (1967:70), Thirsk (1966), and
McCloskey (1975:91).

4. For the late medieval antecedents of the enclosure
movement, see Fox (1975:181-202) and Campbell (1981a).

5. In this context, it should be noted that the main
reason that the villagers of Vila Vila, in the north of
Potosi, abandoned commonfield tillage was that a frost
would kill everyone's potatoes, since all the villagers
planted potatoes in the same great commonfield (Mamani
1973:88).

6. The most usual arrangement is for male co-heirs to
work a holding as a group: each brother receives the
right to work some parcels within each commonfield, and
further plot fragmentation is thereby halted (Mamani
1973:91-92).

7. The complex economics of the changeover from natural to
produced fodder, and thus from ox- to horse-plowing, are
discussed in Boserup (1965:36-39).

8. For agrarian conditions at this time, see Miller and Hatcher (1978).

9. These different British field systems are surveyed in Baker and Butlin (1973).

10. For a fuller specification of the diagnostic features of these different commonfield systems, see Campbell (1981b:112-129).

11. Households will also be faced with a periodic seasonality of agricultural surpluses or deficits, depending upon the amount of land held in the common-fields open to use.

12. This argument is elaborated more fully in Campbell (1981b). On the strength of seigneurial power at the time that European commonfields were crystallizing, see Duby (1974). For an illustration of the coincidence between variations in lordship and variations in field systems, see Harley (1958:8-18) and Roberts (1973:188-231). For the factors that promoted the institutions of serfdom, see Hatcher (1981:3-39).

13. The post-conquest population collapse is discussed in Dobyns (1963:493-515), in Smith (1970:453-464), and in Shea (1976:157-180).

14. For the pattern of rural settlement in Britain, see Roberts (1979).

15. See, for instance, Albo (1977) and Isbell (1978). Earlier echoes of the same theme may be found in the indigenista literature, as in Valcarcel (1925) and Castro-Pozo (1936).

16. These reapportionments seem to date from Inca times, when they were used to ensure that all households had the means of meeting tribute obligations to the kings in Cuzco (Murra 1980a:xv).
   The system was adapted by the Spanish to serve a similar purpose (see Rowe 1957:182). This practice survives in fossilized form today. The shift from true reallotment to a system of nominal or symbolic reallotment, wherein households continue to use the same parcels year after year, probably reflects a growing shortage of land and concomitant increased specification of individual

land rights (Carter 1964:69; Buechler 1969:179; Preston 1973:3).

17. For the existence of unequal holdings among commonfield farmers in Peru, see also Mishkin (1946:421-422), Soler (1958:190), Matos Mar (1964:130-142), and Guillet (1981:146).

18. For a recent review of the literature on this subject, see Smith (1984a).

19. The notion that primitive egalitarian principles may have underlain the emergence in England of corporate commonfield communities has had several influential advocates. The relevant literature is admirably reviewed in Dodgshon (1980:1-7; 1981:130-140).

20. With reference to the link between the development of commonfield systems and exploitative seigneurial systems, it should be noted that mature commonfield systems are unknown in simple tribal societies and have tended to decline with the emergence of capitalist societies.

21. For English documentation of some of these develop-ments, see Havinden (1961); Baker and Butlin (1973); McCloskey (1975).

22. The literature on agricultural progress and enclosure in the 18th and 19th centuries is voluminous. The best general introduction nevertheless remains Chambers and Mingay (1966).

The statistics on crop yields in enclosed and common-field townships come from the 1801 crop returns and are discussed in Turner (1982:489-510).

REFERENCES

Alberti, G. and E. Meyer, eds. 1974. Reciprocidad e
    intercambio en los Andes Peruanos. Lima: Instituto de
    Estudios Peruanos.

Albo, X. 1977. La paradoja aymara. La Paz: CIPCA.

Allison, K. J. 1957. The sheep-corn husbandry of Norfolk
    in the sixteenth and seventeenth centuries.
    Agricultural History Review 5:12-30.

Allison, K. J. 1958. Flock management in the sixteenth
    and seventeenth centuries. Economic History Review
    (2nd series) 11:98-112.

Anonymous. 1980. The open-field village of Laxton. East
    Midland Geographer 7. Nottingham, England: University
    of Nottingham.

Arguedas, J. M., ed. 1964. Estudios sobre la cultura
    actual del Peru. Lima: Universidad Nacional Mayor de
    San Marcos.

Ault, W. O. 1965. Open-field husbandry and the village
    community: a study of agrarian by-laws in medieval
    England. Transactions of the American Philosophical
    Society.

Baker, A. R. H. 1964. Open fields and partible
    inheritance on a Kent manor. Economic History Review
    (2nd series) 17:1-23.

Baker, A. R. H. 1973. Field systems of southeast England.
    Pp. 393-419 in Baker and Butlin 1973.

Baker, A. R. H. and R. A. Butlin, eds. 1973. Studies of
    Field Systems in the British Isles. Cambridge:
    Cambridge University Press.

- 347 -

Baker, A. R. H. and D. Gregory, eds. 1984. Explora-
    tions in Historical Geography: Interpretive Essays.
    Cambridge: Cambridge University Press.

Beresford, M. W. 1948. Ridge and furrow and the open
    fields. Economic History Review (2nd series) 1:
    34-35.

Biddick, K. ed. 1984. Archaeological Approaches to
    Medieval Europe. Kalamazoo, Michigan: Medieval
    Institute, Western Michigan University.

Bidwell, P. and J. Falconer. 1925. History of Agricul-
    ture in the Northern United States 1620-1860. New
    York: Peter Smith.

Bishop, T. A. M. 1935. Assarting and the growth of the
    open fields. Economic History Review 6:13-29.

Bloch, M. 1967. Land and Work in Medieval Europe.
    Berkeley, California: University of California Press.

Boserup, E. 1965. The conditions of agricultural growth:
    the economics of agrarian change under population
    pressure. London: George Allen and Unwin.

Britton, E. 1977. The Community of the Vill: A Study
    in the History of the Family and Village Life in
    Fourteenth Century England. Toronto: Macmillan.

Browman, D. L. n.d. Llama caravan fleteros, and their
    importance in production and distribution. Unpublished
    manuscript.

Brush, S. 1980. The environment and native Andean
    agriculture. America Indigena 40:163.

Brush, S. 1981. Estrategías agrícolas tradicionales en
    las zonas montanosas de America Latina. Seminario
    internacional sobre producción agropecuaria y forestal
    en zonas de ladera de America tropical. Informe
    Técnico 11. Turrialba, Costa Rica: Centro Agronómico
    Tropical de Investigación y Ensenanza.

Buechler, H. C. 1969. Land reform and social revolution
    in the northern altiplano and yungas of Bolivia.
    P. 179 in Heath et al. 1969.

Caballero, J. M. 1981. Economia agraria de la sierre
    Peruana. Lima: Instituto de Estudios Peruanos.

Camino, A., J. Recharte, and P. Bidegaray. 1981.
    Flexibilidad calendarica en la agricultura tradicional
    de las vertientes orientales de los Andes. Pp. 169-194
    in Lechtman and Soldi 1981.

Campbell, B. M. S. 1980. Population change and the
    genesis of commonfields on a Norfolk manor. Economic
    History Review (2nd series) 33:174-192.

Campbell, B. M. S. 1981a. The extent and layout of
    commonfields in eastern Norfolk. Norfolk Archaeology
    38:5-32.

Campbell, B. M. S. 1981b. Commonfield origins--the
    regional dimension. Pp. 112-129 in Rowley 1981.

Campbell, B. M. S. 1981c. The regional uniqueness
    of English field systems? Some evidence from
    eastern Norfolk. Agricultural History Review 29:
    16-28.

Campbell, B. M. S. 1983. Agricultural progress in
    medieval England: some evidence from eastern
    Norfolk. Economic History Review (2nd series)
    36:26-46.

Carter, W. E. 1964. Aymara Communities and the
    Bolivian Agrarian Reform. Social Science Mono-
    graph 24. Gainesville, Florida: University of
    Florida.

Carter, W. and M. Mamani. 1982. Irpa Chico. La Paz:
    Juventud.

Castro-Pozo, H. 1936. Del ayllu al cooperativismo
    socialista. Lima: Juan Mejia Baca.

Chambers, J. D. and G. E. Mingay. 1966. The Agricultural
    Revolution 1750-1880. London: Batsford.

Chevallier, F. 1953. La formation des grands domaines
    au Mexique. Terre et société XVI-XVII sèicles.
    Paris: Institut d'Ethnologie, Musée de l'Homme.

Crawford, R. M. M., D. Wishart, and R. M. Campbell. 1970. A numerical analysis of high altitude scrub vegetation in relation to soil erosion in the eastern Cordilerra. Journal of Ecology 58:173-181.

Custred, G. 1974. Llameros y comercio inter-regional. Pp. 252-289 in Alberti and Mayer 1974.

Custred, G. and B. Orlove. 1974. Sectorial fallowing and crop rotation systems in the Peruvian highlands. Paper presented at the 41st International Congress of Americanists.

Dahlman, C. J. 1980. The Open Field System and Beyond: A Property Rights Analysis of an Economic Institution. Cambridge: Cambridge University Press.

Degregori, C. and J. Golte. 1973. Dependencia y desintegración estructural en la comunidad de Pacaraos. Lima: Instituto de Estudios Peruanos.

Denevan, W. N. ed. 1976. The Native Population of the Americas in 1492. Madison, Wisconsin: University of Wisconsin Press.

Dewindt, E. B. 1972. Land and People in Holywell-cum-Needingworth: Structures of Tenure and Patterns of Social Organization in an East Midlands Village 1252-1457. Toronto: Pontifical Institute of Mediaeval Studies.

Dobyns, H. 1963. An outline of Andean epidemic history to 1720. Bulletin of the History of Medicine 37:493-515.

Dodgshon, R. A. 1980. The Origin of British Fields Systems: An Interpretation. London: Academic Press.

Dodgshon, R. A. 1981. The interpretation of subdivided fields: a study in private or communal interests? Pp. 130-144 in Rowley 1981.

Donkin, R. A. 1979. Agricultural terracing in the aboriginal New World. Tucson, Arizona: University of Arizona Press.

Duby, G. 1974. The Early Growth of the European Economy: Warriors and Peasants from the Seventh to the Twelfth Century. London: Weidenfeld and Nicolson.

Eckholm, E. 1976. Losing Ground. New York: Norton.

Elliott, G. 1973. Field systems of northwest England. Pp. 42-92 in Baker and Butlin 1973.

Eyre, S. R. 1955. The curving ploughstrip and its historical implications. Agricultural History Review 3:80-94.

Figueroa, A. 1982. Production and market exchange in peasant economies: the case of the southern highlands in Peru. Pp. 126-156 in Lehman 1982.

Fox, H. S. A. 1975. The chronology of enclosure and economic development in medieval Devon. Economic History Review (2nd series) 28:181-202.

Fox, H. S. A. 1981. Approaches to the adoption of the midland system. Pp. 64-111 in Rowley 1981.

Fox, H. S. A. 1984. Some ecological dimensions of medieval field systems. Pp. 119-158 in Biddick 1984.

Freeman, P. 1980. Ecologically oriented agriculture. Unpublished manuscript.

Fujii, T. and H. Tomoeda. 1981. Chacra, laime y auquenidos. Pp. 33-63 in Masuda 1981.

Gade, D. 1970. Ecología del robo agrícola en las tierras altas de los Andes centrales. America Indigena 30, No. 1:3-14.

Gade, D. and M. Escobar. 1982. Village settlement and the colonial legacy in southern Peru. Geographical Review 72, No. 4:430-449.

Gade, D. and R. Rios. 1976. La chaquitaclla: herramienta indigena sudamericana. America Indigena 36:359-374.

Godoy, R. A. 1983. From Indian to miner and back again: small scale mining in the Jukumani Ayllu, northern Potosi, Bolivia. Ph.D. dissertation. New York: Columbia University.

Godoy, R. A. 1985. State, ayllu, and ethnicity in northern Potosi. Anthropos 80:53-65.

Godoy, R. A. and B. S. Orlove. Forthcoming. Andean commonfield agriculture. Journal of Ethnobiology.

Goodell, G. 1976. The Elementary Structures of Political Life. Ph.D. dissertation. New York: Columbia University.

Goody, J. R., J. Thirsk, and E. P. Thompson, eds. 1976. Family and Inheritance: Rural Society in Western Europe, 1200-1800. Cambridge: Cambridge University Press.

Guillet, D. 1979. Agrarian Reform and Peasant Economy in Southern Peru. Columbia, Missouri: University of Missouri Press.

Guillet, D. 1981. Land tenure, ecological zone, and agricultural regime in the central Andes. American Ethnologist 8:139-156.

Hall, D. 1981. The origins of open-field agriculture--the archaeological field evidence. Pp. 23-25 in Rowley 1981.

Harley, J. B. 1958. Population trends and agricultural developments from the Warwickshire Hundred Rolls of 1279. Economic History Review (2nd series) 11:8-18.

Harvey, P. D. A., ed. 1984. The Peasant Land Market in Medieval England. Oxford: Oxford University Press.

Hatcher, J. 1981. English serfdom and villeinage: towards a reassessment. Past and Present 90:3-39.

Havinden, M. 1961. Agricultural progress in open-field Oxfordshire. Agricultural History Review 9:73-88.

Heath, D., H. Buechler, and C. Erasmus. 1969. Land Reform and Social Revolution in Bolivia. New York: Praeger.

Homans, G. C. 1941. English Villagers of the Thirteenth Century. Cambridge, Massachusetts: Harvard University Press.

Howell, C. 1975. Stability and change 1300-1700: the socio-economic context of the self-perpetuating family farm in England. Journal of Peasant Studies 2:468-482.

Hoyle, B. S., ed. 1974. Spatial Aspects of Development. London: John Wiley and Sons.

Isbell, B. J. 1978. To Defend Ourselves: Ecology and Ritual in an Andean Village. Austin, Texas: University of Texas Press.

Kerridge, E. 1951. Ridge and furrow and agrarian history. Economic History Review (2nd series) 4:14-36.

Langdon, J. 1983. Horses, oxen and technological innovation: the use of draught animals in English farming from 1066 to 1500. Ph.D. dissertation. Birmingham, England: Birmingham University.

Le Baron, A., L. K. Bond, P. Aitkens, and L. Michaelsen. 1979. An explanation of the Bolivian highlands grazing erosion syndrome. Journal of Range Management 32, No. 39:201-208.

LaBarre, W. 1947. Potato taxonomy among the Aymara Indians of Bolivia. Acta Americana 6:83-103.

Lechtman, H. and A. M. Soldi, eds. 1981. La tecnología en el mundo andino. Mexico City: Universidad Nacional Autonoma de México.

Lehmann, D., ed. 1982. Ecology and Exchange in the Andes. Cambridge Studies in Social Anthropology, 41.

Lewellen, T. 1978. Peasant in Transition: The Changing Economy of the Peruvian Aymara. A General Systems Approach. Boulder, Colorado: Westview Press.

Malaga Medina, A. 1974. Las reducciónes en el Perú durante el Virrey Francisco de Toledo. Anuario de Estudios Americanos 31:819-842.

Mamani, M. P. 1973. El rancho de Vila Vila. La Paz: Consejo Nacional de Reforma Agraria.

Masuda, S., ed. 1981. Estudios etnográficos del Perú meridional. Tokyo: Universidad de Tokyo.

Matos Mar, J. 1958. Las actuales comunidades de indigenas: Huarochiri en 1955. Lima: Instituto de Etnología y Arqueología.

Matos Mar, J. 1964. La propiedad en la isla de Taquile (Lago Titicaca). In Arguedas 1964.

Mayer, E. 1981. Uso de la tierra en los Andes: ecología y agricultura en el valle del Mantaro del Perú con referencia especial a la papa. Lima: Central Internacional de la Papa.

McBride, G. 1921. The Agrarian Indian Communities of Highland Bolivia. New York: Oxford University Press.

McCloskey, D. 1975. The persistence of English common fields. Pp. 73-119 in Parker and Jones 1975.

McCloskey, D. 1976. English open fields as behaviour toward risk. Research in Economic History 1:124-170.

McPherson, M. F. 1983. Land fragmentation in agriculture: adverse? beneficial? and for whom? Development and Discussion Paper 145. Cambridge, Massachusetts: Harvard Institute for International Development.

Metraux, A. 1959. The social and economic structure of the Indian communities of the Andean region. International Labour Review 74:231.

Miller, E. and J. Hatcher. 1978. Medieval England--Rural Society and Economic Change 1086-1348. London: Longman.

Mishkin, B. 1946. The contemporary Quechua. Pp. 411-470 in Steward 1946.

Murra, J. V. 1980a. Waman Puma, etnografo del mundo andino. Pp. xiii-xix in Murra 1980b.

Murra, J. V. 1980b. El Primer Nueva Coronica y Buen Gobierno. Mexico: Siglo Veintiuno.

Orlove, B. 1976. The tragedy of the commons revisited: land use and environmental quality in high-altitude Andean grasslands. Pp. 208-214 in Hill Lands: Proceedings of An International Symposium. Morgantown, West Virginia: West Virginia University Press.

Orlove, B. 1977. Alpaca, Sheep, and Men: The Wool Export
    Economy and Regional Society in Southern Peru. New
    York: Academic Press.

Orwin, C. S. and C. S. Orwin. 1967. The Open Fields.
    Third edition. Oxford: Clarendon Press.

Parker, W. and E. Jones, eds., 1975. European Peasants
    and Their Markets. Princeton, New Jersey: Princeton
    University Press.

Platt, T. 1982. The role of the Andean ayllu in the
    reproduction of the petty commodity regime in northern
    Potosi (Bolivia). Pp. 27-69 in Lehmann 1982.

Popkin, S. 1979. The Rational Peasant. Berkeley,
    California: University of California Press.

Postgate, M. R. 1973. Field systems of East Anglia.
    Pp. 281-322 in Baker and Butlin 1973.

Poyck, A. P. G. 1962. Farm Studies in Iraq. Mededelingen
    van den Landbouwhogeschool te Wageningen, Nederland 62.

Preston, D. 1973. Agriculture in a highland desert: the
    central altiplano of Bolivia. Department of Geography,
    Working Paper 18:6. Leeds, England: University of
    Leeds.

Preston, D. A. 1974. Land tenure and agricultural
    development in the central altiplano, Bolivia.
    Pp. 231-251 in Hoyle 1974.

Rasnake, R. 1981. The 'Kurahkuna'. Ph.D. dissertation.
    Ithaca, New York: Cornell University.

Ravines, R. 1978a. Recursos naturales de los Andes. In
    Ravines 1978b.

Ravines, R., ed. 1978b. Tecnología Andina. Lima:
    Instituto de Estudios Peruanos.

Razi, Z. 1980. Life, Marriage and Death in a Medieval
    Parish: Economy, Society and Demography in Halesowen
    (1270-1400). Cambridge: Cambridge University Press.

Razi, Z. 1981. Family, land and the village community in later medieval England. Past and Present 93:16.

Rhoades, R. E. and S. I. Thompson. 1975. Adaptive strategies in Alpine environments: beyond ecological particularism. American Ethnologist 2:535-551.

Roberts, B. K. 1973. Field systems of the west midlands. Pp. 188-231 in Baker and Butlin 1973.

Roberts, B. K. 1979. Rural Settlement in Britain. London: Hutchinson.

Rodriguez-Pastor, H. 1969. Progresismo y cambios en Llica. Pp. 73-143 in Sabogal Wiesse 1969.

Rowe, J. H. 1957. The Incas under Spanish colonial institutions. Hispanic American Historical Review 37:182.

Rowley, T., ed. 1981. The Origins of Open Field Agriculture. London: Croom Helm.

Sabogal Wiesse, J. R. ed. 1969. La Comunidad Andina. Mexico City, Mexico: Instituto Indigenista Interamericano.

Seebohm, F. 1883. The English Village Community. London: Longmans, Green and Company.

Shea, D. 1976. A defense of small population estimates for the central Andes in 1520. Pp. 157-180 in Denevan 1976.

Sheppard, J. A. 1966. Pre-enclosure field and settlement patterns in an English township: Wheldrake, near York. Geografiska Annaler 48 (Series B):59-77.

Simpson, A. 1958. The East Anglian foldcourse; some queries. Agricultural History Review 6:87-96.

Smith, C. T. 1970. Depopulation of the central Andes in the 16th century. Current Anthropology 11:453-464.

Smith, R. M. 1979. Kin and neighbours in a thirteenth century Suffolk community. Journal of Family History 4:219-259.

Smith, R. M. 1984a. 'Modernization' and the corporate medieval village community in England: some sceptical reflections. Pp. 140-194 in Baker and Gregory 1984.

Smith, R. M., ed. 1984b. Land, Kinship and Life-cycle. Cambridge: Cambridge University Press.

Soler, E. 1958. La comunidad de San Pedro de Huancaire. Pp. 167-257 in Matos Mar 1958.

Steward, J. H. ed. 1946. Handbook of South American Indians. Vol. II. Bulletin 143. Washington, D.C.: Bureau of Ethnology.

Tandeter, E. 1981. Forced and free labour in late colonial Potosi. Past and Present 93:98-136.

Tate, W. E. 1967. The English Village Community and the Enclosure Movements. London: Gollancz.

Thirsk, J. 1964. The common fields. Past and Present 29:3-9.

Thirsk, J. 1966. The origins of the common fields. Past and Present 33:143.

Thomas, B. 1979. Effects of change on high mountain adaptive patterns. Pp. 139-188 in Webber 1979.

Turner, M. 1982. Agricultural productivity in England in the eighteenth century: evidence from crop yields. Economic History Review (2nd series) 35:489-510.

Turner, M. 1984. Enclosures in Britain 1750-1830. London: Macmillan.

Urioste, M. 1977. La economía del campesinado altiplanico en 1976. La Paz: Universidad Católica Boliviana.

Valcarcel, L. 1925. Del ayllu al imperio. Lima: Editorial Garcilaso.

Walcott, R. 1936. Husbandry in colonial New England. New England Quarterly 9:218-252.

Webber, P. J., ed. 1979. High-altitude Geoecology. Boulder, Colorado: Westview Press.

Winterhalder, B., R. Larsen, and B. Thomas. 1974. Dung as an essential resource in a highland Peruvian community. Human Ecology 2:89-104.

Wolf, E. 1966. Peasants. Englewood Cliffs, New Jersey: Prentice-Hall.

Wordie, J. R. 1983. The chronology of English enclosure, 1500-1914. Economic History Review (2nd series) 36:483-505.

Yelling, J. A. 1977. Common Field and Enclosure in England, 1450-1850. London: Macmillan.

Information Problems Involved in Partitioning the Commons for Cultivation in Botswana [1]

Susan G. Wynne

INTRODUCTION TO THE PROBLEM

In 1968, Botswana's central government authorities
assumed responsibility for a major reform of traditional
land and water resource management institutions that had
been in operation since the mid-19th century. The new
administrative system of land boards established by the
Tribal Land Act of 1968 was expected to provide more
professional resource management and end discrimination in
the allocation of use-rights to resources (Hitchcock 1985;
Peters 1983; Roberts 1980). By 1970, twelve main land
boards were in operation. They were responsible for
managing tribal land[2] used for cultivation, grazing,
family housing and commercial purposes, and for all water
resources. Numerous subordinate land boards, which were
assigned responsibility for managing land used for village
housing and cultivation, were authorized in 1973.

Despite the thoughtful attention devoted to the design
of the land board system, substantial conflict continues to
surround the management of land in Botswana (Machacha 1981;
Roe and Fortmann 1982; Werbner 1980). Disregard for the
rules by which cultivation land is supposed to be managed
has emerged as a persistent and widespread problem.
Farmers have cleared and plowed fields not authorized for
such use, illegally extended the boundaries of their
existing fields, and altered new boundary markers erected

by land board members. At the same time, land board
members are known to have refused allocation requests to
protect their own interests or those of relatives in
undeveloped land.

Two different explanations could be advanced to explain
the existence of the conflict and illegal behavior that
followed this institutional reform. One is that the
problems that have arisen are the result of confusion
created by institutional changes--neither officials nor
ordinary citizens understand the intent and substance of
the new procedures and rules. A second explanation is that
the new rules have had the unintended result of creating
situations that offer officials and farmers opportunities
to act in perverse ways that generate conflict.

Sorting out which of these explanations is correct is
an important problem for policymakers in settings where
institutions have been changed.[3] The particular conclusion they reach has major implications for further action.
Acceptance of the first explanation suggests the need only
for additional training and public education. Since this
explanation for the continued conflict has been most widely
accepted by central ministry officials in Botswana,
substantial funds have been spent to improve understanding
of new arrangements. Acceptance of the second suggests the
need for changes in the design of the institutions in order
to restructure incentives.

In this paper, I will use information about land-use
patterns and the administrative problems of the residents
of the village of Lethakeng, located in the Kweneng
District of Botswana, as the basis for my own analysis of
this problem. My conclusion differs from that of the
special interministerial committee established in 1977 by
Botswana's Ministry of Local Government and Lands (the
ministry), the central government authority with principal
responsibility for the land boards, to diagnose the causes
of this illegal behavior. The committee's suggestions to
the ministry reflect the conclusion that conflict has
developed largely as a result of implementation problems
(Botswana Ministry of Local Government and Land 1978).[4]

NATURE OF THE RESOURCE

Land differs in some important respects from other
resources that are frequently managed as common properties.
In this section, I will identify those characteristics of
common lands used for cultivation purposes that pose

particular problems for the design of appropriate management institutions. I will also briefly describe those
features of the physical and social environment of the
central Kweneng District that largely account for the way
grain cultivation is organized in this area. Characteristics of the resource and of the social organization of production strongly influence farmers' strategies in their
interaction with other farmers and with land board members.
They also constitute the physical and social "givens" to
which appropriate land management rules must be fitted.

Nature of a Cultivation Commons

Resources such as underground water basins, fisheries,
forests, bridges, and pastures, though highly diverse,
demonstrate important analytic similarities that are the
basis for their categorization as common-pool resources.
All can be thought of as natural or artifactual systems
that, over time, generate a finite flow (or pool) of
benefits such as water, fish, fuel, crossings, and grazing.
Each resource user consumes a portion of this stream of
benefits. Consumption of benefits is subtractive. The
exclusion of interested users from the pool of benefits is
difficult, in most cases, because of the physical characteristics of the resource systems themselves. The difficulty of exclusion, along with the subtractive nature of
consumption, means that the productivity of resources in
this category may be endangered by inappropriate patterns
of use.

The nature of the distribution of property rights in
both the resource system and the flow of benefits generated
by the system is an artifact of human design created to
preserve the productivity of the resource (V. Ostrom 1980).
Because of the physical characteristics of these systems,
rights in common-pool resource systems are frequently, but
not necessarily, held by a group of people "in common"
rather than by a single individual. As soon as the demand
for benefits produced by the systems exceeds the supply,
consumption of the benefit flow must be limited. This is
usually achieved by partitioning the flow of benefits and
assigning well-specified bundles of rights in a portion of
the flow to specific consumption units. These consumption
units may be individuals or groups. The bundle of rights
assigned to each unit may or may not include the right to
independently transfer rights in the system or in the flow
to others.

In Botswana, land used for cultivation is held in common. Fertile soil is the natural resource system that produces a stream of "cultivation possibilities" that can be realized in the form of crops. Resource consumption is subtractive in that one portion of fertile land cannot be simultaneously cultivated by two producers. The difficulty of excluding interested users from the resource system derives from the strength of long-standing community norms that state that land belongs to all members of a community and that all who wish to cultivate should have rights to a plot of land. Even those who no longer accept this norm, however, believe that altering long-standing and well-known arrangements for resource consumption would entail high social costs. The more isolated portions of Botswana's population may be unaware of alternative ways of distributing rights in land.

Members of Botswana's land boards function as managers of district land. As such they are authorized to assign rights to individuals to appropriate the crops those individuals produce on a portion of this soil system. The "producers" who cultivate and then consume the benefit stream generated by the soil resource are actually groups of kin who form production teams. Land board members are also responsible for assisting the users of each existing field to exclude others from the portion of this resource system already assigned to them.

Common land used for cultivation purposes is an unusual common-pool resource in that it requires the partitioning and the assignment of consumption rights regardless of the level of demand for the benefit flow. This is because the application of human labor is necessary to realize the cultivation possibilities inherent in fertile land. Use of land for cultivation, unlike the use of land for grazing or the open sea for fishing, requires the actual physical division of land into separate plots. Otherwise, producers--whether these be individuals, groups, or an entire community--would have difficulty in appropriating the benefits generated by their work on the resource system. Land cannot be used for cultivation in the absence of rules that assign the production teams rights to the flow of crops from their plots. Fertile land that is being cultivated is, thus, always managed in some sense.

The inappropriate use of common lands for cultivation can lead to an outcome similar to that which follows from the inappropriate use of a commonly held pasture or fishery. The overutilization of a grazing commons not only depletes the existing pool of benefits but also adversely affects edible plants' ability to regenerate. The mismanagement of a cultivation commons decreases the soil's capacity to generate cultivation possibilities; this happens when users are able to mine fertile soil and then move on to other areas.

Poor management of a cultivation commons is often less threatening to the resource system than to the net value to production teams of the crop yields. Recurrent conflict over rights to land is attended by increased costs as more labor is devoted to the surveillance and negotiation needed to prevent incursion or the destruction of crops planted on contested plots. The efficiency of crop production is reduced by virtue of increased costs for equal or reduced levels of agricultural output. Conflict over land may also heighten tension in a community and reduce the possibility of collective agreement on other issues of common concern. Reciprocal hostility can eventually lead to generalized warfare. Land then goes unutilized despite high levels of demand for the crops that the fertile soil could produce.

The Cultivation Commons in Letlhakeng

Characteristics of the natural and social environments in which Letlhakeng residents find themselves have influenced the organization of their agricultural production activities. In turn, the way agricultural production is organized crucially affects the general pattern of demand for land in this area where, in the past, the supply of fertile land has not been a limiting factor. The management authority's operational rules for the commons determine the pattern of supply. The degree of congruence between patterns of demand and supply has had an important impact on the attitudes of villagers toward land management authorities.

The Natural and Social Environments of Central Kweneng

Letlhakeng is the largest settlement located in an extraordinary network of fossil river valleys in central Kweneng District. The fertility of the black soil, the dense vegetation, and the numerous points at which underground water can be tapped with pit wells and boreholes in these valleys contrasts sharply with the sandy soils of the surrounding grass and <u>Acacia</u> brush savanna that contains no perennial water sources.

The harsh climate of the region in which these rich valleys are set, however, makes grain production unreliable. The local, average annual rainfall level of approximately 350 to 400 mm is just sufficient for the rain-fed sorghum cultivation practiced in the area, and then only if the rainfall is not interrupted for lengthy periods during the growing season. The variability of rainfall levels, however, is high. Nighttime winter temperatures low enough for frost bring the single growing season to a very distinct end. The timeliness of plowing is thus a crucial determinant of the size of grain harvests in good rainfall years.

In this arid, tsetse-free region, keeping cattle is the preferred economic activity. Herd owners attempt to keep herd growth rates high by selling off young male animals to buy female calves. Cattle are seldom eaten, however, and, due to the uncertainty of rainfall, grain production has never provided a dependable source of food. Since the 1920s, men from the area have depended upon employment opportunities in the mines of what is now the Republic of South Africa and in Botswana's towns to supplement their grain production activities.

The settlement of Letlhakeng was formed in 1942 when protectorate district administrators asked seven small, scattered communities (<u>makgotla</u>) to move to a central location. These <u>makgotla</u> (singular: <u>lekgotla</u>) are composed largely of fragments of one of three distantly related patrilineages--the Babolaongwe, the Bakgwatheng, and the Bashaga--known collectively as Bakgalagadi (people of the desert). Before 1970, adult males secured rights to land primarily through their membership in a <u>lekgotla</u>. Bashaga-baga-Sekgalo are the only exception, having always cultivated land given originally to the leader of the Baga-Motsoto <u>lekgotla</u>. Fields are still cleared and plowed by men for wives who are responsible for cultivation. Upon her death, a woman's youngest daughter has first claim to her field. Household wealth, held primarily in the form of cattle, continues to be controlled by the head until his death. The inheritance rule for livestock, which once approximated primogeniture, has been gradually abandoned in favor of greater equality of distribution among male and occasionally female heirs.

The inheritance rule has been changed in part in response to the increased financial independence of young men made possible by wage labor opportunities. The prospect of a larger inheritance serves as an incentive for younger sons to forego the higher personal income they could derive from continuous wage employment in order to contribute their labor to their family's cultivation and cattle-raising enterprise. A household owning some cattle whose members live to old age and that is well-endowed with male children who cooperate fully in operating the household enterprise can maintain cultivation simultaneously with cattle raising and wage labor (Henderson 1980). Many households, however, lack one or more of these elements. Survey data show that even married women must frequently rely on members of the extended family for assistance in plowing and supervising livestock.[5]

New wage labor opportunities for men have raised the value of men's labor relative to that of women's and contributed to the decline in polygyny. Social pressure to observe monogamy, accompanied by continued high fertility rates and male preference for younger wives, have produced a "surplus" of women. Some women now produce children but never marry. The divorce rate has also risen. As a result, male household heads today find themselves, for varying periods of time, responsible for several adult women who are not married to them. The productivity of these unmarried, divorced, or widowed women is largely a function of the degree to which a male household head successfully integrates them into his production activity. The improvement of educational facilities in the village has aggravated the agricultural labor problem particularly in those cases where household fields and cattle are located far from the village school (Chernichovsky 1981; Mueller 1981; Froysa 1983).

The Organization of Cultivation and Common Features of the Local Demand for Land

The greater reliability of income from wage labor and from cattle raising in this uncertain environment has drawn adult male labor away from cultivation activity. Young men face substantial short-term opportunity costs in foregoing wage labor opportunities in order to help with household agricultural activities. Households also face high opportunity costs in foregoing the exchange of male for female calves in order to maintain a plowing team of four to six oxen. This has meant that the supply of adult male labor and draft oxen are the scarce inputs into grain production.[6] In view of these constraints, one would

predict that cultivation land, which has been the
relatively abundant input in this area, would be developed
by villagers in ways that economize on the use of the two
scarcest inputs.

The pattern of cultivation in this area is consistent
with this prediction. The cultivation of larger fields
with the aid of the plow dates from the 1930s when diminishing local supplies of game animals could no longer
support the expanding population. Sons cleared fields for
their wives near their mother's field so they could make
use of the oxen team controlled by their father until his
death. Even after a father's death, brothers often kept
the herd together and maintained contiguous grain fields.
This enabled several brothers to share a single plowing
team, thereby reducing the number of male animals that they
had to maintain in their collective cattle holding, while
still plowing all their fields in a timely fashion.
Further, only one son was needed to plow the widowed
mother's field and those of his wife and sisters-in-law
while his brothers worked outside the village.

Earlier patterns of land allocation practiced in the
area were well fitted to this way of organizing production.
Grants of use-rights to cultivation land in the Letlhakeng
area were of varying sizes, but all grants were blocks of
land larger than the size of the single field initially
developed. These blocks of land were allocated to individual heads of households in anticipation of the later
development of additional fields for a second or third wife
and for the wives of sons and grandsons. Buffers of land
between blocks served as a grazing area for cattle kept
near the fields in the growing season. Rights in land were
retained even though the holder did not or could not
cultivate a field for many years because of absence from
the village, illness, or drought.

In the 1950s and 1960s, the size of new allocations
decreased in the more intensely developed plowing areas.
The general pattern of earlier land development, however,
remains popular today. A survey of current land use practices indicates that the fields of sons are often developed
in close proximity to those of their father, as are the
fields of dependent, adult female relatives (see Wynne,
forthcoming). The clustered-fields pattern in current use
closely resembles the clustering of fields belonging to the
wives and daughters-in-law of one man that was characteristic of earlier times. Clustering fields continues to
simplify and expedite plowing in those cases in which one
oxen team is used to plow several fields.

As relative scarcity in the plowing areas has become more severe, the value of undeveloped land surrounding the fields of established farmers has assumed even greater value to household heads who resume responsibility for a widowed or divorced daughter, sister, or sister-in-law. Fields earlier abandoned may acquire new value for similar reasons. New means of providing cultivation opportunities for unskilled female labor have also developed in recent years. A person who has not yet cleared his/her own field may borrow a field belonging to a relative who owns a plowing team. Some widows borrow land for long periods of time. Some also hire plowing services from owners of oxen teams. A partnership owning one of the two tractors in the village is eager to sell plowing services. While these services are as yet above the means of many middle income families in the area, they open up the possibility of substituting capital for labor in plowing in the future.

The absence of adult males, in conjunction with a greater appreciation for the advantages of education, has meant that the supply of labor for day-to-day herd management has been reduced. Survey data indicate that most households owning small- to medium-sized herds keep their animals in or near their cultivation area for much of the year (see Wynne, forthcoming). Even households that graze large herds at distant boreholes may keep plowing oxen and milk cows near their fields.

DECISION-MAKING ARRANGEMENTS

Rules, in combination with the characteristics of the natural and social environments of central Kweneng, shape the context in which land board members and farmers devise strategies of interaction with resources and with each other. In this effort to explain conflict over land in this area, two types of rules have been selected for careful attention out of the dense network of rules that order life in Letlhakeng: (1) authority rules define the structure of the land board system (including the ministry and other institutions of local government) that constitutes the arena in which decisions about operational rules for the cultivation commons are made; and (2) partitioning rules, a subset of operational rules for the cultivation commons, are used by land board members to determine the size and spacing of new field site allocations. Although rules always work in configurations (E. Ostrom 1986), partitioning rules are emphasized here because they are

particularly important in affecting the strategies of farmers and because they are difficult to design for cultivation commons. These rules were also substantially changed
when the land board system of allocation began operation.

The Use of Partitioning Rules

The potential of a cultivation commons cannot be fully
realized in the absence of rules that effectively bound,
determine access to, and divide the common land. Boundary
rules are used to define the physical limits of the soil
surfaces that may be used for cultivation. Entry rules
determine which persons or groups qualify for cultivation
rights within the bounded area. In the case of common land
used for cultivation, partitioning rules direct the
physical division of a soil surface into fields with
attendant streams of cultivation possibilities. Dividing
fertile soil into fields indirectly partitions the future
flow of crops.

Partitioning rules for cultivation commons are
especially difficult to devise because individuals can be
expected to have strong preferences for the use of a specific portion of the commons. Partitioning rules for a
common pasture, in contrast, need make few provisions for
the location of actual consumption. Although the location
of the commons itself in relation to other facilities may
be important for livestock owners, the owners are likely to
be indifferent to where their animals actually graze within
the pasture.

As a consequence of the particular partitioning rule
being applied, each plot assigned to a production team
acquires specific dimensions and spatial relations to
fields owned by others as well as to water sources, grazing pastures, roads, etc. Access to specific locations
within the boundaries of the cultivation commons itself can
assume significance because of differences in soil
fertility and in the ease of achieving cooperation among
producers. In societies where cooperation in stages of
cultivation is widespread, the location of land is as
important as access to land itself.

Partitioning the Cultivation Commons in Letlhakeng

The land boards replaced a land management system in
Kweneng that had been in operation since about 1855. For

the purposes of day-to-day management, chiefdom land had been divided among the leaders of the three major sections of the dominant social group, the Bakwena. Each section leader had further distributed responsibility for large areas to leaders of subordinate makgotla within his section and to leaders of Bakgalagadi makgotla (which were attached at that time to his section as subject people). Leaders of Bakgalagadi makgotla that was settled near Letlhakeng chose overseers who organized the development of each cultivation area as it was established.

Subordinate officials in this system were required to carry out the policies of the Bakwena chief and section leaders. In practice, however, Bakgalagadi managed land and water resources with considerable independence. Because population densities were very low and the cost of moving from one small settlement of kin to another in western Kweneng was also low, Bakgalagadi authorities were considerate of the preferences of others in their cultivation areas. Allocation decisions by overseers could be appealed up the hierarchy of authority to the lekgotla headman, the Bakwena section leader, and finally the Bakwena chief. Most land disputes were, however, settled locally.

By the late 1950s, population densities had increased considerably. Makgotla overseers and headmen began refusing more frequently to allocate new fields; this they did to keep troublesome people out of an area, to preserve access to undeveloped land in the area for the authority or his neighbors, or to punish people for purely personal reasons. Authorities were especially likely to refuse allocations to people from other makgotla. Efforts to reform land management in the late 1960s were intended to reduce discrimination in access to land.

Land Administration Reform

In accordance with the Tribal Land Act of 1968, a single land board began operation in each of Botswana's administrative districts in 1970. By 1973, five subordinate land boards had been established in Kweneng to allocate rights to new housing and field sites. The district board retained authority over all rights to commercial business sites and water sources. Dramatic changes were made in land management jurisdictions and personnel. The six lekgotla headmen and their numerous overseers who had managed the cultivation and grazing land near Letlhakeng

were replaced by the four members of the new subordinate
land board for central Kweneng whose office was established
in Letlhakeng.[7] This board's jurisdiction covers an area
of approximately 7,000 square kilometers. Its members
manage four to five times as much land area as did their
predecessors.[8]

The Ministry of Local Government and Lands, the Kweneng
District Council, the Kweneng District Land Board, and a
meeting of headmen of all villages within the jurisdiction each appoints one member of each subordinate land
board in Kweneng. Members are usually selected so that
four different villages in the jurisdiction are represented. Their five-year term of office runs concurrently
with the terms of office of all national and district-
level elected officials in Botswana. Members may be
reappointed to their positions. The board convenes every
other month for a week or two to process applications and
to make physical demarcations. The members' sitting
allowances are paid out of the district council budget.
The permanent administrative staff members of all boards
belong to the nationwide civil service organization for
district-level personnel, which is administered as part of
the Ministry of Local Government and Lands.

Although the district land board is considered the
principal land management authority in each district, the
minister can veto regulations issued by the district
boards. He is also authorized to issue his own regulations to direct the work of all land boards. Subordinate
land board members are required to apply rules contained in
statutes, ministry regulations, and district land board
instructions. The administrative secretary of each
district land board is responsible for explaining policy
directives to and monitoring the work of the members of the
district and subordinate boards.

The representative bodies at the sub-national level--
the district councils and village development committees--
have no rule-making authority over land management. The
Tribal Land Act requires that district land boards consult
with district councils regarding policies. The ministry
also expects members of subordinate land boards to consult
with the relevant village development committees regarding
allocations, although these bodies have no veto powers.
At the time of the trouble case, only sporadic consultation took place between the Letlhakeng subordinate land
board and the rather inactive village development
committee.

New Partitioning Rules

Before 1970, land in the Letlhakeng area was managed by
makgotla leaders with significant independence as six
makgotla commons.[9] Under the authority of the overseers, production teams cultivating in each plowing area
organized their own affairs with considerable autonomy.
Different partitioning rules were used in the various
cultivation areas before to 1975, due partly to discrimination but also to differing conditions. In older, more
extensively developed areas, it was no longer possible, for
example, for individuals to obtain rights to large blocks
of land that were available in the newer areas. In an
effort to end discrimination in land allocation, the
partitioning rules applied by the subordinate board after
1975 have been much more uniform.

Each district land board is authorized, subject to
possible veto by the minister, to determine the size of
housing and cultivation sites. Subordinate land boards may
adjust these guidelines to take account of circumstances in
their jurisdictions. The first Letlhakeng subordinate
board members used dimensions for its allocations that had
been suggested by the district land board. They would
allocate plots of either 30 or 40 square meters for housing
sites; cultivation sites were allocated in one of three
plots: 400 by 400, 400 by 484, or 484 by 484 meters. Some
space had to be left between fields, but this was space
designed to be used as a roadway.

Now, individuals may have only one legally registered
field. That field can be enlarged with authorized exten-
sions without limit, provided the area is regularly cultivated.[10] If no good reason can be given for a field's
remaining uncultivated for five years or longer, rights to
the field can be confiscated and regranted by the subordinate boards. With some guidance from the district land
board, subordinate board members decide what constitutes a
"good" reason.

Rules determining who qualifies for rights to
cultivate land are closely associated with partitioning
rules. In principle, entry rules used in the Letlhakeng
area did not change with the introduction of the land
boards. Anyone could request land anywhere. Although most
people who cultivated or herded within each of the six
makgotla commons belonged to the lekgotla managing the
area, many cultivation areas today are worked by people
from other makgotla in Letlhakeng and surrounding villages. Some individuals from Thamaga and Molepolole who

are married into Letlhakeng makgotla also cultivate in
these areas. The prospect that Bakwena or others not
related to Letlhakeng residents will secure allocations in
cultivation areas in Letlhakeng is, however, a source of
considerable anxiety to villagers.

PATTERNS OF INTERACTION

Demand for cultivation land in the Letlhakeng area has
been increasing at a moderate but steady rate for decades
as the population of the village has grown. Although
abundant supplies of such land are still available at some
distance from the village, the amount of undeveloped
fertile land located nearby is declining. Rising levels
of conflict over access to increasingly scarce land was
one of the reasons for the reform of land administration.
It was presumed that a more modern administrative
management system would help to reduce earlier inequities
and would reduce conflict levels. The establishment of a
new land management authority in the Letlhakeng area has,
however, been associated with more rather than less
conflict over land in densely developed areas. Inadequate
information is an unexpected but important problem for the
new land authorities.

The Information Variable

Members of subordinate land boards have both executive
and judicial responsibilities that frequently require the
application and interpretation of partition rules. Acting
as executives, subordinate board members are responsible
for the final decision to allocate a new use right, for
physically demarcating new housing and cultivation sites,
and for making a permanent record of the right. Responsibility for all investigations prior to an allocation falls
upon the lekgotla headman who was the former manager of
the area where a new use right is sought. His signature
on an application form purportedly certifies that he
believes that no one currently holds a recognizable right
to the site that is sought and that neighboring cultivators have been consulted about the possibility of
a new field's being created in the area.
Acting as judicial officers, subordinate land
board members serve as a court of first instance for
all disputes over land rights in their jurisdiction.

Judgments reached at this level can be appealed first to the main district land board, then to the ministry, and then, in some cases, to the high court. At issue in most of the disputes heard by subordinate board members is the validity under current law of claims to land that conflict with new allocations of use rights by the boards.

Villagers' compliance with partitioning rules can be achieved with low enforcement costs only if the rules are appropriate (Oakerson 1978, 1984; Taylor 1966) and can, in fact, be applied fairly. Partitioning rules are considered appropriate by a community of resource users if their application allows that community to maintain an array of values simultaneously, including efficiency and equity, within an acceptable range. Subordinate land board members have the difficult task of defining, within the bounds of their discretion, partitioning rules that are uniquely fitted to the circumstances of a farmer's situation. These rules must also be consistent with provisions of the general law (contained in constitutional and national statute law) that define the basic property rights of citizens. The application of partition rules is fair if similar situations are treated similarly. Determining the facts of an allocation situation is a prerequisite for the fair treatment of disputants.

Achievement of all these tasks depends crucially upon information. The types of information that subordinate land board members need to partition the cultivation commons appropriately within their jurisdiction are listed in Table 1. The rules that guide the land boards in tailoring and applying partition rules and in determining the validity of contending claims to land are contained in the Tribal Land Act, ministry regulations, and in district land board guidelines. Board members must know the substance as well as the intent of these rules. In order to apply rules emanating from these sources and to exercise their own discretion appropriately, land board officials must also know the preference for partitioning rules of a community of farmers and be familiar with the general character of land and water resources within their jurisdiction and how people use these resources in production. In order to locate new fields without interfering with the rights of other farmers, members must know the boundaries of legitimate land claims.

Because undeveloped fertile land is still available, a piece of land is now given to the first applicant. After all fertile land has been allocated, board members will be required to determine who among competing applicants "should" get a field that comes vacant. Such decisions will require that board members determine, among other things, the value that access to the land will have for each applicant.

Increased levels of public spending to assist board members in their decision making within the present land board structure could improve members' access to the first three types of information listed in Table 1. Improved

TABLE 1 Types of Information Needed by Subordinate Land Board Members in Partitioning Common Land for Cultivation.

T1 Information regarding the provisions of the national constitution, relevant statutes, ministry regulations, and main land board guidelines regarding partitioning rules and the intent of these provisions.

T2 Information regarding the extent of subordinate land board discretion over the establishment and the application of partitioning rules.

T3 Information regarding the boundaries of use rights in land established by previous land board decisions.

T4 Information regarding the character of land and water resources within their jurisdictions and how, in general, these resources are used as production inputs.

T5 Information regarding the boundaries of use rights in land established by the earlier land administrators.

T6 Information regarding the preferences for partitioning rules of a community of farmers.

T7 Information regarding the value of use rights to a particular field site to a given applicant.

training programs and the attachment of legal specialists
to the boards could provide T1 and T2 information. The
addition of technically trained surveyors and cartographers
could improve the recordkeeping of the boards and provide
T3 information to future boards. The selection of board
members from among long-term residents of a given jurisdiction should ensure that members have T4 information.

The ministry has assumed that T5 information is
available from the present makgotla headmen if land board
members and headmen will only respect and cooperate with
each other. The village development committees are
expected to provide the T6 information to subordinate
board members. No need has yet developed for T7-type
information in central Kweneng. The facts of the trouble
case underscore the critical importance of T5 and T6
information for partitioning decisions and cast doubt on
whether these types of information are available to
subordinate board members.

Farmers' Strategies

Most cases heard by the Letlhakeng land board involve
decisions about the legitimacy of claims to land under
current law. Land board members are told to expect
makgotla leaders and established farmers to attempt to
hoard land, and thus find themselves with access to very
little "disinterested" information about previous allocations of rights. Many villagers now consider land board
members as incompetents who intentionally or unwittingly
sow trouble. They do not like the new partitioning rules,
and they are therefore not very cooperative. Makgotla
headmen attempt to quietly protect themselves and other
makgotla members from new allocations. They try to avoid
uncompensated effort and guilt by association with land
board allocations over which they have no veto. Conscien-
tious board members are frustrated by such a situation but
are determined to uphold the authority of the board to take
control of land affairs.

The absence of authoritative information regarding
the history of allocations in this area creates opportunities for farmers to pursue two undesirable courses of
action: (1) to advance a spurious claim to land where
there is some opportunity to sow doubt about the legitimacy
of another person's claim to it and (2) to collude with
neighbors in a cultivation area to challenge the rightful
claim of another person in order to preserve access to the

land for oneself. Since there are no fees collected by the
land boards for applications, demarcations, or adjudication of disputes, no out-of-pocket cost is associated
with either strategy. The winner gets access to well-
suited land--a prize well worth the effort of asserting a
claim. Without information about prior allocations from
uninvolved parties, the land board members can rely only
upon their own assessment of the validity of the conflicting claims.

AGGREGATE OUTCOMES

The land boards are still recognized by villagers as a
symbol of the efforts to end the petty discrimination of
the earlier land administrators. Nonetheless, the operations of the subordinate land board, in concert with
unpopular actions by the Kweneng District Land Board, have
also increased the villagers' levels of anxiety about land
rights. While there are a few examples of clear and
intentional abuse of authority on the part of a few members
of this board, villagers appear to most fear the unwitting
harm members might do out of ignorance or carelessness. No
one wants to be associated with land board decisions. The
hostile reactions of farmers reinforce the beliefs of some
board members that the land boards are the only champions
of the landless.

In the next section, I will examine the wider social
impact of land management by the land boards. These
outcomes are evaluated using the criteria of equity and
efficiency. In addition, I will consider the extent to
which this administration system is likely to contribute to
the development of the citizenship capabilities of
villagers as well as to the maintenance and extension of
patterns of reciprocity among residents of the settlement.

Equity

The designers of the land boards did not intend that
all Botswana would have rights to an equal quantity of
land at some point in the future. Central government
ministry planners expect many cultivators to continue to
operate near subsistence levels in the short term while
some expand the scale of their cultivation to become
"commercial" producers of food crops. Given climatic
constraints, planners believe that agriculture has a

limited capacity to absorb Botswana's rapidly growing
population. The development of rural industrial enterprises is being strongly encouraged (Botswana Ministry of
Finance and Development Planning 1985). This type of
development would also reduce the pressure on cultivation
land generated by population growth. Progress in this
direction has been slow, however.

A principal objective of those who undertook the design
of the reformed administrative system was to enhance the
equality of opportunity to acquire cultivation land while
protecting the security of existing claims in land. Like
previous land authorities, however, land board members and
their relatives are in a better position to protect claims
in land and to get access to the land they want. They can
better protect themselves and their relatives from illegal
encroachment by persons simply because they know the
history of allocations in these cases. With little
unbiased information about prior allocations in other
cases, their judgments in dispute cases must be largely
subjective. More aggressive individuals may well be
rewarded disproportionately. Board members can also
preserve access for their own purposes to contiguous
undeveloped land. This is usually done by stalling
decisions on allocation requests for the piece of land
until applicants give up and request an alternative site.

Those persons who had no claim to land were the subject
of the special concern of the designers of the land board
system. Few people in Letlhakeng lack claims in land,
although some can claim rights only in land that they
consider "useless" because it is infertile or overgrown by
Cynodon dactylon (motlhwa), a grass with an extensive root
system. However, these people are not helped if they are
given access to land surrounded by the fields of people who
hate them enough to sabotage their crops. Partitioning
rules that ignore the value of access to contiguous land
for some producers do the greatest disservice to poor
households that suffer the most from shortages of labor and
draught power (Henderson 1980).

Efficiency

The further development of strategies of aggression
threatens individual producer efficiency as well as the
efficiency of land administration. Producer efficiency can
be reduced in several ways. Land board allocations using
existing partitioning rules, regardless of whether

they are based on accurate information about prior allocations, may reduce the producer efficiency of family production teams already established in cultivation areas if they make it difficult to group the fields belonging to female relatives. Given the particular constraints on agriculture in this area, the location of cultivation areas is as important to many households as is the absolute size of the holdings. In a situation that rewards aggression, individual land holders incur greater time and effort costs in protecting their claims from encroachments and in securing land board judgments that establish their claim. Individuals who cannot cultivate a contested field until a case has been settled also lose the output from that field.

Aggression also diminishes the efficiency of land administration. The ease with which the land board can exclude illegal claimants from a given field is reduced as uncertainty about the facts in conflict cases rises. At present, land board officials must inquire into the facts of each conflict case even though they have little alter- native but to issue highly subjective decisions in the more complicated cases. Land board members can always lower decision-making costs in adjudication by issuing arbitrary judgments based on no knowledge at all of the facts of the case. Such judgments, however, create serious deprivations for litigants and further undermine conscien- tious board members' efforts to win the respect and cooperation of villagers.

Development of Citizenship Capabilities

The theme of self-help pervades the ministry's public education efforts, but it has been strikingly absent from public discussions of the land boards. Botswana's politi- cal leadership is generally eager to have the citizens take greater initiative in identifying and overcoming local problems through voluntary organizations. The Tribal Land Act, however, requires no direct citizen involvement in land management. The land board operating in central Kweneng has not encouraged groups of citizens to become involved in its decision making. The greatest part of their business is with individual applicants. While the involvement of headmen in making new allocations is required by law, board members suspect that information provided by headmen may be biased toward continuing discrimination. Central ministry officials believe that citizens will be intimidated by "greedy" headmen and

therefore cannot be relied upon to support the management
of land in an even-handed manner.

The creation of the land board system is the last in a
long line of important institutional changes that have
reduced the number of arenas in which makgotla members
could organize important joint undertakings. The pattern
of response by central government leaders to problems of
governance has been to remove authority from makgotla and
villages and give it to authorities at the village,
district, or national level. As the level of conflict over
land increased, ministry officials preempted the necessary
reform of land management institutions in order to ensure
that reform was carried out properly.

As a result, public discussion of the problem of
partitioning and allocating use-rights to common land did
not take place in many villages in Botswana until political
leaders appeared to introduce the land boards. Villagers
in Letlhakeng were pleased that someone was doing something about discrimination, and that they did not have to
struggle with designing the changes. Villagers and headmen alike in Letlhakeng have thus felt free to criticize
the land board system without much thought about how conflict generated by the increasing scarcity of land could be
reduced. They have not tried to reach a collective
decision about what kind of partitioning rules should be
used. Now, however, villagers are faced with a reformed
system that is producing outcomes they do not like. The
considerable self-governing skills, which these people
developed in response to their isolation in the western
desert areas over the past 150 years, are now being put to
use principally by small groups of farmers who organize
ways of outmaneuvering board members to advance their own
interests.

Maintaining and Extending Reciprocity

The levels of conflict between land board members and
villagers in some regions of Botswana, which prompted the
creation of the Interministerial Commission on Land Board
Operations, have not been reached in central Kweneng due in
part to lower population density. The more thoughtful
villagers are anxious, however, about the growing conflict
over land--a new phenomenon for people who have treated
land as an abundant good. Although the land boards were
created to reduce conflict over land, they have become
part of a structure creating incentives to break the

peace. Because bonds of reciprocity are weakest across makgotla in the village, growing conflict will increase rather than decrease the potential for destructive "tribalism."

The maintenance of reciprocity among villagers depends crucially upon the ability of citizens to call fellow citizens and officials alike to account for behavior that violates the climate of trust that is still strong within makgotla. Proper institutional design structures incentives for officials and citizens so that they do what is expected of them. The current management institution is perverse in that it all too often forces officials to reward predatory behavior.

CONCLUSIONS

Peaceful and productive management of cultivation land in the Letlhakeng area is not possible under the existing land management institution. With no means of determining local preferences for partitioning rules and little access to disinterested information about past allocations, the land boards can do little else in extensively developed areas but antagonize people and provide opportunities for some to profit from breaking faith from their fellow citizens. Access to local time and place information is crucial to the appropriate organization of land for cultivation (Hayek 1945). What kinds of considerations bear upon accomplishing this?

The ministry has accepted the recommendation of the Interministerial Commission on Land Board Operations that, in the future, disputes regarding land and water be adjudicated by the traditional court system.[11] This, it is argued, would remove land board members as judges in their own causes. It would also give the responsibility for adjudication to those who presumably know most about the local history of land rights. The separation of judicial and executive functions is vital, but this change would not alter villagers' unhappiness with the partitioning rules being used by the land board members. The popular election of nominees for some positions on the boards, which was introduced in 1984, also fails to provide a means of determining community preferences for partitioning rules.

Residents of Letlhakeng do not trust the leaders of the existing village development committee, which is a purely voluntary organization. Members of each lekgotla

fear other makgotla will free ride on any contributions
they make to joint projects. A new assembly with authority
to determine local rules for resource management would
provide a context in which to aggregate community preferences for operating rules for local common land. The
assembly probably would have little difficulty devising
operating rules for newly developed cultivation areas and
their associated commons grazing areas. It could well have
serious difficulty, however, reaching agreement on
partitioning rules for the extensively developed cultivation areas.

While the situation in these areas is complicated, the
appropriate management of these areas (which are usually
located near the village) is of greatest import for poorer
households. Smaller groups of people--makgotla or new
associations of people who cultivate these areas--would
have the best chance of reaching agreement about rules for
these areas. Existing households of cultivators could use
undeveloped portions on a rotating basis, keep it as a
commons from which to gather wood, thatching grass, etc.,
or divide it into equal shares.

The reallocation of taxing and spending authority in
Botswana to village communities would also likely change
the distribution of primary schools. The concentration of
these schools in villages in accordance with present
district government policy compounds crowding problems in
the cultivation areas surrounding the schools. This
concentration unnecessarily raises the cost to those who
would like to develop fields in new cultivation areas.

Flexibility is an important quality of any management
system for cultivation land. Households now can expand
unexpectedly with the return of widowed or divorced women;
the practice of borrowing land helps cope with these
unanticipated needs for more land, but the introduction of
rights to exchange in land would also help. Market prices
for land in this particular area would not increase enormously because plenty of undeveloped land is available, but
exchange rights would have the effect of encouraging the
development of new cultivation areas and thus relieving
congestion. At this time, virtually all households hold
rights to some land. Even land considered unusable could
become valuable when the advantage of fertilizers is
recognized. The introduction of some market mechanisms now
would have fewer undesirable equity effects than such a
change would have in the future when land scarcity has
increased. Authorizing individuals to sell claims in
fields would not necessarily mean the end of group

management of cultivation areas and attached grazing commons nor group development of new cultivation areas.

Movement in Botswana toward the creation of a widely accepted written record of rights in agricultural land is bound to produce conflict regardless of the structure in which it occurs. The central government has a vital role to play in providing judicial appeal mechanisms that protect basic civil and property rights. The performance of this function is not inconsistent with the empowerment of local resource management groups (Wynne 1980).

NOTES

1. I gratefully acknowledge the many discussions with
Ronald Oakerson, Elinor Ostrom, and Vincent Ostrom; they
have helped me understand the underlying causes of the
conflict I witnessed in Letlhakeng. My field research was
funded by the Fulbright-Hays Doctoral Dissertation Research
Abroad Program. Extensive subsequent support has been
provided by the Workshop in Political Theory and Policy
Analysis, Indiana University. Preparation of this chapter
has been partially funded by the United States Agency for
International Development (USAID) through grant number
DAN-5433-GSS-4052. The views expressed are those of the
author and not those of USAID or the United States
government.

2. There are three categories of land in Botswana: tribal land is administered by the land board system, and
represents 71 percent of the total; state land, which is
administered by the Ministry of Local Government and Lands,
is 23 percent of the total; the remaining 6 percent is held
by individuals as freehold land.

3. I am particularly indebted to Ronald Oakerson for
pointing out the nature of this diagnostic problem.

4. The commission did suggest one important institutional
reform. It recommended that jurisdiction over land and
water conflict cases be transferred from the land boards to
the traditional court system. Consideration was also given
to increasing the control of the popularly elected district
councils over land board policy.

5. Data supporting the description of social organization
and the organization of sorghum production provided here
could not be included because of space limitations. They
are presented in my forthcoming dissertation.

6. Commercial fertilizers are not used in this area and
little conscious effort is made to encourage manuring of
the fields by cattle. Since damage to a borrowed plow is
more easily recognized by the owner than is injury to an
animal, it is much easier to borrow a plow than to borrow
plowing oxen. Animals are normally lent only to persons
trusted by the lender.

7. The Establishment of Subordinate Land Boards Order,
1973, indicates that each subordinate land board shall
consist of five members. The fifth member of these boards
has never been appointed. This member was originally
intended to be a district-level employee of the Ministry of
Agriculture. Reference is made here to six makgotla
commons rather than seven. Members of the Baga-Sekgalo
lekgotla in Letlhakeng were not given any land of their own
in this area. They have always cultivated land controlled
by the Baga-Motsoto.

8. The area of the jurisdiction of the Letlhakeng
Subordinate Land Board, which is approximately 7,000 sq.
km., is actually more than five times as large as the area
earlier controlled by Letlhakeng makgotla, which was
approximately 1,200 sq. km. Portions of this area are
uninhabited or used for grazing, however, and so add
nothing to the work load of management authorities with
authority over cultivation land.

9. There were actually more than six local land
authorities in the Letlhakeng area. The Bakgwathen
lekgotla, Goo-Moiphisi, originally controlled the largest
section of land in the area. Authority equal to that of
the lekgotla headman over two sub-units of this section was
given by the lekgotla to four kinsmen, two of whom remained
in the immediate area. This lekgotla thus had three land
authorities. Because of their close kinship relationship
to the headmen, the other two authorities were sensitive to
the preferences of the headmen regarding allocations. They
were thus not totally independent of his authority.

10. No limit now exists on the size to which a field can
be extended, provided that contiguous land is available.
The ministry is planning, however, to place an upper limit
on the size of fields used for "subsistence" cultivation
purposes. Eventually, a yearly rent will be charged to
users whose fields exceed a specified size. It is presumed
that these larger fields will be used for commercial-scale

agricultural production.

11. Botswana has two judicial systems. The customary court system, which hears probably 90 percent of the cases processed in Botswana, is staffed by chiefs and elected headmen who are part of the tribal administration (still so-called) for each district. These courts rely on un-written customary law and on statutory law. Magistrates courts staffed by law school graduates have jurisdiction over serious criminal cases and civil cases brought to it. The procedures used in this court system, introduced in the colonial era, are similar to those used in British civil and criminal courts.

REFERENCES

Botswana Ministry of Local Government and Lands. 1978.
    Interministerial Committee Report on Land Board
    Operations. Gaborone: Government Printer.

Botswana Ministry of Finance and Development Planning.
    1985. National Development Plan 1985/86-1991.
    Gaborone: Government Printer.

Chernichovsky, D. 1981. Socioeconomic and demographic
    aspects of school enrollment and attendance in rural
    Botswana. Population and Human Resources Division
    Discussion Paper No. 81-47. Washington, D.C.: World
    Bank.

Froysa, T. 1983. School Attendance in Rural Botswana.
    Oslo: Department of Geography, University of Oslo.

Hayek, F. A. 1945. The uses of knowledge in society.
    American Economic Review 35:519-530.

Henderson, W. 1980. Letlhakeng: A Study of Accumulation
    in a Kalahari Village. Ph.D. dissertation. Brighton,
    England: University of Sussex.

Hitchcock, R. K. 1985. Water, land and livestock: the
    evolution of tenure and administration patterns in the
    grazing areas of Botswana. In Picard 1985:96-133.

Machacha, B. N. 1981. Land boards as land management
    institutions. M.A. thesis. Madison, Wisconsin:
    University of Wisconsin.

Mueller, E. 1981. The value and allocation of time in
    rural Botswana. Population and Human Resources
    Division Discussion Paper No. 81-44. Washington,
    D.C.: World Bank.

Oakerson, R. J. 1978. The erosion of public highways: a policy analysis of the eastern Kentucky coal-haul road problem. Ph.D. dissertation, Department of Political Science. Bloomington: Indiana University.

Oakerson, R. J. 1984. Reciprocity: the political nexus. Unpublished manuscript, Department of Political Science. Huntington, West Virginia: Marshall University.

Ostrom, E. 1986. An agenda for the study of institutions. Public Choice 48:3-25.

Ostrom, V. 1980. Artisanship and artifact. Public Administration Review 40:309-317.

Peters, P. E. 1983. Cattlemen, borehole syndicates and privatization in the Kgatleng district of Botswana: an anthropological history of the transformation of a commons. Ph.D. dissertation. Boston, Massachusetts: Boston University.

Picard, L. A. ed. 1985. Politics and Rural Development in Southern Africa. Lincoln, Nebraska: University of Nebraska.

Roberts, S. 1980. Arable land tenure and administrative change in the Kgatleng. Journal of African Law 24:117-130.

Roe, E. and L. Fortmann. 1982. Season and strategy: the changing organization of the rural water sector in Botswana. Rural Development Committee, Center for International Studies. Ithaca, New York: Cornell University.

Taylor, J. F. A. 1966. The Masks of Society. New York: Meredith.

Werbner, R. P. 1980. The quasi-judicial and the experience of the absurd: remaking land law in north-eastern Botswana. Journal of African Law 24:131-151.

Wynne, S. G. 1980. Thinking about redesigning resource management institutions in Botswana: some suggestions from Alexis de Tocqueville. Paper presented at the

Annual Meetings of the Midwest Political Science
Association, Cincinnati, Ohio, April 15-18.

Wynne, S. G. Forthcoming. Bureaucracy and the organization
of knowledge in development: an assessment of the land
boards in Botswana. Ph.D. dissertation. Bloomington:
Indiana University.

BIBLIOGRAPHY

Botswana Ministry of Local Government and Lands. Tribal
    Land Regulations, 1970. Statutory Instrument No. 7 of
    1970.

Botswana Ministry of Local Government and Lands. Tribal
    Land (Subordinate Land Boards) Regulations, 1973.
    Statutory Instrument No. 48 of 1973.

Botswana National Assembly. Tribal Land Act, 1968, as
    Amended by the Tribal Land (Amendment) Act, 1969.

Botswana National Assembly. 1981. Local Government
    Structure in Botswana. Government Paper No. 1 of 1981.

Botswana Office of the President. 1973. Establishment of
    Subordinate Land Boards Order, 1973. Statutory
    Instrument No. 47 of 1973.

Botswana Office of the President. 1979. Report of the
    Presidential Commission on Local Government Structure in
    Botswana.

Kaufman, F. X., G. Majone, and V. Ostrom. 1985. Experience,
    theory, and design. In Guidance, Control, and Evalu-
    ation in the Public Sector, F. X. Kaufmann, G. Majone,
    and V. Ostrom, eds. Berlin, New York: de Gruyter.

Okihiro, G. Y. 1976. Hunters, herders, cultivators, and
    traders: interaction and change in the Kgalagadi,
    nineteenth century. Ph.D. dissertation. Los Angeles,
    California: University of California.

Ostrom, E. 1985. Institutional arrangements for resolving
    the commons dilemma: some contending approaches. Paper
    prepared for the 46th National Conference of the
    American Society for Public Administration,
    Indianapolis, Indiana, March 23-27.

Institutional Dynamics:
The Evolution and Dissolution of Common Property
Resource Management[1]

James T. Thomson
David H. Feeny
Ronald J. Oakerson

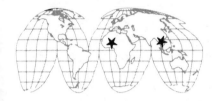

INTRODUCTION

Institutional arrangements for the management of common-pool resources are created and evolve as responses to certain combinations of circumstances. A full understanding of the evolution and survival of such arrangements thus requires dynamic analysis of case studies. The framework presented by Oakerson (this volume) may be applied recursively to examine dynamic sequences of change. Thus, responses to exogenous shocks in one period become part of the existing set of institutional arrangements in the next, affecting the subsequent path of evolution in institutional arrangements.

The dynamic sequences of change in the management of forest resources in Niger (1884-1984) and land resources in Thailand (1850-1980) are the themes of the paper. By applying the model in Oakerson (this volume) iteratively, changes in both individual strategies and decision-making arrangements may be treated as if they were endogenous. The approach is applied at both the local and supra-local levels.

In both Niger and Thailand, exogenous changes in population and market opportunities combined to make the common pool resource more valuable. The response to growing scarcity was the search for new arrangements to manage the resource more effectively.

In each case, the behavior of the state was important in affecting the choice of new arrangements. In Niger, especially in the colonial period, the lack of accountability of the government to constituencies of resource users meant that new socially inefficient arrangements could be gradually imposed. In Thailand, in spite of the general lack of democratic forms of government, indigenous regimes provided new arrangements that better served the interests of the resource users. However, the key difference between the two cases is not merely the type of regime and degree of its accountability to those whom it governed: elite Thai decision makers shared in the gains created by the provision of the new property relations, and consequently their interests affected the innovation possibilities.

Given the existing constitutional structures in each case, basic changes in institutional arrangements relevant to resource management required that the central government take some action. The local arena is, however, also important in shaping the interpretation, enforcement, and operational meaning of the new and existing arrangements. In the Zinder (Niger) woodstock case, arrangements that were extra-legal by national standards, but increasingly legitimate in local eyes, have become relevant as well. In the Thai case, traditional patterns of the exploitation of land resources were retained in spite of the lack of official sanction, and eventually legal compromises were introduced that served to officially recognize actual practices. Formerly extra-legal arrangements were officially sanctioned.

The changes in institutional arrangements occurred within and were linked to the ongoing evolution in the system of resource exploitation. The evolution of each system will be briefly described.

The Zinder Woodstock Case

During the first half century of relative abundance (1884-1935), Zinder's woodstock was subdivided on a de facto basis into three parts: (1) a series of small local common properties around settled areas; (2) an undifferentiated common property resource composed of all remaining undeveloped bushland; and, (3) a de jure statewide commons for one tree, Acacia albida. This species is widely valued and protected for its agroforestry properties (Pélissier 1980; Weber and Hoskins 1983:2-5).

At the beginning of the 40-year period of relative
equilibrium (1935-1974), colonial legislation imposed a de
jure common property status on the 15 most valuable tree
species (including Acacia albida). Management authority
was centralized for the protected species at the colony
level. Colonial foresters created a small force of forest
guards, assisted by local informers, to enforce these rules
in rural areas. But enforcers were so few as to be
virtually ineffective in those places they did patrol. In
other areas, the forest service simply did not make its
presence felt. Nonprotected (rough) species remained a
common property resource, whose management was left to
evolve in light of local concerns. Given extensive
undeveloped bushland in the immediate vicinity, few
residents of the Zinder area perceived any real scarcity of
wood, or any real reason for woodstock management.

In the final 10-year stage of relative scarcity
(1974-1984), the 15-species common property trees remained
a state concern and off limits to unauthorized users. In
consequence, rough species were nearly destroyed, and
pressure was generated by the demands of a growing population to lift bans on protected species. An attempt to
organize common property village woodlots failed because
the technical forestry package was inadequate, commons
regulations remained inchoate, and rules governing management were never specified. Though it is fair to suppose
more elaborate common woodstock management regulations
might have arisen as local people perceived wood shortages,
such rules were not developed because the post-independence
state maintained the preemption and centralization of
management authority. One result has been the recent
emergence of individual attempts by peasants to assert
personal rights to the trees growing on their own land.

The Thai Land Rights Case

The development of a reliable market for surplus paddy
production in the 19th century made land valuable. As a
result, disputes over commons land ownership became
endemic, inducing a series of innovations in institutional
arrangements that resulted in the privatization of arable
land in Thailand. Ultimately, in the early 20th century, a
cadastral survey land titling system was established
through national legislation. This law was the culmina-
tion of successive attempts to reduce or resolve land
disputes.

For land rights in Thailand, neither jointness nor excludability posed prohibitive problems, given the fixed, immovable character of land and the technology available for excluding others, as well as for exploiting it. Divisibility posed no theoretical problem, but as rice cultivation spread in response to world market demand, it became the heart of the issue in efforts to firm up land titles to parts of the original commons.

Institutional Innovation

Pressure for privatization was the result in both the Zinder and the Thai cases. It should be stressed, however, that in the Zinder woodstock case, privatization by peasants is far from a foregone conclusion. Effective subdivision of the woodstock commons into discrete, individually controlled units remains legally impossible and highly problematic today. In the Thai case, continued management of land as a common property resource was improbable, given the combination of factors at work. The world market impact on the local economy during the 19th century stimulated the replacement of usufruct cultivation with intensive exploitation of private arable land.

In addition to examining each of the case studies within the Oakerson framework, the Thai case is explicitly (and the Zinder case is implicitly) analyzed in a simple supply-and-demand model of institutional change.

In the supply-and-demand model, the demand for institutional change arises when some gain cannot be captured under existing institutional arrangements.[2] Changes in relative factor or product prices, changes in the size of markets, changes in technology, and changes in the fundamental decision rules of government are among the important variables that create disequilibrium in the existing institutional arrangements. Whether the demand for change will be met, however, depends on the supply of institutional change--the willingness and capability of the fundamental institutions of government to provide and/or permit and/or prevent new arrangements. The capability depends in part on the cost of institutional innovation, which in turn depends in part on the stock of existing knowledge about the design and operation of institutions. The willingness to provide new arrangements also importantly depends on the private benefits and costs of providing change to the agents who are in a position to do so, the elite decision makers of government. Thus, the

existing set of institutions and initial distribution of
power will have an important impact on the kinds of new
institutional arrangements that are supplied.

Institutional change then arises through the
interactions of the demand for and supply of change in
dynamic sequences. The institutional response in one
period becomes part of the initial conditions in the
next, thus affecting the subsequent path of change.

Institutional innovations in both Zinder and Thailand contrast with those reported by McKean (this volume) in her analysis of Japanese woodlots. In Zinder,
the French colonial state sought to impose a commons
management. Because management was so ineffective,
peasants have recently attempted informal privatization.
In Thailand, by contrast, the state, major landholders,
and peasants all pressured for privatization. In the
Japanese case, local village decision-making authority
and tradition facilitated the continuation of effective
local management of the village's common woodlot, despite
changing circumstances, for more than three centuries.
New rules to exclude potential users of the resource were
officially adopted (Thailand) or attempted on a de facto
basis (Zinder), whereas in Japan the rules governing
inclusion in the group of those who had rights to use
the commons were instead retained and refined.

WOODSTOCK MANAGEMENT IN THE SAHEL

In the arid West African Sahel, around Zinder, Niger,
changing patterns of woodstock management illustrate
several rounds of institutional evolution as population
pressure mounted, supplies of wood as a renewable resource
eroded in the face of growing demand, and various actors
attempted to deal with the problem.

Before woodstock abundance gave way to scarcity in
the Zinder area, trees were managed "passively": people
simply allowed natural regeneration to reclaim fallowed
fields. Though their usefulness was recognized, trees
were generally taken for granted because supplies more
than met demand. Trees on village lands (typically one
to two square miles in all) were apparently dealt with
as a common property resource, but access and use rules
were probably very loose, given the abundance of wood at
that time.

As colonial foresters perceived wood scarcities
elsewhere in the French West African empire, colonial

government fiat declared an important part of the woodstock
to be a common property resource, subject to management at
the colony level. This imposed management system has since
proven to be largely ineffective, and woodstock capital is
under increasingly serious threat.

As a consequence of institutional stalemates within the
forest service and the national government, some peasants
are now moving, often illegally, to privatize parts of the
woodstock. For them, this now appears to be the cheapest
option to preserve their own dwindling wood supplies
against complete destruction.

On the basis of woodstock supply and demand relations,
the century can be divided into three distinct periods:
(1) 1884-1935: relative abundance; (2) 1935-1974:
equilibrium; (3) 1974-1984: increasing scarcity.

Relative Abundance, 1884-1935

Resource Attributes

The physical attributes of the resource and techniques
for controlling and exploiting it remained roughly constant
throughout the three periods. The full description provided here will thus not be repeated for the two later
periods. The local woodstock is clearly a renewable resource, composed of all the woody vegetation in the area
(Thomson 1983:167-71). It can be exploited on a sustained-
yield basis by various users for different purposes, so
long as demand does not cut into woodstock capital and
impair the process of efficient renewal. The limiting
condition here on joint use is set by the productive
capacity of a given woodstock. This capacity may be gradually enriched; it may also be impaired by overcutting.

Unless patrols are mounted (which they have not been),
exclusion is feasible only within an area that can be
enclosed by traditional fences. Such areas will usually
be of limited size (gardens and residential components)
because thorn fences require substantial investment of
labor. Fields are not generally enclosed. However, the
Bugaje agro-silvo-pastoral communities were exceptional
in this regard: they collectively fenced their lands.
Each community was subdivided into a variable number of
quarters or sections, organized over time as new groups
arrived in a village and took up land. Within each
quarter, families resided on their own fields, which were
laid out in long, contiguous, parallel strips. Each family

managed its land as a separate enterprise. But the
residents of each quarter jointly maintained a common
fencing system that both enclosed each quarter field
and separated all the quarter's fields from its fallows
(Nicolas 1962; Thomson 1976:261-64).

Decision-Making Arrangements

Rules and institutions governing woodstock use during
this initial period of excess supply were appropriately
simple. People planted and owned privately at least two
tree species, the baobab (Adansonia digitata) and the date
palm (Phoenix dactylifera), because they produced valued
foods. A third species, Acacia albida (Hausa: gawo, pl.
gawuna) was protected by the fiat ruling of Tenimun, sultan
of Damagaram from 1851-1885. This tree has long been
prized and selectively cultured in many Sahelian arable
areas. It fertilizes the soil, recycling leached nutrients. It also fixes nitrogen and facilitates cereal
crop uptake of phosphorus (National Research Council 1983:
13). Sultan Tenimun reportedly ordered the execution of
those who cut the gawo (Salifou 1971:7).
All other tree species formed an open access resource
that anyone could freely exploit. Trees were relatively
plentiful during this 50-year period (Thomson 1983:169-
171). People viewed them more as a nuisance to cultivation
than as a valuable good, even though they recognized that
leaf litter and wood ashes sharply improved soil fertility.
The woodstock could have been subdivided by allocating
discrete portions to individual owners of land where trees
grow, but this was never done. This would have modified
traditional rules, which instead separated land tenure from
tree tenure, and permitted overlapping property rights and
different systems of effective control of land and woodstock resources within the same piece of real property. As
noted, some peasants are now trying, a century later, to
effect this change. During the period of relative abundance, however, divisibility remained a moot point because
wood was freely available and off-field supplies more than
met demand.

Interactions

There were few conflicts as a result of the imposed
rules because different demands for the wood were not yet

competitive (supply exceeded demand). Indeed, the
only time when use rules might have resulted in conflict
involved the Zinder sultan's fiat ruling against cutting
Acacia albida. It is not clear from available data
whether people generally accepted the sultan's assertion
of authority in this matter as legitimate. At the end
of the period, which came midway through the colonial
era (1899-1960), wood was still plentiful. Much unexploited bushland still existed in the Zinder area.
People continued to found new hamlets in unsettled
regions.

Outcomes

    Interactions changed little between 1884 and 1935.
The dynamics of wood production and consumption appear
to have varied only slightly during the entire period.
We have no information about the extent to which cutting
of gawo seedlings was policed and punished under the
precolonial regime. Under the early colonial government,
presumably little would have been done along those lines.
The impact of consistent population growth was yet to be
felt. In this case, the supply of forest products
generated by passive management of the Zinder-area
woodstock (supplemented by large areas of uncultivated
bush) covered demand. The need for active management
of a renewable resource was not yet perceived by local
residents.

Equilibrium, 1935-1974

Attributes of the Resource

    During the first half of this 40-year period, woodstock
users still did not interfere with each other in exploiting
the common property. Demand could still be satisfied. Nor
did exclusion conditions change: barbed wire appeared in
the area only after 1960, and then only in small amounts
financed by foreign donors. The woodstock was potentially
divisible, but economic considerations militated against
division. Demand for wood did not yet justify the investment in fencing or in patrols to enforce exclusion. In
most of the Zinder hinterland, wood was not sold until well
into the 1960s.

Decision-Making Arrangements

Existing legal (forestry code rules) and political
constraints, which might have hindered subdivision by
individuals, were not tested during this period. Somewhat
larger units, based on either quarters or villages, might
have served as appropriate levels at which to devise common
resource management efforts when scarcity became apparent
toward the end of the period, if state-imposed rules
emasculating local organization had been relaxed. As it
happened, most villages had lost their power of independent
activity as the result of efforts of both the colonial and
independent regimes to establish controls over major forms
of organization in rural areas. Villages (or quarters
within them) had no authority to enforce sanctions against
violators of locally devised use rules. In practice, few
such rules appear to have been made.

The French West Africa forest service was established
in 1935 and charged with overall responsibility for
managing the woodstock. A few French tropical foresters
had concluded that deforestation trends that were then
becoming apparent would threaten and perhaps destroy the
resource if unchecked. Metropolitan French forestry
tradition granted the forestry department relatively
extensive controls over the exploitation of the woodstock
outside national domain lands; accordingly, the colonial
legislation simply arrogated authority to the colonial
regime to regulate wood use in the colonies. Because
colonial subjects--the vast majority of the population in
the Sahelian colonies--had at the time no effective
political or legal recourse against these centralizing
initiatives, and little power to force colonial officials
to take account of local conditions, individual rules
included in the French West African imperial forestry code
reflected precious little sense of the realities of local
agricultural production and woodstock management systems.
Small forestry agencies were set up by French administrators in each colony to implement central policies elaborated through a bureaucratic process and imposed through
the colonial administrative hierarchy.

This legislation defined far-reaching changes in the
regulation of woodstock use. First, it provided for
creation of state forests, subject to exclusive forest
service control concerning woodstock and land use. Second,
and much more important, this legislation centralized the
forestry service's authority to regulate the exploitation
of the 15 most valuable species of trees outside, as well

as inside, the state forests. New regulations prohibited cutting live specimens, or lopping branches above the height of 10 feet without an authorization (provided free by the forestry service if trees were destined for personal use) or a cutting permit (sold to the holder if the wood was to be harvested for sale). Other provisions of the forestry code left intact local customary rights to exploit nonprotected species.

This restructuring of controls on woodstock exploitation amounted, on one level, to a simple broadening of the prerogative to protect valuable trees first asserted in the area by the pre-colonial Sultan Tenimun. Those who wrote the code provisions clearly foresaw the day when wood would become a scarce and valued commodity. They sought to set up rules to reduce consumption, or at least shift demand from valuable to rough tree species.

On another level, however, the French West African imperial forestry code formalized control over the commons; it removed or drastically restricted what had hitherto been fairly broad local-level discretion in dealing with woodstock management. Because wood was plentiful, little, if anything, had been done along these lines before 1935, but the option of developing local management solutions presumably existed before forestry code legislation eliminated the prerogative. As a result of the forestry code, devising new local political solutions to management problems became a much more difficult and expensive process. While most regulations outlined above were enforced sporadically at best, villagers recognized foresters' authority to control woodstock use, and made few (if any) attempts to establish alternative controls on access and use. The independent state of Niger inherited and maintained the common property framework institutionalized in the forestry code imposed by the French.

Interactions

With the creation of the forestry code, and the formalized, colony-level commons, a new series of interactions gradually arose. Nothing changed until the forestry service managed to patrol an area. Once it did, and forest guards began to impose fines, new patterns of behavior arose. As a result, peasants may have left more trees on fields than they otherwise would have. However, aware that they would not subsequently be allowed to cut protected species without special forester-issued

authorizations, they may have done a more systematic job of
surreptitiously destroying seedlings.

Enforcement pressure mounted. Foresters regularly
blamed and fined landowners for any trees illegally felled
on their field. Those who feared fines for harvesting live
trees on their own land cut the wood they needed in
remaining areas of bush. Some cut surreptitiously on
others' land. Eventually, in the early years after independence, some landowners began to discourage cutting on
their property when they found people in the act. Some
simply told cutters to stop; others said they would reveal
violators' names to the forest guards if the guards
threatened the landowners with fines for the code violation. But few landowners ever complained to forest guards
about illegal cutting, or asked their help in controlling
it.

To assist with identification of code violators,
foresters hired local informants. Often these men were
traditional policemen attached to canton chiefs. Peasants
soon realized they could bribe the informants to steer a
touring forester away from a fresh stump. A number of
people adopted this strategy, calculating that it would
in most cases be far cheaper to bribe than to pay the
fine.

A new interaction may be noted: peasants who were
caught by a forest guard did what they could to reduce the
fine. Local people saw this as a process of bribe bargaining. Because almost all were illiterate, few knew
details of the forestry code, and few knew what actually
became of the money. In any case, receipts were rarely
issued by enforcing officers (Thomson 1977:64-71); most
forest guards probably did profit illegally from their
power to fine forestry code violators.

Because they perceived no need, people planted very few
trees until at least the mid-1960s. At most, some planted
shade trees in courtyards, or fruit trees--mangoes, guavas,
and date palms--in gardens where they could be protected
against animal and human damage. But none planted trees in
fields or did very much to preserve natural-regeneration
seedlings there. What fieldowners planted or protected
might be cut by others without permission, so investments
in future woodstock supply made little sense. The
potential still existed for investments to renew the
woodstock once available wood supplies no longer met
demand, or perhaps even earlier, when shortages began to
appear. But the new rules of the game made investments in
augmenting the stock of trees much more problematic.

This is particularly unfortunate when silvo-agricul-
turalists would willingly preserve certain seedlings on
their fields to fertilize soils and improve harvests if
they felt confident they could trim, lop, or cut trees
as needed. Such is not the case, however. Farmers are
unwilling to risk trees' eventually overshadowing their
crops or attracting birds that would destroy ripening
millet and sorghum, so they will simply eradicate seedlings rather than leave themselves with no recourse if
they end up with too many "untouchable" trees on their
fields.

Limited questionnaire data from the area (Thomson 1982)
and in-depth interviews during 1971-72 strongly suggest
that most landowners accepted the proposition that
foresters control the use of trees on lands villagers own
and farm. This division of authority over the two
resources, which reflects traditional land and tree property rules in some African areas, means that they will not
often be managed as an integrated renewable unit.

Outcomes

Neither equity nor distribution terms seemed disrupted
until the very end of this intermediate period of relative
equilibrium between the supply and demand for woodstock
products. The patterns of resource exploitation and
mismanagement that flowed from the structure of decision-
making arrangements had little direct effect on peoples'
lives in the Zinder area. The price of wood did begin to
rise slowly in Zinder, the regional center, and a firewood
market developed in some rural settings, supplementing the
existing markets in building poles. But shortages did not
really appear in the rural area surrounding Zinder.
Furthermore, people did not really see the cause-and-effect
relationship between their actions and the destruction of
the woodstock, whether through direct cutting of mature
trees, or deliberate destruction of seedlings.

Relative Scarcity, 1974-1984

The landscape has changed somewhat since the early
1960s, but few places are totally cleared of trees.
Instead, one still finds rather impressive stands of
Acacia albida, in particular, and other protected and
rough species in scattered, interspersed sites. The

scrub bushes <u>Guira</u> <u>senegalensis</u> and <u>Combretum</u> <u>micranthum</u>
appear everywhere, apparently indestructible and forever a
part of cultivated fields.

Resource Attributes

In general, the limits of jointness have been reached
throughout the Zinder area. Few indeed are the places
where all can find the wood they need. Instead, each
person's harvesting reduces the amount available for other
people, increases the time they spend harvesting, and adds
to the general over-exploitation of the woodstock.

Exclusion through fencing remains largely impossible,
because neither foreign nor adequate local fencing materials are available at reasonable cost. Those who use
branches from protected thorn trees (<u>Acacia</u> <u>albida</u>,
<u>Acacia</u> <u>senegal</u>, <u>Acacia</u> <u>nilotica</u>, etc.) risk fines at the
hands of roving forest guards.

The resource can in fact be subdivided in a few special
situations, e.g., through garden and compound enclosures.
Such plantings have increased recently. Fenced village
woodlots have also been created in some communities since
1974, as a matter of state policy, through foreign-financed
projects.

Decision-Making Arrangements

The central government and donor organizations
introduced common property village woodlots on a trial
basis, beginning in 1974 in the Zinder area. This ever so
slightly changed the character of rules governing woodstock
exploitation. The new system involved creation of a new
set of formal and working rules for the small (one-to-four
hectare) plots fenced with barbed wire financed by foreign
assistance. The land for woodlots was "donated" by villagers. Often the burden for "donations" fell on the village headman, the individual who possessed the most land,
and thus was best able to bear the loss of cropland or
fallow "for the common good."

Formal rules specified by foresters who supervised the
implementation of these projects were minimal: within the
project context, village volunteers, in exchange for token
wage payments (equivalent to about half the daily rate for
field labor), were to clear land, fence the plot, excavate
planting holes and plant seedlings (mainly exotic neem and

eucalyptus, poorly adapted to plantation forestry under local arid conditions). They were then to cultivate peanuts or other leguminous food crops (to ensure that weeds would not smother the newly planted tree seedlings) and generally watch over the plot.

No formal agreement defined the system of distribution. Forest guards who supervised creation of the woodlots asserted that the lots were "for the villagers" and the wood produced there "belongs to the villagers." Villagers remained skeptical. Many assumed that the woodlots really belonged to the government or to the forest service, which they feared would claim the wood at will and without further compensation for villagers' efforts (Thomson 1980).

As far as the rest of the woodstock was concerned, common property rules remain unchanged. The forestry code, as interpreted by local forest guards, still provides for centralized control over use of protected species. Remaining rough species are exploited subject to local use regulations, often highly informal in nature.

Interactions

Because villagers conclude that the new woodlots will benefit the government, not them, they try to minimize their inputs. In most cases, they kill off seedlings by benign neglect: when the fence collapses, or when animals break through it, they do nothing to protect trees. Most trees die quickly, if not from overbrowsing, then from drought. As for protected species, little has changed from earlier periods, although illegal use of wood growing on others' fields may have increased in some villages. In any case, many villagers are beginning to perceive the growing wood shortage.

Some react as usual, allowing the cutting to occur because they feel that the trees do not belong to them. Other landowners, frightened about fines, try either to stop illegal cutting on their land or to identify responsible parties so they can escape paying unjust fines by naming the real violators. Finally, some individuals have begun to defend the trees on their fields when they have the chance; they chase off would-be cutters, asserting a personal right to the trees by virtue of ownership of the land on which the trees grow.[3]

This smaller group of individuals is intent on changing the previously accepted local working rules of wood use, so some take their disputes to village moots, or

before canton chiefs. Others, in an effort to prevent
destruction of trees on their fields, stand up to cutters
authorized by the forestry service to harvest wood for
commercial use. In neighboring areas, individual field
owners have begun to take authorized woodcutters before the
arrondissement forester, to inquire why the latter allow
cutters to chop down trees on their fields. The foresters
generally reply that they never authorize cutting trees on
fields, but only in the bush. But for all practical
purposes, the bush has been destroyed throughout the Zinder
area.

Around Zinder, some field owners have begun during this
period to make use of the Qur'an, considered for this
purpose to be a magical fetish, in order to identify timber poachers and wood stealers, and force return of their
property. A few even go so far as to place a future
Qur'anic prohibition on all unauthorized harvesting of wood
on their fields by other individuals, despite the fact that
this conflicts with recent national-level prohibitions on
such use of the Qur'an.

The village woodlots, as currently organized, are a
fatally flawed experiment in commons management. Those who
established them failed to address the most fundamental
concerns of putative producer/users: they gave no effective guarantees of property rights to the latter, nor did
they provide any information about distribution of trees or
wood produced. Users legitimately concluded they would
derive little or no benefit.

Attempts by individuals to police wood on fields, and
thus in effect to establish private property rights over
those trees, represent efforts to parcel out the commons.
It is not yet clear what, if anything, these efforts will
produce by way of code changes.

Outcomes

State-organized attempts to reforest through a program of village woodlots have demonstrated once again to
Zinder-area villagers that such efforts will not help them,
at least not as these programs are currently operated.
They remain highly suspicious of both the technical feasibility of woodlots and eventual distribution of any wood
produced. Villagers find collective woodlots to be a
losing proposition unless they receive pay equivalent to
or better than the going rate for field labor for the time
they put in.

As for the rest of the woodstock, investment
possibilities are stalemated. This leaves everyone worse
off, because reduction of the woodstock increases the risk
of soil erosion and reduces the likelihood that soil
fertility will be reconstituted through natural regeneration. As people press relentlessly on the remaining trees,
the costs of fuel and building materials rise rapidly.
At the same time, women use more and more animal drop-
pings and crop residues for cooking fuel, so the supply
of organic matter available to restore soil fertility has
dropped off sharply. Failure to increase wood supplies to
keep pace with rising demand in turn translates into a significant lowering of living standards in Zinder's rural
areas.

DEVELOPMENT OF PROPERTY RIGHTS IN LAND IN THAILAND

Among the Western developed nations there is a
centuries-old tradition of well-defined and enforceable
private property rights in land that allow the owner to
exclude others from using the land, pass it on to his/her
heirs, pledge it as security against financial liabilities,
and, within limits (set for instance by zoning regulations), use the land as he sees fit. That system of property rights took centuries to develop and is still
evolving.

Comparable systems are usually of more recent origin
in many of the less developed world. During much of the
19th century (and more recently in some cases), the rights
to land in many countries were usufruct rights. With the
rise of commercial agriculture, this system of property
rights often proved inadequate. Some of the inadequacies
were a consequence of the common property nature of the
usufruct land rights. In a usufruct system, land rights
were use rights and did not apply to the stock; the individual user therefore planned for the flow of services from
the use of the renewable resource over a shorter planning
horizon than he would if his property rights extended to
the stock, the ownership of the resource itself. Because
of the temporal insecurity of land rights, cultivators had
an incentive to overuse the resource because if they took
into account the effects on the future resource service
flow, they could not be sure that they would be able to
capture the gains from stinting.

Commercial agriculture and more profitable opportunities for the sale of the produce from farming the land

were generally associated with a rise in the value of land
and an increase in the rate of return on land clearing and
development activities. Because of the development
of a reliable market for output in excess of subsistence
production, clearing additional land and investments in
leveling, draining, and otherwise developing the land
became more attractive. To fully capture the gains from
the investments as well as the capital gains from the
appreciation in relative land values, the land developer
needed a mechanism whereby he could exclude others from
using or taking possession of the land. Under a usufruct
rights system, the ability to exclude was contingent on
nearly continuous use. Such use conflicted in some cases
with the fallow-rotation system employed to maintain soil
fertility.[4] The developer might also want to capture
some of the gains by using his land as collateral--an
unattractive option to a creditor wanting security if the
ownership rights were conditional on continued use by the
debtor. Land often became open-access property once it was
left idle for a period of time, so the common property
aspect of the system created disincentives for the socially
optimal level of investments in land development during a
period in which, setting aside the prevailing property
rights system, the economic returns on those investments
were in fact increasing.

The generalized case described above applies to a
number of Asian and African countries during the 19th and
20th centuries. The specific changes in the decision-
making arrangements and interactions among the parties
that occurred in Thailand will now be described as a case
study.

Economic Change

In Thailand, the opening of the economy to increased
participation in international trade, population growth,
and generally favorable terms of trade for agricultural
export products led to an appreciation in land prices (see
Table 1). Numerous accounts of the 19th century period
indicate that the expansion of the rice-export economy was
accompanied by an appreciation in real land rents and
prices (see Feeny 1982). For the 20th century period, the
qualitative and fragmentary quantitative evidence is
supplemented by data on land prices derived from mortgage
transactions. The data again document the overall appreciation in real land prices and reveal a pattern in which

TABLE 1 Economic Change in Thailand, 1860 to 1942.

Average Annual Percent Rate of Change

Period	Terms of Trade (1)[a]	Terms of Trade (2)[b]	Period	Real Land Price (3)[c]	Period	Rice Exports Quantity (4)	Rice Exports Value (5)	Period	Population (6)
1865-67 to 1912	1.41	1.55			1864-1910	4.43	5.64	1860-1910	0.85
1912-1925	-3.39	-1.92	1915-1925	-0.31	1910-1925	1.78	4.14	1910-1942	2.08
1925-1940	6.31	6.69	1925-1940	2.58	1925-1940	-0.85	-3.80		
1865-67 to 1940	1.52	1.95	1915-1940	1.41	1864-1940	2.84	3.41	1860-1942	1.33

aExport price of rice divided by import price of white shirting.

bExport price of rice divided by import price of grey shirting.

cLand price deflated by price of rice; similar trends are revealed when the land price is deflated by the price of manufactured goods.

Source: Feeny (1982), pages 17, 20, 21, 33, 127-131.

appreciations in the terms of trade are accompanied by an upward trend in real land prices (for a discussion of a simple general equilibrium model that generates this prediction, see Feeny 1982). The increasing value of land in turn led to disputes over land ownership, and these induced changes in the property rights system, ultimately culminating in the privatization of land rights. The major changes in the system of land rights are summarized in Table 2.

Changes in Land Rights through 1954

Under early 19th century monarchy, the system of property rights in land in Thailand was essentially one of usufruct rights. As long as the cultivator continued to use the land, he (or she) had the right to sell it, to pass it on to heirs, to exclude others from using it, or to use it as collateral to obtain a loan.[5] The maintenance of the rights depended on the payment of land taxes. In addition, if the land were not cultivated for more than three consecutive years, rights were forfeited. Operational rules thus provided for serial jointness.

The provisions created temporal uncertainty in the security of the usufruct land rights in Thailand. Homesteaders were particularly concerned by the insecurity of long-term rights: they wanted to be sure that they could reap the gains of having cleared the land for cultivation. In a monsoonal rain-fed agricultural system, land use was not always predictable, and any lapse in its use could make it fair game for acquisitive neighbors and officials.

The first half of the 19th century saw a gradual increase in the degree of commercialization of the Thai economy.[6] As a consequence, jointness became more problematic. During the fourth reign (1851 to 1868), land rights were made more formal through a change in operational rules: the issuance of title deeds was based on paddy land tax receipts. In 1867 and 1868, titles for paddy land were introduced that based the tax on the area harvested. By 1882/1883, this had been reversed in some major Central Plain rice-producing provinces: titles were based on the area owned rather than harvested. Thus, by paying taxes on land not currently in use, farmers could maintain ownership rights. They could obtain titles by presenting officials with the tax receipts for the previous 10 years. Documents were also available to give cultivators of newly cleared areas the rights to exclude others

TABLE 2 Major Changes in the Thai System of Property Rights
        in Land, 1850-1954.

Period	Institutional Change
Early Nineteenth Century	Usufruct rights, existing system
1867-1868	Title deeds issued based on the area harvested
1882-1883	Title deeds issued based on the area owned
1880s	Standardized forms and procedures prescribed in an effort to reduce land disputes
1892	Comprehensive land law enacted with provision for title deeds and use of land as collateral
1901	Torrens system of land registration instituted and cadastral surveys conducted
1936	1901 law amended to allow for ownership based on registration with the Land Department of claims on unsurveyed lands
1954	New land law enacted providing for a variety of documents and levels of security of land rights

Source: Feeny 1984.

from developing the land for three years, at which time
rights were forfeited if the area had not been developed.

As land prices continued to appreciate, inadequacies in
the property rights system became apparent. Frequent land
disputes occurred. Conflicts over ownership of the same
piece of land became endemic. During the 1880s, the
government responded by issuing standard forms and
prescribing standardized procedures. Although the administrative changes represented improvements, the lack of a
central place for land records meant that more than one set
of titles could be issued for the same piece of land. With
increased commercialization, disputes became increasingly
frequent.

The response was another change in operational rules,
the passage of a more comprehensive land law in 1892. It
created nine types of land, including land held by religious institutions, royal land, residential land, agricultural land, land used for mining, forest and jungle land,
and waterway land. The agricultural land category included
three types of orchards and gardens, upland land, and two
types of paddy land. Provisions were made for transferable
title deeds that could be used as collateral, and there
were documents and procedures for the registration of such
transactions. Homesteading provisions were included as
well as procedures for converting old documents into the
newly created ones. The 1892 land law replaced the earlier
rather ad hoc system with a more comprehensive one.

However, major deficiencies in the legislation and its
administration remained. The continued lack of central
land title offices and precise descriptions of the boundaries of the land in question meant that disputes over
ownership could not be easily resolved and land could not
be unambiguously identified. These problems became very
conspicuous in the Rangsit area (to the northeast of
Bangkok, a major commercial rice exporting region in the
Central Plain) during the boom of the 1890s when a number
of very bitter land disputes arose. Conflictual interactions dominated once the limits of jointness had been
reached. As a result, the Royal Survey Department was
diverted from its work on mapping and in 1896 began cadastral surveys, initially concentrating on the Rangsit
area but later expanding into most of the major rice
exporting areas in the Central Plain.

New operational rules were formally introduced in
1901; the Torrens systems of land titling with central
provincial land record offices and cadastral surveys was
formally adopted. From 1901 to 1909, 11 land record

offices were established. In the Central Plain, 593,069
title deeds had been issued by 1910 (637,001 for the whole
kingdom), and the area surveyed was 1,605,000 ha (1,671,000
ha for the whole kingdom). The work was carried out by
European experts (mainly on loan from the Indian Civil
Service) who, in addition to conducting the survey work,
also provided training to the Thai staff.[7]

The system was not fully realized. A lack of diligent
record keeping and administration reduced the benefits.
Not all farmers obtained or were able to obtain the proper
documents for land that they held. Cadastral surveys in
areas outside the Central Plain were particularly
incomplete.[8]

In 1936, the 1901 law was amended to allow for the
registration of claims on unsurveyed land (see Engel
1978:156; Yano 1968:853 and 856). While claims on
apparently unclaimed lands were traditionally registered
with the village headman, the 1936 law required registration at the Land Department. The 1936 law represented a
compromise between the elaborate European cadastral survey
system of the 1901 law and the incomplete implementation of
that system. The compromise was extended in 1954 when a
new comprehensive land law was enacted. The 1954 code
remains the basis of the current system of land rights in
Thailand. It provides or a variety of land documents that
give different levels of security of land rights. Occupation certificates are issued by village headman and commune
leaders and allow the holder to temporarily exclude others
from using land as long as it is being developed. Reserve
licenses issued by district officers also give rights for
temporary occupation subject to utilization. Exploitation
testimonials (again issued by district officers) confirm
that utilization of previously reserved land has taken
place and confer rights that are transferable and inheri-
table. Finally, full title deeds based on cadastral survey
provide for the recording of land transactions; they are
issued by officials in the provincial capital. Greater
security in land rights thus comes at the expense of higher
transaction cost (both formal and informal). The 1954 code
is the basis of the current system of land rights in
Thailand.

The Land Rights Situation Since 1954

Even within the parameters of the compromise embodied
in the 1954 code, the system is still incomplete. Ingram

(1971) reports estimates for the late 1960s of the area
covered by three types of land documents. Only 12 percent
of the area had full title deeds, 4 percent had reserve
licenses, 18 percent had exploitation testimonials, and
65 percent had no formal legal documentation at all.[9]

The incomplete realization of the system of private
property rights in Thailand, especially in upland areas, is
creating disincentives that hinder efforts to intensify
cultivation in the face of a rapidly shrinking land frontier. Recent World Bank reports have pointed to situations
in which socially profitable investments in land development are being underexploited in favor of continued extensive cultivation systems (such as swidden agriculture).
The reason for the lack of intensification is often that
farmers lack the means to obtain secure property rights,
not that they are unaware of the higher rates of return on
more intensive land development. Thus they make investments in land clearing that have only marginal returns and
in the process contribute to soil erosion. These investments have a certain short-term appeal, however, since
during the first few years the marginal returns exceed
those initially available with more intensive modes of
cultivation (that require larger investments in land
development). In the long run, the outcome is clearly
suboptimal from an efficiency point of view, and because
these farmers are generally members of the lower income
group in Thailand, equity is also not well served.

Disputes over conflicting claims to the same piece of
land played an important role in stimulating the government to develop more systematic and elaborate systems of
private land rights in Thailand. The creation and actual
operation of that system also had distributional consequences. In general, the pre-existing rights of cultivators and homesteaders were formally recognized under the
new system; but differential access to formal procedures
and the ability of powerful government officials to manipulate land records did allow elites in some cases to obtain
ownership of land that, under the traditional system, would
have been controlled by homesteading cultivators. A
striking example of this occurred when the Siam Canals Land
and Irrigation Company successfully evicted 29 previous
occupants in an area along the east bank of the Nakorn
Nayok River to the northeast of the company's Rangsit
development scheme. In 1916, Prince Rabi, then the
Minister of Agriculture (and formerly the Minister of
Justice), reviewed the records of the dispute and concluded that the courts had incorrectly found in favor of

the company and its powerful investors. The previous
occupants had first taken their grievances before local
administrative officials, but after obtaining no satisfaction took their case before the provincial court. They
provided various certificates of occupancy and land tax
receipts as evidence of their prior rights. The company
had, however, been able to use its superior access to
government officials and procedures to have the titles for
the land issued in the company's name.10 Given the high
level of political connections of the company and its
allies, little could be done in this case to protect the
original occupants.

Although the outcome was in this case somewhat
atypical, the process by which external arrangements and
third-party dispute settlement were brought to bear was
not. Initially, disputants typically approached local
administrative officials who attempted to resolve the
dispute. As mentioned above, their ability to do so often
depended upon the precision and accuracy of the land
records; thus the evolution of more precise documentation
and record-keeping systems. When disputes could not be
settled at the district level because the parties were
intractable or the records were incomplete or inaccurate
(whether through deliberate manipulation, carelessness, or
negligence), the provincial courts were then employed to
resolve the dispute.

Today, intrafamilial manipulation of the system has
allowed some heirs to gain at the expense of others (Engel
1978). The traditional system of equal inheritance by all
surviving children is frequently subverted by more literate
and knowledgeable siblings, resulting in a clash between
the use of the modern system and traditional inheritance
practices. Through its provincial courts, the central
government has become increasingly involved in the
adjudication of local disputes that in former times
would have been settled by local officials.

The trend has two important implications. First,
common people can use the court system to inhibit arbitrary
behavior on the part of officials. This advantage, however, comes at the expense of a higher level of transaction
cost than in the traditional system.

Conflicts in frontier areas today share many characteristics with those of the earlier period. First, conflicts
have served to focus the attention of the Thai government
on providing cadastral surveys. A recent World Bank
project in Thailand is specifically aimed at extending the
cadastral survey. Second, differential access of claimants

in land disputes to the Thai bureaucracy, the imperfectly competitive political arena, has distributional consequences. We have already seen that in the early 20th century period elites were sometimes able to successfully manipulate the system. Similarly, today, especially along the mountain slopes in northern Thailand, ethnic Thais are often able to obtain legal claim to lands previously cleared and occupied by non-Thai minorities (Kunstadter et al. 1978).

Institutional Change

In the Thai case, the appreciation of land prices led to an increase in the demand for more systematic procedures for defining property rights in land. The government in fact responded to the demands and a new system of property rights gradually evolved. What factors contributed to the willingness and capability of the government to supply the institutional change?

In part, the new system evolved as a practical solution to the land disputes that became so common as land became more valuable.[11] The cost of supplying a new set of institutions was lowered by the availability of European systems and officials--by the existence of a stock of knowledge and practice on the organization of property rights in land. Over time, that system was increasingly appropriated by Thai institutions. The feasibility of creating private property rights in land in Thailand was enhanced by the concomitant development of a provincial court system; this process began in 1892 when the Ministry of Justice was created; the Law of Provincial Courts was promulgated in 1896, and in 1908, the Law of Courts of Justice transferred control of the provincial court system from the Ministry of Interior to the Ministry of Justice (Engel 1978:24-29). Both Thai officials and foreign experts were engaged in drafting modern civil and criminal codes. Although it has never been vigorously exploited in Thailand, a better cadastral system also gave the government an enhanced land tax revenue base. Finally, private and social interests coincided. Members of the elite, primarily government officials, participated in the land boom and benefited from the more secure system of property rights in land. They had an incentive to supply the new system because they too would share in the gains.

In the case study, one can see that, given the initial common property nature of usufruct land rights and the growing incentive to exploit land resources for commercial agriculture, the existing set of decision-making arrangements generated sub-optimal outcomes. The existence of the unexploited gains and resulting land disputes fed back into the system and produced a series of reasonable administrative changes. Simple and inexpensive remedies were tried first, but when the outcomes were still far from satisfactory, more elaborate and expensive solutions were attempted. A new system of property rights evolved and is still evolving. In this case, a system of private property rights (even if less than ideally implemented) was the solution to the common property resource management problem. Manipulation of the property rights system by elites for their private gain occurred and continues to occur, but in the majority of cases the new system provided more secure rights in arable land to the party who actually cleared and cultivated it. Ownership rights that did not depend on continued use and that were more precisely defined provided cultivators with the assurances necessary to make investments in land development privately profitable. In short, the new system of property rights reduced the divergence between the private and social rates of return on land development.

The discussion may be briefly summarized in the framework provided in Oakerson (this volume).

Resource Attributes

Arable crop land lends itself to excludability; thus the creation of boundaries marking areas for exclusive private use was not prohibitively expensive. Arable land is also divisible. Finally, at low levels of population density, much arable land may be left idle. Jointness may be maintained sequentially.

Decision-Making Arrangements

From the mid-19th century on, land rights and disputes were adjudicated under operational and legislative rules imposed by the Thai government on existing usufruct rights. Both local administration officials and the national government were involved in specifying and enforcing the rules governing land use. Over time, local customary rules increasingly conformed to the national laws as interpreted through the provincial court system. The national laws, however, were also formally modified to reflect the lack of a complete cadastral survey and the long-standing Thai tradition of homesteading on unoccupied lands.

Interactions

Under the traditional usufruct system and in the environment of a largely subsistence economy with a low population density, there was limited competition in land use--in the interactions among cultivators. The usufruct system allowed the cultivator to exclude others from land currently in use. But given the abundance of land and limited outlets for surplus production, there was full jointness and/or little rivalry in the use of waste land.

As the property rights system gradually evolved, individuals made use of the new government-established institutional arrangements to enhance the security and precision of their land rights. Many people, influential and otherwise, shared in the gains. However, differential access to the use of the institutional arrangements did affect the outcomes in terms of who obtained land rights to various tracts of land in a minority of important cases.

Outcomes

The development of more secure property rights in land signalled increased intensification in land use, greater investments in land development (the bunding and leveling of fields to promote the use of transplant varieties instead of the broadcast planting of paddy), and the increased use of land as collateral.

At another level, that of the system as a whole, the result was an evolution of institutional arrangements-- changes in the rules through which individuals interacted. The outcome of the efforts of the landowners to more securely define their rights in land was a gradual evolution of new legislative rules and operational regulations resulting in the privatization of rights in arable land.

CONCLUSIONS

From the two case studies, several propositions concerning the dynamics of common property management emerge. As Oakerson (this volume) stresses, understanding

the dynamics of institutional change involves assessing the
opportunities for individuals to learn from the consequences of their actions. The recursive nature of the
evolution of systems is evident in both cases. An understanding of change also requires an examination of the ways
in which existing institutional arrangements constrain or
enhance individuals' abilities to make adjustments in the
decision-making arrangements. In both the Thai and the
Zinder cases, existing constitutional structures required
action by central government if innovations in institutional arrangements were to be made that would ameliorate common pool resource management problems. In both
cases, peasant farmers in general have limited access and
influence in the political system and few instrumental-
ities of local government or local association. Nevertheless, in the Thai case, the demands of landowners for
innovations in the property rights system were largely met,
apparently because elite and peasant interests largely
overlapped on the issue of land rights.

In both cases, privatization of a common property
resource makes sense for a number of reasons:

o   First, the costs of organizing collective
    management are extremely high and collective
    management creates problems. Privatization does,
    however, risk inequality at the subdivision stage
    when control over the resource itself is allotted
    to particular individuals. If this is a one-time
    allocation, with no easy mechanisms to rectify
    maldistribution, inequities can pose a serious
    problem. It should be noted that maintaining
    common property institutions in no way avoids
    equity problems. They are simply pushed back a
    step, and reappear when annual or other increments
    of production from the resource are harvested and
    distributed to users. Distribution rules specify
    who gets what, when, and how. The potential for
    inequity inherent in such regulations and practices
    is substantial.

o   Second, commons management of any sort depends on a
    situation of perceived scarcity; on the legal
    possibility (that is, legal authority) to manage a
    resource (or at least the lack of a legal prohibi-
    tion on local efforts to manage it); and on the
    perception of some comparative advantage to sus-
    taining common property status for the resource

rather than privatizing it (e.g., prohibitively expensive fencing that makes it reasonable to jointly hire a few guards to protect the resource for everyone). Therefore, it follows that effective commons management depends on: (1) local capacity* to experiment with joint management forms as production-consumption relations deteriorate and resource shortages appear; and (2) low political and economic costs of collective organization to manage the commons.

Zinder-area villages have no authority for, and little tradition of, collective management of any kind of resource. The ethnic Hausa who inhabit this region tend to be highly individualistic, and show little interest in state-organized groups. Collective action groups that could be readily altered to manage a commons effectively simply do not exist. Given the existing institutional arrangements and cultural norms, the transaction costs associated with collective management in this setting are high. Much the same can be said for Thailand, where highly individualistic behavior also generally prevails. In such settings, privatization may minimize transaction costs.

o   Third, population pressure, world or local market opportunities, and changing production technologies will influence the type of management structure local people will prefer. These trends shape the demand for new institutional arrangements.

o   Finally, effective decision makers must perceive that organizing the management enterprise is worthwhile, i.e., that it will benefit them in a personal manner, either directly or indirectly. Incentive compatibility--the congruence of the interests of the individual decision maker and of those affected by his decision--appears to be essential.

---

*In the woodstock case, the state forester lives so far away from most users that they do not consider him a reasonable source of authorization. The national system of common woodstock management thus failed and still fails to function. In Zinder, then, illegal privatization efforts appear critical as indicators of a fundamental change in user perspective. From being producers for their own consumption only, the users in these cases have begun to become producers of wood for sale as well.

NOTES

1. The authors acknowledge the helpful comments of Jere
Gilles, Margaret McKean, Elinor Ostrom, Pauline Peters, and
C. Ford Runge.

2. The specific model employed here is described in more
detail in Feeny (1982, 1984); see also Ruttan and Hayami
(1984) and Hayami and Ruttan (1985).

3. It should be noted that there is a long tradition in
West Africa of a distinction between property rights in
land and in the trees that grow on that land. In part, the
distinction may be a result of the fact that property
rights in land were acquired through the investment of the
labor necessary to clear the land and bring it under
cultivation. Thus, by analogy, the person who invested his
labor in cutting a tree had acquired ownership in the wood,
even if he did not own the land on which it was grown.

4. Furnivall (1909) provides an example of the conflict
between fallow-rotation systems and usufruct rights in
lower Burma in the 19th century.

5. In a usufruct system of land rights, the act of selling
land transfers the use rights from the original user to a
new party; in the process, this new party obtains the
original holder's right to exclude third parties. In many
instances, it is the investments in clearing the land that
are being "sold." Thus, the purchase price compensates the
original owner for improvements in the land.

6. The trends in commercialization in the Thai economy
over the 19th and 20th centuries are discussed in Ingram
(1971) and Feeny (1982). Developments in the Thai property
rights system are discussed in Feeny (1982, 1984).

7. After 1909, the Royal Survey Department was transferred back to its original mapping duties and the rate of

increase in the surveyed area plunged. The number of
title deeds on file (primarily in the Central Plain) did,
however, continue to increase; the rate of increase of
title deeds on file for the whole kingdom was 4.69 percent
per year over the 1905 to 1941 period.

8. After 1909, a number of minor changes were made in the
system. Administrative procedures were changed and fees
were instituted on land transfers. Restrictions were
placed on the sale of public lands in 1916 and 1919 with
the intent of curbing land speculation. Finally, in 1938
and 1939, a new schedule of agricultural land taxes was
established.

9. Ingram (1971:266); see also Feeny (1982), Johnson
(1969), Hooker (1975), Gisselquist (1976), Engel (1978),
Kemp (1981), Yano (1968), and Chalermrath (1972). Reasons
for the incomplete coverage include the lack of a complete
cadastral survey as well as the unwillingness or inability
of farmers to obtain formal documentation of their land
rights. The overwhelming constraint appears to have been
the incomplete coverage of the cadastral survey supplied by
the government.

10. Primary documents relevant to this case are found in
the Thai National Archives, Sixth Reign, Ministry of
Agriculture Documents 5/1 to 5/12; see also Feeny (1982).

11. Unfortunately, archival and other records provide
little evidence on the individual strategies employed among
the competing parties involved in disputes over land use.
Some of the limited available evidence is discussed in
Engel (1978) and Feeny (1982); see also Kemp (1981),
Chalermrath (1972), and Yano (1968).

REFERENCES

Chalermrath, K. 1972. Thailand's Public Law and Policy for
    Conservation and Protection of Land with Special
    Attention to Forests and Natural Areas. Bangkok: The
    National Institute of Development Administration.

Engel, D. M. 1978. Code and Custom in a Thai Provincial
    Court. Tucson, Arizona: University of Arizona Press.

Feeny, D. 1982. The Political Economy of Productivity:
    Thai Agricultural Development 1880-1975. Vancouver,
    Canada: University of British Columbia Press.

Feeny, D. 1984. The development of property rights in
    land: a comparative study. Economic Growth Center,
    Discussion Paper No. 459. New Haven, Connecticut:
    Yale University.

Furnivall, J. S. 1909. Land as a free gift of nature.
    Economic Journal 19:552-562.

Gisselquist, D. P. 1976. A History of Contractual
    Relations in a Thai Rice Growing Village. Ph.D.
    dissertation. New Haven, Connecticut: Yale
    University.

Glantz, M. H. ed. 1977. Desertification: Environmental
    Degradation in and around Arid Lands. Boulder,
    Colorado: Westview Press.

Hayami, Y. and V. W. Ruttan. 1985. Agricultural
    Development: An International Perspective. Revised
    Edition. Baltimore, Maryland: Johns Hopkins
    University Press.

Hooker, M. B. 1975. Legal Pluralism: An Introduction to
    Colonial and Neo-Colonial Law. Oxford: Oxford
    University Press.

Ingram, J. C. 1971. Economic Change in Thailand, 1850-1970. 2d ed. Stanford, California: Stanford University Press.

Johnson, V. W. 1969. Agricultural Development in Thailand with Reference to Rural Institutions. Bangkok: Division of Land Policy, Department of Land Development.

Kemp, J. H. 1981. Legal and informal land tenures in Thailand. Modern Asian Studies 15:1-23.

Kunstadter, P., E. C. Chapman, and S. Sabhasri, eds. 1978. Farmers in the Forest: Economic Development and Marginal Agriculture in Northern Thailand. Honolulu, Hawaii: University Press of Hawaii.

National Research Council. 1983. Agroforestry in the West African Sahel. Washington, D.C.: National Academy Press.

Nicolas, G. 1962. Un village bouzou du Niger: Etude d'un terroir. Les Cahiers d'Outre-Mer 15, No. 58 (April-June 1962):138-165.

Pélissier, P. 1980. L'arbre dans les paysages agraires de l'Afrique Noire, in L'arbre en Afrique tropicale: La fonction et le signe. Cahiers O.R.S.T.O.M., Série Sciences Humaines 17:3-4.

Ruttan, V. W., and Y. Hayami. 1984. Towards a theory of induced institutional innovation. Journal of Development Studies 20:203-223.

Salifou, A. 1971. Le Damagaram ou Sultanat de Zinder au XIX° Siècle. Niamey, Niger: Centre Nigérien de Recherches en Sciences Humaines.

Thomson, J. T. 1976. Law, Legal Process, and Development at the Local Level in Hausa-speaking Niger. Ph.D. dissertation, Department of Political Science. Bloomington: Indiana University.

Thomson, J. T. 1977. Ecological deterioration: local-level rule-making and enforcement problems in Niger. In Glantz 1977:57-59.

Thomson, J. T. 1980. Bois de villages (Niger): Report of
    an Investigation Concerning Socio-Cultural and
    Political-Economic Aspects of the First Phase of the
    Project and Design Recommendations for a Possible
    Second Phase. Report submitted to International
    Development Research Centre, Ottawa, Canada. Centre
    File 3-P-72-0093.

Thomson, J. T. 1982. Peasants, rules and woodstock
    management in Zinder Department, Niger. Washington,
    D.C.: Paper presented at the annual meeting of the
    African Studies Association, November 4-7.

Thomson, J. T. 1983. The precolonial woodstock in
    Sahelian West Africa: the example of central Niger
    (Damagaram, Damergu, Aïr). In Tucker et al. 1983:
    167-177.

Tucker, R. P. and J. F. Richards, eds. 1983. Global
    Deforestation and the Nineteenth-Century World
    Economy. Durham, North Carolina: Duke University
    Press.

Weber, F. and M. W. Hoskins. 1983. Soil Conservation
    Technical Sheets. Washington, D.C.: Office of
    International Cooperation and Development, U.S.
    Department of Agriculture.

Yano, T. 1968. Land tenure in Thailand. Asian Survey
    8:853-863.

Collective Management of Hill Forests in Nepal: The Community Forestry Development Project

J. E. M. Arnold
J. Gabriel Campbell [1]

INTRODUCTION

Forests and forest products have always been of central importance to life in the middle hills of Nepal, a region where villagers are unusually isolated, even today, by the terrain. Fuel and timber, fodder supplies, and tree litter for composting are but the most important products of the forests. The forest has supplied these and other smaller inputs to the household and rural economy, and helped to prevent widespread soil erosion, flooding and damage. But the expanding population has put increasing pressures on the land, with the consequence that forested land is diminishing and with it both the products it has supplied and the protection it has afforded to the ecological balance in the area.

Early attempts by the central government to halt this deteriorating trend were based on measures to bring all forest land under government control. In the late 1970s, however, these measures were reversed in a vigorous new initiative designed to enable, encourage, and support local control, management, and creation of forest resources. In doing so, the government hoped to be able to build upon the tradition of communal management of forests, and of other resources and activities, among the people of the middle hills.

In some areas, this new approach to forest management is being pursued through existing integrated area develop-

ment projects. In the rest of the hills and mountainous
region, about one half of it, the new approach is being
developed through a project of the Community Forestry
Afforestation Division of the Forest Department in the
Ministry of Forests--the Community Forestry Development
Project (CFDP).

This paper reports on progress made in initiating and
institutionalizing communal forestry in the hill areas
through the CFDP, which is supported by technical assistance from the Food and Agriculture Organization of the
United Nations (FAO) and the United Nations Development
Programme (UNDP) and by a loan from the World Bank's
International Development Administration (IDA). During
the initial phase covered here, the project has been
operating in 400 panchayats in 29 administrative districts, spread throughout the middle hill areas of the
four regions of the country (see Figure 1). (A panchayat
is the lowest political and administrative unit.)

This study encompasses an initiative by a government
to provide a widely applicable framework for developing
productive local forest management systems suited to
current needs, and that would build upon local traditions
and practices for forest resource management. Thus, the
concern here is not with a single group or collection of
groups, but rather with a policy.

The newness of the CFDP initiative needs to be
underscored. The project became operational less than
five years ago, and its early years were devoted to
evolving and setting in place the necessary institutional
and physical infrastructures. Transfer of forests to local
control only began to take place on a substantial scale in
1983/84. What is reported here is thus necessarily
confined to the experience gained in the formative stage of
this potentially very large and far-reaching attempt to
establish a sound, sustainable system of common property
resource management.

HISTORICAL BACKGROUND

The Forest Resource

The hill areas of Nepal contain an unusually wide
variety of forest types, reflecting both the wide variations in altitude, climate and terrain, and the fact that
the botanic zones of the eastern and western Himalayas
meet and merge within the country. Stainton (1972)

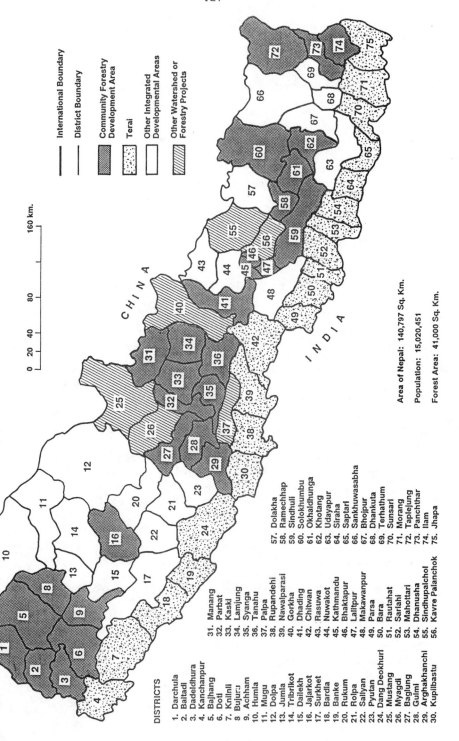

FIGURE 1 Community Forestry Development Program, Nepal.

DISTRICTS

1. Darchula
2. Baitadi
3. Dadeldhura
4. Kanchanpur
5. Bajhang
6. Doti
7. Knilnli
8. Bujurj
9. Achham
10. Humla
11. Mugu
12. Dolpa
13. Jumla
14. Tribrikot
15. Dailekh
16. Jajarkot
17. Surkhet
18. Bardia
19. Banke
20. Rukum
21. Rolpa
22. Sallyan
23. Pyutan
24. Dang Deokhurl
25. Mustang
26. Myagdi
27. Baglung
28. Gulml
29. Arghakhanchl
30. Kupilbastu

31. Manang
32. Parbat
33. Kaskl
34. Lamjung
35. Syanga
36. Tanahu
37. Palpa
38. Rupandehi
39. Nawalparasi
40. Gorkha
41. Dhading
42. Chitwan
43. Rasuwa
44. Nuwakot
45. Kathmandu
46. Bhaktapur
47. Lalitpur
48. Makawanpur
49. Parsa
50. Bara
51. Rautahat
52. Sarlahi
53. Mahottari
54. Dhanusha
55. Sindhupalchol
56. Kavre Palanchok

57. Dolakha
58. Ramechhap
59. Sindhuli
60. Solokhumbu
61. Okhaldhunga
62. Khotang
63. Udayapur
64. Siraha
65. Saptarl
66. Sankhuwasabha
67. Bhojpur
68. Dhankuta
69. Terhathum
70. Sunsari
71. Morang
72. Taplejung
73. Panchthar
74. Ilam
75. Jhapa

Area of Nepal: 140,797 Sq. Km.

Population: 15,020,451

Forest Area: 41,000 Sq. Km.

Legend:
- International Boundary
- District Boundary
- Community Forestry Development Area
- Terai
- Other Integrated Developmental Areas
- Other Watershed or Forestry Projects

CHINA

INDIA

0 20 40   80   160 km.

identifies 6 zones, 13 sub-zones, and 77 forest types. In
general, within the populated range of altitudes, fir and
oak predominate at higher elevations, gradually giving way
to chir pine (Pinus roxburghii), species of Prunus,
Castanopsis, Schima and Alnus at medium elevations, and
sal (Shorea robusta) at lower elevations.

The natural diversity of the forests has been further
modified by prolonged and often heavy local human inter-
vention--which varies considerably both in intensity and
purpose from one area of the hills to another. In the
east, for example, pressures on the forest have been
heavier than in the west. Different mixes of products
drawn from the forest reflect variations in such factors as
the role and management of animal husbandry, type of house
construction, and individual or village preferences.

Changing Patterns of Use of the Forests

Nepal's agricultural economy has always depended on
the farmers' use of several complex economic strategies
to exploit the available natural resources. The principal
source of income has always been crop production from
arable land. But farmers have always supplemented their
incomes through the sale of livestock and livestock products, and have fulfilled their own needs for manure and
draft animals by raising livestock. Thus, farmers have
always depended heavily on forest and pasture land resources to supply fodder for livestock and such forest products
as fuelwood, compost materials, construction, cottage
industry, food, and ritual materials. Indeed, these
resources have traditionally been an indispensable
component of the subsistence systems used by Nepalese
farmers to maintain their livelihood.

So long as there was (and in many parts of Nepal there
still is) a relative abundance of these natural resources,
the traditional methods of exploiting them did not pose a
severe problem. The management systems controlling their
use were primarily concerned with rights of ownership and
the protection and distribution of benefits.

Many villages of Nepal had systems in which forests
and pasture lands were considered community property (such
as the kipat system in eastern Nepal) that could only be
used by noncommunity members through payment of fees or
other commodities. Likewise, many villages (such as in
the far west) had, and continue to have, communal systems
of gathering and harvesting that ensured fairly equal

distribution of and ease of access to such products as
fodder and composting materials. Some communities, like
the Sherpas in Khumbu, even had strict rationing systems
to control the use of construction timber, since trees
regenerated so slowly in their high altitude ecosystem.
In addition, a tradition of temple and monastery forests ensured that trees growing near religious structures
were cut only for religious purposes. However, for
most of the Nepalese hills, the main factor that limited
the amount of deforestation was the relatively small
population and the lack of any commercial exploitation.
In these demographic conditions, it was labor and not
resources that limited agricultural productivity (Campbell
1978).

Given the high intensity of labor required to terrace
fields, build irrigation channels, and transport manure
composts, a farmer could intensively cultivate only a few
fields. This meant that where possible the average farmer
supplemented his main production with labor-efficient
methods such as slash-and-burn agriculture in forest
lands. Similarly, cattle and sheep were extensively herded
in forest and alpine areas. So long as the population was
small and resources exceeded the amount of labor available
to exploit them, this kind of extensive agriculture and
grazing did not produce severe ecological repercussions;
the fields could be left fallow to regenerate naturally,
and the carrying capacity for grazing was not exceeded.

As population dramatically increased from 1850 to the
present, the resources-to-labor equation reversed: land
rather than labor has now become the limiting factor
throughout most of Nepal. This has resulted in a shift to
more intensive farming in which most cultivation is carried
out on terraced fields. It has also resulted in a
reduction in the number of livestock per family, and a
shift from cattle to buffalo, and from sheep to goats.
While these agricultural trends are ecologically beneficial, the benefits are unfortunately offset by the
increasing use of marginal lands for cultivation without
sufficient fallow, and by a continuing pattern of forest
and pasture use that considerably exceeds the carrying
capacity of the environment.

Heavy pressures on the resource base are thus of
relatively recent origin, and there are still important
exceptions and enormous variations in the rate of degradation. People are only now seeing the consequences of
these pressures on a scale sufficient to persuade them to

evolve new methods of resource conservation on common lands.

Forest Legislation

In the face of growing demands for fuel and fodder and other forest products, the government nationalized all nonregistered forest and waste land in 1957, in an attempt to curb the process of deforestation and forest degradation and increase productivity by putting forests under more active management. Later, under the Forest Act of 1961, the definition of forest land was extended to include all land adjoining forest areas and left fallow for two years (Manandhar 1982).

The desirable objectives of this new policy proved very difficult to achieve. Effective government supervision of thousands of patches of forest scattered through remote hill terrain, accessible only with extreme difficulty, proved impossible. For example, one regulation required people to obtain permits from forest rangers to collect each load of firewood. Another required written agreement from a distant forest office (at times, more than a days' walk) for house timber. Obviously, these were difficult for households to obey and nearly impossible for the authorities to enforce. Consequently, people in most places unavoidably resorted to illegal collection of forest produce.

At the same time, nationalization initially had the unforeseen effect of further weakening existing forest conservation and management. Whereas communities previously had sought to protect local forest resources against exploitation by outsiders through their traditional management systems, they now had no legal authority to do so. Furthermore, they now tended to view the forests as government property rather than their own, an attitude that seriously eroded motivation to protect local forest resources. Thus, nationalization apparently inadvertently "hastened the process of deforestation" (Manandhar 1982). Ironically, this alienation of official control also led some communities to intensify protection of their forests from the depredation of outsiders--including, occasionally, the forest department itself.

The forest legislation also tended to obscure the understanding of hill forestry as a component of hill agricultural systems. For example, a regulation that specified that any field left fallow for two years could be appropriated by the state had the effect of discouraging fallowing.

In recognition of these negative consequences, the government took a radically different initiative in 1978 by promulgating new regulations to enable substantial amounts of public forest land to be handed over to local communities to control and manage. Under these regulations, the forest department could enter into agreements to transfer forest to village panchayats. The village panchayat, the lowest level of political and administrative organization, comprises nine wards, usually encompassing several villages with a total population of 2,000 to 4,000 persons. The elected representatives from the constituent wards in turn elect a chairman, the pradhan panch. The village panchayat is the principal institution through which local development activities and funds are channeled.

The 1978 Panchayat Forest and Panchayat Protected Forest (PPF) Rules (as amended in 1980) define the categories of forest that could be transferred to local community control as follows:

o   Panchayat Forest: "Any governmental forest area or any part thereof, which has been rendered waste or contains only stumps, may be entrusted by His Majesty's Government to any village Panchayat on prescribed terms and conditions for reforestation in the interest of the village community, and such forests shall be called Panchayat Forests."

o   Panchayat Protected Forests: "Governmental forests in any area or part thereof may be entrusted by His Majesty's Government to any local Panchayat on prescribed terms and conditions for the purpose of protection and proper management, and such forests shall be called Panchayat Protected Forests."

The new law also made provision for the establishment of Religious Forests to be managed by temple trusts, and for Contract Forests, which could be awarded to either individuals or groups.

As many as 125 hectares of bare land could be handed over to each panchayat for afforestation to create a Panchayat Forest, and approximately 500 hectares of existing forest could be turned over to the panchayat as a Panchayat Protected Forest. It has been estimated that, provided that sufficient forest land is available in each panchayat, a theoretical maximum 1,835,000 hectares could

fall under panchayat control, amounting to almost
45 percent of the existing state forest area (Manandhar
1982).

NATURE OF THE RESOURCE: PEOPLE-FOREST RELATIONSHIPS

Early in 1982, a wide ranging survey was conducted to
provide information that would be used in the design and
implementation of the Community Forestry Development
Project. The information documented prevailing patterns
of forest resource use, particularly fuelwood and fodder,
in relation to local farming systems in different regions
of the country. Information was collected from a sample of
900 households and 180 ward leaders, with the random sample
stratified equally among the four regions in which the
project is operated, and further subdivided by the length
of time the panchayats had participated in the program.
Important features of the people-forest relationship that
emerged are summarized as below (from Campbell and
Bhattarai 1983).

Dependence on Supplies from Public Forests

Fuelwood. Mean annual fuelwood consumption was found to
be 640 kg per capita, varying considerably by region and
source: the consumption level of the central region was
only half that in the east, while use in the other two
regions lay somewhere in the middle (Table 1). Cost was
an important determinant of consumption. In the east, only
one-third of the fuelwood came from public forests, while
this source accounted for over three-quarters of supply in
the far west. On average, public forests provided just
over half of total fuelwood supplies (360 kg of per capita
consumption). With growing fuelwood shortages, more
agricultural residues (except dung) were burned for fuel,
although dung was used in the Kathmandu Valley and the
Terai. Kerosene was reserved almost exclusively for
lighting, and was thus not an alternative to fuelwood.

Fodder. Livestock feed was reported to be insufficient
throughout Nepal; the average of four months of shortage
peaked in March-April. Of the roughly 60 percent of the
households that owned large animals, three-quarters grazed
their cattle for much of the year while two-fifths grazed
their female buffalo; stall feeding accounted for the rest

TABLE 1 Fuelwood Consumption by Source of Supply.

Variable	Value	East	Center	West	Far West	Project	Hill Nepal
Kg/household	mean	4,966	3,198	4,472	3,926	4,126	4,074
	median	4,329	2,600	3,900	2,808	3,444	3,355
Kg/per capita	mean	829	484	743	548	656	640
Kg/public forest	mean	273	234	377	436	327	328
-percentage	mean	33	48	51	80	51	53
Kg/private	mean	205	62	113	27	103	97
-percentage	mean	25	13	15	5	15	14
Kg/twigs and bushes	mean	298	129	251	64	195	181
-percentage	mean	36	27	34	12	29	27
Kg/purchased	mean	54	58	2	19	31	33
-percentage	mean	7	12	0	4	5	6

SOURCE: Campbell and Bhattarai (1983).

of the feed supplies. Of the hand-harvested feed, which was the main source for most households, 17 percent was tree fodder. Of this, less than 25 percent was reported to come from public forest; only one-third of all households used public forest for tree fodder at all.

Other products. Timber and poles for building (and bamboo in the east), and grass for fodder were important additional forest products, followed by green matter for livestock bedding and compost. Overall, the use of such products as forest vegetables, fruits, and herbs was very low, although the proportion of households using some amount was probably quite high.

Thirty-six percent of the ward leaders reported the existence of some form of collective system for protecting an area (or areas) of local public forest. More than half of these collectives had come into existence after the 1957 nationalization of forests, indicating a strong continuing interest in communal solutions to forest-related issues, despite nationalization.

It appears that management systems have developed
in areas where small shortages of fuel and fodder had
emerged, but not where the shortages had become so severe
that they could no longer be remedied by using the
remaining resource, even if it were more effectively
managed. Commitment to management was found to be much
greater where villagers had access to forests that were
rich in desired species, such as sal (Shorea robusta) or
oak. Where the forest contained species that were prized
for fuel and fodder, e.g., chir pine (Pinus roxburghii),
villagers were much less willing to adopt the harvesting
restrictions necessary to preserve it.

Private Tree Growing

The finding that most fodder does not come from public
forests contrasts with earlier assessments, and makes it
more difficult to explain past trends largely in terms of
the use of tree fodder. However, it is consistent with two
other findings from the survey--that livestock numbers are
decreasing in the majority of villages, and that private
sources for tree fodder are increasingly important.
When villages were asked what method they would suggest
to overcome fodder shortages, they most frequently proposed
private planting of fodder trees (by contrast, only
7 percent proposed planting fodder trees on public land).
Apparently, as public sources of fodder have diminished
over the last half century, there has been a major shift
to stall feeding and private fodder trees (Campbell and
Bhattarai 1983).
Each household was found to own an average of 28 trees
of various kinds, and 31 seedlings under 5 years of age.
Ownership was highest in the western and eastern regions.
Three-quarters of all households own some fodder or fuel
timber trees. Although, as is shown in Table 2, the
numbers of both types of trees are roughly equal, the
greater importance of fodder trees is reflected by their
wider distribution (65 percent of households compared with
36 percent with fuel/timber trees), and by their promi-
nence (along with fruit trees) in people's preferences for
additional trees.

TABLE 2   Percentage of Private Tree Ownership by Region.

Type	East	Center	West	Far West	Hill Nepal
Fodder	13.5	9.4	16.7	8.6	12.1
Fuel/timber	12.8	9.2	17.8	7.4	11.9
Fruit	2.2	2.2	1.6	3.9	2.4
Bamboo clumps	5.3	.9	1.3	.03	1.7
Total Trees	33.8	21.7	37.4	20.0	28.1
Total Seedlings	53.0	27.0	36.0	10.0	30.8

SOURCE: Campbell and Bhattarai (1983).

Natural regeneration accounts for most fuel/timber seedlings and half of fodder seedlings. Villagers acquire most of the rest by transplanting naturally occurring seedlings either from elsewhere on their land or from the forest. The study found that nurseries had begun to contribute to supplies, particularly of fruit, bamboo, and particular fodder species that could not be readily obtained from natural regeneration. On average, households expressed a wish for an additional 30 trees, with clear preferences for certain species, although preferences ranged across a large variety of species depending on the region and use.

The 1982 survey thus disclosed a number of factors of considerable importance to the design and implementation of a program to encourage and support collective management of local forest resources. Private trees are an important source of supplies of forest products--the predominant source for some outputs, notably tree fodder. Public forests remain the main source of other products, such as timber, and overall continue to be the mainstay of forest-based activities. Despite the earlier nationalization of the forests, there continues to be widespread interest and willingness to take collective action to maintain--and to extend--remaining forest resources. Eighty-five percent of those surveyed were prepared to make common grazing lands available for tree planting. The basis for strengthened local forest management thus appears to remain very much alive in the existing systems.

DECISION-MAKING ARRANGEMENTS

Pre-Existing Local Forest Management Systems[2]

The size and geographical proximity of the user group
are very important determinants of successful cooperation
in forest management. Common forest use by adjoining
villages and households was found to create strong group
cohesion, even where groups are multicaste in composition.
In all the forest management systems surveyed, areas of
forest are managed by a group comprising only those households that traditionally use the area for fuel, fodder, or
composting material. The management entity is thus almost
always much smaller than the panchayat, and sometimes cuts
across panchayat boundaries.

Group rules governing management of the forest differ
considerably among groups. The bases for group rules used
in various traditional management systems are listed in
Table 3. In general, the use of forests is controlled by
restricting access to certain times of the year, thus
permitting protection and regeneration during the rest of
the year. The length of time during which the forest is
open to member villagers for specified product collection,
the number of times in the year when collection is permitted, and the timing of the periods of access all vary
across groups. These differences reflect the villagers'
perception of the extent to which the forest can be safely
subjected to cutting and collection. As has been noted,
effective management systems are to be found only where
enough accessible forest remains to enable villagers to
meet their fuel or fodder needs by harvesting only in
limited periods of the year.

Systems of spatial control have also been adopted
in some traditional management situations. Within these
systems, areas are delineated that can be harvested at a
specified period. Sometimes these systems cover the whole
resource over the period of one season, and their main
function is to ensure that all members of the community
have equal ease of access to both the nearby and more
distant areas. In other cases, a rotational system is
used that allows a particular resource, such as fuelwood,
to grow again before it is again harvested.

In most of the villages with effective management
systems, the user group employs forest watchers to
discourage breaches of the management rules. These
watchers are paid in grain by every household except
the most poor. The effectiveness of the forest watchers

TABLE 3   Control Systems Used in Traditional Forest
          Management.

Basis of Group Rules	Examples
1. Harvesting only selected products and species	- Trees: timber, fuelwood, food (fruit, nuts, seeds, honey), leaf fodder, fibre, leaf mulch, other minor forest products (gums, resins, dyes, liquor, plate leaves, etc.) - Grass: fodder, thatching, rope - Other wild plants: medicinal herbs, food (tubers, etc.), bamboos, etc. - Other cultivated plants: upland crops (maize, millet, wheat, potatoes, vegetables), fruit, etc. - Wildlife: animals, birds, bees, other insects, etc.
2. Harvesting according to condition of product	- Stage of growth, maturity, alive or dead - Size, shape - Plant density, spacing - Season (flowering, leaves fallen, etc.) - Part: branch, stem, shoot, flower
3. Limiting amount of product	- By time: by season, by days, by year, by several years - By quantity: number of trees, headloads, baskets, number of animals - By tool: sickles, saws, axes - By area: zoning, blocks, types of terrain, altitude - By payment: cash, kind, food or liquor to watchers or village, manure - By agency: women, children, hired labor, contractor, type of animal
4. Using social means for protecting area	- By watcher: paid in grains or cash - By rotational guard duty - By voluntary group action - By making use of herders mandatory

varies with the strength of social sanctions against
forest encroachment, although each village has some system
of fines for villagers who enter the forest illegally.
Generally, villagers were quite willing to pay the forest
watchers with household grain, but they expressed reserva-
tions about increasing the number of watchers, and hence
the burden on households, should the area of communal
forest be increased.

Most traditional management systems tend to be very
conservative, allowing access only to a few products.
If the amount of a resource is too small to be adequately
shared, or if it may be difficult to control an open
harvest, communities prefer to stop collection of the
resource altogether. In an oak forest managed for leaf
litter, for example, all fuelwood cutting will be banned,
even though some trees are overmature or unproductive.

Strong leadership in the locality was found to be
important in starting management systems, but the
villagers' willingness to participate in cooperative
forest management appears to be motivated by perceived
shortages of fuel, fodder, and composting material as
forest resources diminish. Awareness of the problems
created by deforestation is widespread and well understood. However, there is considerable variation in
villagers' conviction that remedial action could be
successful.

Local factionalism impedes successful cooperation in
forest management when opposing factions seek to extend
their power base by discrediting an opposing faction's
forest management initiative. Where factions compete to
be seen as more progressive in their approach to forestry,
the reverse could be the case.

Proximity to markets for forest fuel products also
tends to undermine forest management: where firewood
can be sold nearby at high prices, it is hard to prevent
poaching in panchayats near market centers.

Conflicts between livestock and forest management
are perhaps the most common constraint. Meeting fodder
requirements is a main objective of traditional forest
management, but since grazing prevents natural regeneration, it is one of the principal causes of forest degradation. The most effective systems of forest management were
found to be in areas where animals are largely stall-fed or
under the supervision of herders throughout the year.

In addition, access to forest resources was found to
differ markedly with location, which is in turn linked to

income. Poorer members of the village tend to live in higher and more remote parts of the village, and consequently are likely to depend more on forest grazing and slash-and-burn agriculture to survive.

Existing forest management systems, varying as widely as they do in their form and effectiveness, are not in themselves adapted to the more intensive management now needed. However, they can provide important information about needs and particular constraints that should be accommodated. As has been noted elsewhere,

> [T]he most important lessons to be learned from traditional management systems are that community management of forest resources is possible if the right social unit is self-selected, the objectives are widely understood, and the benefits equitably distributed. In addition, the principles of social control and product distribution encoded in these traditional systems can be successfully incorporated in expanded management programmes. (Pelinck and Campbell n.d.)

The Community Forestry Development Project

The project was established to help the Ministry of Forests, through the Community Forestry Afforestation Division of its forest department, to support the three main elements of local management of forest resources: managed Panchayat Protected Forests (PPFs), planting of Panchayat Forests (PFs), and production of seedlings for private planting. In addition, the project was to develop and distribute more efficient wood fuel stoves for people who were short of fuelwood.

Forest nurseries were to be established in all participating panchayats. Financing and training were to be provided for locally recruited panchayat forest foremen to run the nurseries and panchayat forest watchers to help protect the plantations and managed forests on behalf of the panchayat (in keeping with the tradition of forest watchers in many existing local forest management systems). Finally, a new cadre of forestry staff, community forestry assistants (CFAs), were to provide technical assistance and advice at the panchayat and village level. The CFAs were to help panchayats carry out the preparatory work needed before public lands could be handed over as PFs and PPFs.

The project also sought to help build up the necessary institutional base to service and support this infra-structure. Components included training for forest service field staff and _panchayat_ workers, a system of information and extension materials for communication and training at the village level, a system of field trials to provide basic technical information on choice of species and forest management prescriptions, and a monitoring and evaluation network to provide information about performance of such project activities as nursery production and plantation establishment and about people's needs for project inputs and responses to the project.

During its first five years (1980-85), the project was to extend its operations to 340 _panchayats_ in 29 hill districts. Physical progress has been generally on schedule. By July 1984, the project was working in 381 _panchayats_ and had 430 operational nurseries. Over 8,000 hectares of PF had been planted, more than 1.5 million seedlings distributed for private planting, and 227 PFs and PPFs had been handed over from the government to the _panchayat_.

The performance of individual components and areas within these aggregates has of course varied. Farmers' uptake of seedlings for private planting far outstripped expectations. In contrast, the transfer of existing forests to PPFs, and the development of collaborative management plans, has lagged behind the ambitious initial targets. Although almost half of the _panchayats_ now participating in the project were given PPFs, few such transfers are protected by legal agreements for management and harvesting. Moreover, of the 227 PFs and PPFs that had been transferred by July 1984, 197 were transferred in the last 12 months.

In the remainder of the paper, we examine the PPF experience with regard to the main issues that have had to be tackled to strengthen collaborative forest management in the hill areas of Nepal.

Establishing _Panchayat_ Protected Forests

The process of establishing and operationalizing a PPF involves three principal components. The first is the procedure whereby the _panchayat_ requests that the govern-ment hand over an area as PPF and the government effects the transfer. The second is the establishment and early functioning of the Panchayat Forest Committee, which will be responsible for managing the PPF. The third is drawing up the management plan--the legal agreement between the government, the panchayat and the people within the panchayat who comprise the user group or groups involved.

Within the forest department, the district forest controller is responsible for assisting the panchayats in preparing an application and for carrying out the necessary enquiries and management plan preparation, although the controller generally entrusts most of the on-the-ground work to the community forestry assistant. Authority to approve the handover of a PPF is vested in the regional director within whose territory the district and panchayat fall.

The Panchayat Forest Committee, in addition to its general supervisory and supporting role towards all community forestry activities, also must ensure equitable distribution of products from the PFs and PPFs to all households in the beneficiary group. The following guide-lines[3] were prepared to encourage participation by all sections of the user group in the committee and to specify the committee's duties:

o Users' Group--The committee must represent the primary group of people who use or will use the forest area--the people who call the present grazing land or PPF forest their own. Where appropriate, the formation of subcommittees of users' groups, or even separate committees within the panchayat.

o Nonpartisan--The committee must represent different social and political groups within the local area. The life of a forest is longer than political terms in office. This important common resource must have stable long-term management. Committees are encouraged to elect as chairman someone other than the pradhan panch of the panchayat to represent the users' group and strengthen the nonpartisan character of the committee.

o Flexible Membership--The composition of the committee and the number of members to be included must remain somewhat flexible to adapt to different circumstances. There should be a minimum of 10 persons, one of which includes the local ward leader, and a maximum of 25 as determined by the villagers concerned.

o   Equitable--Although the villagers should be allowed
     to form their own committee, the CFA should try and
     assure that it is representative of all communities
     involved, as well as of both sexes, so that women
     are also included. He should remind the villagers
     that women are usually the primary collectors of
     forest products, and so must be included.

o   Democratic--The formation of the committee should
     take place by election of the full <u>panchayat</u>
     assembly held in users' wards. A decision can only
     be taken if the quorum constitutes a majority of
     the total members.

The CFA is responsible for developing procedures for
agreeing upon management plans for the areas of PPF and for
an appraisal of the resources within the PPF. The CFA is
therefore involved in a continual dialogue with the users,
<u>panchayat</u> officials, and forest committee to arrive at a
management system that best meets their needs through
application of sound, practical silvicultural and
harvesting practices.
     The great diversity of forest types encountered
throughout the hill region makes it difficult establish
straightforward management prescriptions that can be widely
followed. Fortunately, natural productivity is usually
good, and most of the desirable species are hardy, capable
of regenerating vigorously as coppice shoots, and able to
survive heavy and sustained cutting and grazing pressure.
Possible choices for management of each are summarized in
Table 4. In contrast to the single (timber) product focus
of traditional forest management systems, the emphasis in
Nepal is on sustained production of multiple outputs.

                    PATTERNS OF INTERACTION

              Implementation by the Forest Department

     The release of state forest resources for local
community management represents a radical departure from
traditions of government forest management taught to all
forest officers in Nepal (as well as in most other
countries). Relinquishing exclusive control of such a
large natural resource--albeit actual field control over

TABLE 4 Possible Choices for Management of Selected Community Forest Types.

Forest Types	Timber	Poles	Fuel	Tree Fodder	Grazing	Compost	Other
1. Scattered mature sal forest	xxx	xx	x	x	x	x	
2. Heavily lopped small size sal forest		xxx	xx	xx		xx	Plate making
3. Katus-Chilaune coppice bush	x	xx	xxx		x		Roofing
4. Scattered Chilaune	xxx	xx	xx		x		
5. Scattered pine forest	xxx	x	x		x	x	Resin tapping
6. Scattered oak forest	x		xxx	xxx	x	x	
7. Dense lopped oak forest	xxx		xx	xxx		x	

LEGEND: xxx Best choice
xx Good choice
x Possible choice

SOURCE: P.K. Tyystjarvi (1983).

the scattered and degraded forests has been more nominal
than real--has not come easily to officers charged with
the conservation and exploitation of this resource.
Despite notable exceptions, there was substantial resistance to authorizing the large-scale transfer of this
resource during the early years. Government officers
explained this caution as growing from fears that the
local population would destroy the resource once government controls were lessened.

Significantly, not even one such incident has yet
taken place. In the rare instances where PF plantations
have been destroyed, investigation has always shown that
when the area was surveyed the local community did not know
that the purpose of the survey was to transfer the area to
the community. On the contrary, the community believed
that the government intended to usurp their forest.* Thus,
the experience has so far been positive, and has helped to
create a climate of opinion favorable to increasing the
rate of PPF establishment.

Beyond initial resistance from some forest officers,
the major causes for a slow start on this activity can
also be traced to its innovativeness and the difficulty
of adapting traditional working procedures to a completely
new framework. Modern forest management principles used
by professional foresters stress the need for proper
scientific inventories of the existing forest resource
and the application of yield tables to determine harvesting
schedules to meet commercial objectives. In contrast, the
development of PPF management systems rests on jointly
conducting an assessment of the resource with the forest
committee, and jointly arriving at management prescriptions based on meeting locally perceived needs. Harvesting plans must almost always attempt to meet multiple
objectives on an annual basis rather than optimize the
production of a single product over the long run. Plans
have a better chance of working when they are based on
sound socioeconomic principles (as illustrated by the
traditional management systems) than when they follow
textbook procedures. Yield tables for managing scrub
forests for branchwood, fodder, leaf litter, leaf plates,
poles, and other products do not exist.

---

*"Demarcation," a word that has been incorporated in its
English form into the local vocabulary, denotes the
assertion of government rights over areas the villagers
previously considered their own.

The CFAs responsible for the actual field preparation of the plans have found it difficult to meet the silvicultural demands of their superiors and the social demands of the community. Despite training in extension methods and the provision of extensive supporting materials, the youthful and inexperienced CFAs have initially found the task of community organization and collaboration difficult. Existing requirements for scientific inventories, though greatly reduced from those demanded for government forests, are complicated and physically strenuous, and the commensurate rewards are few. For these reasons, the project has continued to examine ways to simplify the management agreement (Troensegaard 1984), and the CFAs have been retained accordingly. Since this kind of forest management is new to all parties involved, experimentation and learning continues, and the CFAs' level of confidence has been steadily increasing.

The bureaucratic procedures involved in processing and approving applications are proving to be an additional impediment to rapid implementation. In the terrain characteristic of most of the hill region of Nepal, even the district forest office can be several days distant from any given panchayat, and regional offices even more remote--up to one week's walk away. Consequently, processing documentation can be very time consuming; field visits to check on queries often must be delayed for long periods. Possibilities for simplifying transfer procedures are therefore also being investigated.

User Group Motivation and Organization

The greatest barrier to community participation during the project's early years was the lack of widespread public knowledge of the details of managing a PPF. Until a community has actually gone through the process of drawing up a plan in a public meeting, villagers remain ignorant of the precise benefits and costs to them individually (Bhattarai and Campbell 1983). Their previous experience with the forest department usually was limited to situations that increased their individual costs by requiring, for example, payments for cutting wood, withdrawal of land previously available for slash-and-burn agriculture, and closure of land for grazing. Demarcation had never been perceived as being beneficial to the community. Villagers sometimes perceive that their panchayat leaders realize some personal gain by forming an

alliance with government authorities. Initially, the
project had to overcome the villagers' widespread suspicion that it was just another way of abrogating their
customary rights.

Project staff early on learned the importance of
widespread public discussion of exactly what the establishment of a PPF involved. Extension messages informing
all members of a community of the provisions of the law
regarding, for example, panchayat-government revenue
sharing, proved insufficient. However, it was remarkable
how quickly group consensus on the value of establishing a
PPF usually materialized when the actual provisions of
specific management plans (spelling out group rules for
protection, harvesting, and benefit sharing) were brought
under group discussion. In annual district meetings held
by the project for pradhan panchas, forest committee
chairmen, and other leaders, it has often been found that
suspicions voiced by panchayats not yet participating in
the project were completely overcome by the enthusiastic
response of villagers from panchayats where the details had
been already worked out. Almost every meeting recommended that similar large public meetings should be held
within the individual panchayats.

The establishment of acceptable PPFs also required
dealing with the central issues involved in upgrading
traditional management systems. Principal among these
were concerns with defining the boundaries of the beneficiary group, improving protection systems, changing grazing patterns, regulating cutting and harvesting, dealing
with offenses, and managing any cash income.

Since the laws governing PPF establishment are written
in terms of panchayats as a whole, many user groups feared
that their local forest resource would be "nationalized"
by the panchayat. Reaching consensus on a PPF thus usually required carefully delineating the boundaries of the
user group by specific product. In many cases, the group
of people who collected specific products (such as bamboo
or fuelwood) were willing to acknowledge the right to
other products (such as timber for house construction)
to the panchayat as a whole so long as the specific
products they previously collected would remain theirs.
It thus became crucial to the success of the program to
specify benefits and responsibilities by product and
beneficiary. To allow PPF plans to build on traditional
management systems, an "Existing Forest Management Survey"
to determine current usages was developed by the project
to replace the earlier survey of needs. This survey,

conducted in a group session, forced communities to make
explicit a number of more or less implicit group management rules, which were then incorporated into a legal
agreement.

Resource Protection

Several key issues arise around the problems of
protecting the resource--particularly from grazing livestock. The most important silvicultural treatment required
by most community forests, including those under explicit
traditional management, is some form of closure of areas to
grazing long enough to allow natural regeneration. The
initial problem has been to obtain consensus on how much to
close and how to enforce compliance. Since no fencing is
used, closure rests on willing consent of all herders to
keep their cattle and goats out of the specified areas.
This requires more intensive guarding than does protection
from cutting and a consequent additional cost (for more
guards) that communities found difficult to bear. Furthermore, most communities felt that the government should
appoint a guard to supplement the local security service,
and have frequently requested financial support to hire
local watchers; the project has recommended that this issue
be considered for the next project phase.

Enrichment planting in PPFs with adequate stocking
for natural regeneration has also contributed to solving
problems of protection. Initially, this planting was done
to assure that yield goals would be met, and so that the
project could finance a guard (money for a guard was
available only if planting had taken place). Subsequently, it has been found that enrichment planting serves an
important symbolic function: when a small number of highly
desirable or visible seedlings are planted in a forest
area, the need to restrict grazing until the seedlings are
established is apparent to all the villagers in the area.
Once planted, the existing natural forest is transformed
from an area that did not depend on humans for its reproduction to a "cultivated" area needing protection from
livestock, and management becomes meaningful to people
who for generations were accustomed to alternative land
use patterns. Furthermore, by agreeing on a phased introduction of plants and rotational grazing areas, people
who were initially suspicious of the loss of their grazing lands were convinced of the value of cooperative
action.

Cutting Regimes

From the perspective of local communities, the most difficult technical issue has been to introduce cutting regimes. The limited number of plans completed to date (86) have tended to be conservative and restrictive in their production prescriptions (de Pater 1984), which evidently reflects the conservative approach of most traditional forest management, an approach whose fundamental tenet is that the only way to prevent abuse and overharvesting by individuals is to ban all cutting of products not specifically controlled by the various methods outlined earlier. This was reinforced by the fact that communities did not previously have legal title to the forests and could not easily institutionalize a system that was vulnerable to government sanction. With the removal of the possibility of government sanction, communities are now theoretically free to design systems based, for example, on selective cutting of diseased and dying trees.

On the basis of extensive discussions with villagers, the following "management systems" appear to be easiest to implement considering local control capabilities and traditional forest management systems:

o   Rotation: some villages conduct product collection (such as branch lopping, grass cutting, grazing) on a rotational basis to control illegal use and ensure regeneration of the area.

o   Limited time period: some forests are opened for only one or two weeks for the collection of particular products so that uncontrolled cutting at other times of the year can be detected and stopped and distribution can be controlled.

o   Equal distribution: to distribute the products, whether hand cut grass, thatch or fuelwood, many villages conduct group harvesting; all users go to the same harvesting area at the same time and obtain roughly equal amounts per household.

However, many communities still opt for avoiding any cutting that would be difficult to control, and sometimes have suggested closing the forest to all product collection. For this reason, rotational cutting of individual areas during prescribed time limits is frequently the method of choice for the local community. This conservative approach to common resource management typically evolves when local communities have been provided with the legal structure and tenural rights within which to take up more active regulation of their existing forests. Because they are extremely aware of the dangers of uncontrolled access, they are cautious about adopting any system of cutting that would be difficult to enforce.

The lesson here is that management prescriptions must answer social requirements first if they are to be widely adopted by the community. But perhaps the more important lesson is that communities themselves will take the responsibility for devising methods for solving the common property problem if they are given sufficient authority, information, and assistance in doing so.

OUTCOMES

Distribution of Benefits

So far, the project has left the exact mode of distribution within the beneficiary groups largely up to the panchayats and user groups involved. The result has been that a number of different systems have emerged that are suited to the size and type of the resource and the communities involved. While fuelwood is usually equally distributed per user household, fodder may be sold on contract or made accessible to a more restricted group during certain periods of the year. Depending on the quantities available, timber may be reserved only for those households who require it for house construction after receiving the permission of the forest committee. While some communities have strong opinions on the mode of disposal, often based on their traditional usage, others have little tradition to draw upon and are open to suggestions from CFAs or village leaders. In this latter case, experience from traditional management systems in other villages has been applied to the setting.

Cash benefits accruing to the user group or panchayat have presented a special problem because of the difficulties arising from the legislation. The 1978 Panchayat Protected Forest Rules are still subject to the provisions of the underlying Forest Act of 1960. The latter requires that harvesting of timber be authorized in advance by the district forest controller. The practical difficulties and delays entailed in trying to observe this requirement discourage local groups from including significant timber production in the management prescriptions.

More important, the Panchayat Protected Forest Regulations themselves mandate that income from timber sales be shared between government and users, and specify a mechanism for handling the funds. This system is proving cumbersome and slow, and is impeding progress at the panchayat level. Twenty-five percent of the income from sales goes to the government and thirty-five percent to the panchayat. Initially, however, the full proceeds of sales accrue to government, and the panchayat's share is supposed to be returned to in due course. Often, a great deal of time elapses before the panchayats receive their repayment, which discourages panchayats and engenders suspicion that the process of PPFs and management plans is intended to generate income for the government, not the user group members.

As a consequence of these difficulties, most established management systems have attempted to avoid cash income from forest products (such as timber) that fall under the forest products sales act and for which the income should go directly to the forest department before being returned. In addition, ambiguities regarding whether or not permits for these products should still be issued by the forest department after a plan has been approved have also inhibited the distribution of these products. The project has recognized that modifications to the legislation, and the establishment of accounting procedures acceptable to all involved, is a priority for improving the program further.

Future Prospects

In April, 1985, 381 panchayats were participating in this project to strengthen collaborative local forest management--and private tree management--in the hill areas of Nepal. Over the next 5 years, 375 panchayats are expected to join the project. If they do, and if the demand to join the project remains strong, the project's coverage will extend over more than half of all the panchayats in the 29 districts that it serves. A continuation of the present momentum could therefore extend the new approaches to common forest management to a significant portion of the hill population.

As has been indicated in this paper, the experience to date, although limited, is nonetheless quite encouraging. Although some of the bureaucratic procedures are seen to be too rigid or poorly adapted to current needs, there do not seem to be insuperable impediments to instituting the necessary changes. For example, experience to date suggests that more may need to be done in some panchayats to ensure that more women participate in the forest committees, that committee leadership is separate from panchayat leadership, that the committee has the proper number of members, and that operating rules are established that permit a quorum of the committee to make decisions. The existence of a committee secretary with some relevant training is also seen to be desirable, as is provision for the committee to directly participate in monitoring and evaluating their panchayat's activities.

At the present time, the key to future success appears to be the management plan, which embodies both the agreement between the government and the community, and the prescriptions to enable the community to make more effective use of its forest resource. Consequently, priority is now being given to resolving those issues that are impeding the process of producing, adopting, and implementing workable and acceptable management plans.

1. J. E. M. Arnold was Chief of the Forestry Policy and Planning Service of the Food and Agriculture Organization of the United Nations (FAO), and headed FAO's Forestry for Local Community Development Programme. He is currently associated with the Oxford Forestry Institute at the University of Oxford. J. Gabriel Campbell was FAO's socioeconomic adviser with the Nepal Community Forestry Development Project from 1980 through 1984, and is now a consultant to the World Bank and FAO on social aspects of community forestry in South Asia.

2. In addition to the survey already cited, this section draws on the report of an enquiry carried out for the project by A. Molnar (1981).

3. Paraphrased from: Guidelines for the Preparation of Management Plan for Panchayat Forests and and Panchayat Protected Forests (Working draft, August 1983 revision), HMB/UNDP/FAO Community Forestry Development Project, Nepal, as modified by: Report of Fifth Annual Meeting of Regional Directors, District Forest Controllers, Associate Experts, Volunteers and CFAD Staff Associated with HMG/WB/UNDP/FAO Community Forestry Development Project. Kathmandu, September 1984.

REFERENCES

Bhattarai, T. N. and J. G. Campbell. 1983. Plantation
    Survival, Private Planting, Improved Stove Use, and
    Increase in Knowledge in Community Forestry: Results
    of On-going Evaluation Surveys, 1983-1983. Miscel-
    laneous Document No. 15. HMG/UNDP/FAO Community
    Forestry Development Project, Nepal.

Campbell, J. G. 1978. Community involvement in conser-
    vation: social and organizational aspects of the
    proposed resource conservation and utilization project
    in Nepal. Report to the U.S. Agency for International
    Development, Nepal.

Campbell, J. G. and T. N. Bhattarai. 1983. People and
    forests in hill Nepal: preliminary presentation of
    findings of community forestry household and ward
    leader survey. Project Paper No. 10, HMG/UNDP/FAO
    Community Forestry Development Project, Nepal.

Manandhar, P. K. 1982. Introduction to policy, legislation
    and programmes of community forestry development in
    Nepal. Field Document No. 19, HMB/UNDP/FAO Community
    Forestry Development Project, Nepal.

Molnar, A. 1981. The dynamics of traditional systems of
    forest management in Nepal: Implications for the
    Community Forestry Development and Training Project.
    Report to the World Bank, February 1981.

de Pater, C. 1984. Summary of initial forest management
    plans prepared for community forest. Miscellaneous
    Document No. 24, HMB/UNDP/FAO Community Forestry
    Development Project, Nepal.

Pelinck, E. and J. G. Campbell. n.d. Management of forest resources in the hills of Nepal. Franco-Nepalese Ecology and Development Seminar.

Stainton, J. D. A. 1972. Forests of Nepal. New York: Hafner Publishing Company.

Troensegaard, J. 1984. Forest management and community forestry in Nepal. Rome: Food and Agriculture Organization of the United Nations.

Tyystjarvi, P. K. 1983. Silvicultural practices in the community forestry development project. Project Paper No. 8, HMB/UNDP/FAO Community Forestry Development Project, Nepal.

People and Resources in Nepal: Customary Resource Management Systems of the Upper Kali Gandaki

Donald A. Messerschmidt [1]

INTRODUCTION

Anthropological interest in indigenous systems of resource management is rising in every part of the world. In the Nepal Himalayas, applied social science and development researchers recently have begun to examine traditional forms of resource management with some care. They have documented forest management systems (the largest share), as well as systems of irrigation and drinking water control, appropriate energy development, and pasture management. The intent of these investigations has been to better understand how and why traditional systems of forest management work. Some experimentation has been conducted to incorporate traditional systems (usually modified to reflect changed or contemporary circumstances) into ongoing renewable resource projects. While results are tentative, the work appears promising (see, for example, Arnold and Campbell, this volume; Martin and Yoder 1983; Messerschmidt 1981, 1983, 1985; Messerschmidt et al. 1984; Williamson 1983).

This paper presents data and analysis of traditional community resource management systems located in two districts along the upper Kali Gandaki river watershed in north central Nepal. Examples of both forest and irrigation water systems are presented side by side--reflecting the local perception that there are great similarities in

their control and management. The discussion focuses on a
60 km transect through the Himalayas from the town of Beni
at 792 m (2,600 ft) in the middle hill district of Myagdi,
north to the sacred pilgrimage site of Muktinath at 3,802 m
(12,475 ft) in the mountainous district of Mustang. The
area is bisected by peaks of the Annapurna and Dhaulagiri
Himalayan massifs.

The climate ranges from monsoonal/subtropical in the
southern Myagdi District, to arid/alpine in northern
Mustang. The area of these two districts is approximately
5,493 km^2 (2,121 mi^2), of which 65 percent is high
mountain, barren, or under perpetual snow. Of the remaining portion, 22 percent is forested (75 percent of which
is found in Myagdi), 10 percent is cultivated (90 percent
in Myagdi), and 3 percent is natural open rangelands
(73 percent in Mustang; Bosken et al. 1977). The higher
ridges, descending from the snow-capped peaks on both sides
of the valley, are forested. The only habitable and arable
land is along the Kali Gandaki river and its tributaries,
where the villagers pursue subsistence farming, herding,
and trading.

The people of the Myagdi District are primarily peasant
farmers, raising upland crops of corn, millet, barley, and
buckwheat. Some also practice transhumant pastoralism,
moving their herds of sheep and goats seasonally between
Myagdi and Mustang along the mountain flanks.

The people of Mustang are agro-pastoralists, raising
mostly wheat and buckwheat under austere oasis-like
conditions along the Kali Gandaki riverside. Their success
in farming is dependent upon extensive irrigation works.
Yak, sheep, and goat herding is also important on high
pasture lands. In addition, a large proportion of Mustang
people engage in seasonal long-distance trade, much of it
in support of trek tourism. Recently, some entrepreneurial
residents of the Mustang District have begun catering to
trek tourism by operating and/or supplying trailside inns.

The people of both districts fall into several distinct
ethnic and caste groups with contrasting social and
cultural traditions. The Myagdi District, with a 1981
population of 96,904, is inhabited predominantly by Magar
ethnic people, with minority Brahmin, Chhetri, and Hindu
artisan caste groups and several communities of ethnic
Thakali. The Magar and Thakali are indigenous to the
region, and their ethos is usually characterized as egalitarian. They are related linguistically and culturally to
other middle hill and upland groups of central Nepal and
more distantly to the ethnic Bhotia (Tibetan border people)

of the north. These ethnic groups have acculturated in
varying degrees to the more hierarchically structured caste
system of the Brahmin and Chhetri people around them.

The Mustang District, with a 1981 population of 12,930,
is dominated in its southern part by Thakali people and a
minority of ethnic Magar and artisan castes. The central
and northern parts are inhabited by various Bhotia ethnic
groups. The Bhotia maintain close affinities in language,
religion, and material culture with Tibet. They are only
distantly related to the upland ethnic groups of the middle
hills of Nepal to their south. While most ethnic groups,
however isolated, have been influenced to some degree by
the Hindus of lower Nepal, the Thakali and Bhotia of
Mustang have historically been able to maintain a strong
sense of independence in social, cultural, and even
political activity; this independence distinguishes their
forms of common property management from other forms
elsewhere in Nepal.

Common Property Resource Management

The history of resource management in Nepal reflects
the impact of two sets of recent legislative activity:
(1) the Village Panchayat Act of 1962 and Decentralization
Act of 1982, and (2) the Private Forests Nationalization
Act of 1957 and National Forest Law of 1976 (and
amendments).[2]

Introduction of the panchayat system was part of an
attempt to unify the Kingdom of Nepal under one multi-
layered form of representative government. The panchayat
is based on earlier concepts of leadership by caste
councils dating far back in the history of South Asia.
Today, the panchayat system operates on three levels--
village, district, and national. The panchayat system is
the focal point of development planning and administration.[3]

The 1982 decentralization legislation builds on the
existing panchayat system, while attempting to relocate
some administrative responsibility at the local district
and village panchayat levels. While much can be said of
the impacts of the panchayat system over two decades,
assessment of decentralization is still premature.

In the 1960s, one immediate result of the new
panchayat system on the ethnic populations of the hills
was the superimposition of a new and essentially alien
political system over pre-existing forms of local and

ethnic (i.e., non-caste) communal governance. It was especially disruptive in traditional non-caste oriented communities where other modes of village leadership existed. In some, for example, leadership was tradition-ally based on the hereditary principle of primogeniture (as among the Magar) or on acquired respect, wisdom, influence, and consensus (as among Thakali and Bhotia).

Also in the early 1960s, and simultaneous with the introduction of the new panchayat system, the Nepal government (with international donor assistance) began investing its modernization energies in rural development. While the focus at first was largely in the agriculture sector, by the 1970s there was increasing interest in natural resource oriented projects, especially in the forestry sector.

The modern history of Nepalese forestry dates only slightly earlier, to 1957, when the government in Kath-mandu enacted the Private Forests Nationalization Act. While this law was designed ostensibly "to protect, manage, and conserve the forest for the benefit of the entire country" it became, in fact, a highly disruptive factor in the overall well-being of the hill forests and related resources (Bajracharya 1983:233; see also Arnold and Campbell, this volume). Partly because of this law, pre-existing and traditional practices of communal resource management in the form of group control over local forests was upset, and existing local political structures in which communal control was embedded, with their customary rights and duties, became irrelevant (Bromley and Chapagain 1984; Chapagain 1984).

It took 19 years and the enactment of the National Forest Act of 1976 for the government of Nepal to formally begin to redress the effects of forest nationalization. The act of 1976 was quickly followed by rules and amend-ments encouraging panchayat-based forestry, ostensibly designed to return some forms of communal management over forests and related resources to the local people.

It is now widely believed and well-substantiated that during the decades of the 1960s and 1970s Nepalese vil-lagers began free riding--systematically overexploiting their forest resources on a large scale. The usual explanations for this free riding are that the villagers felt they had lost control of their forests, and they were distrustful of government officials and national resource policy (particularly forest policy). The forest problem seems to have been especially acute in Nepal's Terai lowlands, where marketing of forest products in India is

relatively easy. But similar behavior occurred in the
hill and mountain regions, albeit with less intensity.
Irrigation water resource management and other common
resources suffered from neglect. Much of the blame rests
on the disruptive changes in patterns of local government
imposed by the central government, resulting in the
abandonment of traditional communal systems of resource
control and allocation.

In some (if not all) locales, the negative effects of
exploitative behavior have been compounded by at least
three other simultaneous events or circumstances. One is
Nepal's rapidly rising population, which places increasing
pressure on the natural resource base. Another is a
dramatic increase in tourism, especially since the 1970s;
the demands that trekkers (and local entrepreneurs catering
to trekkers) place on natural resources are especially
severe. A third came in the form of massive development
aid beginning in the 1960s; much development is aimed at
the rural villages where it is often initially greeted by
euphoria, soon followed, however, by feelings of dependency
and disillusionment. All three trends encouraged the
devaluation of traditional solutions and independent local
group or individual initiative vis-à-vis resource
management (forest and water resources in particular).

In the mid-1970s, Hans Rieger observed in Nepal what
he called a pervasive "tragedy of the hills" (following
closely the theme of Garrett Hardin's [1968] "tragedy of
the commons"). Rieger (1978/79:179) determined that the
people of the middle hills of Nepal held a negative
"social image," this image being the collective knowledge,
beliefs, attitudes, and taboos that affect their view of
themselves and of the natural environment. The predominant
social image of the people of upland Nepal, he wrote, was
one in which many seemingly counterproductive practices
of resource management prevailed. The alarm that he
sounded still echoes among developers and national
planners.

In recent years, however, evidence has emerged to
show that, contrary to a totally negative and pervasive
resource tragedy, rational and conservative resource
management practices have remained strong in some locales.
In some instances, newly organized local systems of
management have sprung up, and in others, older, pre-
existing systems have been rejuvenated or strengthened
despite nationalization and similar disruptive circumstances. The following examples, three from forestry and
two from irrigation, provide supportive cases. Local

perspectives on the two resources--forest and water--are
highlighted side by side because of the inherent similar-
ity in the contexts of their management, each being
seriously affected by exogenous conditions and decisions
imposed by the central government of Nepal. The analysis
of common property resource management issues that concludes the paper is based on the case studies from five
village panchayats (see note 3).

EXAMPLES OF COMMON PROPERTY RESOURCE MANAGEMENT

Case 1: Community Forest Protection in Ghatan
Panchayat (Myagdi)

The "Big Pine Forest" of Ghatan Panchayat is situated
in the south of the Myagdi District, a community predominated by the Chhetri caste. Villagers date the origin of
their forest protection system back three generations, to
a folk hero and visionary named Bala Badra Baniya Chhetri.
Following fires that destroyed earlier natural forests in
the area, this man rallied his neighbors to preserve
approximately 75 hectares of land that had little agricultural value so it could regenerate naturally back to pine
forest. In time, the renewed forest was opened to controlled cutting of dead and fallen trees; villagers paid a
small fee. The fees plus small donations of grain from
neighboring households paid for a watchman to keep the
forest paths clear of pine litter and to watch for fires.
Under the 1950s nationalization legislation, the Ghatan
forest was designated government forest, but traditional
management was maintained until the 1970s. Then, the
divisional forest officer (now district forest controller)
came under pressure to sell timber-cutting permits to
builders in the nearby district headquarters town of Beni.
At that point, local control and customary management
collapsed. More recently, local leaders, forest officers,
and United States Peace Corps Volunteers have begun working
to establish panchayat protected forest (PPF) management
plans incorporating elements of the traditional system.

Case 2: Community Forest Management in Piple and
Rakhu-Bhagwati Panchayats (Myagdi)

Four small local forests in these two panchayats (near
Ghatan) are each managed by traditional "forest management

committees." The inhabitants are predominantly from the
Chhetri, Brahmin, and artisan castes. The members of each
user group work together to plant and fence the forests and
employ a forest watchman. Each watchman is chosen from
among the poorer families; his duties are to patrol the
forest and control access for firewood, fodder, and
building material collection or cutting, and for livestock
grazing (sheep, goat, cattle, and water buffalo) according
to rules set by the user group committee.

Typically, the rules allow for collecting fodder during
winter, harvesting roof thatch during fall, and cutting
wood for house construction as needed. Only those households that are paid-up members of the village forest
protection committee are allowed to use the forest. Fines
are levied in the event of rule violations. Each user
household donates grain in a specified amount annually to
pay the watchman.

Case 3: Forest Protection Committee in Lete Panchayat
(Mustang)

The Thakali villagers of Ghasa in Lete Panchayat,
southern Mustang, recognized in the 1960s that their local
Ramjung Pine Forest was rapidly being depleted by overcutting, indiscriminate grazing, and general abuse. They
closed off approximately five hectares to allow regeneration. Access is controlled and the forest is patrolled by
members of a panchayat forest committee. While the committee functions within the modern panchayat system, it is of
an old style dating to pre-panchayat times (pre-1960s) when
the Thakali exercised much more self-control over local
affairs. The forest is also home for a tutelary deity,
worshipped in an annual ceremony by the Ghasa villagers.

Since 1974, forest access to sheep and goats has been
strictly forbidden, although cattle, water buffalo, horses,
and pack mules are allowed to graze. Cutting fuelwood and
building materials by individuals is prohibited, although
cutting poles and timber for public use (school construction, bridge repair) is permitted on request. Fines are
levied for illegal entry or fuelwood cutting. The district
forest controller's staff regulates permits for thinning
the forest, and cutting large timber by permit will be
allowed with second growth maturity.

Every winter, each Ghasa household is required to
collect debris and litter within the forest. Two persons
from each of approximately 50 user households harvest up to

5 large basketloads of pine needles and litter daily, over a
9- or 10-day period. This reduces the risk of forest fires,
and the litter provides bedding for cattle stalls and
compost for fields.

In the early 1980s, forest officers recommended that
a management plan be prepared and that Ramjung forest be
designated a PPF. Villagers expressed reluctance, however, in the belief that by changing current management
practices, they would lose all local control. As of 1984,
no action had been taken.

Case 4: Irrigation Management System in Marpha Village
(Mustang)

The traditional irrigation control and allocation system
at Marpha, a Thakali ethnic village in Marpha Panchayat, is
an example of the sort of well-organized cooperation and resource management found widely among the Thakali and Bhotia
of the Mustang District. Marpha is a highly nucleated
settlement situated in the rainshadow of Dhaulagiri Himal.
It is subject to the cold, dry climate of the Tibetan
(Xizang) Plateau. Irrigation is essential for farming,
and in the past irrigation management was closely tied to
Marpha's traditional form of government by clan representatives, a system similar to that of Ghasa in Lete Panchayat
(above) and the of Muktinath-Jhong panchayats (below).
Irrigation management in Marpha was closely linked with
forest management, and operated under local custom for many
generations before the panchayat system was introduced.

By long-established custom, the management of all of
Marpha's resources was the business of a committee of 10
workers. Besides controlling the flow and distribution of
irrigation water, the workers also maintained the public
drinking water system and water-powered grinding mills, and
served as forest watchmen and town criers. They were
compensated from mill use fees, fines levied for abuse of
irrigation and forest regulations, and by a small share of
the annual profits from each farmer's irrigated barley crop.

The workers were appointed from the four clans of the
village and were responsible to the headman and his executive and treasury committees. The headman, described as
"the best man in the village" (i.e., the most honest and
influential), was customarily selected for a three-year
period from among the four clans. His executive committee
was composed of four men, one appointed from each clan for
one-year terms.

Marpha's cultivated fields are divided into two
sectors--north and south. The communal workers were
responsible only for the northern sector.

Marpha has two agricultural seasons, one for barley
(planted in winter and harvested in summer), and one for
buckwheat (planted in summer and harvested in fall).
Each crop receives three major waterings during its
growing season.

For barley, the workmen were responsible only for the
first two waterings, and for buckwheat, only the first.
Thereafter, the individual farmer handled his own watering.
To make distribution equitable for all farmers over the
course of the year, the barley crop was watered from the
top of the north fields downward; that is, the fields
closest to the head received first water. Then, for buckwheat, the order was reversed so that the tail-end fields
were watered first. This traditional rule was remembered
in a Thakali rhyme: kar yaalaa, nhaa mhalaa, meaning
"barley from the top, buckwheat from the bottom."

Beginning about 1963, two events led to a reordering
of Marpha's age-old form of village government, economic
life, and overall resource management. The first was the
introduction of the panchayat system. In Marpha, this
meant that a new kind of leader--a panchayat chairman--
replaced the old headman. The new chairman is assisted
by a council representing the nine newly and arbitrarily
designated wards. The clan basis of selection is gone.

The second event was the realization of economic
opportunities outside of Mustang District that attracted
the more entrepreneurial Thakali farmers away from Marpha.
As they left, home farms were placed under tenancy with
Bhotia immigrants, non-Thakalis, and the old system of
irrigation was replaced by a lottery. The Bhotia farmers
and a few remaining Thakali farmers began looking after
water distribution on their own. Nowadays, watering
order is determined by lot and is publicly announced at
periodic meetings quite independent of traditional social
custom.

Case 5:   Irrigation Management in Muktinath and Jhong
Panchayats (Mustang)

The survival of the mountain Bhotia villagers is
critically dependent on the consensual leadership of the
traditional headman and the full and unequivocal cooperation of all adult villagers in managing common properties

in the harsh, arid environment of the northern Mustang
District.

In both Muktinath and Jhong panchayats (and in other
Bhotia villages throughout Mustang), all irrigation canals
are communally constructed and maintained, and water is
distributed according to simple, well-respected, and
customary rules. Forest protection and access are
similarly managed by committee. Periodic public meetings
are called to discuss irrigation management and other
communal resource issues. The head of each household must
attend. Annual irrigation ditch cleaning is a village-
wide responsibility: every able-bodied resident between
the ages of 15 and 56 is required to participate. Absen-
teeism is controlled by fines, and frequent refusal to
participate is countered by social ostracism.

The key to social control among the Bhotia is their
willingness and ability to retain a strong, traditional
system of community governance. Each villager has a part
to play in the daily management of common assets--e.g.,
irrigation water and ditches, forest resources, pastures,
and drinking water systems. But the ultimate responsibility for their management lies with the traditional village
headman. Community members choose this man from among the
most influential in the village, by the consensus of all
household heads.

Over the past few decades, these ethnic Bhotia
communities have succeeded in preserving the ancient and
customary role of headman despite imposition of the caste-
based panchayat system. The Bhotia consider the panchayat
to be a foreign concept, but pay lip service to its
requirements. They elect a chairman and a panchayat council, but beneath this façade the village headman remains in
charge. He manages by consensus and is backed by strong
tradition. His decisions are based on public consensus.
Contrary to the power of many panchayat leaders elsewhere
in the villages of Nepal, the Bhotia headman cannot act
without full support and agreement among his constituent
households.

In the words of one Nepali researcher, a fundamental
fact must be understood by any outsiders who propose to
work here: "The traditional system is the underlying
strength of the communities; the panchayat system serves
[only] as the community mouthpiece to the outside"
(Devkota et al. 1983).

ANALYSIS

I turn now to the Oakerson framework (this volume) for
an analysis of common property issues. A major strength of
the framework is its common and unifying structure, around
which unique case studies can be examined and within which
a multitude of issues can be explored, and to a large
extent, explained. A weakness of the model is a tendency
to ignore or de-emphasize the cultural context of local
understanding and decision making. And while it can be
argued that cultural considerations are in the hands of the
user, the model should, nonetheless, refer to cultural
relevance and cultural context as universally importable
variables.

It is the local villagers' definitions of the resource
that I seek to elucidate first. Their perceptions and
their control and management of common properties and
natural resources are best understood in the context of
culture. "Culture" is herein defined as acquired knowledge that people use to interpret experience and to
generate social behavior (Spradley and McCurdy 1980:2;
emphasis theirs).

Physical and Technical Attributes

Jointness

Oakerson defines "jointness" to mean "that no single
beneficiary of some good subtracts from the ability of
others to derive benefits" (Oakerson, this volume). In
other words, jointness exists to the extent that various
uses are compatible or even complementary; disjointness
reflects incompatible and therefore subtractive uses.
Relative jointness/disjointness, in turn, is a function of cultural perspective or definition, i.e., the
meaningfulness (hence usefulness) of a resource in the
context of the lives, needs, and wants of the various
publics who use it. Meaning, or use, may be as multiple
and variable as the many and various publics who perceive
a resource as a "good" and who demand access to it. When
meanings/uses conflict with one another, as they tend to do
in the face-off between local and national control of
forests in Nepal, for example, then disjointness occurs.

The anthropologist, in determining what a resource
means, and to what use(s) it may be put, whether conflicting or complementary, tends to pose certain fundamental

questions: Who uses the resources? Under what conditions?
How are they managed? By whom? To what end? These questions are designed to consider the fundamental defini-
tion(s) of the resource among the various individuals and
collectivities involved. In short, we ask, "What is -- ?"
(a single tree, a forest, irrigation water, drinking
water). We expect to hear different answers from each
category of user or public whom we ask.

For example, to the question "What is a forest?", we
expect that portion of the relevant public called "scientists" to answer in terms of cover type, species, soil,
aspect, and slope. "Resource managers" and "developers"
might refer to forests in terms of watershed protection,
microclimate amelioration, or soil erosion. "Policy planners" would probably consider ownership, local, regional,
or national needs, and development priorities. "Economists" would talk of access rights and allocation, and of
supply and demand (marketing the resource). Conflict is
inevitable to the extent that these perceptions of "forest"
reflect, for example, a national or regional perspective as
opposed to a local one, or a scientific perspective as
opposed to an indigenous one based on folk wisdom, or use
of the resource for cash production as opposed to subsistence. But, alternative definitions, like these, can also
be complementary.[4]

The local village public, those who have traditionally
kept control of local forest resources for themselves
(whose lives and daily household subsistence economies may
depend on the quality, quantity, accessibility, and utility
of forest products), will answer our question "What is a
forest?" in ways qualitatively distinct from the others.
From Nepalese villagers in the five locations described
above, we can expect to hear answers with at least three
parts. One part concerns the forest's natural products
(e.g., fuelwood, building material, water source, pasture
land, etc.), and the physical and technical attributes
thereof. Another concerns certain supernatural attributes (e.g., the forest as an abode of certain deities
and/or spirits), and beliefs and practices associated with
them. And, while not an attribute of the forest per se,
villagers will also typically describe certain social and
political behaviors associated with those who use and/or
control the forest. Few, however, distinguish clearly
among these seemingly discrete categories of information.
They are all part of the perceptions and knowledge about,
or the definition of "forest" in the local cultural
context. And that, in turn, generates or determines

resource use and management strategies and associated
behaviors (according to our definition of culture).

Furthermore, we tend to find that within each Nepalese
community or social group, the natural attributes vary
considerably by resource type--each is used in distinct
and discrete ways, according to its unique technical and
physical characteristics, in a given cultural context. In
cases 1, 2, and 3 above, for example, local use of the
forest varies among local demand for fuelwood, for litter
to use in composting and stall bedding, and for grass as
fodder in stall feeding or for grazing herds of livestock.
Where extra-local demands have been introduced, e.g., the
demand for construction timbers to supply a booming
government town, definitions of "forest" and "tree" tend to
change and come into conflict, reflecting other needs and
uses complementary to national growth and progress but
contradictory to local custom and understanding.[5]

Traditional Nepalese villagers' definitions of
"fuelwood," an important local forest product, provide a
case in point. By convention, most Nepalese distinguish
two types of fuelwood according to certain physical and
technical characteristics, correlated with cultural and
social activities by season. One type, called _jikra_,
includes old fencing and agricultural residue (stalks,
cobs, etc.) found around households and villagers. The
other, _daura_, consists of fresh (wet or green) wood and
dead wood (dry twigs and branches) collected directly from
the forest. Usually, dead wood is free for the taking from
private lands or from the forest commons, but the cutting
of fresh wood on public land is more often carefully
controlled. _Jikra_ is generally collected any time of the
year, but most often in summer and autumn. _Daura_
collection commences in early winter, when fieldwork is at
a minimum and farmers and householders have more time
(Bajracharya 1983; Fox 1983).

Recent developments in the Myagdi District (case 1),
however, have greatly increased fuelwood demand, just as
they have for building materials from the forest. The
demand comes particularly from new residents (mostly
government civil servants) in the booming district town of
Beni. As their demand rises, local tradition and informal
rules of management and access by season become blurred.
The result is disjointness and "tragedy," in Hardin's
sense, as outsiders begin cutting wood, or buying it from
indiscriminate and uncaring (or unknowing) others, including locals who have abandoned traditional management
custom. The complementarity between physical and technical

attributes and cultural context and seasonal conditions is
lost, especially on outsiders who quite differently define
the product, their use of it, and even the concepts of time
and work associated with it.

A similar case can be made for water resources. As
changes in perspective on the land and on water usage
occurred at Marpha (case 4) with the outmigration of local
Thakali farmers, and as Bhotia farmers arrived to take over
the Thakali lands as tenant farmers, the understanding
and compatibility of pre-existing social customs of local
government and resource management diminished. The old
Thakali management style for the distribution and control
of water was dropped. Likewise, other characteristics
associated with water resources also changed with the new
Bhotia cultural perspectives, and although water is still
assigned to similar categories of use (drinking, bathing,
powering mills, cooking) to the newcomers, the traditional
and culturally distinctively Thakali responses no longer
hold.

The physical and technical attributes of the sociopolitical behaviors associated with particular resources
may vary with the imposition of exogenous changes, but
there is a nearly universal belief in Nepal that certain
resources have supernatural characteristics (uses). These
beliefs tend to appear quite similar despite differences in
ethnic or caste identity, environmental variations, or
religious predilections.[6]

For example, various gods and godlings (local and
regional and of fertility, tutelary, gustatory, or other
definition) are commonly believed to dwell in or be
otherwise closely associated with water sources, forests,
pasture sites, and other resources or natural objects. In
case 2, the residents of Ghasa believe that the Thakali
guardian spirit dwells in the Ramjung forest and that the
people must go there periodically to worship. Similarly,
there are sacred attributes associated with every forest
and water system described in this paper.

At Muktinath (case 5), for example, the springs that
serve as a principal source of irrigation and drinking
water are elaborately enshrined near the source within a
sacred forest of considerable antiquity. This water and
forest place is, furthermore, considered a source of
spiritual power and authority throughout Nepal and Asia as
a major pilgrimage center for Hindus and Buddhists alike.
Such universal reactions toward the supernatural aspects of
forest or water sources are just as much a form of
controlled "use" of such resource as are logging timber,

collecting fuelwood, cutting fodder, grazing meadows, or diverting water into fields.

Belief systems in which nature is sanctified often function to hold resource abuse in check through some combination of respect and fear that disturbance or neglect of the supernatural may cause more harm than good to the resource and to the people associated with it. At various levels, these beliefs serve to remind people of the miraculous (hence fragile) nature of the resource and of the people's own responsibilities to manage it for the sustained public good.

Sociopolitical solutions to resource management needs by the local villagers of the upper Kali Gandaki, and elsewhere across Nepal, also tend to be quite similar. In all cases described, where local traditions have not been totally disrupted by exogenous changes, management actions have been designed by local user groups along egalitarian and participatory lines (although certain historic conditions and styles of communal association vary from place to place). Likewise, rules concerning resource use or abuse tend to be quite similar--fines are charged for misuse, monetary fees or in-kind contributions are collected to pay watchmen, and social ostracism befalls those who neglect communal duties vis-à-vis the resource or who habitually neglect or debase the resource.

In short, these various beliefs and perspectives (meanings and uses), and the rules associated with particular resources all aid in retaining the relative jointness of those resources, all else being equal. When these systems are disrupted by exogenous forces, such as by nationalization and centralization in Nepal, and when other contending definitions are imposed, the result is disjointness.

Indivisibility

The forest and water resources of the upper Kali Gandaki watershed are intrinsically indivisible on physical grounds. But, as noted, a full understanding of indivisibility must take into account both the natural (physical) boundaries of each resource and other meanings/uses in cultural context. While it is conceivable that the forest can be divided into as many units as there are trees, it is not perceived in that manner by its users. Conversely, private trees may grow on private lands, but those trees are not considered as "forest" per se, either by local

farmers or by government forest officers. To villagers,
the forest is a natural unit belonging to the community--
and deviation from that norm results in negative social
sanctions, or (it is widely believed) resource failure
(which some blame on the supernatural).

In the case of irrigation water, divisibility is more
problematic. Farmers perceive water in terms of divisible
time and quantity necessary to serve crop needs. The
farmer cannot subtract water units from the total reserve
in the same manner that one can clandestinely remove single
trees from the forest. Rather, communal control,
reflecting broader styles of local governance, is the
norm. One reason that the old irrigation system in Marpha
broke down was that without the full complement of Thakali
villagers to maintain earlier tradition, the amount of
irrigation time and consequently the quantity of water any
single farmer received was not assured. Local definitions,
hence uses, of the resource changed with the people. The
new lottery system of control operates not on age-old rules
of common and equal access, but on chance in a system
fraught with uncertainties imposed from outside. The
lottery is quite compatible, however, with the cultural
traditions of the Bhotia tenants now operating the Marpha
farms.

Decision-Making Arrangements

Two trends appear in the Nepal data--the first, from
about 1957, toward more national control of resources, or
centralization, and the other, more recent, toward
decentralization.

Centralization is evidenced in an increased level of
control over decision-making by the national government.
In the case of forests, the nationalization legislation of
the 1950s is the prime example of central level policy
planning. In terms of both forestry and irrigation (cases
3, 4, and 5), the imposition of the panchayat system of
local government has provided a centrally defined new
structure of local government, one that has effectively
undermined customary structures and made them irrelevant.

Nationalization, and other related government actions
leading to increased centralization of authority in Nepal,
led quickly to the decline or collapse of local initiatives
for resource management in many communities. One point of
this present discussion, however, is to show that traditional structures do continue to exist, not only in the

upper Kali Gandaki (as the five cases describe) but in
other communities across the country. As Molnar has noted
(based on a sample of forest management systems throughout
the middle hills of Nepal): "Traditional management
systems do exist. Where they do..., they should be
incorporated in the management plans and built upon where
it is feasible" (1981:24).

Decentralization of decision-making authority has
become, in the 1980s, an important goal of the government,
particularly as it relates to the development and maintenance of communal resources. On the one hand, there is a
trend toward strengthening local authority and accountability in communities that have reasserted or have held
tenaciously to "ownership" (in the sense of management
control) over local resources despite nationalization
(cases 3, 4, and 5). On the other hand, both recent reform
legislation in forestry and national development policy
indicate a trend toward more formal control of some
resources (both natural and political). The National
Forest Act of 1976 (and amendments that provide the
mechanism for panchayat-based community forestry), and
the Decentralization Act of 1982 (ostensibly giving more
governing jurisdiction to local district and village
panchayats) are the two principal actions of the national
government toward decentralization.

In the Nepal scene, and I predict elsewhere, the basic
conflict between national and local is (perhaps oversimply
stated) one between formal and customary law. Both
nationalization and "panchayat-ization" are essentially
processes of supplanting preexisting informal and customary
rules based on close interpersonal and largely oral tradition and social control with formal laws or rules that are
based, in part, on the Western tradition of constitutional
law and judicial process and in part on traditional caste
law and governance. The two systems are not likely to be
compatible in any large measure.

The process of decentralization in Nepal implies (it
is not yet well-tested) returning administrative control
to local jurisdiction with, perhaps, tacit allowance for
reinstating some forms of customary resource management.
The difference is that under centralization, formal
national law is brought downward from the center to the
village where it substitutes, in full or in part, for
traditional customary law. The formal law is translated
and transmitted into the rural hinterlands through government offices in district headquarters towns such as Beni in
Myagdi and Jomsom in Mustang.[7] Ostensibly, under the

new legal structure of forest management, formal law and
centralized authority will remain, but some aspects of
customary law and local participation will be encouraged
by a process of selectively melding them with the formal
system. As a development strategy, this has some merit,
giving both systems--national and local, formal and
customary--credibility and acceptability in the eyes of
the rural people.

It is apparent in the data that the farther removed a
resource (or a community) is from the center of power, the
more diminished are the formal, centralized controls over
it. In the most isolated panchayats of the upper Kali
Gandaki watershed, for example, we find greater strength
in customary law (cases 3, 4, 5).[8] The result of close
proximity to the center is clear in the case of Ghatan
(case 1), where the pine forest is controlled from the
district offices in Beni; indeed, the pine forest is
clearly visible from the streets of this government town.
(That Beni is a boom town is also a factor, and gives
credence to the hypothesis that demand, itself, is a
deciding factor in who controls access, for what purpose,
and under what set of rules).[9]

Patterns of Interaction

At root, the behavior of the typical resource user,
with the possible exceptions of contemporary Ghatan
(case 1) and Marpha (case 4), is based on a sense of
reasonably balanced sharing, or reciprocity. Each user has
relatively equal access to the resource, sometimes
calculated according to means or need, sharing it with his
or her neighbor users. Each participating individual is
expected to provide assistance and support in managing the
system. Even leadership roles are shared over the long
term by the most qualified individuals (as locally
defined). In short, access to resources, and the social
relations that grow up around them are developed through a
collection of reciprocal rights, duties, and privileges.

The reciprocal ethic is most clearly demonstrated among
the ethnic groups (e.g., Thakali and Bhotia, in cases 3, 4,
and 5), but also exists more loosely, less formally, among
the castes (cases 1 and 2). Reciprocity in the form of a
relatively egalitarian approach to social and economic
interactions prevails so long as the local people feel a
measure of local control. In Marpha (case 4), local
control was diminished by migration and by a new

form of governance imposed from the central government.
In Ghatan (case 1), local control was usurped by district
forest officials under the aegis of nationalization. These
are only a few examples of the changes in interaction
imposed by national authorities. As often happens in such
instances, disenchanted locals begin to spread rumors
maligning the integrity of certain officials and even some
of their local leaders. It is not uncommon to hear unsup-
ported allegations about local leaders involved in such
fraudulent activities as special timber permit sales with
financial kickbacks or with direct benefits to their own
business enterprises. Such talk, and such beliefs,
effectively undermine or cancel the reciprocity upon
which a well-functioning traditional system depends.

                           Outcomes

     A principal outcome in the Nepal case is a dynamic
tension between local and national interest, particularly
evident in the management of critical natural resources.
While the evidence so far is unclear, it can be reasonably
speculated that the more that local management systems or
customary controls are accommodated in the development of
resource management policy, the more efficient and equitable will be the result; likewise, the health of the
resource will improve. Several development agencies and
resource projects in Nepal recently have been attracted by
the potential opportunities of this assumption (see Arnold
and Campbell, this volume).
     But, even where reciprocity and equity do not appear
strong (as in some instances of hierarchically based Hindu
caste communities), it remains clear that local tradition
"survives" in some form, regardless. It is the strength of
those local systems, their familiarity, their source in
"tradition," and not necessarily their equity, efficiency,
or economy in Western terms, that give them survivability--
even in the face of forces to formalize, nationalize, or
"panchayat-ize" them.
     As has been pointed out before, there is a prevailing
assumption among Western observers, at least, that equality
in communal and cooperative systems is somehow a precondition to success. For a country like Nepal, however,
this expectation may be unrealistic (Messerschmidt 1981,
after Bennett 1979). Rather, cultural diversity and a
diversity of form, function, meaning and use provide
a key to understanding how and why communal systems of

common resource management survive and thrive in the
world. If no other understanding is gained from the Nepal
data, this one should stand--that there are many ways for
communities to organize in dealing with common property and
resource management problems. Each must be studied,
understood, and appreciated in context. Each works well
under its own unique conditions, but none provides a single
model that is applicable to all.[10]

NOTES

1. The author is a development anthropologist with
extensive experience in the Nepal Himalayas since 1963.
The data were collected between 1981-1984 on the
USAID-supported Resource Conservation and Utilization
Project (RCUP). The RCUP was designed to improve forest,
soil, and water resources and their management; its social
science component sought conjunction between development
inputs (of appropriate technology and financial assistance)
and local systems of organization for natural resource
management. Some of the material in this paper was first
developed in a study prepared for the International Centre
for Integrated Mountain Development (ICIMOD) in Kathmandu
(Messerschmidt 1985). The author is indebted to the
directors of the RCUP and the ICIMOD and to their staff for
assistance. Further elaboration may also be found in
Messerschmidt (1986).

2. Sweeping land reform legislation in the mid-1960s
has also had a great effect on the concepts and practice
of private and communal resource control and management,
particularly in relation to such land-related resources
as trees and water. Land reform is not discussed in this
paper, primarily because it is not well-documented in
Nepal. It is clearly an important topic for future
study.

3. A village _panchayat_ comprises a population of
approximately 2,500 to 3,000 people in one or several
villages. It is headed by an elected chairman and vice
chairman and a representative council of nine individuals
selected from each of nine wards. A group of village
panchayats articulates together within an administrative
district, of which there are 75 in Nepal.

4. I am reminded of the contradictory definition of bamboo
as a forest product espoused by an American advisor I knew
in Nepal. In editing an FAO forest survey form to fit the

needs of the resource development project on which he was
engaged, he eliminated a whole section on bamboo. Bamboo,
however, is a product of the forest of immense importance
to Nepalese villagers who put it to an incredibly wide
variety of uses. When the advisor was asked why he had
dropped the questions concerning bamboo, he said: "because
it is not a 'tree'; it is a 'grass'!"

Similarly, a definitional debate--hence a policy debate
concerning access and appropriate use--rages between those
who consider the village forest to be a "national" resource, subject to centralized management and marketing
decisions, or a "local" resource subject to customary
village controls and used in the local subsistence
economy. How a resource is defined has very definite
effects on how it is used (or abused), as well as on its
relative jointness or disjointness in any one place or
time.

5. Donovan (1981) has identified 13 "minor forest
products" including food products, oils, medicinal herbs,
resins and dyes, incense, and such other miscellaneous
products as leaves for smoking, broom material, wicker,
structural bamboo, and beeswax.

6. Furthermore, knowledge about resources is, itself,
frequently held sacred, guarded and preserved by certain
people such as shamans, sorcerers, or diviners and by other
specialists, such as artisans (especially blacksmiths) in
Nepal. These various human repositories of sacred and
profane knowledge sometimes have enviable stores of
environmental information at their disposal. Quite often
such lore is considered as a secret and highly valued
personal resource, propounded and passed along (usually by
oral tradition) only to the initiates or inheritors of the
lore. Often the knowledge is enveloped in semi-secret
ritual, myth, or legend, which functions to keep it
relatively intact and safe. And, in a very real sense,
this lore and folk knowledge is, itself, a communal
resource--entrusted to the specialists to keep secure
for the wider village public. In short, the ritualization
of environmental knowledge serves the distinctly important
purpose of nurturing and preserving knowledge itself as a
communal resource.

7. The question of precisely how to ameliorate the
problems of "formal" versus "informal" and "central" versus
"local" control over forest management, however, is beyond

the scope and prescribed length of this paper. The reader
is encouraged to read Arnold and Campbell (this volume) for
an analysis of one apparently successful attempt to
reinvigorate local communal participation in forest
management under a centralized national forest authority
(see also Messerschmidt 1986).

8.   The historic trend towards local independence from
outside or central government control in the Mustang
District is well-documented (see Bista 1971; von
Fürer-Haimendorf 1966).

9.   It is interesting to note that there are several
similar forest tracts in the Myagdi District, but in those
farther removed from (literally, out of sight of) Beni
headquarters, local leaders have been better able to
maintain customary controls on resource allocation.

10.   Similar conclusions have recently been drawn by
Thompson and Warburton (1985a, 1985b).

REFERENCES

Bajracharya, D. 1983. Deforestation in the food/fuel
context: historical and political perspectives from
Nepal. Mountain Research and Development 3:227-240.

Bennett, J. W. 1979. Agricultural Cooperatives in the
Development Process: Perspectives from Social
Science. Monograph No. 4 of the California
Agricultural Policy Seminar. Davis, California:
Department of Applied Behavioral Sciences, University
of California.

Bista, D. B. 1971. The political innovators of upper
Kali-Gandaki. Man 6, No. 1:52-60.

Bosken, J. J., D. B. Thorud, J. G. Campbell, R. Ehrich, and
J. L. Thames. 1977. Land use practices for the
conservation and development of Nepal's soil and water
resources. Consultant Report. Kathmandu: U.S. Agency
for International Development.

Bromley, D. W. and D. P. Chapagain. 1984. The village
against the center: resource depletion in South Asia.
American Journal of Agricultural Economics 66:868-873.

Chapagain, D. P. 1984. Managing public lands as a common
property resource: a village case study in Nepal.
Unpublished Ph.D. dissertation. Madison, Wisconsin:
University of Wisconsin.

Devkota, B., B. Katuwal, and U. Gurung, 1983. RCUP Social
Science Fieldtrip Report, No. 18. Unpublished project
files. Kathmandu: Resource Conservation and
Utilization Project.

Donovan, D. G. 1981. Focus on minor forest products.
Kathmandu, Nepal: Ministry of Forest and Soil
Conservation Training Wing. Unpublished paper.

Fox, J. M. 1983. Managing public lands in a subsistence economy: the perspective from a Nepali village. Unpublished Ph.D. dissertation. Madison, Wisconsin: University of Wisconsin.

Hardin, G. 1968. The tragedy of the commons. Science 162: 1243-1248.

Martin, E. and R. Yoder. 1983. A farmer-centered approach to irrigation development. In Ministry of Agriculture, 1983:92-99.

Messerschmidt, D. A. 1981. Nogar and other traditional forms of cooperation in Nepal: significance for development. Human Organization 40:40-47.

Messerschmidt, D. A. 1983. Methodology for user group mobilization, and anticipated problems and suggested solutions in user group development in the RCU Project, Nepal. Kathmandu: Resource Conservation and Utilization Project. Unpublished working paper.

Messerschmidt, D. A. 1985. Using human resources in natural resource management: innovations in Himalayan development. Occasional Paper No. 1, Working Group on Watershed Management. Kathmandu: International Centre for Integrated Mountain Development.

Messerschmidt, D. A. 1986. Conservation and society in Nepal: traditional forest management and innovative development. Lands at Risk in the Third World. Proceedings of a conference at the Institute for Development Anthropology, Binghamton, New York). Boulder, Colorado: Westview Press.

Messerschmidt, D. A., forthcoming. Natural and super-natural attributes in the sacred field of Muktinath pilgrimage, Nepal. In Morinis and Stoddard, forth-coming.

Messerschmidt, D. A., U. Gurung, B. Devkota, and B. Katwal. 1984. Gaun Sallah: The 'Village Dialogue' Method for Local Planning in Nepal. Kathmandu: Resource Conservation and Utilization Project.

Ministry of Agriculture. 1983. Water Management in Nepal.
    Proceedings of the Seminar on Water Management Issues,
    Kathmandu, July 31 to August 2, 1983. Kathmandu:
    Agricultural Projects Services Centre and the
    Agricultural Development Council, Ministry of
    Agriculture (HMG/Nepal).

Molnar, A. 1981. The dynamics of traditional systems of
    forest management in Nepal: Implications for the
    Community Forestry Development and Training Project.
    Washington, D.C.: World Bank.

Morinis, A. E., and R. Stoddard, eds. Forthcoming. The
    Geography of Pilgrimage. In Press.

Rieger, H. C. 1978/79. Socio-economic aspects of
    environmental degradation in the Himalayas. Journal of
    the Nepal Research Centre (Kathmandu) 2/3:177-184.

Spradley, J. P. and D. W. McCurdy. 1980. Anthropology:
    The Cultural Perspective. Second edition. New York:
    John Wiley and Sons.

Thompson, M. and M. Warburton. 1985a. Knowing where to hit
    it: a conceptual framework for sustainable development
    of the Himalayas. Mountain Research and Development 5:
    203-220.

Thompson, M. and M. Warburton. 1985b. Decision making
    under contradictory certainties: how to save the
    Himalayas when you can't find out what's wrong with
    them. Journal of Applied Systems Analysis 12:3-34.

von Fürer-Haimendorf, C. 1966. Caste concepts and status
    distinctions in Buddhist communities of western Nepal.
    Pp. 140-160 in C. von Fürer-Haimendorf, ed. Caste and
    Kin in Nepal, India and Ceylon: Anthropological
    Studies in Hindu-Buddhist Contact Zones. Bombay: Asia
    Publishing House.

Williamson, J. 1983. Towards community-managed drinking
    water schemes in Nepal. Waterlines, the Journal of
    Appropriate Water Supply and Sanitation Techniques
    (London) 2, No. 2:8-13.

The Management and Use of Common Property Resources in Tamil Nadu, India

Piers M. Blaikie
John C. Harriss
Adam N. Pain

INTRODUCTION

Tamil Nadu is the state at the southeastern tip of the Indian peninsula. It is traversed from the higher west to the coast by several major river valleys where the culti- vation of irrigated rice predominates. The intervening plateaus also have some irrigated agriculture, dependent upon water stored in surface reservoirs and groundwater, as well as dry cultivation of millets, sorghum, pulses, and oilseeds. Both the valleys and the plateaus have been relatively intensively cultivated over a long historical period. Common property resources play some part in agricultural systems throughout the state, the most important of them being surface water and groundwater for irrigation. These have been the object of some other recent studies, however, and our research1 has been focused rather upon land-based resources: principally fuel, fodder, and grazing, but also construction timber, green manure, and a variety of minor forest products with domestic, craft, or sometimes industrial uses.

All of these products may be obtained, subject to environmental conditions, from one or another of the types of publicly owned lands that are defined by the systems of land and forest administration, and sometimes from private land (see Figure 1). The system of land administration has its roots in the precolonial period but was further developed as a major instrument of British rule, with the objective of maximizing the appropriation of land revenue. The "commons" of Tamil Nadu are now those lands defined under this system as: (a) poromboke: "lands incapable of cultivation or set apart for public or communal purposes," (including, sometimes, public grazing lands) that are not generally liable for revenue; (b) "waste," which may be either "assessed waste" ("cultivable lands which have been left uncultivated, lands relinquished by cultivators, and lands bought in by government in revenue sales") or "unassessed waste" ("lands to which no classification or assessment has been assigned because they are considered unfit for cultivation")[2]; and in addition, (c) areas designated under the terms of the forest act as either reserve forest or revenue forest.

Poromboke and assessed and unassessed waste land fall within village boundaries and are nominally "village lands," while forests are usually outside village limits. None of the lands covered by these official categories should be encroached upon for settlement or cultivation; if they are, then official penalties may be applied. Fuel, fodder, and other products available on poromboke and waste lands may be freely collected, except in the case of designated trees or bushes (such as palmyra palms or tamarind trees), the rights to which are in the control of the local administration and are usually auctioned annually. These products may also be available from designated forests, when rights to collect or cut are under the control of the forest department of the state government. In addition, fuel and fodder may sometimes be obtained quite freely from private land, where there are generally accepted common rights, for example, to dig up the stumps and roots of harvested plants for fuel, to graze animals after harvest, or to cut grass from field edges.

There is a problem in clear labeling of the various resources available and the exact property rights attached to each. Poromboke and waste land, for example, are designated as village land and, as such, would seem to be land on which the resources are common property. However, in many cases, poromboke and waste land are used by persons outside the village too, particularly when they are in large tracts and/or abut roads or other settlements--in which case they are "open access" resources. However, in the majority of cases, users of the poromboke and waste lands close by a village tend to be the villagers themselves. Also, within any one territory, a variety of property rights are attached to specific resources, as

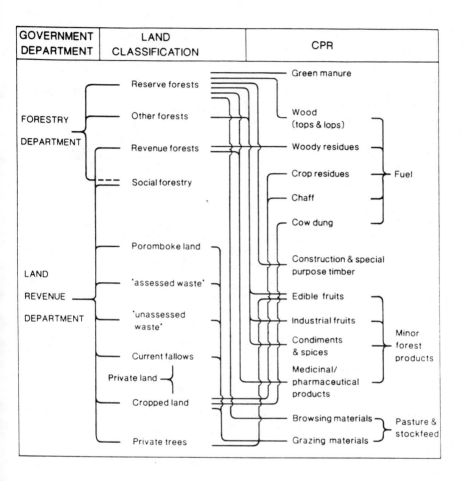

FIGURE 1 Common property resources studied in this paper.

Figure 1 makes plain. For example, a sandalwood tree
in a reserved forest is treated as state property, while
the grass around it is a common property resource for

which users pay the state. The unambiguous label is
threatened by "illegal" use. At what point does poaching
turn state property into an open access resource?

Official data on the areas of land covered by these
official categories give us a measure, though an imprecise
one, of the availability of commons in different parts
of the state, and of the extent to which they are being
depleted. The official land utilization data, shown in
Table 1, gives only an imprecise measure because the
categories employed may lump together both public and private land. It is fair to assume, however, that the major
share of the areas of "forest," "culturable waste" (the sum
of assessed and unassessed waste) and of "permanent pasture" shown in the data is under public ownership, and that
any changes in extent that are recorded are likely to include changes in this "public" area. These figures suggest
that while the forest area has remained constant over the
last 21 years, the areas of culturable waste and of permanent pasture have undergone a general, steady decline.

TABLE 1   Tamil Nadu--Changes in Land Use Patterns Relevant
          to CPRs 1961/62, 1969/70, and 1981/82 (percentage
          geographical area).

	Forest			Culturable Waste			Permanent Pasture		
Year:	61/62	69/70	81/82	61/62	69/70	81/82	61/62	69/70	81/82
Percentage:	14.5	15.5	15.6	5.3	4.1	2.6	2.8	1.7	1.2

SOURCE: Season and Crop Reports.

Field investigations at the village level show that
there is a good deal of diversity in the importance of
common property resources (CPRs) in the economy. But it
seems that we may broadly distinguish in terms of both
area and potential benefits between "CPR-limited" and
"CPR-dependent" villages. In villages in areas of old,
established, and quite intensive cultivation, CPRs may in
fact be of rather marginal importance, where there is no
frontier of "waste" land that can be encroached upon for
cultivation--apart perhaps from limited areas of tank
foreshores; cattle are largely stall-fed with crop residues
and even purchased feeds, and grazing on public or common
lands is of secondary importance; fuel includes dung cakes

made from the manure of privately owned cattle, thorn bush twigs cut on privately owned land, and even purchased firewood (only very poor people collect fuel on poromboke land). Soil fertility depends upon purchased inorganic fertilizers, and even organic manures are purchased from outside; few, if any, minor products supply food or raw materials, apart from the roots of some cacti that provide famine food. These can be termed "CPR-limited" villages.

In contrast with these circumstances are those of villages in more marginal environments such as the hilly areas of Dharmapuri and Salem districts and in the western areas of the state. Here, a "frontier" of waste still exists and offers livelihood possibilities even for poor people. Fuel and fodder are extensively obtained from the "commons" by all classes of people, and soil fertility may be closely bound up with the numbers of livestock that can be maintained. These CPR-dependent villages are often situated in the west of the state where forest still covers a significant percentage of the land area.

TECHNICAL AND PHYSICAL ATTRIBUTES

Tamil Nadu has a wide range of vegetative formations reflecting a diversity of rainfall regimes. This vegetation provides the productive base for CPRs. Although the area of natural vegetation has decreased both quantitatively and qualitatively, the government of Tamil Nadu had listed 1,219 species in the area in 1983, the majority of which are used for one purpose or another (for a detailed list, see Blaikie, Harriss, and Pain 1985).

The technical and physical qualities of these CPRs can be considered in terms of their jointness of supply, excludability and indivisibility (Oakerson, this volume). We will discuss them under the two broad headings of timber and fuel and grazing resources (although for many purposes there is no need to distinguish between them). With regard to jointness of supply of these CPRs, clearly they all can be used by a number of people simultaneously, and that use can subtract from the per capita benefit. However, there are important methodological issues here, since use is not necessarily harmful to productivity: there is evidence that under certain circumstances limited degradation of, for example, climax to secondary vegetation can actually lead to enhancement of productivity. Indeed, continued use of many biological resources is the key to sustained productivity.

Data on the production and productivity of CPRs is very scarce. For example, livestock obtain fodder supplies from crop residues, grazing on village common lands (poromboke and tank foreshores) and from browsing in reserved forests. The relative importance of these various sources is quite variable over space and time, and the intensification of rice production has evidently alleviated problems of fodder supply in some areas. Nevertheless, fodder or browse resources from forests constitute a major source of supply for cattle in western Tamil Nadu, but (as with fuel species) data on natural browse species, on actual and potential productivity, and on carrying capacity of browse areas are almost entirely absent. Thus, precise statements on actual or potential supply and benefits cannot be made. If we knew the sustainable yield of browse species, we could make a determination of what the grazing limits could be. However, one would have to accept a trade-off between fodder and fuel supplies, since maximizing the one would reduce production of the other.

The excludability of CPRs is an issue that is constantly at the centre of contradiction between the rural population and government departments. It is physically feasible to fence off forests, but very expensive. It is estimated that fencing social forestry plantations doubles the costs of establishment (Karnataka State Forestry Department, personal communication). In addition, fences are difficult to guard and are easily cut. It is extremely difficult to guard and to exclude users from small forests entirely surrounded by rural populations. For poromboke land and other major grazing resources, exclusion of non-locals (those from outside the village) might be quite easy through recognition. In practice, little effort is made to exclude outsiders from village poromboke. If a village decided to stint on the poromboke land, it would be fairly easy for people to identify free riders--although not necessarily to exclude them, since effective exclusion is a matter of political power as well as of the physical characteristics of the CPR itself. This point underlines the difficulties of clearly labeling the type of property rights attaching to each resource.

There is another aspect of excludability that depends upon the location of the CPR relative to potential users. The friction of distance derives from relative location and not from the technical attributes of the CPR, but it is an important aspect. Development of the road system even to the remote parts of Tamil Nadu has opened up many forest products to commercial pressures. Pappanaickenpatti (a village in Salem District) has developed a substantial local export industry in green manure for paddy and curry leaves from the curry leaf plant (Murraya koenigi); the former is transported to the Salem district, the latter to the markets of Madras over 100 miles away. The new road to the village laid in the last decade has made this business possible, and has made most CPRs in Tamil Nadu accessible to commercial exploitation.

The physical attributes of CPRs in Tamil Nadu can be summarized, therefore, as broadly accessible and non-excludable, subject to relatively high subtractibility and divisibility, and with a clear set of boundaries.

DECISION-MAKING ARRANGEMENTS

Decision-making arrangements regulating the use of CPRs in Tamil Nadu have these characteristics: first, the development of institutions for collective choice within the groups involved with these "commons" is very restricted indeed; second, there is extensive bureaucratic control under rules that are partial and often unclear, and that leave a great deal to the discretion of field officers in matters of enforcement; and third, following from these features, the arrangements are highly susceptible to manipulation by those with local power.

Conditions of Collective Choice

Few local institutions regulate choices over the use of CPRs in Tamil Nadu. In some instances, purely local, community level councils/committees/informal groups act to regulate surface irrigation, such as those in North Arcot District described by Chambers (1977). A tradition of kudi-maramut, or locally organized collective work in the maintenance of irrigation structures, also can be found to a limited extent in some parts (Harriss 1982: 72-76). But these instances are exceptional and they relate to irri-gation water. We know of no such institutions or arrange-ments for the management of the resources of poromboke and designated waste lands or of forests.

Tamil Nadu, as elsewhere in India, has a history of local institutions (panchayats) with juridical powers (for the resolution of disputes) and executive authority (for certain decisions in the public realm, such as over temple affairs and village religious ceremonies). (We refer here

to village and caste _panchayats_ rather than to the officially constituted _panchayat_, the lowest level of organization in the system of democratic local government adopted
in India in the 1950s and 1960s.) The _panchayats_ still
exist (see Harriss 1982:227-233), but there is little, if
any, evidence that they have been instruments for the
management of resources such as waste land and forest, at
least over the last 200 years. They may be used, however,
to resolve disputes such as those arising from quarrels
over grazing.

The effectiveness of such local dispute resolution and
decision making depends upon local power structures, in
which the extent of the dominance that is exercised by a
particular caste group, and the capacity of that caste
group for taking collective action, are factors of crucial
importance. In circumstances where dominance is disputed
among different groups and/or where the dominant caste
group is itself divided by strong factional rivalries,
collective action may be compromised. Djurfeldt and
Lindberg (1975:125) record an instance of effective action
by locally dominant cultivators to prevent encroachment on
poromboke lands used for grazing, while Hill (1982:131)
documents a case where common grazing lands have been
encroached by richer households. What happens to common
lands in a particular village area is likely to depend
upon the specific interests and politics of richer and
more powerful people. Such effective choice as exists
with regard to CPRs in the highly stratified rural society
of Tamil Nadu is unlikely to involve the entire village
population. It will involve the richer, more powerful
households and will usually reflect their interests. The
mass of rural people may or may not derive some benefit
from their action.[3]

The official _panchayats_ have assumed some responsibility for the management of some CPRs. Palmyra and
tamarind trees, growing on tank bunds or at roadsides
(respectively), thorn bushes used as fuel, and certain
green manure plants all are treated as public property.
Rights to the use of these plants were handed over to the
village _panchayats_, which in turn auctioned them, and put
the money earned into _panchayat_ funds. Though the village
panchayats have been in abeyance in Tamil Nadu since 1975,
it is still said by villagers and by officials that the
panchayat controls the use of these resources. At present,
in practice, use rights are auctioned by a local official
and the proceeds go into official coffers. It is significant, though, that the _panchayat_ should still be referred

to: there is a strong belief in the power and endurance
of popular institutions of local self-government even when
these institutions no longer exist. This belief perhaps
helps to legitimatize state interventions. Under both the
village panchayats and under the current arrangements,
there is evidence that relatively wealthy or powerful
people have been able to obtain rights to CPR produce at
very low rates in auctions, and to sell this produce for
a substantial profit.

In sum, the use of CPRs of fuel, fodder, and other
produce from poromboke, waste and forest lands is subject
to a high degree of personal discretion (individuals are
generally able to act on the basis of personal discretion
in matters of common concern). This discretion, however,
is limited mainly by bureaucratically enforced controls
that can be manipulated, to one degree or another, by each
individual who encounters them. Fieldwork showed a number
of corroborated accounts of bribery: bribes are considered
necessary when users want to gain access to resources to
which the state laid claim, or when they need to extricate
themselves from the consequences of being caught. There
were reported to be considerable variations between
individual officials at all levels, however, as well as
between the way in which the administration operated at
the village, district, and state levels.

Individuals adversely affected by others may turn to
local, unofficial panchayats to adjudicate disputes or
they may find remedies through the law and the local
bureaucracy. All these institutions are susceptible to
influence by those holding local power. In any event, the
extent to which collective decisions are taken at all is
very restricted, and both this and the degree to which
such decisions are binding depends upon the local power
structure, and especially on the politics of the dominant
caste. Powerful individuals both in the village and in the
bureaucracy have extensive powers of veto.

Operational Rules

In circumstances such as those just described, the
operational rules affecting CPR use exist on two levels.
On the one hand, bureaucratic rules regulate access to and
use of poromboke and waste lands and their products; these
are enforced by the revenue department; rules regarding
officially designated forests are enforced by the forest
department. The former include a scale of fines that

should be levied in cases of cultivation of _poromboke_; the latter, such rules as giving rights to collect fallen wood, but not to cut standing trees.

On the other hand, informal rules arise from the nature of the local power structure and the interactions of people with the bureaucracy. Thus the revenue and the forest departments are empowered to enforce rules that, in principle, prevent partitioning of CPRs and establish strong boundary lines. Local officials of the revenue department should prevent encroachment upon the _poromboke_ lands and regulate the use of designated waste, and forest officers control access to the forests. In practice, these rules can be bent systematically in favor of the relatively rich and powerful, for whom the fines imposed by the bureaucracy and/or the bribes paid to local officials for turning a blind eye on infringements may be treated as acceptable "costs of production." For the officials concerned, on the other hand, these payments are part of a kind of bureaucratic rent.

External Arrangements

Our account thus far has emphasized the crucial importance of external arrangements in decision making over CPRs in Tamil Nadu. The commons are actually defined by bureaucratic categorization of land as _poromboke_, or as "waste", or as "forest" (which is then really "state" land and not local "commons"); their boundaries are bureaucratically defined and may or may not correspond to a division based upon vegetational zoning. Rules about access and use are laid down in the standing orders of the departments concerned.

The arrangements in force are mainly bureaucratic, with both highly centralized rule making and, in practice, a great deal of field officer discretion, given the extreme difficulty of supervising their activity very closely. Petty corruption is endemic. But there are also arrangements at other levels, as, for example, with the recent establishment of village social forestry committees that supposedly encourage participation in the management of social forestry plantations. These committees are of such recent origin that it is difficult to assess them. The limited information we have suggests that they are often "paper" organizations characterized by indifference and ignorance on the part of the majority of their members. There is no reason to suppose that they will be any more effective as instruments of participation and collective decision making than are the village panchayats. Their power to make rules is seriously limited. The forestry department can and does coerce villagers to accept social forestry projects on their foreshores (Centre for Research, Extension and IRD 1984). The village level social forestry worker is responsible to the forestry department and not the village; the department selects the species to be planted and the dates when cutting is permitted, and the produce is auctioned off at its wish. Thus, the villagers cannot choose who will use the CPRs or decide upon how the products will be utilized.

Conclusion

In this sphere, as in others in south Indian villages, it seems that the long-standing attempt by the state to exercise close supervision over land use has actively discouraged collective choice and action at the local level (on this in general, see Washbrook 1976). Utilization of CPRs (fodder, fuel, etc.) is extensively controlled in principle by the local officials of several government departments. In practice, the system is subject to manipulation by those with local power and generally works in their favor.

PATTERNS OF INTERACTION

The account of decision-making arrangements for the management of CPRs implies that the consequent patterns of interaction are of two types--those between people and the state with its various functionaries, and those among people themselves who use the CPRs in the village. Since collective choice in the management of CPRs has been reduced to a minimum, the dominant set of interactions concerns the direct users and the state, or more specifically, the state land revenue and forestry departments.

Although these two sets of interactions are distinct, they are often closely related in the way CPRs are actually used. Any group of would-be users of CPRs is heterogeneous in its economic, social, and political resources. Users usually compete for CPRs, and competition among individual households for CPRs is encouraged by the lack of institutions at the local level (or at any other level) to manage the commons in a cooperative way. Each house-

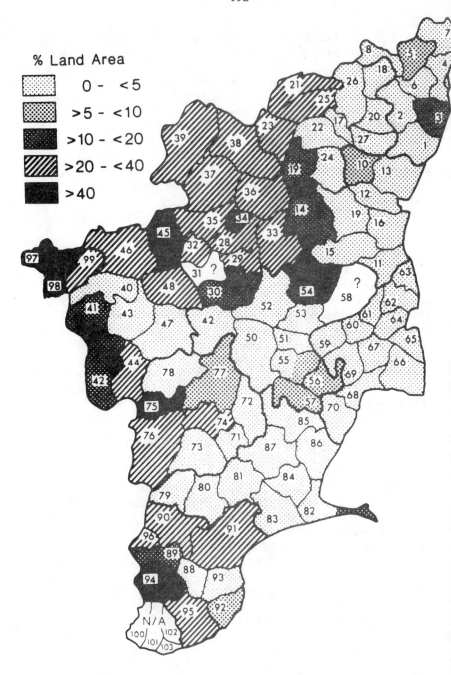

FIGURE 2 Forest cover in Tamil Nadu, 1981-1982.

hold thus competes against the others and against the state, and in this interaction the notion of access is crucial.

Access to CPRs has many dimensions. It implies that the would-be user has sufficient labor to use the resource (this is particularly important for fuel collection and grazing). It also implies that the potential user has spatial proximity to the resource and either the funds to purchase access from state officials (the payment of bureaucratic rent) or sufficient political power and coercion to gain access without paying the fee. Such power usually is the result of land ownership and facilitates dealings with official regulations over CPRs and with other competing households who are also direct users of the CPR. Thus the access position of the user largely determines the choice of strategy to obtain CPRs, and therefore the pattern of interactions among users themselves, and between users and the state.

The first and most common interaction between users and the state is the "legitimate" use of CPRs. This involves the removal of dead wood from both revenue and reserved forests, which is permitted by official regulations for certain forests. In addition, tribal peoples are given special dispensation to graze sheep and cattle (but not goats) in reserved forests. Others pay grazing fees, and there is no restriction on the number of cattle to be grazed. Stock may graze on waste and poromboke lands. As we shall see in the next section, the outcome of legitimate use of CPRs alone (leaving aside "illegitimate" use to be discussed below) has led to extreme pressure on some CPRs, notably grazing land and in some places fuel and construction timber (on the situation in India generally with regard to this point, refer to Government of India 1984). It is not the central contention of this paper that the illegal use of CPRs is necessarily the main culprit in the physical decline of many CPRs, although illegal action certainly is an additional use of CPRs and, as such, contributes to overuse. Illegal use also highlights the contradiction between would-be users and the state (which makes most of the rules).

Patterns of interaction involving illegal use of CPRs are of two major types: (1) instances when the illegal use constitutes overuse or overextraction by an individual of a common resource over and above the limits set by the state, and (2) cases when the illegal use involves a theft of state property (such as sandalwood). The two major resources that are most often overextracted are fuelwood and grazing land for goats, both of which are found on revenue and reserved forests. Those who collect fodder and fuelwood are frequently caught by forest guards; if the wood they have collected is found to have been cut green, the guards will impound their sickles. A fine of Rs. 5/- is common in such circumstances.

The case of theft of state property of timbers (such as sandalwood) is of a different order, since it is so valuable (up to about $10 per kilo of grade 1 timber) that it has long since ceased to be a CPR; rather, it is a much-prized commodity to which the state has laid claim. A few private individuals, often backed by considerable capital and equipment, do mount raids on these trees. The revenue collected by the forest department from this source is so much greater than from all others in certain forest divisions in western Tamil Nadu that much of the resources of staff and transport are committed to protect and harvest sandalwood. This undoubtedly diverts personnel from guarding less valuable resources such as small wood for fuel and other species used for construction purposes.

Bamboo is not such a severe case, although it is commercially valuable enough to provide the forest department with considerable revenue. It is also used by local artisans for weaving winnowing fans and mats, and forest guards often fine artisans not only at the site, but also when the artisans attempt to sell the finished product at the market.

It is difficult to assess how much of the fines levied by forest guards find their way to the official revenues of the department, and how much is appropriated by employees as "bureaucratic rent," but widely corroborated accounts of bribery abound. Villagers informally arrange an annual bribe to local forest guards to facilitate the grazing of goats, for example (by a capitation "fee" of about Rs. 5/- per goat-owning family, which, in one village, provided a sum of some Rs. 600/- [$50] handed over annually). Similarly, artisans using bamboo arrange an annual bribe. In one vil- lage, the collection of green manure from the more productive reserve forests attracts a standardized charge of Rs. 80/-, of which Rs. 36/- is an unreceipted fine to forest guards. The forest guards (and perhaps forest rangers, too) have an informal organization for dividing this rent amongst themselves and for collecting it in a variety of ways. One tribal village, well-endowed with reserve forest, has forest guards who arrive two or three times a year with a lorry, make a spot-check on fuelwood stocks of households, and confiscate and remove any timber that they believe was cut green. The value of a lorryload is estimated to be at least Rs. 1,000/-.

The other main type of interaction between state and user is the privatization of CPRs through encroachment. Successful encroachment of _poromboke_ lands and other common lands (such as uncultivated waste lands) depends upon the access position of the individual encroacher, both with regard to other villagers and to the bureaucracy of the land revenue department. Individuals of widely differing access positions encroach upon _poromboke_ land. Landless and near-landless households are perhaps the most numerous, but their position is threatened by powerful "big-men" and speculators from outside the village who employ strong-arm tactics to evict less powerful people, and who sometimes use the law to have them removed--and then evade the law themselves through bribery to take over the land and register it in their own names (as in the case of Pappanaikenpatti, where the village _munsif_ acquired _patta_--i.e., land to which an individual has title--right over land from which he had evicted tribal encroachers). There is therefore a long, drawn out process of de facto occupation of _poromboke_ land, annual fines for illegal privatization that may go on for many years, and finally change of revenue classification to _patta_ land. Revenue records, therefore, inevitably lag behind the true extent of encroachment. Encroachment clearly has been going on for a very long time, so that opportunities for further encroachment are generally limited. Local revenue records show that most of the encroachment takes place on land designated as _poromboke_, cultivable waste, permanent pastures and other grazing lands, and only to a very limited extent onto land under the jurisdiction of the forest department.

Turning to the interactions among individuals in the use of CPRs, it will by now be plain that there is very little cooperation among individuals in the management of commons that have been taken over by the state. Competition is the dominant relationship in CPR use, rather than free riding. The intensity of competition among users is a function of the supply of CPRs and the demand for them, and of the lack of legitimacy of the rules governing the resources. The state makes the rules but enforces them arbitrarily (from the local users' point of view), and their legitimacy is low.

To summarize the principal patterns of interaction, the chief actors are users and the functionaries of the state, backed by the law that, in official terms, clearly demarcates and sanctions categories of rights and restrictions. The arena of local management and interaction is

thereby drastically limited, and is characterized by
individualistic patterns of use and competition among
users who have differing qualifications for gaining access.

OUTCOMES

Political Economy

The outcomes of the political economy can be summarized
by seven major points discussed below.
It will already be clear that the state has taken
control of virtually all lands on which common property
resources are to be found. The social forestry program,
as it is currently conceived, is merely an extension of the
state's control and a further restriction upon the use of
common property resources. At the local level, too, no
institutions take a major part in managing these resources.
In sum:

(1) The state seeks to regulate most CPRs in Tamil Nadu.

The outcome of CPR management in Tamil Nadu cannot be
analyzed properly without reference to changes in the
ownership and productivity of private property resources
(PPRs). Here there has been a steady reduction in the
average size of landholdings and a considerable degree of
differentiation among rural households has existed for a
long time. Some farmers have managed to increase both the
size and productivity of their farms; others have been
reduced to the status of either landless laborers or sub-
marginal farmers, and have been pushed onto the economic
fringes of cultivation. This sometimes finds spatial
expression in that they illegally squat on poromboke land
and barren wastes, and may be forced to cut and sell firewood to eke out a living. These people are also marginal-
ized in the sense that they cannot usually invest in
productive assets and tend to lose land to more adventur-
ous, unscrupulous, and wealthy people. For the most part,
encroachment is the result of population pressure within a
society with a highly skewed distribution of power. The
exception is encroached land that is irrigable and attracts
speculative purchase by wealthier people.
Other changes in PPRs also affect the use of CPRs;
these come about as a result of irrigation. When an extra
one or two crops a year are produced, crop residues for

feeding livestock and for fuel are more plentiful. In
Tamil Nadu, the double-cropped area has generally increased,
especially as a result of the expansion of groundwater
irrigation (data in Kurien 1980). At the same time, paddy
cultivation may create a demand for green manure, which is
usually obtained from forests where these are accessible.
Thus:

(2) Marginalization of poorer rural people has led to
increased use of CPRs and their encroachment through illegal
squatting.

(3) Increases in irrigated area have tended to ease the
shortage of pastures on common land, but may also have
increased the demand for green manure, particularly near
forests.

     Greatly increased pressure on CPRs has led to rising
costs to users whose travel and collection time have increased; users may also be paying more for bribes and fines.
     In the areas of Tamil Nadu that were studied, there is a
notable exception to encroachment patterns that seem widespread throughout India--namely the unauthorized collection
of fuelwood. There is little evidence of a serious shortage
of fuel in Tamil Nadu. There are a number of reasons for
this. First, there are a fair number of woody residues from
tree crops (for example palmyra and coconut palm), and
annual crops (such as cotton, cassava, and sorghum) that are
not readily recyclable through the agricultural system via
composting, but that are still suitable for burning as
fuel. Second, there is not an appreciable cold season (as
in central or northern India). Third, opportunistic thorn
bushes (such as Lantana spp.) grow rapidly and freely on
poromboke land on roadsides, tank foreshores, and elsewhere,
and provide an adequate source of fuel in many areas. In
eastern districts, Prosopis juliflora provides fuel, since
it is rarely browsed by goats, and it coppices well and
grows fast. This finding is different from that of Jodha
(forthcoming), who found quite acute shortages of fuel in
the drier areas of western India where dung is burned as a
substitute for wood. In Tamil Nadu, dung is burned in areas
far from any available forest, but it is not universal.
Thus, we may summarize our fourth outcome:

(4) There is not yet a widespread nor severe shortage of
combustible fuel.

Increased pressure on grazing is undoubtedly severe, however, and is reflected in reduced numbers of live-stock:

TABLE 2   Changes in Livestock Population in Tamil Nadu, 1961-1982.

	1961	1974	1982	% change 1961-1982
Buffalo	2,594,271	2,853,252	3,212,224	+ 23
Bovines	13,420,174	10,572,378	10,365,500	- 23
Sheep	7,159,956	6,392,821	5,536,514	- 23
Goats	3,428,847	3,954,477	5,246,192	+ 53
TOTAL	26,603,248	23,772,928	24,360,430	+ 8

The views of individual owners of cattle, buffalo, and small stock also support this view. The extension of government-sponsored social forestry onto tank foreshores clearly exacerbates the pressure on remaining land. Thus:

(5) There is severe pressure on grazing land, and this is partly associated with a decline in the numbers of cattle.

Other forest products both for commercial exploitation and for subsistence have also become scarce or unavailable altogether. Exploitation of those that have commercial possibilities (such as gall nuts and curry leaves) have increasingly been organized by contractors who have successfully bid for the rights that are sold by the forestry department or the land revenue department. Medicinal herbs, wild roots, honey, and relishes have long since disappeared from both the forests and minds of those who use the forest (curry leaves are the one exception here). Thus:

(6) Most minor forest products have ceased to be CPRs either because they have been overused to the point of extinction or because they have been commercialized and taken out of the realm of CPRs for local use.

Turning now to the overall extent of land on which CPRs
are or were exploited, encroachment into poromboke land and
unassessed and assessed waste land has reduced the area of
common land to a very small proportion of the whole (see
Table 1). While the remaining poromboke and waste land is
dwarfed by land held in reserve and revenue forests, it
remains the only land that could conceivably be managed by
a committee of users. Thus:

(7) The area of village lands from which CPRs are obtained
has been diminishing over a long period, and has left very
little common land under the control of the village.

Environment

It is difficult to be precise about the efficiency
of use of CPRs in Tamil Nadu because of the general dearth
of accurate physical information on their potential and
actual levels of productivity. Further, if one considers
the interactions among different CPR products obtained from
the same common lands, such as browse or grazing and fuel,
data on how productivity of the one will affect productivity of the other does not exist. Statements of biological
efficiency that concern themselves solely with aggregate
productivity or vegetative material are meaningless without
recourse to exact information on human needs and whether in
fact fuel or grazing products are or should be more significant. Of course, this is not to suggest that there is no
compatibility of use among different CPR products, but one
must recognize the limitations of simply using physical
data in a vacuum.
Verbal reports and some physical evidence do suggest
that overall usage rates of CPRs has led to a depletion of
resources. Productivity has actually increased in one case
where tank foreshores were planted with Acacia nilotica
(babul) under social forestry schemes; however, this has
not necessarily enhanced common benefits.
There are differences among villages in the higher
west of Tamil Nadu and those on the eastern plain. The
Kalrayan hills in Salem district surrounding the village
of Pappanaickenpatti still support a diversity of flora in
a well-structured community, which hardly indicates severe
environmental pressure (see detailed analysis in Blaikie
et al. 1985). In the neighboring district of Dharmapuri
on the common lands of Arakasanahalli, this vegetation

cover is largely gone and the lands are covered by the opportunistic <u>Lantana</u> spp. and thickets of heavily coppiced <u>Albizia</u> <u>amara</u>. But despite the fact that the vegetation is degraded, the village does not suffer from problems of fuel supply. On the other hand, in Dusi, a predominantly paddy village in North Arcot, the remaining 21.56 acres of common grazing lands support no standing timber, and although there is full grass cover, the species composition is such that productivity is low and little benefit is derived by anyone using these lands for grazing. But the fuel situation in Dusi has actually improved over the last decade with the spread of the thorn bush <u>Prosopis</u> <u>juliflora</u>, and the village is almost self-sufficient in its fuel requirements.

In general, production from village grazing lands is minimal, but this has probably been the case for some decades. There is no doubt that many of the forests and their various products are degraded or exploited beyond their natural rate of sustainability, and the overexploitation of bamboo has been well documented.

Livelihoods

CPRs are of varying importance as sources of food, fodder, fuel, manure, and minor products; these products, in turn, are the basis for livelihoods in villages in different parts of Tamil Nadu (see our earlier remarks on "CPR-limited" and "CPR-dependent" villages). The bureaucratic regulation of CPRs is of particular concern in CPR-dependent villages, for this regulation is often subject to manipulation by local power to the disadvantage of poorer people.

But in both CPR-dependent and CPR-limited village economies, CPRs present livelihood opportunities that are either not pursued or that are inefficiently pursued from the point of view of poor peoples' welfare. In the latter category, we would include the current use of tank beds and foreshores for so-called "social" forestry projects; there is often no benefit at all to local people and particularly none to the rural poor, given that they find neither employment nor resources of use to them in the social forestry plantations. In the former category, we would include the possible uses of marginal lands (classified as waste) for forestry conducted by poor people for their own benefit. Clearly the mobilization of opportunities like these is subject to difficulties that should not

be underestimated in circumstances where the powerful and
wealthy have been able to systematically take advantage of
the confusing layering of rights and enforcement, so that
considerable inequalities in access to common resources has
resulted. Any fresh interventions by the state are likely
to be susceptible to manipulation by local power holders.
The point is that opportunities for the production of
livelihoods do still exist and that the means for exploring
them are not available under the current system of
management by a bureaucracy imbued with an ethic of
regulation and control.

NOTES

1. The research on which this paper is based was
essentially of an exploratory kind. The authors undertook field research together in the state of Tamil Nadu in
September 1984, when they collected secondary data and made
studies of six villages, three of them in an area of intensive irrigated agriculture in the North Arcot District.
Thereafter, Adam Pain undertook an additional six weeks of
field work, including some ecological analysis, in the same
villages.

2. Definitions quoted from: Sundararaja Iyengar. 1933.

3. Wade makes this point with regard to some villages in
Andhra Pradesh that display an unusual degree of corpor-
ateness (Wade, forthcoming). The councils in these villages, with their common funds (that are used to pay the
field guards and common irrigators whom they employ),
are essentially institutions of the dominant Reddy caste
community. It may be in this case that low-caste, landless people do derive benefits from the existence of these
institutions because of the higher levels of economic
activity that they are instrumental in bringing about.
But poor and low-ranking people are not participants in
the institutions. Wade's study describes institutions
concerned with collective choice that are certainly unusual
in India, and his account in the end emphasizes just how
exceptional the circumstances are that seem to explain the
existence of corporate activity in this case.

REFERENCES

Blaikie, P., J. Harriss, and A. Pain. 1985. Public Policy and the Utilization of Common Property Resources in Tamil Nadu, India. A report for ESCOR. Norwich, United Kingdom: Overseas Development Administration, School of Development Studies, University of East Anglia.

Blaikie, P. M. and H. C. Brookfield, eds. Forthcoming. Land Degradation and Society. London: Methuen.

Centre for Research, Extension and IRD. 1984. People and Social Forestry: Case Studies in Co-operation and Conflict. Gandhigram, Madurai District, Tamil Nadu, India: Gandhigram Rural Institute.

Chambers, R. 1977. Men and water: the organisation and operation of irrigation. In Farmer 1977.

Djurfeldt, G. and S. Lindberg. 1975. Behind Poverty: the Social Formation in a Tamil Village. London: Curzon Press.

Farmer, B. H. ed. 1977. Green Revolution? London: Macmillan.

Government of India. 1984. Report of the Review Committee on Rights and Access to Forest Areas. New Delhi: Government of India.

Government of Tamil Nadu. 1983. List of More Common Plants of Tamil Nadu and Their Uses. Madras: Statistics and Planning Cell of the Office of the Chief Conservator of Forests.

Harriss, J. 1982. Capitalism and Peasant Farming: Agrarian Structure and Ideology in Northern Tamil Nadu. Bombay: Oxford University Press.

Hill, P. 1982. Dry Grain Farming Families. Cambridge: Cambridge University Press.

Jodha, N. S. Forthcoming. Common property resources and environmental decline in western India. In Blaikie and Brookfield, forthcoming.

Kurien, C. T. 1980. Dynamics of rural transformation: a case study of Tamil Nadu. Economics and Political Weekly. 15:365-390.

Sundararaja Iyengar. 1933. Land Tenures of the Madras Presidency. Madras.

Wade, R. Forthcoming. Village Polities: Collective Action and Common Property Resources in South India. Cambridge: Cambridge University Press.

Washbrook, D. 1976. The Emergence of Provincial Politics: The Madras Presidency 1870-1920. Cambridge: Cambridge University Press.

Minor Forest Products as Common Property Resources in East Kalimantan, Indonesia [1]

Timothy C. Jessup
Nancy Lee Peluso

INTRODUCTION

One way to study the use of biological resources in a diverse ecological setting (such as a forest or fishery) is to consider simultaneously all the exploited species. This is typified by "ecosystem" or "resource system" analyses. Another approach, also holistic but in a different way, is to focus on one or a few resources and their connections to a variety of ecological and economic factors. We take this second approach in our case study of tropical forest resources in the province of East Kalimantan in Indonesian Borneo. We focus on a few so-called "minor" (non-timber) forest products to show how problems of their exploitation are related to: (1) biological and technical characteristics of the exploited species; (2) rules and other formalities of resource use; and (3) interactions among resource users and other relevant actors.

The model for the analysis of common property problems (Oakerson, this volume) is meant to enable us to conduct this analysis in a way that facilitates comparison among case studies. However, we believe Oakerson's identification of problems and the criteria for success or failure of resource management are too narrow in scope. Oakerson discusses one problem said to confront all users of common resources: "how to...attain an optimal rate of production

or consumption for the whole community" (Oakerson, this
volume). This focus on "the" problem of coordination and
the (supposed) community goal of optimal use leads him to
adopt the criteria of efficiency and equity (which are
closely linked in the notion of Pareto optimality) to
evaluate the outcomes of user interactions.[2]

An absence of efficiency and equity may indeed pose
problems for some people in some instances of managing a
resource, but we do not see that the concepts necessarily
help to identify other sorts of problems, especially those
whose scope extends beyond any particular group of users.
One can envisage, for example, situations in which a
resource is exploited equitably and efficiently until it is
exhausted, at which time users can switch to another
resource. No user in the group is harmed (Pareto's
criterion of efficiency) by depletion of the resource in
this case, because an alternate resource is subsequently
available. (Conversely, if all users suffered harm to the
same degree, would that not also be equitable?)

An example of such deplete-and-switch behavior is seen
in the colonization of new land in East Kalimantan by Bugis
pepper farmers from Sulawesi (Vayda and Sahur 1985), some
of whom have abandoned their old farms as productivity
falls in order to exploit opportunities to pioneer in new
areas of forest. To an economist interested principally in
such aspects of coordination as efficiency and equity
within a group of users, there may be no manifest "problem"
in this case. However, others concerned with the conservation or sustainable use of forests will see in this
instance a real problem of resource depletion and environmental degradation. Oakerson says the evaluation of
outcomes is value-laden and dependent on the prior selection of criteria. We would add that the same is true of
the identification of problems (cf. Vayda and McCay 1977).

We shall be explicit, therefore, in stating that our
concern is with environmental problems of resource depletion and forest degradation. By "depletion" we mean the
reduction of a resource to such a low level of abundance
that its renewability is seriously threatened. By "degradation" we mean a decline in the quality of the resource.
We are also interested in how people attempt to sustain
their use of resources despite fluctuations in the circumstances of their availability and exploitation. In these
respects, our criteria for successful management converge
with those of Bromley (this volume), who urges scholars to
"regard the social system and the ecosystem as equally
important and then search for use regimes that...allow both

components to survive, if not prosper."

We differ with Bromley (this volume) and some others in that we do not assume the existence of quasi-autonomous social and ecological systems. By adopting a more integral and nonsystemic approach to the study of resource use, one avoids significant difficulties, both theoretical and practical, in defining and identifying the boundaries and goals of such systems. It is possible instead to focus directly on human actors, their interactions with particular aspects of their environments, and the consequences or outcomes of those actions (Vayda 1983).

Our case study is from the province of East Kalimantan, where we have done human ecological research as part of a U.S.-Indonesian project in the Man and the Biosphere (MAB) Program from 1979 to 1982. The purpose of our research was to investigate the environmental effects of people's forest-related activities (such as shifting cultivation and the collection of forest products) and to identify the contexts in which people engage in or alter those activities.

East Kalimantan was chosen as a site for MAB research because of the rapid social and environmental changes that have accompanied the recent timber boom there, changes that, on the one hand, were believed to seriously threaten forests and, on the other hand, were poorly understood by scientists and development planners (Kartawinata and Vayda 1984). Despite a small population (1,214,604 in 1980, less than 1 percent of Indonesia's total, and a mean density of 5.7 people per sq km [Zimmermann 1982:33]), East Kalimantan had become Indonesia's wealthiest province by the 1970s. Its natural resources--mainly timber and oil, but also rattan and other minor forest products--accounted for almost 25 percent of Indonesia's export earnings in 1976. (The research was conducted before the devastating drought and fire of 1982-83, which particularly affected the middle and lower Mahakam areas and has probably had indirect effects on minor forest products elsewhere in the province.)

MINOR FOREST PRODUCTS

Most useful species in tropical forests provide products other than timber. Though overshadowed in recent times by large-scale commercial logging, products now called "minor"--such as rattan, dammar (resins used in making varnishes and lacquers), and edible birds' nests-- have been traded since antiquity and, until World War II, were comparable in importance to timber. They still contribute more than does timber to the incomes of people living in or near forests.

Most collectors of forest products in Borneo are peasant farmers, whose repertoire of economic activities also includes shifting cultivation; hunting, fishing, and gathering of wild plants for food and materials; production of rubber, pepper, fruit, and other perennial cash crops; and occasional wage labor, e.g., as loggers (Dove 1985; Dransfield 1981; Miles 1976; Jessup 1981; Padoch and Vayda 1983). Other forest-product collectors in East Kalimantan are migrant laborers who flocked to the province during the manual logging boom (1967-1971) and turned to collecting minor forest products when the government restricted logging practices in the 1970s. Among the peasants farmers, the number of forest species collected for subsistence and trade, like the diversity of collectors' economic activities, is substantial.[3]

Indigenous forest product collectors in East Kalimantan, whose forest-related activities are the primary focus of this paper, do not use all available resources or engage in all possible economic activities at any given time. Rather, they switch from one to another or vary the degree of their involvement in response to changing opportunities and problems, including fluctuations in commodity prices and employment as well as environmental variations. Nevertheless, many commercial forest products are over-exploited, often to the point of depletion.

Three circumstances surrounding the overexploitation of forest products may be ascribed to the "modern" economic context of collecting: (1) the concentration of international trade in minor forest products in a relatively small number of species, commonly for luxury uses, with prices (and therefore incentives to collect) rising as the stocks decline; (2) the closing of opportunities to practice some "traditional" activities, such as shifting cultivation, by the designation of large tracts of forest land as logging concessions; and (3) a decline in local employment opportunities in logging with the change from manual to mechanized methods in the 1970s. The combined result of these factors is the specialization of some forest-dwelling people (such as those in Rukun Damai, discussed below) in the collection of a few species.

These observations suggest that the modern commercial context is one of decreasing economic diversity. Yet we do not assume that so-called "traditional" forest-dwelling people were necessarily more conservative users of

resources before the modern boom in tropical forest
exploitation. Other circumstances in the past, including
warfare, demographic changes, and fluctuations in the long-
established trade in minor forest products, may have led
people to deplete certain resources and switch to others;
the switch was not necessarily made at a point that would
conserve the resources.

The most important of East Kalimantan's minor forest
products are rattan, aloes wood, edible birds' nests,
dammar, illipe nuts, beeswax, and reptile skins (Table 1).
We will focus on the first three of these products.[4]

TABLE 1 Export of Forest Products from East Kalimantan, by
Value, as Officially Reported (in Thousands of US
dollars). (Note Rise in Timber Exports in Early
1970s and in Rattan Exports in Late 1970s.)

Year	Timber	Rattan	Birds' nests	Resin	Illipe nuts	Aloes wood	Bees- wax	Reptile skins
1967	600	-	-	-	-	-	-	-
1968	4,000	-	-	-	-	-	-	-
1969	15,000	-	-	-	-	-	-	-
1970	53,000	100	26	1	258	2	-	-
1971	86,000	89	10	8	-	2	-	-
1972	111,000	93	8	12	-	-	1	-
1973	276,000	142	6	6	1	2	2	-
1974	365,000	262	9	19	66	-	-	-
1975	258,000	128	2	8	-	-	-	24
1976	402,000	160	12	2	-	-	-	-
1977	493,000	539	11	7	-	-	0.5	-
1978	525,000	1,313	18	9	-	-	3	-
1979	-	2,912	14	14	3.5	-	-	-
1980	-	2,882	-	6	-	-	-	22

Hyphen indicates no data in source tables.

SOURCES: Daroesman (1979:46) for timber (given to nearest $1 million): Zimmermann
(1982:80-81, 288-289) for minor forest products.

Rattan and aloes wood are typically held as common property within village territories, which is the general pattern of local control over forest resources in Borneo. Birds' nests, in contrast, are often controlled as private property by individuals or families. We shall consider some possible reasons for this difference.

Rattans are a diverse group of climbing palms, highly versatile in their uses. The stems of slender rattans are used in woven mats, baskets, and wickerwork, while large species provide cane for making furniture and other articles. Indonesia produces about 90 percent of the world's rattan, and East Kalimantan is one of the main sources.

Aloes wood, a resinous heartwood found in certain diseased trees, is a component of various Chinese and Malay medicines. Lower grades of the wood are used as incense in the Middle East. Demand for Borneo aloes wood rose sharply around 1977, possibly because the supply from Cambodia and Vietnam had been curtailed (Paul Chai, personal communication). This led to a flurry of collecting in parts of East Kalimantan.

Edible birds' nests, made by cave-dwelling swifts, are the principal ingredient in birds' nest soup and various tonics that are prized in China and parts of Southeast Asia for their supposed restorative and invigorating properties. Birds' nests are the most valuable, per unit of weight, of all Borneo's forest products. One kilogram (about 100 nests) of high quality nests were valued at between U.S. $200 and $400 in 1979 on the Upper Mahakam River in East Kalimantan; the lowest grade sold for about $10. In Singapore, the price was about $1,000 (Peluso 1981).

By comparison, in early 1980 the best grade of aloes wood was bought by upriver traders in the Apo Kayan for $20 per kg and was resold to urban buyers for about $100. Rattan prices are even lower on a per-weight basis: for Calamus caesius, stems of good quality sell for less than $1 per kg on the Upper Mahakam in 1980 and still under $2 at the point of export.[5]

Tables 1 and 2 show forest product exports from East Kalimantan by value from 1967 until 1980 and prices for rattan and birds' nests from 1969 until 1978, the years and products for which we have data. The price trends for birds' nests show substantial increases even as the reported quantities declined. Rattan exports increased in quantity as well as price. (We have more confidence in the trends shown by the data than in the actual value.

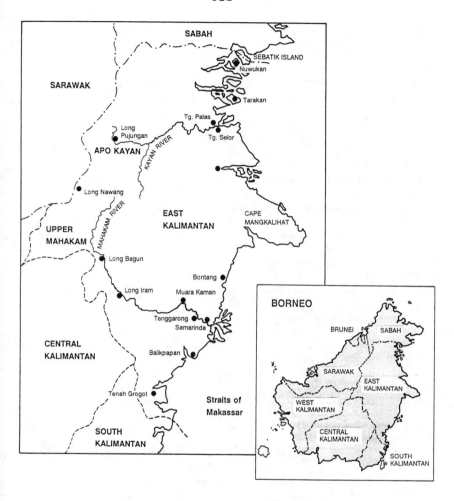

FIGURE 1   Province of East Kalimantan.

TABLE 2   Export Prices of Rattan and Birds' Nests from East
          Kalimantan, 1970-1978.*

YEAR	RATTAN			BIRDS' NESTS		
	Export Volume [Tonnes]	Export Earnings ('000 US$)	Price (US$/Kg)	Export Volume (Tonnes)	Export Earnings ('000 US$)	Price (US$/Kg)
1970	2,979	100	33.57	11.5	26	2.35
1971	3,602	89	24.71	12.9	10	.77
1972	3,703	93	25.11	6.6	8	1.21
1973	5,136	142	27.65	7.0	6	.86
1974	4,634	262	56.54	6.9	9	1.30
1975	2,021	128	63.33	1.0	2	2.00
1976	2,780	160	57.55	5.8	12	2.07
1977	4,787	539	112.59	1.6	11	6.88
1978	3,105	1,313	422.87	1.5	18	12.00

*Official sources often differ on volume and value of
exports. For example, the Kutai District Government
(1974) reported exports of birds' nests in 1970, 1971,
and 1972 as 13.8, 8.9, and 7.8 tonnes, respectively.
Birds' nest prices are purposely undervalued, even by
government officials, to provide an advantage to Indonesian
traders, but the reported price per kilogram provides a
crude indicator of relative value.

SOURCE: Muttaqin (1980).

The true value and quantities of forest products traded are
notoriously under-reported, due to tax incentives given to
exporters and smuggling.)
    Peluso investigated the collection and trade of rattan
and birds' nests in the area of the Upper Mahakam River,
while Jessup did research in the Apo Kayan (see map),
where aloes wood is the most important commercial forest
product. Peluso also visited the Apo Kayan to study the
trade in aloes wood there. The two areas are similar in
many ways, including the kinds of forest products used
locally (such as rattan and dammar), the practice of
shifting cultivation, the ethnic affiliations of the
inhabitants (Kenyah and related Dayak tribes), and the
interior location of both areas. However, they differ
in the greater isolation of the Apo Kayan, the proximity
of commercial logging to the Upper Mahakam, and the
commercial importance of particular forest products.
Birds' nests are important in the Upper Mahakam, and
aloes wood in the Apo Kayan, apparently because each
product is available only in one area or the other.
Rattan occurs in both places but it is not much traded in
the Apo Kayan because of the difficulty of transporting the
bulky stems through the rugged terrain there.

CHARACTERISTICS OF TROPICAL FOREST RESOURCES

    We now consider the biological and technical
characteristics of tropical forest resources in general and
of rattan, aloes wood, and birds' nests in particular.
A general characteristic of tropical forests is their great
diversity of species. Since the number of species in a
given area is high, the number of individuals of any one
species in the area tends to be low. Most are dispersed
throughout the habitats in which they occur rather than
being concentrated in a few locations. Collectors of these
dispersed resources, which include rattan and aloes wood,
must forage widely in search of suitable products.
    Another characteristic of rattan and aloes wood (and
of some other forest products, including timber) is that
the valuable resources are in the stems, rather than in
more easily regenerated parts such as fruit, leaves, or
exudates (gums and resins). The growth of resprouting
stems is relatively slow, if it occurs at all. Some
species only reproduce from seed and, as we have noted,
seed sources (i.e., mature plants) tend to be widely

dispersed. For these reasons, the precise location of collectible rattan and aloes wood is shifting and unpredictable.

In contrast to the pattern just described, edible birds' nests are a highly concentrated and rapidly renewable resource. They are produced by cave-dwelling swifts, which nest year after year in the same locations if the caves have not been seriously disturbed by human predators. These differences in the ecological patterns of forest resources have consequences for the way people manage them (i.e., as common or private property). A more detailed description of the characteristics of each of these resources is presented briefly below.

Rattan

Rattans are spiny, climbing palms, comprising nearly 600 species with their center of abundance in Borneo (c. 150 species) and Malaya. Some rattan is cultivated but most is collected from wild forest stocks. Rattans occur throughout Southeast Asia, mainly in lowland rain forests. The climbing plants reach to the top of the forest canopy, commonly 45-60 m above the ground. Their coiling, sagging stems are often 60-90 m long and some weigh enough to snap tree branches. Pulling down the larger species is arduous work, and most commercial collecting is done by able-bodied men. Most of the thick-stemmed species must be boiled in diesel oil (to remove natural gums and resins) soon after collection, or the cane will spoil. Slender rattans must be dried, before or after they are split into strips and cores, and are usually treated with sulfur to protect them from insects.

Rattan species with multiple stems regenerate after cutting, but single-stemmed ("solitary") species do not. The solitary Calamus manan, a valuable cane species, has consequently suffered badly from overcutting. On the other hand, the slender, multiple-stemmed C. caesius and C. trachycoleus resprout readily, a characteristic that not only makes wild populations somewhat more resilient, but that has also facilitated their cultivation.[6] Even in these species, however, seedling mortality in the forest is high and only a small proportion ever reaches the canopy. Many rattans only grow when seedlings are "released" by light from nearby tree-fall gaps, yet some species cannot survive in large gaps. All these factors contribute to the unpredictability--and vulnerability--of the resource.

Aloes Wood

Aloes wood is a diseased, fragrant heartwood produced
by trees of the genus Aquilaria, which comprises altogether
about 15 species, 5 in Malaya.[7] Only one, A. malaccensis, is widespread, and apparently it is this species
that yields the best grade of aloes wood. The heartwood is
soft, often oily, and lightweight. Once found, it is
easily collected and transported, requires little preparation, and can be stored for long periods. .Little is known
about the biology of these species or the pathogens that
produce aloes wood in them. The data we have suggest they
are restricted to certain localities or habitats, at least
in some areas such as the Apo Kayan.[8] Furthermore, the
diseased wood occurs sporadically; it is not always found
in every tree in a species that can produce aloes wood.
The amount of aloes wood collected from a tree, or even
from many trees during a collecting expedition, is highly
variable. Collectors (and traders seeking to induce people
to collect) tell tales of single trees yielding many
kilograms of high-grade wood worth hundreds of dollars.
Some people in the Apo Kayan have indeed found a kilogram
or more in a single day, but typically a collector
gets less than that from dozens of trees examined during an
expedition of a week or so. Thus, aloes wood is also a
very unpredictable resource.

Birds' Nests

Edible birds' nests are made by cave-dwelling
"swiftlets" belonging to three genera in the Apodidae, or
swift family. Five species occur in Borneo, of which two--
Aerodramus maximus and A. fuciphagus--produce edible
nests.[9] The birds nest in colonies, mainly in limestone
caves, some of which are very large.[10] Swiftlets tend to
breed each year in a fairly regular season, which makes
their nests a temporally as well as spatially predictable
resource.[11] Swiftlets of the two commercially valuable
species require at least 35 days to build a nest and lay
one egg, and some take more than 100 days to complete their
nests. Incubation takes about 25 days and fledging another
43 to 59 days. If nests are taken before fledging, the
parent birds will build another nest.

The birds make their nests and attach them to the
cave walls with a mucin-like protein secreted from
their salivary glands. This protein, commonly called

"nest-cement," is the edible part of the nests. The "white" nests of Aerodramus fuciphagus, which are made purely of nest-cement, fetch the highest prices. "Black" nests, made by A. maximus, contain feathers as an additional structural component and hence are inferior in quality and price. Any nests soiled by feces and other extraneous material, and any that have been allowed to deteriorate with age before being collected, are much reduced in value. Thus, there is a strong incentive for collectors to take nests early in the breeding season while they are still clean and fresh. Collectors studied by Peluso collect nests every forty days, knocking them down with a bamboo pole. A torch or flashlight is needed to find the nests; homemade torches doused with kerosene leave odors and residue on the cave walls, which informants said prevent the birds' returning to the same caves in the next cycle (Peluso 1981). Some East Kalimantan collectors purposely leave the highest nests in a cave to ensure (or so they believe) that a few birds will breed successfully and return later to make new nests. Inaccessible portions of some large caves provide nesting birds with natural refuges from collectors.

Jointness, Exclusion, and Divisibility of Forest Resources

Jointness of use of the resources that we are considering decreases at higher rates of exploitation, not only as a consequence of competition among collectors but also because the intensification of collecting tends to retard or disrupt the reproduction of exploited species. At moderate levels of collection, swiftlets are probably more resilient in this respect than either rattans or Aquilaria. The birds can replace collected nests and still breed in the same year, whereas rattans and Aquilaria require decades to regenerate from seed or (in some rattan species) years to reach commercial size after resprouting.

The spatial distribution and predictability of a resource affect the ease with which users can effectively exclude other potential users. Exclusion is more easily accomplished for a concentrated resource than for a dispersed one as long as the effort required to monitor and guard the resource is proportional to the area, perimeter, or number of entry points that must be covered.[12] This is so for the forest products we have considered; birds' nest caves are more easily watched and guarded than

are the scattered forest populations of rattan and
Aquilaria.

The forest resources we have been discussing are all
inherently divisible, but the scattered distribution of
rattan and aloes wood makes them difficult to privatize.
Only birds' nests occur within discrete natural boundaries
(that is, in caves) and so can easily be apportioned to
private owners.

PROPERTY RIGHTS AND THE REGULATION OF FOREST PRODUCTS

Village and Household Property Rights

Throughout the interior of Borneo, shifting
cultivators (such as the Kenyah of the Apo Kayan and Upper
Mahakam) inhabit village territories, within which residents of each community are entitled to use most forest
products as the common property of the village. In addition, households may have more exclusive rights to certain
forest products or certain uses of forest land within their
village's territory. Territorial boundaries were formerly
established and defended in some instances by force
(warfare and head-hunting), in others by negotiation and
the sale of rights between neighboring groups. These
"boundary rules" (to use Oakerson's terminology) were
sometimes enforced by third parties, such as the paramount
chiefs in the Apo Kayan during the latter part of the 19th
century. More recently, arbitrators' roles have been
divided between traditional leaders and government
officials.

Weinstock (1979) found village territoriality to be a
common principle of land and forest tenure among all groups
of shifting cultivators in Borneo, but he recognized
two types of individual or household land tenure (partitioning rules) within villages: one in which permanent
rights to reclear and cultivate a site are established by
the individual or household that first clears primary
forest (i.e., old-growth or "virgin" forest) from that
site; the other in which the cultivators' land-use rights
lapse after the crops are harvested, and the fallow land
reverts to the village commons. Permanent rights of the
first type are inherited, and they can be loaned between
households. Similar rights to use trees and tree-products
(such as fruit or resin) are found among at least some of
the groups that we or Weinstock (1979) and Appell (n.d.)
have studied. Tree rights are established either by

planting a tree or by marking and tending a wild one. The types of resources (land, fruit-trees, etc.) that can be claimed and owned by households seem to be those that are, like birds' nests, more predictable than most in their locations and temporal availability. (In the case of land under shifting cultivation, there is generally a preferred or minimum fallow period that, though it may vary with site conditions, is fairly predictable to farmers.)

Kinship is an important factor underlying the property rights outlined above. Ethnic groups and villages tend to be identified with more or less inclusive kin groups. Residence in a village, with the rights to common property that it confers, is established by birth or marriage, and so, too, is membership in a household with its more private rights of tenure (whether permanent or temporary). Conversely, property rights are forfeited by a person who permanently leaves a village. These are the "entry and exit" rules of the village community.

Inheritance is also according to kinship. In the so-called "cognatic" societies that predominate in Borneo, male and female descendants share equally in the inheritance of rights to land, trees, and other property. This rule of bilateral inheritance, together with the multiplication of descendants' households as they marry and have children, requires that there be arrangements to distribute property, if necessary, among several eligible claimants. This is done for land by alternating the use of sites among households according to various rules of priority-- notably by the degree of relatedness to the original owner--and for fruit trees by dividing their products. Because inherited rights to property may be distributed over a number of related individuals in several house- holds, this type of property is not strictly "private" but only relatively so in comparison with village-wide rights to common property. In fact, "private" household property lies at the focus of a hierarchy of potential users ordered by degrees of kinship.

It is important to recognize that traditional property arrangements are not stagnant and unchanging, and that adaptations to local circumstances can shift them in unexpected ways. We illustrate this point with two examples of change in the use of forested land for shift- ing cultivation, though similar changes with respect to minor forest products have doubtless occurred as well. The first example is taken from the work of Padoch (1982), who showed how, in some communities of Iban shifting cultivators (in Sarawak), where the formal rules of

land-use are those of permanent household tenure, land
scarcity led to frequent borrowing of land between
households. Although an ideology of relatively private,
circumscribed rights of tenure was maintained, in practice
land was treated more as common property than was the case
in some other, more land-abundant Iban villages.

This is not to say that only land shortages are
correlated with more "common" types of land use. Jessup
(1983, 1984) found that many farm sites in secondary
(previously cut) forest in the Apo Kayan were left
unclaimed when their former owners moved away during a time
of heavy emigration. These sites came to be treated as
common village property under the subsequent conditions of
abundant arable land. Thus, two very different demographic situations led to similar transitions towards a
more common use of a resource. Notice, in these examples,
that the actual coordination of resource use among a group
of users can change considerably even though the formal
rules remain the same.

Ownership of Birds' Nest Caves

Many birds' nest caves are more privately controlled
than are other forest products. Historically, birds' nests
have been more closely regulated than other forest
products, partly because of their great value but also, we
believe, because they are a concentrated and predictable
resource and therefore more easily controlled. What
Oakerson calls "external arrangements," both bureaucratic
and market-oriented, have long been important in East
Kalimantan. During the 19th century, birds' nest caves
along the Mahakam River were owned by the Sultan of Kutai,
whose officials supervised the collection, sale, and
export of nests. Now, the provincial and district governments regulate these activities. In the Kutai district of
East Kalimantan, which includes the Upper Mahakam area,
there are two stages or levels of access rights to nests.
The first is the right to harvest nests in a particular
cave, based on a registered or locally recognized claim of
ownership. The owner of a cave is usually the person who
found and subsequently guarded a previously unclaimed cave,
or an heir of the original owner. The second stage is
the right to buy and export nests from the subdistrict in
which they were collected. This right is granted by the
district government to authorized buyers (_faktar_) at an
annual auction. A buyer may obtain rights to nests in

more than one subdistrict, but he must pay a tax on the
nests taken from each subdistrict.

INTERACTIONS AMONG USERS AND OTHER ACTORS

The basic Agrarian Law of Indonesia, passed in 1960,
made no provision for traditional, village-based control
of forest products. Ownership of all forest land was
claimed by the national government. Although the constitution does recognize the local authority of "customary
law" (adat) in some matters, traditional village rights to
forest land and products were excluded by the 1960 law
(Vargas 1985; Weinstock 1979). In fact, traditional property laws are still important to local people in many
areas, particularly in regard to land tenure, inheritance,
and the collection of forest products. Conflicts often
occur, however, where established residents must compete
with more recent settlers, itinerant collectors, and timber
companies for the use of forest resources.

Effects of Timber Concessions on Forest Product Collection

In the early 1970s, the Indonesian government granted
timber concessions in East Kalimantan to a large number of
foreign and national companies. This had a number of
detrimental effects on local communities in or near the
concessions, such as the village of Rukun Damai in the
Upper Mahakam area. Villagers are permitted, by law, to
collect minor forest products within nearby timber
concessions, but the practice of shifting cultivation there
is strictly prohibited, a rule that is enforced (in this
case) by timber company personnel. Because the infertile soils of the region are not suited to permanent-
field agriculture, the restriction on shifting cultivation
has severely curtailed villagers' ability to produce
sufficient rice for their own needs, let alone to expand
their production of cash crops. Faced with this externally
imposed "cost," villagers have turned increasingly to the
collection and sale of rattan as a source of income or
goods on credit from traders. There are few other opportunities for employment in the area; timber companies are
reluctant to hire local men because of conflicting demands
at home for their labor.
    The people of Rukun Damai began to collect large
quantities of rattan close by their village in 1978, when

prices were rising rapidly. (See Tables 1 and 2.) By the end of 1979, however, the nearby sources had been depleted, and collectors already had to travel for three to six hours upriver by motorized canoe, then walk for another three hours into the forest from the river's edge. Rattan in those distant areas, far from any village, is an open access resource. A group of collectors is entitled to exclude other groups from the locale in which they are harvesting rattan, but only for the duration of a particular expedition.

Despite their legal right to collect minor forest products within timber concessions, villagers have at times been denied entry to those areas, and timber company personnel have otherwise infringed on the rights of local residents. Collectors and traders in various parts of the province complained to Peluso of timber company guards who confiscated rattan from collectors, of loggers who raided caves and sold the stolen birds' nests to unauthorized buyers, and of timber companies that illegally cut Borneo ironwood (Eusideroxylon zwagerii), a species reserved for local use. Some confrontations between loggers and collectors have led to violence, although other conflicts have been settled within the framework of customary law or by ad hoc agreements (Vargas 1985).

An Attempt to Locally Control Aloes Wood in the Apo Kayan

Outsiders can seek permission to collect forest products within a village territory. For example, in the 19th century, traders in upriver areas of East Kalimantan paid fees to village headmen in return for the right to obtain forest products. More recently, new settlers in some relatively densely populated lowland areas have had to pay to collect rattan or hunt within the territories of already established villages. We were able to see how outside collectors of aloes wood were treated in the village of Sungai Barang, in the Apo Kayan, soon after the local collecting boom began in the late 1970s.

Collectors were attracted to Sungai Barang's forests by the availability of high-grade aloes wood there. They used the village as a base from which to travel into the forest on expeditions of a week or more. Virtually all the outside collectors were members of various Kenyah sub-tribes and were considered kin, in some degree or other, of people living in Sungai Barang. Many could also claim a certain amount of reciprocal "generosity," in addition

to the somewhat indefinite obligations of kinship, in
return for past help given Sungai Barang people (for
example, the provision of food, shelter, and other assistance to men on trade expeditions). Indeed, the outsiders
were not excluded from collecting in the Sungai Barang
territory, but they were required (after much deliberation
within the village) (1) to sell the aloes wood they
collected to a local "contractor" (trader's agent) in
Sungai Barang, and (2) to pay a fee (about 10 percent of
the sales value) to the village treasury. The contractor
at the time was a resident of considerable local influence,
who obviously stood to gain personally from the first
rule. The second rule, at least, applied to village
residents as well as outsiders. Most of the aloes wood
collected by residents was, in fact, sold to the local
contractor, but some was taken by collectors to downriver
markets in an attempt to get a better price.

This attempt to control the sale of aloes wood was
disappointing for the community, as the regulations were
largely unenforceable. Apparently, there was a good deal
of smuggling of wood out of the village by the outside
collectors. They were encouraged to do so by contractors
in neighboring villages who offered, at least initially,
higher prices in order to attract sellers and so gain entry
into the market. Peluso (1983a) saw a similar pattern of
competition among rattan traders on the Mahakam River. New
traders not only offered higher initial prices in cash
(especially attractive to indebted collectors), but also
bought immature and inferior grades of rattan in order to
increase their share of the market. They could afford to
do so, first, because they recouped some of their losses by
selling important trade goods back to the collectors, often
on credit; second, because they would later lower the price
paid to collectors once the latter were in debt to the
traders.

Illegal Collection and Trade of Birds' Nests

Owners of birds' nest caves often post guards at the
entrances, especially at the more productive and accessible caves. In the past, supernatural sanctions against
intruders were also invoked. Nevertheless, not all caves
can be adequately guarded all the time, and some nests are
stolen. Raiding caves has become more common in the Upper
Mahakam as the number of outsiders (loggers, immigrants,
and itinerant traders) has increased in recent years and

as the threat of magical protection has become less of a deterrent to thieves.

The exclusion of unauthorized nest buyers from a sub-district is even more difficult to enforce than is the exclusion of thieves from caves. Illegal purchasing and smuggling of birds' nests is common. The incentive for traders is to avoid the tax on nests, while for collectors it is the higher prices offered by unauthorized traders. In general, the high price of birds' nests attracts many casual and short-term collectors and traders who have little interest in the sustained productivity of the caves.

While interactions among collectors or traders in a given locale are often highly competitive, those between collectors and traders are characterized by reciprocity if both parties expect to maintain a long-term trade relationship. Furthermore, reciprocity, loyalty, and "good reputation" are important, not only within small groups as suggested by Runge (this volume), but also in the maintenance of long-distance trade networks. The links in such networks are personal interactions between collectors and upriver traders, between those traders and downriver exporters, and between exporters and overseas buyers of forest products. Information and credit flowing through trade networks can have as great an influence on forest exploitation as do localized interactions within a "user's group" of collectors.

OUTCOMES OF FOREST EXPLOITATION

Commercially valuable forest products in East Kalimantan--and Southeast Asia generally--are rapidly dwindling in abundance and quality as a direct result of exploitation, even as the area of forest in which these species can grow is diminished by logging, shifting cultivation, and other types of conversion (Table 2). Wild populations of rattan seem to have been exhausted in many areas, and others are now disappearing. Until the 1960s, about 20 "elite" Southeast Asian species comprised the bulk of the commercial trade, with six species reported traded in East Kalimantan. (Many more species are used locally, but only in small quantities.) However, as world demand for rattan increased, and natural stocks of the elite species declined, collectors and traders took other, inferior species as well. As Dransfield (1981:184) comments: "It appears now that no species can be classed as useless--a worrying fact for the rattan conservationist."

Collectors also took more immature rattans as the supply of
adult plants declined, thus threatening the natural sources
of regeneration. Peluso found that traders attempting to
enter the highly competitive rattan business offered
relatively good prices for inferior grades of rattan and
accepted bundles containing a mixture of mature and
immature rattan, thereby exacerbating the tendency to
overcollect.

So little is known about the ecology of aloes wood that
we can only speculate about the outcome of its
exploitation. Burkill (1935) suggested that the sporadic
occurrence of **Aquilaria** in some parts of its range reflects
overharvesting in the past. In the vicinity of Sungai
Barang, we have seen the wood depleted in areas of forest
otherwise apparently little disturbed by human activities,
a pattern of exploitation that fits Burkill's scenario.
Aloes wood may soon be found only in the most remote and
inaccessible places.

Bird's nests are commonly overharvested in East
Kalimantan, contrary to existing laws. Only where biologically sound regulations are strictly enforced, as in some
government-owned caves in Malaysian Borneo, has conservation been effective. The great value of nests is, on the
one hand, an incentive to owners to manage their caves for
long-term sustained yields, but, on the other hand, short-
term price fluctuations encourage overharvesting. Thievery
and smuggling are also problems for cave owners and
government regulators.

Thus, despite differences in the biology and property
status of minor forest products, the outcome of commercial
exploitation in each of the three cases we have considered
has been overharvesting and a decline in quality of the
resource.

SUMMARY AND CONCLUSIONS

We have followed the model for the analysis of common
property problems in explicating our case study of three
commercially important minor forest products in East
Kalimantan. We argue that certain biological and technical characteristics of rattan and aloes wood make them
more dispersed and less predictable resources than birds'
nests. This difference in ecological patterns is reflected
in different property rights and controls over the two
types of resources in the context of local communities.
Villagers' rights to clear forest land and harvest

forest products have been restricted since timber concessions have been granted to a few large companies. This policy changed the traditional common property status of many forest resources and increased stresses on local economies and the environment. In addition, commercial incentives to collect forest products and interactions between established villagers and other actors, such as traders, timber company personnel, and recent immigrants, have led to the unfortunate outcomes described above.

Local common property users' organizations cannot by themselves manage forest resources in East Kalimantan, where so many external influences affect forest exploitation. However, traditional village groups and cooperatives can be incorporated into programs of forest conservation and forestry development. For example, in the case of rattan, there are opportunities for rattan processing in upriver collection areas, which might be linked both to locally managed rattan cultivation and to forest reserves as a source of seed for cultivation and cane from noncultivated species (Dransfield 1981; Peluso 1983a). Government can act at the local level, both to assist in the development of such programs and to legitimize and enforce rules of access or exclusion, as appropriate and feasible. One of the greatest difficulties in designing and implementing a policy of "conserving the commons" for minor forest products is to relate the actions and decisions of collectors in a particular locale to the wider context of forest exploitation, trade, and the eventual use of forest products around the world.

NOTES

1. We would like to thank A. P. Vayda, Charles Geisler, John Cordell, Margaret McKean, James Thomson, and David Feeny for their comments, criticism, and encouragement. Our research in East Kalimantan was undertaken in cooperation with the Indonesian Institute of Sciences (LIPI) and Mulawarman University. It was funded by the U.S. Forest Service through the East-West Center as part of a U.S.-Indonesian Man and the Biosphere Program research project.

2. Oakerson does not say that coordination is the only problem faced by users of a commons. However, by asserting that it is a universal one, and by omitting discussion of other actual or potential problems, he implies that the "problem" of coordination is always important, in all situations, even if only as a possibility to be guarded against. Part of our disagreement with Oakerson is in what constitutes a problem to which people must and do respond, a point treated at length by Vayda and McCay (1977).

3. Burkill (1935) lists about 2,432 useful species of plants and animals in Malaya alone. Nearly half of these are native flowering plants with uses other than for timber, comprising about 16 percent of the indigenous flora (Jacobs 1982).

4. Our main sources of information about Southeast Asian forests and forest products are the following: Burkill (1935); Corner (1952, 1966); Cranbrook (1984); Dransfield (1979, 1981); Dunn (1975); Jacobs (1982); Jessup et al. (1982); Medway (1960, 1969); Peluso (1983a, 1983b); Whitmore (1973a, 1973b, 1984). Other references are cited in the text.

5. Rattan is not sold simply by weight, but rather by weighted volume. The initial price of the rattan is determined by its weight, which decreases at each stage of

sale until it is finally dried completely and treated with sulfur by the exporter. However, the cost of shipping rattan overseas depends on its volume and adds considerably to the final price. Volume is not a factor in the shipping cost of birds' nests and aloes wood.

6. These species of rattan have been cultivated for at least a century in Central Kalimantan and for 50 years or more in South and East Kalimantan.

7. The number of Aquilaria species in Borneo is not known, but we suppose it is similar to that in Malaya.

8. The ecology of Aquilaria has received little attention. We summarize here what Jessup learned from Kenyah collectors and his own observations, with the caveat that the data are not from controlled studies and may not be typical of Aquilaria elsewhere. Botanical specimens collected in the Apo Kayan by Jessup and Herwasono Soedjito were identified at the Herbarium Bogoriense (part of the Indonesian National Biological Institute) as A. beccariana, a small to medium-sized tree less widespread than A. malaccensis. Other species may also occur in the area.

9. The genera Aerodramus, Hydrochous, and Collocalia were formerly classified together as Collocalia (Cranbrook 1984).

10. The floor of Niah Cave in Sarawak, one of Borneo's largest, covers 25 acres. Medway (1960) estimated the combined populations of three species living in that cave to be about 2,000,000.

11. Breeding has been disrupted by collection in some areas, however. (See section on "Outcomes.")

12. The possibility of exclusion depends also on the ability of users to defend a resource or to exploit products not easily accessible to other people, such as those in remote or difficult terrain. The latter "strategy" is attributed by Hoffman (1983) to nomadic Punan groups in Borneo.

REFERENCES

Appell, G. N. n.d. Observational procedures for land
tenure and kin groupings in the cognatic societies of
Borneo. Typescript.

Bayliss-Smith, T. P. and R. G. A. Feachem, eds. 1977.
Subsistence and Survival: Rural Ecology in the
Pacific. London: Academic Press.

Burkill, I. H. 1935 (reprinted 1966). A Dictionary of the
Economic Products of the Malay Peninsula. 2 vols.
Kuala Lumpur: Ministry of Agriculture and
Cooperatives.

Corner, E. J. H. 1952. Wayside Trees of Malaya. (2nd ed.)
Singapore: Government Printer.

Corner, E. J. H. 1966. The Natural History of Palms.
Berkeley, California: University of California Press.

Cranbrook, Earl of. 1984. Report on the bird's nest
industry in the Baram District and at Niah, Sarawak.
Sarawak Museum Journal 33 (54 n.s.):145-170. [The Earl
of Cranbrook was formerly Lord Medway.]

Daroesman, R. 1979. An economic survey of East
Kalimantan. Bulletin of Indonesian Economic Studies
15, No. 3:43-82.

Dicastri, F., F. W. G. Baker, and M. Hadley, eds. 1984.
Ecology in Practice: Establishing a Scientific Basis
for Land Management. Vol. 2. Paris: UNESCO.

Dove, M. R. 1985. Swidden Agriculture in Indonesia: The
Subsistence Strategies of the Kalimantan Kantu.
Berlin: Mouton.

Dransfield, J. 1979. A Manual of the Rattans of the Malay Peninsula. Malayan Forest Records No. 29.

Dransfield, J. 1981. The biology of Asiatic rattans in relation to the rattan trade and conservation. In Synge 1981.

Dunn, F. L. 1975. Rain-forest Collectors and Traders: A Study of Resource Utilization in Modern and Ancient Malaya. Monographs of the Malaysian Branch of the Royal Asiatic Society, No. 5.

Golley, F. B. ed. 1983. Tropical Rainforest Ecosystems, Part A: Structure and Function. Amsterdam: Elsevier.

Hoffman, C. L. 1983. Punan. Ph.D. dissertation. Philadelphia: University of Pennsylvania.

Hutterer, K. L. 1982. Interaction between Tropical Ecosystems and Human Foragers: Some General Considerations. EAPI Working Paper. Honolulu, Hawaii: East-West Center.

Jacobs, M. 1982. The study of minor forest products. Flora Malesiana Bulletin 35:3768-3782.

Jessup, T. C. 1981. Why do Apo Kayan shifting cultivators move? Borneo Research Bulletin 13, No. 1:16-32.

Jessup, T. C. 1983. Interactions between people and forests in the Apo Kayan forests. Final report for the 1979-1982 East Kalimantan Man and Biosphere Project, revised version.

Jessup, T. C. 1984. Transitions between common and private property in the use of Apo Kayan forests. Seminar given in the Department of Human Ecology, Rutgers University.

Jessup, T. C., S. S. Hajani, M. Khumaidi, and H. Soedjito. 1982. Forest for food. Phase I: Background report and proposal for research and development. TAD-Materialien 11. Samarinda, Indonesia: Transmigration Area Development Project.

Kartawinata, K. and A. P. Vayda. 1984. Forest conversion in East Kalimantan, Indonesia: the activities and impact of timber companies, shifting cultivators, migrant pepper-farmers, and others. In Dicastri et al. 1984.

Kutai District Government. 1974. Kabupaten Kutai Dalam Masa Pelita I. Samarinda, Indonesia.

Medway, Lord. 1960. Cave swiftlets. In Smythies 1960.

Medway, Lord. 1969. Studies on the biology of the edible-nest swiftlets of South-east Asia. Malayan Naturalist 22, No. 2:57-63.

Miles, D. 1976. Cutlass and Crescent Moon: A Case Study of Social and Political Change in Outer Indonesia. Sydney, Australia: Centre for Asian Studies, University of Sydney.

Muttaqin, Z. 1980. Potensi rotan dan jenis hasil hutan lainnya di propinsi Kalimantan Timur. Paper presented at a Conference on Minor Forest Products, Jakarta, Indonesia.

Padoch, C. 1982. Migration and Its Alternatives Among the Iban of Sarawak. Verhandelingen van het Koninklijk Instituut voor Taal-, Land- en Volkenkunde, No. 98. The Hague: Martinus Nijhoff.

Padoch, C. and A. P. Vayda. 1983. Patterns of resource use and human settlement in tropical forests. In Golley 1983.

Peluso, N. L. 1981. Report on the trade in minor forest products in East Kalimantan. Final report for 1979-1980 portion of East Kalimantan Man and Biosphere project.

Peluso, N. L. 1983a. Networking in the commons: a tragedy for rattan? Indonesia 35 (April):95-108.

Peluso, N. L. 1983b. Markets and Merchants: The Forest Products Trade of East Kalimantan in Historical Perspective. Master's thesis. Ithaca, New York: Cornell University.

Smythies, B. E. ed. 1960. The Birds of Borneo. Edinburgh: Oliver and Boyd.

Synge, H. ed. 1981. The Biological Aspects of Rare Plant Conservation. New York: Wiley.

Vargas, D. M. 1985. The Interface of Customary and National Land Law in East Kalimantan, Indonesia. Ph.D. dissertation. New Haven, Connecticut: Yale University.

Vayda, A. P. 1983. Progressive contextualization: methods for research in human ecology. Human Ecology 11:265-281.

Vayda, A. P. and B. J. McCay. 1977. Problems in the identification of environmental problems. In Bayliss-Smith and R. G. A. Feachem 1977.

Vayda, A. P. and A. Sahur 1985. Forest clearing and pepper farming by Bugis migrants in East Kalimantan: antecedents and impact. Indonesia 39 (April):93-110.

Weinstock, J. A. 1979. Land Tenure Practices of the Swidden Cultivators of Borneo. Master's thesis. Ithaca, New York: Cornell University.

Whitmore, T. C. 1973a. Palms of Malaya. London: Oxford University Press.

Whitmore, T. C., ed. 1973b. Tree Flora of Malaya: A Manual for Foresters. Vol. 2. Kuala Lumpur: Longman.

Whitmore, T. C. 1984. Tropical Rain Forests of the Far East. 2nd ed. Oxford: Clarendon Press.

Zimmermann, G. R. 1982. East Kalimantan (Indonesia): Statistical Guide, 1980 (in English and Indonesian). Samarinda, Indonesia: Transmigration Area Development Project.

Management of Traditional Common Lands *(Iriaichi)* in Japan [1]

Margaret A. McKean

The centuries-old common lands of traditional Japanese villages are particularly worthy of inclusion in our comparative study of common property for several reasons. First, they fall squarely into our most pristine definition of common property--they are common lands with identifiable communities of co-owners, as opposed to being vast open-access public areas used by all and in essence owned by no one, a very different circumstance posing different problems. Second, Japanese villages developed elaborate regulations, even written codes, for their commons; the information available from even a tiny fraction of the many thousands of traditional villages ("classical" or "true" villages, before the amalgamations of the 19th century)[2] offers ample variety on most variables of interest. Third, the documentation and historical records are sufficiently rich to allow us to inquire not only into formal rules but also into their operation and enforcement, thus offering more data than we have in other cases of common property institutions. Fourth, Japanese villages employed threats of ostracism and banishment to control social behavior and as ultimate penalties for abusing the commons; we therefore find a fascinating resemblance between the sanctions they employed and the concept of exclusion that is so important in the public goods theory used in the study of common property.[3] Fifth, from the mid-17th to the mid-19th century, Japan closed its ports

to trade with a formal policy of isolation (sakoku); as
a result, Japanese society spent two centuries in a conveniently isolated "test tube," uncontaminated by the
world economy and living within the limitations imposed
by nature and local technology. Thus, the sources of
those technological and socioeconomic changes that did
occur (which we are gradually discovering to have been
substantial) were internal. This fact may limit the
applicability of the Japanese experience to less developed
nations today, but it also helps us "control" the phenomena
we want to examine so that we can more accurately decipher
what the lessons of that experience might be. Finally,
although economic development and the commercialization
of agriculture threatened the Japanese commons as they
have elsewhere--causing many villages to abandon traditional self-sufficiency in favor of commercial production
and even to privatize the commons--thousands of other
Japanese villages developed management techniques to
protect their common lands for centuries without
experiencing the tragedy of the commons.

Since the political change (known as the Meiji
restoration) in 1868, there has been steady attrition
of common lands.[4] In some cases, the newly modernizing
Japanese government managed to declare that inadequately
documented common land was government property (to be
converted into military bases or national forests). More
recently, many villages have realized handsome profits by
selling their common land for conversion into golf courses,
tourist hotels, shopping centers and other 20th century
monuments. But as late as the 1950s, there were many
expanses of common land in Japan still being managed collectively without ecological destruction. Thus, this case
offers, in our terms, a successful outcome within the
rubric of common property (that is, without privatization).
It may tell us much about how the assurance problem (Runge
1981; this volume) can be solved so that cooperation among
co-owners of a commons is sustained not merely for decades
but for centuries, and thus how tragedies of the commons
may be averted.

Common lands evolved gradually over a period of several
centuries in tandem with other transformations in land
holdings. The slow and steady evolution of these lands is
described below to demonstrate why we can be certain that
the traditional commons in Japan was not simply uninhabited
space claimed by none and used by all--as may often be the
case elsewhere--but rather involved increasingly formalized
use rights. The brief history also describes some of the

conditions external to each village that impinged upon its
decisions about the management of the commons. (Japanese
terms for particular institutions are provided for the
benefit of readers who might want to examine this history
of land transformation in more detail at a later time.)

EMERGENCE OF THE COMMONS

The common lands that we can trace today came into
being gradually during the breakdown of the estate (shōen)
system and the civil wars that followed--essentially
between the 13th and 16th centuries--though the tradition
of the commons may well have begun more than a thousand
years earlier.[5] All land was officially nationalized
(made part of the imperial or public domain) in the 7th
century. Only a century or so later, however, the imperial
court at Kyoto began to decline, and it acknowledged the
rise of vast estates, granting individual court nobles,
Shinto shrines, and Buddhist temples some immunity from
taxation and from the intrusion of police powers. By the
13th century, many nobles and temples retained only titular
possession of the estates; they had lost real control over
both their own estate managers and the land stewards (jitō)
who had been appointed by the Kamakura shogunate (the first
military or feudal government that arose from the emergence
of the warrior class) in an attempt to assert the
shogunate's powers over the land.

With the decline of the Kamakura shogunate in the
14th century, the same process that had allowed imperial
land to devolve into estates recurred within the estates.
Shogunate-appointed military governors (shugo), and particularly the estate managers and land stewards on the
estates, began appropriating land rights for themselves;
they encroached upon the proprietary rights of the absentee
estate holders, and even gathered military bands to defend
these rights as public order deteriorated. With each out-
break of civil war and each decline in central control over
the provinces, real political power slipped away from the
shogunate (controlled by the Ashikaga family from the 14th
to mid-16th century) into the hands of warlords (often
former shugo) or warrior-proprietors (kokujin) (some of
whom descended from Kamakura jitō). These new proprietors
"owned" their land by physically occupying it; they
sometimes acquired additional land in battle and awarded it
as fiefs to their followers, henceforth their vassals.

This was a period of enormous social upheaval, with

much buying, selling, and outright confiscation of proprietary rights as the fortunes of different military families
and coalitions rose and fell. By the 16th century, a
bitter competition for national leadership was raging;
victors absorbed the domains of the losers, consolidated
power, and made and dismantled coalitions until three
national figures emerged in succession: Oda Nobunaga,
Toyotomi Hideyoshi, and finally, Tokugawa Ieyasu.[6]
During this era of transition, the imperial land grant
estates that had been managed by centrally appointed
stewards were replaced by fief and feudal lords (sengoku
daimyō during the 16th century, and finally, kinsei daimyō
after reunification) who had full and independent powers of
taxation over the people living in their domains.

Two important features of the evolution in landholdings during this "feudal" period must be noted: first, the
development of sophisticated notions of property rights,
and second, the eventual assertion of village autonomy in
governing property. The evolution of shiki--multilayered
proprietary rights--in the medieval period and the variety
of ways in which they could be separated, repackaged,
commended, bequeathed, and sold is a very complex matter
that historians are only just beginning to unravel.

During this period, both tenants (e.g., genin, nago,
sakunin) and people who otherwise seemed to be peasant
freeholders (myoshu, hyakusho, dogō) were working land that
was also "owned" by another proprietor or "landlord"
(ryōshu) or by an enfeoffed warrior (jizamurai, zaichi
ryōshu). Conversely, peasants sometimes held long-term
rights to cultivate land even after the right to tax/rent
that land had been traded among different proprietors. The
fact that Japan developed such a complex system of property
rights, along with a legal system to resolve disputes and
thus assure owners of various shiki that their rights were
secure, implies that the Japanese conception of property was
not limited to the simple notion of packaging together all
rights to a piece of land in a privately owned bundle.
Actual experience with other arrangements, coupled with a
legal system to solve "assurance problems," provided a solid
foundation for later experimentation with common property
institutions.

The devolution in land holdings and land rights from
imperial court to land stewards to locally based warriors
that had already taken place proceeded during the years of
disorder finally to the level of the village; this transformation applied both to the arable land that would
eventually become the private property of peasant culti-

vators and to uncultivated land that would eventually
become the commons. Peasant-cultivators' property rights
developed very slowly as the estate system declined, and
may not have been secure until after the national cadastral
surveys (taikō kenchi) that were conducted by Toyotomi
Hideyoshi in the late 16th century. These surveys swept
away the complex system of shiki, assigned most of the
rights that we today consider to be "ownership" to arable
land to peasants who lived on and cultivated that land, and
initiated the process of converting warrior-proprietors
into salaried officials, thereby removing the samurai from
the land and validating the claims of villagers to control
their own lands (Ishii 1980:61-63). (The details of this
transition are still a matter of intense debate: How rapid
was the change? How much credit should be given to
Hideyoshi's surveys for simplifying matters? How progressive was this land reform in terms of its economic impact
on lower layers of the peasantry? [Nagahara 1975; Yamamura
1975; Ishii 1980:59-79; Berry 1982:23-34, 106-126; Wakita
1982; Hall 1983].)

Traditional agriculture in Japan relied heavily on
the availability of fertilizer, fodder, timber, and other
products from the uncultivated land in cultivating arable
land. Thus, there was a need to manage uncultivated lands
and eventually to define property rights to them as well
as to the cultivated areas. Estate proprietors, land
stewards, and eventually the feudal magnates who ended up
with the estates therefore appointed prominent peasants as
their officers and agents in each village, empowering them
to regulate access to uncultivated forests and grasslands,
to summon corvée labor, and to govern the irrigation system
upon which wet-rice agriculture depended. At the outset,
these rights were presumed to reside in the proprietor,
manager, or lord, and all the villagers had to petition him
through his agent for the right to enter the uncultivated
lands. As public order deteriorated, villagers became very
concerned with communal solidarity to protect themselves
from the ravages of war.[7]

The military class obviously became more dependent on
cooperation from the peasants in their areas, and villagers
became more assertive about their right to enter the uncultivated land. Villagers who once paid water charges to the
proprietors or managers of the estates and who entered the
lands only with the proprietor's blessings now received
fees from the proprietors or estate managers for the use of
the same kinds of facilities, and villages wrote their own
codes (complete with penalties for violations) to govern

common lands, irrigation, and corvée labor. Nagahara
documents this transformation in one village where the
estate proprietor refused to pay a water charge demanded
by the village. The village retaliated effectively by
absconding from the land and refusing to pay rent/taxes
to the proprietor (Nagahara and Yamamura 1974:116-118).
Similar changes occurred with respect to uncultivated
areas, with peasants aggressively asserting their rights
to these lands in some regions as early as the 15th century
(Nagahara 1977:108-110). By 1600, when the third of the
great unifiers, Tokugawa Ieyasu, established a military
dictatorship that would control Japan until 1867, most
villages had acquired clear use rights (perpetual usufruct)
to large expanses of uncultivated land, held in common and
shared by all the villagers.

THE PHYSICAL ATTRIBUTES OF THE COMMONS

Two-thirds of Japan is still occupied by forests and
uncultivated mountain plains (about 25 million hectares),
and approximately half of this land was held and managed
in common by rural villages during the Tokugawa period.
(The other half was imperial, Tokugawa, daimyō, or private
land.) Even though about three-fourths of that common
land has been redesignated or sold as public or private
property, more than 3 million hectares of common land
remain in Japan today (Watanabe and Nakao 1975:45-48;
Kawashima 1979).[8] Japan now has one of the highest per capita incomes in the world, and many Japanese
farmers today practice agriculture only on Sundays, rely-
ing on weekday jobs in nearby industries to supply the
income with which they purchase color televisions, cars,
expensive vacations, and elegant houses. Obviously, such
farmers no longer depend on products or income from the
commons; but the infusion of industrial wealth into rural
Japan is a very recent development, and in many parts of
Japan the commons remained a vital part of the rural
economy until economic recovery (in the 1950s) from the
Second World War.

Communities that retained their common land after the
Meiji restoration in 1868 continued to use their land in
the traditional way, but also developed other methods as
their needs changed, especially as subsistence agriculture
increasingly gave way to cash crop agriculture and light
industry. We may group the methods of using the commons
into four rough categories, which are described below.

The classic type of commons use. This type, of
course, prevailed during the Tokugawa period and was
restricted to activities that left the commons essentially
in its natural state. It involved an investment of labor
to harvest natural products that were very important in
daily life: thatch for roofs, fodder for animals, multipurpose bamboo, firewood, charcoal, underbrush and fallen
leaves, compost, wood for furniture and tools, medicinal
herbs, fowl and game to supplement the otherwise vegetarian
diet of the mountains, and edible wild plants that could
not be cultivated but that were much treasured (matsutake,
warabi, and other mountain vegetables [sansai]). Those
with access rights (whom I shall call co-owners of the
commons) could enter the commons to obtain these items
either as individuals, or by households, or in groups, and
either freely or at designated times only, depending on
the particular set of rules devised by that particular
village.

Direct group control of the commons. This prohibited
access by individuals, and was used when the commons was
harvested for cash income. The income earned was either
distributed among co-owners or plowed back into the next
investment in the commons, or some other village project,
as needed. For instance, a village might develop rice
paddies, dry fields, or fruit orchards on the commons
and sell the crop for village income. Some commons were
converted into rock quarries. Many meadows and plains
(perhaps denuded by daimyō during the deforestation of the
16th and 17th centuries before becoming village commons)
have been converted since 1868 into cultivated forests with
the encouragement of the modernizing Japanese government;
the villagers harvest the timber and distribute the income
collectively. Direct group control of the commons as a
source of cash income for the village was used throughout
the last hundred years to supplement village budgets,
especially when compulsory mass education was adopted but
local communities were expected to build the schools.

Divided use of the commons. Common land is actually
divided into pieces for individual co-owners to use as
they see fit. This is akin to privatizing the commons,
except that co-owners do not own their allotments--they
must abide by certain limits in their use of the commons
(they may not build structures on the land, for instance),
and they are not free to sell their pieces to anyone
else.[9] Pieces are usually assigned by lot, and
reassignments are conducted every two or three years
to ensure fairness and to prevent the commons from

degenerating into private property. This method has
obvious appeal for a community in which the collective
decision making required in classic or direct group control of the land has become cumbersome or time-consuming,
or where individual co-owners of the commons have widely
differing needs for timber, cash income, extra paddy land,
private vegetable gardens, or natural products. Direct
group control and divided use of the commons are known to
have appeared occasionally in the management of Tokugawa
and even earlier commons in some regions, but these methods
of management were probably not widespread until the Meiji
period.[10]

    <u>Contracted use</u>. The most modern innovation in common
land use involves contracts that are written when villages
want to hold onto their common land but cannot come up with
the labor to maintain it, so they grant an exploitation
lease to another party. This is particularly true with
forest land--the village leases timber rights to a municipal body or a forestry firm and earns a percentage of the
proceeds as rent.

    Most communities that still possess common land combine
these methods depending on the activity--the classic method
for gathering wild plants and compost, direct group control
for forestry or large-scale farming, divided use for forest
or garden plots, and contracted use for forestry, quarry-
ing, or large-scale farming. In certain areas of Japan,
the classic method has persisted until very recently--
particularly in impoverished areas that did not attract
industry--where the common lands, often substantial in size
and ecological diversity, provided a large share of the
local livelihood.

    The summary of management techniques given below is
drawn from studies of three such villages (Yamanaka,
Hirano, and Nagaike, located on the poor volcanic soils
north of Mount Fuji in Yamanashi Prefecture) that used
the classic method until after World War II.[11] I have
begun my survey of the traditional commons in Japan with
these villages not because they are typical--I will not
know what is typical until I examine the management of the
commons in many other villages as well--but because they
are by far the most carefully studied and can therefore
serve as a solid starting point for further research, and
because they vary in ways that are likely to prove interesting and significant in building hypotheses about
successful management of the commons.

    Studies of Tokugawa documents from these villages
indicate that the use of the commons changed hardly at all

between the 18th century and the early 20th century.
(In fact, in view of pre-Tokugawa records available for
some localities, there is little reason to believe that
the management of the commons changed much from the
14th century on, with the possible exception of the annual
burning of meadowlands [noyaki] explained below that may
have developed in the early Tokugawa period.) Yamanaka,
Hirano, and Nagaike have diverse common lands:[12] forest
and grasslands, large and small expanses of commons, and
rich productive lands and relatively poor lands. Moreover,
each of these villages possesses some common land of its
own, some common land shared with one or both of the other
villages, and access rights to the very large expanse of
land on Mt. Fuji's north slope (Kitafuji) that are shared
among a total of 11 villages.[13]

The villages themselves also vary. Hirano is old and
wealthy, nestled against verdant mountains, hierarchical
in social structure, inegalitarian in income distribution,
crusty in traditional values, and intensely concerned with
family and reputation. Nagaike is a younger (late
Tokugawa), smaller, poorer offshoot of Hirano with very
little difference in social standing or wealth among its
households. Yamanaka is the largest and most impoverished
of the three, located adjacent to the largest but least
productive of the commons (the Kitafuji slope), a large
village in which horizontal organizations known as kumi
are as important a focus of loyalty as is family. In
addition to using the rich social science literature
about these villages, I was able to interview old-timers
whose memories of the commons went back to the 1920s.[14]

The ecological richness of different parcels of common
land in Japan varied enormously, but presumably much of the
land was fragile and vulnerable to degradation if not well
managed: forests could be stripped, and some grass lands
could have been denuded even without the introduction of
grazing animals. Japanese villages obviously altered the
commons from its natural state (with such customs as annual
burning and occasional clear-cutting), but they also clearly operated their commons according to the principle of
sustained yield so as not to degrade the commons as a
productive resource. In Oakerson's sense, then, they
preserved jointness (Oakerson, this volume).

As for the physical and technical possibilities of
exclusion, Japanese society during the Tokugawa period
relied so heavily on natural materials, and lived at such
a generally low standard, that fencing was economically
impossible. Fences were used mostly in urban areas,

immediately surrounding buildings, as if to deter burglars
who might want man-made objects of special value. The only
large expanses of fenced land were the grounds of castles
and Buddhist temples (the latter, one must remember, were
fully comparable in both wealth and political power in
some periods to the great military families). The large
estates, part of which consisted of common land, often
comprised many scattered small parcels of land in any case,
and could not have been fenced very cheaply, no matter how
inexpensive and readily available the fencing materials
might have been. The topography of rural Japan--undulating
mountains for the most part--would also have made fencing
a miserable chore. To this day, cultivated land is not
fenced in Japan; irrigation dikes in between the rice
paddies serve as boundaries, but there are no barriers
to trespassers. Thus we can be fairly comfortable in
asserting that fencing off the commons would have been
inconceivably expensive to villagers who could not afford
to fence off their private land either. In Oakerson's
sense, then, it was not really possible to exclude the
ineligible from the commons with physical barriers.
Instead, as we shall see, Japanese villages had to
substitute rules for physical barriers.

In the same way, just as it was impractical to fence
off land for purposes of exclusion, so private ownership
of the commons was unimaginable in traditional villages as
long as agricultural practices depended so heavily on the
products of the commons. These products were not evenly
distributed throughout the common land, and different
expanses of land were of many grades and sizes and were
used for purposes as varied as timbering and rock quarry-
ing. Given the heterogeneity of the commons, it could not
have been divided equitably. Moreover, a potential private
purchaser of common land would presumably be interested in
buying "prime" land within the commons--precisely the kind
of land that the village governing body overseeing the
commons would be least willing to sell.

As Runge (1981) notes, common property can provide all
its co-owners entitlement to all the resources of the
commons and thus offer some insurance against hard times.
As long as the traditional agricultural economy prevailed
(that is, as long as participants believed that their
investment in maintaining the commons and its rules was a
worthwhile use of time and resources to obtain the products
of the commons), the commons were a sensible and inexpensive form of insurance. Thus we find little privatization
of common land until the rise of commercial agriculture in

the 19th century. Even then, it often happened that villagers simply stopped using the land (as opposed to selling it); rising agricultural labor costs, levels of technology, and agricultural productivity made farmers unwilling to devote long hours to maintaining and collecting resources from the commons when they could substitute commercial inputs for the products of the commons. They did not sell the land to private owners (whether villagers or outsiders) until and unless nonagricultural uses of the land became profitable.

In the three villages involved in this study, most of the common land is still held as a collective asset saleable in the future, and most villagers have abandoned farming and instead work in the hotels and leisure facilities that have bought land from the farmers' private holdings. Nagaike is an exception: faced with a tempting offer, it sold a portion of its commons to a developer who constructed leisure condominiums with a perfect view of Mt. Fuji.

DECISION-MAKING ARRANGEMENTS AFFECTING THE COMMONS

External Constraints

Our chronological account of the evolution of the commons in Japan has taken us to 1600, when Tokugawa Ieyasu established himself as the nation's leader by winning the battle of Sekigahara. His talents were not limited to military strategy or political alliances: he established an effective military dictatorship and complex administrative structure that gave Japan peace for over 250 years.[15]

Japan was divided into 250 to 300 (the number varied) administrative units or domains, each governed by a lord (daimyō). Although these lords had a fairly free hand within their own domains, they were subject to strict constraints designed to prevent the emergence of regional power. These lords also functioned at times as administrative officers of the center and were expected to enforce a body of elaborate laws and decrees from the center within their own domains. The central administra- imposed a four-layered class structure and all manner of sumptuary laws to regulate morality, spending habits, and the behavior of the four classes. It also mandated universal registration of all individuals in the country (to track down illegal Christians) and devised complex

requirements for licenses and official permission to engage
in commerce and even to travel from one domain to another.
All of these were enforced by a nationwide network of
police, spies, and inspection stations at domain borders.
A system of magistrates and domainal and/or shogunal courts
handled disputes not resolved by conciliation at lower
levels.

There is understandable confusion and great controversy among historians over the relationship between this
complex, nearly totalitarian administrative structure
created by the Tokugawa and the newly assertive self-
governing villages below it.[16] For the most part, this
controversy does not affect the governing of common lands,
which were clearly in the hands of the villages and managed
freely and independently by them. But three important
developments in the Tokugawa period did influence the
management of the commons.

First, an administrative innovation of the Tokugawa
regime played a role in enforcing the rules villages
devised to govern their common lands: the notorious
goningumi (literally, five-man groups, but in fact groups
of five to ten households) system of collective responsibility, much like the pao chia system in China (Yanagida
1957; Smith 1959; Chambliss 1965:109-112; Henderson 1965,
1975; Befu 1968:301-314). Villages almost certainly
developed this system of collective responsibility much
earlier than the 1600s (perhaps centuries earlier), and
refined it themselves during the era of civil war when they
had to provide their own law and order and needed internal
spies. Toyotomi Hideyoshi and later Tokugawa Ieyasu
adapted the system for keeping track of Christians, rōnin
(warriors without vassal ties, who often became mercenaries
and sometimes bandits), and tax evaders.

The Tokugawa shogunate and the domains then formalized
this preexisting institution to serve their purposes of
tax collection and social control. This they did by
issuing model five-man registers especially for the
peasantry that consisted of lists of rules governing all
sorts of behavior: from the proper decorum to be shown
to visiting officials (including the stipulation that
they not be given gifts or lavish entertainment that
might influence their judgment), to admonitions about
filial piety, and extending to fair use of the commons
and obedience to all other civil and criminal laws. All
individuals were members of a five-man group and all
were equally responsible and liable for payment of taxes,
obedience to the law, and transgressions by fellow

members. The heads of all households in a village had to
affix their seals to the five-man registers to indicate
their comprehension of the rules and to guarantee their own
compliance and cooperation with the village officers, who
would be considered personally responsible as well for any
misdeeds of the villagers.

We know not only from the circulation of the signed
registers but also from the appearance of cases higher up
in the Tokugawa courts that village chiefs were indeed held
responsible for the behavior of all of the villagers. The
village itself was a juridical body that could sue or be
sued, make contracts, and be held collectively responsible
for misbehavior of its members, whether in tax payment or
in crime. Thus the five-man group system of collective
responsibility created an enormous internal incentive for
villagers to solve their problems and beg, cajole, bribe,
or coerce internal miscreants within the village into
conformity. By almost any standard, this is a very
unpleasant, unjust, but efficient way of frightening
people into policing each other, and it seems to produce
compliance even when people do not view the laws or codes
they are expected to obey as legitimate. There is little
doubt that this fairly totalitarian device enhanced the
communities' ability to enforce rules governing the
commons.

The second important development was that with the Pax
Tokugawa, the new daimyō who had not already done so tried
to acquire more direct control over both their domains and
their vassals by replacing fiefs with stipends of rice drawn
from their own revenues. (We will recall that the daimyō
had originally acquired their positions of power within the
warrior hierarchy through military conquest of the land and
through the award of fiefs to their vassals.) This process
converted landed vassals into salaried bureaucrats and moved
them from the lands that had been their fiefs into the
cities. This freed the villages from direct interference by
a local fief-holder and increased their freedom and independence in the use of all property, including commons.
Moreover, it created a system in which private individuals
and villages had not only usufruct but ownership in all but
the final formal sense, and daimyō had taxation rights but
not ownership.[17] Thus it became possible to distinguish
between land belonging to the daimyō and other lands within
their domains that belonged to peasant freeholders or to
other landlords. In this way, many villages held common
land that was not considered daimyō property, and thus
operated their commons quite independently.

The third noteworthy change was a consequence of the
devastation of widespread civil war in the 16th century.
This was followed by peace and the rapid construction of
cities and castles throughout Japan in the 17th century,
which created a tremendous demand for timber and caused
considerable deforestation (Totman 1982a, 1982b, 1983a,
1983b, 1984; Osako 1983). The problem was initially
most severe in forests owned directly by the Tokugawa
family and the various daimyō engaged in the work of
reconstruction. Their appetite for timber induced the
daimyō to acquire direct control over all prime forests
in their domains, so that the best of the existing timbered
commons passed from villages to the daimyō to become
ohayashi, the lord's forest, thus threatening ever-
widening areas of Japan with deforestation. Eventually,
of course, the daimyō recognized that there was only a
finite supply of timber available, and they began exper-
imenting with conservation. They focused first (and
perhaps inappropriately) on peasants to whom they had
granted access rights to daimyō-owned forests (these rights
are separate from and additional to villagers' perpetual
usufruct on lands not claimed by the daimyō since 1600).
They began regulating these rights more strictly, and along
with the Tokugawa shogunate created forest magistrates to
patrol the daimyō forests, looking for outright theft as
well as for violations of rules governing regulated access
to these forests. The daimyō often granted exclusive
access rights on a long-term basis to particular villages,
in exchange for the villages' assurance that they would
supervise the forests and keep others out. In effect,
then, the daimyō granted these villages increasingly formal
entitlement to still more common lands (this is in addition
to the substantial commons already in existence before the
Tokugawa period and no longer claimed by daimyō at all);
this compensated somewhat for the daimyō's confiscation of
prime forests from village common lands. When the daimyō
finally realized that peasant demand for timber was stable
and occasional, and that the daimyō themselves were the
prime culprits in increasing the demand for timber, they
began to develop principles of management that would not
only sustain their own prime forests but contribute to the
reforestation of Japan during the 18th and 19th centuries.
The daimyō's efforts at regulation may have been mis-
directed, but they did at least provide the villages with
knowledge and experience in designing their own regulations
and institutional arrangements, thus lowering the cost of
institutional design later.

Part of the problem was a conflict of interest between daimyō and peasant as to what type of forest growth to encourage: the daimyō preferred slow-growing conifers for timber, while the peasants preferred broad-leafed deciduous hardwoods because these hardwoods laid down annual additions to a rich underlayer of leaf mold that could be harvested as fertilizer and that offered excellent fuel when the trees were finally cut down. Peasants entitled to use the daimyō forests had little interest in protecting the seedlings of trees prized by the daimyō until land-leasing (nenkiyama) and yield-sharing (buwakebayashi) arrangements were devised to give all of those involved a mutual interest in nurturing slow-growing timber until maturity.

Land-leasing was the advance sale of a stand of timber with final payment on delivery years later. Yield-sharing was a long-term contract to divide the proceeds of a sale of timber as far as 50 years into the future. These arrangements were adopted variously for all kinds of land-- daimyō forest, communal village forest, and private small holdings--and served not only to promote the notion of "multiple use" but also to encourage afforestation during the 18th and 19th centuries (Totman 1982a, 1983a, 1984). We might note that these systems of profit-sharing suggest that separation of land rights from tree rights need not be disastrous at all.[18] Rather, the critical factors seem to be whether the rewards for each party create a mutual interest in nurturing a particular kind of tree growth, and whether there is a legal system that will make a 50-year contract enforceable (the assurance problem). In Japan, this tradition did exist, thanks to the development of customary and codified law and methods of adjudication from a very early period.[19]

The deforestation crisis of the 17th century was not limited to privately owned land; it quite understandably increased environmental pressure on remaining common lands as daimyō commandeered some communal forests and tightened restrictions on lawful use by nearby villagers of daimyō forests. It is very important to note that at this juncture, when theory might predict a tragedy of the commons, neither total environmental destruction nor dissipation of the commons into private hands occurred. To be sure, some commons were seriously degraded, and in fact this encounter with environmental degradation may be the reason that so much common land today turns out to be grassland and meadow--this land was probably prime forest before the 17th century. Similarly, some privatization of

commons did occur. It is apparently much easier to
maintain the environmental quality of commons than it is
to upgrade that quality because the latter requires so much
additional investment of labor and money from co-owners of
the commons. When daimyō wanted to convert meadows to
forests or where villages themselves wanted prime timber
to market later, they (the daimyō or the villages) did
sometimes arrange to divide the commons into private
parcels that were sold to families who then reforested the
land and profited accordingly years later at the harvest.

On the other hand, "de-privatization" also occurred.
Henderson provides information about a village that decided to create a commonly owned forest from privately owned
grassland by buying the land from one of its own residents.
Troost (pers. com. 1984) finds the same sorts of conver-
sions of private land into commons in the villages of
Imabori and Suganoura on Lake Biwa before the Tokugawa
period (also Henderson 1975:76-79).

We also know that frequently the impetus for dividing
the commons into private parcels (an event known as
wariyama or "dividing the mountain") grew from difficulties
of managing conflict among co-owners of the commons, and
not necessarily from the threat of environmental destruction. Wariyama was not always perpetual, and use rights
were not always comprehensive; villages sometimes tried
to maintain a future hold on the land or have it revert to
the village commons after it was afforested. By and large,
the commons that were divided and sold to become privately
owned land in perpetuity were shared by more than one village, and it was conflict among different villages rather
than among residents of a single village that proved unman-
ageable. In effect, the transaction costs involved were
too high with respect to the benefits from the commons to
sustain collective management in this situation. During
the Tokugawa period, there was a clear trend for the
multi-village commons to give way to the single-village
commons (Harada 1969).[20] This suggests that whereas one
Tokugawa-sized village might have been small enough to
manage a commons, several villages were too large, had
too many irreconcilable wishes about how to use their
resources (conflicts between poor mountain villages and
richer lowland villages attempting to share a commons
were especially frequent), and shared no overweening common
goals or communal ethic. Such a finding is consistent with
the theoretical prediction that normative beliefs or ideology will be crucial in preventing cheating against the commons (McKean 1979; North 1981).

For our purposes, the significance of this episode
of deforestation during the 17th century is threefold:
visible deforestation seems to have made villagers aware
of the very real risks of overuse and enabled them to
develop and enforce stricter rules for conservation on
their own initiative to save their forests and commons
from the same fate. Rather than destroying the commons,
deforestation resulted in increased institutionalization
of village rights to common land. And it promoted the
development of literally thousands of highly codified sets
of regulations for the conservation of forests and the use
of all commons.

Conditions of Collective Choice

Our next task is to examine the circumstances
surrounding the development of operational rules for
managing the commons; these rules comprise the
"constitution" that governed day-to-day decision making
on the commons. This requires a look at the structure
of the traditional village in Japan.[21] The historical
evolution of villages and landholding described earlier
gave each village a sturdy internal structure and a strong
sense of identity by the early Tokugawa period. Cadastral
surveys identified particular households with specific
pieces of land; tax records identified property owners;
and the family register (shūmon aratame, intended for
purposes of social control) attached individuals and
families to certain villages. Everyone "belonged" to a
particular place, and mobility from place to place was
tightly controlled--indeed, lodging an out-of-town guest
in one's home or travelling to another village overnight
had to be cleared in advance with the village head (shoya
or nanushi), who then had to seek permission from domain
authorities.

The household, not the individual, was the smallest
unit of accounting, not just for managing the commons but
for all purposes; the household head's name was recorded
in documents to represent the entire household. A village
consisted of a certain number of households, and villages
were governed by an assembly (yoriai) of representatives
(almost always the family head) from each household that
had political rights. This could be variously defined as
households with cultivation rights in land (the hyakusho
class), or perhaps ownership rights in land as determined
by 16th and 17th century cadastres (such people might be

called jinushi, which translates as "landlord"), or perhaps
those with taxpaying obligations (honbyakusho). These three
categories were not coterminous, and each village had its
own rules for participation.

In one case, a document concerning the creation of a
commons to be shared by two adjoining villages was signed
not only by representatives of the landowning households
in both villages but also by representatives of the tenant
families in both villages (Henderson 1975:66-67). Thus,
some villages gave more political rights to tenant families
than did others. In the village of Chiaraijima, rights to
the commons tended to be associated with wealth in private
holdings, but wealth did not guarantee access. While only 2
of the 16 poorest families had rights to the commons, only 6
of the 10 richest families also had such access rights
(Chambliss 1965:44-45). As more documents come to light,
we may eventually acquire a comprehensive picture of what
proportion of the Tokugawa peasantry lacked such political
rights by virtue of belonging to a headless household or one
without any land rights, or falling into such low-status
categories as household servants (genin) or outcaste groups
(eta and hinin, literally "nonhumans"). When we are able to
find multiple records that allow cross-checking, we see that
villages displayed great variety. In some, the great majority of households had something akin to ownership rights in
land and political representation in the village, but in
others the proportion of disenfranchised tenants, household
servants, and outcastes might exceed 50 percent of the total
population. Tenant families who themselves had no political
rights or access to the commons might nonetheless use the
commons via their landlord's rights (Smith 1959:24-25,
1968a:273-274). We also know that as the Tokugawa period
progressed, the tax burden on the peasantry as a whole grew
lighter but that inequalities of wealth within villages
increased over time (Smith 1968b, 1977:41-46).

Villages were usually subdivided into intermediate
groupings called kumi (literally, "group"), each composed
of several households. The kumi was a very important unit
of accounting and distribution of responsibilities and
benefits connected with the commons. In addition, many
other organizations within a village performed collective
functions: they not only managed the commons and the
irrigation canals, but also occasionally built public
works like bridges and roads, took care of the local
shrine, held annual festivals, functioned as a mutual aid
society for destitute villagers, helped at funerals,
thatched roofs, organized the collective labor (yui) for

transplanting rice (an enormously laborious chore that must
be done quickly and has always involved cooperation even
for private paddyland). Dore (1959:352-353) gives a
modern-day example of a village with 401 households and
177 organizations.

On paper, villages were democracies in which each
household that was accorded full participation rights was
equal to any other, and office-holders were either elected
or selected by some principle of rotation. Obviously, the
traditional village assembly was a decision-making unit
with some democratic potential, and there is of course a
raging debate over whether this potential was ever realized
in fact. The conventional view is that the traditional
village has always been a bastion of hierarchy, elitism,
and authoritarianism. Recently, however, scholars espous-
ing the ideas and research methods of folklorist Yanagida
Kunio have argued that, before and perhaps during the
Tokugawa period, Japanese villages may have operated as
idyllic communal democracies in which horizontal bonds
were more important than vertical ones, and in which the
young men's association often became a focal point for
challenges to village elders.[22] It is quite possible
that in villages where the distribution of wealth was
fairly egalitarian (such as Nagaike, described below), each
household was nearly equal in power. But the most common
circumstance was that a few families held far more land
than any of the others, and it is almost certain that the
poor deferred to the rich, that the elders (toshiyori)
tended to make decisions on behalf of the assembly most of
the time, and that they themselves came only from the
wealthiest "major" families. (Hirano used the term
"meimon" to identify these families, and the term may
indicate descent from those who once possessed land rights
that were called myō in the medieval period.) Similarly,
wherever the group of villagers in charge of maintaining
the local shrine (miyaza) had broad jurisdiction, the
miyaza turned out to be an elitist decision-making group
and reflected a very unequal and hierarchical arrangement
of power in the village.

That households and not individuals were the unit
of accounting, and that villages possessed the power to
determine which households were eligible to participate in
politics (and to extend rights of access to the commons
only to such households) are facts of great significance.
First, large households had no advantage over small
ones--they had no extra votes in decisions, no extra
representation, no enlarged share of benefits from the

commons; indeed, their household benefits were the same
size as the smaller households, but had to be apportioned
among a larger number of family members. Large households
could not obtain advantages by splitting into several
households; permission to form a branch household (bunke)
from the main household (honke) had to be obtained from
village authorities, who recognized that creating an
additional household would enlarge the number of claimants
on the commons without enlarging the commons, and so were
reluctant to create a new bunke. Smith reports that
creating a branch household was actually viewed as a
honke's selfish attempt to increase its power over the
commons (Smith 1959:82-183). New households sometimes
were grudgingly accommodated and were awarded incomplete
political rights--for example, no entitlement to hold
village office, or less than one regular household's share
of benefits.

Of course, households were also constrained from
forming a bunke because they would then have to split up
their private property and thus dissipate the family's
wealth. This fact no doubt played a part in the early
emergence of family planning (through birth control,
abortion, and infanticide) in Tokugawa Japan that permitted
steady increases in per capita income during the latter
half of the period.[23] Recent scholarship takes this
argument one step further and suggests that this combination of low aggregate population growth over an extended
period (only 0.025 percent per year between 1721 and 1846)
with rising per capita income permitted much more capital
accumulation in Tokugawa Japan than has been acknowledged
in the past, and thus set the conditions for industrial
take-off in Meiji Japan.[24]

Thus, users of the commons did not try to increase
their numbers in order to increase their share of the
commons, nor did anyone count on the benefits from the
commons to bail them out after a period of irresponsible
procreation. Villages and total population did grow during
the Tokugawa period, to be sure, but slow judicious growth
was the rule. It seems eminently clear, not only from
these indirect kinds of evidence but also from the contents of village and domain legal codes, that everyone was
conscious of a sense of "limits." Records from some villages show that after a certain point--about midway through
the Tokugawa period--no new arable land was brought into
cultivation and the number of formally constituted (politically participant) households did not increase, because no
new households were permitted unless an old one died

out for lack of heirs. There is every reason to believe
that these villages had "filled up" their legal and
topological boundaries and consciously concluded that,
given the level of available technology, it simply was
not worth trying to bring new lands into cultivation. The
commons could produce fertilizer and equipment for cultivating only a certain amount of land, and turning some
uncultivated commons into cultivated land would violate
that sacred ratio and be useless anyway.

One final source of information about the unwritten
"constitution" governing decision making in the villages
is the village codes (sompō) from the Tokugawa period,
studied by Maeda Masaharu and further analyzed by Harumi
Befu (1968:307-310). These were generated from within
the village, and, in contrast with shogunate codes and
exhortations that emphasized maximizing production, they
focused on resolving disputes. Some codes clearly
protected the interest of a village elite, but most
provided that the assembly as a whole rather than the
village head was empowered to enforce the rules. The
village codes were streamlined, brief, and clearly based
on centuries of knowledge and experience at maximizing the
collective good by keeping internal conflict to a minimum.
We will now turn to a consideration of the specific rules
for managing the commons that were used in Hirano, Nagaike,
and Yamanaka to defuse conflict and prevent abuse of the
commons.

Rules Governing Rights of Access to the Commons

The villages of Hirano, Nagaike, and Yamanaka relied
on the commons as a source of several products. Kaya is a
grass grown to produce thatch for roofs. When it is still
young, it is good as horse fodder and for weaving into
containers for charcoal and other household items. After
it has fruited, it is good for thatch. After winter,
when only the dried stalk (saguri) remains, it is good for
weaving stiffer products, for racks to dry root vegetables,
and for certain purposes in sericulture. In order to
prevent the kaya from being cut at an immature stage for
horse fodder, villagers usually designated an area with
kaya as "closed" during the growing season.

Magusa was a grass used as fodder for draft animals
and pack horses. Combined with animal excrement, it
also made excellent fertilizer. During the growing season,
each household had to cut a fresh supply daily for its

animals. At the end of the growing season, an entire
winter's supply had to be cut, dried, and preserved
(called <u>hoshikusa</u> or <u>kaiba</u>) so it could be parceled out
to the animals during the winter months. To ensure that
daily cutting of fresh fodder did not deplete the supply
available for winter, villagers, like those in Hirano,
usually designated one open area for daily cutting of fresh
grass and another closed area as a source of grass to be
dried into fodder for the winter. Most households,
particularly those with more horses than usual, had to
supplement their share of the common supply of winter
fodder with grass collected and dried from their own
private holdings.

In Nagaike, the animals were allowed to roam within a
certain area and pasture at will, but it was more customary
for villagers to forbid the use of commons as a pasture and
insist instead that people cut the grass and bring it to
the horses. This rule may have been devised to eliminate
the temptation for a household that relied on common
pasturage to acquire more animals than it could supply
with fresh-cut fodder; it may have thus been an effort to
prevent overgrazing. I was told that villagers wanted to
supervise what the horse ate--in particular to make sure
that they did not eat grass or plants intended for other
purposes. In any case, the role of animals in Japanese
agriculture was as a precious form of equipment that had
work to do each day, and not as a product in itself, so
there never was any need for vast pasturage to fatten up
large herds. Those Japanese who violated Buddhism's
vegetarian customs generally ate game. A household's need
for animals was limited by the amount of land it had to
work. It was not until the late 19th and especially early
20th century that the production of animals become a lucrative activity in itself; families in all three villages
began to earn extra income by breeding horses and leasing
them as pack animals for transporting freight along the
rough mountain roads in the Fuji area. As we shall see,
horse breeding placed stress on the commons and caused
villagers to tighten the rules.

Firewood and charcoal came from two locations. There
were patches of forest that villagers could enter at any
time as long as they obeyed rules about taking fallen wood
first, cutting only certain kinds of trees and then only
those that were smaller than a certain diameter, and only
with cutting tools of limited strength (to guarantee that
no tree of really substantial size could be cut). In
addition, all three villages conducted a joint annual tree

cutting: on this occasion they clear-cut everything
but the pines, and each household in each village got
an equal-sized stack of wood.

Different villages arrived at different arrangements
for guaranteeing an adequate supply of the products from
the commons. For items that were needed regularly and
that the commons yielded in abundance, a village might
allow co-owners free and open entry as long as they abided
by certain rules to make sure that a self-sustaining
population of mature plants or animals was left behind.
To enter the commons, one might need to go to village
authorities to obtain an entry permit, carved on a little
wooden ticket and marked "entrance permit for one person."
The rules would probably restrict a villager's choice of
cutting tools or the size of the sack or container used
to collect plants. Everyone would be expected to abide by
the village headman's instructions about leaving so much
height on a cut plant so that it could regenerate, or
taking only a certain portion of a cluster of similar
plants to make sure the parent plant could propagate
itself, or collecting a certain species only after
flowering and fruiting, and so on.

Villagers usually set aside closed reserves (tomeyama
or "closed mountains") for items that had to be left
undisturbed until maturity and harvested all at once at
just the right time, or that the commons supplied in only
adequate, not abundant, amounts. The village headman
would be responsible for determining when the time had
come to harvest thatch or winter fodder or other products,
and would schedule the event (literally, yama no kuchi ake
or "mountain-mouth-opening"). The rules for mountain-
opening day varied with the village and even the product
being collected. If the reserve had been closed merely
to assure that the plants were allowed to mature but
there was more than enough to go around, opening day
might simply mark the annual transition from a closed
mountain to an open one, allowing individuals and
households to enter at will and collect as much as they
wanted. On the other hand, if the supply were limited,
the reserve might be declared open for a brief period (two
or three days) and households allowed to send in only one
able-bodied adult to collect only what could be cut in
that time. If the item were limited in supply and had to
be collected all at once in a massive effort to prevent
spoilage, then the villagers would all enter the reserve
together, work until the job was done, and divide the
proceeds.

Even among the three villages in this study, there was great variation in the rules applied on mountain-opening days for harvesting different products from closed reserves. In Hirano, for instance, every household had to send one able-bodied adult (two after 1910) and a maximum of one horse to carry what was cut on the day scheduled for opening the closed thatch reserve. Hirano was divided into five kumi (groups), and each kumi was assigned to a par-ticular zone within the thatch reserve.[25] To preserve equality, the kumi changed zones according to a fixed rotational sequence each year. Household representatives from each kumi gathered in their kumi zone in the morning, with the kumi chiefs standing guard to make sure no one started cutting prematurely (anyone who did would be fined). At the sound of the great temple bell, everyone started cutting. One could cut only in the zone assigned to one's kumi, but could keep whatever one cut. A strong person could cut an adequate supply in a day (say, 10-15 units), but many would stay until after dark and even come back the next day. After two days, the mountain would be closed again and households would be required to donate two units of thatch to the common village reserve used in emergencies. The punishment for entering the thatch reserve before opening day was loss of the right to cut thatch or to receive a share from the kumi or the village for that year. These rules appeared to be a judicious combination that rewarded strength and hard work but also severely limited the circumstances in which cutting was allowed, which ensured that the total supply was not threatened and no extreme inequality appeared among households in a given year or among kumi over time.

The same village used different rules for collective harvesting of winter fodder for the animals from another closed mountain set aside for that type of grass. As with thatch, each kumi was assigned a zone according to an annual rotation scheme, and each household had to send one, but only one, adult. On the appointed day, each representative reported to the appropriate kumi zone in the winter fodder commons and waited for the temple bell as the signal to begin cutting. However, this grass was cut with large sickles, and since it would be dangerous to have people distributed unevenly around their kumi zone swinging sickles in all directions, the individuals in each kumi lined up together at one end of their zone and advanced to the other end, whacking in step with each other like a great agricultural drill team. The grass was left to dry for two or three days (when it became much

lighter), and then two representatives from each household
entered the fodder commons to tie the grass up into equal
bundles. The haul for each _kumi_ was grouped together and
then divided evenly into one cluster per household. Each
household was then assigned its cluster by lottery. This
extremely scrupulous division into equal lots per household was done not merely to prevent competitive cutting
or to assure an equal amount per household: bundles of
grass varied enormously in quality according to how thickly
the grass grew in different spots and how much extraneous
undesirable plant matter was included, so they were assigned randomly to eliminate the bad feelings that would
otherwise result in households that discovered their
bundles to be of poor quality. Random assignment of
bundles to households also ensured that household
representatives, unsure which bundles would become,
theirs would try to assemble bundles of equal size and
quality.

In Nagaike, the rules for cutting and division of
thatch and winter fodder from closed reserves were at one
time the opposite of those in Hirano. In Nagaike, households kept for themselves the supply of winter fodder that
they managed to cut on mountain-opening day to feed their
horses, but thatch was divided equally among the households after cutting. The equal division of thatch may
have originated in the fairly egalitarian distribution of
income among Nagaike households, meaning that households
had dwellings of similar size, and therefore similar needs
for thatch. Moreover, because all of the thatch for
roofing jobs came from the village reserve, there was
little value in amassing a private supply. Nagaike had
a highly routinized arrangement for collecting a common
reserve of thatch to provide a new roof for an outbuilding
or barn for two households per year and a complete
re-roofing job for all buildings for two more households
per year. By the time this communal system had provided a
new roof to all of Nagaike's 38 households, it was time to
start all over again. In 1923, the growing population of
horses in Nagaike was beginning to create much competitive
pressure for winter fodder on opening day, so Nagaike
switched from the "keep-what-you-cut" system to equal
division by _kumi_ and by household, much like the practice
in Hirano. (In fact, there is reason to believe that
Hirano had originally used the "keep-what-you-cut" system
for fodder too, like Nagaike, and that competitive cutting
as well as fear of swinging sickles had produced the change
to equal division by _kumi_ and household.)

From this brief sketch of the rules for closed reserves in Hirano and Nagaike, one might conclude that the poorer the village or the more dependent it was on its commons, the greater the likelihood that it would set aside closed reserves and develop stricter rules. However, a review of Yamanaka's practices toward the commons indicates that this was not the case.

Yamanaka was the poorest of the three villages, the least endowed with privately owned land, the most dependent on day labor and pack horses and carriage trade to supplement subsistence agriculture; its common lands were scruffy and dismal compared with those of Hirano and Nagaike. Nonetheless, Yamanaka's own commons combined with the huge Kitafuji slope that it shared with 11 villages made up in quantity what it lacked in quality: Yamanaka was located immediately adjacent to the Kitafuji slope and could conveniently use it, whereas the other villages that shared it were located far away and could not easily take advantage of their access rights. Then, in 1939, the Japanese government expropriated the Kitafuji slope, and even though the government was supposed to honor the villages' rights of access, the routine conduct of military exercises on the slope damaged the ecosystem and further reduced the productive potential of the Kitafuji commons. Yamanaka therefore grew more heavily dependent on another piece of common land that it held in its own right, and was forced to set aside a portion of that as a closed reserve for horse fodder. Even then, Yamanaka did not need to set aside a closed reserve for thatch. The supply of thatch on Kitafuji was sufficient, though so sparsely distributed that the hunt-and-peck method required 10 to 15 times the investment of time that was needed in Hirano to collect the same quantity.

A more appropriate conclusion, then, would be that as demand for the products of the commons--whether that demand reflected wealth or poverty--approached the maximum sustainable yield of the commons, portions of the commons would be set aside as reserves and the rules would be progressively tightened.

Thus far we have examined the benefits that villagers drew from the commons, but equally important is the contribution of labor to the maintenance of the commons. In the classic type of commons, villagers did not till the soil or sow seeds, but they often engaged in a systematic program of harvesting and weeding of certain plants in a particular sequence to increase the natural production of the plants they wanted.

One very dramatic technique of this sort was the annual burning of the grasslands, or noyaki. Originally practiced on a small scale on private holdings, the Tokugawa villagers gradually extended this custom; throughout Japan many of the common meadowlands were burned completely clear once a year. The burning undoubtedly altered the ecosystem drastically from its previous state, but the apparently altered ecosystem absorbed this custom of annual burning, and common lands survived in spite of it.[26] Noyaki was carefully timed in the early spring to burn off hard and woody grasses and thorny plants, along with "bad" insects, before the shoots of desirable grasses emerged. Noyaki essentially converted the previous season's leftover dried grass and the current season's early but undesirable grasses into a layer of ash (rich, desirable fertilizer to nourish the desirable vegetation) without the effort of hand weeding, manual composting, or manual redistribution of fertilizer. Even though the furious winds around Mt. Fuji caused the fire to race across the entire Kitafuji slope in just a few hours, somehow the game population was able to evacuate safely, to return later after delicious new shoots of grass had appeared.

There were written rules about the obligation of each household to contribute a share to the collective work to maintain the commons--to conduct the annual burning (which involved cutting nine-foot firebreaks ahead of time, carefully monitoring the blaze, and occasional fire-fighting when the flames jumped the firebreak), to report to harvest on mountain-opening days, or to do a specific cutting of timber or thatch. Accounts were kept about who contributed what to make sure that no household evaded its responsibilities unnoticed. Only illness, family tragedy, or the absence of able-bodied adults whose labor could be spared from routine chores were recognized as excuses for getting out of collective labor. (Temporary absences from the village were not acceptable; all healthy adults had to make themselves available.)[27] In such cases, others in the unrepresented family's kumi might cut a share of thatch or fodder for the missing family and the accounts would be evened out later. But if there were no acceptable excuse, punishment was in order.

PATTERNS OF INTERACTION IN THE COMMONS

As we have just seen, villages had elaborate rules to govern both open and closed commons. Abuses were

possible: taking too much or taking unallowed items
from an open commons, entering a closed commons before
mountain-opening day, violating the strict rules for
mountain-opening days, and failing to contribute labor.
What actually happened? What were the real behavioral
responses to rules and circumstances? What do we learn
from these responses about both individual and collective
agendas for using and abusing the commons?

Enforcement of Rules

One mechanism for enforcement of the rules about the
commons, as well as the rules about everything else, was
the general atmosphere of mutual dependence and collective
responsibility in the village. Japanese villages observed
a universal small-town rule that everything was everybody's
business, so everyone understood that a transgression in
one area of life--from serving cheap tea to building a
pretentious house to cheating on the commons--might cause
damage in another. In economic terms, this arrangement
served to internalize within the household most of the
costs that the household might otherwise have been able to
impose on others. To the extent that the formal system of
collective responsibility (five-man groups) was effective
in a village, all potential violators of rules knew that
those near them had strong incentives to advocate compliance as a general rule (or, when persuasion failed, to
snitch on one's colleagues rather than be implicated with
them). For most people most of the time, obedience to the
rules was probably the path of least resistance.

But villages did not rely entirely on formal collective
responsibility, or on social pressure from peers, or even
on the individual's sense of identification with the
welfare of the community to protect the precious commons.
Villagers were not so naive as to imagine that there would
never be temptations to violate the commons, so they
created groups of detectives to patrol them. This task
might be assigned to the young men's association or to the
village fire brigade (also composed of young men), which
would in turn delegate the job to its members on the basis
of annual rotation. The detectives would patrol the
commons on horseback every day looking for intruders, in
effect enforcing exclusionary rules.

In Hirano, the detectives (tantei) had to come from
families that could spare a young man's labor and a horse
for an entire year, and the job was considered one of the

most prestigious and responsible available to a young man.
In Nagaike, these positions (called wakashū there)
changed hands more frequently, but all eligible males had
to take a turn, so that no family was without its full
labor supply for very long but all would have to serve.
It is extremely interesting to note that Nagaike, which
was the smallest, most egalitarian of the three villages
and which also happened to depend completely on the commons
for the thatch and animal fodder that private holdings
simply did not produce, appears to have had virtually no
violations of the commons by Nagaike residents. The
detectives there had to deal only with intruders from
villages on the other side of the mountain.

Interestingly, Yamanaka had no system of detectives to
patrol its commons, although it did observe the principle
of "citizen's arrest"--anyone, not merely a designated
detective, could report violations. Yamanaka had no
closed reserve until 1939, and fewer rules to enforce on
the open commons. It may also have been too poor to spare
the labor of those who might serve as detectives. In any
case, the commons to which Yamanaka had exclusive access
rights (not the Kitafuji slope it shared with other
villages) had been formally registered as property of a
Shinto shrine during the Meiji land reform (this was
one of the few available ruses by which a village could
preserve common land), and the elders among the parish-
ioners performed functions akin to patrolling the shrine
commons for violators.

Violating rules that protected the commons was
viewed as one of the most terrible offenses a villager
could commit against his peers, and the penalties were
very serious. Most villages had written codes to govern
the commons, and these stipulated specific punishments for
specific violations, with a built-in scheme of escalating
penalties for noncooperation. Most violations were handled
quietly and simply by the detectives, who would set the
penalty. It was considered perfectly appropriate for the
detectives to demand cash and saké from violators and to
use that as their own entertainment cache. Anyone found
violating the rules of an open commons or illegally
entering a closed commons was instantly deprived of his
equipment, his horse, and whatever he had cut. To
retrieve his equipment and horse he would have to pay a
fine--usually a bottle or two of saké--and apologize to
the detectives who apprehended him. (Such saké given as
payment of a fine was referred to by special terms
indicating the humility of the giver and fine-payer:

ayamarizaké [apology wine], kotowarizaké [refusal wine],
or more quaintly ashiaraizaké [foot-washing wine].) The
contraband harvest was of course retained by the village.
If the offense were relatively large or the apology unsatisfactory, the head of the culprit's household or
his kumi or temple priest would have to make the apology
on his behalf and offer a larger fine in his stead. To
prevent the stain of collective responsibility and humili-
ation from spreading to them, the culprit's family or kumi
members would exert powerful pressure on him to make
adequate amends. If the intruder were a resident of
another village, the leaders of his village would have
to travel to the village whose commons had been violated
and apologize. Very rarely did a village have to go
beyond these first three stages of punishment to obtain
satisfaction.[28]

When necessary, though, the village could threaten
to employ its more powerful sanctions: ostracism in
increasingly severe stages, followed by banishment. The
Japanese term for ostracism, murahachibu, signifies that
the village cuts off all contact with the offender except
for assistance at funerals and fire-fighting. In fact,
it was usually employed in gradual stages, starting with
social contact and only escalating to economic relations
if the offender did not express remorse and modify his
behavior. To ensure that the villagers would remember
to shun contact with someone subjected to ostracism, that
person might be expected to wear distinctive clothing (a
flashy red belt or pair of unmatched socks. [Minzokugaku
kenkyūjo 1951:472]). Ostracism was a horrible punishment
for the Japanese villager, not only because it cut him
off from a highly group-oriented society and made daily
life unpleasant, but because it actually deprived the
villager of tangible services essential to daily living:
village water supplies, irrigation for his rice paddies,
and, of course, access to the commons. A villager of
ordinary means would never jeopardize the survival of
his household and his family's reputation for many generations when a simple apology could extinguish the controversy, and when strict obedience to the rules could
guarantee that such possibilities would not arise in the
first place. Only families of great wealth and pride
could afford to risk ostracism--often gambling that their
social status would win them enough allies that they could
either defeat the established village leadership in a
political contest or secede from the village and form a
new one.

Compliance and Violations

It is very difficult to ascertain how well the rules were obeyed, how well the threatened penalties discouraged violations, and how honestly the rules were enforced, especially when the offender was a resident of the governing village and the locals wished to keep the offense from going to the local magistrate's office and thus becoming a matter of public record. Those who have studied primary documents on Tokugawa villages and the commons have not been very interested in these questions in the past, so it is virtually impossible to arrive at reliable generalizations about Tokugawa villages on the basis of the written record. Moreover, this is a matter about which loyal villagers then and now would be understandably defensive and reticent, and one is forced to be skeptical when the available evidence suggests that all worked well. At the risk of exaggerating dysfunction in the enforcement system, then, I will take special note below of examples of violations of the commons in these three villages that have been so carefully studied.[29]

It would appear that villagers' reluctance to incur the disfavor of their peers was usually enough to keep violations of the commons at a manageable level--that is, offenses by outsiders were far more numerous than offenses by village residents, and all offenses taken together were usually minor in degree and did not threaten the ecological health of the commons. Moreover, the villagers--certainly village elders and kumi chiefs, and probably heads of all households--thoroughly understood the direct relationship between the rules and the preservation of the commons. These people lived with the seasons and natural cycles and knew their commons very well. Every time I asked about the reason for a particular rule, my informants gave a sophisticated and sensible explanation in terms of environmental protection and fair treatment of all the villagers, never, "Well, we've always done it that way." Even if the village elders were the prime repositories of accumulated scientific knowledge, this information circulated regularly through the village. Obedience to the rules was almost certainly based on an appreciation of their value, not merely on compliance to avoid penalties.

In these three villages taken together, there has been only one case in which violation against the commons led eventually to ostracism. The original violation was a minor one: entering an open commons to cut fresh grass on an official work holiday (essentially a compulsory vacation to give everyone a rest but to prevent any single family from gaining an advantage over others by working). This would have had no impact on the health of the commons and could have been taken care of quickly with an apology. However, the person who committed the violation was very proud and argued, in effect, that the rules did not apply to him because he was a village elder and former village chief. This claim, of course, was a more serious threat to the rule of law in the village than was the act itself. The man refused to apologize, he rejected his relatives' efforts at mediation, and the controversy and punishments escalated to the point where he had to travel to distant towns to do all of his trading and marketing. Finally, the village deprived him even of assistance at funerals and fire-fighting services, in effect turning murahachibu into murajūbu (in effect, he lost all rights instead of only some of them, as is implied by the term murahachibu).[30]

Certain more ordinary violations, however, were almost routine. For instance, in the weeks and days preceding mountain-opening days, impatient households would occasionally enter closed reserves prematurely. The detectives ordinarily collected one bottle of saké per minor violation, but during this "peak season" the young men collected more liquor than even they could drink, and they usually had to give it away. Similarly, the detectives were young men with predictable weaknesses, and some households intentionally sent their attractive young daughters into the commons to collect grass in violation of the rules of the commons. The detectives might then be disposed to look the other way, or even to ignore repeated offenses in exchange for sexual favors. Except for this single instance, there is no evidence of detectives exploiting their position by co-opting bits of the commons and concealing their own violations, or by terrorizing suspected offenders against the commons, or by concealing others' violations in exchange for favors. Certainly, there was an intrinsic pride in the importance of doing one's duty by the commons and in preserving the village's well-being; a young man brought credit to his family and future by doing the job properly (which included showing no favoritism). However, these internal incentives were augmented by the system of collective responsibility, since the detectives patrolled in teams. Any detective who felt tempted to violate the rules had to answer to his colleagues and risk the possibility that they would rather report him than be caught later as co-conspirators in an

offense. Apparently, not only violations of the rules
but abuse of power by the "police" appointed to search
out those violations was expected, and correctives were
built into the system. (When the village of Shiwa suffered
a drought, farmers at the downstream end of the irrigation
system, including the water guards on patrol, were sorely
tempted to alter the dikes so as to receive more than their
allocated share of water. During such times, the
collective response was for all adult males to patrol the
dikes all night long in mutual surveillance. [Shimpo 1976:
9-17.])

Violations of rules to protect the commons would also
increase noticeably in response to certain special circumstances. First, there might be a real challenge to the
wisdom of a village chief who, for instance, set mountain-
opening day too late. In this instance, an entire faction
of disgruntled villagers might violate the rules together
in an act of civil disobedience; this would clearly be a
protest against an error in the leadership rather than
disrespect for the rules to protect the commons. One
former detective in Hirano, now a respected village elder,
described how he had been patrolling a closed commons
one day and came upon not one or two intruders but thirty,
including some of the heads of leading households. It was
not yet mountain-opening day, but they had entered the
commons en masse to cut a particular type of pole used
to build trellises to support garden vegetables raised
on private plots. If they could not cut the poles soon
enough, their entire vegetable crop might be lost, and
they believed that the village headman had erred in setting
opening day later than these crops required. Out-classed
in both numbers and status, the detectives were unable to
resolve this episode quietly and had to go through channels
"all the way to the top." By way of apology, the thirty
offenders were ordered to make a donation to the village
school (rather than giving the huge quantity of saké that
would otherwise be called for to the five detectives).

Second, sudden changes in the economy or in the supply
of certain products that increased dependence on the
commons as a source of some particular item would increase
violations. This seems to have been the case in Yamanaka,
which experienced a fairly severe breakdown of the rules
during the depression of the 1930s. Almost all the
villagers knew that almost all the other villagers were
breaking the rules: sneaking around the commons at night,
cutting trees that were larger than the allowed size, even
using wood-cutting tools that were not permitted. This is

precisely the behavior that could get a tragedy of the commons started, but it did not happen in Yamanaka.

Instead of regarding the general breakdown of the rules as an opportunity to become full-time free riders and cast caution to the winds, the violators themselves tried to exercise self-discipline out of deference to the preservation of the commons, and stole from the commons only out of desperation. Inspectors or other witnesses who saw violations maintained silence out of sympathy for the violators' desperation and out of confidence that the problem was temporary and could not really hurt the commons. Yamanaka was also fortunate to have ready access to the Kitafuji slope, so that when its own commons was endangered the villagers could switch to its more widely shared commons instead. Finally, I strongly suspect that the rules villages adopted for the commons were very conservative and left wide margins for error, so that the violations that did occur did not often pose a serious threat to the commons. Interestingly, villagers did not question the rules themselves or become more casual about obeying them when they observed that violations did not damage the commons; the system of rules, and the values they embodied, seem to have been perceived as entirely legitimate and not subject to being challenged as unnecessarily cautious.

However, when villagers felt that the rules were too lax, or when they began to fear the environmental consequences of too many violations, they modified their management techniques in the direction of still greater caution in order to save the commons. For instance, when Yamanaka found in 1939 that the Kitafuji slope was no longer very productive, it converted its own commons--from which it had silently conspired to steal earlier that decade--into a closed reserve to make enforcement of the rules and identification of violators much easier. Similarly, when Hirano and Nagaike discovered that competitive cutting even on a closed reserve became a problem, they removed the incentives for individuals to race against each other on mountain-opening day by abolishing "keep-all-you-cut," instituting equal distribution, and assigning the harvest to households by lottery, which automatically reduced the frantic pace of cutting and thus the total quantity cut in a season.

OUTCOMES AND LESSONS

We have explored the experience of these three villages in governing access to their commons in order to diagnose the factors that help and hinder a community in dealing with common property. I must point out that, in addition to the rules and enforcement schemes, these three villages had other factors--their small size, their very strong community identity, and a sense of mutual interdependence that was reinforced by a formal structure of collective responsibility--that almost certainly enhanced their ability to make _any_ regulatory scheme work, even a very badly designed one. Nonetheless, we can extract a few themes and suggestions about the necessary and sufficient ingredients of successful management of common property, all else being equal, since there was variation among the villages in the types of commons they possessed, in their respective risks of producing a tragedy of the commons, and in the economic changes they endured over time. Naturally, it is early to generalize from just three villages, and hazardous to extrapolate from the commons in a closed agrarian society in the historical past to common property problems today, but I will still take the liberty of presenting tentative conclusions that can serve as hypotheses to be tested and refined in later studies. I will organize these evaluations around four questions suggested by the facts themselves and by Oakerson's analytical framework.

Efficiency of Use of Common Property

One might handily dismiss the value of the Japanese experience with common property by arguing that the natural environment was never hard-pressed in Tokugawa Japan, and that communities never created tragedies on their commons because they were never very close to any trouble--that they would have succeeded at managing the commons no matter what they did because they imposed so little on their common resources. However, we must remember that in the 17th century the Japanese did face the threat of massive deforestation, and there is good reason to believe that within the limits of local preindustrial technology the Japanese were actually pressing their natural environment--their agricultural potential--to its limits by the late Tokugawa period.

Villagers knew how much forest they had to leave intact
to produce the fertilizer they needed for their cultivated
plots. It is not clear whether villagers got as much from
the commons as the commons could have spared without
deterioration, but to extract more from the commons would
have required a still greater investment of labor. Village
resistance to shogunal pressures to reclaim more arable
land from the forest suggests that villagers viewed the
reclamation of additional upland fields from the forest
(inevitably of poorer quality than what they already had)
to be an inefficient use of their labor, especially later
in the period when conditions of labor shortage arose.

Villages sensed that they might be pushing the commons
too far when they let the rules break down, and they did
alter the rules to relieve pressure on the commons at
various times, suggesting that Tokugawa and later peasants
were indeed pressing the commons, and, by extension, that
managing the commons did require both skill and planning.
In other words, it seems clear that they did have to be
concerned about an efficient use of their commons and were
aware that haphazard control or management would threaten
their resources.

Equity Among Co-owners of the Commons

It is quite apparent that Japanese villagers were
deeply concerned with some notion of fairness. This can
be concluded from the rules, the sanctions for violations
of rules, the kinds of disputes over the commons that
reached the courts, and from the explanations of behavior
that are still offered today. Fairness was not synonymous
with equality in material possessions--many villages had
considerable inequality in holdings of private property
and did not seem troubled by this.

But there was an overriding sense that access to the
commons should be distributed according to some principle
of fairness that ignored existing maldistributions in
private wealth. Hence the frequent use of random distributions, assignment to parcels or products of the commons
by lottery, frequent rotations to move the good and the
bad around, and scrupulous attention to bookkeeping to
keep track of contributions and exchanges and offsetting
aid offered by one household to another. Such methods
provided assurance to each co-owner that the sacrifices
and gains of other co-owners would be similar, and offered
the additional advantage of removing the competitive

impulse (which is very dangerous when it becomes a race to
see who can deplete the commons first) and thus relieving
pressure on the commons. Yet laziness was not rewarded,
because someone who failed to do his share of the work lost
entitlement to a share of the proceeds altogether. Nor did
this notion of fairness mean that entitlement was automatic
for all comers (the way food stamps or food aid sometimes
are); a household had to earn its eligibility through some
period of established residence in the village, and casual
drifters were ignored.

Enforceability of the Rules

Violations of the rules and conflicts over use of
the commons suggest that any rules for the commons must be
designed to have an obvious and direct relationship to the
goal of preserving the commons. Co-owners of the commons
will not obey regulations that they regard as frivolous or
arbitrary. They will obey regulations that are quite
clearly based on maximum-sustainable-yield principles.
They will consent to being deprived of certain products of
the commons if they can be convinced that what they do not
extract from the commons is truly needed for the long-term
maintenance of the commons and that others will exercise
similar self-restraint.

The Japanese experience also demonstrates that no
rules are self-enforcing. Japanese villagers had a strong
community identity and were very concerned about social
reputation and bonds with the group, and they internalized
the preservation of the commons as a vital goal. Nevertheless, even this most cooperative, compliant group of
people were vulnerable to temptations to bend, evade, and
violate the rules governing the commons. Thus there had
to be a scheme of penalties, and these had to be enforced.
The rules and the penalties had to be aimed directly at
free riding, and to make enforcement possible at all they
had to be designed to distinguish handily between good and
bad behavior. It was hard to enforce the rules governing
open commons without individual inspection of each user's
activities. Therefore, as pressure on the commons
increased, it became necessary to close off the commons
so that any intruder could be instantly and automatically
designated as a violator.

Moreover, villages not only assumed that violations
could occur but that even the police or detectives who
patrolled the commons would be tempted to stray and steal

from the commons or abuse their privileged position in
other ways. Even though traditional Japanese were about
as far from being libertarians as anyone might imagine,
they too worried about who would watch the watchers.
Correctives for this problem were built into the system:
the watchers watched each other, collective responsibility
applied to the watchers as well as to the watched, and the
duty of watching rotated through the body of co-owners so
that everyone got his turn to exercise power, to be
suspected of abusing his power, and finally to prove
himself innocent by exercising exemplary behavior on
duty. All of this also suggests that small intimate
communities of co-owners united not only by their mutual
interest in the commons but by other social relationships
were essential. The ever-present anxiety about preservation of the commons and the expectation that violators
would harm the commons seemed in itself to operate as
some sort of deterrent. (I am reminded of modern urban
Japanese, who have the safest cities in the world and are
simultaneously nervous wrecks about crime. They put bars
on their first floor windows, build walls--sometimes topped
with chipped glass--around their houses, and almost never
leave their houses totally unoccupied. Asked why they
exert themselves so over a nearly nonexistent problem,
they offer the same reply as the man who snaps his fingers
to keep the elephants away--"it works, doesn't it?")

Although the system of collective responsibility by
community, kumi, and household is not at all attractive
to someone who values liberty, we have to admit that it
was a very cheap tool for enforcement because it encouraged
each village, each kumi, and each household to monitor its
own recalcitrant members. A somewhat more palatable lesson
may be in the use of a unit other than individuals for
calculating contributions to and benefits from the commons: this practice seemed to induce each unit (here, the
household) to restrict its own size--and by extension to
restrain its own demand for products of the commons.

Finally, these villages had an escalating scale of
penalties that began with confiscation of the contraband
taken from the commons--instantly negating the advantage
of violating the rules--and proceeded through gradual
stages of exclusion from the commons and eventually from
all contact and exchange with other co-owners of the
commons. This scale of punishments may seem harsh, but in
fact it operated rather gently, most violators confessing
and apologizing quickly rather than having to suffer more
severe consequences. This graduated scheme of punishments

to fit the offense may be very important in controlling repeat offenders: the desperate know that they may be forgiven this once, but the malicious know that they will suffer severely.

Legitimacy of the Rules

In conclusion, it is also important to point out that the villagers themselves invented the regulations, enforced them, and meted out punishments, indicating that it is not necessary for regulation of the commons to be imposed coercively or from the outside. This, along with the fact that villagers could change their own rules through a process of consultation and consensus that was democratic in form if not always in fact, almost certainly increased the legitimacy of the regulations. Although the Tokugawa social order was very oppressive toward individuals whom it classified as "deviant," the village itself was largely self-regulating in this regard, and did not require intervention by an autocratic state to protect the commons. The implications for democratic processes and individual liberties in societies that face tragedies of the commons are mixed: there is, indeed, something ominous and inequitable about a system of collective responsibility that victimizes innocent members of groups that contain free riders, and about the village's power to impose ostracism to the point where life is threatened. The importance of uniform and impartial applications of law, the restraint exercised before harsh penalties are employed, and the room for democratic rule making and rule amending are more assuring.

NOTES

1. I would like to thank David Feeny, Pauline Peters,
and Kristina Kade Troost for very helpful comments on an
earlier version of this paper. I am also grateful to the
Joint Committee on Japanese Studies of the Social Science
Research Council and the American Council of Learned
Societies, as well as the Duke University Research
Council, for the support that allowed me to gather
material for this study.

2. Estimates are that there were between 70,000 and
150,000 villages before amalgamation.

3. For a summary of the literature on free rider and
public goods problems, see McMillan (1979). Other major
works are G. Hardin (1968); R. Hardin (1982); Olson
(1965); Brubaker (1975); Buchanan (1968a, 1968b); Coase
(1974); Demsetz (1964); Frohlich et al. (1975); Furubotn
and Pejovich (1972); Groves and Ledyard (1977); Sweeney
(1973, 1974); Mishan (1971); and Stigler (1974). James
Buchanan (1975) reaches the unhappy conclusion that
exclusion must be used.

4. The great body of Japanese scholarship on common
lands is devoted to this process of attrition and the
legal and social controversies it engendered.
Fortunately, Japanese scholars tend to be meticulous
about publishing early documents and gathering details
as they go, and as a result the primary materials
compiled by these scholars serve as a catalog of
management practices and even of disputes over how
to deal with abuse and abusers of the commons.

5. The brief history of the nationalization and
decentralization of landholding that follows is based on
two studies by Asakawa (1914, 1929a) that are reprinted
in Asakawa (1965); and Asakawa (1918); Arnesen (1979);
Duus (1969); Hall (1966:99-295, 1968, 1981); Smith

(1968a, 1968b); Sato (1974); Mass (1974); Wintersteen (1974); Miyagawa and Kiley (1974); Nagahara and Yamamura (1974; 1981); Ishii (1980); Sansom (1958:339-389); Totman (1979); Wakita (1982).

6. Kurosawa Akira's well-known recent film, Kagemusha, is a reasonably accurate account of the rise and fall of Takeda Shingen and his son Katsuyori, very serious competitors during the final stages of this struggle for political leadership during the 16th century. Shingen's double, the shadow warrior who is the centerpiece of the film, is fictional.

7. Another Kurosawa film, The Seven Samurai, is a plausible depiction of the struggle of one such village to protect itself against ravaging bands of warriors and thieves during the 15th and 16th centuries.

8. On the attrition of common lands since the Meiji period, see Furushima et al. (1966); Hōjō (1979b); Kainō (1958, 1964); Kawashima et al. (1959-61); Watanabe (1972).

9. A crucial distinction between owning a share of the commons and owning any other form of property jointly with others is that traditional co-ownership rights to the commons are conferred only on households of long standing in the village, and they cannot be sold to anyone else. Each household possesses one share in the commons and no more, and households or persons not invited into the group of co-owners (iriai shūdan) are simply not entitled to a share. For a brief explanation of the current legal status of ownership of common access rights, see Watanabe and Nakao (1975:67-97).

10. Kristina Kade Troost's (pers. com. 1984) dissertation research (in progress) on the indigenous development of village governance for three villages on Lake Biwa near Kyoto that kept their own documents has uncovered examples of all three of these forms of management (classic, direct group control, and divided use) well before the Tokugawa period.

11. The most important general work on the history of the evolution of common access rights is Furushima (1955). The major works on the history of the common lands in the particular area studied here--Kitafuji--

are Hōjō and Fukushima (1964); Hōjō (1977:191-433, 1978, 1979a); Kamimura (1979); Ōshima (1978); Watanabe and Hōjō (1975).

12. These three communities were three independent villages or _mura_ during the Tokugawa period, and I will continue to use the term "village" to refer to the classical Tokugawa-period village. Since 1868, the Japanese government has encouraged administrative amalgamation of villages. The three villages of Yamanaka, Hirano, and Nagaike have in fact been amalgamated once so that together they now compose one modern village, called Yamanaka-mura, but they have rejected further amalgamation with additional communities in the area.

13. The Japanese government expropriated Mount Fuji's north slope in 1939 for use as a military base but guaranteed that it would continue to honor traditional access rights. Villagers recently fought a lawsuit claiming that the government frequently denied them access without cause and that military practice on the land has disrupted the ecosystem and damaged the trees so that certain plants are no longer available. The villagers won, and now receive regular compensation from the government for damage to their commons. During the trial, the Japanese Self Defense Forces (SDF) continued to use the land for practice, and at that time the villagers entered the land in nonviolent protest to prevent these military operations. Many who follow the news in Japan are familiar with these Kitafuji protests against the SDF, but do not realize that the cause of the protesters is not pacifism so much as it is the tradition of centuries-old rights of access to commons. Similar arguments underlie the famous farmers' protest against the construction of Narita Airport on an expropriated commons.

14. The following descriptions draw principally on the work of Hōjō Hiroshi, Kamimura Masana, and the interviews that they arranged for me. A shorter version appears in McKean (1982).

15. The Tokugawa administrative structure, established in the early 1600s, is sometimes called "centralized feudalism," a bewildering and misleading label for a political system that was at once federalist,

authoritarian, highly bureaucratic, and perhaps even totalitarian in the extent to which the state controlled information and monitored individual lives. On the Tokugawa political order, see Duus (1969); Hall and Jansen (1968); Ishii (1980); Totman (1967). Berry (1982) suggests that Hideyoshi began much of what Ieyasu has been given credit for.

16. One aspect of this confusion is just how long the Tokugawa shogunate really exercised the peremptory powers and tight administrative controls that are implied in the formal structure it created. Recent evidence on the relationship between the shogunate and its supposedly most loyal subgroup of daimyō suggests that after the first three shoguns, central control began to decline. The Tokugawa gradually lost the ability to enforce the use of their currency in the domains and to extract the tax revenue they expected from the domains, and they never were able to exert control over the seemingly irrepressible growth of commerce. See Bolitho (1974). However, even if the daimyō acquired considerable independence from the shogunate, we cannot be sure that the daimyō were any less autocratic toward their subjects than the shogunate controls had been.

17. After the Meiji restoration, all land was re-registered so that it could be taxed anew by the young government. At this point, much of the land that had been held and used in common by villages all over Japan was registered as public (national or government-owned) land, and the system of commons was greatly reduced. Villages were able to protect their commons against expropriation by the land-hungry Meiji government only if they had ample documentation of use rights acknowledged by Tokugawa-period daimyō or revealed in legal decisions made when disputes over land use arose during the Tokugawa period.

18. For the consequences of such a separation of land rights from tree ownership in Niger, see Thomson et al., this volume.

19. On the early development of Japanese law, see Asakawa (1929b); Bock (1970); Mass (1979); Grossberg and Kanamoto (1981); Wigmore (1969).

20. An interesting exception to this trend is available

in Henderson (1975:66-67), in which two villages that
could not agree on the precise location of a boundary
between them decided to create a joint commons for grass
in the area in dispute instead.

21. On the traditional village, see Asakawa (1909-11);
Befu (1968); Smith (1959, 1968a); Nagahara and Yamamura
(1974); Chambliss (1965). For twentieth-century survi-
vals of these traditional forms of organization and
cooperation, see Embree (1939); Fukutake (1967); Shimpo
(1976); Marshall (1984).

22. Tsurumi Kazuko (1975) summarizes these views of the
traditional village. See also Irokawa (1973a, 1973b:
508-564); and Gluck (1978).

23. The argument that slow population growth in the
Tokugawa period was a result of natural disasters and
famines--these definitely did occur--has been thoroughly
trounced. Detailed studies of family size and income
based on the shūmon aratame for villages with fairly
complete series of registers for the Tokugawa period
demonstrate that Japanese farm families chose not to
reproduce rapidly after famine, that they limited family
size even during good economic times, and that wealthy
families and wealthy villages as well as poor ones
limited family size. Hanley and Yamamura (1977) and
Smith (1977) conclude that the effort to limit family
size was a conscious one intended to increase the
family's standard of living. Kalland and Pedersen (1984)
agree but argue that the family's motives might have had
a darker side as well: to increase the family's standard
of living and therefore its potential for savings and
accumulation as insurance against potential destitution
in the future. These are essentially the glass-half-full
and the glass-half-empty versions of the same argument.
See Smith (1977); Hanley and Yamamura (1977); Kalland and
Pedersen (1984).

24. Smith (1977:1-14) and Hanley and Yamamura (1977:
92-334) point out that Tokugawa Japan's low population
growth rates came not from high death rates but from a
combination of low death rates and low birth rates (20-30
per thousand). Combined with a reasonable average life
expectancy for preindustrial society (to the early 40s),
this meant that throughout the Tokugawa period two-thirds
of the population were productive adults supporting a

dependent population of children and elderly one half
their own number. Such conditions have been matched in
history only in preindustrial Europe, where low
birthrates were due in part to some attempts at birth
control but more importantly to even later female
marriage than in Japan (the late 20s in Europe), and
most critically of all to the very high rates (more than
50 percent of the adult female population in some times
and places) of celibacy thanks to Catholic nunneries.
Kelley and Williamson (1971) concluded in one of their
early studies that the low population growth rate in the
Tokugawa period was the single most important factor
permitting the later rise of the Meiji. Later, however,
they retreated from their earlier stress on low population growth as a factor in economic growth; experimental simulations of Meiji economic models had shown
that Japan could have sustained almost as much economic
growth in the Meiji period as it in fact experienced even
with the very high rates of population growth that we are
familiar with today in developing countries. However,
their counterfactual simulation run tested the effect on
Meiji economic growth of a higher Meiji population growth
rate (starting in 1887), and did not concern the role of
low Tokugawa population growth rates in permitting
capital accumulation during the Tokugawa period at all.
It is quite possible that high population growth rates
during the Tokugawa period would have produced very
different conditions for the Meiji economy to work with,
quite possibly absent the potential for subsequent
take-off. See Kelley and Williamson (1974).

25. Kumi are sometimes considered survivors of the
Tokugawa five-man groups. See Embree (1939:112-157);
Fukutake (1967:96-104). The major work on kumi and other
horizontal organizations in the traditional village has
been done by followers of Yanagida Kunio's school of
folklore, particularly by Segawa Kiyoko and Sakurai
Tokutaro.

26. I am assured by students of forestry that brief
brushfires of this sort that do not penetrate the soil to
burn roots do not tax the ability of a natural system to
restore itself.

27. Gradually, with the commercialization of agriculture, it occasionally became possible for a household
to buy its way out of these obligations by contributing

equipment instead of labor, or cash for some needed collective purchase, or even to hire someone else to stand in; on the other hand, this was regarded in some villages as dereliction of duty and the unfair exploitation of economic advantage, so substitution of material contributions for labor was not allowed.

28. If the offender belonged to another village, the village whose commons was violated would have to take its case to the local magistrate for adjudication, and indeed we find many such disputes in Tokugawa records. Villages might make reciprocal claims of violations against each other, and the documents presented and the decisions rendered formed part of the documentary record by which villagers were later able to establish their claims to commons in the Meiji period.

29. I have drawn these examples from Kamimura Masana's research and from several interviews with former commons detectives who were remarkably forthcoming about matters that would not ordinarily be revealed to outsiders. I am very grateful to Professor Hōjō Hiroshi for giving me the introductions that allowed these candid discussions to take place.

30. When the ostracized man's children went out to play, other children threw stones at them. When the grandfather of the household drowned in Lake Yamanaka, no one would come to help recover the body. At the funeral, rather than helping to carry the coffin, the village fire brigade actually tried to block the path to the cemetery until prefectural police arrived. Then finally the man's house burned down--it is said that village officials actually started the fire intentionally--and no one came to his assistance. When other villagers felt sympathy for the man's perfectly innocent family, village officials pointed out that having any contact with a family that was the target of ostracism would destroy the effectiveness of the sanction and make the contactor subject to ostracism, too. The fear of spreading ostracism was so powerful that even though prefectural police arrested some of the onlookers at the fire for negligence (standing idly by was actually a violation of fire laws), no one offered to help extinguish the fire. This episode of ostracism

lasted 5-6 years, and it took four generations for the
family to shake off the taint of having been ostracized.
See Kamimura (1979:219-222).

Arnesen, P. J. 1979. The Medieval Japanese Daimyō: The Ouchi Family's Rule of Suo and Nagato. New Haven, Connecticut: Yale University Press.

Asakawa Kan'ichi. 1909-11. Notes on village government in Japan after 1600. Parts 1 and 2. Journal of the American Oriental Society 30:259-300, 31:151-216.

Asakawa Kan'ichi. 1914. The origin of feudal land tenure in Japan. The American Historical Review 20, No. 1:1-23.

Asakawa Kan'ichi. 1918. Some aspects of Japanese feudal institutions. Transactions of the Asiatic Society of Japan 46, No. 1:77-102.

Asakawa Kan'ichi. 1929a. The early shō and the early manor: a comparative study. Journal of Economic and Business History 50, No. 2:177-207.

Asakawa Kan'ichi. 1929b. The Documents of Iriki, Illustrative of the Development of the Feudal Institutions of Japan. New Haven, Connecticut: Yale University Press.

Asakawa Kan'ichi. 1965. Land and Society in Medieval Japan. Tokyo: Japan Society for the Promotion of Science.

Befu, Harumi. 1968. Village autonomy and articulation with the state. In Hall and Jansen 1968.

Berry, M. E. 1982. Hideyoshi. Cambridge, Massachusetts: Harvard University Press.

Bock, F. G., trans. 1970. Engishiki: Procedures of the Engi Era. Tokyo: Sophia University.

Bolitho, H. 1974. Treasures among Men: The Fudai Daimyō in Tokugawa Japan. New Haven, Connecticut: Yale University Press.

Brubaker, E. 1975. Free ride, free revelation, or golden rule? Journal of Law and Economics 18, No. 1:147-161.

Buchanan, J. M. 1968a. Congestion on the common: a case for government intervention. Il Politico: Rivista Italiana di Scienze Politiche 33, No. 4:776-778.

Buchanan, J. M. 1968b. The Demand and Supply of Public Goods. Chicago: Rand McNally.

Buchanan, J. M. 1975. The Limits of Liberty: Between Anarchy and Leviathan. Chicago: University of Chicago Press.

Chambliss, W. J. 1965. Chiaraijima Village: Land Tenure, Taxation, and Local Trade 1818-1884. Tuscon: University of Arizona Press.

Coase, R. H. 1974. The lighthouse in economics. Journal of Law and Economics 17, No. 2:357-376.

Demsetz, H. 1964. Toward a theory of property rights. American Economic Review 54, No. 3:347-359.

Dore, R. P. 1959. Land Reform in Japan. London: Oxford University Press.

Duus, P. 1969. Feudalism in Japan. New York: Alfred E. Knopf.

Elison, G. and B. L. Smith, eds. 1981. Warlords, Artists, and Commoners: Japan in the Sixteenth Century. Honolulu, Hawaii: University Press of Hawaii.

Embree, J. F. 1939. Suye Mura: A Japanese Village. Chicago, Illinois: University of Chicago Press.

Frohlich, N., T. Hunt, J. Oppenheimer, and R. H. Wagner. 1975. Individual contributions for collective goods: alternative models. Journal of Conflict Resolution 19, No. 2:310-329.

Fukutake Tadashi. 1967. Japanese Rural Society. Ithaca,
New York: Cornell University Press.

Furubotn, E. G. and S. Pejovich. 1972. Property rights
and economic theory: a survey of recent literature.
Journal of Economic Literature 10:1137-1162.

Furushima Toshio. 1955. Kinsei iriai seido ron [On the
common access system of the early modern period].
Tokyo: Nihon hyoron shin shuppan.

Furushima Toshio, Ushiomi Toshitaka, and Watanabe Yōzō.
1966. Rin'ya iriaiken no honshitsu to yōsō [The
Appearance and Reality of Common Access Rights to
Forests]. Tokyo: Tokyo University Press.

Gluck, C. 1978. The people in history: recent trends
in Japanese historiography. Journal of Asian Studies
38, No. 1:25-50.

Grossberg, K. and Kanamoto Nobuhisa, trans. 1981.
Laws of the Muromachi Bakufu. Tokyo: Sophia
University Press.

Groves, T. and J. Ledyard. 1977. Optimal allocation of
public goods: a solution to the "free rider"
problem. Econometrica 45:783-809.

Hall, J. W. 1966. Government and Local Power in Japan,
500 to 1700: A Study Based on Bizen Province.
Princeton, New Jersey: Princeton University Press.

Hall, J. W. 1968. Foundations of the modern Japanese
daimyō. In Hall and Jansen 1968.

Hall, J. W. 1981. Japan's sixteenth-century revolution.
In Elison and Smith 1981.

Hall, J. W. 1983. Terms and concepts in Japanese
medieval history: an inquiry into the problems of
translation. Journal of Japanese Studies 9, No.
1:1-32.

Hall, J. W. and M. B. Jansen, eds. 1968. Studies in the
Institutional History of Early Modern Japan.
Princeton, New Jersey: Princeton University Press.

Hall, J. W. and J. P. Mass, eds. 1974. Medieval Japan: Essays in Institutional History. New Haven, Connecticut: Yale University Press.

Hall, J. W., Nagahara Keiji, and Yamamura Kozo, eds. 1981. Japan before Tokugawa: Political Consolidation and Economic Growth, 1500 to 1650. Princeton, New Jersey: Princeton University Press.

Hall, J. W. and Toyoda Takeshi. 1974. Japan in the Muromachi Age. Berkeley, California: University of California Press.

Hanley, S. B. and Yamamura Kozo. 1977. Economic and Demographic Change in Preindustrial Japan, 1600-1868. Princeton, New Jersey: Princeton University Press.

Harada Toshimaru. 1969. Kinsei iriai seido keitai katei no kenkyū: Yamawari seido no hassei to sono henshitsu [A Study of the Process of the Dissolution of the Early Modern Common Access System: Genesis and Change in the "Mountain-Division System"]. Tokyo: Hanawa shobō.

Hardin, G. 1968. The tragedy of the commons. Science 162:1243-1248.

Hardin, R. 1982. Collective Action. Baltimore: Johns Hopkins University Press (for Resources for the Future, Washington, D.C.).

Henderson, D. F. 1965. Conciliation and Japanese Law. Vol. 1: Tokugawa. Seattle: University of Washington Press.

Henderson, D. F. 1975. Village "Contracts" in Tokugawa Japan: Fifty Specimens with English Translations and Comments. Seattle: University of Washington Press.

Hōjō Hiroshi. 1977. Rin'ya iriai no shiteki kenkyū (jō) [Historical Research on Common Access to Forests (volume 1)]. Tokyo: Ochanomizu shobō.

Hōjō Hiroshi. 1978. Mura to iriai no hyakunen shi:
Yamanashi ken sonmin no iriai tōsōshi [A Hundred
Years' History of a Village and Its Common Access:
The History of the Common Access Struggle of the
Villagers of Yamanashi Prefecture]. Tokyo:
Ochanomizu shobō.

Hōjō Hiroshi. 1979a. Kinsei ni okeru iriai no shokeitai
[The Various Forms of Common Access in the Early
Modern Period]. Tokyo: Ochanomizu shobō.

Hōjō Hiroshi. 1979b. Rin'ya hōsei no tenkai to sonraku
kyodotai [The Development of Forestry Law and Village
Community]. Tokyo: Ochanomizu shobō.

Hōjō Hiroshi and Fukushima Masao. 1964. Meiji 26 nen
zenkoku sanrin gen'ya iriai kankō shiryō shū:
Yamanashi ken [Collected Documents from the Meiji 26
National Survey of Customary Common Access to
Virgin Mountain Forests: Yamanashi Prefecture].
Tokyo: Rin'yachō.

Irokawa Daikichi. 1973a. Japan's grass-roots tradition:
Current issues in the mirror of history. Japan
Quarterly 21, No. 1:78-86.

Irokawa Daikichi. 1973b. Shinpen Meiji seishin shi [A
New Spiritual History of the Meiji Period]. Tokyo:
Chūō kōronsha.

Ishii Ryōsuke. 1980. A History of Political Institutions
in Japan. Tokyo: University of Tokyo Press.

Kainō Michitaka. 1958. Iriai no kenkyū [A Study of
Common Access]. Tokyo: Ichiryūsha.

Kainō Michitaka. 1964. Kotsunagi jiken: sandai no
wataru iriaiken funsō [The Kotsunagi Incident: A
Struggle over Common Access Rights that Spans Three
Generations]. Tokyo: Iwanami shoten.

Kalland, A. and J. Pedersen. 1984. Famine and
population in Fukuoka domain during the Tokugawa
period. Journal of Japanese Studies 10 (Winter):
31-72.

- 585 -

Kamimura Masana. 1979. Sonraku seikatsu no shūzoku,
kanshū no shakai kōzō [The Social Structure of the
Folkways and Customs of Village Life]. Tokyo:
Ochanomizu shobo.

Kawashima Takeyoshi. 1979. Iriai ken kenkyū no genjō to
mondaiten [The Current State and Problems in Research
on Common Access Rights]. Parts 1 and 2. Jūrisuto
682:70-76, 683:120-127.

Kawashima Takeyoshi, Ushiomi Toshitaka, and Watanabe
Yōzō. 1959-61. Iriaiken no kaitai [The Dismemberment
of Common Access Rights]. 2 vols. Tokyo: Iwanami
shoten.

Kelley, A. C. and J. G. Williamson. 1971. Writing
history backwards: Meiji Japan revisited. The
Journal of Economic History 31, No. 4.

Kelley, A. C. and J. G. Williamson. 1974. Lessons from
Japanese Development: An Analytical Economic
History. Chicago: University of Chicago Press.

Marshall, R. C. 1984. Collective decision making in
rural Japan. University of Michigan Center for
Japanese Studies Papers in Japanese Studies, no. 11.
Ann Arbor: University of Michigan Press.

Mass, J. P. 1974. Jitō land possession in the thirteenth
century: The case of Shitaji chubun. In Hall and
Mass 1974.

Mass, J. P. 1979. The Development of Kamakura Rule,
1180-1250: A History with Documents. Stanford,
California: Stanford University Press.

McKean, M. 1982. The Japanese experience with
scarcity: management of traditional common lands.
Environmental Review 6, No. 2:63-88.

McKean, R. N. 1979. Economic aspects of ethical-
behavioral codes. Political Studies 27, No. 2:251-
265.

McMillan, J. 1979. The free-rider problem: a survey.
The Economic Record 55, No. 149:95-107.

Minzokugaku kenkyūjo [Folklore Research Institute].
1951. Minzokugaku jiten [Dictionary of Folklore].
Tokyo: Tokyodo shuppan.

Mishan, E. J. 1971. The post-war literature on
externalities: an interpretive essay. Journal of
Economic Literature 9, No. 1:1-28.

Miyagawa Mitsuru, and C. J. Kiley. 1974. From shōen to
chigyo: proprietary lordship and the structure of
local power. In Hall and Toyoda 1974.

Nagahara Keiji. 1975. Landownership under the
shōen-kokugaryō system. Journal of Japanese
Studies 1, No. 2:269-296.

Nagahara Keiji. 1977. Chūsei nàiranki no shakai to
Minshū [Society and People During the Medieval Civil
Wars]. Tokyo: Yoshikawa kobunkan.

Nagahara Keiji and Yamamura Kozo. 1974. Village
communities and daimyō power. In Hall and Toyoda
1974.

Nagahara Keiji and Yamamura Kozo. 1981. The Sengoku
daimyō and the kandaka system. In Hall et al. 1981.

North, D. C. 1981. Structure and Change in Economic
History. New York: W. W. Norton.

Olson, M. 1965. The Logic of Collective Action: Public
Goods and the Theory of Groups. Cambridge,
Massachusetts: Harvard University Press.

Osako, Masako M. 1983. Forest preservation in Tokugawa
Japan. In Tucker and Richards 1983.

Oshima Mario. 1978. Kinsei ni okeru mura to ie no shakai
kōzō [The Social Structure of Village and Household
in Early Modern Japan]. Tokyo: Ochanomizu shobō.

Runge, C. F. 1981. Common property externalities:
isolation, assurance, and resource depletion in a
traditional grazing context. American Journal of
Agricultural Economics 63, No. 4:595-606.

Sansom, George. 1958. A History of Japan to 1334. Stanford, California: Stanford University Press.

Sato, E. 1974. The early development of the shōen. In Hall and Mass 1974:91-108.

Shimpo Mitsuru. 1976. Three Decades in Shiwa: Economic Development and Social Change in a Japanese Farming Community. Vancouver, Canada: University of British Columbia Press.

Smith, T. C. 1959. The Agrarian Origins of Modern Japan. New York: Atheneum Press.

Smith, T. C. 1968a. The Japanese village in the seventeenth century. In Hall and Jansen 1968.

Smith, T. C. 1968b. The land tax in Tokugawa Japan. In Hall and Jansen 1968.

Smith, T. C. 1977. Nakahara: Family Farming and Population in a Japanese Village, 1717-1830. Stanford, California: Stanford University Press.

Stigler, G. J. 1974. Free riders and collective action: an appendix to theories of economic regulation. Bell Journal of Economics and Management Science 5(2):359-365.

Sweeney, J. W., Jr. 1973. An experimental investigation of the free-rider problem. Social Science Research 2(3):277-292.

Sweeney, J. W., Jr. 1974. Altruism, the free rider problem, and group size. Theory and Decision 4(3-4):259-275.

Totman, C. 1967. Politics in the Tokugawa Bakufu 1600-1843. Cambridge, Massachusetts: Harvard University Press.

Totman, C. 1979. English-language studies of medieval Japan: An assessment. Journal of Asian Studies 38, No. 3:541-551.

Totman, C. 1982a. Kinsei Nihon no ringyō ni tsuite
no ikkōsatsu [A perspective on early modern Japanese
forestry]. Kenkyū kiyō [Research Notes, annual
publication of Tokugawa rinseishi kenkyūjo], 377-399.

Totman, C. 1982b. Forestry in early modern Japan,
1650-1850: A preliminary survey. Agricultural
History 56, No. 2:415-425.

Totman, C. 1983a. The forests of Tokugawa Japan: a
catastrophe that was avoided. Transactions of the
Asiatic Society of Japan (3d series) 18:1-15.

Totman, C. 1983b. Logging the unloggable: timber
transport in early modern Japan. Journal of Forest
History 27, No. 4:190-191.

Totman, C. 1984. Land-use patterns and afforestation
in the Edo period. Monumenta Nipponica 39, No. 1:1-
10.

Tsurumi Kazuko. 1975. Yanagida Kunio's work as a model
of endogenous development. Japan Quarterly 22, No.
3:223-238.

Tucker, R. P. and J. F. Richards, eds. 1983. Global
Deforestation and the Nineteenth-Century World
Economy. Durham, North Carolina: Duke University
Press.

Wakita Osamu. 1982. The emergence of the state in
sixteenth-century Japan: from Oda to Tokugawa.
Journal of Japanese Studies 8, No. 2:343-367.

Watanabe Yōzō. 1972. Iriai to hō [Common Access and the
Law]. Tokyo: Tokyo University Press.

Watanabe Yōzō, and Hōjō Hiroshi. 1975. Rin'ya iriai to
sonraku kōzō: Kitafuji sanroku no jirei kenkyū
[Common Access to Forests and Village Structure: A
Case Study from the North Fuji Slope]. Tokyo: Tokyo
University Press.

Watanabe Yōzō and Nakao Hidetoshi. 1975. Nihon no
shakai to hō [Law and Society in Japan]. Tokyo:
Nihon hyōronsha.

Wigmore, J. 1969. Law and Justice in Tokugawa Japan
    (eventually to comprise ten sections). Tokyo:
    University of Tokyo Press.

Wintersteen, P. B., Jr. 1974. The Muromachi Shugo
    and Hanzei. In Hall and Mass 1974.

Yamamura Kozo. 1975. Introduction. Journal of Japanese
    Studies 1, No. 2:255-268.

Yanagida Kunio, ed. 1957. Japanese Manners and Customs
    in the Meiji Era. Tokyo: Ōbunsha.

PART THREE: **Conclusions**

25

Closing Comments at the Conference on Common Property Resource Management

Daniel W. Bromley

After a week of stimulating exchange we are left
with the following question: are there useful activities
in which the development assistance community might engage
that can enhance resource management regimes in the developing countries? The prior question, of course, is whether
we know enough about resource situations and the structure
of resource management regimes to: (1) recommend a
specific regime in a particular resource situation; or
(2) analyze the fact situation in a particular resource
setting and make pertinent statements about needed change
to solve an observed problem?

Each of the systems under discussion this week has a
fixed capacity to support humans. However, too often we
see these systems criticized because they will not continue
to support ever-increasing populations. In fact, agriculture practiced on private lands also has a finite
capacity to absorb more people. With conventional agriculture, fewer and fewer people are able to be supported as
"progress" occurs, and the surplus production is used to
support consumption in urban places. It is certainly no
fault of a particular resource--nor of its management
regime--that a finite population is required; it is wrong
to think otherwise.

If we escape the logical trap of expecting ever-
increasing populations to be supported by these natural
resource complexes, then we are free to ask more

pertinent questions. I suggest that one of these concerns
the sustainability of a particular use regime pending
further articulation of ultimate resource and user
disposition. If there is a decision to overexploit the
resource, then let that be a conscious one, not one made
by default. If there is to be a decision to exclude
people from using the resource, then let that decision
be a conscious one, not one that follows inexorably from
resource exhaustion.

The problem, quite often, is that these resource
systems are asked to absorb the very people who cannot be
absorbed by the more conventional agricultural regimes
found on private lands. In essence, people are marginal-
ized, and the marginal ecosystems are asked to take on
those sloughed off from the highly commercialized lands;
the exclusion rights that run with fee-simple land
redirect people to the marginal ecosystems. It hardly
seems fair to condemn these resource complexes for failing
to do what the commercialized ecosystems cannot do.

A common property regime is really a people management
regime. The presumption of a private property regime is
that people management is not an interest of the collective. Indeed, the premise is that the sum of actions
taken by a large number of atomistic entrepreneurs will
contribute to the larger public good. With common
property regimes, the presumption is that the interests
of the group transcend the individual interests--at least
with respect to the use of certain resources during
particular times of the year.

Turning to a discussion of the performance of common
property regimes, I suggest that we consider a management
goal to be a level of sustainability of such renewable
resources that gives future generations the option to
continue such management or to liquidate the resource.
This goal does not advocate sustained yield for its own
sake, but rather casts sustained yield as an explicit
human choice that passes on to the future what we have
inherited from our past. Each successive generation
retains the option of destroying the resource, but carries
the burden of breaking the "golden rule" of resource use.
This management goal says, in effect, let us not exhaust
natural resources by accident or by default; if we do
exhaust the resource, then let it be explicitly, so that
we might then have a plan for what we will do when the
resource is gone.

I support purposeful sustainability as well as
purposeful exhaustion, if that should be the social

decision. As resources are sustained, future generations have the option of continued sustainability or of purposeful exhaustion. Of course there are economically optimal plans for utilizing both renewable and nonrenewable resources, but that must be understood as only one of several possible management strategies.

While our focus this week has often been with the management and protection of natural resources rather than with those who depend on such resources, we should recall that development assistance is equally to be concerned with preventing a continued decline in human welfare within degraded resource regimes. In most instances, improved resource management can restore or improve human welfare. In a sense, we are dealing with problems of human relations in common property regimes. This degradation of the management regime is often less visible than is the degradation of the physical resource. If development assistance can correct the degraded management regimes, then human welfare will surely increase.

ON CONCEPTS AND LANGUAGE

Throughout the week I have observed a persistent and potentially troublesome problem with language and concepts. I would start by asking that we ought to be very careful in our use of the terms "common pool resources" and "common property resources." We have not yet arrived at a consistent definition of what is, and what is not, a common pool resource. More seriously, to talk of common property resources may leave the impression that there are certain natural resources that are only controlled by common property arrangements. After all, do we ever talk of "private property resources?"

I believe that is preferable to talk of resource management regimes. There are natural resources that are managed (even mismanaged) by common property regimes, just as there are natural resources managed (and, yes, mismanaged) by private property regimes. But to talk generically of common property resources is to suggest that there are resources that belong uniquely to a particular control/management/institutional regime. Of course this is false.

Hence, let us talk of alternative management regimes--really institutional structures--and then explore the efficacy of those regimes for a specific natural

resource in a particular situation. We then have four
candidate regimes: (1) open access regimes; (2) common
property regimes; (3) private property regimes; and
(4) state property regimes.

Moving to the more detailed matter of language and
concepts, I believe it would lend continuity to our future
discussions of common property regimes if we adopted some
consistent definitions.

I would propose that we regard a primary decision
unit as one that is the basic economic decision unit
in a society with respect to managing assets, allocating
resources, and for managing risk. The primary decision
unit (PDU) is a domain of redistribution of the most
primitive sort; it is the minimal management unit in the
society under study. For some societies, the PDU may be
the individual, in others it may be the family, and in
still others it may be the kinship group. Of course the
PDU will vary depending upon the particular management
decision under consideration. This unit is worthy of
definition because the very essence of the "common" is
that more than one PDU is involved in its use. We must
also recognize that for different times of the year, and
with respect to different assets, the primary decision
unit will differ. In the Swiss Alps, for example, the
family is the PDU for arable lands, but the co-equal
owners of the alp become the relevant decision unit
during the summer grazing season. When multiple families come together to make decisions regarding summer
grazing, we might regard this as a resource decision
unit.

A resource decision unit is a constellation of primary
decision units that are jointly involved in the management
and control of a common resource. In common property
regimes, it is the resource decision unit (RDU) that will
determine rules for deciding who is in the group and who
is not, as well as the rules controlling use rates of
those recognized as being "in."

The discussion this week has also suffered by persistent yet inconsistent use of the term "property."
Property is a secure expectation over some benefit stream,
with the security arising from collective sanctions and
enforcement. Property represents the owner(s), and the
thing(s) owned, against all others with an interest in the
thing(s). Property is the social convention that
precludes all others from converting their interest in the
asset (or income stream) into a claim. These others have
duties to observe the rights of the owners.

Once this basic truth is apprehended, it becomes logically impossible to denote open access situations as common property. For where group size is not controlled, and/or any potential user may make unrestricted claims on the asset, then it is not possible for any particular user to have a claim to a benefit stream; all the users have is access. The popular phrase "everybody's property is nobody's property" is thus seen to be nonsense. What should be said is that "everybody's access is nobody's property."

We have heard much this week about free riding, yet it is not yet clear what we have meant. I propose that we regard free riding as the shifting costs others bear as a result of actions I take either: (1) because I expect others will do the same; (2) because I do not know (or care) what others will be doing; or (3) because I am convinced that I will be the only one to do so and thus will not be noticed.

Transaction costs play a prominent role in the use of common pool resources. By transaction costs economists mean the real or monetary costs of: (1) gathering information; (2) arranging bargains with others; and (3) enforcing bargains that have been struck.

Property regimes represent specific aspects of the broader institutional structure in a society. By institutions we mean the structure of rules and conventions that define individuals vis-à-vis others, as well as with respect to objects of value. An example of institutions would be the rights and duties that define users with respect to a common resource. Organizations, then, which are often confused with institutions, become entities that exist pursuant to an institutional structure--examples would be a water-user's association, a panchayat, or a fishermen's group.

Consider now the four types of management regimes over natural resources. Under private property, it is the primary decision unit that retains ownership. This means that PDUs can independently determine use rates, can reap the income from the asset, and can alienate it at will. The institutional structure is such that PDUs retain exclusive rights over the resource.

Under common property, resource decision units (RDUs) are formed when multiple PDUs unite with respect to the management and control of the particular resource. Each PDU retains important rights in the service flows from the resource (the income stream), yet each PDU also has certain duties with respect to other PDUs that are considered part

of the resource decision unit. The essence of common
property is that a certain number of PDUs have explicit
rights to be included in the management of the resource, as
well to share the income stream arising from the resource.
But with those rights also come duties to respect the
rights of other PDUs. Common property can often be thought
of as "private property with consensus" among the relevant
PDUs.

State property gives no rights to primary decision
units, yet each PDU has duties. A military reservation is
an example of state property.

An open access regime is one in which each PDU has
access to the resource. There is no property in an open
access situation since there are no secure claims on
resource services.

In essence, the management regimes under study this
week have consisted of a constellation of rights and
duties, and privileges and exposures. These institutional
arrangements give rise to patterns of interaction among
resource users that will determine the ultimate fate of the
resource base--and so of the dependent populations.
Management regimes are not successful when those institutional arrangements lead to counterproductive patterns of
interaction vis-à-vis the resource. The problem for the
scientific community is to learn as much as we can of the
intricate relationships that exist among the ecosystem,
technique, and the institutional arrangements that
influence human interactions. This has been an inspiring
session, but the real work still lies ahead.

26

Issues of Definition and Theory: Some Conclusions and Hypotheses
Elinor Ostrom

Pauline Peters made some perceptive comments last evening that have stimulated some of these remarks. She first indicated that it was important to recognize that many seemingly different resource systems, previously described with different terminologies, share central characteristics of common-pool resource systems. Pauline stressed, however, that it was also important to recognize that different types of resource systems had been brought together under this broad unifying concept; she urged us to be careful to distinguish among the systems we examine.

This is the way that I view the scientific endeavor. The world in which we live is so complex that our first problem is how to cluster phenomena so that we can understand some processes in the most general way. It is hard to develop theoretically useful ways of clustering phenomena, but once we've done so, we must be careful not to let the use of terms that focus on similarities fool us into thinking that everything clustered together is similar on all dimensions.

In our discussion yesterday, Ford Runge talked about culture and the specific rules used by individuals to organize contractual arrangements; he characterized both as being important in reducing the time and effort required to organize joint activities. Without cultural norms and rule systems, every pair of individuals would have to

organize each and every activity using a short-term contract. Today, they would have to agree to form a team to
go hunting. Tomorrow, they would have to agree to build a
house. Still later, they would have to agree on ways to
bring water to the village. Instead of spending substantial time and effort in negotiating each of these short-
term contracts, individuals can develop generally accepted
rules governing community life. Such rules state who will
do the hunting, and how the hunt will be shared, as well as
who will build the houses, and how housing will be
allocated. Specialization of labor and definite rules
for allocating tasks and benefits save lots of time in unpleasant haggling over how individuals organize their
efforts to survive.

The classification of the world into classes and
subclasses of events is also a great economizer. Once the
concept of a tree is developed, one does not have to treat
each tree as a unique event. By giving things general
names, many properties of these unique events can be viewed
as the same. General ways of relating to the specific
instances could be developed.

We are attempting to classify the world into the most
economical set of concepts to enable us to understand the
similarities and differences of processes associated with
broad classes of individual events. No single method of
classifying events will serve all purposes. Many of those
attending this conference have developed different, but
effective, scientific classification systems based on major
attributes of biological systems. It took a long time for
biologists to develop the most economic and effective way
of classifying biological species and the process continues. After many trials and much scholarly conflict,
biologists have developed a relatively useful general
scheme for organizing phenomena into an inclusive,
conceptual hierarchy.

Knowing that an animal is a mammal immediately conveys
substantial information about expected behavior. We
immediately know, for example, that young mammals are
dependent upon the mother for a long period of time before
they are ready to go forth and seek their own food. Being
told that an animal is a mammal is not, however, the last
of the knowledge that can be obtained from biological
classification systems. All members are further subdivided into an inclusive, conceptual hierarchy. While
some theoretical generalizations can be made about all
mammals, other propositions are made only about a subset of

mammals. Still other propositions can be made about only
a subset of a subset of mammals.

Returning to our task, we are trying to understand
how difficult property systems affect the incentives of
participants, their interdependent behavior, and the outcomes they produce for themselves and others. Several of
us have been trying to develop a system for identifying a
broad class of resource systems, which we have called
common pool resource systems. We have then attempted to
ascertain the problems of organizing human behavior in
relation to this entire class of resource systems. We will
initially make two types of errors in this endeavor, since
we are still relatively new at it. This is the thrust of
Pauline Peters' cautionary note (see this volume). The
two types of errors are:

1. A wrong assertion that a proposition about relationships between resource systems and property
   systems holds for all common pool resource systems
   when in fact the proposition holds only for a
   subset of such systems.

2. A wrong assertion that a proposition about relationships between resource systems and property
   systems holds for only a subset of such systems
   when the proposition actually holds for the entire
   class.

Peters is concerned that the emphasis on a general
level would lead to the first type of error. She is wise
to warn of the dangers of an overemphasis on the similarities of all common pool resources. However, too much
emphasis on the particular leads to the second type of
error. In this instance, scholars assume that a proposition is related only to a specific type of situation when
it actually holds for a broader class of situations. As
long as scientific discourse develops around very specific
situations, we are apt to make errors of the second type.

My strategy to cope with these epistemological threats
would be to urge that we first try to develop broad, conceptual definitions and theoretical propositions stated at
as broad a level as possible. When we conduct research and
find that such propositions do not hold at the broadest
level, we can begin to proceed downward to ascertain how
many further conditions must be met before the proposition
appears to have scientific warrant. Eventually we either

reject the proposition as describing no "real" situation, or find the appropriate level of generality. I think this is a better strategy than starting with a discretely stated proposition.

Let us then begin to identify the relevant character-istics needed to most economically identify classes and subclasses of common pool resources on the one hand, and of organizational forms on the other. First we turn to the world of events. For a long time, economists classi-fied the world of events--commodity space--into two broad classes: "pure private goods" and "pure public goods." This classification was based on variation along two analytical dimensions: exclusion and jointness of use. Purely private goods can be excluded at relatively low cost from those who did not produce the good. Such goods are consumed individually and not jointly. My consumption of a private good subtracts that particular item completely from your set of options. Pure public goods have the opposite characteristics. Once such a good is produced, it is difficult or costly to exclude others from consumption. Further, my consumption of a pure public good does not subtract from the availability of that good to you. The concepts of "pure private goods" and "pure public goods" group broad classes of phenomena that share the extreme points along two dimensions of exclusion and jointness.

Dividing the world into two classes of events based on two (rather than a single) dimension, should have hinted that a dichotomy may not be the most useful way to classify phenomena for the purpose of understanding how organiza-tional arrangements work. Further, referring to the events in the world--the phenomena--by names ("private" and "public") that are most closely related to the presumed "optimal" organizational arrangements for their pro-vision has also created confusion. The phenomena in the world were given names that were too similar to those of the organizational arrangements that many thought were needed to make the best decisions related to their provision.

Looking briefly at this earlier classification, we can see somewhat better where we were. As shown in Figure 1, the concepts of exclusion and jointness were used to define two types of phenomena: private goods and public goods. Similarly, the concept of free entry was used to distinguish two broad types of organizational arrangements: the private market sector and the public sector.

The market has been conceptualized as an area in which

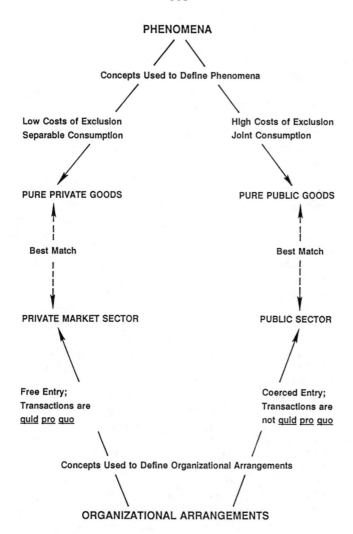

FIGURE 1 The dichotomous view of phenomena and organizational
         arrangements.

individuals--both buyers and sellers--are free to enter
and exit. Contracts are made by mutual consent. Transactions involved quid pro quo relationships: something
specific is exchanged for something else specific. The
public sector has also been characterized using entry
rules. Here the fundamental relationship is that one can

be coerced into a jurisdiction and may find it costly to leave. In a modern "state," there is no place to go to escape coerced payment to some public jurisdiction or, most likely, several jurisdictions. Choice of a residence carries with it membership in a set of public juris- dictions to which one will pay taxes. We cannot engage in quid pro quo relationships with our public jurisdictions at the individual level. We cannot directly tell the U.S. government that we would like so much national defense this year and so many social services. We must try to do some of this through the imperfect mechanism of electing representatives to articulate our preferences for us.

Microeconomic theory concludes that market arrange- ments lead to optimal patterns of production and allocation of pure private goods, but that some form of organization in the public sector is necessary to obtain optimal levels of public goods. When the opposite organization is used to produce either type of good, institutional failure is predicted. Dichotomizing both the world of phenomena and the world of organizational arrangements proved to be a useful initial strategy for considerable theoretical development. But these dichotomies are not sufficient to analyze the problems of concern to those of us interested in common pool resource systems and common property organizational arrangements.

We are grappling with a mixed phenomenon that has attributes of both pure private goods and pure collective goods. Similarly, common property management arrangements are neither simple market nor public sector arrangements. A definition of a broad class of phenomena called "common pool resources" is: a natural or man-made facility that produces a flow of use units per unit of time (or several flows of different types of use units) where exclusion from the resource is difficult or costly to achieve and the resource can potentially be utilized by more than one individual or agent simultaneously or sequentially.[1]

This is still a working definition and needs further refinement, but it seems to capture the broad class of phenomena that have been discussed at this conference. And it clearly separates the phenomena from the institutions used to regulate its use. Institutional arrangements will be discussed below.

By distinguishing between the resource system and the flow of use units produced by such a system, one can use the attributes of jointness and exclusion to identify a third, broad class of events relatively well. The problem

of exclusion is related to the resource system itself:
the ocean fishery, the common pasture, the forest lands,
the large irrigation system, etc. Once exclusion is
conceptualized as a variable, one recognizes that the cost
of excluding individuals from resource systems varies
across different types of common pool resources, and even
within types of common pool resources, such as fisheries.
The problem of devising a system of enforceable rules to
exclude anyone from an ocean fishery, as contrasted to an
offshore fishery, is obviously of a different order of
magnitude.

While many individuals can jointly consume use units
from the same common pool resource, the actual consumption
by one person is subtractive in terms of the use units.
The problems of congestion and degradation illustrate the
subtractive nature of using a common pool resource; these
problems are not characteristic of pure public goods. My
consumption of scientific knowledge, or any other pure
public good, does not subtract from your consumption of the
same knowledge. On the other hand, my gathering morel
mushrooms on the commons subtracts from the number of
mushrooms left for you. Congestion and degradation are the
key problems of interest across all of the case studies.
Viewed this way, common pool resources share one attribute
in common with pure public goods (cost of exclusion) and
one attribute with pure private goods (separable
consumption).

Turning to the organizational or institutional
spectrum, it is also possible to identify organizational
arrangements in addition to the private market sector and
public sector (see Figure 2). Common property management
systems are those that have some clear-cut role for who is
and is not a member: the "ins" and the "outs." As I have
thought about these entry rules during the week, it seems
to me that entry into a common property organization
arrangement is either by rights or by invitation. By
right, you were born, or otherwise incorporated, into this
tribe, village, extended family, or other collectivity.
Thus, you have a right to the use of property held by the
collectivity. When entry is by invitation, it means that
both you and those whom you are joining must agree that you
can become a member. Entry into a cooperative is of this
latter fashion.[2] Further, common property management
systems involve some form of regulated use patterns.

The open access sector is characterized by unrestricted
entry and unregulated use. Unfortunately, many scholars

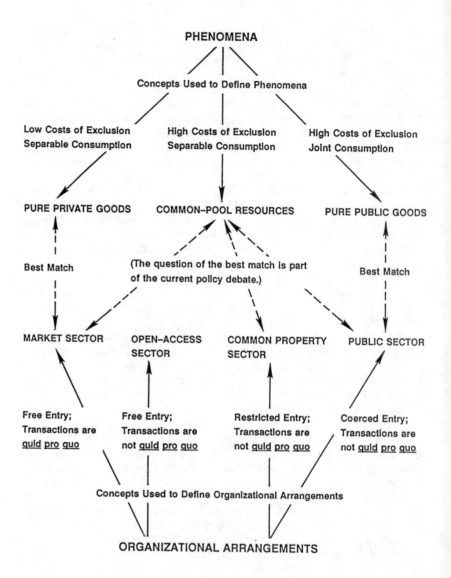

FIGURE 2   A more complex view of phenomena and organizational
           arrangements.

confuse open access arrangements with common property
arrangements. As Bromley and Runge have argued in this
volume, this confusion needs to be alleviated. Open

access arrangements lead to many perverse results when used with any type of good. Common property arrangements may, on the other hand, work very well in helping individuals to manage some common pool resource systems. Thus, we can think of at least four types of arrangements that could be used in relationship to phenomena in the world.[3]

The key question is that of a good match between the resource system and the organizational arrangements used to manage the resource. In regard to common pool resource systems, different prescriptions are made. Some analysts focus entirely on the separability of consumption of these resources and argue that rights to specific quantities of use units should be defined and managed by arrangements similar to a private market; this is the privatization camp. Others focus entirely on the problem of exclusion from these resources and argue that the management of these resources should be turned over to central government authorities; this is the central government camp. Others, including some of the participants at this conference, argue that in regard to many, but not necessarily all, common pool resources, it is possible to use common property management methods. I tend to identify with this third camp.

The successful case studies discussed here demonstrate that some common property management systems work very well. The cases also provide evidence that more common property systems exist than central government and donor agency officials presume. On the other hand, considerable evidence exists of common pool resource systems that have not been successfully managed. Major fisheries have disappeared. Traditional grazing areas have become deserts. Irrigation systems have been neglected.

Thus, the question of how organizational arrangements are well-matched to common pool resource systems is key to the further understanding of the management of such resources. How such organizational arrangements survive over time is the next question requiring further work. Finally, the question of what factors enhance the performance of common property management systems must be raised.

Let me turn first to the issue of origin. To examine this question, let us first define the concept of a user group. A user group is a set of individuals that makes (or has claims to make) use of a particular common pool resource. A user group may live in or nearby the common pool resource or live far away and travel to the resource (which itself may shift locations) to harvest use units.

Jim Roumasset used the term "latent group" at the conference to describe the same concept. A user group is
"latent as a group" until those in the group establish
rules to define membership and order activities within the
group. Entry rules can be used as a distinguishing characteristic between latent user groups, with no organizational
arrangements, and some form of a user group organization
(UGO) that may be able to undertake some form of common
property management.

A UGO has at least a minimal rule for defining who is
and who is not a member. When membership is associated
with access to a common pool resource, a UGO is a minimal
form of organization that may be able to undertake common
property management. In addition to making and enforcing
entry and exit rules, UGOs frequently also engage in other
activities, such as: (1) making and enforcing rules to
regulate patterns of use of the resource (e.g., partitioning rules--who, how much, and when various individuals with
particular types of claims can consume use units);
(2) assessing penalties on outsiders and insiders for rule
infractions and developing conflict resolution mechanisms;
and (3) organizing investment in the enhancement of the
common pool resource as well as raising revenue through
diverse arrangements.

A major, though tentative, finding coming from the
conference is that it is highly likely that any relatively
small residential group that has lived for a long period of
time in close proximity to and dependent upon a common pool
resource system of moderate scarcity (given the demands
made by users) will have organized some type of UGO.

This tentative finding formed the underlying premise
for our recommendation to policymakers: that host country
and donor officials should assume the local organization
exists until they establish otherwise, instead of assuming
that no local organization exists in relationship to common
pool resource systems. This recommendation, which reverses
the burden of proof currently in vogue, is based on an
implicit proposition. The underlying proposition is this:

o   If not prevented from exercising local
    organizational capacities by central governments,
    UGOs will be organized by user groups whenever:

    -- the user group is relatively small and has
        lived in close proximity and dependent upon a
        common pool resource for a long time;

-- the flow of use units is moderately scarce
   when compared with the demands that individuals
   within the user group make upon the common pool
   resource; and

-- the resource is subject to multiple uses
   (simultaneous and sequential) and hence
   requires careful coordination and management
   of use.

Now we have the beginnings of a testable proposition of
the type that Roumasset pushed us toward last evening. The
proposition, as stated, applies to most smaller, common pool
resources that exist on land or near to a shore.[4] By
definition, it excludes ocean fisheries. If we now find
situations meeting these conditions and no UGO, the proposition will have to be revised to add further restrictions
based on further evidence.

This proposition is arrived at inductively from the
cases and discussion this past week. It would be possible
to derive this proposition from a relatively simple theory
of the type that Ford Runge sketched here yesterday,
focusing on the relative benefits and costs of different
types of contracts among individuals to organize production
activity in diverse ways.

This initial proposition states that, given particular
conditions, a UGO will eventually be organized. It is also
possible to generalize further from our cases and discussion
about the relative difficulty or ease that diverse user
groups may face in attempting to create UGOs. The fewer
difficulties that a user group faces, the faster the group
should form a UGO. Thus, these propositions are related
to the speed of organizing. When scarcity of a common
pool resource becomes apparent to user groups, the speed
with which they are able to organize is dependent upon:

1. Some heterogeneity of asset structure. Remember our
    discussion of the need for some entrepreneur-
    ship to get an organization started even though
    homogeneity may help later. The relevant example is
    the businessman who helped start the fisher-
    man's cooperatives in Turkey.

2. Some prior or concurrent experience with other
    local organizations that provide an easy model to
    copy. Negotiating the constitution of a UGO from

scratch is much costlier than borrowing the basic structure of a constitution from an extant organization. The "model" UGO may be in the immediate neighborhood or may be in a neighboring village--I assume that organizational innovation and diffusion behave somewhat like technological innovation and diffusion--spreading out from some central locations.

3. The availability of a general purpose UGO that may be able to take on additional purposes. Many village organizations do several different activities, including the management of local common pool resource systems.

4. The homogeneity in the community in terms of the uses made of the common pool resource system. Two different groups who see their task as using the CPR in conflicting manners would make it more difficult for a UGO to develop.

5. The users' shared perceptions that the risks involved in continued open access arrangements may be reduced or better spread across the community by such an organization. The users' shared perception of the nature of their common situation may itself be enhanced by cultural homogeneity, value systems, and potentially by the size of the group. Communication costs are much lower in a smaller group and information about scarcity needs to be shared and discussed.

6. The physical unity of the user community. It is harder for two fishing villages located on either side of a large lake to organize into one user group organization. Two UGOs may develop with considerable intergroup conflict over the lake.

The above propositions all need to be more carefully stated and to be integrated into a more general theoretical framework.[5] Right now, they are simply an initial effort to summarize many of the relationships discussed at this conference.

Additional discussions at the conference turned to the identification of factors that participants thought would enhance the likelihood of UGOs' surviving. Some factors discussed included:

1. Development of a clear-cut and unambiguous set of rules that all participants can know and agree upon. The fewer rules used to organize activities, relative to the complexity of the activities, the more likely that individuals can understand them, remember them, and follow them, and the more likely that infractions will be interpreted by all as infractions. Thus, punishment will be perceived to be meted out to those who have broken the rules and not to others. Remember our discussion of the multiple functions of the simple rule: "you have to live locally to use this system." That rule leads to enhanced local knowledge, reciprocity and trust, lower decision-making costs and solves the problem of exclusion.

2. Clear enforcement of rules by officials backed up by social enforcement by users. I think this is very important. Social enforcement needs to be there at all times. One's co-workers are ever-present. If they are willing to impose mild social sanctions on infractions swiftly and clearly, then the cost of guards or other officials can be much lower.

3. Slow exogenous changes. Or, if rapid external changes come, they should come one change at a time--not population growth, and major changes in technology, and hostile government, etc.

4. Internally adaptive institutional arrangements. One of our discussions focused on the necessity for a creative use of conflict so that the source and extent of problems could be discovered. The creative uses of conflict could lead participants in a UGO to make new rules governing use patterns when the old rules do not appear to serve the community of users well.

5. Different decision rules for different purposes, if many purposes are involved. A single decision maker may be most effective in regard to some types

of rapidly changing variables. A council may be most effective when concerns exist over equity or distribution. A broad consensus or extraordinary majority may be most effective in deciding on actions that involve major sacrifice or penalties.

6. The capacity of a UGO to nest into a set of larger organizations for dealing with the external environment or for dealing with a larger segment of a common pool resource. If the UGO has effectively organized a tertiary irrigation distribution channel, for example, users of this channel need to be able to communicate with the operations of the headwaters from time to time.

Having now started to identify some factors that may be associated with survival of a UGO, it is important to bear in mind that simple survival is not a sufficient condition for effective performance. The survival of a UGO over a long period leads one to presume that the UGO is doing something well. However, the key question is, "what is it doing well?" For some UGOs, the answer may be that the only thing it is doing well is surviving. Unless UGOs are in highly competitive environments where selection pressures tend to eliminate inefficient and inequitable UGOs, we cannot assume that those that survive are performing well. If UGOs were firms in a highly competitive market, the theory of market processes would enable us to infer that survivors use efficient, long-term strategies (even though the survivors may not have consciously selected these strategies through a full analysis).

Some UGOs have extraordinary powers not available to private firms in a competitive market. These powers enable such UGOs to survive even though performing poorly. UGOs that can coerce membership and contributions to collective actions (e.g., they have public powers) can survive even when most of their members do not evaluate them as performing efficiently or equitably. It is even possible for a UGO that has survived for a long time to generate more costs than benefits. The latter can occur when membership is coerced and the costs of existence are high. Consequently, it is especially important not to assume that surviving UGOs, which have full governmental powers, automatically perform well.

UGOs operating over a long period without full governmental powers--established and maintained primarily through voluntary agreement--are more likely to generate benefits that exceed costs. Unless the users badly misperceive benefits and costs, it is hard to imagine how strictly voluntary UGOs could survive unless net benefits were positive. In a strictly voluntary association, members can leave the UGO at any point when they perceive that costs of participation exceed the benefits.

We discussed several factors at these meetings--in addition to those identified as conducive to emergence and to survival--that some participants thought should enhance the performance of UGOs in maintaining withdrawal of use units below maximum sustainable yield in an efficient and equitable manner. One broad set of conditions was concerned with the "match" of the membership of the UGO and that of the user group. A second consideration involved the relationship between the incidence of benefits and the incidence of costs derived from the operation of the UGO. A third factor was the knowledge generated by users about the CPR and about user preference,
benefits, and costs.

These ideas and concerns deserve further attention, and should be explored more thoroughly in the future.

NOTES

1. Given the importance of developing a set of technical
terms that scientists trained in many different disciplines (biology, political science, economics, anthropology, sociology, forestry, management, and history) could
use to communicate with one another about common property
resource management, I circulated several versions of some
of the definitions and propositions contained herein.
During the conference, I received thoughtful and critical
responses to these initial efforts from Fikret Berkes,
Piers Blaikie, Edwin Connerly, David Feeny, Timothy Jessup,
Ronald Oakerson, Pauline Peters, Emery Roe, and Ford Runge.

2. It must be pointed out that a private firm or any
corporate entity is also of this type, and that the model
that Ford Runge has explicated during our meetings is
similar to the model used by Coase and Williamson to show
the benefits of establishing firms to reduce the contractual costs of market arrangements. So, by formulating the
problem in this fashion, we already have models of human
organization available that we can "try on" to see how well
they fit the general class of phenomena of interest to us.

3. This classification of organizational arrangements is
similar to that presented by Daniel Bromley in his final
summary. Bromley relied on the distribution of rights and
duties to arrive at his classification.

4. The size of the common property resource (CPR) is a
factor. A small residential group using only a small
portion of a large CPR (such as the Great Lakes) may not
organize to manage the CPR because of its incapacity to
affect the resource system. On the other hand, small user
group organizations (UGOs) may manage parts of a large CPR,
such as grazing lands, relatively effectively for long
periods of time if they are able to exclude others from
their territory.

5. Since the conference, I have tried to develop the
rudiments of such a theory. A working paper describing
these efforts is available by writing to me at the Workshop
in Political Theory and Policy Analysis, 513 North Park,
Indiana University, Bloomington, Indiana 47405, U.S.A.

27

Concluding Statement
Pauline E. Peters

The papers by Bromley and Ostrom presented their views of the major findings and conclusions that emerged from the conference. In this final brief section, we wish to summarize some of the main points and directions for future research and action raised in our plenary sessions and in the smaller groups' discussions that were organized by resource type and by topical theme.

PERFORMANCE

The studies demonstrated the widespread use of resources managed under common property regimes, and the important role these resources play in the diversified income-producing strategies used by a substantial majority of the world's population. Common property regimes are especially important for the large numbers of poor peasants and small farmers, but others benefit as well.
   A central topic at the conference was that uses of resources are as often competitive as they are complementary. For example, the practice of allowing cattle to graze postharvest stubble does not interfere with cultivation based on a single crop season, but where permanent water sources enable double cropping, grazing livestock can endanger the crops. Similarly, where newly introduced

water sources facilitate year-round pasturing of cattle,
the transhumant movements of other herds will compete with
year-round users of the pastures. It was made clear that
where there are competing uses and/or users, and where the
economic and other values of the resources are changing--
circumstances that are connected--there has tended to be
increased stress on both the management regime and on the
resource(s) being used. It thus becomes important, in any
situation of perceived environmental or social stress, to
untangle the relations among uses, among users, and among
the varying influences on use (such as rapid increase or
decrease in human or animal populations, change in technology, political and administrative organization, and so
forth).

Measures of performance were considered to be
difficult to specify; more work is needed in conceptual-
izing and operationalizing them for each type of resource.
Participants also emphasized that measures of performance
must be selected carefully in relation to the appropriate unit of analysis, which will vary from the individual user, through a particular common property regime,
to a set of such regimes. The questions to be asked,
then, are whose equity and whose efficiency, or whose
success and whose failure are we measuring in assessing
performance?

Among the relations that were hypothesized as being
crucial to performance were:

o   The size of regime and the size of the management
    and/or user group
o   Relative scarcity
o   Homogeneity and/or heterogeneity*
o   Legitimacy
o   Clarity of rules
o   Interaction between rules and practices
o   Place of the regime in wider social and political
    structures.

---

*Several dimensions were noted--one use by different
groups, multiple uses by one group, multiple uses
by different groups, type and extent of
social/political/economic differentiation among
users/managers.

RESEARCH

Several topics were considered pertinent for further research. These are summarized below:

o   Cross-resource linkages and interactions
     (e.g., agro-pastoral; irrigation and fisheries;
     forestry and irrigation or pastoral). The issues
     here are: (1) to understand the way in which a
     common property regime operates within systems of
     production, rather than seeing it as an isolate;
     and (2) to document the implications of these
     interactions for levels of livelihood and
     consumption among different categories of resource
     users.

o   Bureaucratic administration and cross-sector
     linkages and interactions. For example, the
     management and use of resources are frequently
     affected by different administrative structures
     that are often at cross purposes or act in
     ignorance of each other. These relations are
     critical to an understanding of how a common
     property regime is working, yet often are not
     included in such an assessment.

o   Indigenous or local knowledge concerning different
     resources, regimes, rules and practices. A
     frequent observation in the conference papers and
     discussions was that local users of common property
     resources are often more competent and
     knowledgeable as resource managers than are highly
     trained technicians from elsewhere, because local
     residents and users know the exact local physical
     conditions and local history of the resource so
     well (as opposed to knowing only general principles
     of resource management that may not apply smoothly
     to local conditions). In addition, the definitions
     of resources often differ between local users and
     outside experts (see, for example, the paper by
     Messerschmidt) and, unless this difference is
     recognized, misunderstanding and misdirection are
     the frequent results.

o   The relations between national legal systems
     regulating resource use and nongovernment systems.
     It is important to note that the use of

the term "informal" to refer to nongovernmental and/or noncodified systems of resource management is inappropriate and misleading. As many of the cases demonstrate, these systems are usually highly formalized in the sense of including rules, expected and conventional practices, dispute-settling mechanisms, and sanctions, even though codification may be absent. Two foci for research seem important: (1) the reciprocal influence between the rules and practices of the national legal systems and local systems including actual and potential conflict; and (2) the role of government recognition of local systems of management and resolution, including enabling legislation, as well as more indirect administrative action such as taxation.

o   Comparative contemporary studies are needed. These should be both within a region and cross-regional, and should examine institutional alternatives and critical conditions of performance.

o   Coordinated, cross-disciplinary research is also important. It would facilitate more fully considered studies of common property regimes. For example, the study of a rangeland-forestry resource system might be carried out by a team including plant and animal biologists, ecologists, economists, sociologists, anthropologists, and policy and law specialists.

o   Time-related studies must be conducted. These would give comparative insights and provide a foundation for valid generalizations about common property regimes. The question here is how are we to study and learn from changes over time in these institutional arrangements? First, historical studies (such as the Japanese case presented by McKean, and that comparing the English and Andean systems by Campbell and Godoy) are invaluable for providing comparative evidence and hypotheses. Second, longitudinal data can be gathered by systematic observation of particular systems over extended periods of time. Both of these methods would increase our knowledge base and our ability to test hypotheses.

ACTION

Most action would be specific to the resource, regime, and situation. However, the following general points were made:

o   Provide small-scale infrastructure (such as communications or processing technologies) that facilitates management in common property regimes.

o   Establish data collection and monitoring procedures for the communication of technical and other necessary information as well as mechanisms for communication of the views, opinions, and problems of the users of common property resources.

o   Build the administrative capacity for handling the diversity that typifies common property regimes; in particular, combine a capacity for decentralized management structures with a centralized information system.

o   Be particularly wary of inappropriate legal imposition (in legislative and judicial form). Common property management systems often will be found to require legal recognition. Also, enabling legislation may be useful, both direct (e.g., recognizing and providing support or sanctions for existing management systems) and indirect (e.g., taxation, group organization, limited liability regulation). But extreme caution is urged: the burden of proof that systems are not working and will benefit from interference from outside must rest with the potential intervenors.

o   Prepare training manuals intended to inform and sensitize donor agencies and project officers with reference to current knowledge, analytical frameworks, and critical questions about understanding common property regimes.

AUTHORS AND PARTICIPANTS

Conference on Common Property Resource Management
Governor Calvert House
Annapolis, Maryland
April 21-26, 1985

J. E. M. Arnold*
Oxford Forestry Institute
University of Oxford
South Parks Road
Oxford   OX1 3RB
ENGLAND

Neal E. Artz*
Department of Range Science
Utah State University
Logan, Utah   84322
U.S.A.

Joan Atherton
Office of Policy Development and Program Review
Bureau for Program and Policy Coordination
Agency for International Development
Washington, D.C.   20523
U.S.A.

David Atwood
Office of Rural and Institutional Development
Bureau for Science and Technology
Agency for International Development
Washington, D.C.   20523
U.S.A.

---

*Authors of proceedings papers.

Fikret Berkes*
Institute of Urban and Environmental Studies
Brock University
St. Catherines, Ontario   L2S 3A1
CANADA

Piers M. Blaikie*
School of Development Studies
University of East Anglia
Norwich   NR4 7TJ
ENGLAND

Clem B. Bribitzer
Fisheries Management
National Oceanic and Atmospheric Administration
Department of Commerce
Washington, D.C.   20230
U.S.A.

Daniel Bromley*
Department of Agricultural Economics
University of Wisconsin
427 Lorch Street
Madison, Wisconsin   53706
U.S.A.

Bruce Campbell*
Department of Geography
Queen's University of Belfast
University Road
Belfast   BT7 1NN
NORTHERN IRELAND

J. Gabriel Campbell*
c/o Ford Foundation
55 Lodi Estate
New Delhi   110 003
INDIA

Kenneth M. Chomitz
Department of Population Health and Nutrition
Policy and Research Division
The World Bank
1818 H Street, N.W.
Washington, D.C.   20433
U.S.A.

Edwin F. Connerley
National Association of Schools of Public Affairs
  and Administration
Suite 520
1120 G Street, N.W.
Washington, D.C. 20005
U.S.A.

John C. Cordell*
The Ethnographic Institute
21 Glen Drive
Sausalito, California 94965
U.S.A.

Wilfrido D. Cruz*
Center for Policy and Development Studies
University of the Philippines at Los Banos
College, Laguna 3720
PHILIPPINES

Michael McD. Dow
Board on Science and Technology for
  International Development
National Research Council
2101 Constitution Avenue, N.W.
Washington, D.C. 20418
U.S.A.

Ahmed Driouchi
Department of Social Sciences
Ecole Nationale d'Agriculture
B.P. S/40
Meknès
MOROCCO

K. William Easter*
Department of Agricultural and Applied Economics
University of Minnesota
1991 Buford Avenue
St. Paul, Minnesota 55108
U.S.A.

M. Taghi Farvar
International Union for Conservation of Nature
  and Natural Resources
Avenue du Mont-Blanc
1196 Gland
SWITZERLAND

David H. Feeny*
Department of Clinical Epidemiology and Biostatistics
McMaster University
Hamilton, Ontario L8S 4M4
CANADA

Shirley Fisk
Office of the Administrator
National Oceanic and Atmospheric
  Administration
Department of Commerce
Washington, D.C. 20230
U.S.A.

Louise R. Fortmann*
Department of Forestry
  and Resource Management
145 Mulford Hall
University of California
Berkeley, California 94720
U.S.A.

Jere L. Gilles*
Department of Rural Sociology
University of Missouri
Columbia, Missouri 65211
U.S.A.

Ricardo A. Godoy*
Institute for International Development
Harvard University
1737 Cambridge Street
Cambridge, Massachusetts 02138
U.S.A.

John A. Grayzel
Office of Rural and Institutional Development
Bureau for Science and Technology
Agency for International Development
Washington, D.C. 20523
U.S.A.

Anil K. Gupta*
Indian Institute of Management
Vastrapur
Ahmedabad 380 015
INDIA

Abdellah Hammoudi*
Bloc des Sciences Humaines
Institut Agronomique et
  Vétérinaire Hassan II
B.P. 6202
Rabat - Instituts
MOROCCO

John C. Harriss*
School of Development Studies
University of East Anglia
Norwich   NR4 7TJ
ENGLAND

Abdellah Herzenni*
Office Regional du Mise en Valeur Agricole du Haouz
B.P. 22
Marrakech
MOROCCO

Robert C. Hunt*
Department of Anthropology
Brandeis University
415 S Street
Waltham, Massachusetts   02154
U.S.A.

Peter Jacobs
Faculté de l'Aménagement
Université de Montréal
5620 avenue Darlington
Montréal, Québec   H3T 2T1
CANADA

Timothy C. Jessup*
Department of Human Ecology
Cook College
Rutgers University
P.O. Box 231
New Brunswick, New Jersey   08903
U.S.A.

Emizet Kisangani*
P.O. Box 1504
Iowa City, Iowa   52244
U.S.A.

Barbara J. Lausche
World Wildlife Fund
1255 23rd Street, N.W.
Washington, D.C.   20037
U.S.A.

Michael Lipton
Institute of Development Studies
University of Sussex
Brighton   BN1 9RE
ENGLAND

Margaret A. McKean*
Department of Political Science
Duke University
Durham, North Carolina   27706
U.S.A.

Mohamed Mahdi*
Bloc des Sciences Humaines
Institut Agronomique et Vétérinaire
   Hassan II
B.P. 6202
Rabat - Instituts
MOROCCO

Donald A. Messerschmidt*
Department of Anthropology
Washington State University
Pullman, Washington   99164-4910
U.S.A.

Norman K. Nicholson
Office of Development Planning
Bureau for Asia and Near East
Agency for International Development
Washington, D.C. 20523
U.S.A.

Brien E. Norton*
Department of Range Science
Utah State University
Logan, Utah   84322
U.S.A.

Ronald J. Oakerson*
Advisory Commission on Intergovernmental Relations
1111 20th Street, N.W.
Washington, D.C.   20036
U.S.A.

James T. O'Rourke*
Box 600
Story, Wyoming   82842
U.S.A.

Elinor Ostrom*
Workshop in Political Theory and Policy Analysis
Indiana University
513 North Park
Bloomington, Indiana   47405
U.S.A.

Adam N. Pain*
School of Development Studies
University of East Anglia
Norwich   NR4 7TJ
ENGLAND

K. Palanisami*
Department of Agricultural Economics
Tamil Nadu Agricultural University
Coimbatore   641 003
Tamil Nadu
INDIA

Pauline E. Peters*
Institute for International Development
Harvard University
1737 Cambridge Street
Cambridge, Massachusetts   02138
U.S.A.

Nancy Lee Peluso*
Department of Rural Sociology
Cornell University
Ithaca, New York   14853
U.S.A.

Michael Q. Philley
Office of Project Development
Bureau for Asia
Agency for International Development
Washington, D.C.   20523
U.S.A.

Robert Repetto
World Resources Institute
1735 New York Avenue, N.W.
Washington, D.C.   20006
U.S.A.

Emery M. Roe*
Graduate School of Public Policy
University of California
2607 Hearst Avenue
Berkeley, California   94720
U.S.A.

C. Ford Runge*
Department of Agricultural and Applied Economics
332 Classroom Office Building
University of Minnesota
1994 Buford Avenue
St. Paul, Minnesota   55108
U.S.A.

Steven Edward Sanderson
The Ford Foundation
Caixa Postal 49
Rio de Janeiro - ZC-00
Brasil CEP 22210
BRAZIL

Courtland L. Smith
Department of Anthropology
Oregon State University
Corvallis, Oregon   97331
U.S.A.

Randy Stringer
Land Tenure Center
University of Wisconsin
1300 University Avenue
Madison, Wisconsin   53706
U.S.A.